Henry Morley, John Gower

Tales of the Seven Deadly Sins

being the Confessio amantis.

Henry Morley, John Gower

Tales of the Seven Deadly Sins
being the Confessio amantis.

ISBN/EAN: 9783337023645

Printed in Europe, USA, Canada, Australia, Japan

Cover: Foto ©Thomas Meinert / pixelio.de

More available books at **www.hansebooks.com**

THE CARISBROOKE LIBRARY.

THE UNIVERSAL LIBRARY, now completed in sixty-three cheap shilling volumes, has included English versions of the "Iliad," of all extant plays of the Greek tragedians, and of some plays of Aristophanes, of Sanskrit fables, and of Virgil's "Æneid." It has followed the course of time with English versions of the most famous works of Dante, Boccaccio, Machiavelli, Rabelais, Cervantes, Molière, as recast by English dramatists, of Goethe's "Faust" and of Schiller's Poems. It has given currency also to a series of the works of English writers, representative, as far as limits would allow, of our own literature, from Richard of Bury's "Philobiblon" to Sheridan's Plays and Emerson's Essays. In the sequence of publication variety was aimed at, but in the choice of books to be republished there was always the unity of purpose that now allows the volumes to be arranged in historical order, illustrating some of the chief epochs of European literature, and especially of English literature, in the long course of time.

THE CARISBROOKE LIBRARY, now begun, will continue the work of its predecessor, with some changes of form and method. It will include books for which the volumes of the former series did not allow sufficient room. Sometimes in the "Universal Library" a large book—Hobbes's "Leviathan," for example—was packed into small type.

In the "Carisbrooke Library" there will be no small type. The volumes will be larger; each of about four hundred and fifty pages. They will be handsome library volumes, printed with clear type upon good paper, at the price of half-a-crown, and they will be published in alternate months. In the "Universal Library" the editor's introduction to each volume was restricted to four pages, and there was no annotation. In the "Carisbrooke Library," with larger leisure and a two months' interval between the volumes, it will be possible for the editor to give more help towards the enjoyment of each book. There will be fuller introductions, and there will be notes.

Since changes of method and form in the old Library mean the beginning of a new Library with change of name, a simple change is made from the universal to the particular; from the purpose to the one who purposes; from the wide world that yields fruitage for the mind, to the small spot of earth where, if God please, in shades of evening one fruit-gatherer will find new leisure to unburthen himself of his little store.

In the "Carisbrooke Library," as in the predecessor of which it is an extension, there will be order in disorder. Variety will still be aimed at in sequence of the volumes, while the choice of books to be issued will be still guided by the desire to bring home to Englishmen, without unfair exclusion of any form of earnest thought, as far as may be, some living knowledge of their literature along its whole extent, and of its relations with the wisdom and the wit of the surrounding world.

HENRY MORLEY.

CONFESSIO AMANTIS.

Tales of the Seven Deadly Sins

BEING THE

CONFESSIO AMANTIS

OF

JOHN GOWER

EDITED BY

HENRY MORLEY, LL.D.

PROFESSOR OF ENGLISH LITERATURE AT UNIVERSITY COLLEGE
LONDON

LONDON
GEORGE ROUTLEDGE AND SONS
BROADWAY, LUDGATE HILL
GLASGOW, MANCHESTER, AND NEW YORK
1889

Ballantyne Press
BALLANTYNE, HANSON AND CO.
EDINBURGH AND LONDON

INTRODUCTION.

JOHN GOWER'S book of old stories is here at last made current among Englishmen of every degree. The first way of its wider diffusion was by recitation of the story-tellers. It was their business to give pleasures of imagination to the people through their ears, when even the few who could read would also listen with enjoyment to a tale recited with dramatic energy. When the play of "Pericles" brought one of Gower's tales upon our stage in Shakespeare's time, John Gower himself was supposed to speak its Prologue in his chosen measure of eight-syllabled verse. His words then recalled to mind the old way of reciting as well as reading. The actor who, dressed as Gower, came before the people, said to them :—

"To sing a song that old was sung,
From ashes ancient Gower is come;
Assuming man's infirmities
To glad your ear and please your eyes.
It hath been sung at festivals,
On ember eves and holy ales;
And lords and ladies in their lives
Have read it for restoratives."

To all of us Gower may now go on to repeat other lines of the same Prologue :—

"If you, born in these latter times,
When wit's more ripe, accept my rhymes;
And that to hear an old man sing
May to your wishes pleasure bring,
I life would wish, and that I might
Waste it for you, like taper light."

For my own part, I have long wished to make it possible that in these times his countrymen might again be pleased to hear John Gower's song.

In the few editions of these tales hitherto published, Gower's taper has burnt dimly, because they have been so presented as to blur his light. The first edition was Caxton's, printed at Westminster, and dated 1493 [by mistake for 1483]. The second edition was "Imprinted at London in Flete strete by Thomas Berthelette, Printer to the King's grace," in the year 1532. Berthelette published another edition in 1544. These were the editions of Gower's English poem read—and it was read—in the good time of Queen Elizabeth. A copy of one of Berthelette's editions was priced in a recent catalogue at £14. There was not another edition until 1810, when the "Confessio Amantis," printed from Berthelette's edition, was included, with other works, in the second of the twenty-one volumes of Chalmers's English Poets. Next came in 1857, and last of all, three handsome volumes of large print, the "Confessio Amantis of John Gower, edited and collated with the best Manuscripts by Dr. Reinhold Pauli." Dr. Pauli's edition of the text was based upon Berthelette. But there were some corrections made by reference to MSS. for supply of omissions and revision of the metre.

Here let me interpolate a word or two in hearty recognition of Dr. Reinhold Pauli's services to English Literature. He was born on the 25th of May 1823, and died on the 3rd of June 1882. He was born in Berlin, studied at Berlin and Bonn, and came to England in 1847. For several years Pauli was private secretary to Bunsen, and he did not return to Germany until 1855, after publishing here, in 1851, a study of King Alfred and his place in English History. After returning to Germany he went on with a continuation to Lappenberg's History, of which he published the first volume in 1853, the third and last in 1858. In 1857, the year in which his edition of this poem appeared, Pauli obtained a Professorship in Rostock. In 1859 he was transferred to the University of Tübingen, from which he was degraded for the independent spirit shown by him in an article on the condition of Würtemberg, and sent down to teach in the Schönthal Seminary. In 1864 he had begun a History of England since Waterloo, of which the third and last volume appeared in 1875. In 1867 he became a Professor at Marburg, and in 1870 he went to the University of Göttingen. Pauli was essentially historian, with right qualification for his work in breadth of culture and a clear sense of the debts of the present to the past, which made him the more ready to understand our duty to the future.

Old texts of the "Confessio Amantis" often destroy the music of the verse. There are careless transpositions of words, droppings or additions of words, substitutions of later for earlier forms, and frequent omissions of the final *e* where English of Gower's time required it. There are also in all the texts destructions of sense by errors of punctuation. Dr. Pauli's edition was an improvement upon those that went before. It is not a fault, but a merit, that he was unwilling to make any change without MS. authority. Yet this fidelity obliged him to leave many broken lines. For example, recognition of the fact that in Gower's English an adjective used definitely took a final *e* at once restores to music many scores of lines that want a syllable in Caxton's, Berthelette's, and Dr. Pauli's texts. Dr. Pauli's text has also, like Caxton's and Berthelette's, now and then a full stop in what should be the middle of a sentence.

But in all these texts, and especially in Dr. Pauli's, most of the lines are right for those whose previous training has enabled them to read Old English. There is really nothing wanted but a little help to right accentuation to enable any reader, with or without previous training in Old English, to enjoy the "Confessio Amantis." Of course a fallible and mortal editor cannot avoid some slips in the line for line accentuation of a poem of 30,000 lines. I believe, however, that the reader here has Gower's song more nearly than in any former edition given as he sang it himself, nothing modernised, but rather with a few words carried back to their original form for the recovery of the right rhythm of a line. Gower's poem in this edition is so far from being jagged and unmusical that, I hope, there is not a broken line in it from first to last.

Many lines of the "Confessio Amantis" that, in the modern way of reading them, would seem to halt, run easily when read with their own old accentuation. In the present volume this accentuation has been marked throughout, wherever it varied from that of the present day. Gower's verse, as we may now see, was, in fact, noticeable for its easy flow. His octosyllabics have some of the freedom that long afterwards gave grace and power to blank verse, by the interlacing of sentences and making frequent pauses and breaks of sense within the lines and not at their close only. Gower's frequent rhyming of words differing in sense but spelt alike we must regard now as a blemish. He found, indeed, difference enough for a rhyme between identical words of which one was used as a verb, one as a noun. But we may feel also that he does this because he is at ease, and not because he is hard pressed. He pours out his ready rhymes with animation by the thousand. He runs them into shrewd and homely couplets. He varies their dramatic effect by interlacing sentences with what Milton calls "the sense variously drawn out from one verse into another."

If this text, meant to be popular and yet not modernised, adds, as of course it must, some errors of its own, it has removed so many current errors that to the student as well as to the general reader it should bring Gower's Story Book much nearer home than it has been able to come hitherto. I have avoided, except in the case of manifest deviations from the first sense, all interference with the spelling of those old words which are most likely to be mangled by transcribers and printers. Names of persons were very often broken on the rack. In all the editions of the "Confessio Amantis," from Caxton to Pauli, the Phrygian Dares appears as Frigidilles; and Epicurus, obviously paired in a line with his friend Menander, is called Epyloquorus. In all the editions from Caxton to Pauli we read also of the plant under the star 'Cor Scorpionis,' that "His herbe is Astrology," where Astrology is a misprint for Aristolochy, Aristolochia. I have corrected one or two such errors, but have not meddled with forms of names which are as Gower may possibly himself have written them. But who was Gower?

John Gower, Chaucer's friend and fellow poet, may have been born about the year 1327. He died in the year 1408, and was blind during the last eight years of his life. His work as a writer for the outside world was ended by his blindness in the year 1400, the year of Chaucer's death.

John Gower was a country gentleman, of the kindred of a Sir Robert Gower who lies buried in Brabourne Church, about five miles from Ashford in Kent. A manor of Kentwell in Suffolk, which had belonged to Sir Robert Gower, found its way through a series of family arrangements into the possession of John Gower the poet. John Gower acquired also a manor of Feltwell in Norfolk; a manor of Moulton in Suffolk; and lands in Kent in the parishes of Throwley and Stalesfield. He was a feoffee of the Kentish manor of Aldington; he had a rental of ten pounds out of the manor of Wigborough in Essex; and he signed a will in the year 1373 at his own house in Kent, which was at Otford by the river Darent. From 1390 until 1397, John Gower, described not as priest but as clerk, held the rectory of Great Braxted in Essex. This was within a mile of that manor of Wigborough from which he drew ten pounds a year rental.

Gower's social position gave him access to the Court. He was known personally to the King, and he held his rectory of Great Braxted as a grant from Richard the Second. He wrote *Balades* in French, which were designed chiefly for the pleasure of the Court. But he was in his own way very much of a philosopher, and liked life best in his own home with his own thoughts and friends of his own choosing. He wrote three large poems, which agreed in having Latin titles. One of them—"Speculum Meditantis"—was in French; one—"Vox Clamantis"—was in Latin; one—this our "Confessio Amantis"—was in English: these being the three languages then used by English writers.

Of Gower's French poem—"Speculum Meditantis," the Mirror of one Meditating—no copy can now be found.* Some day, perhaps, a MS. of it will be discovered abroad in some quiet old monastic library. A description of it was given in a MS. of the English poem as "divided into twelve parts, and treating of the Vices and the Virtues, and of the various degrees of this age." It is added that the poem sought "to teach, by a right path, the way whereby a transgressed sinner ought to return to the knowledge of his Creator."

It may have been especially this book which caused Chaucer to attach to his friend's name the epithet which has represented during many years for many a reader almost his whole stock of knowledge about John Gower;—that he was called "moral" by Geoffrey Chaucer. John Locke four or five times in an essay on Civil Government, written just after the English Revolution, with a half playful seriousness delivered shots from Richard Hooker out of a book which Locke's opponents looked upon as one of their own great fortress guns. When doing so he took pleasure in citing his author again and again as "the judicious Hooker." Since that time "the judicious Hooker" has kept company with "the moral Gower."

Chaucer's adjective was very naturally used in the dedication of his Troilus and Cressida to two of his own intimate friends, a poet and a philosopher, John Gower and Ralph Strode.

"O morall Gower, this book I direct
To thee and the philosophicall Strode,
To vouchen safe there need is to correct,
Of your benignités and zeles good."

That the friendship between Chaucer and Gower was intimate is proved by the fact that, in 1378, when Chaucer was sent with Sir Edward Berkeley to Lombardy on a political mission, he left John Gower as one of two representatives who were to act for him in his absence, appearing for him in the courts if any legal proceedings should chance to be instituted.

Gower's "Confessio Amantis" was not written when Chaucer in the close of Troilus and Cressida dedicated that poem to him; and Troilus and Cressida seems also to have been written earlier than Gower's Latin poem, "Vox Clamantis," the Voice of One Crying. This poem was suggested by the Jack Straw Rebellion of May 1381, which began at Gower's own doors, including people who lived on estates of his own in Kent and Essex.

Now John Gower was a country gentleman averse to all violent change. His bias was conservative. He looked with no favour on the Lollards, as passages in the "Confessio Amantis" show, and he felt keenly the danger of a triumph of mob law. But he said in his "Vox Clamantis" that no blind Fortune governs the affairs of men; our world is as we make it; whatever happens to us, "nos sumus in causa." The disorder in his time, however dangerous, must have its exciting causes in the life of the community, and he resolved to look through the whole framework of our social system. This he would do in a poem that should speak through Latin to the educated, boldly pointing out wrongs to be righted without shaping war-cries for the ignorant. All England would have echoed to that bold crying out on the condition of the clergy and the people if it had been heard in English, free as the Latin verses poured out with as much facility as if Gower were writing in his mother-tongue. In those verses Gower—a good orthodox Churchman—was outspoken in condemning all corruption, even that by which the Papacy was tainted. He was vigorous with calm invective of a righteous man who had wit and humour at command for use in homeliest plain speaking. "I do not," he said, "affect to touch the stars, or write the wonders of the poles; but rather, with the common human voice that is lamenting in this land, I write the ills I see. God knows, my wish is to be useful; that is the prayer that directs my labour. No hatred urges me. In the Voice of my Crying there will be nothing doubtful, for every man's knowledge will be its best interpreter." He prays that his verse may not be turgid; that there may be in it no word of untruth; that each word may answer to the thing it speaks of pleasantly and fitly; that he may flatter in it no one, and seek in it no praise above the praise of God. "Give me that there shall be less vice and more virtue for my speaking." That is the true homeliness of the best English literature, and in that spirit he wrote the "Confessio Amantis."

Gower's English poem, the "Confessio Amantis," was, like Chaucer's "Canterbury Tales," a device for the stringing of a large number of stories upon some slender thread of narrative that should run through them all, in the way that had been made popular by the great recent success of Boccaccio's "Decameron." Gower probably had written much of the "Confessio Amantis" before Chaucer planned his "Canterbury Tales." Both poets worked sometimes on the same material; while, now and then, Gower seems to have inspired Chaucer with a desire to tell again one of his friend's good stories. It is difficult to know precisely when Gower's "Confessio Amantis" was first written. In its earliest form, as set forth in the Harleian MS., 3490, Gower said—without then naming as a date "the yere sixtenthe of King Richard"—that he wrote it at the request of Richard the Second. He had met the King's barge when rowing on the Thames, and Richard, having invited him on board, asked—

> "That to his highé worthynesse
> Some newé thing I shuldé boke,
> That he himself it mighté loke
> After the forme of my writíng."

Gower adds that although he had long been out of health, he did his best for the king—

> "To make a boke after his heste,
> And write in such a manner wise
> Which may be wisdom to the wise,
> And play to hem that list to play."

Professor John W. Hales has reasoned that the work could only have been thus undertaken, and completed—as it is in that first form—with a loyal dedication to Richard II., at a time when Gower had yet hope in the young King. Such hope was possible only before the year 1386. In 1386 the great barons of England were active under the lead of the King's uncle, the Duke of Gloucester, whom Gower in the Latin verse of a "Tripartite Chronicle" has honoured as the Swan. Richard was then compelled to establish a Regency for twelve months. Professor Hales, looking for a date before 1386, finds several allusions that suggest to him the end of 1383 and the year 1384 as the time when the poem may have been first written. Afterwards in "the yere sixtenthe of King Richard," homage to the King was struck out of the beginning and end of the poem. Bolingbroke—Henry of Lancaster—was addressed in his place, and Gower, like Langland, had turned his back upon an evil King whose deposition was the best hope of the country.

The sixteenth year of King Richard, in which Gower changed the dedication of his poem, was the year 1393. In 1393–4

Henry of Lancaster presented a collar to Gower, possibly in recognition of the dedication thus transferred to him. Gower is represented on his tomb as wearing the collar of SS with a small Swan chained; but Henry of Lancaster did not assume the Swan as his badge until after the murder of Gloucester in 1397. The collar of SS must, therefore, have been a later gift.

In 1397, the year of Gloucester's murder, for which Richard was responsible, Gower resigned his Essex rectory, and resigned the world. Being then about seventy years old, he married Agnes Groundolf in a chapel of his own, under rooms to which he retired with her for the rest of his life within the Priory of St. Mary Overies, now known as St. Saviour's, on the Southwark side of London Bridge. The old Priory was then being for the second time rebuilt, and Gower contributed so liberally to the building works that upon his death in 1408, after eleven years of residence among them—during eight of the years blind—the brethren built for him a handsome tomb, on which they carved his figure in effigy. They represented him with his head resting on the three books he had written, in French, Latin, and English. They also paid him pious honour on a painted window which another kind of piety has since destroyed. The tomb remains. The effigy upon it helps us to recall him in his habit as he lived. But in this volume his mind lives again for friendly and familiar speech among all classes of his countrymen.

In the "Confessio Amantis" Gower, of course, so chose his connecting matter that he might bring his tales into distinct groups, with each group armed for battle against one of the Seven Deadly Sins. He added one book more, based on a work popular in the Middle Ages, the "Secretum Secretorum," ascribed to Aristotle. It set forth the Duties of a King, and Gower inserted it because he was writing the poem for King Richard the Second, who was in much need of such instruction. Gower contrived also to mix with his stories much knowledge upon matters of philosophy and science. Indeed if we add all the record of what Aristotle taught Alexander to the other good doctrine of the Confessor, we have the substance of a fair education for any modern reader who does not mind being five hundred years behind the day. The book will have for many readers an interest, apart from its tales, in its pleasant record of the kind of knowledge that a well-trained man thought worth diffusing in the latter half of the fourteenth century.

The reader to whom old English is new English will after experience of a few pages slip into Gower's music, and find his lines easier reading than some even of the good verse published in our time.

In reading aloud these differences between old and new English should be remembered:

(1) The old pronunciation of the vowels was nearer than it now is to the practice abroad, as its survival in our country dialects will help to show.

(2) Words added to our vocabulary from the Norman French were nearer to their source, and usually had their accents near the close, as they are placed in French.

(3) As a general rule a vowel at the end of a word was sounded if the next word began with a consonant, and had no separate sound if the next word began with a vowel.

(4) Verbs in 'eth,' like 'cometh,' were pronounced often, but not necessarily, without regarding the 'eth' as more of a syllable than the 'es' in comes.

(5) Where 'th' or 'v' came between two short syllables, as in whether, other, ever, there was usually an elision. In the text here given 'whether' was generally written 'where' (whe'er); in other such words the reader makes the contraction for himself. The metre tells him when to do so.

(6) The conjunction 'and' was not necessarily placed at the beginning of a clause connected by it with preceding matter. It may stand within the clause as the word 'also' does in modern English.

Some of Gower's commonest forms, like 'sigh' for saw, will become quickly familiar. Because an equivocal word like 'not' for 'ne wot'—know not—might cause a stumble now and then, I have interpreted that and other such words rather often in the footnotes, the purpose of those notes being to interrupt the text as little as possible, while enabling the eye to take in at once the meaning of an obsolete word or form. Where the same word often recurs, the explanation is repeated often but not always: often enough, it is hoped, for the convenience of a reader who dips into the book for a tale or two, and has not yet read it through. The only modernised word is the pronoun 'thee' in a few earlier pages of the volume. It had in Gower's time, like 'me,' only one 'e.' This of course gives readers the trouble of discriminating between pronoun and article. Wherever in the early pages of the book the word 'thee' is found, the second 'e' is of my adding; but after those earlier pages I have avoided making even that slight alteration.

A few notes on the sources of Gower's Tales will be found in the Table of Contents. Of John Gower himself and of his works a fuller account than it is here possible to give will be found in the fourth volume of my "English Writers."

H. M.

CARISBROOKE, *March* 1889.

CONTENTS.

PAGES

Book III.

OF WRATH.

Against this story Chaucer protested in the Prologue to the Man of Lawes Tale, where he made the Man of Lawes, after giving a list of tales that had been told by Chaucer, add—

"But certainly no word ne writeth he
Of thilké wicke ensample of Canacé,
That lovéd here owen brother sinfully;
Of all swiche curséd stories I say fy."

Book VI.

OF GLUTTONY.

Book VII.

Book VIII.

CONFESSIO AMANTIS.

CONFESSIO AMANTIS.

Prologue.

Of hem, that writen us to-fore,
The bokés dwelle, and we therfore
Ben taught of that was writen tho.[1]
Forthý good is, that we also
In ouré time amonge us here
Do write of newé some matere
Ensampled of the oldé wise,
So that it might in suche a wise,.
Whan we be dede and ellés where,
Belevé[2] to the worldés ere
In timé comend after this.
But for men sain, and sothe it is,
That who that al of wisdom writ
It dulleth ofte a mannés wit
To hem that shall it allday rede,
For thilké cause if that ye rede
I woldé go the middel wey
And write a boke betwene the twey
Somwhat of lust, somwhat of lore,
That of the lasse or of the more
Som man may like of that I write.
And for that fewé men endite
In oure englisshe, I thenké make[3]
A boké for Englondés sake

1 *Tho*, then. 2 *Beleve*, remain.

3 This was the original form of the passage, MS. Harl. 3490:

In our englisshe I thenké make
A boké for king Richardes sake,
To whom belongeth my legeaúnce
With all min hertés obeisaúnce
In all that ever a legé man
Unto his king may don or can,
So ferforth, and me recommaunde
To him which all me may commaunde,

The yere sixtenthe of King Richárd,
What shall befalle here afterward
God wote, for nowe upon this side
Men seen the worlde on every side

Preiend unto the highé regne
Which causeth every king to regne
That his coroné longé stonde.
I thenke and have it understonde,
As it befell upon a tide,
As thing which shuldé tho betide,
Under the town of newé Troy,
Which toke of Brute his firsté joy,
In Themsé, whan it was flowénd,
As I by boté came rowénd
So as Fortúne her timé sette,
My legé lord perchaunce I mette.
And so befell as I came nigh
Out of my bote, whan he me sigh,
He bad me come into his barge.
And whan I was with him at large,
Amongés other thingés said
He hath this charge upon me laid
And bad me do my besinesse,
That to his highé worthynesse
Some newé thing I shuldé boke,
That he him self it mighté loke
After the forme of my writing.
And thus upon his commaunding
Min herte is well the moré glad
To writé so as he me bad.
And eke my fere is well the lasse,
That none envié shall compasse
Without a resonable wite[1]
To feigne and blamé, that I write.
A gentil herte his tungé stilleth
That it malicé none distilleth
But preisé that is to be preised.
But he that hath his worde unpeised
And handleth out wrong any thing,
I pray unto the heven king
Fro suché tungés he me shilde.
And netheles this world is wilde
Of suche jangling, and what befalle.
My kingés hesté shall nought falle,
That I in hopé to deserve
His thank ne shall his will observe
And ellés were I nought excused.

1 *Wite*, blame.

In sondry wisé so diversed,
That it wel nigh stant all reversed.
Als for to speke of time ago,
The causé why it chaungeth so
It nedeth nought to specifie,
The thing so open is at eye,
That every man it may beholde.
And nethéles by daiés olde,
Whan that the bokés weren lever,[1]
Writingé was belovéd ever
Of hem that weren vertuous.
For here in erthe amongés us,
If no man writé howe it stood,
The pris of hem that weré good
Shulde, as who saith, a great partie,
Be lost; so for to magnifie
The worthy princes that tho were
The bokés shewen here and there
Wherof the worlde ensampled is,
And tho that diden then amis
Through tiranny and crueltė,
Right as they stonden in degre
So was the writinge of the werke.
Thus I which am a borel[2] clerke
Purpósé for to write a boke
After the worlde that whilom toke
Long time in oldé daiés passed.
But for men sain it is now lassed[3]
In worsé plight than it was tho,

For that thing may nought be refused
What that a king him selfé bit.[4]
Forthý the simplesse of my wit
I thenke if that I may availe
In his servicé to travaile,
Though I sikenesse have upon honde
And longe have had, yet woll I fonde,[5]
So as I madé my beheste,
To make a boke after his heste
And write in such a maner wise,
Which may be wisdome to the wise
And play to hem that list to play.
But in proverbe I have herde say,
That who that wel his werk beginneth,
The rather a good end he winneth.
And thus the prologue of my boke
After the world that whilom toke,
And eke somdele[6] after the newe
I woll beginné for to newe.

1 *Lever*, better loved.
2 *Borel*, rough homespun.
3 *Lassed*, become smaller.
4 *Bit*, prays for.
5 *Fonde*, try.
6 *Somdele*, some part.

I thenké for to touche also
The world which neweth every day,
So as I can, so as I may.
Though I sikenesse have upon honde
And longe have had, yet wol I fonde[1]
To write and do my besinesse,
That in some part, so as I gesse,
The wisé man may ben advised.
For this Prologue is so assised,
That it to Wisdome all belongeth;
That wise man that it underfongeth
He shal drawe into remémbraunce
The fortune of this worldés chaunce,
The which no man in his persone
May knowé, but the God alone.
Whan the Prológue is so dispended,
This boke shall afterward ben ended
Of Lové, which doth many a wonder
And many a wise man hath put under;
And in this wise I thenke to treate
Towardés hem, that now be greate,
Betwene the vertue and the vice
Which longeth unto this office.
But for my wittés ben to smale
To tellen every mannés tale,
This boke, upon amendément,
To stonde at his commaundément,
With whom min herte is of accorde,
I sende unto min owné lorde
Which of Lancastre is Henry named.
The highé god hath him proclamed
Full of knighthód and allé grace.
So wolde I now this werke embrace
With hol truste and with hol beleve:
God graunte I mote it well acheve.
If I shall drawe into my minde
The timé passéd, than I finde
The worldé stode in al his welthe,
Tho[2] was the life of man in helthe,
Tho was plenté, tho was richésse,
Tho was the fortune of prowésse,

1 *Fonde*, try.
2 *Tho*, then.

Tho was knighthóde in pris by
name,
Wherof the widé worldés fame
Write in croniques is yet witholde.[1]
Justíce of lawé tho was holde,
The privelege of regalie
Was sauf, and all the baronie
Worshipéd was in his estate.
The citees knewen no debate,
The people stode in obeisaúnce
Under the reule of governaúnce,
And pees, with rightwisnessé keste,
With charité tho stode in reste,
Of mannes herté the corâge
Was shewéd than in the visâge.
The word was liche to the conceipte
Withouté semblaunt of deceipte;
Tho was there unenvíëd love,
Tho was vertúë set above,
And vicé was put under fote.
Now stant the crope under the
rote,
The worlde is chaungéd overall,
And therof moste in speciall
That Love is falle into discorde.
And that I take into recorde
Of every lond for his partie
The comun vois, which may nought
lie,
Nought upon one, but upon alle
It is that men now clepe and calle
And sain, that regnés ben devided,
In stede of love is haté guided,
The werré[2] wol no pees purchace,
And lawe hath take her double
face,
So that justíce out of the wey
With rightwisnesse is gone awey.
And thus, to loke on every halve,[3]
Men sene the soré without salve,
Whiche al the worlde hath overtake.
Ther is no regne of alle out take,[4]

1 *Witholde*, held or kept with us.
2 *Werre*, war.
3 *On every halve*, on all sides.
4 *Out take*, excepted.

For every climat hath his dele[1]
After the turninge of the whele
Which blindé Fortune overthrow-
eth,
Wherof the certain no man knoweth.
The heven wot what is to done.
But we that dwelle under the mone
Stonde in this worlde upon a
were,[2]
And namély but[3] the powér
Of hem that ben the worldés guides,
With good counseil on allé sides
Ben kept upright in suche a wise,
That Haté breké nought thassise
Of Lové, whiche is all the chefe
To kepe a regne out of mischefe:
For allé reson woldé this,
That unto him, which the' heved[4] is,
The membrés buxóm shall bowe,
And he shulde eke here trouth alowe
With all his hert, and make hem
chere,
For good counseil is good to here:
All though a man be wise him selve,
Yet is the wisdome more of twelve.
And if they stonden both in one,
To hope it weré than anone
That God his gracé woldé sende
To make of thilké werre an ende,
Whiche every day now groweth
newe,—
And that is gretely for to rewe,
In speciáll for Cristés sake,
Which wolde his owné life fórsake
Amonge the men to yeven pees.[5]
But nowe men tellen nethéles,
That Love is fro the world departed,
So stant the pees uneven parted
With hem that liven now a daies.
But for to loke at all assaies,
To him, that woldé reson seche
After the comun worldés speche,

1 *Dele*, share.
2 *Upon a were*, in conflict and confusion.
3 *But*, unless. 4 *Heved*, head.
5 *To yeven pees*, to give peace.

It is to wonder of thilké werre,
In which none wote who hath the werre.[1]
For every lond him self deceiveth
And of disese his parte receiveth,
And yet ne také men no kepe.[2]
But thilké Lorde, whiche al may kepe,
To whom no counseil may be hid
Upon the world, whiche is betid,
Amendé that wherof men pleine
With trewé hertés and with pleine,
And reconcilé Love agayne,
As he, whiche is king soverayne
Of all the worldés governaunce,
And of his highé purveiance
Affermé pees bitwene the londes
And take herecause into his hondes,
So that the world may stande appesed
And his godhede also be plesed !.

To thenke upon the daiés olde
The life of clerkés to beholde,
Men sain, how that they weré tho
Ensample and reule of allé tho
Which of wisdóm the vertue soughten.
Unto the God first they besoughten
As to the substaunce of here scole,
That they ne sholden nought befole
Her witte upon none erthly werkes,
Whiche were ayein th'estate of clerkes,
And that they mighten flee the vice,
Which Simon hath in his offíce,
Wherof he taketh golde in honde.
For thilké time, I understonde,
The Lumbarde madé non eschaunge
The bisshoprichés for to chaunge,
Ne yet a letter for to sende
For dignité ne for provende

1 That war in which none knows who has the worse.
2 *No kepe*, no heed.

Or curéd or withouté cure,
The chirché keie in adventúre
Of armés and of brigantaille[1]
Stood no thing than upon bataille,
To fight or for to maké cheste[2]
It thought hem thanné nought honéste.
But of simplesce and paciénce
They maden thanné no defence.
The courte of worldly regalie
To hem was thanné no bailie.
The vain honóur was nought desired,
Which hath the proudé herté fired.
Humilité was tho witholde
And pridé was a vicé holde.[3]
Of holy chirché the largesse
Yaf thanne and didé great almesse
To pouer men that hadden nede.
They were eke chast in word and dede,
Wherof the people ensample toke.
Their lust was al upon the boke,
Or for to preche or for to preie
To wissé[4] men the righté weie
Of such as stode of trouth unlered.
Lo, thus was Peters bargé stered
Of hem that thilké timé[5] were.
And thus came first to mannés ere
The feith of Criste, and allé good
Through hem that thanné weren good
And sobre and chaste and large and wise.
And now, men sain, is other wise.
Simon the cause hath undertake,
The worldés swerde on hond is take.
And that is wonder nethéles,
Whan Criste him self hath bodé[6] pees
And set it in his Testamént,
How now that holy chirche is went
Of that here lawé positife,

1 *Brigantaille*, armour. 2 *Cheste*, strife.
3 *Holde*, esteemed. 4 *Wisse*, teach.
5 *Thilke time*, in that time.
6 *Bode*, commanded.

Hath set to maké werre and strife
For worldés goods which may nought last ! [1]
God wote the causé to the last
Of every right and wronge also.
But while the lawe is reuled so
That clerkés to the werre entende,
I not [2] how that they shall amende
The woful worlde, in other thinges
To maké pees betwen the kinges
After the lawe of charité,
Which is the propré dueté
Belongend unto the presthode.
But as it thinketh to manhode,
The heven is fer, the worlde is nigh,
And vainglorye is eke so sligh, [3]
Which covetise hath now witholde, [4]
That they none other thing beholde
But only that they mighten winne.
And thus the werrés they beginne,
Wherof the holy chirche is taxed,
That in the point as it is axed
The dismé [5] goth to the bataile,
As though Crist mighté nought availe
To don hem right by other weie.
Into the swerd the chirché keie
Is tornéd, and the holy bede
Into cursinge, and every stede
Whiche sholdé stonde upon the feith
And to this cause an eré leyth
Astonéd is of the quarele.
That [6] sholdé be the worldes hele
Is now, men sain, the pestilénce,
Which hath exiléd paciënce
Fro the clergie in speciáll.
And that is shewéd overall
In any thing whan they be greved.
But if Gregoiré be beleved

[1] For the transitory goods of this world.
[2] *I not*, I know not.
[3] *Sligh*, cunning.
[4] *Witholde*, held with, had for comrade.
[5] *Disme*, tithe.
[6] *That*, that which.

As it is in the bokés write,
He dothe us somdele for to wite [1]
The cause of thilké prelacie,
Where God is nought of compaignie.
For every werke as it is founded
Shall stonde, or ellés be confounded.
Who that only for Cristés sake
Desireth curé for to take
And nought for pride of thilke estate
To beare a name of a preláte,
He shal by reson do profite
In holy chirche, upon the plite
That he hath set his consciënce.
But in the worldés reverence
Ther ben of suché many glade
Whan they to thilke estate ben made,
Nought for the merite of the charge
But for they wolde hem self discharge
Of pouérte and becomé grete ;
And thus for pompe and for beyete [2]
The scribe and eke the pharisee
Of Moïses upon the see
In the chaire on high ben set,
Wherof the feith is ofté let [3]
Whiche is betaken [4] hem to kepe.
In Cristés cause all day they slepe,
But of the worlde is nought foryete.
For wel is him that now may gete
Office in court to be honoúred.
The strongé cofre hath al devoured
Under the keie of avarice
The tresor of the benefice,
Wherof the pouer [5] shulden clothe
And ete and drinke and housé bothe.
The charité goth all unknowe,
For they no greine of pité sowe,
And slouthé kepeth the librarie
Which longeth to the seintuarie.

[1] *Doth us somdele for to wite*, causes us in some part to know.
[2] *For beyete*, for what they can get.
[3] *Let*, hindered. [4] *Betaken*, entrusted.
[5] *The pouer*, the poor.

To studie upon the worldés lore
Sufficeth now withouté more.
Delícacié his sweté tothe
Hath soffred so that it fordothe
Of abstinence al that ther is.
And for to loken over this,
If Etna brenne in the clergie,
Al openly to mannés eye
At Avignon thexperiénce
Therof hath yove an evidénce
Of that men seen hem so devided.
And yet the cause is nought decided,
But it is saide and ever shall:
Bitwen two stoolés is the fall,
Whan that men wenen best to sitte.
In holy chirche of suche a slitte
Is for to rewe unto us alle.
God graunte it moté wel befalle
Towardés him which hath the trouth.
But ofte is seen, that mochel slouth,
Whan men ben drunken of the cuppe,
Doth mochel harme whan fire is uppe,
But if[1] somwho the flammé staunche;
And so to speke upon this braunche
Which proud envie hath made to springe
Of scismé, causeth for to bringe
This newé secte of Lollardie,
And also many an heresie,
Among the clerkés in hem selve.
It weré better dike and delve
And stonde upon the righté feith
Than knowe al that the Bible saith
And erre as somé clerkés do.
Upon the hond to were a shoe
And set upon the foot a glove,
Accordeth nought to the behove
Of resonáble mannés use.
If men behelden the vertuse,
That Criste in erthé taught us here,
They shulden nought in such manere

[1] *But if*, unless.

Among hem that ben holden wise
The papacíë so desguise
Upon divérs electiön,
Whiche stant aftér thaffectiön
Of sondry londés al aboute.
But whan God wol it shal were oute,
For trouth mot stonden atté laste.
But yet they argumenten faste
Upon the Pope and his estate,
Wherof they fallen in great debate.
This clerk saith yea, that other nay,
And thus they drivé forth the day;
And eche of hem him self amendeth
Of worldés good: but none entendeth
To that which comun profite were.
They sain, that God is mighty there,
And shal ordeiné what he wille;
There maké they none other skille,
Where is the perill of the feith:
But every clerke his herté leith
To kepe his worlde in speciall;
And of the causé generáll
Whiche unto holy chirché longeth,
Is none of hem that underfongeth[1]
To shapen any resisténce.
And thus the right hath no defence,
But there I lové, there I holde.
Lo, thus to-broke is Cristés folde,
Wherof the flock withouté guide
Devouréd is on every side,
In lacke of hem that ben unware
Shepherdés, which here wit beware[2]
Upon the worlde in other halve.
The sharpé pricke in stede of salve
They usen now, wherof the hele[3]
They hurte of that they shulden hele.[4]
And what sheep that is full of wulle
Upon his backe they toose and pulle
While ther is any thinge to pille.
And though there be none other skille,

[1] *Underfongeth*, undertakes.
[2] *Beware*, spend.
[3] *Hele*, heel.
[4] *Hele*, heal.

But onely for they woldé winne,
They levé nought whan they beginne
Upon here acté to procede,
Whiche is nogood shephérdés dede.
And upon this also men sain
That fro the leesé whiche is pleine,
Into the brerés they forcacche
Here orf, for that they wolden lacche
With such duresse and so bereve
That shal upon the thornes leve
Of wulle whiche the brere hath tore,[1]
Wherof the sheep ben al to-tore,
Of that the herdés make hem lese.[2]
Lo, how they feignen chalk for chese!
For though they speke and teché wel,
They don hem self therof no dele.
For if the wolf come in the wey,
Their gostly staf is then awey,
Wherof they shulde her flock defende.
But if the pouer sheep offende
In any thing, though it be lite,[3]
They ben al redy for to smite;
And thus, howe ever that they tale,
The strokés falle upon the smale,
And upon other that bene greate
Hem lacketh herté for to beate,
So that undér the clerkés lawe
Men seen the merel al misdrawe.[4]
I wol nought say in generall,
For there ben somme in speciall,
In whome that al vertúë dwelleth,
And tho ben, as thapostel telleth,
That God of his electiön
Hath clepéd to perfectiön
In the manér as Aaron was.
They be nothínge in thilké cas
Of Simon, which the foldés gate
Hath lete and goth in othergate,
But they gone in the righté weie.
There bene also somme as men saie,
That folwen Simon atté heles
Whose carté goeth upon wheles
Of covetise and worldés pride,
And holy chirché goth beside,
Whiche sheweth outwarde a viságe
Of that is nought in the coráge.
For if men loke in holy chirche
Betwene the worde and that they wirche,
There is a ful great differénce.
They prechen us in audiénce,
That noman shall his soule empeire,[1]
For al is but a chery feire[2]
This worldés good, so as they telle.
Also they sain there is an helle,
Whiche unto mannés sinne is due,
And bidden us therfore escheue
That wicked is, and do the good.
Who that her wordés understood
It thinketh they wolden do the same;
But yet betwene ernést and game
Ful oft it torneth other wise.
With holy talés they devise,
How meritóry is thilké dede
Of charité to clothe and fede
The pouer folke, and for to parte
The worldés good, but they departe
Ne thenken nought[3] fro that they have.
Also they sain, good is to save
With penaunce and with abstinence
Of chastité the continence.
But pleinly for to speke of that,
I not[4] how thilke body fat,
Which they with deinté metés kepe,
And lein it softé for to slepe,

1 *That fro the leese*, &c. That from the meadow which is open plain they hunt their flock into the briars, because they would seize profit by such hard treatment and so rob them of wool that the briar has torn.
2 *Lese*, lose. 3 *Lite*, little.
4 *The merel al misdrawe*, the world all drawn awry.

1 *Empeire*, damage.
2 *Chery feire*, charivari.
3 *They departe ne thenken nought*, they do not think of distributing.
4 *Not*, ne wot, know not.

Whan it hath ellés of his wille,
With chastité shall stondé stille.
And nethéles I can nought say
In aunter[1] if that I missay
Touchend of this, how ever it stonde,
I here and wol nought understonde,
For therof have I nought to done.
But he that madé first the mone,
The highé God of his goodnésse,
If ther be cause, he it redresse.
But what as any man can accuse,
This may resón of trouthe excuse.
The vice of hem that ben ungood
Is no reproef unto the good.
For every man his owné werkes
Shall beare, and thus as of the clerkes
The goodé men ben to commende,
And all these other God amende!
For they ben to the worldés eye
The mirrour of ensamplarie
To reulen and to taken hede
Betwene the men and the Godhede.

Now for to speke of the comúne
It is to drede of that fortúne
Whiche hath befalle in sondry londes.
But often for defaute of bondes
Al sodeinlich er it be wist
A tonné, whan his lie arist,[2]
To-breketh, and renneth al aboute
Whiche ellés sholdé nought gone oute.
And eke ful ofte a litel scar
Upon a banke, er men be ware,
Let in the streme which with gret paine,
If ever, man it shal restraine.
Where lawé lacketh errour groweth,
He is nought wise who that ne troweth,
For it hath provéd oft ér this.
And thus the comun clamour is

[1] *In aunter*, peradventure.
[2] *Whan his lie arist*, when its lees rise, when its contents are fermenting.

In every lond where people dwelleth
And eche in his compleinté telleth,
How that the worlde is al miswent.
And therupon his argument
Yeveth every man in sondry wise.
But what man wolde him self avise
His consciénce and nought misuse,
He may well at the first excuse
His God, whiche ever stant in one,
In Him there is defauté none.
So must it stonde upon us selve,
Nought only upon ten ne twelve,
But plenerlich[1] upon us alle,
For man is cause of that shal falle.
And nethéles yet som men write
And sayn Fortune is to wite;[2]
And som men holde opinión
That it is constellación,
Which causeth al that a man dothe;
God wot of bothé whiche is sothe.
The worlde as of his propre kinde
Was ever untrew, and as the blinde
Improperlich he demeth fame,
He blameth that is nought to blame
And preiseth that is nought to preise.
Thus whan he shall the thingés peise,[3]
Ther is deceipte in his balaúnce
And al is that the variaunce
Of us, that shulde us better avise.
For after that we fall and rise
The worlde ariste and falleth with al,
So that the man is over al
His owné cause of wele and wo.
That we Fortúné clepé so
Out of the man him selfe it groweth.
And who that other wisé troweth
Beholde the people of Israël.
For ever while they deden wel
Fortúné was hem debonaire;
And whan they deden the contraire
Fortúné was contrariende.
So that it proveth wel at ende,

[1] *Plenerlich*, fully. [2] *To wite*, to blame.
[3] *Peise*, weigh.

Why that the worlde is wonderful
And may no whilé stondé ful,
Though that it semé wel besein ;
For every worldés thinge is vain
And ever goth the whele aboute
And ever stant a man in doute,
Fortúné stant no whilé stille.
So hath ther no man al his wille,
Als far as ever a man may knowe
There lasteth no thing but a throwe.[1]
The world stant ever upon debate,
So may be siker none estate,
Now here now there, now to now fro,
Now up now down, the world goth so
And ever hath done and ever shal.
Wherof I finde in special
A talé writen in the Bible,
Which must nedés be credíble,
And that as in çonclusión
Saith, that upon división
Stant why no worldés thing may laste
Til it be drivé to the laste,
And fro the firsté regne of all
Unto this day how so befall
Of that the regnés be meváble,
The man him self hath be coupable,
Whiche of his propre governaunce
Fortúneth al the worldés chaunce.
The high almighty purveiaunce,
In whose eterné rémembraúnce
From first was every thing presént,
He hath his prophecië sent
In suche a wise, as thou shalt here,
To Daniél of this matere,
How that this world shal torne and wende
Till it be falle unto his ende ;—
Wherof the talé tell I shal
In which it is betokenéd al.

[1] *But a throwe*, but for a space of time.

As Nabugodonosor slepte
A sweven[1] him toke, the whiche he kepte
Til on the morwe he was arise,
For he therof was sore agrise.
Til[2] Daniél his dreme he tolde
And praid him fairé, that he wolde
Aredé what it token may,
And saide : a beddé where I lay
Me thought I sigh[3] upon a stage,
Where stood a wonder straunge ymage.
His hed with al the necke also
They were of fine gold, bothé two
His brest, his shulders and his armes
Were al of silver, but the armes,
The wombe and al down to the kne
Of bras they were upon to se,
His leggés were al made of steel,
So were his feet also somdele,
And somdele part to hem was take
Of erthé, which men pottés make.
The feble meind[4] was with the strong,
So might it nought wel stonde long.
And tho me thoughté, that I sigh
A great stone from an hill on high
Fell down of sodein aventure
Upon the feet of this figure,
With which stone al to-broké was
Gold, silver, erthé, steel and bras,
That al was into pouder brought
And so forth tornéd into nought.
This was the sweven which he had,
That Daniel anone arad
And saidé him : that figure straunge
Betokeneth how the world shal chaunge
And waxé lassé worth and lasse,
Til it to nought all over passe.
The necke and hed, that weren golde,
He saide how that betoken sholde

[1] *Sweven*, dream.
[2] *Til*, to.
[3] *Sigh*, saw.
[4] *Meind*, mixed.

A worthy worlde, a noble, a riche
To which none after shal be liche.
Of silver that was over forthe
Shal ben a worlde of lassé worthe.
And after that the wombe of bras
Token of a wers worlde it was.
The steel which he sigh afterward
A world betokeneth more hard.
And yet the werste of every dele
Is last, than whan of erth and steel
He sigh the feet departed[1] so,
For that betokeneth mochel wo.
Whan that the world devided is,
It mot algaté fare amis,
For erth which meined is with steel
To-gider may nought lasté wele,
But if that one that other waste,
So mot it nedés fail in haste.
The stone, whiche fro the hilly stage
He sigh down falle on that ymage
And hath it into pouder broke,
That sweven hath Daniel unloke
And said, that it is Goddes might,
Which, whan men wené most upright
To stondé, shal hem over caste.
And that is of this world the laste,
And than a newé shal beginne,
From whiche a man shal never twinne
Or al to paine or al to pees,
That world shal laste endéles.
Lo, thus expoundeth Daniël
The kingés sweven faire and wel
In Babiloiné the citee,
Wher that the wisest of Caldee
Ne couthen wité[2] what it mente,
But he tolde al the hole entente,
As in partie it is befalle.
Of goldé the first regne of alle
Was in that kingés timë tho,
And lasté many daiés so.
There whilés that the monarchíe
Of al the worlde in that partie

[1] *Departed*, divided. [2] *Wite*, know.

To Babiloiné was subgite
And helde him still in suche a plight,
Til that the world began diverse.
And that was, whan the kinge of Perse,
Which Cyrus hight, ayein the pees
Forth with his soné Cambisés
Of Babiloine all that empire,
Right as they wolde hem self desire,
Put under in subjectión
And toke it in possessión,
And slain was Baltazar the king,
Which lost his regne and all his thing.
And thus whan they it haddé wonne,
The worlde of silver was begonne
And that of gold was passéd oute;
And in this wise it goth aboute
Into the regne of Dariús,
And than it fell to Persé thus.
There Alisaundre put hem under,
Which wroght of armés many a wonder,
So that the monarchíë lefte
With Grecs and here estate up lefte,
And Persiens gone under fote,
So suffre they that nedés mote.
And tho the world began of bras,
And that of silver ended was,
But for the timé thus it laste,
Til it befellé, that at laste
This king, whan that his day was come,
With strength of deth was overcome.
And nethéles yet or he dide[1]
He shope his regné to devide
To knightés, which him haddé served,
And after that they have deserved
Yaf the conquestés that he wanne,
Wherof great werré tho beganne
Among hem that the regnes had,
Through proud envíë which hem lad,

[1] *Or he dide*, ere he died.

Til it befelle ayein hem thus.
The noble Cesar Julius,
Which tho was kinge of Romé-londe,
With great bataile and with strong honde
All Grecé, Perse and eke Caldee
Wan and put under, so that he
Nought al only of th'orient
But al the marche of th'occident
Govérneth under his empire
As he that was hole lord and sire
And heldé through his chivalrie
Of al this worlde the monarchie
And was the first of that honoúr
Which taketh name of Emperoúr.
Where Romé thanné wolde assaile,
There mighté no thing contrevaile,
But every contré must obeie:
Tho goth the regne of bras aweie
And comen is the worlde of steel,
And stode above upon the whele.
As steel is hardest in his kinde
Above al other that men finde
Of metals, such was Romé tho
The mightiest and lasté so
Long time amongés the Romains,
Til they becomé so vilains,
That the fals emperoúr Leo
With Constantin his sone also
The patrimonie and the richésse,
Which to Silvester in pure almesse
The firsté Constantinus lefte,
Fro holy chirché they berefte.
But Adrian, which Popé was
And sawe the mischef of this cas,
Goth into Fruncé for to pleine
And praieth the great Charlemaine
For Cristés sake and soulé hele,
That he wol také the quarele
Of holy chirche in his defence,
And Charlés, for the reverence
Of God, the cause hath undertake
And with his host the waie hath take
Over the mountes of Lumbardie.
Of Rome and al the tirannie
With blody swerd he overcome
And the citee with strengthé nome [1]
In suche a wise and there he wroughte,
That holy chirche ayein he broughte
Into fraunchise, and doth restore
The Popés luste and yaf him more.
And thus whan he his God hath served,
He toke, as he hath well deserved,
The diademe and was coróned
Of Rome, and thus was abandóned
Thempire, whiche camé never ayeine
Into the hande of no Romaine.
But a long time it stode so stille
Under the Frensshé kingés wille,
Til that Fortúne her whele so lad,
That afterward Lumbárdes it had,
Nought by the swerd, but by suffraunce
Of him that tho was king of Fraunce,
Whiche Carlé Calvus clepéd was;
And he resigneth in this cas
Thempire of Rome unto Lowis
His cousin, which a Lumbarde is,
And so it laste into the yere
Of Alberte and of Berenger.
But than upon dissensiön
They felle and in divisiön
Among hem self that weré grete,
So that they losté the beyete [2]
Of worship and of worldés pees.
But in proverbé nethéles
Men sain: ful seldome is, that welthe
Can suffre his owne estate in helthe,
And that was in the Lumbardes sene,
Suche comun strife was hem betwene

1 *Nome*, took. 2 *Beyete*, possession.

Through covetise and through envie,
That every man drough his partie,
Which mighté leden any route
Withinné bourgh and eke withoute.
The comun right hath no felawe,
So that the governaunce of lawe
Was lost; and for necessité
Of that they stode in suche degré
Al only through divisiön
Hem nedeth in conclusiön
Of straungé londés helpe beside,
And thus for they hem self divide
And stonden out of reule uneven,
Of Alemainé princes seven
They chose, in this condiciön,
That upon here electiön
Thempire of Romé sholdé stonde.
And thus they left it out of honde
For lacke of grace, and it forsoke
That Alemains upon hem toke.
And to confermen here estate
Of that they stoden in debate,
They token the possessiön
After the composiciön
Among hem self, and ther upon
They made an Emperour anon,
Whos name as the croniqué telleth
Was Othes, and so forth it dwelleth,
Fro thilke daie yet unto this,
Thempire of Rome hath ben and is
To thalemains: and in this wise
As ye to-fore have herd devise [1]
How Daniel the sweven [2] expoundeth
Of that ymáge, on whom he foundeth
The world which after sholdé falle,—
Comen is the last token of alle.
Upon the feet of erthe and steel
So stant the world now every dele
Departed,[3] which began right tho
Whan Romé was devided so.

[1] *Devise*, relate. [2] *Sweven*, dream.
[3] *Every dele departed*, every part divided.

And that is for to rewé sore,
For alwey sithé [1] more and more
The worlde empeireth [2] every day,
Wherof the sothé shewé may.
At Romé first if we beginne,
The walle and al the citee withinne
Stant in ruine and in decás,
The feld is where the palais was,
The town is wast, and over that
If we beholden thilke estate
Whiche whilome was of the Romains,
Of knighthod and of citizeins,
To peisé [3] now with that beforne,
(The chaf is take for the corne.)
And for to speke of Romés might
Unnethés [4] stant ther ought upright
Of worship or of worldés good,
As it beforé timé stood.
And why the worship is away
If that a man the sothe shall say,
The cause hath ben devisiön,
Which moder of confusiön
Is, where she cometh overall
Nought only of the temporall
But of the spiritual also.
The dedé proveth it is so,
And hath do many daies er this,
Through venim which that medled [5] is
In holy chirche of erthely thing.
For Crist him self maketh knowleching,
That no man may togeder serve
God and the World but if [6] he swerve
Froward that one, and stonde unstable:
And Cristés word may nought be fable.
The thing so open is at theye,
It nedeth nought to specifie

[1] *Sithe*, since.
[2] *Empeireth*, grows worse.
[3] *Peise*, weigh. [4] *Unnethes*, hardly.
[5] *Medled*, mixed.
[6] *But if*, unless.

Or speke ought more in this matere.
But in this wise a man may lere[1]
How that the worlde is gone aboute,
The whiche wel nigh is weréd out
After the forme of that figúre,
Which Daniël in his scriptúre
Expoundeth as to-fore is tolde:
Of bras, of silver and of golde
The worlde is passéd and agone,
And nowe upon his oldé tone[2]
It stant, of brutel[3] erthe and steel
The whiche accorden never a dele,[4]
So mot it nedés swerve aside
As thing the which men seen divide.
Thapostel writ unto us alle
And saith, that upon us is falle
Thend of the world, so may we knowe
This ymage is nigh overthrowe
By which this world was signified,
That whilom was so magnified
And nowe is olde and feble and vile,
Full of mischéfe and of perile,
And stant divided eke also
Lyke to the feet, that weré so
As I tolde of the statue above.
And thus men seen, through lacke of Love
Where as the lond divided is,
It mot algaté fare amis.
And now, to loke on every side,
A man may se the world divide:
The werrés ben so generall
Amonge the Cristen overall,
That every man now secheth wreche,[5]
And yet these clerkés alday preche
And sain, good dedé may none be
Whiche stant nought upon charite.

[1] *Lere*, learn.
[2] *Tone*, toes. [3] *Brutel*, brittle.
[4] *Never a dele*, never a bit.
[5] *Wreche*, wreaking of vengeance.

I not[1] how charité sholde stonde
Where dedly werre is taken on honde,
But al this wo is cause of man
The which that wit and reson can;
And that in token and in witnesse,
That ilke ymágé bare liknesse
Of man, and of none other beste.
For first unto the mannés heste
Was every creätúre ordeigned,
But afterward it was restreigned;
Whan that he fel they fellen eke,
Whan he wex seke they wexen seke;
For as the man hath passiön
Of sikenesse, in comparison
So suffren other creätúres.
Lo, first the hevenly figures.
The sonne and mone eclipsen both
And ben with mannés sinne wroth;
The purest air, for sinne, alofte
Hath ben and is corrupt ful ofte;
Right now the highé windés blowe
And anon after they ben lowe,
Now cloudy and now clere it is;
So it may proven wel by this,
A mannés sinne is for to hate[2]
Which maketh the welken to debate.
And for to se the properté
Of every thinge in his degré,
Benethé forth amonge us here
Al stant a like in this matere.
The see nowe ebbeth and nowe it floweth,
The lond now welketh and now it groweth;
Now be the trees with levés grene,
Now they be bare and no thing sene;
Now be there lusty somer floures,
Now be there stormy winter shoures;

[1] *Not*, know not.
[2] *For to hate*, to be hated.

Now be the daiés, now the nightes,
So stant there no thing al uprightes:
Nowe it is light, nowe it is derke,
And thus stant al the worldés werke
After the disposiciön
Of man, and his condiciön.
Forthý[1] Gregoire in his moráll
Saith, that a man in speciáll
The lassé worlde[2] is properly;
And that he proveth redily.
For man of soulé resonáble
Is to an angel resembláble;
And lyke to beste, he hath felíng;
And lyke to tres, he hath growíng.
The stonés ben, and so is he,
Thus of his propre qualite
The man, as telleth the clergie,
Is as a worlde in his partie;
And whan this litel world mistorneth
The greté worlde al overtorneth.
The lond, the see, the firmament
They axen allé jugément
Ayein the man, and make him warre,
Ther while him selfe stant out of harre[3]
The remenaunt wol nought accorde:
And in this wise as I recorde
The man is cause of allé wo,
Why this worlde is divided so.
Divisiön the gospel saith
One house upon an other laith,
Til that the regne al overthrowe.
And thus may every man wel knowe
Divisiön aboven alle
Is thing which maketh the world to falle
And ever hath do, sith it began;
It may firste prove upon a man.
The which for his complexiön
Is made upon divisiön

[1] *Forthý*, for that.
[2] *The lasse worlde*, the microcosm.
[3] *Out of harre*, unhinged, out of order.

Of cold of hot of moist of drie,
He mot by verry kinde[1] die.
For the contraire of his estate
Stant evermore in such debate,
Til that a part be overcome
There may no final pees be nome.[2]
But otherwise if a man were
Made al togeder of one matere
Withouten interrupciön,
There shuldé no corrupciön
Engendre upon that unité;
But for there is diversité
Within him selfe, he may nought laste
That he ne deieth at the laste.
But in a man yet over this
Full great divisiön there is,
Through which that he is ever in strife
While that him lasteth any life.
The body and the soule also
Among hem ben divided so,
That what thing that the body hateth
The soulé loveth and debateth.
But nethéles ful ofte is sene
Of werré which is hem betwene,
The feble hath wonné the victoire;
And whoso draweth into memoire
What hath befalle of olde and newe
He may that werré soré rewe;
Which first began in paradis:
For there was provéd what it is
And what disesé there it wrought,
For thilké werré tho[3] forth brought
The vice of allé dedly sinne
Through which divisiön came inne
Among the men in erthé here,
And was the cause and the matere,
Why God the greté flodés sende
Of all the world and[4] made an ende

[1] *Kinde*, nature.
[2] *Nome*, taken.
[3] *Tho*, then.
[4] *And*. The place of "and" in a sentence might be varied, as we vary the place of "also."

But Noe with his felaship,
Which only weren sauf by ship.
And over that through sinne it come,
That Nembroth such emprisé nome,
Whan he the touré Babel on hight
Let make, as he that woldé fight
Ayein the highé goddés might,
Wherof devided anon right
Was the languáge in suche entent
There wisté non what other ment,
So that they mighten nought procede.
And thus it stant of every dede
Where sinné taketh the case on honde
It may upright nought longé stonde,
For sinne of her condiciön
Is mother of divisiön,
And token whan the world shall faile.
For so saith Crist withouté faile,
That nigh upon the worldés ende
Pees and accorde away shall wende
And allé charité shall cease
Among the men, and hate encrease.
And whan these tokens ben befall
All sodeinly the stone shall fall,
As Daniël it hath beknowe,
Which all this world shal overthrowe:
And every man shall than arise
To joie or elles to juise,[1]
Where that he shall for ever dwell,
Or straight to heven or straight to hell.
In heven is pees and al accorde,
But helle is full of such discorde
That there may be no Lové day.[2]
Forthý[3] good is, while a man may,

[1] *Juise*, judgment.
[2] *Love-day*, day of peacemaking by submitting quarrels to the judgment of a Christian minister.
[3] *Forthý*, for that.

Echone to setté pees with other
And loven as his owné brother,
So may he winné worldés welthe
And afterwarde his soulé helthe.
But woldé god that now were one
An other suche as Arione,
Whiche had an harpe of such temprúre,
And therto of so good mesúre
He song, that he the bestés wilde
Made of his noté tame and milde,
The hinde in pees with the león,
The wolfe in pees with the motton,[1]
The hare in pees stood with the hounde,
And every man upon this grounde
Whiche Arion that timé herde,
As well the lorde as the shepherde,
He brought hem all in good accorde,
So that the comun with the lorde
And lord with the común also
He sette in Lové bothé two
And put awey maléncolie.
That was a lustie mėlodie
Whan every man with other lough.[2]
And if ther were suche oné now
Whiche coudé harpe as he tho[3] ded
He might availe in many a stede
To maké pees where nowe is hate.
For whan men thenken to debate
I not[4] what other thinge is good;
But wher that wisdom waxeth wood[5]
And reson torneth into rage,
So that mesúre[6] upon outrage
Hath set this worlde, it is to drede;
For that bringeth in the comun drede
Whiche stant at every mannés dore.
But whan the sharpnesse of the spore
The horsé sidé smit to sore
It greveth ofte. And now no more

[1] *Motton*, sheep.
[2] *Lough*, laughed.
[3] *Tho*, then.
[4] *Not*, know not.
[5] *Wood*, mad.
[6] *Mesure*, moderation.

As for to speke of this matere,
Which none but only God may stere.
So weré good if at this tyde
That every man vpon his syde
Besought and prayéd for the peace
Whiche is the cause of all in-
cresse
Of worshippe and of worldés welthe,
Of hertes reste and soulés helthe,
Without peace stondé nothing good,
Forthy to Christ which shed his
blood
For peace byseketh alle men.
Amen, Amen, Amen, Amen.

CONFESSIO AMANTIS.

Book I.

I may nought strecche up to the
heven
Min hond, ne setten al in even
This world, whiche ever is in bal-
aunce;
It stant nought in my suffisaunce
So greaté thingés to compásse.
But I mote lette it over passe
And treaten upon other thinges:
Forthý the stile of my writínges
Fro this day forth I thenké chaunge,
And speake of thinge is nought so
strange,
Whiche every kinde hath upon
honde,
And wherupon the world mote
stonde
And hath done sithen [1] it began
And shall while there is any man,
And that is Love; of whiche I mene
To treate, as after shall be sene,
In whiche there can no man him
reule
For Lovés lawe is out of reule
That of to moche or of to lite [2]
Wellnigh is every man to wite.[3]
And nethéles there is no man
In all this world so wise, that can
Of Lové temper the mesúre
But as it falleth in aventure.

[1] *Sithen*, since. [2] *Lite*, little.
[3] *To wite*, to blame.

For wit ne strengthé may nought
helpe
And he which ellés wolde him
yelpe [1]
Is rathest [2] throwen under foote,
Ther can no wight therof do bote.[3]
For yet was never such covíne [4]
That couth ordeine a medicíne
To thing which God in lawe of
kinde [5]
Hath set, for there may no man
finde
The righté salve for suche a sore.
It hath and shal be evermore
That Love is maister where he will,
There can no life make other skill,[6]
For where as ever him list to set
There is no might which him may
let.
But what shall fallen atté laste,
The sothé can no wisedom caste,
But as it falleth upon chaunce,
For if there ever was balaunce
Whiche of Fortúné stant governed,
I may well leve as I am lerned [7]
That Love hath that baláunce on
honde
Whiche wol no reson understonde.

[1] *Yelpe*, boast. [2] *Rathest*, soonest.
[3] *Bote*, remedy. [4] *Covíne*, contrivance.
[5] *Kinde*, Nature. [6] *Skill*, distinction.
[7] *Leve as I am lerned*, believe as I am taught.

For Love is blinde and may nought se,
Forthý there may no certeinté
Be sette upon his jugément.
But as the whele abouté went
He yeveth his graces undeserved,
And fro that man which hath him served
Ful ofte he taketh awey his fees;
As he that plaieth at the dies[1]
And therupon what shal befall
He not,[2] til that the chauncé fall
Where[3] he shall lese or he shal winne.
And thus full ofté men beginne
That if they wisten what it ment
They woldé chaunge all here entent.
And for to prove that it is so
I am my selfé one of tho[4]
Whiche to this scole am underfonge.[5]
For it is sithé go nought longe[6]
As for to speake of this matere
I may you telle, if ye woll here,
A wonder hap which me befelle,
That was to me bothe harde and felle,
Touchend of Love and his fortúne,
The which me liketh to commúne
And pleinly for to telle it oute
To hem that lovers ben aboute;
Fro point to pointe I wol declare
And writen of my woful care,
My woful day, my woful chaunce,
That men mow také rémembraúnce
Of that they shall here after rede.
For in good feith this wolde I rede,[7]
That every man ensample take
Of wisedom which is him betake,[8]
And that he wote of good apprise[9]
To teche it forth, for suche emprise

[1] *Dies*, dice. [2] *Not*, knows not.
[3] *Where*, whether. [4] *Tho*, them.
[5] *Underfonge*, received.
[6] Since not long ago.
[7] *Rede*, counsel. [8] *Betake*, entrusted.
[9] And that which he knows to be worth learning.

Is for to preise: and therfore I
Wol write and shewe all openly,
How love and I togider mette,
Wherof the worlde ensample fette
May[1] after this, whan I am go,
Of thilke unsely jolif wo,
Whose reulé stant out of the wey,
Now glad, and now gladnesse awey,
And yet it may nought be withstonde
For ought that men may understonde.
Upon the point that is befalle
Of love, in which that I am falle,
I thenké tellé my matere.
Now herken, who that woll it here,
Of my fortúne how that it ferde
This enderday,[2] as I forth ferde
To walke, as I you tellé may.
And that was in the moneth of May,
Whan every brid hath chose his make
And thenketh his merthés for to make
Of lové, that he hath acheved.
But so was I no thíng releved,
For I was further fro my love
Than erthe is fro the heven above.
And for to speke of any spede[3]
So wiste I me none other rede,[4]
But as it were a man forfare[5]
Unto the wood I gan to fare,
Nought for to singé with the briddes,
For whan I was the wood amiddes
I fonde a swoté grené pleine,
And there I gan my wo compleine
Wisshinge and wepinge all min one[6]
For other mirthés made I none.
So hard me was that ilké throwe,[7]
That ofte sithes[8] overthrowe

[1] *Ensample fette may*, may fetch example.
[2] *This enderday*, this past day, lately.
[3] *Spede*, success. [4] *Rede*, counsel.
[5] *Forfare*, undone.
[6] *All min one*, all by myself.
[7] *Throwe*, throe.
[8] *Ofte sithes*, many times.

To grounde I was, withouté brethe ;
And ever I wisshéd after dethe,
Whan I out of my peine awoke,
And caste up many a pitous loke
Unto the heven and saidé thus :
'O thou Cupíde, O thou Venús,
Thou god of love and thou goddesse,
Where is pité? where is mekenésse?
Now doth me[1] pleinly live or die,
For certés suche a maladie
As I now have, and longe have had,
It mighté make a wise man mad,
If that it shuldé longe endure.
O Venus, quene of lovés cure,
Thou life, thou lust, thou mannés hele,
Beholde my cause and my quarele
And yef me some part of thy grace,
So that I may finde in this place,
If thou be graciós or none !'
And with that worde I sawe anone
The Kinge of Love and Quené bothe.
But he, that king, with eyen wrothe
His chere aweiward fro me caste
And forthe he passéd atté laste
But nethéles er he forth wente
A firy dart me thought he hente[2]
And threwe it through min herté rote.[3]
In him fonde I none other bote,[4]
For lenger list him nought to dwelle.
But she, whiche is the source and welle
Of wele or wo that shal betide
To hem that loven, at that tide
Abode, but for to tellen here
She cast on me no goodly chere,
Thus nethéles to me she saide :
'What art thou, sonne?' And I abraide[5]

[1] *Doth me*, cause me to.
[2] *Hente*, seized.
[3] *Min herte rote*, the root of my heart.
[4] *Bote*, remedy.
[5] *Abraide*, started.

Right as a man doth out of slepe,
And therof toke she right good kepe[1]
And bad me nothing be adradde,
But for all that I was nought gladde,
For I ne sawe no causé why.
And eft[2] she asketh, what was I?

I saide : 'A caitif that lyth here.
What woldé ye my lady dere?
Shall I be hole or ellés die?'

She saidé : 'Telle thy maladie.
What is thy sore of which thou pleinest,
Ne hide it nought, for if thou feignest
I can do thee no medicíne.'

'Madame, I am a man of thine
That in thy Court have longé served
And axé that I have deserved,
Some wele after my longé wo.'

And she began to louré tho
And saidé : 'There be many of you
Faitours,[3] and so may be that thou
Art right suche one, and by faintise
Saist, that thou hast me do service.'
And nethéles she wisté wele
My word stood on an other whele
Withouten any faiterie.
But algate of my maladie
She bad me tell and say her trouthe.

'Madame, if ye wolde havé routhe,'
Quod I, 'than wolde I tellé you.'

'Say forth,' quod she, 'and telle me how,
Shewe me thy sikenesse every dele.'

'Madamé, that can I do wele,
Be so my life therto wol laste.'

With that her loke on me she caste
And saide : 'In aunter[4] if thou live
My wille is first, that thou be shrive ;

[1] *Kepe*, heed.
[2] *Eft*, again.
[3] *Faitours*, dissemblers.
[4] *In aunter*, if it happen.

And nethéles how that it is
I wot my selfe, but for all this
Unto my Prest which cometh anone
I wol thou telle it one and one,
Both al thy thought and al thy werke.
O Genius, min owné clerke,
Come forth, and here this mannés shrifte,'
Quod Venus tho. And I uplifte
Min hede with that, and gan beholde
The selfé Prest, whiche as she wolde
Was redy there and fet him doune
To heré my Confessiön.

This worthy prest, this holy man
To me spekend thus began
And saidé: "Benedicite
My sone, of the felicité
Of Love and eke of all the wo
Thou shalt be shrive of bothé two.
What thou er[1] this for lovés sake
Hast felt, let nothing be forsake;
Tel pleinly as it is befalle."

And with that worde I gan down falle
On knees, and with devoción
And with full great contrición
I saidé thanné! "Dominus
Min holy fader Genius,
So as thou haste experience
Of Lové, for whose reverence
Thou shalt me shriven at this time,
I pray thee let me nought mistime
My shrifté, for I am destourbed
In all min herte and so contourbed,
That I ne may my wittes gete;
So shal I moché thing foryete.[2]
But if thou wolt my shrifte oppose[3]
Fro point to pointe, than I suppose
There shall nothing be left behinde.
But now my wittés be so blinde,

[1] *Er*, ere. [2] *Foryete*, forget.
[3] *Oppose*, test by argument.

That I ne can my selfé teche."
Tho[1] he beganne anon to preche,
And with his wordés debonaire
He saidé to me softe and faire:
"My sone, I am assignéd here
Thy shrifté to oppose and here
By Venus the goddésse above,
Whose prest I am touchend of love.
"But nethéles for certain skill[2]
I mote algate[3] and nedés will
Nought only maké my spekinges
Of Lové, but of other thinges
That touchen to the cause of Vice.
For that belongeth to thoffice
Of Prest, whose ordre that I bere:
So that I wol nothing forbere
That I the Vices one and one
Ne shall thee shewen everichone,
Wherof thou might take evidence
To reulé with thy consciënce.
But of conclusiön finál
Conclude I wolde in speciáll
For Lové, whose servaúnt I am
And why the cause is that I cam.
So thenke I to do bothé two,—
First that[4] min ordre longeth to
The Vices for to telle a rewe;[5]
But nexte, above all other, shewe
Of Love I wol the propretés,
How that they stondé by degres
After the disposiciön
Of Venus, whose condiciön
I must folwe as I am holde,
For I with Love am al witholde,[6]
So that the lasse I am to wite,[7]
Though I ne conné but a lite[8]
Of other thingés that bene wise;
I am nought taught in suche a wise.

[1] *Tho*, then; from an indeclinable *thá*. When it means 'those,' it is from *thá*, plural of 'that.'
[2] *Skill*, discrimination.
[3] *Mote algate*, must always.
[4] That which belongs to my calling.
[5] *A rewe*, in row, in their order.
[6] *Witholde*, retained.
[7] *To wite*, to blame. [8] Know but a little.

For it is nought my comun use
To speke of vices and vertúse,
But all of Love and of his lore,
For Venus bokés of no more
Me techen, nouther text ne glose.
But for als moche as I suppose
It sit a Prest to be wel thewed [1]
And shame it is if he be lewed,[2]
Of my presthode after the forme
I wol thy shrifté so enforme,
That at the lasté thou shalt here
The Vices, and to thy matere
Of Love I shal hem so remeve
That thou shalt knowé what they
meve.
For what a man shall axe or saine
Touchend of shrifte, it mot be
pleine ;[3]
It nedeth nought to make it queinte,[4]
For Trouth his wordés wol nought
peinte.
That I wol axe of thee forthý,
My sone, it shal be so pleinly
That thou shalt knowe and under-
stonde
The pointes of Shrift how that they
stonde."

[*The Senses: Sight and Hearing.*]

Betwene the life and death I
herde
This Prestés tale er I answérde ;
And than I praid him for to say
His will, and I it wolde obey
After the forme of his apprise.
Tho spake he to me in such wise
And bad me, that I sholdé shrive
As touchende of my wittés five,
And shapé that they were amended
Of that I haddé hem mispended.

[1] *Well thewed*, of good manners.
[2] *Lewed*, unlearned as the common people.
[3] *Pleine*, plain.
[4] *Queinte*, ingeniously elaborated.

For tho [1] be properly the gates,
Through which as to the hert
algates [2]
Cometh all thing unto the feire
Which may the mannes soule em-
peire.[3]
And now this matter is brought in,
"My sone, I thenké first beginne
To wit [4] how that thin eye hath
stonde,
The whiche is as I understonde
The mosté principál of alle
Through whom that peril may be-
falle.
And for to speke in Lovés kinde,
Full many suche a man may finde
Whiche ever caste aboute here eye
To loke if that they might aspie
Ful ofté thing which hem ne touch-
eth,
But only that here herte soucheth [5]
In hindringe of an other wight.
And thus ful many a worthy knight
And many a lusty lady bothe
Have be full ofté sithés wrothe ;
So that an eye is as a thefe
To Love, and doth ful great mes-
chéfe ;
And also for his owné part
Ful ofté thilké firy dart
Of lové, which that ever brenneth,
Through him [6] into the herté ren-
neth.
And thus a mannés eyé ferst
Him selfé greveth altherwerst,[7]
And many a timé that he knoweth
Unto his owné harme it groweth.
My soné, herken now forthý
A talé, to be ware therby

[1] *Tho*, those. [2] *Algates*, always.
[3] *Empeire*, impair, injure.
[4] *To wit*, to know.
[5] *Soucheth*, suspecteth.
[6] *Him*, (the eye). 'It' was used only in the nominative and accusative. 'His' and 'him' are both masculine and neuter.
[7] *Altherwerst*, worst of all.

Thin eyé for to kepe and warde,
So that it passé nought his warde.
"Ovidé telleth in his boke
Ensample touchend of misloke
And saith, how whilom ther was one
A worthy lord, whiche Acteon
Was hote,[1] and he was cousin nigh
To him that Thebés first on high
Upsetté,[2] which king Cadmé hight.
This Acteón, as he wel might,
Above all other cast his chere,[3]
And used it from yere to yere
With houndés and with greté hornes
Among the wodés and the thornes
To make his hunting and his chace;
Where him best thought, in every place,
To findé gamen in his way,
There rode he for to hunte and play.
So him befelle upon a tide[4]
On his hunting as he gan ride
In a foréste alone he was;
He sigh[5] upon the grené gras
The fairé fresshé flourés springe;
He herd among the levés singe
The throstel with the nightingale.
Thus, er he wist, into a dale
He came, wher was a litel pleine
All rounde abouté wel beseine
With busshes grene and cedres high,—
And there within he caste his eye.
Amid the plaine he saw a welle
So fairé there might no man telle,
In which Diana naked stood,
To bathe and play her in the flood,
With many a nimphé which her serveth.
But he his eye awey ne swerveth
Fro heré, which was naked all.
And she was wonder wroth withall,
And him, as she which was goddésse,
Forshope[1] anone, and the likenesse
She made him him taken of an herte,
Which was tofore his houndés sterte,
That ronné besilich aboute
With many an horne and many a route,
That maden mochel noise and crie:
And atté laste unhappilie
This hert his owné houndes slough
And him for vengeaunce all todrough.[2]
"Lo now, my soné, what it is
A man to caste his eye amis,
Which Acteón hath dere abought;
Beware forthý[3] and do it nought.
For ofté, who that hedé toke,
Better is to winké than to loke.
And for to proven it is so
Ovidé the poete also
A talé, whiche to this matere
Accordeth, saith, as thou shalt here.
In Methamor[4] it telleth thus,
How that a lord whiche Phorceus
Was hoté,[5] haddé doughters thre.
But upon their nativité
Such was the constellaciön,
That out of mannés naciön
For kindé they be so miswent,
That to the likenésse of a serpént
They weré bothe, and so that one
Of hem was clepéd Stellibone,
That other suster Suriale,
The thrid, as telleth in the tale,
Medusa hight; and nethéles
Of comun namé Gorgonés
In every contre there about,
As monstres whiché that men doute,[6]

[1] *Hote*, called.
[2] *Upsette*, set up.
[3] *Cast his chere*, lifted his face.
[4] *Upon a tide*, upon a time.
[5] *Sigh*, saw.

[1] *Forshope*, transformed.
[2] *All to-drough*, pulled to pieces.
[3] *Forthy*, therefore.
[4] *Methamor*, (Ovid's) Metamorphoses.
[5] *Was hote*, was called.
[6] *Doute*, fear.

Men clepen[1] hem ; and but one eye
Among hem thre in purpartie[2]
They had of which they mighté se,
Now hathe it this, nowe hath it
she.
After that cause and nede it ladde
By throwés eche of hem it hadde.[3]
A wonder thing yet more amis
There was, wherof I telle al this :
What man on hem his cheré caste[4]
And hem behelde, he was als faste
Out of a man into a stone
Forshape,[5] and thus ful many one
Deceivéd were, of that they wolde
Misloké where that they ne shulde.
But Perseus that worthy knight,
Whom Pallas of her greté might
Halpe, and toke him a shield therto,
And eke the god Mercúry also
Lent him a swerde, he, as it fell,
Beyond Athlans the highé hill
These monstres sought, and there
he fonde
Diversé men of thilké londe
Through sight of hem mistornéd
were
Stondend as stonés here and there.
But he,—which wisdome and prow-
ésse
Hath of the god and the goddesse,—
The shielde of Pallas gan embrace,
With which he covereth sauf[6] his
face,
Mercuries swerde and out he
drough,
And so he bare him that he slough
These dredfull monstres allé thre.
"Lo now, my sone, avisé the,
That thou thý sight nought misuse ;
Cast nought thin eye upon Meduse

1 *Clepen*, name. 2 *Purpartie*, share.
3 As cause and need directed, each of them had it at times.
4 *His chere caste*, turned his face.
5 *Forshape*, transformed.
6 *Sauf*, safely.

That thou be tornéd into stone.
For so wise man was never none
But if he woll his eyé kepe
And take of foul delite no kepe,[1]
That he with lusté nis[2] ofte nome
Through strengthe of love, and over-
come.
Of mislokinge how it hath ferde,
As I have told, now hast thou herde.

"My godé soné, take good hede,
And over this yet I thee rede,[3]
That thou beware of thin hering,
Which to the herté the tiding
Of many a vanité hath brought
To tarie with[4] a mannés thought.
And nethéles good is to here
Such thing, wherof a man may lere
That[5] to vertue is accordaúnt ;
And toward all the remenaúnt
Good is to torne his eré fro,
For elles but a man do so
Him may ful ofté misbefalle.
I rede ensample amongés alle,
Wherof to kepé wel an ere
It oughté put a man in fere.
"A serpent, which that aspidis
Is clepéd, of his kinde hath this,
That he the stone noblést of alle
The which that men carbuncle calle
Berethin his heed above on heighte
For which whan that a man by
sleighte,
The stone to winne and him to
daunte
With his carecte[6] him wolde en-
chaunte,
Anone as he perceiveth that,
He lith down his one ere al plat
Unto the ground, and halt it faste,
And eke that other ere als faste

1 *No kepe*, no heed. 2 *Nis*, is not.
3 In addition to this I counsel you.
4 *To tarie with*, wherewith to corrupt, French 'tarer.'
5 Learn that which.
6 *Carecte*, magic spell.

He stoppeth with his tail so sore,
That he the wordés lasse or more
Of his enchauntément ne hereth.
And in this wise him selfe he skiereth,[1]
So that he hath the wordés weived[2]
And thus his ere is nought deceived.
"An other thing who that recordeth
Lyke unto this ensample accordeth,
Whiche in the tale of Troye I finde.
Sirenés of a wonder kinde
Ben monstres, as the bokés tellen,
And in the Greté See[3] they dwellen,
Of body bothe and of viságe
Like unto women of yonge age
Up fro the navel on high they be,
And down benethe, as men may se,
They bere of fisshes the figúre.
And over this, of such natúre
They ben, that with so swete a steven[4]
Like to the melodie of heven
In womannishé vois they singe,
With notés of so great likínge,
Of suche mesúre, of suche musíke,
Wherof the shippes they beswike[5]
That passen by the costés there.
For whan the shipmen lay an ere
Unto the vois, in here avis[6]
They wene it be a paradis,
Whiche after is to hem an helle.
For reson may nought with hem dwelle
Whan they the greté lustés[7] here,
They conné nought here shippes stere;
So besilich upon the note
They herken and in such wise assote,[8]

[1] *Skiereth*, secureth. [2] *Weived*, set aside.
[3] *The Grete See*, was the name of the Mediterranean.
[4] *Steven*, voice. [5] *Beswike*, betray.
[6] *Here avis*, their opinion.
[7] *Lustes*, delight.
[8] *Assote*, become besotted.

That they here righté cours and weie
Foryete, and to their ere obeie,
And sailen till it so befalle
That they into the perill falle
Where as the shippés ben to-drawe
And they ben with the monstres slawe.
But fro this peril nethéles
With his wisdóm king Ulixés
Escapeth and it over passeth,
For he to-fore the hond[1] compásseth
That no man of his compaignie
Hath power unto that folie
His eré for no lust to caste.
For he hem stoppéd allé faste,
That non of hem may here hem sing.
So whan they comen forth sailíng,
There was such governaunce on honde
That they the monstres have withstonde,
And slain of hem a great partie.
Thus was he sauf with his navie
This wisé king through governaunce.
"Herof, my sone, in rémembraúnce,
Thou might ensample taken here
As I have tolde, and what thou here
Be wel ware, and yef no credence
But if[2] thou se more evidence.
For if thou woldest také kepe[3]
And wisely couthest warde and kepe
Thine eye and ere, as I have spoke,
Than haddest thou the gatés stoke[4]
Fro such folý as cometh to winne
Thin hertés wit whiche is withinne.
Wherof, that now thy love excedeth
Mesúre, and many a peiné bredeth:

[1] *To-fore the hond*, before hand.
[2] *But if*, unless.
[3] *Take kepe*, take heed.
[4] *Stoke fro*, barred against.

But if thou couthest sette in reule
Tho two, the thre were eth [1] to reule.
Forthy as of thy wittés five
I wol as nowe no moré shrive,
But only of these ilké two.
Tel me, therfore, if it be so,—
Hast thou thine eyé nought mis-
throwe?"
"My fader yea, I am beknowe,
I have hem cast upon Meduse,
Therof I may me nought excuse.
Min hert is growén into stone,
So that my lady there upon
Hath suche a printe of Lové grave,
That I can nought my selfé save.'
'What saist thou sone, as of thin
ere?"
"My fader, I am gilty of there,
For whanne I my lady here,
My wit with that hath lost his stere.
I do nought as Ulixes dede,
But falle anon upon the stede [2]
Where as I se my lady stonde.
And there I do you understonde [3]
I am to-pulléd in my thought,
So that of reson leveth [4] nought
Wherof that I me may defende."
"My godé sone, God the amende.
For as me thenketh by thy speche
Thy wittés ben right far to seche.
As of thin ere and of thin eye
I wol no moré specifie,
But I woll axen over this
Of other thing how that it is.

[*Of the Seven Deadly Sins: and* PRIDE, *the First of them.*]

My sone, as I thee shall enforme,
There ben yet of another forme
Of Dedly Vices, Seven applied,
Wherof the herte is ofté plied [1]
To thing which after shal him greve.
The first of hem thou shalt beleve
Is Pridé, whiche is principall,
And hath with him in speciall
Ministrés fivé ful divérse,
Of which as I thee shal reherse
The first is said Ypocrisie.
If thou art of his compaignie
Tel forth, my sone, and shrive thee
clene."
"I wote nought, fader, what ye
mene,
But this I woldé you beseche,
That ye me by somweié teche
What is to ben an ypocrite.
And than if I be for to wite [2]
I wol beknowen [3] as it is."
"My sone, an ypocrite is this,—
A man which feigneth consciénce
As though it were al innocénce
Without, and is nought so withinne;
And doth so, for he wolde winne
Of his desire the vein estate:
And whan he cometh anone thereat,
He sheweth thanné what he was;
The corne is tornéd into gras,
That was a rose is than a thorne,
And he that was a lamb beforne
Is than a wolfe; and thus malíce
Under the colour of justíce
Is had, and, as the people telleth,
These Ordres witen [4] where he
dwelleth
As he that of her [5] counseil is;
And thilké world, which they er this
Forsoken, he draweth in ayeine;
He clotheth richesse, as men saine,
Under the simplest of pouérte
And doth to seme of great deserte

1 *Eth*, easy. 'The two' are sight and hearing, which have been discussed; if you could rule those two of the Five Senses, it would be easy to rule the other three. Therefore of the rest of the five, &c.
2 *Stede*, place.
3 Make you to understand.
4 *Leveth*, remaineth.

1 *Plied*, bent.
2 *To wite*, to blame.
3 *Beknowen*, acknowledge and confess.
4 These religious orders know.
5 *Her*, their.

Thing whiche is litel worth withinne,
He saith, in open, fy ! to sinne,
And in secré there is no vice
Of which that he nis a norſce.[1]
And ever his chere is sobre and softe,
And where he goth he blesseth ofte.
Wherof the blindé world he drecheth,[2]
But yet all only he ne strecheth
His reule upon religiön.
But next to that condicion,
In suche as clepe hem holy cherche,
It sheweth eke howe he can werche
Amonge tho widé furréd hodes
To geten hem the worldés goodes.
And they have self ben thilké same
That setten most the world in blame,
But yet in contraire of here lore
There is nothíng they loven more ;
So that, feignend of light, they werke
The dedés whiche are inward derke,
And thus this double Ypocrisie
With his devoute apparancie,
A viser set upon his face
Wherof toward this worldés grace
He seméth to be right wel thewed,
And yet his herte is all beshrewed
But nethéles he stant beleved
And hath his purpos ofte acheved
Of worship and of worldés welthe,
And taketh it as who saith by stelthe
Through coverture of his fallas.[3]
And right so in semblable cas
This Vice hath eke his officers
Among these other seculers
Of greté men,—for of the smale
As for to accompt he set no tale,[4]
But they that passen the comúne
With suche him liketh[5] to comune ;

[1] *Norice*, nurse.
[2] *Drecheth*, troubleth.
[3] *Coverture of his fallas*, concealment of his deceit.
[4] *Set no tale*, makes no account.
[5] *Him liketh*, it pleases him.

And where he saith he wol socoure
The people, there he wol devoure.
For now-a-day is many one
Which speketh of Peter and of John
And thenketh Judas in his herte ;
There shall no worldés good asterte[1]
His honde, and yet he yeveth almesse
And fasteth ofte and hereth messe
With *mea culpa*, whiche he saith ;
Upon his brest ful ofte he leith
His hond and cast upwárd his eye,
As though he Cristés facé seie,
So that it semeth atté sight
As he alone al other might
Rescué with his holy bede.[2]
But yet his herte in other stede
Among his bedés most devoute
Goth in the worldés cause aboute,
How that he might his warison[3]
Encrese, and in comparison
There ben lovérs of suche a sorte,
That feignen hem an humble porte,
And al is but Ypocrisie,
Which with deceipte and flaterie
Hath many a worthy wife beguiled.
For whan he hath his tunge affiled
With softé speche and with lesínge
Than with his fals pitóus lokinge
He woldé make a woman wene
To gon upon the fairé grene,
Whan that she falleth in the mire.
For if he may have his desire,
How so falle of the remenaunt,
He halt[4] no worde of covenaunt,
But er the timé that he spede
There is no sleighte at thilké nede,
Which any lovés faitour[5] may,
That he ne put it in assay
As him belongeth for to done.
The colour of the reiny mone

[1] *Asterte*, escape from. [2] *Bede*, prayer.
[3] *Warison*, advantage.
[4] *Halt*, holds. [5] *Faitour*, dissembler.

With medicine upon his face
He set, and than he axeth grace,
As he which hath sikenessé feigned;
Whan his viságe is so disteigned,
With eye up cast on her he siketh
And many a continaunce he piketh [1]
To bringen her into beleve
Of thing which that he wold acheve,
Wherof he bereth the pale hewe,
And for he woldé semé trewe
He maketh him sike, whan he is
heil.
But whan he bereth lowest sail,
Than is he swiftest to beguile
The woman which that ilké while
Set upon him feith or credénce.
"My sone, if thou thy consciénce
Entaméd [2] hast in such a wise,
In shrifté thou the might avise
And telle it me, if it be so."
"Min holy fader, certés no.
As for to feigné such sikenésse
It nedeth nought, for this witnésse
I take of God, that my coráge [3]
Hath ben more sike than my viságe.
And eke this may I well avowe,
So lowé couthe I never bowe
To feigne humilité withoute
That me ne listé better loute
With all the thoughtés of min herte.
For that thing shall me never
asterte,
I speke as to my lady dere,
To make her any feignéd chere;
God wot well there I lié nought,
My chere hath been such as my
thought.
For in good feith, this leveth wele, [4]
My wil was better a thousand dele
Than any cheré that I couthe. [5]
"But sire, if I have in my youthe
Done other wise in other place,
I put me therof in your grace.
For this excusen I ne shall,
That I have ellés over all
To Love and to his compaignie
Be plein without ypocrisie.
But there is one, the whiche I serve,
All though I may no thank deserve,
To whom yet never unto this day
I saide onlich or 'ye' or 'nay,'
But if it so were in my thought
As touchend other say I nought
That I nam somdele for to wite [1]
Of that ye clepe an ypocrite."
"My sone, it sit wel every wight
To kepe his worde in trouth upright
Towardés Love in allé wise.
For who that wold him wel avise
What hath befalle in this matére,
He shuldé nought with feignéd chere
Deceivé Love in no degre.
To Love is every herté fre,
But in deceipt if that thou feignest
And therupon thy luste atteignest,
That thou hast wonné with thy wile,
Though it thee liké for a while,
Thou shalt it afterward repente.
And for to provê min entente
I finde ensample in a cronique
Of hem that Lové so beswike. [2]
It fell by oldé daiés thus,
Whil themperour Tiberius
The monarchie of Romé ladde,
There was a worthy Romain hadde
A wife, and she Pauliné hight,
Which was to every mannés sight
Of al the cité the fairést
And as men saiden eke the best.
It is and hath ben ever yit
That so strong is no mannés wit,
Which through beauté ne may be
drawe
To love, and stonde under the lawe

1 *Piketh*, pitches, sets up.
2 *Entamed*, subdued.
3 *Corage*, disposition of the heart.
4 Believe well.
5 Than any face that I could put on.

1 That I am not some part to blame.
2 *Beswike*, deceive.

Of thilké boré [1] freilé kinde,
Which maketh the hertés eyen blinde,
Where no resón may be communed.
And in this wisé stode fortúned
Of whiche I wol this talé mene,
This wife, whiche in her lustés grene
Was faire and fressh and tender of age.
She may nought letté the corage
Of him that wol on her assote.[2]
There was a Duke, and he was hote [3]
Mundus, which had in his baillie [4]
To ledé the chevalérie
Of Rome, and was a worthy knight.
But yet he was nought of such might
The strength of lové to withstonde,
That he ne was so brought to honde,
That malgré where [5] he wol or no
This yongé wife he loveth so,
That he hath put all his assay
To winné thing which he ne may
Get of her graunt in no manere,
By yefte of gold, ne by praiere.
And whan he sigh,[6] that by no mede [7]
Toward her love he mighté spede,
By sleighté feignend than he wrought:
And therupon he him bethought,
How that there was in the cité
A temple of suche auctorité,
To which with great devociön
The noble women of the towne
Most comunlich a pelerináge
Gone for to prayé thilke ymáge,
Which the goddesse of childing is
And clepéd was by name Ysis.
And in her temple thanné were
To reule and to minístre there

1 *Bore*, born—born of that frail nature.
2 *Assote*, dote.
3 *Hote*, called.
4 *Baillie*, office.
5 *Where*, whether.
6 *Sigh*, saw.
7 *Mede*, means, mode.

After the lawé which was tho,
Above all other prestés two.
This Duke, which thought his lové get,
Upon a day hem two to mete
Hath bede, and they come at his heste,
Where that they had a riché feste.
And after mete in privé place
This lord, which wold his thank purcháce,
To eche of hem yaf thanne a yift
And spaké so by waie of shrift,
He drough hem into his covíne [1]
To helpe and shape, how he Pauline
After his lust deceivé might.
And they her [2] trouthés bothé plight,
That they by night her shulden winne
Into the temple, and he therinne
Shall have of her all his entent.
And thus accorded forth they went.
Now list, through which Ypocrisie
Ordeignéd was the trecherie,
Wherof this lady was deceived.
These prestés hadden wel conceived,
That she was of great holinesse.
And with a counterfeit simplesse,
Which hid was in a fals corâge,
Feignend an hevenly messáge
They cam and saide unto her thus:
Pauliné, the god Anubus
Hath sent us bothé prestés here
And saith, he wol to the appere
By nightés time him selfe alone,
For love he hath to thy persone.
And therupon he hath us bede,
That we in Ysis temple a stede
Honestly for thee purveie,
Where thou by night as we thee saie
Of him shalt take a visión.

1 *Covine*, secret treacherous agreement.
2 *Her*, their.

For upon thy condiciόn,
The whiche is chaste and full of feith,
Suche price, as he us tolde, he leith,
That he wol stonde of thin accorde;
And for to beare herof recorde
He sende us hider bothé two.
Glad was her innocéncé tho
Of suché wordés as she herd,
With humble chere and thus answerd
And saidé, that the goddés will
She was all redy to fulfill,
That by her husébondés leve
She wolde in Ysis temple at eve
Upon her goddés grace abide
To serven him the nightés tide.
The prestés tho gon home ayeine,
And she goth to her sovereine;
Of goddes will and as it was [1]
She tolde him all the plainé cas,
Wherof he was deceivéd eke,
And bad that she her shuldé meke
All hole unto the goddés heste.
And thus she, which was all honeste
To godward, after her entent
At night unto the temple went
Where that the falsé prestés were.
And they recefvén her there
With suche a token of holinesse,
As though they seén a goddesse;
And all within in privé place
A softé bedde of largé space
They haddé made and encortíned,
Where she was afterward engíned.[2]
But she, whiche all honóur supposeth,
The falsé prestés than opposeth
And axeth by what observaúnce
She mighté most to the plesaúnce
Of god that nightés reulé kepe.
And they her bidden for to slepe

[1] And she told all the plain case, of how it was the god's will. 'And' was not always placed at the beginning of a clause.
[2] *Engined*, trapped by a crafty contrivance.

Liggend upon the bedde a loft,
For, so they said, al still and soft
God Anubus her wolde awake.
The counseil in this wisé take
The prestés fro this lady gone.
And she that wiste of guilé none
In the manér as it was said
To slepe upon the bedde is leid,
In hopé that she sholde acheve
Thing which stode than upon beleve
Fulfilléd of all holinesse.
But she hath failéd as I gesse,
For in a closet fasté by
The Duke was hid so privelý,
That she him mighté nought perceive.
And he that thoughté to deceive
Hath suche array upon him nome,[1]
That whan he wold unto her come
It shuldé semen at her eye,
As though she verriliché seie
God Anubus, and in suche wise
This Ypocrite of his queintise
Awaiteth ever til she slept.
And than out of his place he crept
So stillé, that she nothing herde,
And to the bed stalkénd he ferde
And sodeinly, er she it wiste,
Beclipt in armés he her kiste,
Wherof in womannisshé drede
She woke and niste what to rede.[2]
But he with softé wordés milde
Comforteth her and saith, with childe
He wolde her make in suche a kinde,
That al the world shall have in minde
The worshippe of that ilké sone;
For he shall with the goddes wone [3]
And ben him selfe a god also.
With suché wordés and with mo,

[1] *Nome*, taken.
[2] Knew not what counsel to take.
[3] *Wone*, dwell.

The which he feigneth in his speche,
This ladies wit was al to seche,[1]
As she which alle trouthe weneth.
But he, that all untrouthé meneth,
With blindé talés so her ladde,
That all his will of her he hadde.
And whan him thought it was inough,
Ayein the day he him withdrough
So prively, that she ne wiste
Where he be come, but as him liste
Out of the temple he goth his way.
And she began to bid and pray,
Upon the baré ground knelende,
And after that made her offrende
And to the prestés yeftés great
She yaf, and homeward by the strete
The Duke her mette and saidé thus:
'The mighty god, whiche Anubus
Is hote, he savé the Pauline,
For thou art of his discipline
So holy, that no mannés might
May do that he hath do to night,
Of thing which thou hast ever
eschued.
But I his grace have so pursued,
That I was made his lieutenaúnt.
Forthy by way of covenaúnt
Fro this day forth I am all thine,
And if thee liké to be mine
That stant upon thin owné wille.'
She herde his tale and bare it stille
And home she went as it befell
Into her chambre and there she fell
Upon her bed to wepe and crie
And saide: O derke Ypocrisie,
Through whose dissimulatiön
Of false ymaginatiön
I am thus wickedly deceived!
But that I have it apperceived
I thonke unto the goddés alle.
For though it onés be befalle
I shall never eft while that I live,
And thilke avow to god I yive.
And thus wepéndé she compleigneth
Her fairé face and all disteigneth
With wofull terés of her eye,
So that upon this agonie
Her husébónde is inné come
And sigh[1] how she was overcome
With sorwe, and axeth her what
her eileth.
And she with that her self beweileth
Well moré than she didde afore
And said: 'Alas, wifehode is lore
In me which whilom was honést,
I am none other than a beste
Nowe I defouléd am of two!'
And as she mighté speaké tho
Ashaméd with a pitous onde,[2]
She tolde unto her husébonde
The soth of all the holé tale,
And in her speché dead and pale
She swouneth well nigh to the laste.
And he her in his armés faste
Upheld and ofté swore his oth,
That he with her is nothing wroth,
For wel he wot she may there
nought.
But nethéles within his thought
His hert stode in a sory plite
And said, he wolde of that despite
Be vengéd how so ever it falle;
And send unto his frendes alle,
And whan they weré come infere,[3]
He tolde hem upon this matere
And axeth hem what was to done.
And they aviséd weré sone
And said, it thought hem for the
beste
To setté first his wife in reste
And after pleiné to the king
Upon the matter of this thing.
Tho was his wofull wife comfórted

[1] *All to seek*, all away, as she who believes all to be truth. 'To seek' was a phrase long used to represent want of knowledge. So the elder brother in Milton's Comus—
'I do not think my sister so *to seek*
Or so undisciplined in virtue's book.'

[1] *Sigh*, saw.
[2] *Onde*, anger.
[3] *Infere*, together.

By alle waiés and dispórted,
Til that she was somdele amended.
And thus a day or two dispended
The thriddé day she goth to pleine
With many a worthy citezeine
And he with many a citezein.
Whan themperoúr it herde saine
And knew the falsehed of the vice,
He said he woldé do justíce.
And first he let the prestes take,
And for they shulde it nought forsake[1]
He put hem into questión.
But they of the suggestión
Ne couthé nought a word refuse,
But for they wold hem self excuse
The blame upon the Duke they laide.
But thereayein the counseil saide,
That they be nought excuséd so
For he is one and they be two,
And two have moré wit than one,
So thilke excusément was none.
And over that, was said hem eke
That whan men wolden vertue seke
Men shulden it in the prestés finde,
Their ordre is of so high a kinde,
That they be dívisers[2] of the wey.
Forthý if any man forswey[3]
Through hem, they be nought excusáble,
And thus by lawé resonáble
Among the wisé jugés there
The prestés bothé dampned were,
So that the privé trecherý
Hid under false Ypocrisie
Was thanne all openliché shewed,
That many a man hem hath beshrewed.
And whan the prestés weren dede,
The temple of thilk horríble dede
They thoughten purge and thilke ymage

[1] *Forsake*, deny. [2] *Divisers*, tellers.
[3] *Forswey*, swerve aside, go wrong.

Whose causé was the pelrinágе
They drowen out and also faste
Fer into Tiber they it caste,
Where the rivér it hath defied.[1]
And thus the temple purified
They have of thilke horríble sinne,
Which was that timé do[2] therinne.
Of this point such was the divise.
But of the duke was otherwise;
For[3] he with lové was bestad
His dome was nought so hardé lad.
For lové put resón awey
And can nought se the righté wey.
And by this cause he was respíted,
So that the deth him was acquíted,
But for all that he was exiled,
For he his love had so beguiled,
That he shall never come ayeine.
For he that is to trouth unpleine
He may nought failen of vengeaunce
And eke to také remembraunce
Of that Ypocrisie hath wrought.
On other half, men shuldé nought
To lightly leve all that they here,
But thanné shulde a wiseman stere
The ship, whan suché windés blowe;
For first though they beginné lowe,
At endé they be nought meváble,[4]
But all to-broken mast and cable,
So that the ship, with sodain blast
Whan men leste wene, is overcast.
As now full ofte a man may se,
And of old time how it hath be
I finde a great experience,
Wherof to take an evidence
Good is, and to beware also
Of the períll er him be woo.[5]

"Of hem that ben so derk withinne
At Troie also if we beginne,

[1] *Defied*, digested. So in 'The Vision of Piers Plowman,' 'wyn the roste to defye.'
[2] At that time done.
[3] *For*, because.
[4] *Mevable*, to be moved.
[5] Before woe betides him.

Ypocrisie it hath betraied.
For whan the Grekes had all assaied
And foundé that by no bataile
Ne by no siege it might availe
The town to winné through prowesse,
This Vicé feignéd of simplesse,
Through sleight of Calcas and of Crise
It wan by such a maner wise :—
An horse of brass they let do forge
Of suche entaile,[1] of suche a forge,
That in this world was never man
That such an other werk began.
The crafty werkeman Epius
It made, and for to tellé thus,
The Grekes that thoughten to beguile
The king of Troie in thilké while
With Antenór and with Enee,
That weré bothe of the citee
And of the counseil the wisést,
The richest and the mightiest,
In privé placé so they trete
With fair beheste and yeftes grete
Of gold, that they hem have engínod
To-gider and whan they be covined,
They feignen for to maké pees,
And under that yet nethéless
They shopen the destructión
Bothe of the king and of the town.
And thus the falsé pees was take
Of hem of Grece and undertake,
And therupon they founde a way,
Where strengthé mighté nought away,
That sleighté shuldé helpé thanne,
And of an inche a largé spanne,[2]
By colour of the pees they made :
And tolden how they weré glade
Of that they stoden in-accorde,
And, for it shall ben of recórde,

[1] *Entaile*, carving.
[2] An ell should be got out of an inch under outward show of the peace made.

Unto the king the Gregois saiden
By way of love and thus they praiden,—
As they that wolden his thank deserve,
A sacrifice unto Minerve
The pees to kepe in good entent
They must offre, or that they went.
The King, counseiléd in the cas
By Antenór and Eneás,
Therto hath yoven his assent.
So was the pleiné trouthé blent [1]
Through counterfeit Ypocrisie.
Of that they shulden sacrifie
The Grekes under the holinesse
Anone with alle besinesse
Here hors of brass let fairé dight,
Which was to sene a wonder sight.
For it was trappéd of him selve
And had of smalé whelés twelve,
Upon the whiché men inowe
With craft toward the town it drowe,
And goth glistrénd ayein the sonne.
Tho was there joie inough begonne,
For Troie in great devoción
Came also with processión
Ayein this noble sacrifice
With great honóur, and in this wise
Unto the gatés they it broughte :
But of here entré whan they soughte,
The gatés weren all to smale.
And therupon was many a tale ;
But for the worship of Minerve,
To whom they comen for to serve,
They of the town which understood
That all this thing was done for good,
For pees, wherof that they ben glade,
The gatés that Neptunus made
A thousand winter ther to-fore
They have anone to-broke and tore,
The strongé wallés down they bete,
So that into the largé strete

[1] *Blent*, blinded.

This horse with great solempnité
Was brought withinné the cité,
And offred with great reverence,
Which was to Troie an evidence
Of love and pees for evermo.
The Gregois token levé tho
With all the holé felaship,
And forth they wenten into ship,
And crossen sail, and made hem yare,[1]
Anone as though they wolden fare.[2]
But whan the blacké winter night
Withouté mone or sterré light
Bederkéd hath the water stronde,
Al privély they gone to londe
Full arméd out of the navie.
Sinon, whiche made was here espie
Withinné Troie, as was conspired,
Whan timé was, a tokne hath fired,
And they with that here waié holden
And comen in, right as they wolden,
There as the gaté was to-broke.
The purpose was full take and spoke
Er any man may teké kepe,
Whil that the citee was aslepe;
They slowen al that was withinne
And token what they mighten winne
Of such good as was suffisaunt
And brenden[3] up the remenaunt.
And thus come out the trecherie,
Which under false Ypocrisie
Was hid, and they that wendé[4] pees
Tho mighten findé no releese
Of thilké swerd whiche al devoureth.
Full ofte and thus the swеté soureth
Whan it is knowé to the taste,
He spilleth many a worde in waste
That shal with such a people trete,
For whan he weneth most beyete[5]
Than is he shapé most to lese.

[1] *Yare*, ready.
[2] As though they would go.
[3] *Brenden*, burnt.
[4] *Wendé*, hoped for, expected.
[5] When he expects to get most.

And right so if a woman chese[1]
Upon the wordés that she hereth,
Som man whan he most true appereth
Than is he furthest fro the trouthe.
But yet full ofte, and that is routhe,
They speden that ben most untrue
And loven every day a newe,
Wherof the life is after lothe
And love hath causé to be wrothe.
But what man that his lust desireth
Of love and therupon conspireth
With wordés feignéd to deceive,
He shall nought failé to receive
His peine as it is ofté sene.
"Forthy my sone, as I the mene,
It sit thee well to taken hede,
That thou escheue of thy manhede
Ypocrisie and his semblaunt,
That thou ne be nought deceivaunt
To make a woman to beleve
Thing whiche is nought in thy beleve.
For in suche feint Ypocrisie
Of Love is all the trecherie,
Through which love is deceivéd ofte.
For feignéd semblaunt is so softe,
Unnethés[2] Lové may be ware.
Forthy my sone, as I well dare,
I chargé the to flee that vice,
That many a woman hath made nice,
But loke thou delé nought withall."—
"Iwis[3] my fader, no more I shall."—
"Now, soné, kepe that thou hast swore.
For this that thou hast herd before
Is said the firsté point of Pride.
And next upon that other side

[1] *Chese*, choose.
[2] *Unnethés*, not easily.
[3] *Iwis* ("gewis") certainly.

To shrive and speken over this,
Touchend of Pridé, yet there is
The Point Secónde I thee behote,[1]
Which Inobedience is hote.

Inobedience.

This Vice of Inobedience
Ayein the reule of consciénce
All that is humble he disaloweth,
That he toward his God ne boweth
After the lawés of his heste.[2]
Nought as a man, but as a beste
Whiche goth upon his lustés wilde
So goth this proudé Vice unmilde,
That he disdeigneth allé lawe.
He not[3] what is to be felawe,
And servé may he nought for pride.
So is he ledde on every side
And is that selve of whom men speke,
Which woll nought bowe er that he breke.
I not[3] if Lové might him plie,[4]
For ellés for to justifie
His herte, I not[3] what might availe.
Forthý[5] my sone, of suche entaile
If that thin herté be disposed,
Telle out and let it nought be glosed.
For if that thou unbuxome[6] be
To love, I not[3] in what degre
Thou shalt thy goodé worde acheve."—
"My fader, ye shal well beleve,
The yongé whelpe which is affaited[7]
Hath nought his maister better awaited
To couché whan he saith: go lowe,
Than I anone as I may knowe
My lady will me bowé more.

1 *Behote*, promised.
2 *Heste*, commandment.
3 *Not*, knows not.
4 *Plie*, bend.
5 *Forthý*, therefore.
6 *Unbuxome*, unbending, un-bow-some.
7 *Affaited*, bound to some object, tamed.

But other while I grucché sore
Of somé thingés that she doth,
Wherof that I woll tellé soth.
For of two pointes I am bethought,
That though I wolde I mighté nought
Obeie unto my ladies hest;
But I dare maké this behest
Sauf only of that ilké two,
I am unbuxome of no mo."
"What ben tho two, tell on," quod he.
"My fader, this is one, that she
Commaundeth me my mouthe to close,
And that I shulde her nought oppose
In love, of whiche I ofte preche,
And plenerlich[1] of suche a speche
Forbere and suffre her in pees.
But that ne might I nethéles
For all this worlde obey iwis.[2]
For whan I am there as she is,
Though she my talés nought allowe,
Ayein her will yet mote I bowe
To seche if that I might have grace.
But that thing may I nought embrace
For ought that I can speke or do.
And yet full ofte I speké so,
That she is wroth and saith: be stille.
If I that hesté shall fulfille
And therto ben obediént,
Than is my causé fully shent,
For spechéles may no man spede.
So wote I nought what is to rede.[3]
But certés I may nought obeie,
That I ne mote algaté[4] saie
Some what of that I woldé mene,
For ever it is aliché grene
The greaté lové which I have,
Wherof I can nought bothé save
My speche and this obedience.

1 *Plenerlich*, fully, wholly.
2 *Iwis*, certainly.
3 I know not what is to be counselled.
4 *Algate*, always.

And thus full ofté my silence
I breke, and is the firsté point
Wherof that I am out of point
In this, and yet it is no Pride.
"Now than upon that other side
To tell my disobeïsaunce,
Full sore it stant to my grevaunce
And may nought sinke into my wit.
Full ofté timé she me bit[1]
To leven her and chese a newe;
And saith, if I the sothé knewe
How fer I stondé from her grace,
I shuldé love in other place.
But therof wol I disobeie,
For also wel she mighté saie
'Go take the moné there it sit,'
As bringé that into my wit.
For there was never rooted tree
That stood so faste in his degree,
That I ne stondé moré faste
Upon her love, and may nought caste
Min herte awey all though I wolde.
For God wote though I never sholde
Sene her with eye after this daie,
Yet stant it so, that I ne maie
Her love out of my brest remue.'
This is a wonder retenue,
That malgré where[2] she woll or none
Min herte is evermo in one,
So that I can none other chese,
But whether that I winne or lese
I must her loven till I deie;
And thus I breke, as by that weie,
Her hestés and her cómmaundinges.
But trulich in none other thinges.
Forthý my fader, what is more
Touchende unto this ilké lore
I you beseche, after the forme
That ye pleinly me wolde enforme,
So that I may min herté reule
In Lovés cause after the reule."

[1] *Bit*, prays.
[2] *Where*, whether.

Murmur and Complaint.

Toward this Vice of which we trete
There ben yet tweie of thilke estrete,[1]
Her[2] name is Murmur and Compleinte.
Ther can no man her cheré peinte
To sette a glad semblaunt therinne:
For though Fortuné make hem winne,
Yet grucchen they; and if they lese
There is no waié for to chese
Wherof they mighten stonde apesed.
So ben they comunly disesed,
There may no welth ne no pouerte
Attempren hem to the deserte[3]
Of buxomnessé by no wise.
For ofté timé they despise
The goodé fortune as the badde,
As they no mannés reson hadde,
Through Pridé wherof they be blinde.
And right of such a maner kinde
Ther be lovérs, that though they have
Of love all that they woldé crave,
Yet woll they grucché by some weie,
That they wol nought to love obeie
Upon the trouth, as they do sholde.
And if hem lacketh that they wolde,
Anon they falle in such a peine,
That ever unbuxomly they pleine
Upon Fortúne and curse and crie,
That they wol nought her hertes plie
To suffre, till it better falle.
Forthý if thou amongés alle

[1] *Of thilke estrete*, of the same street, neighbours.
[2] *Her*, their.
[3] *Deserte*, merit.

Hast uséd this condición,
My sone, in thy Confessión
Now tell me pleinly what thou
art."—
"My fader, I beknowe[1] a part
So as ye tolden here above
Of Murmur and Compleint of Love;
That for I se no spede coménde,
Ayein Fortúné compleignénde
I am, as who saith, evermo
And eke full ofté time also.
Whan so as that I se or here
Of hevy word or hevy chere
Of my lady, I grucche anone,
But wordés dare I speké none
Wherof she mighté be displesed.
But in min herte I am disesed
With many a Murmur god it wote,
Thus drinke I in min owné swote.[2]
And though I maké no semblaunt,
Min herte is all disóbeisaúnt,
And in this wise I me confesse
Of that ye clepe Unbuxomnesse.
Now telleth what your counseil
is."—
"My sone, as I thee redé this,
What so befall of other weie,
That thou to lovés hest obeie
Als fer as thou it might suffise.
For ofté sith[3] in such a wise
Obedience in love availeth,
Where all a mannés strengthé
faileth:
Wherof if that thee list to wit,
In a cronique as it is writ
A great ensample thou might finde,
Which now come is into my minde.
There was whilom by daiés olde
A worthy knight, and as men tolde
He was neveu to themperóur
And of his court a courteóur:
Wifeles he was, Florent he hight,
He was a man that mochel might.

[1] *Beknowe*, confess. [2] *Swote*, sweat.
[3] *Ofte sith*, oftentimes.

Of armés he was desiróus,
Chiváleróus and amoróus,
And for the fame of worldés speche
Straunge aventúrés for to seche
He rode the marches all aboute.
And fell a time, as he was oute,
Fortúné, which may every threde
To-breke[1] and knitte of mannés
spede,[2]
Shope, as this knight rode in a pas,
That he by strengthé taken was,
And to a castell they him ladde,
Where that he fewé frendés hadde.
For so it fell that ilké stounde,
That he hath with a dedly wounde,
Fightend, his owne hondes slain
Branchus, whiche to the Capitain
Was sone and heire, wherof ben
wrothe
The fader and the moder bothe.
That knight Branchus was of his
honde
The worthiest of all his londe,
And fain they wolden do vengeaúnce
Upon Florent, but remembraúnce
That they toke of his worthinesse,
Of knighthode and of gentilesse,
And how he stood of cousinage
To themperour, made hem assuage,
And dorsté nought slaine him for
fere.
In great desputeson they were
Among hem selfe, that[3] was the
best.
There was a lady, the sliest
Of allé that men knewen tho,
So olde she might unnethés go,
And was grauntdamé to the dede.
And she with that began to rede[4]
And saide hem she wol bring him
inne,
That she shal him to dethé winne

[1] *To-breke*, break up altogether. To- is an intensive prefix.
[2] *Spede*, prosperity.
[3] What. [4] *Rede*, counsel.

All only of his owné graunt
Through strength of verray covenaunt [1]
Withouté blame of any wight.
Anone she sendé for this knight
And of her soné she alleide [2]
The deth, and thus to him she saide:
'Florent, how so ever thou be to wite [3]
Of Branchus deth, men shal respite
As now to také vengément,
Be so thou stonde in jugément
Upon certein condición,
That thou unto a questión
Which I shall axé shait answére.
And over this thou shalt eke swere,
That if thou of the sothé faile,
There shal non other thinge availe,
That thou ne shalt thy deth receive;
And for men shal thee nought deceive
That thou therof might ben avised,
Thou shalt have day and time assised
And levé saufly for to wende,
Be so that at thy daiés ende
Thou come ayein with thin avise.'
This knight, which worthy was and wise,
This lady praieth, that he may wit
And have it under sealés writ,
What questión it sholdé be
For which he shall in that degre
Stonde of his life in jeopartie.
With that she feigneth compaignie
And saith: 'Florent, on love it hongeth
All that to min axingé longeth:—
What allé women most desire—
This woll I axe, and in thempire
Where thou hast mosté knowleching

[1] *Verray covenaunt*, a true agreement.
[2] *Alleide*, alleged.
[3] *To wite*, to blame.

Také counséil of this axinge.'
Florent this thing hath undertake;
The day was set and timé take;
Under his seale he wrote his othe
In such a wise, and forth he gothe
Home to his emés [1] courte ayein,
To whom his aventúré plein
He tolde, of that is him befalle.
And upon that they weren alle
The wisest of the londe assent,
But nethéles of one assent
They mighté nought accordé plat,
One saidé this, an other that;
After the dispositiön
Of natural complexiön
To some woman it is plesaúnce
That to another is grevaúnce,
But suche a thinge in speciáll
Whiche to hem alle in generall
Is most plesaunt and most desired
Above all other and most conspired,
Suche o [2] thing conné they nought finde
By constellatión ne kinde.[3]
And thus Florent withouté cure
Mot stonde upon his aventúre
And is al shape unto the lere,[4]
And in defaulte of his answere
This knight hath lever for to deie
Than breke his trouth, and for to lie
In placé wheré he was swore,
And shapeth him gone ayein [5] therfore.
"Whan timé cam he toke his leve
That lenger wolde he nought beléve [6]
And praieth his eme he be nought wroth,
For that is a point of his oth,

[1] *Eme*, uncle.
[2] *O*, one.
[3] *Kind*, nature.
[4] *Lere*, learning (finding the answer to the question).
[5] Makes himself ready to go back again.
[6] *Beleve*, remain.

He saith, that no man shal him wreke,[1]
Though afterward men heré speke
That he perάventuré deie.
And thus he wenté forth his weie
Alone as a knight aventurόus
And in his thought was curiόus
To witté what was best to do.
And as he rode aloné so
And cam nigh there he woldé be,
In a forést there under a tree
He sigh[2] where sat a creätúre,
A lothly womannissh figúre,
That for to speke of flesshe and bone
So foule yet sigh he never none.
This knight behelde her redily,
And as he wolde have passéd by
She clepéd him and bad abide.
And he his hors hevéd[3] aside
Tho[4] tornéd and to her he rode
And there he hovéd[5] and abode
To witté[6] what she woldé mene.
And she began him to bemene[7]
And saidé: 'Florent, by thy name
Thou hast on hondé such a game
That but thou be the better avised
Thy deth is shapen and devised,
That al the world ne may thee save,
But if[8] that thou my counseil have.'
Florent whan he this talé herde,
Unto this oldé wight answérde
And of her counseil he her praide.
And she ayein to him thus saide:
'Florent, if I for thee so shape,
That thou through me thy deth escape
And také worship of thy dede,
What shall I havé to my mede?'
'What thing,' quod he, 'that thou wolde axe.'

[1] *Wreke*, avenge.
[2] *Sigh*, saw.
[3] *Hevéd*, head.
[4] *Tho*, then.
[5] *Hovéd*, waited.
[6] *To witté*, to know.
[7] *Bemene*, bemoan.
[8] *But if*, unless.

'I bid never a better taxe,'
Quod she, 'but first, or thou be sped,
Thou shalt me levé suche a wed[1]
That I woll have thy trouth on honde,
That thou shalt be min husébonde.'
'Nay,' saith Florent, 'that may nought be.'
'Ridé thanne forth thy way,' quod she,
'And if thou go withouté rede,
Thou shalt be sekerliché dede.'
Florent behight[2] her good inough
Of londe, of rent, of parke, of plough,
But all that compteth she at nought.
Tho fell this knight in mochel thought,
Now goth he forth, now cometh ayein,
He wot nought what is best to sain,
And thought as he rode to and fro,
That chese he mote one of the two—
Or for to take her to his wife
Or ellés for to lese his life.
And than he caste his avauntáge,
That she was of so great an age
That she may livé but a while,
And thought to put her in an ile
Where that no man her shuldé knowe
Til she with deth were overthrowe.
And thus this yongé lusty knight
Unto this oldé lothly wight
Tho said: 'If that none other chaunce
May maké my deliveraunce
But only thilké samé speche
Which as thou saist thou shalt me teche,
Have here min honde, I shal thee wedde.'

[1] *Wed*, pledge.
[2] *Behight*, promised.

And thus his trouth he leith to
wedde.
With that she frounceth up the
browe:
'This covenaunt woll I allowe,'
She saith, 'if any other thing
But that thou hast of my teching
Fro deth thy body may respite,
I woll thee of thy trouth acquite,
And elles by none other waie.
Now herken me what I shall saie:
Whan thou art come into the
place,
Where now they maken great
manáce
And upon thy comíng abide,
They wol anone the samé tide
Opposé thee of thine answére.
I wot thou wolt no thing forbere
Of that thou wenest be thy beste,
And if thou might so findé reste
Wel is, for than is ther no more.
And ellés this shall be my lore,
That thou shalt saie:—Upon this
Molde
That allé Women levest wolde
Be Soverein of Mannés Love:—
For what woman is so above
She hath, as who saith, all her wille,
And ellés may she nought fulfille
What thinge her weré levest have.
With this answeré thou shalt save
Thy self, and other wisé nought.
And whan thou hast thy endé
wrought,
Come here ayein, thou shalt me
finde,
And let nothínge out of thy minde.'
He goth him forth with hevy chere,
As he that not[1] in what manere
He may this worldés joie atteigne:
For if he deie he hath a peine;
And if he live he mote him binde
To suche one which of allé kinde

[1] *Not*, knows not.

Of women is the unsemlieste.
Thus wot he nought what is the
beste.
But be him lief or be him loth
Unto the castel forth he goth
His full answeré for to yive
Or for to deïe or for to live.
Forth with his counseil came the
lorde,
The thingés stoden of recorde,
He send up for the lady sone,
And forth she cam that oldé mone.[1]
In presence of the remenaunt
The strengthe of all the covenaunt
Tho was rehersé̆d openly,
And to Florent she bad forthý
That he shall tellen his avise
As he that wot what is the prise.
Florent saith all that ever he couth,
But such word cam ther none to
mouth,
That he for yefte or for beheste
Might any wise his deth areste.
And thus he tarieth longe and late,
Til that this lady bad algate
That he shall for the dome finâll
Yef[2] his answere in speciall
Of that she had him first opposed.
And than he hath trulý supposed,
That he him may of nothing yelpe,[3]
But if so by tho wordés helpe
Which as the woman hath him
taught,
Wherof he hath an hopé caught
That he shall be excusé̆d so,
And tolde out plein his willé tho.
And whan that this matróné herde
The maner how this knight an-
swerde,
She said: 'Ha, treson! Wo thee be
That hast thus tolde the priveté,
Whiche allé women most desire!
I woldé that thou were afire!'

[1] *Mone*, wicked one, hag.
[2] *Yef*, give. [3] *Yelpe*, boast.

But nethéles in suche a plite
Florent of his answére is quite.
And tho began his sorwé newe,
For he mot gone or ben untrewe
To hiré which his trouthé hadde.
But he, which allé shamé dradde,
Goth forth in stede of his penaunce
And taketh the fortune of his chaunce
As he that was with trouth affaited.[1]
This olde wight him hath awaited
In placé where as he her lefte.
Florent his wofull hed up lifte
And sigh this vecke[2] where that she syt,
Which was the lothliesté wyght,
That ever man cast on his eye.
Her nasé bass,[3] her browés high,
Her eyen smal and depé set,
Her chekés ben with terés wet
And rivelin[4] as an empty skin
Hangend down unto the chin,
Her lippés shrunken ben for age,
There was no grace in her viságe,
Her front was narwe, her lockés hore,
She loketh forth as doth a more,[5]
Her necke is short, her shulders courbe,
That might a mannés lust distourbe,
Her body great and no thing small,
And shortly to descrive her all
She hath no lith[6] without a lack;
But liche unto the wollé sack
She profreth her unto this knight
And bad him, as he hath behight,
So as she hath by his warránt,
That he her holdé covenaúnt.
And by the bridell she him seseth,

[1] *With trouth affaited*, bound to truth only. Goods and chattels might be promised in Old French 'pour estre et demourer affaiz et ypothequez.'
[2] *Vecke*, old woman. [3] *Bass*, low.
[4] *Rivelin*, wrinkled, shrunk.
[5] Witch, hag. [6] *Lith*, limb.

But god wot how that she him pleseth
Of suché wordés as she speketh:
Him thenketh wel nigh his herté breketh
For sorwe that he may nought fle
But if[1] he wolde untrewé be.
Loke, how a seke man for his hele
Taketh baldemoin with canele[2]
And with the mirré taketh the sucre,
Right upon such a maner lucre
Stant Florent, as in this diete
He drinketh the bitter with the swete,
He medleth sorwe with likíng
And liveth so as who saith dyíng.
His youthé shall be cast awey
Upon suche one, which as the wey
Is olde and lothly overall.
But nede he mot that nedé shall
He wolde algate his trouthé holde
As every knight therto is holde
What hap so him is ever befalle,
Though she be the foulést of alle.
Yet to thonoúr of womanhed
Him thought he shuldé taken heed,
So that for puré gentilesse
As he her couthé best adresse,
In raggés as she was to-tore
He set her on his hors to-fore,
And forth he taketh his way softe.
No wonder though he siketh[3] ofte.
But as an oulé fleeth by nighte
Out of all other briddés sighte,
Right so this knight on daiés brode
In close him held, and shope his rode
On nightés timé till the tide
That he come there he wolde abide,
And prively withouté noise
He bringeth this foulé greaté coise[4]

[1] *But if*, unless.
[2] *Baldemoin with canele*, gentian with cinnamon.
[3] *Siketh*, sigheth. [4] *Coise*, mistress.

To his castell in suche a wise,
That no man might her shape avise,
Til she into the chambre came,
Where he his privé counseil name
Of[1] suché men as he most truste
And told hem, that he nedés muste
This besté[2] weddé to his wife,
For ellés had he lost his life.
The privé women were assent[3]
That sholden ben of his assent.
Her raggés they anone of drawe
And as it was that timé lawe
She haddé bath, she haddé rest,
And was arraiéd to the best.
But with no craft of combés brode
They might her horé lockés shode,[4]
And she ne woldé nought be shore
For no counseil, and they therfore
With suche attire as tho was used
Ordeinen,[5] that it was excused
And had so craftilich aboute
That no man mighté seen hem oute.[6]
But whan she was fullich arraied
And her attire was all assaied,
Tho was she fouler unto se.
But yet it may non other be,
They weré wedded in the night;
So wo begone was never knight
As he was than of mariáge.
And she began to pleie and rage
As who saith, I am well inough;
But he therof nothing ne lough.[7]
For she toke thanné chere on honde
And clepeth him her husébonde
And saith: 'My lord, go we to bedde,
For I to that ententé wedde
That thou shalt be my worldés blisse.'
And profreth him with that to kisse,
As she a lusty lady were.
His body mighté well be there,
But as of thought and memorie
His hert was in purgátorie.
But yet for strengthe of matrimóine
He mighté maké non essóine,
That he ne mote algatés plie
To gon to bed of compaignie.
And whan they were a beddé naked
Withouté slepe he was awaked,
He torneth on that other side
For that he wolde his eyen hide
Fro loking of that foulé wight.
The chamber was all full of light,
The courtines were of sendall thinne,
This newé bride which lay withinne,
Though it be nought with his accorde,
In armés she beclept her lorde
And praid, as he was tornéd fro
He wolde him torne ayeinward tho.
'For now,' she saith, 'we be both one.'
But he lay stille as any stone,
And ever in one she spake and praide
And bad him thenke on that he saide,
Whan that he toke her by the honde.
He herd and understood the bonde,
How he was set to his penaunce.
And as it were a man in traunce
He torneth him all sodeinly
And sigh a lady lay him by
Of eightené winter age,
Which was the fairest of visage,
That ever in all this world he sigh.
And as he wolde have take her nigh,
She put her hond, and by his leve
Besought him that he woldé leve,
And saith, that for to winne or lese
He mot one of two thingés chese,

[1] Took private counsel with.
[2] This beast.
[3] *Assent*, sent to her.
[4] Part her hoary locks.
[5] Set it in order.
[6] So craftily surrounded with the customary headgear that one could see any grey locks peep out of it.
[7] *Lough*, laughed.

Where[1] he woll have her such on night
Or ellés upon daiés light,
For he shall nought have bothé two.—
And he began to sorwe tho
In many a wise and caste his thought,
But for al that yet couth he nought
Devise him self which was the best.
And she that wolde his hertés rest
Praieth that he shulde chese algate,
Til at the lasté longe and late
He saide: 'O, ye my livés hele,
Say what ye liste in my quarele.
I not[2] what answere I shall yive,
But ever while that I may live
I woll that ye be my maistresse;
For I can nought my selfé gesse
Which is the best unto my chois,
Thus graunt I you min holé vois,
Chesé for us bothe, I you praie,
And what as ever that ye saie,
Right as ye wollé so woll I.'
'My lord,' she saidé, 'graunt mercy,
For of this word that ye now sain
That ye have made me Soverein
My destiné is overpassed,
That never hereafter shall be lassed[3]
My beauté which that I now have,
Til I be take into my grave.
Both night and day as I am now
I shall all way be such to you.
The kingés daughter of Cecile
I am; and fell but sith a while,[4]
As I was with my fader late,
That my stepmoder for an hate,
Which toward me she hath begonne,
Forshope[5] me, till I haddé wonne
The love and the sovéreinté
Of what knight that in his degré
All other passeth of good name.
And as men sain ye ben the same
The dedé proveth it is so;
Thus am I yourés evermo.'
Tho was plesaunce and joie inough,
Echone with other pleid and lough,
They livé longe, and well they ferde,
And clerkés that this chauncé herde
They writen it in evidence
To teche how that obedience
May well fortúne a man to love
And set him in his luste above,
As it befell unto this knight.
"Forthý, my sone, if thou do right,
Thou shalt unto thy love obeie
And folwe her will by allé weie."—
"Min holy fader, so I will.
For ye have told me such a skill
Of this ensample now to-fore,
That I shall evermo therfore
Here afterward min observaunce
To love and to his obeissaunce
The better kepe, and over this[1]
Of Pride if there ought ellés is
Wherof that I me shrivé shall,
What thing it is in speciall,
My fader, axeth, I you pray."—
"Now list, my sone, and I shall say.
For yet there is Surquederie,[2]
Which stant with Pride of compaignie,
Wherof that thou shalt here anone
To knowe if thou have gult or none,
Upon the forme as thou shalt here;
Now understond well the matere.

Surquederie.

Surquederie is thilké Vice
Of Pridé which the third office

1 *Where*, whether.
2 *Not*, know not.
3 *Lassed*, lessened.
4 *Sith a while*, a while since.
5 *Forshope*, transformed.

1 *Over this*, beyond this.
2 *Surquederie*, presumption.

Hath in his court and wol nought knowe
The trouthé till it overthrowe.
Upon his fortune and his grace
Cometh *had I wist*[1] full ofte a place,
For he doth all his thing by gesse
And voideth allé sikernesse ;
None other counseil good him semeth
But such as he him selfé demeth.
For in such wise as he compásseth
His wit alone all other passeth,
And is with Pride so thorough sought
That he all other set at nought,
And weneth of him selven so
That such as he there be no mo
So fair, so semely, ne so wise,
And thus he woldé beare a prise
Above all other, and nought forthý
He saith nought onés graunt mercy[2]
To God, which allé gracé sendeth,
So that his wittés he despendeth
Upon him selfe, as though there were
No God which might availé there,
But all upon his owné wit
He stant, till he fall in the pit
So fer that he may nought arise.
"And right thus in the samé wise
The Vice upon the cause of Love
So proudely set the hert above
And doth him pleinly for to wene,
That he to loven any quene
Hath worthinesse and suffisaunce.
And so withouté purveiaunce
Full ofte he heweth up so highe,
That chippés fallen in his eye ;
And eke full ofte he weneth this,
There as he nought belovéd is
To be belovéd altherbeste.
Now, soné, telle what so thee leste
Of this that I have told thee here."—
"Ha fader, be nought in a were.[1]
I trowé there be no man lesse
Of any maner worthinesse
That halt him lesse worthý than I
To be beloved, and nought forthý
I say in excusing of me
To allé men, that love is fre.
And certés that may no man werne.[2]
For love is of him selfe so derne,[3]
It luteth[4] in a mannes herte.
But that ne shall me nought asterte[5]
To wené for to be worthy
To loven, but in her mercy.
But sir, of that ye woldé mene,
That I shulde other wisé wene
To be belovéd than I was,
I am beknowe as in this cas."—
"My godé soné, telle me how."—
"Now list, and I woll tellé you,
My godé fader, how it is.
Full ofte it hath befalle er this
Through hopé, that was nought certein,
My wening hath be set in vein
To trust in thing that helpe me nought
But onlich of min owné thought.
For as it semeth that a bell
Like to the wordés that men tell
Answereth right so, no more ne lesse,
To you, my fader, I confesse
Such will my wit hath over set,
That what so hopé me behet[6]
Full many a time I wene it soth,
But finally no spede it doth.
Thus may I tellen, as I can,
Wening beguileth many a man.

[1] *Had I wist*, if I had only known. "Had-I-wist" was a popular phrase for the repentance of the rash. So in Spenser's "Mother Hubbard's Tale"—

> "Most miserable man, whom wicked Fate
> Hath brought to court, to sue for Had-y-wist!"

[2] *Graunt mercy*, gramercy, great thanks!

[1] *In a were*, in confusion or doubt.
[2] *Werne*, refuse. [3] *Derne*, secret.
[4] *Luteth*, lies hidden.
[5] Drive me to think myself worthy of love, but through her mercy.
[6] *Me behet*, promises me.

So hath it me, right wel I wot,
For if a man wol in a bote
Whiche is withouté botmé rowe,
He must nedés be overthrowe.
Right so weníng hath fard by me,
For whan I wendé next have be
As I by my wening caste,
Than was I furthest atté laste,
And as a fool my bowe unbende
Whan all was failéd that I wende.
Forthý, my fader, as of this
That my weníng hath gone amis
Touchend unto surquederie,
Yef me my penaunce or I die.
But if ye wolde in any forme
Of this matér a tale enforme,
Which were ayein this Vicé set,
I shuldé faré well the bet."—
"My sone, in allé maner wise
Surquederie is to despise,
Wherof I findé writé thus:—
The proudé knight Capaneus
He was of suche surquederie,
That he through his chivalerie
Upon him self so mochel triste,[1]
That to the goddés him ne liste
In no quarelé to beseche,
But saide it was an idel speche
Which causé was of puré drede,
For lacke of hert and for no nede.
And upon such presumptión
He held this proude opinión,
Till atté laste upon a day
Abouté Thebés, where he lay,
Whan it of siegé was belaine,
This knight, as the croníqués saine,
In allé mannés sighté there,
Whan he was proudest in his gere
And thought how nothing might him dere,[2]
Full arméd with his shield and spere
As he the cité wolde assaile,
God toke him selfé the bataile
Ayein his pride, and fro the sky
A firy thonder sodeinly
He sende and him to pouder smote.
And thus the Pridé, which was hote
Whan he most in his strengthé wende,
Was brent and lost withouten ende.
So that it proveth well therfore
The strength of man is soné lore,[1]
But if[2] that he it well govérne.
And over this a man may lerne,
That eke full ofté time it greveth
What that a man him self beleveth,
As though it shulde him well beseme
That he all other men can deme[3]
And hath foryete his owné vice.
A tale of hem that be so nice
And feigne hem self to be so wise
I shall thee telle in suche a wise,
Wherof thou shalt ensample take,
That thou no such thing undertake.
I finde upon surquederie,
How that whilom of Hungarie
By oldé daiés was a king
Wise and honést in allé thing.
And so befell upon a daie,
And that was in the month of May,
As thilké time it was usaúnce,
This king with noble purveiaúnce
Hath for him selfe his chare[4] arraied,
Wherin he woldé ride amaied[5]
Out of the cite for to pleie
With lordés and with great nobleie
Of lusty folk that weré yonge,
Where somé pleide and somé songe,
And somé gone and somé ride,
And somé prick her horse aside
And bridlen hem now in now oute.
The kinge his eyé cast aboute,
Til he was atté lasté ware
And sigh coménd ayein his chare

[1] *Triste*, trusted. [2] *Dere*, hurt.

[1] *Lore*, lost. [2] *But if*, unless.
[3] *Deme*, judge. [4] *Chare*, chariot.
[5] *Amaied*, a-Maying. Professor Skeat, in explaining this peculiar construction, started from the phrase in "Piers Plowman" "they gon a begged" for "they go a begging."

Two pilgrimés of so great age,
That lich unto a drie ymage
They weren pale and fadé hewed,
And as a busshe, whiche is be-
snewed,
Here berdés weren hore and white,
There was of kindé [1] but a lite
That they ne semen fully dede.
They comen to the king and bede [2]
Some of his good, pur [3] charité.
And he with great humilité
Out of his chare to groundé lepte
And hem in both his armes kepte
And kist hem bothé foot and honde
Before the lordés of his londe
And yaf hem of his good therto.
And whan he hath this dedé do
He goth into his chare ayeine.
Tho [4] was murmúr, tho was dis-
deine,
Tho was compleinte on every side,
They saiden of their owné pride
Echone till other, 'What is this?
Our king hath do this thing amis
So to abesse [5] his roialté,
That every man it mighté se,
And humbled him in such a wise
To hem that were of none emprise.'
Thus was it spoken to and fro
Of hem that weré with him tho
All privély behinde his backe.
But to him selfé no man spake.
The kingés brother in presénce
Was thilké time, and great offence
He toke therof and was the same
Above all other which moste blame
Upon his legé lord hath laid,
And hath unto the lordés said
Anone as he may timé finde,
There shall nothing be left behinde,
That he wol speke unto the king.
Now list what fell upon this thing.

1 *Of kinde*, by nature *lite*, little.
2 *Bede*, pray.
3 *Pur (pour)*, for.
4 *Tho*, then.
5 *Abesse*, abase.

The weder was merie and fair
inough,
Echone with other pleid and lough
And fellen into talés newe,
How that the fresshé flourés grewe,
And how the grené levés spronge,
And how that love amonge the
yonge
Began the hertés thanne awake,
And every brid hath chose his
make.
And thus the Maiés day to thende
They lede, and home ayein they
wende.
The king was nought so soné come,
That whan he had his chambre
nome,
His brother ne was redy there
And brought a tale unto his ere
Of that he diddé such a shame
In hindring of his owné name,
Whan he him selfé woldé dreche [1]
That to so vile a pouer wrecche
Him deigneth shewé such simplesse
Ayein the state of his noblesse.
And saith, he shall it no more use
And that he mot him selfe excuse
Toward his lordés everichone.
The king stood still as any stone
And to his tale an ere he laide
And thoughté moré than he saide.
But nethéles to that he herde
Well curteisly the king answerde
And tolde, it shuldé ben amended.
And thus whan that here tale is
ended,
All redy was the bord and cloth,
The king unto his souper goth
Among the lordés to the halle.
And whan they haddé soupéd alle,
They token leve and forth they go.
The king bethought him selfé tho,
How he his brother may chastie,
That he through his surquederie

1 *Dreche*, trouble.

Toke upon hondé to dispreise
Humilité, which is to preise,
And therupon yaf such counseil
Toward his king, that was nought heil,
Wherof to be the better lered
He thenketh to make him afered.
It fell so, that in thilké dawe[1]
There was ordeignéd by the lawe
A trompé with a sterné breth,
Which was clepéd the Trompe of Deth.
And in the court where the king was
A certein man this trompe of brass
Hath in kepíng and therof serveth,
That whan a lord his deth deserveth,
He shall this dredfull trompé blowe
To-fore his gate, and make it knowe
How that the jugément is yive
Of deth, which shall nought be foryive.
The king whan it was night anone
This man assent[2] and bad him gone
To trompen at his brothers gate.
And he, which mot so done algate,
Goth forth and doth the kingés hest.
This lord, which herde of this tempest
That he to-fore his gaté blewe,
Tho wist he by the lawe and knewe
That he was sekerliché dede.
And as of helpe he wist no rede,
But sendé for his frendés all
And tolde hem how it is befalle.
And they him axé causé why,
But he the sothé nought forthý
Ne wist, and there was sorwe tho.
For it stood thilké timé so,
This trompé was of such sentence,
That there ayein no resisténce
They couthe ordeiné by no weie,
That he ne mot algaté deie,
But if so that he may purcháce
To get his legé lordés grace.
Here wittés therupon they caste
And ben appointed atté laste.
This lorde a worthy lady had
Unto his wife, whiche also drad
Her lordés deth, and children five
Betwene hem two they had alive,
That weren yonge and tender of age
And of statúre and of viságe
Right faire and lusty on to se.
Tho casten they, that he and she
Forth with their children on the morwe,
As they that weré full of sorwe,
All naked but of smock and sherte
To tendre with the kingés herte
His gracé shulden go to seche
And pardon of the deth beseche.
Thus passen they that wofull night,
And erly whan they sigh it light
They gone hem forth in suche a wise,
As thou to-fore hast herd divise,
All naked but here shertés on
They wepte and madé mochel mone.
Here hair hangénd about here eres,
With sobbing and with sory teres
This lord goth than an humble pas
That whilom proud and noble was,
Wherof the cité sore a flight[1]
Of hem that sawen thilké sight.
And nethéless all openly
With such wepíng and with such cry
Forth with his children and his wife
He goth to praié for his life.
Unto the court whan they be come
And men therin have hedé nome,
There was no wight, if he hem sigh,
From water mighté kepe his eye
For sorwé which they maden tho.
The king supposeth[2] of this wo
And feigneth as he nought ne wiste,
But nethéles at his upriste

[1] *Dawe*, day. [2] *Assent*, sent to.

[1] *A flight*, was afflicted, grieved.
[2] *Supposeth*, makes believe.

Men tolden him, howe that it ferde.
And whan that he this wonder
herde,
In hast he goth into the halle.
And all at onés down they falle,
If any pité may be founde.
The king, which seeth hem go to
grounde,
Hath axéd hem what is the fere,
Why they be so dispuiled there.
His brother said: 'Ha, lord, mercy!
I wote none other causé why,
But only that this night full late
The trompe of deth was at my gate
In token that I shuldé deie;
Thus we be comé for to preie
That ye my worldés deth respite.'
'Ha, fool, how thou art for to
wite,'[1]
The kinge unto his brother saith,
'That thou art of so litel feith,
That only for a trompés soun
Hath gone dispuiled through the
town
Thou and thy wife in such manere
Forth with thy children that ben here
In sight of allé men aboute.
For that thou saist, thou art in
doubte[2]
Of deth which standeth under the
lawe
Of man, and man it may withdrawe,
So that it may perchauncé faile,
Now shalt thou nought forthý mer-
veile,
That I down from my chare alight,
Whan I beheld to-fore my sight
In hem that were of so great age
Min owné deth through here
ymáge,
Which God hath set by lawe of
kinde,
Wherof I may no boté[3] finde.

[1] *To wite*, to blame. [2] *Doubte*, fear. [3] *Boté*, remedy.

For well I wot, suche as they be
Right suche am I in my degré,
Of flesshe and blood, and so shall
deie.
And thus though I that lawe obeie
Of which that kingés ben put under,
It ought ben well the lassé wonder
Than thou, which art withouté nede
For lawe of londe in suche a drede,
Which for to accompte is but a jape
As thing which thou might over-
scape.
Forthy, my brother, after this
I rede that sithen it so is
That thou canst drede a man so
sore,
Drede God with all thin herté more.
For all shall deie and all shall passe,
As well a leon as an asse,
As well a begger as a lorde,
Towardés dethe in one accorde
They shullen stonde.' And in this
wise
The kingé with his wordés wise
His brother taught and all foryive.
Forthý, my sone, if thou wolt live
In Vertue, thou must Vice escheue
And with lowe herte humblessé sue,
So that thou be nought surque-
dous."—
"My fader, I am amorous,
Wherof I woldé you beseche
That ye me some ensample teche,
Which might in Lovés causé
stonde."—
"My soné, thou shalt under-
stonde
In Love and other thingés alle,
If that surquederié falle,
It may to him nought well betide
Which useth thilke Vice of Pride,
Which torneth wisdom to wening
And sothfastnesse into lesing
Through foll imaginatión.
And for thin énformatión,

That thou this Vice as I thee rede
Escheué shalte, a tale I rede,
Which fell whilom by daiés olde,
So as the clerke Ovídé tolde.
There was whilom a lordés sone,
Which of his Pride a nicé wone[1]
Hath caught, that worthy to his liche[2]
To sechen all the worldés riche
There was no woman for to love.
So high he set him selfe above
Of stature and of beauté bothe,
That him thought allé women lothe.
So was there no comparisón
As towarde his conditión.
This yongé lord Narcizus hight.
No strength of Lové bowé might
His herté, whiche is unaffiled.[3]
But atté laste he was beguiled.
For of the goddés purveiaúnce
It felle him on a day perchaunce,
That he in all his proudé fare
Unto the forest gan to fare
Amonge othér, that theré were,
To hunten and disporte him there.
And whan he cam into the place,
Where that he woldé make his chace,
The houndés weren in a throwe
Uncoupled and the hornés blowe,
The greté herte anone was founde
With swifté feet set on the grounde.
And he with spore in horsé side
Him hasteth fasté for to ride,
Till allé men be left behinde.
And as he rode under a linde
Beside a roche, as I thee telle,
He sigh where spronge a lusty welle.
The day was wonder hote withalle,
And suche a thurst was on him falle,
That he must outher deie or drinke.
And downe he light and by the brinke
He tide his hors unto a braunche
And laid him lowé for to staunche
His thurst. And as he cast his loke
Into the welle and hedé toke,
He sigh the like of his viságe
And wendé there were an ymáge
Of suche a nimphe, as tho was say,[1]
Wherof that love his herte assay
Began, as it was after sene
Of his sotie[2] and made him wene
It were a woman, that he sigh.[3]
The more he cam the wellé nigh,
The neré cam she to him ayein,
So wist he never what to sain;
For whan he wepte he sigh her wepe,
And whan he cried he toke good kepe,
The samé worde she cried also;
And thus began the newé wo,
That whilom was to him so straunge.
Tho made him Love an harde eschaunge
To set his herte and to beginné
Thing whiche he might never winné.
And ever amonge he gan to loute,[4]
And praith that she to him come oute.
And other while he goth afer
And other while he draweth ner
And ever he founde her in one place.
He wepeth, he crieth, he axeth grace,
There as he mighté geté none.
So that ayein a roche of stone,
As he that knewe none other rede,
He smote him self til he was dede.

[1] *Wone*, custom. [2] *Liche*, body.
[3] *Unaffiled*, attached to no one.

[1] *Tho was say*, then was seen.
[2] *Sotie*, folly. [3] *Sigh*, saw.
[4] *Loute*, bow.

Wherof the nimphés of the welles
And other that there weren elles
Unto the wodés belongénde
The body, which was dede ligénde,
For puré pité that they have
Under gravé they begrave.[1]
And than out of his sepulture
There spronge anone perâventúre
Of flourés suche a wonder sight,
That men ensample také might
Upon the dedés whiche he dede.
And tho was sene in thilké stede,
For in the winter fressh and faire
The flourés ben, whiche is contraire
To kinde, and so was the folie
Which felle of his Surquederie.
"Thus he which Love had in disdeigne,
Worst of all other was beseine,
And as he set his prise most hie,
He was lest worthy in Lovés eye
And most bejapéd in his wit,
Wherof the remembraunce is yit;
So that thou might ensample take,
And eke all other, for his sake."—
"My fader, as touchénd of me
This Vice I thenké for to fle,
Whiche of his wening overthroweth
And namélich[2] of thing which groweth
In Lovés cause or well or wo,
Yet prided I me never so.
But woldé God that gracé sende,
That toward me my lady wende
As I towardés hiré wene,
My lové shuldé so be sene
There shuldé go no Pride a place.
But I am fer fro thilké grace
And for to speke of timé nowe
So mote I suffre and praié you
That ye woll axe on other side,
If there be any point of Pride
Wherof it nedeth me to be shrive."—

[1] *Begrave*, bury. [2] *Namelich*, especially.

"My soné, God it thee foryive,
If thou have any thing misdo
Touchend of this, but evermo
Ther is another yet of Pride
Which couthé never his wordés hide,
That he ne wold him selfe avaunt.
There may nothing his tungé daunt,
That he ne clappeth as a belle,
Wherof if thou wolt that I telle
It is behovely for to here,
So that thou might thy tungé stere
Toward the worlde and stonde in grace,
Which lacketh ofte in many a place
To him that can nought sitté stille,
Whiche ellés shuld have all his wille

Boasting.

The vice clepéd Avauntánce[1]
With Pride hath take his ácquein-tánce,
So that his owné prise he lasseth
Whan he such mesure overpasseth,
That he his owné herald is.
That first was wel is thanné mis,
That was thankworthy is than blame,
And thus the worship of his name
Through pride of his avauntarie
He torneth into vilenie.
I rede, how that this proudé Vice
Hath thilké wind in his office
Which through the blastés that he bloweth
The mannés fame he overthroweth
Of vertue which shulde ellés springe
Unto the worldés knoulechinge.
But he fordoth it all to sore,
And right of such a maner lore
There ben lovérs; forthý if thou
Art one of hem, tell and say how,

[1] *Avauntánce*, vaunting, boasting.

Whan thou hast taken any thinge
Of lovés yefte or ouche[1] or ringe,
Or toke upon thee for the colde
Some goodly word that thee was tolde
Of frendly chere or token or letter,
Wherof thin herté was the better,
Of that she sendé thee gretinge,
Hast thou for pride of thy likinge
Made thin avaunt where as thee liste?"—
"I woldé, fader, that ye wiste
My consciëncé lith not here.
Yet had I never such matere,
Wherof min herté might amende,
Nought of so mochel as she sende
By mouth and saidé, 'grete him wel.'
And thus for that there is no dele
Wherof to maké min avaunt,
It is to reson accordaunt,
That I may never, but I lie,
Of lové make avauntarie.
I wote nought what I shulde have do
If that I had encheson so
As ye have said here many one;
But I found causé never none,
But Daunger which me welnigh slough.
Therof I couthé telle inough
And of none other avauntaunce.
Thus nedeth me no repentaunce.
Now axeth further of my life,
For herof am I nought gultife."—
"My sone, I am wel paid withall.
For wite it wel in speciall,
That love of his verray justice
Above all other ayein this Vice
At allé timés most debateth
With all his hert and most it hateth.
And eke in allé maner wise
Avauntarie is to despise,
As by ensample thou might wite,
Whiche I finde in the bokés write.

[1] *Ouche*, jewel in its setting.

Of hem that we Lombárdes now calle
Albinus was the firste of alle
Which baré crowne of Lombardie,
And was of great chivalerie
In werre ayeïnst divers kinges.
So felle it amonge other thinges
That he that time a werré had
With Gurmund which the Geptes lad,[1]
And was a mightie kinge also.
But nethéles it fell him so
Albinus slough him in the felde,
Ther halpe him nouther spere ne shelde,
That he ne smote his heved of thanne,
Wherof he toke awey the panne,
Of whiche he saide he woldé make
A cuppé for Gurmundés sake
To kepe and drawe into memoire
Of his batailé the victoire.
And thus when he the felde had wonne,
The londe anon was overronne
And seséd in his owné honde;
Where he Gurmundés doughter fonde,
Which maidé Rosemundé hight,
And was in every mannés sight
A fair, a fressh, a lusty one.
His herté fell to her anone,
And suche a love on her he cast,
That he her wedded atté last.
And after that long time in reste
With her he dwelleth, and to the beste
They love eche other wonder wele.
But she that kepeth the blindé whele,
Venus, when they be most above
In all the hottest of her love,
Her whele she torneth: and they felle

[1] *Lad*, led.

In the manér, as I shall telle.
This king which stood in all his welth
Of pees, of worship and of helth,
And felt him on no sidé greved
As he that hath his worlde acheved,
Tho thought he wolde a festé make
And that was for his wivés sake,
That she the lordés atté feste,
That were obeisaunt to his heste,
May knowe. And so forth there upon
He lette ordeigne and send anon
By letters and by messengers
And warnéd all his officers,
That every thing be well arraied,
The greaté stedés were assaied
For justinge and for tornement,
And many a perléd garnément
Embrouded was ayein the day.
The lordés in her beste array
Be comen at the timé set;
One justeth well, an other bet,
And other whilé they torney;
And thus they casten care awey
And token lustés upon honde.
And after thou shalt understonde
To mete into the kingés halle
They comen, as they be bidden alle.
And whan they weré set and served
Than after, as it was deserved
To hem that worthy knightés were,
So as they setten here and there,
The prise was yove and spoken out
Among the heralds all about.
And thus benethe and eke above
All was of armés and of love,
Wherof abouten atté bordes
Men had many sondry wordes,
That of the mirthé which they made
The kinge him self began to glade
Within his hert and toke a Pride
And sigh the cuppé stonde aside,
Which made was of Gurmundés hed,
As ye have herd, when he was ded,
And was with golde and riché stones
Beset and boundé for the nones,
And stode upon a fote on highte
Of burnéd golde, and with great slighte
Of werkmenship it was begrave
Of such worke as it shuldé have
And was polisséd eke so clene
That no signe of the scull was sene
But as it were a gripés[1] eye.
The king bad bere his cuppe awey
Which stood before him on the borde
And fetté thilke.[2] Upon his worde
The sculle is fette and wine therinne,
Wherof he bad his wife beginne:
'Drink with thy fader, dame,' he said.
And she to his biddíng obeid
And toke the sculle, and what her list
She drank, as she which nothing wist
What cup it was. And than all out
The kinge in audiénce about
Hath tolde, it was her faders sculle,
So that the lordés knowé shulle
Of his bataile a soth witnésse,
And made avaunt through what prowésse
He hath his wivés lové wonne,
Whiche of the sculle hath so begonne.
Tho was there mochel pride alofte,
They spoken all, and she was softe,
Thenkend on thilke unkindé Pride,
Of that her lord, so nigh her side,
Avaunteth him that he hath slaine
And pikéd out her faders braine
And of the sculle had made a cuppe.
She suffreth all till they were uppe,
And tho she hath sekenessé feigned
And goth to chambre and hath compleigned

[1] *Gripes*, eagle's.
[2] *Fette thilke*, fetch that one.

Unto a maidé which she triste,[1]
So that none other wight it wiste.
This maidé Glodeside is hote,
To whom this lady hath behote[2]
Of ladiship all that she can
To vengen her upon this man,
Which did her drink[3] in suche a plite
Among hem allé for despite
Of her and of her fader bothe,
Wherof her thoughtés ben so wrothe,
She saith, that she shall nought be glad,
Till that she se him so bestad
That he no moré make avaunt.
And thus they felle in covenaunt,
That they accorden atté laste
With suché wilés as they caste,
That they wol get of here accorde
Some orpéd[4] knight to sle this lorde.
And with this sleighté they beginne,
How they Helmegé mighten winne,
Which was the kingés botéler,
A proude and lusty bachiler,
And Glodeside he loveth hote.
And she to make him more assote[5]
Her lové graunteth, and by nighte
They shape how they to-gider mighte
A beddé mete. And done it was
This samé night. And in this cas
The quene her self the night seconde
Went in her stede and there she fonde
A chambre derké without light
And goth to beddé to this knight.
And he to kepe his observaunce
To lové doth his obeisaunce
And weneth it be Glodeside.
And she than after lay a side

1 *Triste*, trusted.
2 *Behote*, promised.
3 *Did her drink*, caused her to drink.
4 *Orpéd*, bold.
5 *Assote*, to dote.

And axeth him what he hath do,
And who she was she tolde him tho
And said: 'Helmege, I am thy quene,
Now shall thy lové well be sene
Of that thou hast thy willé wrought;
Or it shall soré ben abought,
Or thou shalt worche, as I thee saie.
And if thou wolt by suche a waie
Do my plesaúnce and holde it stille,
For ever I shall ben at thy wille
Bothe I and all min heritáge.'
Anone the wildé lovés rage,
In which no man him can govérne,
Hath made him that he can nought werne,[1]
But felle all hole to her assent,
And thus the whele is all miswent,
The which Fortúne hath upon honde.
For how that ever it after stonde,
They shope among hem such a wile
The king was ded within a while.
So slily came it nought aboute,
That they ne ben discovered out,
So that it thought hem for the beste
To fle, for theré was no reste.
And thus the tresor of the kinge
They trusse, and mochel other thinge,
And with a certaine felaship
They fled and went awey by ship
And heldé her right cours from thenne
Till that they comen to Ravenne,
Where they the dukés helpé sought.
And he, so as they him besought,
A placé graunteth for to dwelle.
But after, whan he herdé telle
Of the manér how they have do,
The duke let shapé for hem so,
That of a poison which they drunke
They hadden that they have beswunke.[2]

1 *Werne*, refuse.
2 *Beswunke*, laboured for.

And all this made Avaunt of Pride.
Good is therfore a man to hide
His owné prise, for if he speke,
He may lightlý his thanké breke.
In armés lith none avauntánce
To him, which thenketh his name avaunce
And be renoméd of his dede.
And also who that thenketh to spede
Of Love he may nought him avaunte.
For what man thilké Vicé haunte,
His purpose shall full ofté faile.
In armés he that woll travaile
Or ellés Lovés grace atteigne,
His losé tunge he mot restreigne,
Whiche bereth of his honóur the keie.
"Forthy my sone, in alle waie
Take right good hede of this matere."—
"I thonké you, my fader dere,
This scole is of a gentil lore.
And if there be ought ellés more
Of Pridé whiche I shall escheue,
Nowe axeth forth, and I woll sue[1]
What thing, that ye me woll enforme."—
"My sone, yet in other forme
There is a Vice of Pridés lore,
Which like an hawk whan he will sore,
Fleeth up on high in his delíces
After the likinge of his vices
And woll no mannés reson knowe
Till he down falle and overthrowe.
This vicé Vayngloríe is hote,
Wherof, my sone, I thee behote
To trete and speke in suche a wise,
That thou thee might better avise.

Vainglory.

The proudé Vice of Veinglorie
Remembreth nought of purgatorie,

[1] *Sue*, follow.

His worldés joiés ben so grete,
Him thenketh of heven no beyete.[1]
This livés pompe is all his pees,
Yet shall he deié nethéles,
And therof thenketh he but a lite,[2]
For all his lust is to delite
In newé thingés, proude and veine,
Als ferforth as he may atteine.
I trowe, if that he mighté make
His body newe, he woldé take
A newé forme and leve his olde.
For what thing that he may beholde
The which to comun use is straunge,
Anone his oldé guisé chaunge
He woll, and fallé therupon
Lich unto the camelión,
Whiche upon every sondry hewe
That he beholt he moté newe
His colour; and thus unavised
Ful ofté time he stant desguised.
More jolif than the brid in Maie,
He maketh him ever fressh and gaie
And doth all his array desguise,
So that of him the newé guise
Of lusty folke all other take.
And eke he can carollés make,
Roundel, baláde and virélay.
And with all this, if that he may
Of lové gete him avauntage
Anone he wext of his coráge
So over glad, that of his ende
He thenketh there is no deth coménde.
For he hath than at allé tide
Of lové such a maner Pride,
Him thenketh his joy is endéles.
"Now shrive thee, sone, in Goddés pees
And of thy lové tell me plein,
If that thy glorie hath be so vayne."—
"My fader, as touchénd of all
I may nought well ne nought ne shall

[1] *Beyete*, gain. [2] *Lite*, little.

Of vayn glorie excusé me,
That I ne have for lové be
The better addresséd and arraied.
And also I have ofte assaied
Roundel, baláde and virélay
For her on whom min herté lay,
To make and also for to peinte
Carollés with my wordés queinte
To setté my purpós alofte.
And thus I sang hem forth full ofte
In halle and eke in chambre aboute
And madé merie among the route:
But yet ne ferde I nought the bet.
Thus was my glorie in vayn beset
Of all the joié that I made.
For when I woldé with her glade
And of her lové songes make,
She saide, it was nought for her sake,
And listé nought my songés here,
Ne witen what the wordés were.
So for to speke of min array
Yet couth I never be so gay
Ne so well make a songe of love,
Wherof I mighté ben above
And have enchéson[1] to be glad.
But rather I am ofte adrad
For sorwé, that she saith me nay.
And nethéles I woll nought say,
That I nam glad on other side
For famé that can nothing hide.
All day woll bringe unto min ere
Of that men speken here and there,
How that my lady berth the prise,
How she is faire, how she is wise,
How she is womanlich of chere.
Of all this thing whan I may here,
What wonder is though I be fain.
And eke whan I may heré sain
Tidíngés of my ladis hele,
All though I may nought with her dele,
Yet am I wonder glad of that.
For whan I wote her good estate,

[1] *Encheson*, occasion.

As for that time I dare well swere,
None other sorwé may me dere.
Thus am I gladed in this wise.
But, fader, of your lorés wise,
Of whiché ye be fully taught,
Now tell me if ye thenketh ought,
That I therof am for to wite."[1]—
"Of that there is, I thee acquite,
My sone," he saide, "and for thy good
I wollé that thou understood,
For I thenke upon this matere
To tell a tale, as thou shalt here,
How that ayein this proudé Vice
The highé God of his justíce
Is wrothe and great vengeaúncé doth.
Nowe herken a talé, that is soth,
Though it be nought of Lovés kinde.
A great ensample thou shalt finde
This Veingloríé for to fle,
Whiche is so full of vanité.
There was a king, that mochel might,
Which Nabugodonosor hight,
Of whom that I spake here to-fore.
Yet in the bible this name is bore,
For all the worlde in thorient
Was hole at his commaundément,
As than of kingés to his liche
Was none so mighty ne so riche,
To his empire and to his lawes
As who saith all in thilké dawes
Were obeisaúnt and tribute bere,
As though he god of erthé were.
With strengthe he putté kingés under
And wrought of Pridé many a wonder,
He was so full of Veinglorie,
That he ne hadde no memorie,
That there was any God but he
For pride of his prosperite.

[1] *To wite*, to blame.

Till that the highé King of Kinges,
Which seeth and knoweth allé thinges,
Whose eyé may nothínge asterte
The privetés of mannés herte,[1]
They speke and sounen in his ere
As though they loudé windés were,
He toké vengeaunce of his Pride.
But for he wolde a while abide
To loke if he wolde him amende,
To him aforé token he sende.
And that was in his slepe by night
This proudé kinge a wonder sight
Had in his sweven[2] there he lay.
Him thought upon a mery day,
As he beheld the world aboute,
A tre full growe he sigh[3] there oute
Which stood the world amiddés even,
Whos heighté straught up to the heven.
The levés weren faire and large,
Of fruit it bore so ripe a charge,
That allé men it mighté fede.
He sigh also the bowés sprede
Above all erth, in whiché were
The kinde of allé briddes there.
And eke him thought he sigh also
The kinde of alle bestés go
Under the tre abouten round
And fedden hem upon the ground.
As he this wonder stood and sigh,
Him thought he herde a vois on high
Criende, and saide aboven alle:
'Hewe down this tree and let it falle,
The levés let defoule in haste
And do the fruit destruie and waste;
And let ofshreden every braunche,
But atté roote be let it staunche.
Whan all his Pride is cast to grounde
The rooté shall be fasté bounde;
And shall no mannés herté bere,
But every lust he shall forbere
Of man, and lich an oxe his mete
Of gras he shall purcháce and ete,
Till al the waters of the heven
Have wasshen him by timés seven,
So that he be through-knowe aright
What is the hevenliché might,
And be made humble to the wille
Of Him which may all save and spille.'
This king out of his sweven abraide[1]
And he upon the morwe it saide
Unto the clerkés which he hadde.
But none of hem the soth aradde,
Was none his sweven couth undo.
And it stood thilké timé so,
This kinge had in subjectión
Judee and of affectión
Above al other one Daniél
He loveth, for he couthé well
Diviné that none other couthe.
To him were allé thingés couthe,
As he it hadde of Goddes grace.
He was before the kingés face
Assent and bodé[2] that he shulde
Upon the point the kinge of tolde[3]
The fortune of his sweven expounde,
As it shulde afterward be founde.
Whan Daniél this sweven herde,
He stood long time, er he answérde,
And made a wonder hevy chere.[4]
The king toke hede of his manere
And bad him tellé that he wiste
As he to whome he mochel triste,[5]
And said, he woldé nought be wroth.
But Daniél was wonder loth

1 From whose eye the secrets of man's heart may in no wise escape.
2 *Sweven*, dream.
3 *Sigh*, saw.

1 Awoke suddenly from his dream.
2 Sent for and commanded.
3 *Of tolde*, told of.
4 *Hevy chere*, sad face.
5 *Triste*, trusted.

And said: 'Upon thy fomen alle,
Sir king, thy sweven moté falle.
And nethéles touchénd of this
I woll thee tellen howe it is,
And what disese is to thee shape,
God wote if thou it shall escape.
The highé tre which thou hast sein,
With lef and fruit so wel besein,
The which stood in the world amiddes,
So that the bestés and the briddes
Govérnéd were of him alone,
Sir King, betokeneth thy persóne
Which stonde above all erthely thinges.
Thus regnen under thee the kinges
And all the people unto thee louteth[1]
And all the worlde thy person douteth,[2]
So that with vein honoúr deceived
Thou hast the reverencé weived[3]
Fro him whiche is thy kinge above,
That thou for dredé ne for love
Wolt nothing knowen of this God,
Which now for thee hath made a rod,
Thy Vayngloric and thy folie
With greté peinés to chastie.
And of the vois thou herdest speke,
Which bad the bowés for to breke
And hewe and fellé down the tre,
That word belongeth unto thee.
Thy regné shall be overthrowe,
And thou despuiléd for a throwe.[4]
But that the rooté shuldé stonde,
By that thou shalt wel understonde,
There shall abiden of thy regne
A time ayein whan thou shall regne.
And eke of that thou herdest saie
To take a mannés hert aweie
And setté there a bestiáll,
So that he lich an oxé shall

1 *Louteth*, bows.
2 *Douteth*, fears.
3 *Weived*, put aside.
4 *Throwe*, space of time.

Pastúre, and that he be bereined
By timés seven and soré peined,
Till that he knowe his Goddes mightes,
Than shall he stond ayein uprightes.
All this betokeneth thine estate,
Which now with God is in debate:
Thy mannés formé shall be lassed,
Till seven yere ben overpassed,
And in the likenesse of a beste
Of gras shall be thy roiall feste,
The weder shall upon thee rayne.
And understonde, that all this payne
Which thou shalt suffre thilké tide,
Is shape all only for thy Pride
Of Vayngloric and of the sinne
Which thou hast longé stonden inne.
So upon this condición
Thy sweven hath exposición.
But er this thing befalle in dede,
Amendé thee, this wold I rede,
Yif and departé[1] thin almésse,
Do mercy forth with rightwisnésse,
Beseche and praie the highé grace,
For so thou might thy pees purcháce
With God and stonde in good accorde.'
But Pride is loth to leve his lorde
And wol nought suffre Humilité
With him to stonde in no degré.
And whan a ship hath lost his stere,
Is none so wise that may him stere
Ayein the wawés in a rage.
This proudé king in his corágé
Humilité hath so forlore,
That for no sweven he sigh to-fore
Ne yet for all that Daniél
Him hath counséiléd every dele,
He let it passe out of his minde
Through Vayngloric, and as the blinde
He seth no weie er him be wo.
And fel withinne a timé so,

1 *Departe*, divide, distribute.

As he in Babiloiné wente,
The Vanité of Pride him hente.[1]
His hert aros of vayn glorie,
So that he drough to memorie
His lordship and his regalie
With wordés of surquederie.
And whan that he him most avaunteth,
That Lord, which Vaynglorié daunteth,
All sodeinlich, as who saith treis,[2]
Where that he stood in his paleis
He toke him fro the mennés sight.
Was none of hem so ware that might
Set eyé where that he becom.
And thus was he from his kingdóm
Into the wildé forest drawe,
Where that the mighty Goddés lawe
Through his powér did him transforme
Fro man into a bestés forme.
And lich an oxe under the fote
He graseth as he nedés mote
To geten him his livés fode.
Tho thought him coldé grasses goode,
That whilome ete the hoté spices,
Thus was he tornéd fro delices.
The wine which he was wont to drinke,
He toke than of the wellés brinke
Or of the pit or of the slough,
It thought him thanné good inough.
In stede of chambres well arraied
He was than of a bussh well paied;
The hardé ground he lay upon,
For other pilwés had he non,
The stormés and the reinés fall,
The windés blowe upon him all,
He was tormented day and night.
Such was the highé Goddes might,
Till seven yere an endé toke.
Upon him self tho gan he loke:

[1] *Hente*, seized.
[2] *As who seith treis*, in a trice.

In stede of meté gras and streis;
In stede of handés longé cleis;[1]
In stede of man a bestés like;[2]
He sigh,[3] and than he gan to sike[4]
For cloth of golde and of perrie.[5]
Which him was wont to magnifie.
When he beheld his cote of heres
He wepte and with full wofull teres
Up to the heven he caste his chere[6]
Wepénd and thought in this manere;
Though he no wordés mighté winne,
Thus said his hert and spake withinne:
'O mighty God, that all hast wrought
And all might bring ayein to nought,
Now knowe I wel but all of thee
This world hath no prosperité,
In thin aspect ben alle aliche
The pouer man and eke the riche,
Withouté thee there may no wight,
And thou above all other might.
O mighty Lord, toward my vice
Thy mercy medle[7] with justice,
And I woll make a covenaunt
That of my life the remenaunt
I shall it by thy grace amende
And in thy lawé so dispende,
That Vaynglorie I shall escheue,
And bowe unto thin heste, and sue
Humilité, and that I vowe.'
And so thenkend he gan down bowe,
And though him lacké vois of speche,
He gan up with his fete areche
And wailend in his bestly steven[8]
He made his plaint unto the heven.
He kneleth in his wise and braieth
To seché mercy and assaieth

[1] *Cleis*, claws.
[2] *Like*, body.
[3] *Sigh*, saw.
[4] *Sike*, sigh.
[5] *Perrie*, precious stones.
[6] *Chere*, countenance.
[7] *Medle*, mix, join.
[8] *Steven*, voice.

His God, which made him nothing straunge.[1]
Whan that he sigh his Pridé chaunge
Anone as he was humble and tame
He found toward his God the same,
And in a twinkeling of a loke
His mannés forme ayein he toke
And was reforméd to the regne
In whiche that he was wont to regne,
So that the Pride of Vaynglorie
Ever after out of memorie
He lett it passe. And thus is shewed
What is to ben of Pride unthewed [2]
Ayein the highé Goddés lawe,
To whom no man may be feláwe.
"Forthy my sone, také good hede
So for to ledé thy manhede,
That thou ne be nought lich a beste.
But if thy life shall ben honéste
Thou must Humblessé take on honde,
For thanné might thou siker stonde,
And for to speke it other wise
A proud man can no love assise.[3]
For though a woman wolde him plese,
His Pridé can nought ben at ese.
There may no man to mochel blame
A Vicé which is for to blame.
Forthy men shulden nothing hide
That mighte fall in blame of Pride,
Whiche is the worsté Vice of alle,
Wherof so as it was befalle
The tale I thenke of a cronique
To telle, if that it may thee like,
So that thou might Humblessé sue
And eke the Vice of Pride escheue,

1 Showed himself no whit estranged—did not turn from him.
2 *Unthewed*, showing want of discipline against the law of the high God to whom, &c.
3 *Assise*, be in session with.

Wherof the glorie is false and vaine,
Which God him self hath in disdeine,
That though it mounté for a throwe,[1]
It shall down falle and overthrowe.
A king whilom was yonge and wise,
The which set of his wit great prise.
Of depe ymaginatións
And straunge interpretatións,
Problemés and demaundés eke
His wisedom was to finde and seke,
Wherof he wolde in sondry wise
Opposen hem that weren wise.
But none of hem it mighté bere
Upon his word to yive answére
Out taken [2] one, which was a knight,
To him was every thing so light,
That al so sone as he hem herde
The kingés wordés he answerde,
What thing the king him axe wolde,
Whereof anone the trouth he tolde.
The king somdele had an envie
And thought he wolde his wittés plie
To seté some conclusión,
Which shuldé be confusión
Unto this knight, so that the name
And of wisdóm the highé fame
Toward him sèlfe he woldé winne.
And thus of all his wit withinne
This king began to studie and muse
What straungé mater he might use
The knightés wittés to confounde,
And atté last he hath it founde:
And for the knight anon he sente,
That he shall tellé what he mente.
Upon thre points stood the matere
Of questións as thou shalte here.
"The firsté point of allé thre
Was this: 'What thing in his degré

1 *Throwe*, space of time.
2 *Out taken*, except.

Of all this world hath nedé lest
And yet men helpe it allthermest.'[1]
The seconde is: 'What moste is worth
And of costage is lest put forth.'
The thrid is: 'Which is of most cost
And lest is worth and goth to lost.'
The king these thre demaundés axeth,
To the knight this law he taxeth,
That he shall gone and comen ayein
The thriddé weke and tell him pleine
To every point, what it amounteth.
And if so be that he miscounteth
To make in his answere a faile,
There shall none other thinge availe,
The king saith, but he shall be dede
And lese his goodés and his hede.
This knight was sory of this thinge
And wolde excuse him to the kinge;
But he ne wolde him nought forbere,
And thus the knight of his answere
Goth home to take avisément.
But after his entendément
The more he cast his wit aboute,
The more he stant therof in doubte.
Tho wist he well the kingés herte,
That he the deth ne shulde asterte[2]
And suche a sorwe to him hath take,
That gladship he hath all forsake.
He thoughté first upon his life,
And after that upon his wife,
Upon his children eke also,
Of whiché he had doughteres two.
The yongest of hem had of age
Fourtené yere, and of visage
She was right faire and of stature
Lich to an hevenlich figure,
And of manér and goodly speche;
Though men wolde allé londés seche,
They shulden nought have founde her like.
She sigh her fader sorwe and sike
And wisté nought the causé why.
So cam she to him prively
And that was, wher he made his mone
Within a gardin all him one.[1]
Upon her knees she gan down falle
With humble herte and to him calle
And saide: 'O goodé fader dere,
Why maké ye thus hevy chere
And I wot nothinge how it is?
And well ye knowé, fader, this,
What aventúré that you felle
Ye might it saufly to me telle,
For I have ofté herd you saide,
That ye such truste have on me laide,
That to my suster ne to my brother
In all this worlde ne to none other
Ye dursté telle a priveté
So well, my fader, as to me.
Forthý,[2] my fader, I you praie
Ne casteth nought that hert awaie,
For I am she, that woldé kepe
Your honour.' And with that to wepe
Her eyé may nought be forbore,
She wissheth for to ben unbore,
Er that her fader so mistriste
To tellen her of that he wiste.
And ever among 'Mercý' she cride,
That he ne shulde his counseil hide
From hiré, that so wolde him good
And was so nigh in flesshe and blood.
So that, with weping, atté laste
His chere[3] upon his childe he caste
And sorwefullý to that she praide
He tolde his tale and thus he saide:

1 *Alltherwest*, most of all.
2 *Asterte*, escape from.

1 *All him one*, by himself alone.
2 *Forthy*, therefore.
3 *Chere*, countenance.

'The sorwe, doughter, which I make
Is nought all only for my sake,
But for thee bothe and for you alle.
For suche a chaunce is me befalle,
That I shall er this thriddé day
Lese [1] all that ever I lese may,
My life and all my good therto.
Therfore it is I sorwe so.'
'What is the cause, alas,' quod she,
'My fader, that ye shulden be
Dede and destruied in suche a wise?'
And he began the points devise,[2]
Which as the king tolde him by mouthe
And said her pleinly, that he couthe
Answéren to no point of this.
And she, that hereth howe it is,
Her counseil yaf and saidé tho: [3]
'My fader, sithen [4] it is so,
That ye can se none other weie,
But that ye must nedés deie,
I woldé pray you of o thinge,—
Let me go with you to the kinge,
And ye shall make him understonde,
How ye, my wittés for to fonde,[5]
Have laid your answere upon me,
And telleth him in such degré
Upon my worde ye wol abide
To life or deth what so betide.
For yet perchaunce I may purcháce
With some good word the kingés grace,
Your life and eke your good to save.
For ofté shall a woman have
Thing whiche a man may nought areche.[6]
The fader herd his doughters speche
And thought there was no reson in,
And sigh his owné life to winne

[1] *Lese*, lose. [2] *Devise*, relate.
[3] *Tho*, then. [4] *Sithen*, since.
[5] *Fonde*, try. [6] *Areche*, reach to.

He couthé done him self no cure.
So better him thought in aventúre
To put his life and all his good,
Than in the maner as it stood
His life incertein for to lese.
And thus thenkénd he gan to chese [1]
To do the counseil of his maid
And toke the purpose, which she said.
The day was comen and forth they gon,
Unto the court they come anon,
Where as the kinge in his jugemént
Was set, and hath this knight assent.
Arraiéd in her besté wise
This maiden with her wordés wise
Her fader leddé by the honde
Into the placé, where he fonde
The king with other which he wolde,
And to the king knelénd he tolde
As he enforméd was to-fore,
And praith the king, that he therfore
His doughters wordés woldé take,
And saith that he woll undertake
Upon her wordés for to stonde.
Tho was ther great merveile on honde,
That he, which was so wise a knight,
His life upon so yonge a wight
Besetté wolde in jeopartie,
And many it helden for folie.
But at the lasté nethéles
The king commaundeth ben in pees,
And to this maide he cast his chere
And saide, he wolde her talé here,
And bad her speke, and she began:
'My legé lord, so as I can,'
Quod she, 'the pointés which I herde,
They shull of reson ben answerde.
The first I understonde is this,
What thinge of all the worlde it is,

[1] *Chese*, choose.

Which men most helpe and hath lest nede.
My legé lord, this wolde I rede
The erthe it is, whiche evermo
With mannés labour is bego
As well in Winter as in Maie.
The mannés honde doth what he may
To helpe it forth and make it riche,
And forthý men it delve and diche
And eren[1] it with strength of plough,
Wher it hath of him self inough
So that his nede is atté leste.
For every man and birde and beste
Of flour and gras and roote and rinde
And every thing by way of kinde
Shall sterve,[2] and erthe it shall become;
As it was out of erthé nome
It shall to therthé torne ayein.
And thus I may by reson sein
That erthe is mosté nedéles
And most men helpe it nethéles,
So that, my lord, touchénd of this
I have answerde how that is.
'That other point I understood,
Which most is worth and most is good
And costeth lest a man to kepe,
My lorde, if ye woll také kepe,
I say it is Humilité,
Through whiché the high Trinite
As for deserte of puré Love
Unto Marié from above
Of that he knewe her humble entente
His owné sone adown he sente,
Above all other and[3] her he chese
For that vertu which bodeth pees.
So that I may by reson calle
Humilité most worthe of alle,

[1] *Eren*, till. [2] *Sterve*, die.
[3] And he chose her above all other. "And" used in the middle of a clause, as we might now use "also."

And lest it costeth to mainteine
In all the worlde, as it is seine.
For who that hath humblesse on honde
He bringeth no werrés into londe,
For he desireth for the best
To setten every man in reste.
Thus with your highé reverence
Me thenketh that this evidence
As to this point is suffisaúnt.
'And touchend of the remenaúnt,
Whiche is the thridde of your axinges,
What lest is worth of allé thinges
And costeth most, I telle it Pride,
Which may nought in the Heven abide.
For Lucifer with hem that felle
Bar Pridé with him into helle.
There was Pride of to grete cost,
Whan he for Pride hath Heven lost;
And after that in paradise
Adam for Pridé lost his prise
In middel-erth. And eke also
Pride is the cause of allé wo,
That all the world ne may suffise
To staunche of Pridé the reprise.[1]
Pride is the hevéd[2] of all sinne,
Which wasteth all and may nought winne.
Pride is of every mis[3] the pricke,
Pride is the worste of allé wicke,
And costeth most and lest is worth
In placé where he hath his forth.
'That have I said that I woll say
Of min answére and to you pray,
My legé lorde, of your office,
That ye such grace and suche justíce
Ordeigné for my fader here,
That after this whan men it here,

[1] *Reprise*, reproach. [2] *Hevéd*, head.
[3] *Mis*, thing amiss; wrong.

The world therof may speké good.'
The king, which reson understood
And hath all herde how she hath said,
Was inly glad and so well paid,
That all his wrath is over go.
And he began to loké tho
Upon this maiden in the face,
In which he found so mochel grace,
That all his prise on her he laide
In audiénce and thus he saide:
'My fairé maidé, well thee be
Of thin answére, and eke of thee
Me liketh well, and as thou wilte
Foryivé be thy faders gilte.
And if thou were of such lignáge,
That thou to me were of parágе
And that thy fader were a pere,
As he is now a bachelére,
So siker as I have a life,
Thou sholdest thanné be my wife.
But this I saié nethéles,
That I woll shapé thin encrese,
What worldés good that thou wolt crave
Are of my yift, and thou shalt have.'
And she the king with wordés wise
Knelendé thonketh in this wise:
'My legé lord, god mot you quite.[1]
My fader here hath but a lite
Of warison,[2] and that he wende
Had all be lost, but now amende
He may well through your noble grace.'
With that the king right in his place
Anon forth in that fresshé hete
An erldome, which than of eschete
Was laté falle into his honde,
Unto this knight, with rent and londe,

[1] *Quite*, requite.
[2] Little of reward for service done.

Hath yove and with his chartre sesed.[1]
And thus was all the noise appesed.
This maiden, which sate on her knees
To fore the kingés charitees,
Commendeth and saith evermore:
'My legé lord, right now to-fore
Ye saide, and it is of recórde,
That if my fader were a lorde
And pere unto these other grete,
Ye wolden for nought ellés lette,
That I ne sholdé be your wife.
And thus wote every worthy life
A kingés worde mot nede be holde.
Forthý my lord, if that ye wolde
So great a charité fulfille,
God wote it weré well my wille.
For he, which was a bachelere,
My fader, is now made a pere;
So whan as ever that I cam,
An erlés doughter nowe I am.'
"This yongé king, which peiséd all
Her beauté and her wit withall,
As he which was with lové hente,
Anone therto yaf his assente.
He mighté nought the place asterte
That she nis lady of his herte.
So that he toke her to his wife
To holdé while that he hath life.
And thus the king toward his knight
Accordeth him as it is right.
And over this, good is to wite[2]
In the cronique as it is write
This noble kinge, of whom I tolde,
Of Spainé by tho daiés olde
The kingdom had in governaunce,
And as the boke maketh remembraúnce
Alphonsé was his propre name.
The knight also, if I shall name,

[1] *Sesed*, "seisin" (possession), given.
[2] *To wite*, to know.

Danz Petro hight, and as men telle
His doughter wisé Petronelle
Was clepéd, which was full of grace.
And that was sene in thilké place,
Where she her fader out of tene [1]
Hath brought, and made her selfe
a quene,
Of that she hath so well desclosed
The points wherof she was opposed.
"Lo now, my sone, as thou might
here,
Of all this thing to my matere
But one I take, and that is Pride,
To whom no gracé may betide.
In Heven he fell out of his stede,
And Paradise him was forbede;
The goodé men in erthe him hate,
So that to helle he mote algate,
Where every Vertue shall be weived [2]
And every Vicé be resceived.
But Humblesse is all other wise,
Which most is worth, and no re-
prise [3]
It taketh ayein, but softe and faire
If any thing stant in contraire
With humble speche it is redressed.
Thus was this yongé maiden blessed,
The whiche I spake of now to-fore,
Her faders life she gat therfore

1 *Tene*, anxious grief.
2 *Weived*, put aside.
3 *Reprise*, reproach.

And wan withall the kingés love.
Forthý my sone, if thou wolt love,
It sit thee well to levé Pride
And taken Humblesse on thy side,
The more of gracé thou shalt
gete."—
"My fader, I woll nought foryete
Of this that ye have told me here,
And if that any such manere
Of humble port may love appaie,
Here afterwarde I thonke assaie.
But now forth over I beseche,
That ye more of my shrifté
seche."—
"My godé sone, it shall be do.
Now herken and lay an eré to,
For as touchénd of Pridés fare
Als ferforth as I can declare
In cause of Vice, in cause of Love
That hast thou pleinly herde above,
So that there is no more to saie
Touchénd of that; but other waie
Touchend Envie I thenké telle,
Whiche hath the propre kinde of
helle,[1]
Withouté causé to misdo
Toward him self and other also;
Hereafterward as understonde
Thou shalt the spieces,[2] as they
stonde.

1 Which hath from hell its proper nature.
2 Species, classification into its several kinds.

Book II.

OF ENVY.

Now after Pridé the secoúnde
There is, which many a wofull stounde,
Towardés other berth aboute
Within him self and nought withoute.
For in his thought he brenneth ever,
Whan that he wote an other lever[1]
Or moré vertuós than he,
Which passeth him in his degré;
Therof he taketh his maladie.
That Vice is clepéd hot Envie.
Forthý, my sone, if it be so,
Thou art or hast ben one of tho,[2]
As for to speke in Lovés cas
If ever yet thin herté was
Seke of another mannes hele?"[3]—
"So god ávauncé my quaréle,
My fader, ye[4] a thousand sithe.
Whan I have sene another blithe
Of love and hadde a goodly chere,
Ethna, which brenneth yere by yere,
Was thanné nought so hote as I
Of thilké sore which privély
Mine hertés thought withinné brenneth.
The ship, which on the wawes renneth
And is forstorméd and forblowe,[5]

[1] *Lever*, more belovéd.
[2] *Tho*, those.
[3] Sick of another man's health.
[4] *Ye*, yea.
[5] "For" is an intensive prefix.

Is nought more peined for a throwe[1]
Than I am thanné whan I se
Another which that passeth me
In that fortúne of Lovés yifte.
But fader, this I telle in shrifte,
That is no where but in o place.
For who that lese or findé grace
In other stede, it may nought greve.
But this ye may right well beleve,
Toward my lady that I serve,
Though that I wisté for to sterve,
Min hert is full of such folý,
That I my selfe may nought chastý,
Whan I the Court se of Cupíde
Approche unto my lady side
Of hem that lusty ben and fresshe,
Though it availe hem nought a resshe,[2]
But only that they ben of speche,
My sorwe is than nought to seche.
But whan they rounen[3] in her ere,
Than groweth all my mosté fere.
And namely[4] whan they talen longe,
My sorwes thanné be so stronge,
Of that I see hem well at ese
I can nought tellé my disese.
But, sire, as of my lady selve,
Though she have wowers, ten or twelve,

[1] *Throwe*, space of time.
[2] *Resshe*, rush.
[3] *Rounen*, whisper.
[4] *Namely*, especially.

For no mistrust I have of her
Me greveth nought, for certés, sir,
I trowe in all this world to seche
Nis woman, that in dede and speche
Woll better avise her what she doth,
Ne better, for to saie a sothe,
Kepe her honóur at allé tide
And yet get her a thank beside.
But nethéles I am beknowe,
That whan I se at any throwe [1]
Or elles if I may it here,
That she make any man good chere,
Though I therof have nought to done,
My thought woll entermete [2] him sone.
For though I be my selven straunge
Envié maketh min herté chaungc,
That I am sorwefully bestad
Of that I se another glad
With hiré, but of other all
Of Lové what so may befall,
Or that he faile or that he spede,
Therof take I but litel hede.
Nowe have I said, my fader, all,
As of this point in speciall
As ferforthly as I have wiste.[3]
Nowaxeth, fader, what you liste."—
"My sone, ere I axe any more
I thenké somdele for thy lore
Tell an ensample of this matére
Touchend Envý, as thou shalt here.
"Write in Civilé this I finde,
Though it be nought the houndés kinde
To eté chaff, yet woll he werne
An oxe, which cometh to the berne,
Therof to taken any fode.
And thus who that it understode
It stant of Love in many a place,
Who that is out of Lovés grace
And may him selven nought availe,
He wold an other sholdé faile.
And if he may put any lette,
He doth al that he may to lette.
Wherof I finde, as thou shalt wit,
To this purpós a talé write.
"There ben of suché mo than twelve,
That ben nought able as of hem selve
To getté love, and for Envie
Upon all other they aspie.
And for [1] hem lacketh that they wolde,
They kepé that none other sholde
Touchend of love his causé spede;
Wherof a great ensample I rede,
Whiche unto this matére accordeth,
As Ovide in his boke recordeth,
How Poliphemus whilom wrought,
Whan that he Galathé besought
Of lové, whiche he may nought lacche,[2]
That made him for to waite and wacche
By allé waiés howe it ferde;
Till at the last he knewe and herde
How that an other haddé leve
To lové there, as he mot leve
As for to speke of any spede;
So that he knew none other rede
But for to waiten upon alle
Till he may se the chauncé falle,
That he her lové mighté greve,
Whiche he him self may nought acheve.
This Galathé, saith the poéte,
Above all other was unmete [3]
Of beauté, that men thanné knewe,
And had a lusty love, and trewe

1 *Throwe*, space of time.
2 *Entermete*, go apart from.
3 As far forth as I have known.

1 *For*, because.
2 *Lacche*, catch, secure.
3 *Unmete*, beyond measure.

A bacheler in his degré,
Right such an other as was she;
On whom she hath her herté set,
So that it mighté nought be let[1]
For yifté ne for no beheste,
That she ne was all at his heste.[2]
This yongé knight Acís was hote,[3]
Whiche her ayeinwarde also hote[4]
All only loveth and no mo.[5]
Herof was Poliphemus wo
Through pure Envíe and ever aspide
And waiteth[6] upon every side,
Whan he to-gider mighté se
This yonge Acís with Galathé.
So longe he waiteth to and fro,
Till at the laste he founde hem two
In privé placé, where they stood
To speke and have her wordés good.
The placé, where as he hem sigh,[7]
It was under a banké nigh
The greaté se, and he above
Stood and behelde the lusty love,
Whiche eche of hem to other made
With goodly chere and wordés glade
That all his hert hath sette a fire
Of pure Envíe. And as a vire[8]
Which flieth out of a mighty bowe,
Away he fleddé for a throwe,[9]
As he that was for lové wode,
Whan that he sigh how that it stode.
This Polipheme a geaunt was,
And whan he sigh the sothé cas,
How Galathé him hath forsake
And Acis to her lové take,
His herté may it nought forbere
That he ne roreth as a bere
And as it were a wildé beast
In whom no reson might areste.
He ranne Ethná the hill about,
Where never yet the fire was out,

[1] *Let*, hindered. [2] *Heste*, command.
[3] *Hote*, named. [4] *Hote*, hotly.
[5] *No mo*, no more, no one else.
[6] *Waiteth*, watcheth. [7] *Sigh*, saw.
[8] *Vire*, arrow. [9] *Throwe*, space of time.

Fulfilled of sorwe and great disese
That he sigh Acis well at ese.
Till atté last he him bethoughte
As he which all Envié soughte,
And torneth to the banke ayein
Where he with Galathé hath sein
That Acis, whom he thoughté greve,
Though he him self may nought releve.
This geaunt with his rudé might
Part of the banke he shof down right,
The whiche even upon Acis fille,[1]
So that with falling of this hille
This Poliphemus Acis slough,
Wherof she madé sorwe inough.
And as she fleddé from the londe,
Neptúnus toke her by the honde
And kept her in so faste a place
Fro Polipheme and his manáce,
That he with al his false Envie
Ne might atteigne her compaignie.
This Galathé, of whom I speke,
That of her self may nought be wreke,[2]
Withouten any semblaunt feigned
She hath her lovés deth compleigned,
And with her sorwe and with her wo
She hath the goddés moved so,
That they of pité and of grace
Have Acis in the samé place,
There he lay dede, into a welle
Transforméd, as the bokes telle,
With fresshé stremés and with clere,
As he whilom with lusty chere
Was fressh his lové for to queme.[3]
And with this rudé Polipheme
For his Envie and for his hate
They weré wroth. And thus algate,

[1] *Fille*, fell. [2] *Wreke*, avenged.
[3] *Queme*, please.

"My soné, thou might understonde,
That if thou wolt in gracé stonde
With Lové, thou must leve Envie:
And as thou wolt for thy partie
Toward thy lové stondé fre
So must thou suffre another be,
What so befalle upon thy chaunce.
For it is an unwise vengeaúnce
Which to none other man is lefe
And is unto him selvé grefe."[1]—
"My fader, this ensample is good,
But how so ever that it stood
With Poliphemus love as tho,[2]
It shall nought stondé with me so
To worchen any felonie
In lové for no suche envie.
Forthý if there ought ellés be,
Now axeth forth, in what degré
It is, and I me shall confesse
With shrifte unto your holinesse.
"My godé soné, yet there is
A Vicé revers unto this,
Whiche envioús taketh his gladnésse
Of that he seeth the hevinesse
Of other men. For his welfare
Is, whan he wote another care
Of that an other hath a falle,
He thenketh him selfe arist[3] with alle.
Suche is the gladship of Envie
In worldés thing and in partie
Full ofté timés eke also
In Lovés cause it stant right so.
If thou, my sone, hast joié had,
Whan thou an other sigh unglad,
Shrive thee therof."—"My fader, yis.
I am beknowe[4] unto you this

1 Which pleases no other man and grieves oneself.
2 *Tho*, then.
3 *Arist*, lifted up.
4 *Beknowe*, to confess.

Of these lovérs that loven streite,[1]
And for that point which they coveite
Ben pursuaúntes from yere to yere
In Lovés court, when I may here
How that they climbe upon the whele,
And whan they wene all shall be wele
They ben down throwen atté laste,
Than am I fed of that they faste,
And laugh of that I se hem loure.
And thus of that they brewé soure
I drinké swete, and am well esed
Of that I wote they ben disesed.
But this whiche I you tellé here
Is only for my lady dere,
That for none other that I knowe
Me recheth nought who overthrowe
Ne who that stonde in love upright;
But be he squier, be he knight,
Which to my lady warde[2] pursueth
The more he lost of that he sueth,
The more me thenketh that I winne,
And am the moré glad withinne
Of that I wote him sorwe endure;
For ever upon suche aventure
It is a comfort, as men sain,
To him the which is wo besein.[3]
To sene an other in his peine,
So that they bothé may compleine.
Where I myself may nought availe,
To sene an other man travaile
I am right glad if he be let.[4]
And though I faré nought the bet,
His sorwe is to min herte a game,
Whan that I knowe it is the same
Which to my lady stant enclined
And hath his lové nought termíned,[5]
I am right joyfull in my thought.
If such Envié greveth ought,

1 *Streite*, strictly, intensely.
2 *To my lady warde*, toward my lady.
3 *Wo besein*, clothed in sorrow.
4 *Let*, hindered.
5 *Termíned*, brought to the desired end.

As I beknowé me coupable,
Ye that be wise and resónable,
My fader, telleth your avise."—
"My sone, Envie in to no prise
Of such a forme I understonde
Ne mighté by no reson stonde.
For this Envie hath such a kinde,
That he woll set himself behinde
To hinder with another wight,
And gladly lese[1] his owné right
To make another lesé his.
And for to knowen how so it is
A talé lich to his matere
I thenké telle, if thou wolte here,
To shewé properlý the Vice
Of this Envie and the malíce.
"Of Jupiter thus I finde iwrite,
How whilom that he woldé wite[2]
Upon the pleinté[3] whiche he herde
Among the men, how that it ferde,
As of her wrong condición
To do justificación.
And for that causé down he sent
An aungel, which abouté went
That he the sothé knowé may.
So it befell upon a day
This aungel which him shuld enforme
Was clothéd in a mannés forme
And overtoke, I understonde,
Two men that wenten over londe,
Through which he thoughté to aspie
His cause and goth in compaignie.
This aungel with his wordés wise
Opposeth hem in sondry wise,
Now loudé wordés and now softe,
That made hem to desputen ofte.
And eche of hem his reson hadde,
And thus with talés he hem ladde
With good examinación
Till he knew the condición
What men they weré bothé two;

[1] *Lese*, lose. [2] *Wite*, know.
[3] *Pleinte*, complaint.

And sigh wel atté lasté tho,
That one of hem was coveitoús,
And his felaw was envioús.
And thus, whan he hath knoulech-ing,
Anone he feignéd departíng
And said he mote algaté wende.
But herken now what fell at ende,
For than he made hem understonde,
That he was there of Goddés sonde;[1]
And said hem for the kindéship
That they have done him felaship
He woldé do some grace ayein,
And bad that one of hem shuld sain
What thinge him is levést to crave,
And he it shall of yifté have.
And over that[2] eke forth with all
He saith that other havé shall
The double of that his felawe axeth:
And thus to hem his grace he taxeth.
The coveitous was wonder glad,
And to that other man he bad
And saith, that he first axé sholde;
For he supposeth that he wolde
Make his axíng of worldés good;
For than he knewe well howe it stood,
That he him self by double weight
Shall efté take; and thus by sleight
By causé that he woldé winne
He badde his felaw first beginne.
This envioús, though it be late
Whan that he sigh[3] he mote algate
Make his axíngé first, he thought
If he worshíp or profit sought,
It shall be doubled to his fere:[4]
That wold he chese in no manere.
But than he sheweth what he was
Towarde Envíe, and in this cas
Unto this aungel thus he saide
And for his yifté this he praide,

[1] *Sonde*, sending.
[2] *Over that*, beyond that.
[3] *Sigh*, saw.
[4] *Fere*, companion.

To make him blinde on his one eye,
So that his felaw no thing sigh.
This word was nought so soné spoke,
That his one eye anon was loke,
And his felaw forth with also
Was blinde on both his eyen two.
Tho was that other gladde inough,
That oné wept, that other lough,
He set his one eye at no cost
Wherof that other two hath lost.
Of thilke ensample, which fell tho,
Men tellen now full ofté so.
The worlde empeireth [1] comunly
And yet wot none the causé why;
For it accordeth nought to kinde [2]
Min owné harme to seche and finde,
Of that I shall my brother greve
I mighté never wel acheve.
What saist thou, sone, of this folie?"—
"My fader, but [3] I shuldé lie
Upon the point which ye have saide,
Yet was min herté never laide
But in the wise as I you tolde.
But evermore if that ye wolde
Ought ellés to my shrifté saie
Touchend Envie, I woldé praie."—
"My soné, that shall well be do.
Now herken and lay thin ere to.
"**Touchend** as of envíous brood
I wot nought one of allé good,
But nethéles suche as they be
Yet there is one, and that is he,
Which clepéd is Detractión.
And to conferme his action
He hath witholde Malebouche, [4]
Whose tunge nouther pill ne crouche [5]
May hiré so that he pronounce

[1] *Empeireth*, grows worse.
[2] *Kinde*, nature. [3] *But*, unless.
[4] *Witholde Malebouche*, held with Evil Mouth.
[5] *Pill ne crouche*, plunder nor coin.

A plein good word withouten frounce, [1]
Where behinde a mannés backe;
For though he preise he find some lacke,
Whiche of his tale is ay the laste
That all the prise shall overcaste.
And though there be no causé why,
Yet woll he jangle nought forthý,
As he whiche hath the heraldie
Of hem that usen for to lie.
For as the nettle whiche up renneth
The fresshé redé roses brenneth
And maketh hem fade and pale of hewe,
Right so this fals envíous hewe [2]
In every placé where he dwelleth
With falsé wordés where he telleth
He torneth preising into blame
And worship into worldés shame.
Of such lesínge as he compásseth
Is none so good that he ne passeth
Betwene his tethe and is backbited
And through his falsé tunge endited.
Lich to the sharnebudés [3] kinde,
Of whose natúré this I finde,
That in the hotest of the day,
Whan comen is the mery May,
He spret his winge and up he fleeth
And under all aboute he seeth
The fairé lusty flourés springe.
But therof hath he no likínge.
But where he seeth of any beste
The filthé, there he maketh his feste
And there upon he woll alighte,
There liketh him none other sighte
Right so this jangler envioús,
Though he a man se vertuoús
And full of good condición,
Therof maketh he no mención.
But ellés, be it nought so lite, [4]
Wherof that he may set a wite, [5]

[1] *Frounce*, frown. [2] *Hewe*, servant.
[3] *Sharnebudes*, shard-beetle's.
[4] *Lite*, little. [5] *Wite*, blame.

There renneth he with open mouth
Behinde a man and maketh it couth.[1]
But all the vertue whiche he can
That woll he hide, of every man,
And openly the vicé telle,
As he which of the scole of helle
Is taught, and fostred with Envie
Of housholde and of compaignie,
Where that he hath his propre office
To sette on every man a vice.
How so his mouth be comélý,
His wordé sit e'ermore awry
And saith the worsté that he may.
And in this wisé now a daye
In Lovés court a man may here
Full ofté pleine of this matere;
That many envious tale is stered,[2]
Where that it may nought be answered
But yet full ofte it is beleved;
And many a worthy love is greved
Through backbitinge of false Envie.
"If thou have made suche janglerie
In Lovés court, my sone, er this,
Shrive thee therof."—"My fader, yis.
But wite ye how, nought openly
But otherwhilé prively,
Whan I my deré lady mete
And thenke how that I am nought mete
Unto her highé worthinesse,
And eke I se the besinesse
Of all this yongé lusty route
Which all day púrsue her aboute,
And eche of hem his time awaiteth,
And eche of hem his tale affaiteth,[3]
All to deceive an innocent
Which woll nought be of her[4] assent.

[1] *Couth*, known.
[2] *Stered*, stirred up.
[3] *Affaiteth*, submitteth.
[4] *Her*, their.

And for men sain 'unknowen unkiste,'
Her thombé she holt in her fiste
So close within her owné honde
That theré winneth no man londe;
She leveth nought all that she hereth
And thus ful ofte her self she skiereth[1]
And is all ware of *had I wist*.[2]
But for all that min hert ariste
Whan I these comun lovers see
That wol nought holden hem to thre
But well nigh loven over al,
Min hert is envioús with all,
And ever I am adrad of guile,
In aunter if with any wile
They might her innocence enchaunte.
Forthý my words full ofte I haunte
Behindé hem so as I dare,
Wherof my lady may beware.
I say what ever cometh to mouth,
And wers I wolde if that I couth.
For whan I come unto her speche
All that I may enquere and seche
Of such deceipte I telle it all,
And ay the worst in speciall.
So faine I woldé that she wist
How litel they ben for to trist,
And what they wold and what they mente
So as they be of double entente,
Thus toward hem that wické mene[3]
My wicked word was ever grene.
And nethéles the soth to telle
In certein if it so befelle
That althertrewest man ibore[4]
To chese amonge a thousand score,
Which were all fully for to triste,
My lady loved, and I it wiste,

[1] *Skiereth*, secureth.
[2] Had I known. Old phrase to express a repentance come too late.
[3] Those who mean wickedly.
[4] The truest of all men born.

Yet rather than he shuldé spede
I woldé suché talés sprede
To my ladý, if that I might,
That I shuld all his love unright,
And therto wolde I do my peine.
For certés though I shuldé feigne
And tellé that was never thought,
For all this worlde I mighté nought
To suffre an other fully winne
There as I am yet to beginne;
For be they good or be they bad
I woldé none my lady had.
And that me maketh full ofte aspie
And usen wordés of Envié,
And for to make hem bere a blame—
And that is but of thilké same—
The whiche unto my lady drawe,
For ever on them I rounge[1] and gnawe
And hinder hem all that ever I maie.
And that is, sothly for to saie,
But only to my lady selve;
I telle it nought to ten ne twelve,
Therof I wol me well avise
To speke or jangle in any wise
That toucheth to my ladies name,
The whiche in ernest and in game
I woldé save, in to my deth;
For me were lever to lacke breth
Than speken of her name amis.
Now have ye herd touchénd of this,
My fader, in Confession
And therfore of Detraction
In Love, of that I have mispoke,
Tell how ye will it shall be wroke.
I am all redy for to bere
My peine, and also to forbere
What thing that ye woll nought allowe;
For who is bounden, he must bowe.
So woll I bowe unto your hest,
For I dare maké this behest,

[1] *Rounge*, nip.

That I to you have nothing hid,
But told right as it is betid,
And otherwise of no misspeche
My consciéncé for to seche.
I can nought of Envié finde
That I misspoke have ought behinde,
Wherof love oughté be mispaide.
Now have ye herde and I have saide,
What woll ye fader, that I do?"—
"My soné, do no moré so,
But ever kepe thy tungé still,
Thou might the moré have thy will.
For as thou saist thy selven here,
Thy lady is of such manere,
So wise so ware in allé thinges,
It nedeth of no bakbitínges,
That thou thy lady misenforme:
For whan she knoweth all the forme,
How that thy self art enviońs,
Thou shalt nought be so gracioús,
As thou paraunter[1] shuldest be elles.
There wol no man drinke of the welles,
Whiche as he wote[2] is poison inne.
And ofté suche as men beginne
Towardés other, such they finde,
That set hem ofté fer behinde
Whan that they wenen be before.
My godé sone, and thou therfore
Be ware and leve thy wicked speche,
Wherof hath fallen ofté wreche[3]
To many a man before this time.
For who so wol his hondés lime,[4]
They musten be the more unclene.
For many a moté shall be sene,
That woldé nought cleve ellés there;
And that shulde every wise man fere.
For who so woll another blame,
He seketh ofte his owné shame,

[1] *Paraunter*, peradventure.
[2] *Wote*, knows. [3] *Wrecke*, revenge.
[4] Take birdlime in his hands.

Which ellés mighté be right stille.
Forthý if that it be thy wille
To stonde upon amendément,
A tale of great entendément
I thenké tellé for thy sake,
Wherof thou might ensample take.
"A worthy knight in Cristés lawe
Of greaté Rome, as is the sawe,
The sceptre haddé for to right,
Tibéry Constantin he hight,
Whos wife was clépe Italie.
But they to-gider of progenie
No children haddé but a maide,
And she the God so wel apaide[1]
That al the widé worldés fame
Spake worship of her godé name.
Constance, as the croniqué saith,
She hight, and was so full of faith
That the greatést of Barbarie,
Of hem whiche usen marchandie,
She hath converted, as they come
To her upon a time in Rome
To shewen such thing as they brought
Which worthely of hem she bought.
And over that[2] in suche a wise
She hath hem with her wordés wise
Of Cristés feith so full enformed,
That they therto ben all conformed,
So that baptismé they receiven
And all her[3] falsé goddés weiven.
"Whan they ben of the feith certéin,
They gone to Barbaríe ayein,
And there the Souldan for hem sente
And axeth hem to what entente
They have her firsté feith forsake.
And they, whiche hadden undertake
The righté feith to kepe and holde,
The mater of her talé tolde
With all the holé circumstaúnce.

[1] *Apaide*, pleased.
[2] *Over that*, beyond that.
[3] *Her*, their.

And whan the Souldan of Constaunce,
Upon the point that they answerde,
The beauté and the gracé herde,
As he which thanné was to wedde,
In allé haste his causé spedde
To sendé for the mariágc,
And furthermore with good coráge
He saith, be so[1] he may her have,
That Crist, that came this world to save,
He woll beleve, and thus recorded
They ben on either side accorded.
And there upon to make an ende
The Souldan his hostáges sende
To Rome, of princes sonés twelve.
Wherof the fader in him selve
Was glad, and with the Pope avised.
Two Cardinales he hath assised
With other lordés many mo,
That with his doughter shulden go
To se the Souldan be converted.
"But that which never was wel herted
Envïé tho gan to travaile
In disturbaúnce of this spousaile
So privély that none was ware.
The Moder which the Souldan bare
Was than alive, and thoughté this
Unto her selfe: if it so is,
My sone him wedde in this manere,
Than have I lost my joiés here,
For min estate shall so be lassed.
Thenkend thus, she hath compássed
By sleight how that she may beguile
Her sone, and fell within a while,
Betwene hem two whan that they were,
She feignéd wordés in his ere
And in this wisé gan to say:
'My sone, I am by double way
With all min herté glad and blithe,
For that my selfe have ofté sithe[2]

[1] *Be so*, if so be.
[2] *Ofté sithe*, oftentimes.

Desiréd thou wolte, as men saith,
Receive and take a newé feith,
Which shall be forthringe of thy
life.
And eke so worshipfull a wife
The doughter of an emperoúr
To wedde, it shall be great honoúr.
Forthý [1] my sone, I you beseche,
That I such gracé might areche,
Whan that my doughter comé shall,
That I may than in speciáll,
So as me thenketh it is honéste,
Be thilké which the firsté feste
Shall make unto her welcominge.'
"The Souldan graunteth her
axinge.
And she therof was gladde inough,
For under that anone she drough
With falsé wordés that she spake
Covin [2] of dethe behinde his backe.
And therupon her ordinaunce
She madé so, that whan Constance
Was comen forth with the Romains,
Of clerkés and of citezeins
A riché festé she hem made.
And mosté whan they weren glade
With falsé covin, which she hadde,
Her close Envié tho she spradde.
And allé tho, that hadden be
Or in appert or in privé
Of counseil to the mariáge,
She slough hem in a sodein rage
Endlong the borde as they be set,
So that it mighté nought be let.
Her owné soné was nought quite,[3]
But died upon the samé plite.
But what the highé God woll spare
It may for no perfll misfare.
This worthy maiden which was
there
Stode than as who saith dede for
fere

1 *Forthý*, therefore.
2 *Covin*, secret contrivance.
3 *Quite*, acquitted.

To se the fest how that it stood,
Whiche all was tornéd into blood.
The dissh forth with the cuppe and
all
Bebled [1] they weren over all;
She sigh hem die on every side,
No wonder though she wepte and
cride
Makend maný a wofull mone.
When all was slain but she al one,
This oldé fend, this Sarazin
Let take anone this Constantin
With all the good she thider brought
And hath ordeignéd as she thought
A naked ship withouté stere,
In which the good and her in fere,
Vitáléd full for yerés five,
Where that the winde it woldé
drive,
She put upon the wawés wilde.
"But he, which allé thinges may
shilde
Thre yere til that she cam to londe
Her ship to stere hath take on
honde,
And in Northumberlond arriveth;[2]
And happeth thanné that she
driveth
Under a castell with the flood,
Whiche upon Humber banké stood.
And was the kingés owne also
The whiche Allee was clepéd tho;
A Saxon, and a worthy knight,
But he beleveth nought aright.
Of this castéll was castellaine
Elda the kingés chamberlaine,
A knightly man after his lawe.
And whan he sigh upon the wawe [3]
The ship drivénd aloné so,
He badde anone men shulden go
To se what it betoken may.
This was upon a somer day

1 *Bebled*, covered with blood.
2 *Arriveth*, touches shore.
3 Saw upon the waves.

The ship was lokéd and she founde.
Elda within a litel stounde[1]
It wist, and with his wife anone
Toward this yongé lady gone,
Where that they foundé great richesse.
But she her woldé nought confesse,
Whan they her axen what she was.
And nethéles upon the cas
Out of the ship with great worshíp
They toke her into felashíp
As they that weren of her glade.
But she no maner joié made,
But sorweth sore of that she fonde
No christendome in thilké londe;
But ellés she hath all her will,
And thus with hem she dwelleth still.
Dame Hermegild, which was the wife
Of Elda, liche her owné life
Constancé loveth; and fell so
Spekend all day betwene hem two
Through grace of Goddés purveiaúnce
This maiden taughté the creaúnce
Unto this wife so parfitly,
Upon a day that fasté by
In presence of her husébonde,
Where they go walkend on the stronde,
A blindé man which cam ther ladde
Unto this wife criénd he badde
With bothe his hondés up and praide
To her, and in this wise he saide:
'O Hermegilde, which Cristés feith
Enforméd as Constancé saith
Receivéd hast: yif me my sight!'
"Upon this worde her herte aflight
Thenkend what was besté to done,
But nethéles she herde his bone[2]
And saide: 'In trust of Cristés lawe,

[1] *Stounde*, interval, hour. [2] *Bone*, petition.

Which done was on the crosse and slawe,[1]
Thou blindé man beholde and se!'
With that, to God upon his kne
Thonkend, he toke his sight anone,
Wherof they merveil everychone,
But Elda wondreth most of alle;
This open thing whiche is befalle
Concludeth[2] him by suche a way
That he the feith mo nede obey.
"Now list what fell upon this thinge.
This Elda forth unto the kinge
A morwé toke his way and rode,
And Hermegild at home abode
Forth with Constancé well at ese.
Elda, which thought his king to plese,
As he that than unwedded was,
Of Constance all the pleiné cas,
As godélich as he couth, tolde.
The king was glad, and said he wolde
Comé thidér in suche a wise,
That he him might of her avise.[3]
The time appointed forth withall
This Elda truste in speciall
Upon a knight which fro childhode
He had updrawe into manhode,
To him he tolde all that he thought;
Wherof that after him forthought.[4]
And nethéles at thilké tide
Unto his wife he bad him ride
To maké redy allé thinge
Ayeinst the cominge of the kinge;
And saith that he him self to-fore
Thenketh for to come, and bad therfore
That he him kepe,[5] and tolde him whan.

[1] The law of Christ who was put upon the cross and slain.
[2] *Concludeth*, decides.
[3] *Him avise*, take note.
[4] *Him forthought*, it repented him.
[5] *Him kepe*, have care for him, look for him.

This knight rode forth his waié than.
And soth was, that of timé passed
He had in all his wit compássed,
Howe he Constancé mighté winne.
But he sigh tho no spede[1] therinne.
Wherof his lust began to abate,
And that was love is thanné hate.
Of her honoúr he had Envie,
So that upon his trecherie
A lesinge[2] in his herte he cast.
Til he come home he hieth fast,
And doth his lady to understonde
The message of her husébonde.
And therupon the longé daie
They setten thingés in arraie,
That all was as it shuldé be
Of every thinge in his degre.
And whan it came into the night,
This wife with her hath to beddé dight
Where that this maiden with her lay.
This falsé knight upon delay,
Hath taried till they were aslepe,
As he that woll his timé kepe
His dedly werkés to fulfille.
And to the bed he stalketh stille,
Where that he wisté was the wife,
And in his honde a rasour knife
He bar, with whiche her throte he cut
And privély the knife he put
Under that other beddés side,
Where that Constancé lay beside.
Elda come hom the samé night
And stillé with a privé light,
As he that woldé nought awake
His wife, he hath his waié take
Into the chambre, and there ligénd
He fonde his dedé wife bledénd,
Where that Constancé fasté by
Was falle aslepe; and sodeinly

[1] *Sigh tho no spede*, saw then no success.
[2] *Lesinge*, falsehood.

He cried aloude, and she awoke,
And forth with all she cast a loke
And sigh this lady bledé there,
Wherof swounéndé dede for fere
She was, and stille as any stone
She laie, and Elda therupon
Into the castell clepeth out,
And up sterte every man about;
Into the chambre forth they went.
But he whiche all untrouthé ment
This falsé knight among hem all
Upon this thing whiche is befall
Saith that Constánce hath don this dede.
And to the bed with that he yede
After the falsehed of his speche
And made him theré for to seche,[1]
And fond the knife where he it laid.
And than he cried and than he said:
'Lo, se the knife all bloody here,
What nedeth more in this matere
To axe?' and thus her innocénce
He sclaundreth there in audiénce
With falsé wordés, whiche he feigneth.
But yet for al that ever he pleineth.
"Elda no full credéncé toke.
And happéd that there lay a boke,
Upon the which, whan he it sighe,
This knight hath swore, and said on highe
That allé men it mighten wite,[2]—
'Now by this boke which here is write,
Constance is gultif well I wote.'
With that the honde of Heven him smote
In token of that he was forswore,
That he has bothe his eyen lore,[3]
Out of his hed the samé stounde
They stert, and so they weré founde.

[1] *Seche*, seek.
[2] *Wite*, know.
[3] *Lore*, lost.

A vois was herd whan that they fel,
Which saide: 'O dampnéd man to helle,
Lo, thus hath God thy sclaunder wroke,
That thou ayein Constánce hath spoke:
Beknowe the sothe[1] er that thou deie.'
And he tolde out his felonie
And starf forth with his tale anone.
Into the grounde where allé gone,
This dedé lady was begrave.
Elda, which thought his honour save
All that he may, restreigneth sorwe.
"For by the second day a morwe
The king came, as they were accorded,
And whan it was to him recorded,
What God hath wrought upon this chaunce,
He toke it into remembraúnce
And thoughté moré than he saide;
For all his holé herte he laide
Upon Constánce, and saide he shulde
For love of her, if that she wolde,
Baptismé take and Cristés feith
Beleve, and over that he saith
He wol her wedde, and upon this
Assuréd eche til other is.
And for to maké shorté tales
There came a bisshop out of Wales
Fro Bangor, and Lucie he hight,
Which through the grace of God almight
The king with many an other mo
He cristnéd, and betwene hem two
He hath fulfilled the mariáge.
But for no lust ne for no rage
She tolde hem never what she was.
And nethéles upon this cas
The king was glad, how so it stood,
For well he wist and understood
She was a noble creätúre.
The highé Maker of Natúre
Her hath visíted in a throwe,
That it was openliché knowe
She was with childé by the kinge,
Wherof above all other thinge
He thonketh God and was right glad.
And fell that time he was bestad
Upon a werre, and musté ride.
And while he shuldé there abide
He left at home to kepe his wife
Suche as he knewe of holy life,
Elda forth with the bisshop eke.
And he with power go to seke
Ayein the Scottes for to fonde[1]
The werré whiche he toke on honde.
The timé set of kinde is come,
This lady hath her chambre nome[2]
And of a soné boré fulle,
Wherof that she was joiéfull,
She was delivered sauf and sone.[3]
The bisshop, as it was to done,
Yaf him baptisme and Moris calleth.
And therupon as it befalleth
With letters writen of recórde
They send unto her legé lorde
That kepers weren[4] of the quene.
And he, that shuldé go betwene,
The messanger to Knarésburgh
(Which town he shuldé passé thurgh)
Ridendé cam the firsté daie;
The kingés moder theré lay,
Whose righté namé was Domilde,
Whiche after all the causé spilde.
For he, which thonk deservé wolde,
Unto this lady goth and tolde

[1] Confess the truth.

[1] *Fonde*, try issues in.
[2] *Nome*, taken.
[3] Safe and sound.
[4] They that were keepers of the queen sent to their liege lord.

Of his messáge al how it ferde.
And she with feignéd joie it herde
And yaf him yeftés largélý,
But in the night al privély
She toke the letters whiche he had,
Fro point to point and overrad [1]
As she that was through out untrewe,
And let do writen other newe
In stede of hem, and thus they speke.
'Our legé lord, we thee beseke,
That thou with us ne be nought wroth,
Though we such thing as is thee loth
Upon our trouthé certifie.
Thy wifé, whiche is of fairie,
Of suche a child delivered is,
Fro kindé,[2] which stant all amis.
But for it shuldé nought be saie
We have it kept out of the waie
For drede of puré woridés shame,
A pouer childe, and in the name
Of thilké whiche is so misbore,
We toke and therto we be swore,
That none but only you and we
Shall knowen of this priveté.
Morice it hat, and thus men wene
That it was boren of the quene
And of thine owné bodie gete.
But this thing may nought be foryete,
That thou ne sende us worde anone,
What is thy willé therupon.'
"This letter, as thou hast herd devise,
Was counterfet in suche a wise,
That no man shulde it apperceive.
And she which thoughté to deceive
It laith where she that other toke.
This messanger, whan he awoke,
And wist nothíngé how it was,
Arose and rode the greaté pas
And toke his letter to the kinge.
And whan he sigh [1] this wonder thinge,
He maketh the messanger no chere,
But nethéles in wise manere
He wrote ayein, and yaf him charge
That they ne suffre nought at large
His wife to go but kepe her still,
Till they have herd more of his will.
"This messanger was yeftéles,
But with his letter nethéles,
Or be him lefe or be him loth,
In allé haste ayeine he goth
By Knaresburgh, and as he went,
Unto the moder his entent
Of that he fond toward the kinge
He tolde, and she upon this thinge
Saith, that he shulde abide all night
And made him feste and chere aright,
Feignend as though she couthe him thonke.[2]
But he with strong wine which he dronke
Forth with the travaile of the day
Was drunke aslepe, and while he lay
She hath his letters oversay,
And forméd in an other way
There was a newé letter write,
"Which saith: 'I do you for to wite,
That through the counseil of you two
I stonde in point to ben undo,
As he whiche is a king deposed,
For every man it hath supposed
How that my wife Constánce is fay.
And if that I, they sain, delay
To put her out of compaignie,
The worship of my regalie
Is lore, and over this they telle
Her child shal nought among hem dwelle

1 And read them over from point to point.
2 *Fro kinde*, contrary to nature.

1 *Sigh*, saw.
2 *Couthe him thonke*, paid him thanks.

To claimen any heritáge.
So can I se none avauntáge,
But all is lost, if she abide.
Forthý to loke on every side
Toward the mischefe as it is
I chargé you and biddé this,
That ye the samé ship vittaile,
In which that she toke arrivaile,
Therin and putteth[1] bothé two
Her self forth with her childe also,
And so forth brought into the depe
Betaketh her the see[2] to kepe.
Of fouré daiés time I set
That ye this thing no lenger let,[3]
So that your life be nought forfete.'
"And thus this letter counterfete
The messanger, which was unware,
Upon the kingés halvé bare
And where he shulde it hath betake.
But whan that they have hedé take
And rad that writen is withinne,
So great a sorwé they beginne,
As they her[4] owné moder sighen
Brent in a fire before her[4] eyen.
There was wepinge and there was wo,
But finallý the thinge is do.
Upon the see they have her brought,
But she the causé wisté nought,
And thus upon the flood they wone[5]
This lady with her yonge sone.
And than her hondés to the heven
She straught, and with a mildé steven[6]
Knelend upon her baré kne
She saide: 'O highé mageste,
Which seest the point of every trouth,
Take of thy wofull woman routh
And of this child that I shal kepe!'[1]
And with that word she gan to wepe
Swounénd as dede, and there she lay.
But he, whiche allé thingés may,
Confórteth her, and atté laste
She loketh, and her eyen caste
Upon her childe, and saydé this:
'Of me no maner charge it is
What sorwe I suffre, but of thee
Me thenketh it is great pitee,
For if I stervé thou shalt deie,
So mote I nedés by that weie
For moderhed and for tendernesse
With all min holé besinesse
Ordeigné me for thilke office
As she which shall be thy norice.'
Thus was she strengthed for to stonde.
And tho she toke her childe in honde
And yaf it souke and ever amonge
She wepte and otherwhilé songe
To rocké with her childe aslepe;
And thus her owné childe to kepe
She hath under the Goddes cure.
"And so fell upon aventúre,
Whan thilké yere hath made his ende,
Her ship, so as it mosté wende,
By strength of wind which God hath yive
Estward was into Spainé drive
Right fast under a castell walle
Where that an hethen admiralle
Was lorde, and he a steward had
One Theloús, whiche al was bad,
A fals knight and a renegate.
He goth to loke in what estate
The ship was comen, and there he fonde

[1] *Therin and putteth*, and put therein.
[2] *Betaketh her the see*, commit her to the sea.
[3] *Let*, delay.
[4] *Her*, their.
[5] *Wone*, dwell.
[6] *Steven*, voice.

[1] *Shal kepe*, have to take care of (shall, with the sense of obligation).

Forth with a childe upon her honde
This lady where she was alone.
He toke good hede of the persóne
And sigh she was a worthy wight,
And thought he wolde upon the night
Demene her at his owné wille;
And let her be therinné stille,
That no man sigh she nought[1] that day.
At Goddes wille and thus she lay
Unknowé what her shall betide.
And fell so that by nightés tide
This knight withouté felaship
Hath take a boot and cam to ship
And thought of her his lust to take,
And swore, if she him daunger make,
That certainlý she shuldé deie.
She sigh there was none other weie
And saide he shulde her well confórte,
That he first loked out at porte,
That no man weré nigh the stede
Which mighté knowé what they dede,
And than he may do what he wolde.
He was right glad that she so tolde,
And to the port anone he ferde.
"She praieth God, and he her herde.
And sodeinlich he was out throwe
And dreint,[2] and tho[3] began to blowe
Windé meváble fro the londe,
And thus the mighty Goddes honde
Her hath conveiéd and defended.
And whan thre yere ben full despended,
Her ship was drive upon a daie,
Where that a great navié laie
Of shippés, all the worlde at ones.
And as God woldé for the nones

1 She saw not any man.
2 *Dreint*, drowned. 3 *Tho*, then.

Her ship goth in amonge hem alle
And stint nought er it be befalle
And hath that vessel under gete
Which maister was of all the flete;
But there it resteth and abode.
This greté ship on anker rode,
The lord come forth, and whan he sigh
That other ligge on bord so nigh
He wondreth what it mighté be,
And bad men to go in and se.
This lady tho was crope a side
As she that wolde her selven hide,
For she ne wisté what they were.
They sought about and fond her there
And broughten up her childe and her.
And therupon this lord to spire[1]
Began fro whenné that she came
And what she was. Quod she: 'I am
A woman wofully bestad.
I had a lorde and thus he bad,
That I forth with my litel sone
Upon the wawés shuldé wone.
But why the causé was I not,[2]
But he whiche allé thingés wot
Yet hath, I thonk him, of his might
My childe and me so kepte upright,
That we be saufé bothé two.'—
This lorde her axeth evermo
How she beleveth, and she saith:
'I leve and trust in Cristés feith,
Which died upon the rodé tre.'—
'What is thy namé?' tho quod he.
'My name is Custé,' she him saide.
But furthermore for nought he praide
Of her estaté to knowe pleine,
She wolde him nothing ellés saine
But of her namé, which she feigned,
All other thingés she restreigned,
That o word moré she ne tolde.
This lord than axeth if she wolde

1 *Spire*, enquire, "speir." 2 *Not*, know not.

With him abide in compaignie,
And saide, he came from Barbarie
To Romé ward and home he went.
Tho she supposeth what it ment
And saith, she woldé with him wende
And dwelle unto her lives ende,
If it so be to his plesaúnce.
And thus upon her ácqueintaúnce
He tolde her pleinly as it stood,
Of Rome how that the gentil blood
In Barbarïé was betraied
And therupon he hath assaied
By werre, and taken such ven-
geaúnce
That none of thilke euil alliaúnce,
By whom the treson was compássed,
Is from the swerd alivé passed.
But of Constancé how it was
That couthe [1] he knowé by no cas
Where she becam, so as he said;
Her ere unto his word she laid,
But furthermore made she no chere.
And nethéles in this matére
It happed that ilké timé so
This lord with whom she shuldé go
Of Romé was the senatoúr
And of her fader themperoúr
His brother doughter hath to wive,
Which hath her fader eke on live,[2]
And was Salustés clepéd tho,
His wife Heleiné hight also,
To whom Constáncé was cousìne.
Thus to the sike a medicine
Hath God ordeignéd of his grace,
That forthwith in the samé place
This senatour his trouthé plight
For ever while he livé might
To kepe her in worshíp and in wele,
Be so that God woll yive her hele,
This lady, which Fortúne him sende.
And thus by shippé forth sailénde
Her and her childe to Rome be
brought,
And to his wife tho he besought

[1] *Couthe*, could. [2] *On live*, alive.

To take her into compaigníe.
And she, which couth of curtesie
All that a good wife shuldé conne,[1]
Was inly glad, that she hath wonne
The felaship of so good one.
This emperoúrés doughter Custe
Forth with the doughter of Saluste
Was kept, but no man redély
Knew what she was, and nought
forthý
They thoughten well she haddé be
In her estate of high degré,
And every life her loveth wele.
"Now herken: thilke unstable
whele,
Whiche ever torneth went aboute.
The king Allee, while he was oute,
As thou to-fore hast herd this cas,
Deceivéd through his moder was.
But whan that he come home ayein,
He axeth of his chamberlain
And of the bisshop eke also,
Where they the quené hadden do.
And they answerdé there he bad
And have him thilké letter rad
Whiche he hem sendé for warránt,
And tolde him pleinly as it stant,
And sain, it thought hem great pité
To se a worthy one as she
With suche a childe as there was
bore
So sodeinly to be forlore.
He axeth hem, what child that
were.
And they him saidé, that no where
In all the world, though men it
sought,
Was never woman that forth
brought
A fairer child than it was one.
And than he axeth hem anone,
Why they ne hadden writen so.
They tolden, so they hadden do.

[1] Who knew all that a good wife should know of courtesy.

He saidé, nay. They saiden, yis.
The letter shewéd, rad[1] it is,
Which they forsoken every dele.[2]
Tho was it understondé wele
That there is treson in the thinge.
The messanger to-fore the kinge
Was brought and, sodeinlich opposed
As he which no thinge hath supposed
But allé wel, began to saie,
That he no where upon the waie
Abode but only in a stede,[3]
And causé why that he so dede,
Was, as he wenté to and fro,
At Knaresburgh by nightés two
The kingés moder made him dwelle.
And when the king it herdé telle,
Within his hert he wiste als faste
The treson whiche his moder caste;
And thought he woldé nought abide
But forth right in the samé tide
He toke his hors and rode anone,
With him there riden many one,
To Knaresburgh, and forth they wente
And lich the fire which thonder hente[4]
In suche a rage, as saith the boke,
His moder sodeinlich he toke
And saide unto her in this wise:
'O beste of helle, in what juſse[5]
Hast thou deservéd for to deie,
That hast so falsely put aweie
With treson of thy backbitínge
The trewest at my knoulechinge
Of wivés and the most honést?
But I wol maké this behest,

1 *Rad*, read.
2 *Forsoken*, denied in every part.
3 *A stede*, one place.
4 *Hente*, pursued and seized, *i.e.*, lightning, the fire on which the thunder pounced.
5 *Juſse*, judgment.

I shall be vengéd or[1] I go.'
And let a firé do make tho
And bad men for to caste her inne.
But first she tolde out all the sinne,
And did hem allé for to wite
How she the letters haddé write,
Fro point to point as it was wrought.
And tho she was to dethé brought
And brent to-fore her sonés eye,
Wherof these other, whiche it sighe
And herden how the causé stood,
Sain, that the jugément was good
Of that her sone her hath so served;
For she it haddé wel deserved
Through treson of her falsé tunge,
Which through the lond was after songe,
Constance and[2] every wight compleineth.
But he, whom allé wo distreigneth,
This sorwefull king, was so bestad
That he shall never more be glad,
He saith, eftsoné for to wedde
Till that he wist how that she spedde
Which haddé ben his firsté wife;
And thus his yonge unlusty life
He driveth forth so as he may.
"Till it befel upon a day,
Whan he his werrés hadde acheved
And thought he woldé be releved
Of soulé hele upon the feith
Whiche he hath také, than he saith,
That he to Rome in pelrinage
Wol go, where Popé was Pelage,
To take his absolución.
And upon this condición
He made Edwin his lieutenaúnt,
Whiche heir to him was apparaúnt,
That he the lond in his absénce
Shall reule. And thus by providénce
Of allé thingés well begonne
He toke his leve and forth is gone.

1 *Or*, ere.
2 And every one laments for Constance.

"Elda, which was with him tho there,
Er they fulliche at Romé were,
Was sent to-foré to purveie,
And he his guide upon the weie,
In helpé to ben herbergeour[1]
Hath axéd who was senatour,
That he his namé mighté kenne.
Of Capadoce, he saide, Arcenne
He hight and was a worthy knyght.
To him goth Elda tho forth right
And tolde him of his lord tiding
And praidé, that for his cominge
He wolde assigne him herbergáge.
And he so did of good coráge.
"Whan all is do that was todone,
The kinge him self cam after sone.
This senatoúr whan that he come
To Custe and to his wife at home,
Hath tolde how suche a Kinge Allee
Of great array to the citee
Was come, and Cust upon his tale
With herté close and colour pale
A swouné[2] felle, and he merveileth
So sodeinly what thinge her eileth,
And caught her up, and whan she woke
She siketh with a pitous loke
And feigneth sikenesse of the see,
But it was for the kinge Allee,
For joié which fell in her thought,
That God him hath to towné brought.
This King hath spoké with the Pope
And tolde all that he couthé grope
What greveth in his consciénce,
And than he thought in reverence
Of his estate, er that he went
To make a feste, and thus he sent
Unto the senatoúr to come
Upon the morwe and other some

[1] *Herbergeour*, one sent before to provide lodgings for a stately company.
[2] *A swouné*, in swoon.

To sitté with him at the mete.
This tale hath Custé nought foryete,
But to Morsce her soné tolde
That he upon the morwe sholde
In all that ever he couth and might
Be present in the Kingés sight,
So that the Kinge him ofte sigh.
Morsce to-fore the Kingés eye
Upon the morwe, where he sat,
Full ofté stood, and upon that
The King his chere upon him caste
And in his face him thought als faste
He sigh his owné wife Constánce,
For Nature, as in resemblaúnce
Of face, him liketh so to clothe
That they were of a suité bothe.
The King was movéd in his thought
Of that he sigh, and knew it nought;
This childe he loveth kindély,
And yet he wot no causé why;
But wel he sigh and understode,
That he toward Arcenné stode,
And axeth him anone right there
If that this childe his soné were.
He saidé: 'ye,[1] so I him calle,
And wolde it weré so befalle,
But it is all in other wise.'
And tho[2] began he to devise,
How he the childés moder fonde
Upon the see, from[3] every londe,
Within a ship was steréles;
And how this lady helpéles
Forth with her childe he hath forth drawe.
The Kinge hath understood his sawe
The childés name and axeth tho,
And what the moder hight also,
That he him woldé telle he praide.

[1] *Ye*, yea. [2] *Tho*, then.
[3] *From*, away from.

'Morice this childe is hote,'[1] he
saide,
'His moder hatté Custe, and this
I not[2] what maner name it is.'
But Allee wiste wel inough,
Wherof somdele smilénd he lough.
For Custe in Saxon is to saine
Constance upon the word Romaine.
But who that couthé specifie,
What tho fell in his fantasie,
And how his witte abouté renneth
Upon the love in which he bren-
neth
It were a wonder for to here.
For he was nouther there ne here,
But clene out of him selfe awey,
That he not what to thenke or say,
So faine he wolde it weré she;
Wherof his hertés priveté
Began the werre of ye and nay,
The whiche in such balaúncé lay
That contenaúncé for a throwe[3]
He losté, till he mighté knowe
The soth. But in his memorie
The man which lieth in purgatorie,
Desireth nought the Heven more
That he ne longeth also sore
To wité what him shall betide.
And whan the bordés were aside
And every man was rise aboute,
The Kinge hath weivéd all the route
And with the senatoúr alone
He spake and praid him of a bone,[4]
To se this Custé where she dwelleth
At home with him, so as he telleth.
The senatoúr was wel apaide;
This thing no lenger was delaide.
To se this Custé goth the Kinge,
And she was warnéd of the thinge,
And with Heleiné forth she came
Ayein the Kinge, and he tho name[5]

[1] *Hote*, called.
[2] *Not*, know not.
[3] *Throwe*, space of time.
[4] *Bone*, petition.
[5] *Name*, took.

Good hede, and whan he sigh his
wife,
Anone with all his hertés life
He caught her in his armes and
kiste.
Was never wight that sigh ne wiste[1]
A man that moré joié made,
Wherof they weren allé glade
Which herdé tellen of this chaunce.
This King tho with his wife Con-
stánce,
Whiche had a great part of his will,
In Romé for a timé still
Abode and made him well at ese.
But so yet couth he never plese
His wife, that she him woldé saine
Of her estate the trouthé pleine,
Of what contré that she was bore
Ne what she was, and yet therfore
With all his wit he hath done seke.
Thus as they ligh in bedde and
speke,
She praith him and counselleth
both,
That for the worship of hem both
So that her thought it were honéste
He wolde an honourable feste
Make er he went in that citee,
Where themperoúr him self shall
be.
He graunteth all that she him
praide.
But as men in that timé saide,
This emperoúr, fro thilké day
That first his doughter went away,
He was than after never gladde,
But what that any man him badde
Of gracé for his doughter sake
That gracé wolde he nought for-
sake,[2]
And thus ful great almésse he dede,
Wherof he haddé many a bede.[3]

[1] *Sigh ne wiste*, saw or knew.
[2] *Forsake*, refuse.
[3] *Bede*, prayer.

"This Emperoúr out of the towne,
Within a ten mile enviroúne,
Where as it thought him for the beste
Hath sondry places for to reste,
And as fortúné woldé tho
He was dwellénd at one of tho.
The kinge Allee forth with thassent
Of Custe his wife hath thider sent
Moríce his sone, as he was taught,
To themperoúr, and he goth straught
And in his fader halve[1] he sought
As he whiche of his lordship sought,
That of his highé worthinesse
He woldé do so great mekenesse
His owné town to come and se
And yive a time in the citee,
So that his fader might him gete
That he wolde onés with him ete.
This lorde hath graunted his requeste.
And whan the day was of the feste,
In worship of her[2] Emperoúr
The kinge and eke the senatoúr
Forth with her wivés bothé two,
With many a lorde and lady mo,
On hors gan riden him ayeine,
Till it befell upon a pleine
They sigh where as he was coménd.
With that Constance anone praiénd
Spake to her lord that he abide,
'So that I may to-foré ride
To ben upon his bienvenue[3]
The firsté which shall him salue.'
And thus after her lordés graunte
Upon a mulé white amblaúnte
Forth with a fewé rode this quene.
They wondred what she woldé mene,
And riden after softé pas.
But whan this lady comen was
To themperoúr, in his presence

[1] On his father's behalf. [2] *Her*, their.
[3] *Bienvenue*, welcome.

She saide aloude in audience:
'My lord, my fader, wel you be!
And of this timé that I se
Your honour and your godé hele,
Whiche is the helpe of my quarele,
I thonke unto the goddés might.'
For joie his herté was aflight
Of that she tolde in remembraunce.
And whan he wiste, it was Constánce,
Was never fader half so blithe.
Wepend he kiste her often sithe,
So was his hert all overcome,
For though his moder weré come
Fro deth to life out of the grave,
He might no moré wonder have
Than he hath whan that he her sigh.
With that her owné lord come nigh
And is to themperoúr obeied.
And whan the fortune is bewreied,[1]
How that Constánce is come aboute,
So harde an herté was none oute
That he for pité tho ne wepte.
Arcennus which her fonde and kepte
Was thanné glad of that is falle,
So that with joie among hem alle
They riden in at Romé gate.
This Emperoúr thought all to late,
Till that the Popé weré come
And of the lordés sendé some
To pray him that he woldé haste.
And he cam forth in allé haste,
And whan that he this talé herde,
How wonderly this chauncé ferde,
He thonketh god of his mirácle,
To whos might may be none obstácle.
The King a noble feste hem made,
And thus they weren allé glad.
A parlément er that they went
They setten, unto this entent,

[1] *Bewreied*, disclosed.

To putten Rome in full espeire,[1]
That Morſce was apparant heire
And shulde abidé with hem stille,
For such was all the londés wille.
"Whan every thing was fully spoke
Of sorwe and queint[2] was all the smoke,
Tho toke his leve Allee the Kinge
And with full many a riché thinge
Which themperoúr him hadde yive
He goth a gladdé life to live.
For he Constance hath in his honde,
Which was the comfort of the londe.
For whan that he cam home ayein,
There is no tungé that might sain,
What joié was that ilké stounde
Of that he hath his quené founde,
Which first was sent of Goddés sonde[3]
Whan she was driven upon the stronde,
By whom the misbeleve of sinne
Was lefte and Cristés feith came inne
To hem that whilome weré blinde.
But he, which hindreth every kinde
And for no gold may be forbought,
The Deth, coménd er he besought
Toke with this king such acquein-taúnce
That he with all his retenaúnce
Ne mighté nought defend his life;
And thus he parteth from his wife
Which thanné madé sorwe inough.
And therupon her herté drough
To leven Engélond for ever
And go where that she haddé lever,
To Romé whanné[4] that she came.
And thus of all the lond she nam[5]

[1] *Espeire*, hope.
[2] *Queint*, quenched; and all the smoke of sorrow was quenched.
[3] *Sonde*, sending.
[4] *Whanne*, whence.
[5] *Nam*, took.

Her leve, and goth to Rome ayein.
And after that the bokés sain
She was nought theré but a throwe
Whan Deth, of kinde,[1] hath over-throwe
Her worthy fader, which men saide
That he betwene her armés deide.
And afterward the yere suénde
Tho God hath made of her an ende,
And fro this worldés fairie[2]
Hath take her into compaignie.
"Morſce her soné was coroúned,
Which so ferforth was abandoúned
To Cristés feith that men him calle
Morſce the Christenest of alle.
And thus the whel meving of Love
Was atté lasté set above.
And so, as thou hast herd to-fore,
The falsé tungés weren lore[3]
Whiche upon Lové wolden lie.
Forthý touchénd of this Envie,
Which longeth unto Bakbitſnge,
Be wáré thou make no lesſnge
In hindring of another wight.
And if thou wolt be taught aright,
What mischefe Bakbitingé doth,
By other waie a talé soth
Now might thou heré next suénde,
Which to this Vice is accordénde.
"**In a cronique** as thou shalt wite
A great ensample I finde write,
Whiche I shall telle upon this thinge.
Philip of Macedoiné Kinge
Two sonés haddé by his wife,
Whose famé yet in Grece is rife.
Demetrius the firsté brother
Was hote[4] and Perseús that other.
Demetrius men saiden tho[5]
The better knight was of the two,

[1] *Of kinde*, in the course of Nature.
[2] *Fairie*, changes and illusions.
[3] *Lore*, lost.
[4] *Hote*, called.
[5] *Tho*, then.

To whom the lond was attendánt
As he, whiche heir was apparánt
To regne aftér his faders day.
But that thing which no water may
Quenche in this world, but ever brenneth,
Into his brothers hert it renneth,
The proud Envie of that he sighe[1]
His brother shuldé climbe on highe
And he to him mot than obeie;
That may he suffre by no waie,
With strengthé durst he no thing fonde,[2]
So toke he lesinge upon honde
When he sigh time, and spake therto.
For it befell that timé so
His fader greté werrés hadde
With Romé, whiche he streité ladde
Through mighty hond of his manhód,
As he which hath inough knighthód,
And ofte hem haddé fore greved.
But er the werré were acheved,
As he was upon ordenaunce
At home in Grece, it fell par chaunce
Demetrius, whiche ofte aboute
Ridénd was, stodé that time out,
So that this Perse in his absénce,
Which bar the tunge of pestilénce
With falsé wordés whiche he feigneth
Upon his owné brother pleineth
In privété behinde his bake,
And to his fader thus he spake:
'My deré fader, I am holde
By way of kinde, as reson wolde,
That I fro you shall nothing hide
Which mighté torne in any side
Of youre estate into grevaúnce.
Forthý min hertés obeísaúnce
As toward you I thenké kepe.

[1] *Sighe*, saw.
[2] *Fonde*, try.

For it is good ye také kepe[1]
Upon a thing whiche is me tolde.
My brother hath us allé solde
To hem of Rome, and you also,
For thanné they behote[2] him so
That he with hem shall regne in pees.
Thus hath he cast, for his encrés,
That your estate shall go to nought.
And this to prov: shall be brought
So ferforth that I undertake
It shall nought wel mow be forsake.'[3]
"The kinge upon this tale answerd
And said, 'If this thing which he herd
Be soth and may be brought to prove,
It shall nought be to his behove[4]
Which so has shapen us the werste,
For he him self shall be the ferste
That shall be dede, if that I may.'
Thus afterwarde upon a day,
Whan that Demetrius was come,
Anone his fader hath him nome[5]
And bad unto his brother Perse,
That he his talé shall reherse
Of thilké treson whiche he tolde.
And he whiche all untrouthé wolde
Counseileth that so high a nede
Be treted where as it may spede,
In comun place of jugément.
The King therto yaf his assent.
"Demetrius was put in holde,
Wherof that Perseús was bolde.
Thus stood the trouth under the charge
And the falsehedé goth at large,
Which through behest hath overcome
The greatest of the lordés some,

[1] *Také kepe*, take heed.
[2] *Behote*, promised.
[3] *Forsake*, denied.
[4] *Behove*, advantage.
[5] *Nome*, taken.

That priveliche of his accorde
They stonde as witnesse of recórde,
The juge was madé favouráble;
Thus was the lawé deceiváble
So ferforth that the trouthé fonde
Rescoussé [1] none, and thus the
londe
Forth with the King deceivéd were:
The giltéles was dampnéd there
And deide upon accusément.
But suche a fals conspirément,
Though it be privé for a throwe,[2]
God woldé nought it were unknowe,
And that was afterward wel proved
In him which hath the deth con-
troved
Of that his brother was so slaine.
This Perseús was wonder faine
As he that tho was apparánt
Upon the regne [3] and expectant,
Wherof he wax so proude and veine
That he his fader in disdeigne
Hath take, and sette at none ac-
compte,
As he which thought him to sur-
mounte,
That where he was first debonaire
He was tho rebell and contraire,
And nought as heir but as a kinge
He toke upon him allé thinge
Of malice and of tirannie
In cóntempte of regalitie
Livénd his fader, and so wrought
That whan the fader him bethought
And sighe to whether side it drough,
Anone he wisté well inough
How Perse aftér his falsé tonge
Hath so thenvious bellé ronge,
That he hath slain his owné brother;
Wherof as thanne he knew none
other
But sodeinlý the juge he nome [4]

[1] *Rescoussé*, rescue.
[2] *Throwe*, space of time.
[3] Heir apparent to the kingdom.
[4] *Nome*, took.

Which corrupt sat upon the dome,[1]
In suche a wise and [2] hath him
pressed
That he the soth him hath con-
fessed
Of all that hath ben spoke and do.
More sory than the king was tho
Was never man upon this molde,
And thought in certain that he
wolde
Vengeauncé take upon this wronge.
But thother partie was so stronge,
That for the lawe of no statúte
There may no right ben execute.
And upon this división
The lond was tornéd up so downe,
Wherof his herte is so distraught
That he for puré sorwe hath caught
The maladie of which nature
Is queint [3] in every creature.
"And whan this King was passéd
thus,
This falsé tungéd Perseús
The regiment [4] hath underfongé.
But there may nothing stondé longe
Whiche is nought upon trouthé
grounded.
For God, which hath al thingé
bounded
And sigh [5] the falsehed of his guile,
Hath set him but a litel while
That he shall regne upon depose,
For sodeinlich right as a rose
So sodeinliché down he felle.
"In thilké timé, so it befelle,
This newé King of newé pride
With strengthé shope him for to
ride [6]
And saide he woldé Romé waste;
Wherof he made a besy haste,

[1] *Upon the dome*, in judgment.
[2] And in such a wise.
[3] *Of which nature is queint*, by which nature is extinguished (caught his death).
[4] *Regiment*, rule.
[5] *Sigh*, saw.
[6] *Ride*, make raid.

And hath assembled him an host
In all that ever he might most,
What man that mighté wepen bere
Of all he woldé none forbere.
So that it mighté nought be nombred
The folké which was after encombred
Through him that God wolde overthrow.
"Anon it was at Romé know
The pompé, which that Persé lad,
And the Romainés that time had
A consul which was clepéd thus
By namé Paul Emilius,
A noble, a worthy knight withalle,
And he which chef was of hem alle
This werre on honde hath undertake.
And whan he shulde his levé take
Of a yong doughter which was his,
She wepte, and he what cause it is
Her axeth, and she him answérde,
'That Perse is dede;' and he it herde
And wondreth what she mené wolde.
And she upon childehód him tolde,
That Perse, her litel hounde, is dede.
With that he pulleth up his hede
And madé right a glad viságe
And said, how it was a preságe
Touchénd unto that other Perse,
Of that Fortúne him shulde adverse.
He saith for suche a prénostike
Most of an hound was to him like,
For as it is an houndés kinde
To berke upon a man behinde,
Right so behinde his brothers bake
With falsé wordés whiche he spake
He hath do slaine, and that is routh.
But he whiche hateth all untrouth
The highé God it shall redresse,
For so my doughter prophetesse
Forth with her litel houndés dethe
Betokeneth; and thus forth he geth
Comfórted of this evidénce
With the Romains in his defence
Ayein the Grekes that ben coménde.
This Perseus, as nought seënde
This mischef which that him abode,
With all his multitudé rode
And prided him upon this thinge,
Of that he was become a Kinge,
And howe he had his regné gete.
But he hath all the right foryete
Which longeth unto governaunce,
Wherof through Goddés ordenaunce
It felle upon the winter tide
That with his hoste he shuldé ride
Over Danubie thilké flood,
Whiche all befrosé thanné stood
So hardé, that he wendé wele
To passé. But the blindé whele,
Which torneth ofte er men be ware
Thilke ice which that the horsmen bare
To-brake, so that a great partie
Was dreint [1] of the chivalérie;
The reréwarde it toke aweie,
Came none of hem to londé drey.[2]
"Paulus, this worthy knight Romain,
By his aspie it herdé sain,
And hasteth him all that he may,
So that upon that other day [3]
He came where he this host behelde,
And that was in a largé felde,
Wherein the banners ben displaied.
He hath anone his men arraied,
And whan that he was embatailed
He goth and hath the felde assailed
And slough and toke all that he fonde,
Wherof the Macedonie londe

[1] *Dreint*, drowned. [2] Dry land.
[3] *That other day*, the second day.

Which, through king Alisaundre honoúred
Long timé stood, tho was devoured;
To Perse and all that infortúne
They wité,[1] so that the comúne
Of all the londe his heire exile:
And he dispeired[2] for the while
Desguiséd in a pouer wede
To Romé goth; and there, for nede,
The craft which thilke timé was
To worche in laton[3] and in bras
He lerneth for his sustenaúnce.
Such was the sonés purveiaunce.
And of his fader it is saide,
In strong prisón that he was laide
In Albé, where that he was dede
For hunger and defaulte of brede.
The hounde was token and prophecie
That liche an hounde he shuldé deie
Which lich was of conditión
Whan he with his detractión
Barke on his brother so behinde.
"Lo, what proffit a man may finde,
Which hinder woll an other wight.
Forthý with all thin holé might,
My sone, escheué thilké vice."—
"My fader, ellés were I nice.
For ye therfore so well have spoke,
That it is in min herté loke
And ever shall; but of Envie,
If there be more in his bailie[4]
Towardés Lové, say me what."—
"My sone, as guile under the hat
With sleightés of a tregetour[5]
Is hid, Envie of such coloúr
Hath yet the fourthé deceivaúnt,
The whiche is clepéd Fals Semblaunt,
Wherof the mater and the forme

[1] And to Perseus they give the blame for all that misfortune.
[2] *Dispeired*, in despair.
[3] *Laton*, latten, brass with an alloy of tin.
[4] *Bailie*, government.
[5] *Tregetour*, sleight-of-hand man.

Nowe herken, and I thee shall enforme.
"**Of fals semblaunt** if I shall telle
Above all other it is the welle
Out of the which deceipté floweth.
There is no man so wise that knoweth
Of thilké flood whiche is the tide,
Ne howe he shulde him selven guide
To také sauf passágé there.
And yet the wind to mannés ere
Is softe, and as it semeth oute
It maketh clere weder all aboute.
But though it seme, it is nought so.
For Fals Semblaunt hath ever mo
Of his counseil in compaignie
The derke untrewe Ypocrisie
Whose word discórdeth to his thought.
Forthý they ben to-gider brought
Of one covíne, of one houshólde,
As it shall after this be tolde.
Of Fals Semblaunt it nedeth nought
To telle of olde ensamples ought.
For all day in experiénce
A man may see thilke evidénce
Of fairé wordés, whiche he hereth.
But yet the barge Envié stereth
And halt[1] it ever fro the londe,
Where Fals Semblaunt with ore in honde
It roweth and will nought arrive
But let it on the wawés drive
In great tempést and great debate,
Wherof that Love and his estate
Empeireth.[2] And therfóre I rede,
My soné, that thou fle and drede
This Vice and, what that other sain,
Let thy semblaúnt be trewe and plein.
For Fals Semblaunt is thilké Vice,
Which never was without office,

[1] *Halt*, holds. [2] *Empeireth*, are impaired.

Where that Envié thenketh to guile
He shall be for that ilké while
Of privé counseil messagére.
For whan his semblaunt is most clere
Than is he most derke in his thought;
Though men him se, they knowe him nought.
But as it sheweth in the glas
Thing which therinné never was,
So sheweth it in his viságe
That never was in his corâge.[1]
Thus doth he all his thing by sleighte.
Now lith thy consciénce in weighte,
My godé sone, and shrive thee here
If thou were ever custumére
To Fals Semblaunt in any wise."—
"For ought I can me yet avise,
My godé fader, certes no;
If I for love have ought don so,
Now axeth, I woldé pray you.
For ellés I wot never how
Of Fals Semblaunt that I have gilt."[2]—
"My sone, and sithen[3] that thou wilt
That I shall axé, gabbé nought,
But telle if ever was thy thought
With Fals Semblaunt and Coverture
To wite of any creature
How that he was with lové ladde,
So were he sory, were he gladde.
Whan than thou wistest howe it were,
All that he rounéd[4] in thin ere
Thou toldest forth in other place

[1] That which never was in the thought of his heart. *Courage* was any feeling from the heart. When the small birds make melody, says Chaucer, 'so pricketh hem Nature in her corages,' that is, they sing with all their hearts.
[2] *Gilt*, been guilty. [3] *Sithen*, since.
[4] *Rounéd*, whispered.

To setten him fro Lovés grace
Of what womán that thee best liste,
There as no man his counseil wiste
But thou, by whom he was deceived
Of love, and from his purpose weived,[1]
And thoughtest that his disturbaúnce
Thin owné causé shuld avaúnce,
As who saith I am so sely[2]
There may no mannés privetć
Ben heléd[3] half so well as min.
Art thou, my sone, of suche engín?
Tell on."—"My godé fader, nay,
As for the moré part, I saie.
But of somedele I am beknowe[4]
That I may stonde in thilké rowe
Amongés hem that saundres[5] use.
I woll nought me therof excuse,
That I with such coloúr ne steine,
Whan I my besté semblant feigne
To my felów, till that I wote
All his counseil both colde and hote.
For by that cause I make him chere
Till I his lové knowe and here.
And if so be min herté soucheth[6]
That ought unto my lady toucheth
Of lové that he woll me telle,
Anon I renne unto the welle
And casté water in the fire,
So that his cart amid the mire
By that I have his counseil knowe
Full ofté sith[7] I overthrowe
Whan that he weneth best to stonde.
But this I do you understonde,[8]
If that a man love ellés where,
So that my lady be nought there,
And he me tell, I will it hide,
There shall no worde escape aside.
For with deceipt of no semblaunt

[1] *Weived*, put aside. [2] *Sely*, simple.
[3] *Heléd*, concealed.
[4] I confess as to some part.
[5] *Saundres*, sandal wood (as a dye).
[6] *Soucheth*, suspects.
[7] *Ofté sith*, oftentimes.
[8] *Do you*, make you to understand.

To him breke I no covénaunt.
Me liketh nought in other place
To letté no man of his grace,
Ne for to ben inquisitife
To knowe an other mannés life,
Where that he love or lové nought
That toucheth nothing to my thought,
But all it passeth through min ere
Right as a thing that never were
And is foryete and laid beside.
But if it toucheth any side
My lady, as I have er spoken,
Min erés ben nought thanné loken.
For certés whanné that betit,[1]
My will, min herte and all my wit
Ben fully set to herken and spire [2]
What any man woll speke of hire.
Thus have I feignéd compaignie
Full ofté for[3] I wolde aspie
What thinge it is that any man
Tell of my worthy lady can.
And for two causes I do this.
The firsté causé wherof is,
If that I might of herken and seke
That any man of her misspeke,
I woll excuse her so fullý
That whan she wist it inderly,[4]
Min hopé shuldé be the more
To have her thank for evermore.
That other cause, I you assure,
Is, why that I by coverture
Have feignéd semblaunt ofté timé
To hem that passen all day by me
And ben lovérs als well as I,
For this I wené truély,
That there is of hem allé none,
That they ne loven everychone
My lady. For sothlích I leve [5]
And durste setten it in preve,
Is none so wise that shulde asterte,[6]

1 *Betit*, betides.
2 *Spire*, speir, seek narrowly.
3 *For*, because. 4 *Inderly*, thoroughly.
5 *Leve*, believe. 6 *Asterte*, escape.

But [1] he were lustles in his herte,
For why and he my lady sigh,[2]
Her visage and her goodlich eye,
But he her lovéd er he went.
And for that suche is min entent,
That is the cause of min aspie,
Why that I feigné compaignie
And maké felowe over all.
For gladly wolde I knowen all
And holdé me covért alway,
That I full ofté ye or nay
Ne list answére in any wise,
But feignen semblaunt as the wise
And herken talés, till I knowe
My ladies lovers all arowe.
And whan I here how they have wrought,
I fare as though I herd it nought
And as I no worde understood.
But that is nothing for her good,
For leveth well, the soth is this,
That whan I knowe all how it is,
I woll nought furthren hem a lite
But all the werste I can endite
I tell it unto my lady plat
For furthering of min own estate
And hinder hem all that I may.
But for all that yet dare I say
I finde unto my self no bote,
All though min herté nedés mote,
Through strength of love, all that I here
Discover unto my lady dere.
For in good feith I have no might
To helé [3] fro that sweté wight
If that it toucheth her any thinge.
But this wote wel the heven kinge,
That sithen first the world began
Unto none other straungé man
Ne feignéd I semblaúnt ne chere
To wite or axe of his matere,
Though that he lovéd ten or twelve
Whan it was nought my ladies selve.

1 *But*, unless. 2 If he saw my lady.
3 *Helé*, conceal.

But if he wold axe any rede
Alonlich of his owné hede,
How he with other lové ferde,
His talés with min eres I herde
But to min herté came it nought
Ne sank no deper in my thought,
But held counseil as I was bede,
And tolde it never in other stede,[1]
But let it passen as it come.
Now fader, say, what is thy dome,
And how thou wolt that I be peined[2]
For such semblaunt as I have feigned."—
"My sone, if reson woll be peised,[3]
There may no Vertue ben unpreised
Ne Vicé none be set in prise.
Forthy, my sone, if thou be wise
Do no visér upon thy face
Which woldé nought thin hert embrace.
For if thou do, within a throwe
To other men it shall be knowe,
So might thou lightly fall in blame
And lese a great part of thy name.
And nethéles in this degré
Full ofté timé thou might se
Of suché men as now a day
This Vicé setten in assay,
I speke it for no mannes blame
But for to warné thee the same.
My sone, as I may heré talke
In every placé where I walke,
I not[4] if it be so or none
But it is many daiés gone
That I first herdé tellé this,
How Fals Semblaunt hath be and is
Most comunly from yere to yere
With hem that dwelle among us here
Of suche as we Lumbardés calle.

[1] *Stede*, place. [2] *Peined*, put to penance.
[3] *Peised*, weighed. [4] *Not*, know not.

For they ben the sliést of alle
So as men sain in towne about
To feigne and sheué thing without
Whiche is revers to that withinne,
Wherof that they full ofté winne
Whan they by reson shuldé lese.
They ben the last, and yet they chese,
And we the firste, and yet behinde
We gone there as we shulden finde
The profit of our owné londe,
Thus gone they free withouten bonde
To done her profit all at large,
And other men bere all the charge.
Of Lumbardes unto this covine
Whiche allé londés conne engine[1]
May Fals Semblaunt in éspeciáll
Be likened, for they over all
Where that they thenken for to dwelle,
Among hem self, so as they telle,
First ben enforméd for to lere[2]
A craft which cleped is Facrere.[3]
For if Facreré come about
Than afterward hem stant no doubt
To voidé with a subtil honde
The besté goodés of the londe,
And bringé chaffe and také corne.
Where as Facreré goth beforne
In all his waie he fint no lette,
That doré can none ussher shette,
In whiche he list to take entré.
And thus the counseil most secré
Of every thing Facreré knoweth
Whiche into straungé place he bloweth
Where as he wote[4] it may most greve.
And thus Facreré maketh beleve.
So that full ofte he hath deceived
Er that he may ben apperceived.

[1] To this secret contrivance of the Lombards, who can outwit all nations.
[2] *Lere*, learn. [3] *Facrere*, dissimulation.
[4] *Wote*, knows.

Thus is this Vicé for to drede,
For who these oldé bokés rede
Of suche ensamples as were er,
Him oughté be the moré ware
Of allé tho that feigné chere,
Wherof thou shalte a talé here.
"Of fals semblant whiche is beleved,
Ful many a worthy wight is greved
And was long time or[1] we were bore.
To thee, my sone, I will therfore
A talé tell of Fals Semblaunt
Which falseth many a covenaúnt
And many a fraude of fals counséil
There ben hangénd upon his sail.
And that aboughten giltéles
Both Deianire and Hercules,
The whiche in great disesé fell
Through Fals Semblaunt, as I shall tell.
"Whan Hercules within a throwe
All only hath his herté throwe
Upon this fairé Deianire,
It fell him on a day desire,
Upon a river as he stood,
That passe he wolde over the flood
Withouté bote and with him lede
His lové, but he was in drede
For tendresse of that sweté wight,
For he knewe nought the forde aright.
There was a geaunt thanné nigh,
Which Nessus hight, and whan he sigh
This Hercules and Deianire,
Within his herte he gan conspire
As he which through his trecherie
Hath Hercules in great envie,
Whiche he bare in his herté loke,
And than he thought it shall be wroke.
But he ne dursté nethéles
Ayein this worthie Hercules

[1] *Or*, ere.

Fall in debate as for to feight,
But feigned semblaunt all by sleight
Of frendship and of allé good,
And cometh where as they both stood
And maketh hem all the chere he can
And saith, that as her[1] owné man
He is all redy for to do
What thinge he may; and it fel so,
That they upon this semblaunt triste[2]
And axen him, if that he wiste
What thinge hem weré best to done,
So that they mighten sauf and sone
The water passé, he and she.
And whan Nessús the privété
Knew of her herté what it ment,
As he that was of double entent
He made hem right a glad viságe.
And whan he herde of the passáge
Of him and her, he thoughté guile
And feigneth semblant for a while
To done hem plesaunce and servíse,
But he thought all an other wise.
"This Nessus with his wordés sligh
Yaf such counseil to-fore her eye,
Which semeth outward profitáble
And was withinné déceiváble.
He bad hem of the stremés depe
That they beware and také kepe,
So as they knowé nought the pas.
But for to helpe in suche a cas
He saith him self, that for her ese
He wolde, if that it mighte hem plese,
The passage of the water take
And for this lady undertake
To bere her to that other stronde
And sauf to set her up a londe,
And Hercules may than also
The waié knowe, how he shall go.
And herto they accorden all.
But what as after shall befall

[1] *Her*, their. [2] *Triste*, trust.

Well paid was Hercules of this.
And this geaunt also glad is
And toke this lady up alofte
And set her on his shulder softe
And in the flood began to wade
As he which no grucchingé made,
And bare her over sauf and sounde.
But whan he stood on drié grounde
And Hercules was fer behinde,
He set his trouth all out of minde,
Who so therof be lefe or loth
With Deianiré forth he goth,
As he that thoughté to dissever
The compaignie of hem for ever.
Whan Hercules therof toke hede,
As faste as ever he might him spede
He hiéth after in a throwe.
And hapneth that he had a bowe,
The whiche in allé hast he bende,
As he that wolde an arwé sende,
Whiche he to-fore had envenímed.
He hath so well his shotté timed,
That he him through the body smette
And thus the falsé wight he lette.[1]
But list now, suche a felonie.
Whan Nessus wist he shuldé deie,
He toke to Deianire his sherte,
Which with the blood was of his herte
Through out disteignéd over all,
And tolde how she it kepé shall
And privély to this entent,
That if her lorde his herté went
To love in any other place,
This shert, he saith, hath suche a grace,
That if she may so mochel make
That he the sherte upon him take,
He shall all other lette in veine
And torne unto her love ayeine.
"Who was so glad but Deianire?
Her thought her herte was on a fire,

[1] *Lette*, delayed, stopped.

Till it was in her cofre loke,
So that no word therof was spoke.
"The daiés gone, the yerés passe,
The hertés waxen lasse and lasse
Of hem that ben to love untrewe.
This Hercules with herté newe
His love hath set on Eolen,
And therof speken allé men.
This Eolen, this fairé maide
Was as men thilké timé saide
The kingés doughter of Eurice.
And she made Hercules so nice
Upon her love and so assote,[1]
That he him clotheth in her cote,
And she in his was clothéd ofte,
And thus feblésse is set alofte
And strengthé was put under fote.
There can no man therof do bote.
Whan Deianire hath herd this speche,
There was no sorwe for to seche,
Of other helpé wot she none
But goth unto her cofre anone,
With wepend eye and wofull herte
She toke out thilke unhappy sherte,
As she that wendé wel to do,
And brought her werke abouté so,
That Hercules this shert on dede
To suche entent as she was bede
Of Nessus, so as I said er.
But therof was she nought the ner,
As no fortúné may be weived,
With Fals Semblant she was deceived.
But whan she wendé best have wonne,
She lost all that she hath begonne.
For thilké shert unto the bone
His body sette a fire anone
And cleveth so it may nought twinne[2]
For the venim, that was therinne.

[1] *Assote*, made to dote.
[2] *Twinne*, be separated.

And he than as a wildé man
Unto the highé wode he ran,
And as the clerke Ovidé telleth,
The greté trees to grounde he felleth
With strengthe al of his owné might
And made an hughé fire upright
And lept therin him self at ones
And brent him self both flessh and bones;
Which thingé cam through Fals Semblaúnt
That falsé Nessus the geaunt
Made unto him and to his wife,
Wherof that he hath lost his life,
And she sorý for evermo.
"Forthy my sone, er thee be wo
I redé be wel ware therfore.
For whan so great a man was lore,[1]
It ought to yive a great conceipt
To warne all other of such deceipt."—
"Graunt mercy, fader; I am ware
So fer, that I no moré dare
Of Fals Semblaunt take ácqueintaúnce,
But rather I wol do penaúnce,
That I have feignéd chere er this.
Now axeth forth, what so there is
Of that belongeth to my shrifte."—
"My soné, yet there is the fifte,
Whiche is conceivéd of envie
And clepéd is supplantarie,
Through whos compassément and guile
Ful many a man hath lost his while
In love as wel as other wise,
Here after as I shall devise.
The Vice of Supplantáción
With many a fals collación
Whiche he conspireth áll unknowe,
Full ofté time hath overthrowe
The worship of another man.
So wel no life awaité can

[1] *Lore*, lost.

Ayein his sleighté for to caste,
That he his purpose atté laste
Ne hath, er that it be withset.[1]
But most of all his hert is set
In court upon these great offices
Of dignités and benefíces.
Thus goth he with his sleighte about
To hinder and shove another out
And stonden with his sligh compás
In stedé there another was,
And so to set him selven inne.
He recheth nought be so he winne
Of that another man shall lese,
And thus full ofté chalk for chese
He chaungeth with full litel coste,
Wherof another hath the loste
And he the profit shall receive.
For his Fortúne is to deceive
And for to chaunge upon the whele
His wo with other mennés wele;
Of that another man availeth
His own estate thus he up haileth
And taketh the brid to his beyete,[2]
Where other men the busshes bete.
My sone, and in the samé wise
There ben lovérs of suche emprise,
That shapen hem to be relieved
Where it is wronge to ben acheved,
For it is other mannés right
Whiche he hath taken, day and night,
To kepé for his owné store,
Toward him self for evermore
And is his proper[3] by the lawe,
Which thing that axeth no felawe,
If Lové holde his covenaunt.
But they that worchen by supplant,
Yet wolden they a man supplant
And take a part of thilké plant,
Whiche he hath for him sèlvé set.
And so ful ofte is all unknet

[1] *Withset*, upset.
[2] Takes the bird for his own profit.
[3] *Proper*, property.

That some man weneth be right faste.
For Súpplaunt with his slié caste
Full ofté happeneth for to mowe
Thing which another man hath sowe,
And maketh común of propreté
With sleighte and with subtilité,
As men may sen from yere to yere.
Thus claimeth he the bote to stere
Of whiche another maister is.
"Forthý my sone, if thou er this
Hast ben of such professión,
Discover thy confessión.
Hast thou supplanted any man?"—
"For ought that I you tellé can,
Min holy fader, as of dede
I am withouten any drede
And giltéles but of my thought,
My consciénce excuse I nought.
For were it wronge or were it right,
Me lacketh no thingé but might
That I ne woldé longe er this
Of other mannés love iwis[1]
By way of súpplantatión
Have made appropriatión
And holde that I never bought,
Though it another man forthought.[2]
And all this speke I but of one,
For whom I let all other gone.
But her I may nought overpasse
That I ne mote alway compásse,
Me rought nought by what queïntise,[3]
So that I might in any wise
Fro suché that my lady serve,
Her herté maké for to swerve
Withouten any part of love.
For by the goddés alle above
I wolde it mighté so befalle,
That I aloné shuld hem alle
Supplant and welde her at my wille.
And that thing may I nought fulfille,

[1] *Iwis*, certainly. [2] *Forthought*, grieved.
[3] I should not care by what ingenious device.

But if I shuldé strengthé make.
And that I dare nought undertake
Though I were as was Alisaunder,
For therof might arise a sclaunder.
And certés that shall I do never,
For in good feith yet had I lever
In my simplessé for to deie,
Than worché such supplantarie.
Of other wise I woll nought say
That, if I founde a siker way,
I wolde as for conclusion
Worche after supplantacion
So highe a lové for to winne.
Now fader, if that this be sinne,
I am all redy to redresse
The gilt, of whiche I me confesse."—
"My godé sone, as of Supplant
Thee theré nought drede *tant ne quant*
As for no thing that I have herde,
But only that thou haste misferde
Thenkend, and that me liketh nought,
For God beholt[1] a mannes thought.
And if thou understood in soth
In Lovés causé what it doth
A man to ben a supplantoúr,
Thou woldest for thin own honoúr
By double waié také kepe.
"First for thin own estate to kepe,
To be thy self so well bethought
That thou supplanted weré nought.
And eke for worship of thy name
Towardés other do the same
And suffre every man have his.
But nethéles it was and is
That in awaite[2] at all assaies
Supplant of love is in our waies;
The lief full ofté for the lever
Forsaketh,[3] and so it hath done ever.
Ensample I finde therupon,
At Troie how that Agámemnón

[1] *Beholt*, beholds. [2] *Awaite*, watch.
[3] Leaves the loved for the more loved.

Supplanted hath the worthy knight
Achilles for that sweté wight,
Which naméd was Brisseïda;
And also of Criseïda,
Whom Troilus to lové ches,[1]
Supplanted hath Diómedés.
Of Geta and Amphitrióne,
That whilom weré both as one
Of frendship and of compaignie,
I rede how that Supplantarſe
In Love, as it betidé tho,
Beguiléd hath one of hem two.
For this Getá, that I of mene,
To whom the lusty ſaire Alcmene
Assuréd was by way of love,
Whan he best wende have ben above
And sikerest of that he hadde,
Cupído so the causé ladde,
That while he was out of the way,
Amphitrion her love away
Hath take, and in this forme he wrought.
By night unto the chambre he sought
Where that she lay, and with a wile
He counterfeteth for the while
The vois of Get in suche a wise,
That made her of her bedde arise
Wenéndé, that it weré he,
She wendé, that it weré soth.
Lo, what supplant of Lové doth.
This Geta forth bejapéd went,
And yet ne wist he what it ment.
Amphitrion him hath supplanted
With sleight of love and her enchaunted,
And thus put every man out other.
The ship of Love hath lost his rother,
So that he can no reson stere.
And for to speke of this matere
Touchendé Love and his supplaunt
A talé, whiche is accordaúnt,
Unto thin ere I thenke enforme.
Now herken, for this is the forme.

[1] *Ches*, chose.

"Of thilke citee chefe of alle,
Which men the noble Romé calle,
Er it was set to Cristés ſeith,
There was, as the croniqué saith,
An emperoúr, the whiche it ladde
In pees, that he no werrés hadde.
There was no thing disóbeisaúnt,
Which was to Rome appertenaúnt,
But all was tornéd into rest.
To some it thought hem for the best,
To some it thought nothíngé so.
And that was only unto tho
Whose herté stood upon knighthode.
But most of allé his manhode
The worthy sone of themperóur,
Which woldé ben a werrióur,
As he that was chivalerous,
Of worldés fame and desiroús,
Began his fader to beseche,
That he the werrés mighté seche
In straungé marchés for to ride.
His fader saide he shulde abide
And woldé grraunté him no leve.
But he, which woldé nought beleve,[1]
A knight of his to whom he trist,
So that his fader nothing wist,
He toke and tolde him his corage,[2]
That he purpóseth a viage,
If that Fortúné with him stonde.
He said how that he woldé fonde[3]
The Greté See[4] to passe unknowe
And there abidé for a throwe[5]
Upon the werrés to travaile.
And to this point withouté faile
This knight, whan he hath herde his lorde,
Is swore and stant of his accorde.
And they that bothé yongé were,
So that in privé counseil there

[1] *Beleve*, remain.
[2] *His corage*, the thought of his heart.
[3] *Fonde*, try.
[4] *Grete See*, Mediterranean.
[5] *For a throwe*, for a time.

They ben assented for to wende;
And therupon to make an ende
Tresúre inough with hem they token.
And whan the time is best they loken
That sodeinlich in a galeie
Fro Romé-lond they went their waie
And lond upon that other side.
"The worldé fell so thilké tide,
Whiche ever his happés hath divérse,
The greté Souldan than of Perse
Ayein the Caliphe of Egípte
A werré, which that him beclipte,[1]
Hath in a marché costeaúnt.[2]
And he, which was a pursuivaunt
Worshíp of armés to atteigne,
This Romain, let anon ordeigne
That he was redy every dele.
And whan he was arraiéd wele
Of every thing which him belongeth,
Straught unto Kaire his wey he fongeth,[3]
Wher he the Souldan thanné fonde
And axeth that within his londe
He might him for the werré serve
As he which woll his thank deserve.
The Souldan was right glad withall
And well the more in speciáll,
Whan that he wist he was Romain.
But what was ellés incertaín
That might he wité by no way.
And thus the knight of whom I say
Toward the Souldan is belefte
And in the marches now and efte,
Where that the dedly werrés were,
He wroughté such knighthodé there,
That every man spake of him good.
"And thilké timé so it stood,

1 *Beclipte*, surrounded.
2 *Marché costeaúnt*, border country.
3 *Fongeth*, takes.

This mighty Souldan by his wife
A doughter hath, that in this life
Men saidé there was none so faire;
She shuldé ben her faders heire,
And was of yerés ripe inough,
Her beauté many an herté drough
To bowen to that ilké lawe,
Fro which no life may be withdrawe.
And that is Lové, whose natúre
Set life and deth in a ventúre
Of hem that knighthode undertake.
This lusty peine hath overtake
The hert of this Romaín so sore,
That to knighthodé more and more
Prowésse avaunteth his coráge.
Lich to the leon in his rage,
Fro whom that alle bestés fle;
Such was this knight in his degre.
Where he was arméd in the felde,
Ther dursté none abide his shelde.
Great price[1] upon the werre he hadde.
"But she, whiche all the chauncé ladde,
Fortúné shope the marchés so,
That by thassent of bothé two
The Souldan and the Caliphe eke
Bataile upon a day they seke,
Which was in suche a wisé set,
That lenger shulde it nought be let.
They made hem stronge on every side,
And whan it drough toward the tide,
That the batailé shuldé be,
The Souldan in great priveté
A gold ringe of his doughter toke
And made her swere upon a boke
And eke upon the goddés all,
That if fortúné so befall
In the batailé that he deie,—
That she shall thilké man obeie
And take him to her husébonde,
Which thilké samé ring to honde

1 *Price*, praise.

Her shuldé bringe after his deth.
"This hath she swore, and forth he geth
With all the power of his londe
Unto the marché, where he fonde
His enemy full embatailed.
The Souldan hath the feld assailed.
They that ben hardy sone assemblen,
Wherof the dredfull hertés tremblen.
That one sleeth, and that other sterveth,[1]
But above all his prise deserveth
This knightly Romain; where he rode
His dedly swerd no man abode,
Ayein the which was no defence,
Egipté fledde in his presénce,
And they of Perse upon the chace
Pursuen, but I not[2] what grace
Befell, an arwe out of a bowe
All sodeinly within a throwe
The Souldan smote, and there he lay.
The chas is left for thilké day,
And he was bore into a tent.
The Souldan sigh how that it went,
And that he shulde algaté deie.
And to this knight of Romainie,
As unto him whome he most triste,
His doughters ring, that none it wiste,
He toke and tolde him all the cas,
Upon her othe what token it was
Of that she shuldé ben his wife.
Whan this was said, the hertés life
Of this Souldán departeth sone.
And therupon, as was to done,
The dedé body well and faire
They carry till they come at Kaire,
There he was worthely begrave.
"The lordés, whiche as wolden save

1 *Sterveth*, dies. 2 *Not*, know not (ne wot).

The regné, which was desolate,
To bringe it into good estate
A parlément they set anone.
Now herken what fell therupon.
This yougé lord, this worthy knight
Of Rome upon the samé night
That they a morwe treté sholde,
Unto his bacheler he tolde
His counseil, and the ring with al
He sheweth, through which that he shall,
He saith, the kingés doughter wedde,
For so the ring was leid to wedde,[1]
He tolde, into her faders honde,
That with what man that she it fonde
She shulde him take unto her lorde.
'And thus,' he saith, 'stant of recorde.
But no man wot who hath this ring.'
This bacheler upon this thing
His ere and his ententé laid
And thoughté moré than he said;
And feigneth with a fals viságe,
That he was glad, but his coráge
Was all set in another wise.
These oldé philosóphres wise
They writen upon thilké while,
That he may best a man beguile
In whom the man hath most credénce.
And this befell in evidence
Toward this yongé lord of Rome.
His bacheler, which haddé come
Whan that his lord by nighté slepte,
This ring, the which his maister kepte,
Out of his purs awey he dede
And put another in the stede.
"A morwe whan the court is set
The yongé lady was forth fet,

1 *To wedde*, as pledge.

To whom the lordés done homáge,
And after that of mariáge
They treten and axen of her wille.
But she, which thoughté to fulfille
Her faders hest in this matére,
Said openly, that men may here,
The chargé whiche her fader bad.
Tho was this lorde of Romé glad
And drough toward his purs anone,
But all for nought, it was agone.
His bacheler it hath forth drawe
And axeth therupon the lawe,
That she him holdé covenaunt.
The token was so suffisaúnt,
That it ne mighté be forsake..
And nethéles his lorde hath take
Quaréle ayein his owné man,
But for no thing that ever he can
He might as thanné nought be herde,
So that his claime is unanswérde,
And he hath of his purpos failed.
"This bacheler was tho counseiled
And wedded and of thilke empíre
He was coroúnéd lord and sire,
And all the lond him hath received;
Wherof his lord, which was deceived,
A siknesse er the thriddé morwe
Conceivéd hath of dedly sorwe.
And as he lay upon his deth,
There while him lasteth speche and breth
He sendé for the worthiést
Of all the londe and eke the best
And tolde hem all the sothé tho,
That he was sone and heire also
Of themperoúr of greté Rome,
And how that they to-gider come,
This knight and he, right as it was
He tolde hem all the pleiné cas.
And for that he his counseil tolde,
That other hath all that he wolde
And he hath failéd of his mede.
As for the good he taketh none hede
He saith, but only of the love,
Of which he wend have ben above.
And therupon by letter write
He doth his fader for to wite
Of all the mater how it stode.
And thanné with an hertely mode
Unto the lordés he besought
To tell his lady howe he bought
Her love, of whiche another gladdeth.
And with that worde his hewé fadeth
And saide: 'a dieu my lady swete.'
The life hath lost his kindely hete,
And he lay dede as any stone,
Wherof was sory many one,
But none of allé so as she.
"This falsé knight in his degre
Arested was and put in holde.
For openly whan it was tolde
Of the tresón, whiche is befalle,
Throughout the lond they saiden alle,
If it be soth that men suppose
His owne untrouth him shall depose.
And for to seche an evidence
With honour and great reverence,
Wherof they mighté knowe an ende,
To themperoúr anon they sende
The letter whiche his soné wrote.
And whan that he the sothé wote,
To tell his sorwe is endéles;
But yet in hasté nethéles
Upon the talé whiche he herde,
His steward into Persé ferde
With many a worthy Romain eke
His legé tretour[1] for to seke.
And whan they thider comé were,
This knight him hath confesséd there,
How falsly that he hath him bore,
Wherof his worthy lord was lore.[2]

[1] *His legé tretour*, his traitorous liegeman.
[2] *Lore*, lost.

"Tho saiden some he shuldé deie,
But yet they founden such a weie,
That he shall nought be dede in Perse,
And thus the skillés ben diverse.
By causé that he was coróned,
Of that the lond was abandóned
To him, all though it were unright,
There is no peiné for him dight,
But to this point and to this ende
They graunten wel, that he shall wende
With the Romaíns to Rome ayein.
And thus accorded full and plein
The quické body with the dede
With levé také[1] forth they lede,
Where that supplant hath his juise.[2]
Wherof that thou thee might avise
Upon this enformaciön
Touchend of Supplantaciön,
That thou, my soné, do nought so
And for to také hede also
What Súpplant doth in other halve,
There is no man can finde a salve
Pleinly to helen suche a sore.
It hath and shall ben evermore,
Whan Pride is with Envié joint,
He suffreth no man in good point,
Where that he may his honour let.
And therupon if I shall set
Ensample, in holy chirche I finde
How that Supplant is nought behinde.
God wote, if that it now be so.
For in croníque of time ago
I finde a talé concordáble
Of Supplant, which that is no fable,
In the manér as I shall telle
So as whilóm the thingés felle.
At Rome as it hath ofté falle
The Viker Generall of alle
Of hem that leven Cristés feith
His lasté day,—which none withsaith,—
Hath shette as to the worldes eye;
Whos name, if I shall specifie,
He highté Popé Nicholas.
And thus whan that he passéd was,
The Cardinals, that wolden save
The forme of lawe in the conclave,
Gon for to chese a newé Pope,
And after that they couthe agrope
Hath eche of hem said his entent.
Til atté lasté they assent
Upon an holy clerk recluse,
Which full was of gostlý vertuse.
His paciënce and his simplesse
Hath set him into highe noblesse.
Thus was he Popé canonised
With great honoúr and intronised.
And upon chaunce, as it is falle,
His namé Celestin men calle;
Which notifiéd was by bulle
To holy chirche, and to the fulle
In allé londés magnified.
But every worship is envíed,
And that was thilké timé sene.
For whan this Pope, of whome I mene,
Was chose and other set beside,
A Cardinal was thilké tide,
Which the papate long hath desired
And therupon gretely conspired.
But whan he sigh fortúne is failed,
For which long time he hath travailed,
That ilké fire whiche Ethna brenneth
Throughout his wofull herté renneth,
Whiche is resembled to Envie,
Wherof Supplant and Trecherie
Engendred is. And nethéles
He feigneth love, he feigneth pees.
Outward he doth the reverénce,
But all within his consciënce
Through fals ymaginaciön
He thoughté Supplantaciōn.

[1] *Levé také*, leave taken.
[2] *Juise* (judicium), judgment.

And therupon a wonder wile
He wroughté. For at thilké while
It fel so, that of his lignáge
He hadde a clergeon of yonge age,
Whom he hath in his chambre affaited.[1]
"This Cardinal his time hath waited
And with his wordés sly and queint,
The whiche he couthé wisely peint,
He shope this clerke, of whiche I telle,
Toward the Popé for to dwelle,
So that within his chamber a night
He lay, and was a privé wight
Toward the Pope on nightés tide;
May no man fle that shall betide.
"This Cardinal, which thoughté guile,
Upon a day, whan he hath while,
This yongé clerke unto him toke
And made him swere upon a boke
And tolde him what his willé was.
And forth with al a trompe of bras
He hath him take and bad him this:
'Thou shalt,' he saidé, 'whan time is
Awaite and také right good kepe,
Whan that the Pope is fast aslepe
And that none other man be nigh.
And thanné that thou be so sligh
Through out the trompe into his ere,
Fro heven as though a vois it were,
To soune of such prolaciön,
That he his meditaciön
Therof may take, and understonde
As though it were of Goddés sonde.
And in this wisé thou shalt say,
That he do thilk estate away
Of Pope, of whiche he stant honoúred,
So shall his soulé be socoúred
Of thilké worship atté last
In heven which shall ever last.'
"This clerk, whan he hath herd the form,
How he the Popé shuld enform,
Toke of the Cardinal his leve
And goth him home, till it was eve.
And privély the trompe he hedde,
Til that the Popé was a bedde.
And at the midnight, whan he knewe
The Popé slepté, than he blewe
Within his trompé through the wall
And tolde, in what manér he shall
His Papacíë leve, and take
His firste estate. And thus awake
This holy Pope he madé thries,
Wherof diversé fantasies
Upon his greté holinésse
Within his hert he gan impresse.
The Popé full of innocénce
Conceiveth in his consciënce
That it is Goddés wil he cesse.[1]
But in what wise he may relesse
His highe estate, that wote he nought.
And thus within him selfe be thought,
He bare it stille in his memoire,
Till he cam to the consistoire,
And there in presence of hem alle
He axeth if it so befalle,
That any Popé cessé wolde,
How that the lawe it suffré sholde.
They seten allé stille and herde,
Was none, which to the point answérde;
For to what purpos that it ment
There was no man knew his entent
But only he which shope the guile.
"This Cardinal the samé while
All openly with wordés pleine
Saith if the Popé woll ordeigne,

[1] *Affaited*, adapted to his purpose.

[1] *Cesse*, abdicate.

That there be sucho a lawé wrought,
Than might he cesse, and elles
nought.
"And as he saidé, done it was.
The Pope anone upon the cas
Of his papáll auctorité
Hath made and yové the decré.
And whan the lawé was confermed
In dué forme and all affermed,
This innocent which was deceived
His papacie anone hath weived,[1]
Renouncéd and resignéd eke.
That other was no thing to seke,
But undernethé suche a jape
He hath so for him selfé shape,
That how as ever it him beseme
The mitre with the diademe
He hath through Supplantaciön
And in his confirmaciön,
Upon the fortune of his grace,
His name was clepéd Boneface.
"Under the viser of Envie,
Lo, thus was hid the trecherie
Whiche hath beguiléd many one.
But such counseil there may be none
Which treson, whan it is conspired,
That it nis lich the sparké fired
Up in the roof, which for a throwe
Lith hid til, whan the windés blowe,
It blaseth out on every side.
This Boneface, which can nought
hide
The trecherie of his supplaunt,
Hath openly made his avaunt,
How he the papacie hath wonne.
But thing which is with wrong be-
gonne
May never stondé wel at ende.
Where Pridé shall the bowé bende,
He shet[2] ful oft out of the way.
And thus the Pope, of whom I say,
Whan that he stood on high the
whele,

[1] *Weived*, put aside.
[2] *Shet*, shoots.

He can nought suffre himself be
wele.
Envië, whiche is lovéles,
And Pridé, whiche is lawéles,
With such tempésté made him erre,
That charité goth out of herre.[1]
So that upon misgovernaunce
Ayein Lewfis the King of Fraunce
He toké quarell of his oultrage
And said, he shuldé don homáge
Unto the chirché bodély.
But he, that wist no thingé why
He shuldé do so great servíce
After the worlde in suche a wise,
Withstood the wrong of that
demaunde,
For nought the Popé may com-
maunde
The King woll nought the Pope
obeie.
This Popé tho by allé weie
That he may worche of violénce,
Hath sent the bulle of his senténce
With cursinge and with enterdite.
The king upon this wrongfull plite
To kepe his regné from servage,
Counseiléd was of his barnáge,[2]
That might with might shall be
withstond.
Thus was the causé tak on hond,
And saiden, that the papacie
They wolden honoúr and magnifie
In all that ever is spirituáll,
But thilké Pridé temporáll
Of Boneface in his persone
Ayein that ilké wronge alóne
They woldé stonden in debate,
And thus the man and nought the
state
The Frensshé shopen by her might
To greve. And fel there was a
knight
Sire Guilliam de Langharet,
Which was upon this causé set.

[1] Goes off its hinges. [2] *Barnage*, baronage.

And therupon he toke a route
Of men of armés and rode oute,
So longe and [1] in awaite he lay,
That he aspied upon a day
The Popé was at Avinon
And shuldé ride out of the town
Unto Pontsorgé, the whiche is
A castell in Provence of his.
Upon the way and as he rode,
This knight, whiche hovéd and abode
Embuisshéd upon horsébake,
All sodeinlich upon him brake
And hath him by the bridell sesed
And said: 'O thou, which hast disesed
The courte of Frauncé by thy wronge,
Now shalt thou singe an other songe.
Thin enterdite and thy senténce
Ayein thin owné consciénce
Hereafter thou shalt fele and grope.
We pleigné nought ayein the Pope,
For thilké name is honouráble,
But thou, whiche hast be deceiváble
And trecherous in all thy werke,
Thou Boneface, and proudé clerke,
Misleder of the papacie,
Thy falsé body shall abie [2]
And suffre, that it hath deserved.'
"Lo, thus this supplantór was served.
For they him ladden into Fraunce
And setten him to his penáunce
Within a toure in hardé bondes,
Where he for hunger both his hondes
Ete of and diéd, God wote how.
Of whome the writinge is yet now
Registred as a man may here,
Which speketh and saith in this maner:
'Thin entré lich a fox was sligh,
Thy regne also with pride on high
Was lich the leon in his rage,
But atté laste of thy passáge
Thy deth was to the houndés like.'
"Suche is the letter of his cronique
Proclaméd in the court of Rome,
Wherof the wise ensample nome. [1]
And yet as ferforth as I dare,
I rede all other men beware
And that they loké well algate,
That none his owne estate translate
Of holy chirche in no degre
By fraudé ne by subtilté.
For thilke honoúr whiche Aaron toke
Shall none receive as saith the boke,
But he be clepéd, [2] as he was.
What shall I thenken in this cas
Of that I heré nowe a day?
I not, [3] but he which can and may
By reson both and by natúre
The helpe of every mannés cure
He kepé Simon fro the folde.
"For Joachim, thilke abbot tolde,
How suché daiés shulden falle,
That comunlich in places alle
The chapmen of such mercerie
With fraude and with supplantarie
So many shulden beie and selle,
That he ne may for shamé telle
So foule a sinne in mannés ere.
But God forbedé that it were
In ouré daiés, that he saith.
For if the clerk beware [4] his faith
In chapmanhode at suche a faire
The remenaunt mot nede empeire [5]

[1] *So longe and*, and so long. This way of placing "and" occurs frequently throughout the poem. Here it recurs six lines lower down.

[2] *Abie*. "Abye" means buy, that is, "pay for." "Abide" would mean "wait for," as this knight "hoved" (hovered about a spot) and abode, waited for, Pope Boniface.

[1] *Nome*, took.

[2] *But he be clepéd*, unless he be called.

[3] *Not*, know not.

[4] *Beware*, barter.

[5] *Empeire*, grow worse.

Of all that to the world belongeth.
For whan that holy chirché wrongeth,
I not what other thing shall righte.
And nethéles at mannés sighte
Envíë for to be preferred
Hath consciëncé so differred,
That no man loketh to the Vice
Whiche is the moder of malíce,
And that is thilké fals Envie,
Which causeth many a trecherie.
For where he may another se
That is more gracïoús than he,
It shall nought stonden in his might
But if he hinder suche a wight.
And that is well nigh over all
This Vice is now so generall.
"Envíë thilke unhap indrough,
Whan Joab by deceipté slough
Abner, for drede he shuldé be
With king David such as was he.
"And through Envíe also it felle
Of thilké fals Achitofelle,
For his counseil was nought acheved
But that he sigh Cusy beleved
With Absolon and him forsake,
He henge him selfe upon a stake.
"Senec witnésseth openly,
How that Envíë properly
Is of the Court the comun wenche.
And halt taverné for to schenche [1]
That drink which maketh the herté brenne,
And doth [2] the wit abouté renne
By every waié to compásse
How that he might all other passe,
As he which through unkindéship
Envíeth every felaship.
So that thou might well knowe and se,
There is no Vicé suche as he
First toward God abhomináble
And to mankinde unprofitáble.

[1] *Schenche*, pour out. [2] *Doth*, causes.

And that by wordés but a fewe
I shall by reson prove and shewe.
"Envie if that I shall descrive,
He is nought shaply for to wive
In erth among the women here.
For there is in him no matere
Wherof he mighté do plesaunce.
First for his hevy contenaunce
Of that he semeth ever unglad
He is nought able to be hadde,
And eke he brenneth so withinne,
That kindé may no profit winne,
Wherof he shulde his lové plese.
For thilké blood, which shuld have ese
To regne among the moisté veines,
Is drie of thilke unkindly peines
Through which Envie is firéd ay.
And this by reson prove I may,
That toward Love Envie is nought;
And other wise if it be sought,
Upon what side as ever it falle
It is the werstė Vice of alle,
Which of him self hath most malíce.
For understond that every Vice
Some causé hath wherof it groweth.
But of Envíë no man knoweth
Fro whenne he cam, but out of helle.
For thus the wisé clerkés telle,
That no spirít but of malíce
By way of kinde upon a Vice
Is tempted, and by such a way
Envíe hath kindé [1] put away
And of malíce hath his steríng,
Wherof he maketh his bákbitíng,
And is him self therof disesed;
So may there be no kindé plesed.
For ay the more that he envieth,
The more ayein him self he plieth.
Thus stant Envíe in good espeire
To ben him self the divels heire
As he whiche is his nexté liche
And furthest from the heven riche.

[1] *Kindé*, nature.

For theré may he never wone.[1]
"Forthý my godé deré sone,
If thou wolt finde a siker way
To lové, put Envíe away."—
"Min holy fader, reson wolde,
That I this Vice escheué sholde.
But yet to strengthen my coráge
If that ye wolde in avauntáge
Therof set a recoverir,
It were to me a great desir,
That I this Vicé mighté flee."—
"Now understond, my sone, and see,
There is phisiqué for the seke
And Vertues for the Vices eke.
Who that the Vices wolde escheue,
He mot by reson thanné sue[2]
The Vertues. For by thilké way
He may the Vices done away;
For they to-gider may nought dwelle.
For as the water of the welle
Of fire abateth the malíce,
Right so Vertu fordoth the Vice.
"Ayein Envíe is Charité,
Whiche is the moder of pité,
That maketh a mannés herté tender,
That it may no malíce engender
In him that is inclined therto.
For his coráge is tempred so,
That though he might him self releve
Yet wolde he nought another greve,
But rather for to do plesaúnce
He bereth him selven the grevaúnce,
So fain he wolde another ese.
Wherof, my soné, for thin ese
Now herken a talé, whiche I rede,[3]
And understonde it well I rede.[4]
"Among the bokés of Latín
I finde it writ of Constantín,
The worthy emperoúr of Rome,
Such infortúnés to him come

[1] *Wone*, dwell.
[2] *Sue*, follow.
[3] *Rede*, read.
[4] *Rede*, advise.

Whan he was in his lusty age,
The lepre caught in his viságe
And so forth over all aboute
That he ne mighté riden oute.
So left he bothé shield and spere,
As he that might him nought bestere,
And helde him in his chamber close.
Through all the world the fame arose.
The greté clerkés ben assent
And com at his commaundémént
To tret upon this lordés hele.
So longé they to-gider dele,
That they upon this medicíne
Appointen hem and determíne,
That in the maner as it stood
They wolde him bath in childés blood
Withinné seven winter age.
For as they sain, that shulde assuage
The leper and all the violénce,
Which that they knewe of accidence
And nought by way of kinde is falle.
And therto they accorden alle
As for finâll conclusiön,
And tolden her opiniön
To themperoúr. And he anone
His counseil toke, and therupon
With letters and with sealés out
They send in every londe about
The yongé children for to seche,
Whose blood, they said, shuldé be leche
For themperoúrés maladie.
"There was inough to wepe and crie
Among the moders, whan they herde
How wofully this causé ferde.
But nethéles they moten bowe,
And thus womén there come inowe,
With children soukend on the tete;
Tho was there many terés lete.
"But were hem liefe or were hem loth,

The women and the children both
Into the paleis forth be brought
With many a sory hertés thought
Of hem whiche of her[1] body bore
The children hadde, and so forlore
Within a whilé shulden se.
The moders wepe in her degre
And many of hem a swouné falle,
The yongé babies crieden alle.
This noise arose, this lorde it herde
And lokéd out, and how it ferde
He sigh, and as who saith abraide
Out of his slepe and thus he saide:
'O thou diviné purveaúnce,
Which every man in the balaúnce
Of kinde hast forméd to be liche,—
The pouer is bore as is the riche
And dieth in the samé wise;
Upon the fole, upon the wise,
Siknésse and hele entér comune;
May none escheué that fortúne
Which kinde hath in her lawé sette;
Her strengthe and beauté ben besette
To every man aliché free;
That she preferreth no degree
As in the disposiciön
Of bodely complexiön.
And eke, of soulé resonáble,
The pouer childe is bore as able
To vertue as the kingés sone.
For every man his owné wone [2]
After the lust of his assay
The Vice or Vertue chesé may.
Thus stonden allé men fraunchísed,
But in estate they ben devísed;
To somé worshíp and richésse,
To somé pouérte and distresse;
One lordeth and an other serveth:
But yet as every man deserveth
The world yeveth nought his yeftés here.
And certés he hath great matere

[1] *Her*, their.
[2] *His owné wone*, according to his own usage.

To ben of good condiciön,
Whiche hath in his subjectiön
The men that ben of his semblaúnce.'
And eke he toke his remembraúnce,
How he that madé lawe of kinde
Wolde every man to lawé binde,
And bad a man, suche as he wolde
Toward him self, right such he sholde
Toward an other done also.
"And thus this worthy lord as tho[1]
Set in balaúnce his owne estate
And with him self stood in debate
And thoughté, howe it was nought good
To se so mochel mannés blood
Be spilt by cause of him alone.
"He sigh also the greté mone
Of that the moders were unglad,
And of the wo the children made
Wherof that all his herté tendreth,
And such pité within engendreth
That him was lever for to chese
His owné body for to lese,
Than se so great a mordre wrought
Upon the blood which gilteth nought.
Thus for the pité whiche he toke,
All other lechés he forsoke
And put him out of aventúre
Al only into Goddés cure
And saith: 'Who that woll maister be
He mot be servaunt to pité.'
So ferforth he was overcome
With charité, that he hath nome
His counseil and his officérs,
And badde unto his tresorérs,
That they his tresour all about
Departe[2] among the pouer route
Of women and of children bothe,
Wherof they might hem fede and clothe

[1] *As tho*, as then. [2] *Departe*, part out, divide.

And saufly tornen home ayein
Withoute loss of any grein.
Through Charité thus he dispendeth
His good, wherof that he amendeth
The pouer people and countrevaileth
The harm that he hem so travaileth.
And thus the wofull nightés sorwe
To joie is tornéd on the morwe.
All was thanking, all was blessing,
Whiche erst was wepinge and cursing.
These women gone home glad inough,
Echone for joie on other lough
And praiden for this lordés hele,
Whiche hath reieséd the quaréle
And hath his owné will forsake
In Charite for Goddés sake.
But now hereafter thou shalte here
What God hath wrought in this matére,
As he that doth all equité.
To him that wroughté Charité
He was ayeinward charitoús
And to pité he was pitoús.
For it was never knowé yit,
That Charité goth unaquit.
The night whan he was laid to slepe,
The highé God, which wold him kepe,
Saint Peter and saint Poule him sende,
By whom he wolde his lepre amende.
They two to him slepénd appere
Fro God, and said in this manére:
'O Constantin, for thou hast served
Pité, thou hast pité deserved.
Forthý thou shalt such pité have,
That God through pité woll the save.
So shalt thou double helé finde,
First for thy bodeliché kinde,
And for thy wofull soule also.
Thou shalt ben hole of bothé two.
And for thou shalt the nought despeire,
Thy lepré shall no more empeire
Till thou wolt sendé therupon
Unto the mount of Celión,
Where that Silvéster and his clergie
To-gider dwelle in compaignie
For drede of the, which many a day
Hast ben a fo to Cristés lay[1]
And hast destruied to mochel shame
The prechours of his holy name.
But now thou hast somdele appesed
Thy God and with good dedé plesed,
That thou thy pité hast bewared
Upon the blood which thou hast spared.
Forthý to thy salvaciön
Thou shalt have informaciön,
Such as Silvéster shall the teche,
The nedeth of none other leche.'
This emperour, whiche all this herde:
'Graunt mercý Lorde, he answerde,
I woll do so as ye me say.
But of o thing I woldé pray,
What shall I telle unto Silvéstre
Or of your name or of your estre?"[2]
And they him tolden what they hight
And forth with all oute of his sight
They passen up into the heven.
And he awoke out of his sweven[3]
And clepeth, and men come anone
And tolde his dreme, and therupon
In suche a wise as he hem telleth
The mount wher that Silvester dwelleth
They have in allé hasté sought,
And founde he was, and with hem brought
To themperoúr, which to him tolde

[1] *Lay*, law, faith. [2] *Estre*, being. [3] *Sweven*, dream.

His sweven and ellés what he wolde.
And whan Silvéster hath herd the king
He was right joyfull of this thing,
And him began with all his wit
To techen upon Holy Writ.
First how mankindé was forlore,
And how the híghe God therfore
His Soné sendé from above,
Which boré was for mannés love;
And after of his owné chois
He toke his deth upon the crois;
And how in grave he was beloke,
And how that he hath hellé broke
And toke hem out that were him leve.[1]
And for to make us full beleve
That he was verray Goddes Sone
Ayein the kinde of mannés wone
Fro deth he rose the thriddé day.
And whan he wolde, as he well may,
He stigh up to his Father even
With flessh and blood into the heven;
And right so in the samé forme,
In flessh and blood, he shall retorne,
Whan timé cometh, to quicke and dede
At thilké wofull Day of Drede,
Where every man shall take his dome
Als well the maister as the grome.
The mighty kingés retenue
That Day may stonde of no valúe
With worldés strengthé to defende;
For every man mot than entende
To stond upon his owné dedes
And leve all other mennés nedes.
That Day may no counséil availe,
The pledour and the plee shall faile;
The sentence of that ilké day
May none appele sette in delay;

[1] *Leve*, dear.

There may no gold the jugé plie
That he ne shall the sothé trie
And setten every man upright,
As well the plowman as the knight.
The leudé man, the greté clerke
Shall stonde upon his owné werke;
And suche as he is foundé tho,
Such shall he be for evermo,
There may no peiné be relesed,
There may no joié ben encresed,
But endéles as they have do
He shall receivé one of two.
"And thus Silvester with his sawe
The ground of all the newé lawe
With great devociön he precheth
Fro point to point and plainly techeth
Unto this hethen emperóur
And saith: 'The highe Creatour
Hath underfonge his Charité
Of that he wroughté suche pité,
Whan he the children had on honde.'
"Thus whan this lord hath understonde
Of all this thing how that it ferde,
Unto Silvéster he than answérde
With all his holé herte and saith,
That he is redy to the feith.
And so the vessell, which for blood
Was made, Silvéster, there[1] it stood
With clené water of the welle
In allé haste he let do felle
And setté Constantin therinne
All nakéd up unto the chinne.
And in the while it was begunne,
A light, as though it were a sunne,
Fro heven into the placé come
Where that he toke his christendome,
And ever amonge the holy tales
Lich as they weren fisshes scales
They fellen from him now and efte,
Till that there was nothing belefte

[1] *There*, where.

Of all this greté maladie.
For he that wolde him purifie
The highé God hath made him clene,
So that there lefté nothing sene.
He hath him clenséd bothé two
The body and the soule also.
Tho [1] knew this emperoúr in dede,
That Cristés feith was for to drede,
And sende anone his letters out
And let do crien all aboute
Up pein of deth, that no man weive,
That he baptismé ne receive.
After his moder quene Eleine
He sende, and so betwene hem tweine
They treten, that the citee all
Was christnéd, and she forth with all.
This emperoúr, which hele hath found,
Withinné Rome anone let founde
Two churches, which that he did make [2]
For Peter and for Poulés sake,
Of whom he hadde a visión
And yaf therto possessión
Of lordship and of worldés good.
And how so that his will was good
Toward the Pope and his fraunchise,
Yet hath it provéd otherwise
To se the worching of the dede.
For in croniqué thus I rede
Anone as he hath made the yefte
A vois was herde on high the lefte,[3]
Of which all Romé was adradde
And said: 'This day is venim shadde
In Holy Chirche, of temporall

[1] *Tho*, then.
[2] *Did make*, caused to be made.
[3] *Lefte*, air.

Which medleth [1] with the spirituall.'
And how it stant of that degré
Yet a man may the sothe se,
God may amende it, whan he wille,
I can therto none other skille.
But for to go there I began,
How Charité may helpe a man
To bothé worldés, I have saide.
And if thou have an eré laide,
My soné, thou might understonde,
If Charité be take on honde,
There folweth after mochel grace.
Forthý if that thou wolt purcháce
How that thou might Envié flee,
Acqueinté the with Charite,
Which is the Vertue Sovereine."—
"My fader, I shall do my peine.
For this ensample whiche ye tolde
With all min herte I have witholde,
So that I shall for evermore
Escheue Envíë well the more.
And that I have er this misdo
Yive me my penaunce er I go.
And over that to my matere
Of shrifté, why we sitten here
In priveté betwene us twey,
Now axeth what there is I prey."—
"My godé sone, and for thy lore
I woll the tellé what is more,
So that thou shalt the Vices knowe.
For whan they be to thee full knowe,
Thou might hem wel the better eschue.
And for this cause I thenké sue
The formé bothe and the matere,
As now suendé thou shalt here,
Which Vicé stant nexte after this.
And whan thou wost how that it is,
As thou shalt heré my devise,
Thou might thyself the better avise.

[1] *Medleth*, mingleth.

Book ·III.

OF WRATH.

If thou the Vices list to knowe,
My sone, it hath nought be unknowe
Fro first that men their swerdés grounde,
That there nis one upon this grounde
A Vicé foreine fro the lawe,
Wherof that many a good felawe
Hath be destraught by sodein chaunce.
And yet to kindé no plesaúnce
It doth, but where he most acheveth
His purpose, most to kinde he greveth,
As he whiche out of consciénce
Is enemy unto paciénce.
And is by name one of the Seven,
Whiche oft hath set the world uneven,
And clepéd is the cruel Ire,
Whose herte is evermore on fire
To speke amis, and to do, bothe,
For his servaúnts ben ever wrothe."
"My godé fader, tell me this
What thinge is Iré?"—"Sone, it is
That in our englissh Wrath is hote,
Whiche hath his wordés ay so hote,
That all a mannés paciénce
Is firéd of the violence.
For he with him hath ever five
Servaunts, that helpen him to strive.
The first of hem Maléncoly
Is clepéd, whiche in compaignie
An hundred timés in an houre
Woll as an angry besté loure,
And no man wot the causé why.
My soné, shrive the now forthý,
Hast thou be Malencolien?"—
"Ye fader, by saint Julien.
But[1] I untrewé wordés use
I may me nought therof excuse.
And all maketh Lové, well I wote,
Of which min herte is ever hote,
So that I brenne as dothe a glede
For wrathé that I may nought spede.
And thus full oft a day for nought
Saufe onlich of min owné thought
I am so with my selven wroth,
That how so that the gamé goth
With other men, I am nought glad
But I am well the more unglad;
For that is other mennés game
It torneth me to puré grame.[2]
Thus am I with my self oppressed
Of thought the whiche I have impressed,
That all wakénd I dreme and mete,[3]
That I with her alone mete[4]
And pray her of some good answére.
But for she wol nought gladly swere,
She saith me 'Nay' withouten othe.
And thus waxe I withinné wrothe

[1] *But*, unless.
[2] *Grame*, vexation.
[3] *Mete*, dream.
[4] *Mete*, meet

That outward I am all affraied
And so distempred and so esmaied,
A thousand timés on a day
There souneth in min eres 'Nay,'
The which she saidé me to-fore.
Thus be my wittés all forlore.
And namély[1] whan I beginne
To reken with my self withinne,
How many yerés ben agone,
Sith I have truely lovéd one
And never toke of her other hede,
And ever a liché for to spede
I am, the more I with her dele,
So that min hap and all min hele
Me thenketh is ay the lenger the ferre.[2]
That bringeth my gladship out of herre,
Wherof my wittés ben empeired
And I, as who saith, all dispeired,
For finally whan that I muse
And thenke, how she woll me refuse,
I am with Anger so bestad,
For al this world might I be glad.
And for the whilé that it lasteth
All up so down my joie it casteth,
And ay the further that I be
Whan I ne may my lady se,
The more I am redý to Wrathe,
That for the touching of a lath
Or for the torning of a stre[3]
I wode[4] as doth the wildé see
And am so malencolioús,
That there nis servaunt in min house
Ne none of tho that be aboute,
That eche of hem ne stant in doute
And wenen that I shuldé rave,
For anger that they se me have.
And so they wonder more and lasse,
Til that they seen it overpasse.
But fader, if it so betide,
That I approche at any tide
The placé where my lady is,
And thanné that her like iwis
To speke a goodly word untó me,
For all the gold that is in Romé
Ne couth I after that be wroth,
But all min anger overgoth.
So glad I am of the presénce
Of hiré, that I all offence
Foryete, as though it weré nought
So over glad is than my thought.
And nethéles, the soth to telle,
Ayeinward if it so befelle,
That I at thilké timé sigh
On me that she miscaste her eye,
Or that she listé nought to loke,
And I therof good hedé toke,
Anone into my first estate
I torne and am with that so mate,[1]
That ever it is aliché wicke.
And thus min honde ayein the pricke
I hurte and have don many a day,
And go so forth as I go may
Full ofté biting on my lippe
And make unto my self a whippe
With whiche in many a chele and hete
My wofull herte is so tobete,[2]
That all my wittés ben unsofte,
And I am wrothe I not[3] how ofte.
And all it is maléncolie,
Which groweth on the fantasie
Of Lové that me woll nought loute.[4]
So bere I forth an angry snoute
Full many timés in a yere.
But fader, now ye sitten here
In Lovés stede, I you beseche,
That some ensample ye me teche,
Wherof I may my self appese."—
"My soné, for thin hertés ese

[1] *Namély*, especially. [2] *Ferre*, farther.
[3] *Stre*, straw. [4] *Wode*, rage madly.

[1] *Mate*, deadened in spirit.
[2] *Tobete*, *to* is an intensive prefix.
[3] *Not*, know not.
[4] Love that will not bow to me.

I shall fulfillé thy praiere,
So that thou might the better lere,
What mischefe that this Vicé stereth,
Whiche in his anger nought forbereth,
Wherof that after him forthenketh,
Whan he is sobre, and that he thenketh
Upon the folie of his dede.
But if thou ever in cause of Love
Shalt deme, and thou be so above
That thou might lede it at thy wille,
Let never through thy Wrathé spille
Whiche every kindé shuldé save.
For it sit every man to have
Reward to love and to his might,
Ayein whos strengthé may no wight.
What Nature hath set in her lawe,
Ther may no mannés might withdrawe,
And who that worcheth thereayein,
Full ofté time it hath be sein,
There hath befallé great vengeaúnce,
Wherof I finde a remembraunce.
"Ovide after the timé tho
Tolde an ensample and saide so,
How that whilóm Tiresias,
As he walkéndé goth par cas,
Upon an high mountein he sigh
Two serpentés in his waie nigh.
And they so, as natúre hem taught,
Assembled were, and he tho cought
A yerdé, which he bare on honde,
And thoughté, that he wolde fonde[1]
To letten hem, and smote hem bothe,
Wherof the goddes weren wrothe.
And for he hath destourbéd kinde
And was so to Natúre unkinde,
Unkindelich he was transformed,
That he, which erst a man was formed,
Into a woman was forshape;
That was to him an angry jape.

[1] *Fonde*, try.

But for that he with anger wrought
His anger angerliche he bought.
"Lo, thus my sone, Ovide hath write,
Wherof thou might by reson wite
More is a man than suche a beste,
So might it never ben honéste
A man to wrathen him to sore
Of that another doth the lore
Of kinde, in whiche is no malice,
But only that it is a Vice.
And though a man be resonáble,
Yet after kinde he is meváble
To lové where[1] he woll or none.
Thenk thou, my soné, therupon
And do Maléncolie awey,
For love hath ever his lust to pley
As he which wold no lifé greve."—
"My fader, that I may well leve[2]
All that ye tellen it is skille,[3]
Let every man love as he wille,
Be so it be nought my ladý,
For I shall nought be wroth thereby.
But that I wrath and fare amis
Alone upon my self it is,
That I with bothé love and kinde
Am so bestad, that I can finde
No wey howe I it may astert,
Which stant upon min owné hert
And toucheth to none other life
Sauf onely to that sweté wife,
For whom, but if it be amended,
My gladdé daiés ben dispended,
That I my self shall nought forbere
The Wrath the whiché now I bere,
For therof is none other liche.
Nowe axeth forth I you beseche
Of Wrathe, if there ought ellés is,
Wherof to shrivé."—"Sone yis.
Of Wrathé the secónd is Chest,[4]
Which hath the windés of tempest
To kepe, and many a sodein blast
He bloweth, wherof ben agast

[1] *Where*, whether.
[2] *Leve*, believe.
[3] *Skille*, reason.
[4] *Chest*, strife.

They that desiren pees and rest.
He is that ilke ungoodliest,
Which many a lusty love hath twinned,
For he bereth ever his mouth unpinned,
So that his lippés ben unloke
And his corage is all to-broke,
That every thing whiche he can telle,
It springeth up as doth a welle,
Which may none of his stremés hide,
But renneth out on every side.
So boilen up the foulé sawes,
That Chesté wote [1] of his felawes.
For as a sivé [2] kepeth ale,
Right so can chesté kepe a tale;
All that he wote he woll disclose
And speke er any man oppose.
As a citee withoute a walle,
Where men may gon out overalle
Withouten any resisténce,
So with his crokéd eloquence
He speketh all that he wot withinne,
Wherof men lesé more than winne.
For often time of his chidíng
He bringeth to housé such tidíng
That makéth werre at beddés hede.
He is the levein of the brede
Which soureth all the past [3] about.
Men ought well suché one to doute.[4]
For ever his bowe is redy bent,
And whome he hit I tell him shent,[5]
If he may perce him with his tonge.
And eke so loude his belle is ronge,
That of the noise and of the soune
Men feren him in all the towne
Well moré than they done of thonder;
For that is cause of moré wonder.
For with the windés, which he bloweth,

[1] *Wote*, knows. [2] *Sive*, sieve.
[3] The leaven of the bread that turns all the paste sour.
[4] *Doute*, fear.
[5] *I tell him shent*, I count him put to shame.

Full ofté sith he overthroweth
The citees and the polecie,
That I have herd the people crie
And echone saide in his degre:
'Ha, wické tungé, wo thou be!'
For men sain, that the hardé bone—
All though him selvé havé none—
A tungé braketh it all to pieces.
He hath so many sondry spieces [1]
Of Vicé, that I may nought wele
Descrive hem by a thousand dele.[2]
But whan that he to Chesté falleth,
Full many a wonder thing befalleth,
For he ne can no thing forbere.
Now tell, my soné, thin answére,
If it hath ever so betid,
That thou at any time hast chid
Toward thy lové."—"Fader, nay.
Such Chesté yet unto this day
Ne made I never, God forbede.
For er I singé suche a crede,
I haddé lever to be lewed,
For thanne were I all beshrewed
And worthy to be put abacké
With all the sorwe upon my backe,
That any man ordeigné couthe.
But I spake never yet by mouthe
That unto Chesté mighté touche.
And that I durst right wel avouche
Upon her selfe as for witnesse.
For I wote of her gentilesse,
That she me woldé wel excuse,
That I no suché thingés use.
And if it shuldé so betid,
That I algatés must chid,
It mighté nought be to my Love.
For so yet was I never above
For all this widé world to winne,
That I durst any word beginne,
By which she might have ben amoved,
And I of Cheste also reproved.
But rather if it might her like,

[1] *Spieces*, species, kinds.
[2] By a thousandth part.

The besté wordés wolde I pike [1]
Whiche I couthe in min herté chese
And serve hem forth in stede of chese,
For that is helpelich to defie; [2]
And so I wolde my wordés plie,
That mighten Wrath and Cheste
avale [3]
With telling of my softé tale.
Thus dar I maken a forwárd,
That never unto my lady ward
Yet spake I word in suche a wise,
Wherof that Chesté shulde arise.
Thus say I nought that I full ofte
Ne havé, whan I spake most softe,
Par cas said moré than inough;
But so well halt no man the plough,
That he ne balketh other while;
Ne so wel can no man affile
His tungé, that somtime in rape [4]
Him may some light word overscape,
And yet ne meneth he no cheste.
But that I have ayein her heste
Full ofté spoke, I am beknowe. [5]
And how, my wille is that ye knowe;
For whan my timé cometh about
That I dar speke and say all out
My longé love of which she wot,
That ever in one aliché hot
Me greveth, than all my disese
I telle, and though it her displese
I speke it forth and nought ne leve.
And though it be beside her leve
I hope and trowé nethéles,
That I do nought ayein the pees.
For though I telle her all my thought,
She wot well that I chidé nought.
Men may the highé God beseche,
And he wol here a mannés speche
And be nought wroth of that he saith,
So yiveth it me the moré feith
And maketh me hardy soth to say,
That I dar wel the better prey
My lady, whiche a woman is.
For though I telle her that er is
Of lové, which me greveth sore,
Her oughté nought be wroth the
more,
For I withouté noise or cry
My plainté make all buxomly,
To putten allé Wrath away,
This dar I say unto this day
Of Cheste, in ernest or in game,
My lady shall me no thing blame.
"But ofté time it hath betid,
That with my selven I have chid,
That no man couthé better chide,
And that hath ben at every tide,
Whan I cam to my selve alone.
For than I made a privé mone,
And every talé by and by
Whiche as I spake to my ladý,
I thenke and peise in my balaúnce
And drawe into my remembraunce.
And than, if that I finde a lacke
Of any word that I misspake,
Which was to moche in any wise,
Anone my wittés I despise
And make a chiding in min herte
That any word me shulde asterte [1]
Whiche as I shulde have holden inne
And so forth after I beginne
And loke if there was ellés ought
To speke, and I ne spake it nought.
And than if I may seche and finde,
That any word ben left behinde,
Whiche as I shuldé more have spoke,
I wold upon my self be wroke
And chidé with my selven so,
That all my wit is over-go.
For no man may his timé lore
Recover, and thus I am therfore
So overwroth in all my thought,
That I my self chide all to nought.
Thus for to moche, or for to lite,
Full ofte I am my self to wite. [2]

[1] *Pike*, pick.
[2] *Defie*, digest. This belief was the origin of the old custom of ending dinner with cheese.
[3] *Avale*, bring down. [4] *Rape*, haste.
[5] I confess.

[1] *Asterte*, escape. [2] *Wite*, blame.

But all that may me nought availe,
With Chesté though I me travaile,
But oule on stoke and stoke on oule
The moré that a man defoule,
Men witen wel which hath the werse.
And so to me nis worth a kerse,[1]
But torneth unto min owné hede,
Though I till that I weré dede
Wolde ever chide in suche a wise
Of Love, as I to you devise.
But fader, now ye have all herd
In this manér, howe I have ferd
Of Cheste and of Dissension,
Yif me your absolucion."—
"My sone, if that thou wistest all,
What Chesté doth in speciall
To love and to his welwilling,
Thou woldest fleen his knowleching
And lerné to be debonaire.
For who that most can speké faire
Is most accordend unto love.
Fair speche hath ofté brought above
Full many a man, as it is knowe,
Whiche ellés shuld have ben right
lowe
And failéd mochel of his wille.
Forthý hold thou thy tungé stille
And let thy wit thy will areste
So that thou fallé nought in cheste,
Whiche is the source of great dis-
taúnce,
And take into thy rémembraúnce,
If thou might geté paciënce,
Which is the leche of all offence,
As tellen us these oldé wise.
For whan nought ellés may suffise
By strengthé ne by mannés wit,
Than paciënce it over sit
And over cometh it at laste.
But he may never longé laste,
Which woll nought bow er that he
breke.
Take hedé, sone, of that I speke."—
"My fader, of your goodly speche
And of the wit, whiche ye me teche,
I thonké you with all min hert.
For that word shall me never astert,
That I ne shall your wordés holde
Of paciënce, as ye me tolde,
Als ferforth as min herté thenketh
And of my Wrath it me forthenketh.
But fader, if ye forth with all
Some good ensample in speciáll,
Me wolden teche of some cronique,
It shuldé well min herté like
Of paciëncé for to here,
So that I might in my matére
The more unto my love obey
And putten my disese awey."—
"**My sone**, a man to bye him
pees
Behoveth suffre as Socrates
Ensample lefté, whiche is write,
And for thou shalt the sothé wite
Of this ensample, what I mene,
All though it be now litel sene
Among the men thilke evidence,
Yet he was upon paciënce
So set, that he him self assay
In thing, which might him most
mispay,
Desireth and a wicked wife
He weddeth, which is sorwe and
strife
Ayein his esé was contraire.
But he spake ever soft and faire,
Till it befell, as it is tolde,
In winter, whan the day is colde,
This wife was fro the wellé come,
Where that a pot with water nome[1]
She hath and brought it into house,
And sigh how that her sely spouse
Was set and lookéd on a boke
Nigh to the fire, as he which toke
His ese as for a man of age.
And she began the wodé rage
And axeth him, what divel he thought
And bare on hond, that him ne rought

[1] *Kerse*, cress.

[1] *Nome*, taken.

What labour that she toke on honde,
And saith, that suche an husébonde
Was to a wife nought worth a stre.[1]
He saidé nouther nay ne ye,
But helde him stille and lete her chide.
And she, which may her self nought hide,
Began withinné for to swelle
And that she brought in fro the welle,
The water pot, she hent a lofte
And bad him speke, and he all softe
Sat stille and nought a word answérd.
And she was wroth that he so ferd,
And axeth him, if he be dede,
And all the water on his hede
She poured out and bad him awake.
But he, whiche woldé nought forsake
His paciëncé, thanné spake
And said, how that he fond no lake
In nothing which she haddé do,
For it was winter timé tho,
And winter, as by wey of kinde,
Which stormy is as men it finde,
First maketh the windés for to blowe
And after that, within a throwe,
He reineth and the water gates
Undoth, and thus my wife algates,
Which is with reson well besein,
Hath made me bothé winde and rein
After the seson of the yere.
And than he set him ner the fire
And as he might his clothés dreide,[2]
That he nomore o word ne saide,
Wherof he gat him somdele rest,
For that him thought was for the best.
"I not[3] if thilke ensample yit
Accordeth with a mannés wit
To suffre as Socrátes dede.
And if it fal in any stede
A man to lesé so his galle,
Him ought among the women alle
In Lovê court by jugément
The namé bere of paciënt
To yive ensample to the good
Of paciënce how that it stood,
That other men it mighté knowe.
And, sone, if thou at any throwe
Be tempted ayein paciënce,
Take hede upon this evidence,
It shall par cas the lassé greve."—
"My fader, so as I believe
Of that shall be no maner nede,
For I woll také so good hede,
That er I fall in suche assay
I thinke escheue, if that I may.
But if there be ought ellés more,
Wheref I mighté také lore
I praié you, so as I dare,
Now telleth, that I may beware,
Some other tale of this mater."—
"Sone, it is ever good to lere
Wherof thou might thy word restreigne
Er that thou falle in any peine.
For who that can no counseil hide,
He may nought faile of wo beside,
Which shall befalle, er he it wite,
As I finde in the bokés write.
Yet cam there never good of strife
To seche in all a mannés life,
Though it beginne on puré game
Full ofte it torneth into grame
And doth grevaúnce on somé side.
Wherof the greté clerk Ovide
After the lawé which was tho,
Of Jupiter and of Juno
Maketh in his bokés menciön,
How they felle at dissenciön,
In manner as it were a borde,[1]
As they begunné for to worde
Among hem self in privété.
And that was upon this degré,
Whiche of the two more amorous is
Or man or wife. And upon this

[1] *Stre*, straw.
[2] Dried his clothes as well as he could.
[3] *Not*, know not.

[1] *Borde*, jest.

They mighten nought accorde in one
And toke a jugé therupon,
Which clepéd is Tiresias
And bede him demen in this cas.
And he withoute avisément
Ayein Junó yaf jugément.
This Goddesse upon his answére
Was wroth and woldé nought forbere,
But tok awey for evermo
The light from both his eyen two.
Whan Jupiter this harm hath sein
Another bienfait there ayein
He yaf and suche a grace him doth
That, for he wiste he saidé soth,
A soth-saier he was for ever.
But yet that other weré lever
Have had the loking of his eye
Than of his word the prophecie.
But how so that the sothé went,
Strife was the cause of that he hent
So great a peiné bodily.
"My soné, be thou ware thereby
And hold thy tungé stillé close,
For who that hath his word disclose
Er that he wité what he mene
He is full ofte nigh his tene [1]
And leseth full many timé grace,
Wher that he wold his thank purcháce.
And over this, my soné dere,
Of other men, if thou might here
In privité what they have wrought,
Hold counseil and discover it nought,
For Chesté can no counseil hele,[2]
Or be it wo or be it wele,
And take a tale into thy minde,
The which of olde ensample I finde.
Phebus, which maketh the daiés light,
A love he haddé, which tho hight
Cornidé, whom aboven alle
He pleseth. But what shall befalle
Of lové, there is no man knoweth.

[1] *Tene*, vexation. [2] *Hele*, conceal.

But as fortúne her happés throweth,
So it befell upon a chaunce,
A yong knight toke her ácqueintaunce
And had of her all that he wolde.
But a fals bird, which she hath holde
And kept in chambre of puré youthe
Discovereth all that ever he couthe.
The briddés namé was as tho
Corvus, the which was than also
Well moré white than any swan,
And he, the shrewe, al that he can
Of his ladý to Phebus saide.
And he for wrath his swerd out braide,
With which Cornide anone he slough.
But after, him was wo inough
And toke a full great repentaúnce,
Wherof in token and remembraúnce
Of hem whiche usen wické speche,
Upon this brid he toke his wreche,
That there he was snow-white to-fore
Ever afterward cole black therfore
He was transforméd, as it sheweth.
And many a man yet him beshreweth
And clepen him into this day
A raven, by whom yet men may
Take evidencé, whan he crieth,
That some mishap it signifieth.
Beware therfore and say the best,
If thou wolt be thy self in rest,
My godé sone, as I the rede.
And suche a daiés be now fele [1]
In Lovés Courte, as it is saide,
That let her tungé's gone unteide.
My soné, be thou none of tho
To jangle and telle talés so,
And namély [2] that thou ne chide,
For Chesté can no counseil hide,
For Wrathé saidé never wele."—
"My fader, sothe is every dele,
That ye me teche, and I woll holde,
The reulé to whiché I am holdé,

[1] *Fele*, many. [2] *Namely*, especially.

To fle the Cheste, as ye me bidde:
For well is him, that never chidde.
Now telle me forth if there be more,
As touchinge unto wrathés lore."—
"Of wrathe yet there is another,
Whiche is to Cheste his owné brother,
And is by namé clepéd Hate,
That suffreth nought within his gate,
That there come other love or pees,
For he woll maké no relese
Of no debate whiche is befalle.
Now speke, if thou arte one of alle,
That with this Vice hath be witholde."[1]—
"As yet for ought that ye me tolde,
My fader, I not what it is."—
"In good feith, sone, I trowé yis."—
"My fader, nay, but ye me lere."—
"Now list, my sone, and thou shalt here.
Hate is a Wrathé nought shewend,
But of long timé gaderénd,
And dwelleth in the herté loken
Till he se timé to be wroken.
And than he showeth his tempést
More sodein than the wildé beste,
Which wot nothing, what mercy is.
My sone, art thou knowen of this?"—
"My gode fader, as I wene,
Now wote I somedele what ye mene,
But I dare saufly make an othe,
My lady was me never lothe.
I woll nought sweré nethéles,
That I of Hate am giltéles.
For whan I to my lady ply
Fro day to day and mercy cry,
And she no mercy on me laith,
But shorté wordés to me saith,
Though I my lady love algate,
Tho wordés mote I nedés hate,
And woldé they were all dispent
Or so fer out of londé went
That I never after shuld hem here:
And yet love I my lady dere.
Thus is there Hate, as ye may se,
Betwene my ladies word and me.
The worde I hate and her I love,
What so me shall betide of love.
But furthermore I woll me shrive,
That I have hated all my live
These janglers, whiche of her envíe
Ben ever redy for to lie.
For with her fals compássément
Full often they have made me shent
And hindred me full ofté timé,
Whan they no causé wisten by me,
But onlich of her owné thought.
And thus have I full ofté bought
The lye and drank nought of the wine.
I wolde her hap were such as mine.
For how so that I be now shrive,
To hem ne may I nought foryive,
Untill I se hem at debate
With Love, and thanné min estate
They mighten by her owné deme
And loke how wel it shuld hem queme[1]
To hinder a man, that loveth sore.
And thus I hate hem evermore,
Til Love on hem wold done his wreche;
For that I shall alway beseche
Unto the mighty Cupido,
That he so mochel woldé do,
So as he is of Love a god,
To smite hem with the samé rod,
With whiche I am of Lové smiten,
So that they mighten know and witen,
How hindring is a wofull peine
To him that lové wold atteigne.
Thus ever on hem I wait and hope,
Till I may se hem lepe a lope[2]

[1] *Witholde*, held with.

[1] *Queme*, be pleasing.
[2] *Lepe a lope*, take a leap.

And halten on the samé sore,
Whiche I do now for evermore.
I woldé thanné do my might
So for to stonden in her light,
That they ne shulden have a wey
To that they wolden put awey.
I wolde hem put out of the stede
Fro Lové, right as they me dede
With that they speke of me by mouthe,
So wolde I do, if that I couthe
Of hem, and thus so God me save
Is all the Haté that I have
Toward these janglers every dele,
I wolde all other ferdé wele.
Thus have I, fader, said my wille.
Say ye now forth, for I am stille."—
"My sone, of that thou hast me said
I holdé me nought fully paid,[1]
That thou wold haten any man
To that accorden I ne can,
Though he have hindred thee tofore.
But this I tellé thee therfore,
Thou might upon my benison
Well haten the condiciön
Of tho janglérs, as thou me toldest,
But furthermore, of that thou woldest
Hem hinder in any other wise,
Suche Hate is ever to despise.
Forthý my sone, I wold thee rede,
That thou drawe in by frendly hede
That thou ne might nought do by Hate,
So might thou geté love algate
And setté thee, my sone, in rest.
For thou shalt finde it for the best,
And over this so as I dare
I redé, that thou be right ware
Of other mennés Hate about,
Whiche every wise man shuldé dout,
For Hate is ever upon await.

[1] *Paid*, satisfied.

And as the fissher on his bait
Sleeth, whan he seeth the fisshes faste,
So whan he seeth time atté last
That he may worche an other wo,
Shall no man tornen him ther fro,
That Haté nill his felonie
Fulfill and feigné compaignie.
Yet nethéles for fals semblaunt
Is toward him of covenaunt
Witholdé, so that under bothe
The privé wrathé can him clothe,
That he shall seme a great beleve.
But ware thee well, that thou ne leve
All that thou seest to-fore thin eye,
So as the Gregois whilom sigh;
The boke of Troié who so rede,
There may he finde ensample in dede.
"Sone, after the destructión,
Whan Troy was allé beté down
And slain was Priamus the king,
The Gregois, which of all this thing
Ben causé, tornen home ayein.
There may no man his hap withsain,
It hath ben sene and felt full ofte,
The hardé time after the softe.
By see as they forth homeward went,
A rage of great tempést hem hent.[1]
Juno let bende her partie bow,
The sky wax derke, the wind gan blow,
The firy welken gan to thonder,
As though the world shuld al asonder.
From heven out of the water gates
The reiny storm fell down algates,
And all her tacle made unwelde,
That no man might him self bewelde.
There may men heré shipmen crie
That stood in aunter for to die.
He that behindé sat to stere

[1] *Hent*, seized.

May nought the foré stempne[1] here;
The ship arose ayein the wawes,
The lodésman hath lost his lawes,
The see bet in on every side,
They nisten what fortúne abide,
But setten hem all in goddes will,
Where[2] he wolde hem save or spill.
And it fell thilké timé thus,
There was a kingé, which Nauplus
Was hote, and he a soné hadde
At Troié, which the Gregois ladde
As he that was made prince of alle,
Till that Fortúné let him falle.
His namé was Palámidés,
But through an Haté nethéles
Of som of hem his deth was caste
And he by treson overcaste.
His fader, whan he herde it telle,
He swore, if ever his timé felle,
He wolde him venge if that he might,
And therto his avow he hight.
And thus this king through privé Hate
Abode upon a waite algate,
For he was nought of suche emprise,
To vengen him in open wise.
"The famé, which goth widé where,
Maketh knowe, how that the Gregois were
Homwárd with al the felaship
Fro Troy upon the see by ship.
Nauplus, whan he this understood
And knew the tidés of the flood
And sigh the wind blow to the londe,
A great deceipt anone he fonde
Of privé Hate, as thou shalte here,
Wherof I telle all this matére.
"This king the weder gan beholde
And wisté well, they moten holde
Her cours endlonge his marché right,
And made upon the derké night
Of greté shidés[3] and of blockes

1 *Foré stempne*, voice in the bows.
2 *Where*, whether. 3 *Shides*, logs.

Great fire ayeine the greaté rockes,
To shew upon the hillés high,
So that the flete of Grece it sigh.
And so it fell right as he thought,
This fleté, which an haven sought,
The brighté firés sighe a fer,
And they ben drawen ner and ner
And wendé well and understood
How all that fire was made for good
To shewé where men shulde arrive.[1]
And thiderward they hasten blive.[2]
In semblaunt as men sain is guile,
And that was provéd thilké while.
The ship, which wend his helpe accroche,[3]
Drof all to pieces on the roche.
And so there deden ten or twelve
There no man mighté helpe him selve,
For there they wenden[4] deth escape
Withouten helpe her deth was shape.
Thus they that comen first to-fore
Upon the rockés ben forlore.
But through the noise and through the cry
The other weren ware therby,
And whan the day began to rowe,[5]
Tho mighten they the sothé knowe,
That where they wenden frendés finde,
They fondé frendship all behinde.
The londé than was soné weived,
Where that they hadden be deceived,
And toke hem to the highé see,
Therto they saiden alle ye,
Fro that day forthe and ware they were
Of that they had assaiéd there.
"My sone, herof thou might avise,
How fraudé stant in many wise
Amongés hem that guilé thinke.
There is no scrivener with his inke,

1 *Arrive*, come to the shore.
2 *Blive*, quickly. 3 *Accroche*, increase.
4 *Wenden*, hoped. 5 *Rowe*, dawn.

Whiche half the fraudé writé can,
That stant in suche a maner man.
Forthý the wisé men ne demen
The thingés after that they semen,
But after that they knowe and finde.
The mirrour sheweth in his kinde
As he had all the world withinne,
And is in soth nothing therinne.
And so fareth Haté for a throwe,[1]
Till he a man hath overthrowe;
Shall no man knowé by his chere,
Whiche is avaunt ne whiche arere.
Forthý my soné, thenke on this."—
"My fader, so I woll iwis,[2]
And if there more of Wrathé be,
Nowe axeth forth pour charité,
As ye by your bokés knowe,
And I the sothé shall beknowe."—
"My sone, thou shalt understonde,
That yet towardé Wrathé stonde
Of dedly Vices other two.
And for to telle her namés so
It is Contek and Homicide,
That ben to drede on every side.
Contek so as the bokés sain
Foolhast hath to his chamberlain,
By whose counsell all unavised
Is paciëncé most despised,
Till Homicidé with him mete.
Fro mercy they ben all unmete
And thus ben they the worst of alle
Of hem whiche unto Wrathé falle
In dedé both and eke in thought.
For they accompte her Wrath at nought
But if there be shedíng of blood.
And thus liche to a besté wode
They knowen nought the god of life,
Be so they havé swerde or knife
Her dedly wrathé for to wreke,
Of pité list hem nought to speke.
None other reson they ne fonge,
But that they ben of mightés stronge.

[1] *Throwe*, space of time. [2] *Iwis*, certainly.

But ware hem well in other place,
Where every man behoveth grace;
For there I trowe it shall him faile,
To whom no mercy might availe,
But wroughten upon tirannie,
That no pité ne might hem plie.
Now tell, my sone."—"My fader, what?"—
"If thou hast be coupáble of that?"
"My fader, nay, Crist me forbede;
I onliché speke of the dede
Of which I never was coupáble
Withouten causé resonáble.
But this is nought to my matére
Of shrifté, why we sitten here.
For we ben set to shrive of Love,
As we beganné first above.
And nethéles I am beknowe,
That as touchénd of lovés throwe,
Whan I my wittés overwende,
Min hertés Contek hath none ende,
But ever stant upon debate
To great disese of min estate,
As for the timé that it lasteth.
For whan my fortune overcasteth
Her whele and is to me so straunge,
And that I se she woll nought chaunge,
Than cast I all the worlde about
And thenk howe I at home in dout
Have all my time in vein despended
And se nought how to be amended,
But rather for to be empeired,
As he that is well nigh despeired.
For I ne may no thank deserve,
And ever I love and ever I serve
And ever I am a liché nere,
Thus, for I stonde in suche a weré,
I am as who saith out of herre.[1]
And thus upon my self I werre,
I bringe and put out allé pees.
That I full ofte in such a rees[2]
Am wery of min owné life,

[1] *Out of herre*, unhinged.
[2] *Rees*, stir of battle.

So that of Contek and of Strife
I am beknowe and have answérde,
As ye, my fader, now have herde.
Min herte is wonderly begone
With counseil, wherof wit is one,
Whiche hath resón in compaignie
Ayein the whiché stant partie
Will, which hath Hope of his accorde.
And thus they bringen up discorde,
Witte and Resón counseilen ofte,
That I min herté shuldé softe
And that I shuldé Will remue [1]
And put him out of retenue
Or elles holde him under fote.
For as they sain, if that he mote
His owné reule have upon honde,
There shall no Wit ben understonde
Of Hope; also they tellen this,
That over all where that he is
He set the herte in jeopartie
With wishing and with fantasie,
And is nought trewe of that he saith,
So that there is on him no feith.
Thus with Resón and Witte avised
Is Will and Hope all day despised.
Resón saith, that I shuldé leve
To lové, where there is no leve
To spede, and Will saith there ayein
That such an herte is to vilain
Which dare nought love till that he spede;
Let Hopé serve at suché nede.
He saith eke, where an herte sit
All holé governed upon Wit,
He hath this livés lust forlore.
And thus min herte is all to-tore
Of suche a Contek, as they make.
But yet I may nought Will forsake
That he nis maister of my thought,
Or that I spede, or spedé nought."—
"Thou dost, my sone, ayeinst the right,
But Love is of so great a might,

[1] *Remue*, remove.

His lawé may no man refuse,
So might thou there the better excuse.
And nethéles thou shalt be lerned,
That thy Will shuldé be govérned
Of Reson moré than of Kinde;
Wherof a talé write I finde.
A philosophre of which men tolde
There was whilom by daiés olde,
And Diogénes than he hight,
So olde he was that he ne might
The world travaile, and for the best
He shope him for to take his rest
And dwelle at home in suche a wise,
That nigh his house he let devise
Endlonge upon an axel tree
To set a tonne in suche degree
That he it mighté torne aboute;
Wherof one heed was taken oute
For he therinne sitte shulde
And torné him selve as he wolde
And také the eire and se the heven
And deme of the planetés seven
As he which couthé mochel what.[1]
And thus full ofté there he sat
To muse in his philosophie
Solé withouten compaignie;
So that upon a morwe tide
A thing which shuldé tho betide.
Whan he was sette here as him list
To loke upon the sonne arist,
Wherof the propertie he sigh,
It fellé, there cam ridend nigh
King Alisaundré with a route.
And as he cast his eye aboute
He sigh this tonne, and what it ment
He woldé wite, and thider sent
A knight, by whom he might it knowe.
And he him self that ilké throwe
Abode and hoveth theré stille.
This knight after the kingés wille

[1] *Couthe mochel what*, knew a good deal, much what, a formation similar to somewhat.

With sporé made his horse to gone
And to the tonne he came anone,
Where that he fonde a man of age,
And he him toldé the message,
Suche as the kinge him haddé bede,
And axeth why in thilké stede[1]
The tonné stood and what it was.
And he, which understood the cas,
Sat still and spake no worde ayein.
The knight bad speke and saith: 'Vilain,
Thou shalt me telle, er that I go,
It is thy king, whiche axeth so.'
'My king,' quod he, 'that were unright.'
'What is he thanné?' saith the knight,
'Is he thy man?' 'That say I nought,'
Quod he, 'but this I am bethought,
My mannés man how that he is.'
'Thou liest, falsé cherle, iwis,'[2]
The knight him said and was right wroth,
And to the kinge ayein he goth
And told him, how this man answérde.
The king whan he this talé herde
Bad that they shulden all abide,
For he him self wold thider ride.
And whan he came to-fore the tonne,
He hath his talé thus begonne:
'Al heil,' he saith, 'what man art thou?'
Quod he: 'Such one as thou seest now.'
The king, which haddé wordés wise,
His agé woldé nought despise
But saith: 'My fader, I thee pray,
That thou me wolt the causé say,
How that I am thy mannés man?'
'Sire king,' quod he, 'and that I can,
If thou wilt.'—'Yea,' saith the king.—

[1] *Stede*, place. [2] *Iwis*, certainly.

Quod he: 'This is the sothé thing:
Sith I first reson understood
And knew what thing was evil and good,
The Will, whiche of my body moveth,
Whos werkés that the god reproveth,
I have restreignéd evermore
Of him which stant under the lore
Of Reson, whos subjéct he is,
So that he may nought done amis.
And thus by wey of covenaunt
Will is my Man and my Servaunt
And ever hath be and ever shall.
And thy Will is thy Principal
And hath the lordship of thy wit,
So that thou couthest never yit
Take a day rest of thy labour.
But for to be a conqueroúr
Of worldés good, which may nought laste,
Thou hiést ever a liché faste,
Where thou no Reson hast to winne.
And thus thy Will is cause of sinne
And is thy Lord to whom thou servest,
Wherof thou litel thank deservest.'
The king, of that he thus answérd,
Was nothing wroth, but when he herd
The highé wisedom, whiche he saide,
With goodly wordés this he praide,
That he him woldé tell his name.
'I am,' quod he, 'that ilké same,
Which that men Diogénes calle.'
Tho was the king right glad with alle,
For he had herd ofté to-fore
What man he was, so that therfore
He saide: 'O wisé Diogéne,
Now shall thy greté wit be sene,
For thou shalt of my yifté have,
What worldés thingé thou wolt crave.'

Quod he: 'Than hove out of my sonne
And lete it shine into my tonne,
For thou benimst me[1] thilké yifte,
Which lith nought in thy might to shifte:
None other good of thee me nedeth.'
"The king, whom every contré dredeth,
Lo, thus he was enforméd there;
Wherof, my soné, thou might lere,
How that thy Wil shal nought be leved,
Where it is nought of Wit releved.
And thou hast said thy self er this,
How that thy Wil thy maister is,
Through which thin hertés thought withinne
Is ever of contek to beginne,
So that it greatly is to drede,
That it no homicidé brede.
For Love is of a wonder kinde
And hath his wittés ofté blinde,
That they fro mannés Reson falle.
But whan that it is so befalle,
That Will shall his corágé lede
In Lovés cause, it is to drede;
Wherof I finde ensample write,
Whiche is behovely for to wite.
"**I rede a tale**, and telleth this,
The citee which Semiramis
Encloséd hath with walle about
Of worthy folk with many a rout
Was inhabíted here and there.
Amongé the which two there were
Above all other noble and great,
Dwellend tho within a strete
So nigh to-gider, as it was sene,
That there was nothing hem betwene
But wowe[2] to wowe and walle to walle.

[1] *Benimst me*, takest away from me.
[2] *Wowe*, wall. "Wowe" and "wall" are equivalent, like "follow" and "sue" fourteen lines later.

This o lord hath in specialle
A sone, a lusty bacheler,
In all the towne was none his pere.
That other had a doughter eke
In all the lond that for to seke
Men wisten none so faire as she.
And fell so, as it shuldé be,
This fairé doughter nigh this sone,
As they to-gider thanné wone,[1]
Cupíd hath so the thingés shape.
That they ne might his honds escape
That he his fire on hem ne caste,
Wherof her herts he overcaste
To folwé thilké lore and sue,
Which never man yet might escheue.
And that was Love, as it is happed,
Whiche hath her hertés so betrapped,
That they by allé waiés seche,
How that they mighten winne a speche
Her wofull peiné for to lesse.
Who loveth wel, it may nought misse,
And namély[2] whan there ben two
Of one accord, how so it go,
But if that they some waié finde,
For Love is ever of suche a kinde
And hath his folk so wel affaited,
That how so that it be awaited,
There may no man the purpos let.[3]
And thus betwene hem two they set
An hole upon a wal to make
Through which they have her counseil take
At allé timés, whan they might.
This fairé maiden Tisbé hight
And he, whom that she lovéd hote,
Was Piramus by namé hote.
So longe her lesson they recorden,
Til atté lasté they accorden
By nightés timé for to wende
Alone out fro the townés ende,

[1] *Wone*, dwell. [2] *Namély*, especially.
[3] *Let*, hinder.

Where was a welle under a tree,
And who cam first, or she or he,
He shuldé stillé there abide.
So it befell the nightés tide
This maiden which desguiséd was,
All privély the softé pas
Goth through the largé town unknowe,
Till that she cam within a throwe
Where that she likéd for to dwelle
At thilke unhappy freshé welle,
Which was also the forest nigh;
Where she coménd a leon sigh
Into the feld to take his pray
In haste. And she tho fledde away,
So as Fortúné shuldé falle,
For fere, and let her wimpel[1] falle
Nigh to the wel upon therbage.
This wildé leon in his rage
A besté whiche he found there out
Hath slain, and with his bloody snout
Whan he hath eten what he wolde,
To drinke of thilké stremés colde
Come to the wellé, where he fonde
The wimpel, whiche out of her honde
Was falle, and he it hath to-drawe,
Bebledde aboute and all forgnawe.
And than he straught[2] him for to drinke
Upon the fresshé wellés brinke,
And after that out of the plein
He torneth to the wode ayein.
And Tisbé dursté nought remewe,
But as a brid which were in mewe,[3]
Within a bussh she kept her close
So stillé that she nought arose
Unto her self and pleigneth ay.
And fell, while that she theré lay,
This Piramus cam after sone
Unto the welle and by the mone
He found her wimpel bloody there.
Cam never yet to mannés ere

[1] *Wimpel*, neck-covering.
[2] *Straught*, stretched.
[3] *Mewe*, cage for moulting birds.

Tidingé ne to mannés sight
Merveillé which so sore aflight[1]
A mannés herte, as it tho dede
To him, whiche in the samé stede
With many a woful cómpleigninge
Began his hondés for to wringe
As he which deemeth sikerly
That she be dede. And sodeinly
His swerd all naked out he braide
In his Foolhaste and thus he saide:
'I am cause of this felonie,
So it is reson that I deie,
And she is dede by cause of me.'
And with that worde upon his kne
He fell, and to the goddés alle
Up to the heven he gan to calle
And praié, sithen[2] it was so
That he may nought his love as tho[3]
Have in this world, that of her grace
He might her have in other place,
For heré wolde he nought abide,
He saith. But as it shall betide,
The pomel of his swerd to ground
He set and through his hert a wound
He made up to the baré hilte,
And in this wisé him self spilte
With his Foolhaste, and deth he nam.[4]
For she within a whilé cam,
Where he lay dede upon his knife,
So woful yet was never life
As Tisbé was. Whan she him sigh,
She mighté nought one worde on high
Out speké, for her herté shette,
That of her life no pris she sette
But dedé swounend down she felle;
Till after whan it so befelle,
That she out of her traunce awoke,
With many a wofull pitous loke
Her eye alwey among she caste
Upon her love and atté laste
She caught her breth and saide thus:

[1] *Aflight*, afflicted. [2] *Sithen*, since.
[3] *Tho*, then. [4] *Nam*, took.

'O thou, which clepéd art Venús,
Goddesse of Love, and thou Cupide,
Which Lovés cause hast for to guide,
I wot now wel that ye be blinde,
Of thilke unhap whiche I nowe finde
Only betwene my love and me.
This Piramus, whiche here I se
Bledend, O, what hath he deserved?
For he your hest hath kept and served,
And was yonge and I both also,
Alas, why do ye with us so?
Ye set our hertés both on fire
And made us suché thing desire
Wherof that we no skillé couthe.
But thus our freshé lusty youthe
Withouten joy is all despended,
Which thing may never ben amended.
For as for me this woll I say,
That me is lever for to deie
Than live after this sorwefull day.'
And with this word where as he lay
Her love in armés she embraseth
Her owné deth and so purchaseth,
That now she wepte and now she kiste,
Till atté laste, 'ere she it wiste,
So great a sorwe is to her falle
Whiche overgoth her wittés alle,
And she, which mighté nought asterte,
The swerdés pointe ayein her herte
She set and fell down therupon,
Wherof that she was dede anone.
And thus both on a[1] swerd bledend
They weré founden dede liggend.
"Now thou, my sone, hast herd this tale
Beware that of thin owné bale
Thou be nought cause in thy Fool-haste,
And kepe that thou thy Wit ne waste
Upon thy thought in aventúre,

[1] *A*, one.

Wherof thy livés forfetúre
May falle. And if thou have so thought
Er this, tell on and hide it nought."—
"My fader, upon Lovés side
My consciënce I wol nought hide,
How that for love of puré wo
I have ben ofté moved so
That with my wishes if I might
A thousand timés, I you plight,
I haddé storven[1] in a day.
And therof I me shrivé may,
Though Lové fully me ne slough,
My will to deié was inough.
So am I of my Will coupáble,
And yet is she nought merciáble
Which may me yivé life and hele,
But that her list nought with me dele
I wot by whos conséil it is
And him wolde I long time er this,
And yet I wolde and ever shall,
Sleen and destruie in speciáll.
The golde of niné kingés londes
Ne shulde him savé fro min hondes,
In my powér if that he were.
But yet him stant of me no fere,
For nought that ever I can manáce
He is the hinderer of my grace,
Til he be dede I may nought spede.
So mote I nedés taken hede
And shape how that he were awey,
If I therto may finde a wey."—
"My soné, tell me now forthý
Whiche is that mortal enemy,
That thou manácest to be dede."—
"My fader, it is suche a quede[2]
That where I come, he is to-fore
And doth so that my cause is lore."
"What is his name?" "It is Daunger,
Whiche is my ladies counseiler,
For I was never yet so sligh
To come in any placé nigh

[1] *Storven*, died.
[2] *Quede*, foul one.

Where as she was, by night or day,
That Daunger ne was redy ay,
With whom for speché ne for mede
Yet might I never of Lové spede.
For ever I this findé soth,
All that my lady saith or doth
To me Daunger shall make an ende.
And that maketh al my world mis-
wende,
And ever I axe his helpe, but he
May be wel clepéd sauns pité.
For ay the more I to him bowe,
The lasse he woll my tale allowe.
He hath my lady so engleued [1]
She woll nought, that he be re-
meued.
For ever he hongeth on her saile
And is so privé of counseile,
That ever whan I have ought bede,
I findé Daunger in her stede
And min answere of him I have.
But for no mercy that I crave,
Of mercy never a point I hadde.
I find his answer ay so badde,
That worsé might it never be.
And thus betwen Daungér and me
Is ever werré til he deie.
But might I ben of such maistrie,
That I Daungér had overcome,
With that were all my joié come.
Thus wolde I wonde for no sinne
Ne yet for all this world to winne,
If that I mighté finde a sleight
To lay all min estate in weight
I wolde him fro the Court desever
So that he come ayeinward never,
Therfore I wisshe and woldé fain
That he were in some wisé slain,
For while he stant in thilké place
Ne gete I nought my ladies grace.
Thus hate I dedely thilké Vice
And wolde he stood in none office
In placé where my lady is.
For if he do, I wot wel this,

[1] *Engleued*, fastened to him.

That outher he shall deie or I
Within a while, and nought forthý
On my ladý full ofte I muse,
Now that she may her self excuse.
For if I deie in suche a plite
Me thenketh she might nought be
quite,[1]
That she ne were an homicide.
And if it shuldé so betide,
As god forbede it shuldé be,
By double way it is pité.
For I, which all my Will and Wit
Have yove and servéd ever yit,
And than I shuld in suche a wise,
In rewardíng of my servíce
Be dede, me thenketh it were routh.
And furthermore I tellé trouth,
She that hath ever be wel named,
She were worthý than to be blamed
And of resón to ben appeled,
Whan with o word she might have
heled
A man, and suffreth him to deie.
Ha, who sigh ever such a way?
Ha, who sigh ever such destresse?
Withouté pité gentilesse,
Withoute mercy womanhede,
That woll so quite [2] a man his mede
Whiche ever hath be to Lové trewe.
"My godé fader, if ye rewe
Upon my talé, tell me now,
And I wol stinte and herken
you."—
"My sone, attempre thy corâge
Fro Wrath and let thin hert assuage,
For who so wol him underfonge,
He may his grace abidé longe
Or he of Lové be received
And eke also, but it be weived,[3]
There mighté mochel thing befalle
That shuldé make a man to falle
Fro Love, that never afterwarde
Ne durst he loké thiderwarde.

[1] *Quite*, acquitted. [2] So requite.
[3] Unless it (Wrath) be put aside.

In hardé waiés men gon softe,
And er they climbe avise hem ofte,
And men seen all day, that rape[1] reweth.
And who so wicked alé breweth
Full ofte he mot the worsé drinke;
Better it is to flete than sinke;
Better is upon the bridel chewe
Than if he fel and overthrewe
The hors and stickéd in the mire;
To casten water in the fire
Better is than brenne upal the hous.
The man whiche is malicioús
And foolhastif, full ofte he falleth.
And selden is whan Love him calleth.
Forthý better is to suffre a throwe[2]
Than to be wilde and overthrowe.
Suffraunce hath ever be the best
To wishen him that secheth rest.
And thus if thou wolt Lové spede,
My soné, suffre, as I the rede.
What may the mous ayein the cat?
And for this cause I axé that,
Who may to Lové make a werre,
That he ne hath him self the werre?
Love axeth pees and ever shall,
And who that fighteth most withall,
Shall lest conquere of his emprise.
For this they tellen that ben wise,
Whiche is to strive and have the werse
To hasten, is nought worth a kerse.[3]
Thing that a man may nought acheve,
That may nought wel be done at eve,
It mot abidé till the morwe.
Ne hasté nought thine owné sorwe,
My sone, and take this in thy witte,
He hath nought lost that wel abitte.[4]
Ensample, that it falleth thus,

[1] *Rape*, haste. Icelandic "hrapa," headlong hurry. It is the word used in the phrase "rap out an oath."
[2] *A throwe*, for a time.
[3] *Kerse*, cress.
[4] *Abitte*, abides, waits (like our "everything comes to him who waits").

Thou might well take of Piramus,
Whan he in haste his swerd out drough
And on the point him selven slough
For love of Tisbé pitously
For[1] he her wimpel fond bloodý
And wende a beste her haddé slain,
Where as him ought have be right fain,
For she was there al sauf beside.
But for he woldé nought abide,
This mischef fell. Forthý beware,
My sone, as I thee warné dare,
Do thou no thinge in suche a rees,[2]
For suffraunce is the well of pees,
Though thou to Lovés Court pursue,
Yet sit it wel that thou escheue
That thou the Court nought overhaste,
For so thou might thy timé waste.
But if[3] thin hap therto be shape,
It may nought helpé for to rape,
Therfore attempre thy corage,
Foolhasté doth none avauntage,
But ofte it set a man behinde
In cause of love, and thus I finde
By olde ensample as thou shalt here
Touchend of love in this matere.

A maiden whilom there was one,
Which Daphné hight, and such was none
Of beaute thán, as it was saide.
Phebús his love hath on her laide,
And therupon to her he sought
In his Foolhaste and so besought
That she with him no resté hadde,
For ever upon her love he gradde,[4]
And she said ever unto him nay.
So it befelle upon a day
Cupidé, whiche hath every chaunce
Of love under his governaunce,
Sigh Phebus hasten him so sore,
And for he shulde him hasté more

[1] *For*, because.
[2] *Rees*, rush.
[3] *But if*, unless.
[4] *Gradde*, cried out.

And yet nought speden atté laste
A dart throughout his hert he caste,
Which was of golde and all a fire,
That made him many fold desire
Of lové moré than he dede.
To Daphne eke in the samé stede
A dart of led he caste and smote,
Which was all colde and no thing
hote.
And thus Phebús in lové brenneth
And in his haste abouté renneth
To loken if that he might winne.
But he was ever to beginne,
For ever away fro him she fled,
So that he never his lové sped.
And for to make him full beleve,
That no Foolhasté might acheve
To geté love in such degre,
This Daphne into a lorer tre
Was tornéd, whiche is ever grene
In token, as yet it may be sene,
That she shall dwelle a maiden stille
And Phebus failen of his wille.
By suche ensamples as they stonde,
My soné, thou might understonde
To hasten love is thing in vein
Whan that Fortúne is there ayein,
To také where a man hath leve
Good is, and ellés he mot leve.
For whan a mannés happés failen,
There is none hasté may availen."—
"My fader, graunt mercý of this.
But while I se my lady is
No tree, but holde her owné forme,
There may me no man so enforme,
To whether part Fortúné wende,
That I unto my livés ende
Ne wol her serven evermo."—
"My soné, sithen it is so,
I say no more, but in this cas
Beware, howe it with Phebus was.
Nought only upon Lovés chaunce,
But upon every governaunce,
Which falleth unto mannés dede,
Foolhaste is ever for to drede,
And that a man good counseil take
Er he his purpose undertake,
For counseil put Foolhaste awey."—
"Now godé fader, I you prey,
That for to wissé me the more,
Some good ensample upon this lore
Ye wold me telle, of that is writ,
That I the better mighté wit,
Howe I Foolhasté shulde escheue
And the wisdóme of counseil sue."—
"My sone, that thou might
enforme
Thy paciënce upon the forme
Of olde ensamples as they felle,
Nowe understond, what I shall telle.
"When noble Troié was belein
And overcome, and home ayein
The Gregois tornéd fro the siege,
The kingés found her owné liege
In many places, as men saide,
That hem forsoke and disobeide.
Among the whiché fell this case
To Demephon and Athemas,
That weren kingés bothé two
And bothé weren servéd so,
Her leges wolde hem nought re-
ceive,
So that they mote algatés weive [1]
To seché londe in other place
For theré foundé they no grace.
Wherof they token hem to rede
And soughten frendés atté nede,
And eche of hem assureth other
To helpe as to his owné brother
To vengen hem of thilke oultráge
And winne ayein her heritáge.
And thus they ride abouté faste
To geten hem helpe, and atté laste
They hadden power suffisaunt
And maden than a covenaunt,
That they ne shuldé no life save,
Ne prest, ne clerk, ne lord, ne
knave,
Ne wife, ne childe of that they finde

[1] *Weive*, turn aside.

Which bereth viságe of mannés kinde,
So that no life shall be socoúred,
But with the dedely swerd devoúred.
In such Foolhaste her ordinaunce
They shapen for to do vengeaunce.
Whan this purpóse was wist and knowe
Among here host, tho was there blowe
Of wordés many a speche aboute.
Of yongé men the lusty route
Were of this talé glad inough,
There was no caré for the plough;
As they that weren foolhastif
They ben accorded to the strife
And sain, it may nought ben to great
To vengen hem of such forfét.
Thus saith the wilde unwisé tonge
Of hem that theré weren yonge.
"But Nestor, which was olde hore,
The salvé sigh to-fore the sore
As he that was of counseil wise.
So that anone by his advise
There was a privé counseil nome,
The lordés ben to-gider come.
"This Demephon and Athemas
Her purpos tolden as it was.
They setten allé still and herde,
Was non but Nestor hem answérde.
He badde hem, if they wolden winne,
They shulden se, er they beginne,
Her ende and set her first entent
That they hem after ne repent.
And axeth hem this questiön,
To what fináll conclusiön
They woldé regné kingés there,
If that no people in londé were?
And saith, it were a wonder wierd[1]
To seen a king become an hierd,
Where no life is but only beste
Under the legeaunce of his heste.[2]

[1] *Wierd*, destiny.
[2] Only beasts under allegiance to his command.

For who that is of man no kinge
The remenaunt is as no thinge.
He saith eke, if they pourpose holde
To slee the people, as they two wolde,
Whan they it mighté nought restore,
All Grece it shulde abeggé sore[1]
To se the wildé besté wone[2]
Where whilom dwelt a mannés sone.
And for that cause he bad hem trete
And stint of tho manáces grete.
'Bet is to winne by fairé speche,'
He saith, 'than such vengeaúncé seche.
For whan a man is most above,
Him nedeth most to gete him love.'
"Whan Nestor hath this talé saide,
Ayein him was no word withsaide;
It thought hem all he saidé wele;
And thus Fortúne her dedly whele
Fro werré torneth into pees.
But forth they wenten nethéles,
And whan the contrees herdé sain,
How that her kingés be besein
Of suche a power as they ladde,
Was none so bold that hem ne dradde
And for to seché pees and grith[3]
They sende and praide anon forthwith,
So that the kingés ben appesed
And every mannés hert is esed.
All was foryete and nought recorded,
And thus they ben to-gider accorded.
The kingés were ayein received,
And pees was take and wrathé weived
And all through counseil which was good
Of him that reson understood.
"By this ensample, sone, attempre
Thin hert and let no Will distempre

[1] *Abegge sore*, abye,—pay for—it sorely.
[2] *Wone*, dwell.
[3] *Grith* was a secured interval of peace; "frith" was peace generally.

Thy Wit, and do no thing by might,
Which may be do by love and right.
Foolhaste is cause of mochel wo,
Forthý my soné, do nought so.
And as touchénd of homicide,
Which toucheth unto Lovés side,
Ful ofte it falleth unavised
Through Will which is nought wel assised,
Whan Wit and Reson ben awey
And that Foolhaste is in the wey,
Wherof hath fallé great yengeaunce.
Forthý take into remembraunce
To love in suche a maner wise,
That thou deservé no juise.
For well I wot, thou might nought lette,
That thou ne shalt thin herté sette
To lové, where[1] thou wolt or none.
But if thy wit be overgone,
So that it torne unto malíce,
There wot no man of thilké Vice,
What perill that there may befalle.
Wherof a tale amongés alle
Whiche is great pité for to here
I thenké for to tellen here,
That thou such mordre might withstonde,
Whan thou the tale hast understonde.

Of Troie at thilké noble towne,
Whose famé stant yet of renowne
And ever shall to mannés ere,
The siegé lasté longé there
Er that the Grekes it mighté winne,
While Priamús was king therinne.
But of the Grekes that lien aboute,
Agámenon lad all the route.
This thinge is knowen overall,
But yet I thenke in speciall
To my matéré therupon
Telle in what wise Agámenon

[1] *Where*, whether.

Through chauncé which may nought be weived
Of love untrewé was deceived.
An oldé sawe is : who that is sligh
In placé where he may be nigh
He maketh the ferré levé loth[1]
Of love, and thus ful ofte it goth.
There while Agámenon bátáilleth
To winné Troie and it assaileth
From home and was long timé fer,
Egistus drough his quené ner
And with the leiser whiche he hadde
This lady at his will he ladde.
Climestré was her righté name,
She was therof greatlý to blame
To lové there it may nought laste,
But fell to mischefe atté laste.
For whan this noble worthy knight
Fro Troié came, the firsté night
That he at home a beddé lay
Egistus longe er it was day,
As this Climestre him had assent
And weren bothe of one assent,
By treson slough him in his bed.
But morder, which may nought ben hed,
Sprong out to every mannés ere,
Wherof the lond was full of fere.

Agámenon hath by this quene
A sone, and that was after sene.
But yet as than he was of youth
A babé which no reson couth.
And as God wolde, it felle him thus,
A worthy knight Taltibius
This yongé childe hath in keepíng.
And whan he herde of this tidíng,
Of this tresón, of this misdede,
He gan within him self to drede
In aunter if this false Egiste
Upon him come er he it wiste
To take and morther of his malice
This child whiche he hath to norice;
And for that cause in allé haste

[1] The cunning man who can come near makes loathed the loved one who is farther off.

Out of the londe he gan him haste
And to the kinge of Crete he straught
And him this yongé lorde betaught[1]
And praid him for his faders sake,
That he this child wolde undertake
And kepe him till he be of age,
So as he was of his lignage,
And told him over all the cas,
How that his fader morthred was,
And how Egistus, as men saide,
Was king, to whom the londe obeide.
"And whan Ydomeneus the kinge
Hath understonding of this thinge,
Which that this knight him haddé told,
He madé sorwé manyfold
And toke the childe unto his warde
And saide he wolde him kepe and warde,
Till that he were of such a might
To handle a swerde and ben a knight
To venge him at his owné will.
And thus Horestes dwelleth still,
Such was the childés righté name,
Whiche after wroughté mochel shame
In vengeaunce of his faders deth.
"The time of yerés overgeth
That he was man of brede and lengthe,
Of wit, of manhode, and of strengthe,
A fair persone amongés alle.
And he began to clepe and calle
As he which comé was to man,
Unto the kinge of Creté than
Praiéndé that he wold him make
A knight and power with him take,
For lenger wolde he nought beleve,[2]
He saith, but praith the kinge of leve
To gone and claim his heritáge
And vengen him of thilke oultráge
Which was unto his fader do.
The kinge assenteth well therto
With great honoúr and knight him maketh
And great powér to him betaketh.[1]
And gan his journé for to caste
So that Horestes atté laste
His levé toke and forth he goth
As he that was in herté wroth.
His firsté pleinté to bemene[2]
Unto the citee of Athene
He goth him forth and was received,
So theré was he nought deceived.
The duke and tho that weren wise
They profren hem to his servíce,
And he hem thonketh of her proffer
And saith him self he wol gone offer
Unto the goddés for his spede,
And allé men him yivé rede.
So goth he to the temple forth,
Of yiftés that be mochel worth
His sacrifice and his offrínge
He made. And after his axínge
He was answerde, if that he wolde
His state recover, than he sholde
Upon his moder do vengeaunce
So cruel, that the rémembraúnce
Therof might evermore abide,
As she that was an homicide
And of her owné lord mordrice.
Horestes, whiche of thilke office
Was nothing glad, as than he praide
Unto the goddés there and saide,
That they the jugément devise,
How she shall také the juíse.[3]
And therupon he had answére,
That he her pappés shulde of-tere
Out of her breast his owné hondes,
And for ensample of allé londes
With hors she shuldé be to-drawe,
Till houndés had her bonés gnawe
Withouten any sepultúre.
This was a wofull aventúre.

[1] *Betaught*, entrusted. [2] *Beleve*, remain.

[1] *Betaketh*, entrusteth. [2] *Bemene*, bemoan. [3] *Juise*, judgment (judicium).

"And whan Horestes hath all herde,
How that the goddés have answérde,
Forth with the strengthé whiche he lad,
The duke and his powér he had
And to a citee forth they gone,
The which was clepéd Cropheone,
Where as Phorcús was lord and sire,
Which profreth him withouten hire
His helpe and all that he may do,
As he that was right glad therto
To greve his mortal enemy,
And tolde him certain causé why,
How that Egiste in mariáge
His doughter whilom of full age
Forlay and afterward forsoke,
Whan he Horestes moder toke.
Men sain : old sinné newé shame.
Thus more and more arose the blame
Ayein Egiste on every side.

"Horestes with his host to ride
Began, and Phorcus with him wente,
I trowe Egist him shall repente.
They riden forth unto Micene,
There lay Climestré thilké quene,
The whiche Horestes moder is.
And whan she herdé telle of this,
The gatés weré fasté shette,
And they were of her entré lette.[1]
Anone this citee was withoute
Belain and siegéd all aboute,
And ever among they it assaile
Fro day to night, and so travaile
Till atté lasté they it wonne;
Tho was there sorwe inough begonne.

"Horestes did his moder calle
Anone to-fore the lordés alle
And eke to-fore the people also,
To her and tolde his talé tho
And saide: 'O cruel beste unkinde,
How mightest thou thin herté finde,
For any luste of lovés draught
That thou accordest to the slaught
Of him which was thin owné lorde?
Thy treson stant of such recórde,
Thou might thy werkés nought forsake,
So mote I for my faders sake
Vengeaúnce upon thy body do,
As I commaunded am therto.
Unkindély for thou hast wrought,
Unkindélich it shall be bought:
The soné shall the moder slee,
For that whilom thou saidest ye
To that thou shuldest nay have said.'
And he with that his honds hath laid
Upon his moder breast anone
And rent out from the baré bone
Her pappés both and caste away
Amiddés in the carté way,
And after toke the dedé cors
And lete it be drawe awey with hors
Unto the hounde, unto the raven,
She was none other wise graven.[1]

"Egistus, which was ellés where,
Tidingés comen to his ere,
How that Micené was belain,
But what was more herd he nought sain.
With great manáce and mochel boste
He drough powér and made an hoste
And came in the rescousse[2] of the town.
But all the sleight of his tresón
Horestes wist it by a spie
And of his men a great partie
He made in busshément abide
To waite[3] on him in suche a tide,
That he ne might her hond escape.
And in this wise as he hath shape
The thing befell, so that Egist
Was take er he him selfe it wist,
And was forth brought his hondés bonde,

1 Hindered from entering.

1 *Graven*, buried. 2 *Rescousse*, rescue. 3 *Waite*, watch.

As whan men have a traitor fonde.
And tho that weren with him take,
Whiche of tresón were overtake,
To-gider in one sentence falle.
But false Egiste above hem alle
Was deméd to diversé peine,
The worsté that men couthe ordeigne,
And so forth after by the lawe
He was unto the gibet drawe,
Where he above all other hongeth,
As to a traitor it belongeth.
The Famé with her swifté winges
Abouté fligh and bare tidinges
And made it couth in allé londes,
How that Horestes with his hondes
Climestre his owné moder slough.
Somé sain, he did well inough,
And somé sain, he did amis,
Divérs opiniön there is;
That she is dede they speken alle,
But pleinly howe it is befalle
The matere in so litel throwe [1]
In sothé there might no man knowe
But they that weren at the dede.
And comunlich in every nede
The worsté speche is rathest herde
And levéd,[2] till it be answerde.
The kingés and the lordés great
Begonne Horestes for to threat
To putten him out of his regne,—
He is nought worthy for to regne,
The child which slough his moder so,
They said; and therupon also
The lordés of común assent
The timé sette of parlément,
And to Athenés king and lorde
To-gider come of one accorde,
To knowe how that the sothé was,
So that Horestes in this cas
They senden after, and he come.
"King Menelay the wordés nome
And axeth him of this matere.
And he, that all it mighten here,

1 In so short a time. 2 *Levéd*, believed.

Answérde and tolde his tale at large,
And how the goddés in his charge
Commaunded him in suche a wise
His owné hond to do juise.[1]
And with this tale a duke arose,
Which was a worthy knight of lose,[2]
His namé was Menesteús,
And saide unto the lordés thus:
'The wreché [3] whiche Horestes dede,
It was thinge of the goddés bede
And nothinge of his cruelté:
And if there were of my degre
In all this placé suche a knight
That woldé sain it was no right,
I woll it with my body prove.'
And therupon he cast his glove
And eke this noble duke alleide
Full many an other skill[4] and saide,
She haddé well deservéd wreche,
First for the cause of spousé breche,[5]
And after wrought in suche a wise,
That all the worlde it ought agrise,[6]
Whan that she for so foul a vice
Was of her owné lord mordrice.
They sitten allé still and herde,
But therto was no man answérde,
It thought hem all he saidé skille,
There is no man withsay it wille.
Whan they upon the reson musen
Horestes allé they excusen,
So that with great solempnité
He was unto his dignité
Receivéd and corounéd kinge.
And tho befell a wonder thinge.
Egfona whan she it wiste,
Which was the doughter of Egiste
And suster on the moder side
To this Horest, at thilké tide,
Whan she herde how her brother sped,
For puré sorwé whiche her led,

1 *Juise*, judgment. 2 *Lose*, praise, fame.
3 *Wreche*, vengeance. 4 Alleged . . . reason.
5 *Spousé breche*, adultery.
6 *Agrise*, to terrify.

That he ne haddé ben exiled,
She hath her owné life beguiled
Anone and henge her selfé tho.
It hath and shall ben evermo
To mordre who that woll assente
He may nought failé to repente.
This false Egfona was one
Whiché to mordre Agámenon
Yaf her accorde and her assent,
So that by goddés jugement,
Though other noné man it wolde,
She toke her juise as she sholde,
And as she to an other wrought
Vengeaúnce upon her self she sought
And hath of her unhappy wit
A modre with a modre quit.
Suche is of modre the vengeaunce.
"Forthy my sone, in remembraunce
Of this ensample take good hede.
For who that thenketh his lové spede
With mordre, he shall with worldés shame
Him self and eke his lové shame."—
"My fader, of this aventúre,
Whiche ye have tolde, I you assure
My herte is sory for to here;
But onely for I woldé lere
What is to done and what to leve,
And over this now by your leve.
That ye me woldé telle I pray,
If there be leful any way
Withouté sinne a man may slee."—
"My sone, in sondry wisé ye.[1]
What man that is of traiterie
Of mordre or ellés robberie
Atteint, the jugé shal not let
But he shal seen of puré det[2]
And doth great sinne if that he wonde.[3]
For who, that lawe hath upon honde,
And spareth for to do jústice
For mercy, doth nought his office,

[1] *Ye*, yea. [2] *Det*, debt, obligation. [3] *Wonde*, turn aside.

That he his mercy so bewareth,[1]
Whan for o shrewé, whiche he spareth,
A thousand godé men he greveth;
With such mercý who that beleveth
To plesé God, he is deceived
Or ellés reson mot be weived.
The lawé stoode or[2] we were bore,
How that a kingés swerde is bore
In signé that he shall defende
His trué people and make an ende
Of suche, as wolden hem devoure.
"Lo, thus my soné, to succoúr
The lawe, and comun right to winne,
A man may slee withouté sinne
And do therof a great almesse
So for to kepé rightwisnesse.
And over this[3] for his contree
In time of werre a man is free
Him self, his house, and eke his londe
Defendé with his owné hondé
And sleen, if that he may no bet,
After the lawé whiche is set."—
"Now fader, than I you beseche
Of hem that dedly werrés seche
In worldés cause and sheden blood,
If suche an homicide is good?"—
"My sone, upon thy questiön
The trouth of min opiniön,
Als ferforth as my wit arecheth
And as the pleiné lawé techeth,
I wol thee telle in evidence
To reulé with thy consciënce.
The highé god of his justice
That ilké foul horrible Vice
Of Homicide he hath forbede
By Moïses, as it was bede.
Whan Goddés sone also was bore
He sent his aungel down therfore,
Whom the shephérdés herden singe:
'Pees to the men of welwillinge
In erthé be amonge us here.'

[1] *Bewareth*, expends. [2] *Or*, ere. [3] *Over this*, beyond this.

So for to speke in this matére
After the lawe of charité,
There shall no dedly werré be.
And eke Natúre it hath defended
And in her lawé Pees commended,
Whiche is the chefe of mannés welth,
Of mannés life, of mannés helth.
But dedly Werre hath his covíne
Of Pestilence and of Famíne,
Of Pouerte and of allé wo,
Wherof this world we blamen so
Which now the werre hath under fote,
Till God him self therof do bote.[1]
For allé thing, which God hath wrought,
In erthé, Werre it bringeth to nought.
The chirche is brent, the prest is slain,
The wife, the maide is eke forlain,
The lawe is lore and God unserved:
I not[2] what mede he hath deserved,
That suché werrés ledeth inne.
If that he do it for to winne,
First to accompte his greté coste,
Forth with the folke that he hath loste
As to the worldés reckeninge,
There shall he findé no winninge.
And if he do it to purcháce
The heven, mede of suche a grace
I can nought speké, nethéles
Crist hath commaunded Love and Pees.
And who that worcheth the revers,
I trowe his mede is full divers.
And sithen thanné that we finde,
That werrés in her owné kinde
Ben toward God of no deserte
And eke they bringen in pouerte
Of worldés good, it is merveile
Among the men what it may eile
That they a pees ne connen sette.
I trowé Sinné be the lette,

[1] *Do bote*, cause remedy. [2] *Not*, know not.

And every mede of Sinne is deth.
So wote I never howe it geth.
But we, that ben of o[1] beleve
Among us self, this wolde I leve,[2]
That better it were Pees to chese
Than so by double weié lese.
I not if that it now so stonde,
But this a man may understonde,
Who that these oldé bokés redeth,
That covetise is one which ledeth
And broughté first the werrés inne.
At Grece if that I shall beginne,
There was it provéd howe it stood
To Persé, whiche was full of good.
They maden werre in speciall
And so they didden over all
Where great richessé was in londe,
So that they leften nothing stonde
Unwerréd, but onliche Archade.
For theré they no werrés made
Because it was barein and pouer,
Wherof they mighté nought recouer
And thus pouerté was forboré,
He that nought had nought hath loré.
But yet it is a wonder thinge,
Whan that a riché worthy kinge
Or other lord, what so he be,
Woll axe and claimé properté
In thing to whiche he hath no right
But only of his greté might.
For this may every man well wite,
That bothé Kinde and Lawé write
Expressely stonden there ayein.
But he mot nedés somewhat sain,
All though there be no reson inne,
Which secheth causé for to winne.
For Wit that is with Will oppressed,
Whan covetise him hath adressed
And allé reson put away,
He can well findé such a way
To werré where as ever him liketh,
Wherof that he the worde entriketh,[3]

[1] *O*, one. [2] *Leve*, believe.
[3] *Entriketh*, deceives by intrigue.

That many a man of him compleigneth.
But yet alway some cause he feigneth
And of his wrongfull herte he demeth
That all is well what ever him semeth
Be so that he may winne inough.
For as the true man to the plough
Only to the gaignáge entendeth,
Right so the werrioúr despendeth
His time and hath no consciënce.
And in this point for evidence
Of hem that suché werrés make,
Thou might a great ensample take
How they her tirannie excusen
Of that they wrongful werrés usen,
And how they stonde of one accorde,
The souldeoúr forth with the lorde,
The pouér man forth with the riche,
As of corágé they ben liche
To maké werrés and to pille
For lucre and for none other skille,[1]
Wherof a propre tale I rede,
As it whilom befelle in dede.

"Of him, whom all this erthé dradde
Whan he the world so overladde
Through werré, as it fortuned is,
King Alisaundre, I redé this,
How in a marché where he lay
It fell parchaunce upon a day
A rover of the see was nome,[2]
Which many a man had overcome
And slain and take her good away.
This pilour as the bokés say,
A famous man in sondry stede
Was of the werkés whiche he dede.
This prisoner to-fore the kinge
Was brought, and therupon this thinge
In audiénce he was accused,

[1] *Skille*, reason. [2] *Nome*, taken.

And he his dede hath nought excused
And praid the king to done him right
And said: 'Sire, if I were of might,
I have an herté liche to thine;
For if thy power weré mine,
My wille is most in speciall
To rifle and geten over all
The largé worldés good about.
But for I lede a pouer route
And am as who saith at mischefe,
The name of pilour and of thefe
I bere, and thou which routés great
Might lede and také thy beyete[1]
And dost right as I woldé do,
Thy name is nothing clepéd so,
But thou art naméd emperoúr.
Our dedés ben of one coloúr
And in effecte of one desérte,
But thy richesse and my pouérte
They be nought taken evenliche,
And nethéles he that is riche
This day, to morwe he may be pouer,
And in contrarie also recouer
A pouer man to greté richesse.
Men sain forthý let rightwisenesse
Be peiséd even in the balaúnce.'

"The king his hardy contenaunce
Behelde, and herd his wordés wise,
And said unto him in this wise:
'Thin answere I have understonde,
Wherof my will is, that thou stonde
In my servíce and stille abide.'
And forth with al the same tide
He hath him terme of life witholde
The more and for he shuld ben bolde,
He made him knight and yaf him lond,
Whiche afterward was of his honde
An orpéd[2] knight in many a stede
And great prowésse of armés dede,
As the croníqués it recorden.
And in this wisé they accorden,
The whiche of her condición
Be set upon destructión,

[1] *Beyete*, gains. [2] *Orpéd*, distinguished.

Such capitain such retenue.[1]
But for to see to what issúe
The king befalleth at the laste,
It is great wonder that men caste
Her herte upon such wrong to winne
Where no beyeté may ben inne
And doth disese on every side;
But whan Resón is put aside
And Will govérneth the corâge,
The faucon which fleéth ramâge[2]
And suffreth no thing in the way
Wherof that he may take his pray,
Is nought more set upon ravine
Than thilké man whiche his covine
Hath set in suche a maner wise.
For all the world ne may suffise
To Wil whiche is nought reson-
 áble.
 Wherof ensample concordáble
Lich to this point of which I mene
Was upon Alisaundre sene,
Whiche haddé set all his entent
So as Fortúné with him went,
That Reson might him non govérne,
But of his Wille he was so sterne,
That all the worlde he overran
And what him list he toke and wan.
In Yndé the superioúr
Whan that he was full conqueroúr
And had his wilfull pourpos wonne
Of all this erth under the sonne,
This king homward to Macedoine
Whan that he cam to Babiloine
And wendé moste in his empire,
As he which was hole lorde and
 sire,
In honour for to be received,
Most sodenliche he was deceived
And with strong poison envenímed.
And as he hath the world mistimed
Nought as he shuldé with his wit,
Nought as he wolde it was acquit.
Thus was he slain that whilom
 slough,
And he which riché was inough
This day, tomorwe he haddé nought.
And in such wise as he hath wrought
In disturbaúnce of worldés pees,
His werre he fond than endéles,
In which for ever discomfíte
He was. Lo, now for what profite
Of werre it helpeth for to ride,
For covetíse and worldés pride
To slee the worldés men aboute
As bestés, whiché gone there oute.
For every life which reson can[1]
Oweth wel to knowé that a man
Ne shuldé through no tirannie
Lich to these other bestés deie
Til Kindé[2] woldé for him sende.
I not how he it might amende
Which taketh awey for evermore
The life that he may nought restore.
 "Forthy my sone, in allé wey
Be wel aviséd I thee prey
Of slaughter that thou be coupáble
Withouté causé resonáble."—
 "My fader, understonde it is,
That ye have said, but over this
I pray you telle me nay or ye,
To passe over the greaté see
To werre and sle the Sarasin
Is that the lawé?"—"Soné min,
To preche and suffre for the feith
That I have herd the gospel saith,—
But for to sle, that here I nought.
Crist with his owné deth hath bought
All other men and made hem fre
In token of parfit charité,
And after[3] that he taught him selve
Whan he was dede these other twelve
Of his apostles went aboute
The holy feith to prechen oute,
Wherof the deth in sondry place
They suffre, and so God of his grace
The feith of Crist hath made arise.
But if they wolde in other wise

[1] Like master like man. [2] *Ramâge*, wild.

[1] Everybody capable of reason.
[2] *Kindé*, Nature. [3] *After*, according to.

By werre have brought in the creaúnce,
It haddé yet stonde in balaúnce.
And that may proven in the dede;
For what man the croníqués rede,
Fro first that Holy Chirche hath weived[1]
To preche and hath the swerd received,
Wherof the werrés ben begonne,
A great partie of that was wonne
To Cristés feith stant now miswent.
God do therof amendément
So as he wot what is the best.
But sone, if thou wilt live in rest
Of consciëncé well assised,
Er that thou slee, be wel avised;
For man, as tellen us the clerkes,
Hath God above all erthly werkes
Ordeignéd to be principáll,
And eke of soule in speciáll
He is made lich to the godhede:
So sit it wel to taken hede
And for to loke on every side
Er that thou falle on homicide,
Which sinne is now so generall
That it wel nigh stant overall
In Holy Chirche and elles where.
But all the while it is so there,
The world mot nedé fare amis.
For whan the well of pité is
Through covetíse of worldés good
Defouléd with shedíng of blood,
The remenaunte of folke about
Unnethé stonde in any doubt
To werre eche other and to slee,
So it is all nought worth a stre,[2]
The Charité wherof we prechen,
For we do no thing as we techen.
And thus the blindé consciënce
Of Pees hath lost thilke evidence
Which Crist upon this erthé taught.
Now may men se mordre and manslaught

[1] *Weived*, put aside. [2] *Stre*, straw.

Liche as it was by daiés olde,
Whan men the sinnés bought and solde.
"**In Grece** aforé Cristés feith,
I rede as the cronísqué saith
Touchend of this matéré thus,
In thilké time how Peleús
His owné brother Phocus slough.
But for he haddé gold inough
To yive, his sinné was despensed
With golde wherof it was compensed.
Achastus, which with Venus was
Her prest, assoiléd[1] in that cas
Al weré there no répentaunce.
And as the boke maketh rémembraúnce,
It telleth of Medee also,
Of that she slough her sonés two
Egeús in the samé plite
Hath made her of her sinné quite.[2]
The sone eke of Amphíoras,
Whose righté name Almeús was,
His moder slough Eriphelé,
But Achilo the prest and he,
So as the bokés it recorden,
For certain some of golde accorden
That thilke horríble sinfull dede
Assoiléd was; and thus for mede
Of worldés good it falleth ofte,
That homicide is set alofte
Here in this life: but after this
There shall be knowe, how that it is
Of hem that suché thingés wirche,
And how also that Holy Chirche
Let suché sinnés passé quite,
And how they wolde hem self acquite
Of dedely werrés, that they make.
For who that wold ensample take,
The lawé whiche is naturel,
By wey of Kindé sheweth wel
That homicide in no degre
Which werreth ayein charité
Among the menné shuldé dwelle.

[1] *Assoiléd*, absolved. [2] *Quite*, acquitted.

For after that the bokés telle,
To seche in all the worldé riche
Men shall nought finde upon his
liche[1]
A besté for to take his prey,
And sithen Kind hath suche a wey,
Than is it wonder of a man,
Which kindé hath and reson can,
That he woll outher more or lasse
His kinde and reson óverpasse
And slee that is to him sembláble.
So is the man nought resonáble
Ne kinde, and that is nought
honéste,
Whan he is worsé than a beste.
"Among the bokés which I finde
Solins speketh of a wonder kinde
And saith of foulés there is one,
Whiche hath a face of blood and
bone
Like to a man in resemblaúnce.
And if it fallé so parchaunce,
As he whiche is a foule of pray,
That he a man finde in his way,
He woll him sleen if that he may.
But afterward the samé day
Whan he hath eten all his felle
And that shall be beside a welle
In whiché he woll drinké take
Of his viságe and seeth the make
That he hath slain, anone he
thenketh
Of his misdede, and it forthenketh
So greatly that for puré sorwe
He liveth nought till on the morwe.
By this ensample it may well sue,
That man shall homicide escheue,
For ever is mercy good to take.
But if the lawe it hath forsake
And that justíce is there ayein,
Ful oftetime I have herd sain
Amongés hem that werrés hadden,
That they somwhile her causé
ladden

[1] Upon his own kind.

By mercy, whan they might have
slain,
Wherof that they were after sain.
And sone, if that thou wolt recorde
The vertue of misericorde,
Thou sighé never thilké place,
Where it was uséd lacké grace;
For every lawe and every kinde
The mannés wit to mercy binde,
And namély the worthy knightes,
Whan that they stonden most up-
rightes
And ben most mighty for to greve,
They shulden thanné most releve
Him whom they mighten over-
throwe,
And by ensample a man may
knowe
He may nought failen of his mede
That hath mercý. For this I rede.
In a cronique I findé thus,
Whan Áchillés with Thelaphus
His soné toward Troié were,
It fell hem er they comen there
Ayein Theucér the kinge of Mese
To maké werre and for to sese
His lond as they that wolden regne
And Theucer put out of his regne.
And thus the marches they assaile,
But Theucer yaf to hem bataile.
They foughten on both sidés faste,
But so it hapneth atté laste
This worthy Greke this Áchillés
The king amonge all other ches,
As he that was cruél and felle,
With swerd in honde on him he felle
And smote him with a dethés
wounde,
That he unhorséd fell to grounde.
Achilles upon him alight
And wolde anone, as he wel might,
Have slain him fulliche in the place,
But Thelaphus his faders grace
For him besought, and for pité
Praith that he woldé let him be,

And cast his shield betwene hem two.
Achilles axeth him why so.
And Thelaphus his causé tolde
And saith, that he is mochel holde,
For whilom Theucer in a stede
Great grace and socour to him dede,
And saith that he him wolde acquite
And praith his fader to respite.
Achilles tho withdrough his honde;
But all the power of the londe
Whan that they sigh her king thus take
They fled and han the feld forsake.
The Grekes unto the chacé fallé
And for the mosté part of alle
Of that contré the lordés great
They toke and wonne a great beyete.
Anone after this victorie,
The king, whiche haddé memorie,
Upon the greté mercy thought
Which Thelaphus toward him wrought,
And in presénce of all the londe
He toke him fairé by the honde
And in this wise he gan to say:
'My sone, I mot by double way
Love and desiré thin encrees,
First for thy fader Áchilles
Whilom full many a day ere this
Whan that I shulde have fare amis
Rescoussé did in my quarele
And kept all min estate in hele,
How so there fallé now distaúnce
Amongés us, yet rémembraúnce
I have of mercy whiche he dede
As than, and thou nowe in this stede
Of gentilesse and of fraunchise
Hast do mercý the samé wise;
So woll I nought that any timé
Be lost of that thou hast do by me,
For how so this fortúné falle
Yet stant my truste aboven alle,
For the mercý whiche now I finde,
That thou wolt after this be kinde;
And for that suche is min espeir
And for my sone and for min heire
I thee receive, and all my londe
I yive and sese into thin honde.'
And in this wisé they accorde,
The causé was misericorde,
The lordes do her obeisaúnce
To Thelaphus, and purveaúnce
Was madé so that he was coróned
And thus was mercy reguerdóned
Whiche he to Theucer did to-fore.
"Lo, this ensample is made therfore,
That thou might také rémembraunce,
My sone, and, whan thou seest a chaunce,
Of other mennés passiön
Take pité and compassiön,
And let nothing to the be lef
Which to another man is gref.
And after this if thou desire
To stonde ayein the Vice of Ire,
Counseilé thee with paciënce
And take into thy consciënce
Mercý to be thy governour,
So shalt thou felé no rancour,
Wherof thin herté shall debate
With Homicidé ne with hate
For Cheste or for Maléncolie.
Thou shalt be softe in compaignie
Withouté Contek or Foolhaste,
For ellés might thou longé waste
Thy time, er that thou have thy wille
Of Lové; for the weder stille
Men preise, and blamé the tempestes."—
"My fader, I woll do your hestes,
And of this point ye have me taught
Toward my self the better saught [1]
I thinké be while that I live.
But for als mochel as I am shrive
Of Wrath and all his circumstaunce,
Yef what ye list to my penaunce

[1] *Saught*, reconciled.

And axeth further of my life,
If other wise I be giltif
Of any thing, that toucheth sinne."—
"My sone, er we depart a twinne,[1]
I shall behindé no thing leve."—
"My gode fader, by your leve
Than axeth forth what so ye liste,
For I have in you such a triste[2]
As ye that be my soulé hele,
That ye fro me nothing wol hele,[3]
For I shall tellé you the trouthe."—
"My sone, art thou coulpable of Slouthe
In any point, which to him longeth?"—
"My fader, of tho points me longeth[4]
To wité pleinly what they mene,
So that I may me shrivé clene."—
"Now herken, I shal tho points devise,
And understond well min apprise.
For shrifté stant of no valúe
To him that woll him nought vertue
To leve of Vicé the folie,
For worde is wind, but the maistrie
Is that a man him self defende
Of thing whiche is nought to commende,
Whereof ben fewé now a day.
And nethéles so as I may
Make unto thy memórie know
The points of Slouthé thou shalt knowe.

[1] *A twinne*, separated. [2] *Triste*, trust.
[3] *Hele*, conceal.
[4] I long to know plainly.

Book IV

OF SLOTH.

Upon the Vices to procede
After the cause of mannés dede
The firsté point of Slouth I calle
Lachesse,[1] and is the chefe of alle
And hath this properlich of kind
To leven allé thing behind,
Of that he mighté do nowe here
He tarieth all the longé yere
And evermore he saith: 'To morwe,'
And so he woll his timé borwe
And wissheth after: God me sende,[2]
That whan he weneth have an ende,
Than is he furthest to beginne.
Thus bringeth he many a mischefe inne
Unware, till that he be mischéved
And may nought thanné be releved.
And right so nouther more ne lesse
It stant of Love and of Lachesse.
Some time he sloutheth on a day,
That he never after geté may.
"Now, sone, as of this ilké thing
If thou have any knouleching
That thou to Love hast done er this,
Tell on."—"My godé fader, yis.
As of Lachesse I am beknowe,
That I may stonde upon his rowe,
As I that am clad of his suite,
For whanne I thoughté my pursuite
To make, and therto set a day

[1] *Lachesse*, slackness. [2] For a godsend.

To speke unto that sweté may,[1]
Lachessé bad abidé yit
And bare on honde it was no Wit
Ne timé for to speke as tho.[2]
Thus with his talés to and fro
My time in tarieng he drough;
Whan there was timé good inough,
He said another time is better,
Thou shalt now senden her a letter
And par cas writé moré plein
Than thou by mouthé durstest sain.
Thus have I letté timé slide
For slouthe, and kepté nought my tide,
So that Lachessé with his vice
Full oft hath made my wit so nice,
That what I thought to speke or do
With tarieng he held me so
Til whan I wolde and mighté nought.
I not what thing was in my thought
Or it was drede, or it was shame,
But ever in ernest and in game
I wit there is long timé passed,
But yet is nought the lové lassed,
Whiche I unto my lady have;
For though my tunge is slow to crave
At allé time, as I have bede,
Min hert stant ever in o stede
And axeth besiliché grace,
The whiche I may nought yet embrace,

[1] *May*, maid. [2] *Tho*, then.

And god wot that is malgré min.
For this I wot right well afin,[1]
My gracé cometh so selde aboute,
That is the Slouthé, which I doubte
More than of all the remenaunt
Whiche is to Love appartenaunt.
"And thus as touchend of Lachesse,
As I have tolde, I me confesse
To you, my fader; I beseche
That furthermore ye wol me teche,
And if there be to this matere
Some goodly talé for to here,
How I may do Lachesse awey,
That ye it wolden telle, I prey."—
"To wisséthe, my sone, and rede,[2]
Among the talés whiche I rede,
An olde ensample therupon
Now herken, and I wol telle on.
"**Ayein lachesse** in Lovés cas
I finde, how whilom Eneás,
Whom Ánchisés to soné hadde,
With great navié, which he ladde,
Fro Troie arriveth at Cartage.
Wherfore a while his herbergage
He toke, and it betiddé so
With her which was a quené tho
Of the citee, his ácqueintaúnce
He wan, whos name in remembraunce
Is yet, and Dido was she hote,
Which loveth Éneás so hote
Upon the wordés whiche he saide,
That all her hert on him she laide
And did all holy what he wolde.
But after that, as it be sholde,
Fro thenne he goth toward Itaile
By ship and there his arrivaile
Hath take and shope him for to ride.
But she, which may nought longe abide
The hoté peine of lovés throwe,[3]

[1] *Afin*, at last. [2] *Rede*, counsel. [3] *Throwe*, throe.

Anon within a litel throwe[1]
A letter unto her knight hath write
And did him pleinly for to wite
If he made any tarieng
To drecche[2] of his ayein comming,
That she ne might him fele and se,
She shuldé stonde in such degre
As whilom stood a swan to-fore
Of that she hadde her maké lore[3]
For sorwe a fether into her brain
She shof and hath her selvé slain.
As king Menander in a lay
The soth hath foundé, where she lay
Spraulend with her wingés twey
As she which shuldé thanné deie
For love of him which was her make.
And so shal I do for thy sake
This quené saidé, wel I wote.
"Lo, to Eneë thus she wrote
With many another word of pleint.
But he which had his thoughtés feint
Towardés Love and full of Slouthe,
His timé let, and that was routhe.
For she, which loveth him to-fore,
Desireth ever more and more
And whan she sigh him tary so,
Her herté was so full of wo,
That compleignend manyfolde
She hath her owné talé tolde
Unto her self and thus she spake:
'Ha, who found ever suche a lacke
Of Slouth in any worthy knight?
Now wote I well my deth is dight
Through him, which shuld have be my life.'
But for to stinten all this strife
Thus whan she sigh none other bote,
Right even unto her herté rote
A naked swerd anone she threste
And thus she gat her selvé reste
In remembraúnce of allé slowe.
"Wherof, my soné, thou might knowe,

[1] *Throwe*, space of time. [2] *Drecche*, delay. [3] *Maké lore*, lost her mate.

How tarieng upon the nede
In Lovés cause is for to drede.
And that hath Dido sore abought,
Whose deth shall ever be bethought.
And evermore if I shal seche
In this matere another speche
In a cronſque I finde write
A talé, whiche is good to wite.
"At Troie whan king Ylixés
Upon the siege, among the pres
Of hem that worthy knightés were,
Abodé long time stillé there,
In thilké time a man may se,
How goodly that Penelope,
Which was to him his trewé wife,
Of his Lachessé was pleintife,
Wherof to Troié she him sende
Her will by letter, thus spekende:
'My worthy love and lord also,
It is and hath ben ever so,
That where a woman is alone
It maketh a man in his persone
The moré hardy for to wowe,
In hopé that she woldé bowe
To such thinge as his willé were,
While that her lord were ellés where.
And of my self I tellé this,
For it so longé passéd is
Sith first that ye fro homé wente,
That well nigh every man is wente
To there I am while ye be oute,
Hath made and eche of hem aboute
Which lové can my lové seche
With great praiére and me beseche.
And somé maken great manáce,
That if they mighten come in place,
Where that they mighten her[1] will have,
There is no thing me shuldé save,
That they ne woldé werché thinges.
And somé tellen me tidinges,
That ye ben dede, and somé sain,
That certainly ye ben besain[2]

[1] *Her*, their. [2] *Besain*, resolved.

To love a newe and levé me.
But how as ever that it be,
I thonke unto the goddés alle
As yet for ought that is befalle,
May no man do my chekés rede.
But nethéles it is to drede,
That Lachesse in continuaunce
Fortuné mighté suche a chaunce,
Which no man after sholde amende.'
"Lo, thus this lady compleignénde
A letter unto her lord hath write
And praid him, that he woldé wite
And thenke how that she was al his,
And that he tarié nought in this,
But that he wold his love acquite
To her ayeinward, and nought write
But come him self in allé haste,
That he none other paper waste,
So that he kepe and holde his trouthe
Withouté let of any Slouthe.
"Unto her lord and lové liege
To Troié, where the greté siege
Was laid, this letter was conveied.
And he, which wisdome hath purveied
Of all that to resón belongeth,
With gentil herte it underfongeth.
And whan he hath it overrad,
In parte he was right inly glad
And eke in parte he was disesed.[1]
But love his hert hath so through sesed
With pure ymaginación,
That for none occupación
Whiche he can take on other side
He may nought flit his herte aside
Fro that his wife him had enformed,
Wherof he hath him self conformed
With all the will of his corâge
To shape and také the viâge
Homeward, what timé that he may.
So that him thenketh of a day
A thousand yere till he may se

[1] *Disesed*, made uneasy.

The visage of Penelope,
Whiche he desireth most of alle.
And whan the time is so befalle
That Troié was distruied and brent,
He madé non delaiément,
But goth him home in alle hie,[1]
Where that he found to-fore his eye
His worthy wife in good estate,
And thus was cesséd the debate
Of Love, and Slouthé was excused;
Which doth great harm wher it is
used,
And hindreth many a cause honést.
"For of the greté clerk Grostest
I rede how busy that he was
Upon the clergie an heved[2] of bras
To forge and make it for to telle
Of suché thingés as befelle.
And seven yerés besinesse
He laidé, but for the Lachesse
Of half a minute of an houre
Fro firsté he began laboúre
He lost all that he haddé do.
And other while it fareth so
In Lovés causé, who is slowe,
That he without under the wowe[3]
By nighté stant full oft a colde,
Which mighte, if that he haddé
wolde
His timé kept, have be withinne.
But Slouthé may nought profit
winne,
But he may singe in his caróle,
How latewar camé to the dole,[4]
Where he no good receivé might.
And that was provéd well by night
Whilome of the maidens five,
Whan thilké lord came for to wive,
For that her[5] oilé was awey
To light her lampés in his wey,
Her Slouthé brought it so aboute
Fro him that they be shet withoute.

"Wherof, my soné, be thou ware,
Als ferforth as I tellé dare.
For Lové musté ben awaited,
And if thou be nought well affaited[1]
In Lové to escheué Slouthe,
My soné, for to tellé trouthe
Thou might nought of thy self ben
able
To winné love or make it stable,
All though thou mightest love
acheve."—
"My fader, that I may well leve.
But me was never assignéd place
Where yet to geten any grace,
Ne me was non such time appointed,
For than I wolde I were unjointed
Of every limmé that I have
And I ne shuldé kepe and save
Min houré bothe and eke my stede,
If my ladý it haddé bede.
But she is otherwise avised
Than graunté suche a time assised.
And nethéless of my Lachesse
There hath be no default I gesse
Of timé loste, if that I mighte.
But yet her liketh nought alighte
Upon no luré which I caste.
For ay the more I crié faste
The lasse her liketh for to here.
So for to speke of this matere
I seché that I may nought finde,
I haste and ever I am behinde
And wot nought what it may
amounte.
But fader, upon min accompte,
Whiche ye ben set to examíne
Of shrifte after the disciplíne,
Say what your besté counseile is."—
"My soné, my counseil is this.
How so it stonde of timé go,
Do forth thy besinessé so,
That no Lachesse in thee be founde,
For Slouthe is mighty to con-
founde

1 *Hie*, haste. 2 *Heved*, head.
3 *Wowe*, wall.
4 Late-aware came to the sharing.
5 *Her*, their.

1 *Affaited*, adapted to the purpose.

The spede of every mannés werke.
For many a Vice, as saith the clerke,
There hongen upon Slouthés lappe
Of suche as make a man mishappe
To pieigne and tell of had-I-wist.[1]
And therupon if that thee list
To knowe of Slouthes causé more
In speciál yet overmore
There is a Vicé full grevable
To him which is therof coulpable,
And stant of allé Vertue bare
Here after as I shall declare.
"Touchend of slouth in his degré,
There is yet Pusillamité,
Which is to say in this langáge
He that hath litel of coráge
And dare no mannés werk beginne;
So may he nought by reson winne.
For who that nought dare undertake
By right he shall no profit take.
But of this Vicé the natúre
Dare nothing set in aventúre,
Him lacketh bothé worde and dede,
Wherof he shuld his causé spede.
He woll no manhode understonde,
For ever he hath drede upon honde
All is perill that he shall say,
Him thenketh the wolfe is in the way.
And of ymaginación
He maketh his excusación
And feigneth cause of puré drede
And ever he faileth atté nede
Till all be spilt that he with deleth.
He hath the sore which no man heleth,
The whiche is clepéd lacke of herte;
Though every grace about him sterte,
He woll nought onés stere his fote,
So that by reson lese he mote
That woll nought aunter for to winne.

[1] *Had-I-wist*, if I had only known. See note 1, page 75.

"And so forth, sone, if we beginne
To speke of Love and his servíce,
There ben truantes in suche a wise,
That lacken herté whan best were
They speken of Love, and right for fere
They waxen dombe and dare nought telle,
Withouten soun as doth the belle
Whiche hath no clapper for to chime.
And right so they as for the time
Ben hertélés withouté speche
Of Love and dare nothíng beseche:
And thus they lese and winné nought.
Forthý, my sone, if thou art ought
Coulpáble as touchend of this Slouthe,
Shrive thee therof and tell me trouthe."—
"My fader, I am all beknowe
That I have ben one of the slowe
As for to telle in Lovés cas.
Min herte is yet and ever was
As though the world shuld al tobreke,
So ferful that I dare nought speke
Of what purpós that I have nome
Whan I toward my lady come,
But let it passe and overgo."—
"My soné, do no moré so.
For after that a man pursueth,
To Lové so Fortúné sueth
Ful oft and yiveth her happy chaunce
To him which maketh continuaunce
To preié love and to beseche,
As by ensample I shall the teche.
I finde, how whilom there was one,
Whose namé was Pigmaleón,
Which was a lusty man of youthe.

The werkés of entaile[1] he couthe
Above all other men as tho.
And through Fortúne it felle him so
As he, whom Lové shall travaile,
He made an ymage of entaile
Lich to a woman in semblaunce
Of feture and of contenaunce,
So faire yet never was figúre.
Right as a livés creatúre
She semeth, for of yvor white
He hath it wrought of such delite,
That she was rody on the cheke
And rede on both her lippés eke,
Wherof that he him self beguileth,
For with a goodly loke she smileth:
So that through pure impressiön
Of his ymaginatiön
With all the herte of his corágc
His love upon this faire ymáge
He set, and her of lové preide.
But she no worde ayeinward said.
The longé day what thing he dede
This ymage in the samé stede[2]
Was ever by, that atté mete
He wold her serve and praide her ete
And put unto her mouth the cup.
And whan the bord was taken up,
He did as he would her embrace.
And ever among he axeth grace,
As though she wisté what it mente.
And thus him self he gan tormente
With such disese of lovés peine,
That no man might him moré peine.
But how it were of his penaúnce
He madé such continuaunce
Fro day to night and praid so longe,
That his praiére is underfonge,
Which Venus of her gracé herde
By night, and whan that he worst
ferde
And it lay in his naked arme,
The cold ymáge he feeleth warme
Of flesshe and bone and full of life.
Lo, thus he wanne a lusty wife,

[1] *Entaile*, carving, sculpture. [2] *Stede*, place.

Whiche obeisaúnt was at his will.
And if he wolde have hold him still
And nothing spoke, he shuld have
failed.
"By this ensample thou might
finde,
That word may worche abové
kinde.
Forthý, my sone, if that thou spare
To speké, lost is all thy fare,
For Slouthé bringeth in allé wo.
"And over this to loke also,
It semeth Love is welwilléndc
To hem that ben continuénde
With besy herté to pursue
Thing which that is to Lové due.
Wherof, my sone, in this matere
Thou might ensample taken here,
That with thy greté besinesse
Thou might atteigné the richesse
Of Lové, that there be no Slouth."—
"But fader, so as it is right
In forme of shrifté to beknowe
What thing belongeth to the
slowe,
Your faderhode I woldé pray,
If there be further any way
Touchend unto this ilké Vice."—
My sone, ye, of this office
There serveth one in speciál,
Which lost hath his memoriál,
So that he can no wit witholde
In thing which he to kepe is holde,
Wherof full ofte him self he gre-
veth.
And who that most upon him leveth,
Whan that his wittés ben so weived,
He may full lightly be deceived.
To serve Accidie in his office,
There is of Slouth an other Vice,
Which cleped is Foryetelnesse,
That nought may in his herte im-
presse
Of vertue, which resón hath set,
So clene his wittés he foryete.

For in the tellinge of his tale
No more his herté than his male [1]
Hath remembraúnce of thilké forme
Wherof he sholde his wit enforme
As than, and yet ne wot he why.
Thus is his purpos nought forthý
Forlore, of that he woldé bidde,
And scarsely if he saith the thridde [2]
To love of that he haddé ment.
Thus many a lover hath be shent.
Telle on therefore, hast thou ben one
Of hem that Slouth hath so begonne?"—
"Ye fader, ofte it hath ben so,
That whan I am my lady fro
And thenké me toward her drawe,
Than cast I many a newé lawe
And all the world torne up so down
And so recorde I my lessoun
And write in my memoriall
What I unto her tellé shall,
Right all the mater of my tale.'
But all nis worth a nuttéshale.
For whan I comé there she is,
I have it all foryete iwis
Of that I thoughté for to telle;
I can nought than unnethés spelle
That I wende altherbest have rad,
So sore I am of her adrad.
For as a man that sodeinly
A gost beholdeth so fare I,
So that for fere I can nought gete
My wit, but I my self foryete,
That I wot never what I am,
Ne whider I shall, ne whenne I cam,
But muse as he that were amased.
Lich to the boke in whiche is rased
The letter and may nothíng be rad
So ben my wittés overlad,
That what as ever I thought have spoken,
It is out of min herté stoken,

[1] *Male*, bag. [2] *Thridde*, third.

And stonde as who saith doumbe and defe,
That all nis worth an yvy lefe
Of that I wendé well have saide.
And atté last I make abraide, [1]
Cast up min heed and loke aboute
Right as a man that were in doubte
And wot not where he shall become.
Thus am I oft all overcome
There as I wendé best to stonde.
But after, whan I understonde
And am in other place alone,
I make maný a wofull mone
Unto my self and speke so:
'Ha fool, where was thine herté tho
Whan thou thy worthy lady sigh,
Were thou aferéd of her eye?
For of her hond there is no drede,
So well I knowe her womanhede,
That in her is no more oultrage
Than in a childe of thre yere age.
Why hast thou drede of so good one,
Whom allé vertue hath begone, [2]
That in her is no violence
But goodlyhede and innocence
Withouten spot of any blame.
Ha, nicé herté, fy for shame,
A cowarde herte of love unlered,
Wherof art thou so sore afered,
That thou thy tungé suffrest frese
And wolt thy godé wordés lese,
Whan thou hast foundé time and space:
How sholdest thou deservé grace,
Whan thou thy self darst axé none,
But all thou hast foryete anone?'
And thus dispute in Lovés lore,
But helpe ne finde I nought the more,
But stomble upon min owné treine
And make an eking [3] of my peine.

[1] *Make abraide*, start suddenly, as from sleep.
[2] *Begone*, gone round about, wholly occupied, as in "woe-begone."
[3] *Eking*, increasing.

For ever whan I thenke amonge,
Howe all is on my self alonge
I say: 'O fool of allé fooles
Thou farest as he betwene two stoles
That woldé sit and goth to grounde.
It was ne never shall be founde
Betwene Foryetelnesse and Drede,
That man shulde any causé spede.'
And thus, min holy father dere,
Toward my self, as ye may here,
I pleigne of my foryetelnesse.
But ellés all the businesse,
That may be take of mannés thought,
My herté taketh and is through
sought
To thenken ever upon that swete
Withouté Slouthe I you behete.
For what so falle or wel or wo,
That thought foryete I neverno,
Where so I laugh or so I loure
Nought half a minute of an houre
Ne might I lette out of my minde
But if I thought upon that ende:
Therof me shall no Slouthé lette,
Till Deth out of this world me fette,
All though I had on suche a ring,
As Moises through his énchauntíng
Sometime in Ethiopé made,
Whan that he Tharbis wedded had,
Which ringé bare of oblivión
The name, and that was by resón,
That were it on a finger sate,
Anone his Love he so foryate,
As though he had it never knowe.
And so it fell that ilké throwe,
Whan Tharbis had it on her honde,
No knouleching of him she fonde,
But all was clene out of memoire,
As men may reden in histoire.
And thus he wenté quite away,
That never after that ilké day
She thought, that there was such a
one;
All was foryete and overgone.
But in good feith so may nought I.
For she is ever fasté by
So nigh, that she min herté toucheth
That for no thing that Slouthé
voucheth
I may foryete her, lefe ne loth.
For over all where as she goth,
Min herté folweth her aboute.
Thus may I say withouten doubte,
For bet, for wers, for ought, for
nought
She passeth never fro my thought.
But whan I am there as she is,
Min hert, as I you said er this,
Sometime of her is sore adrad
And sometime it is overglad
All out of reule and out of space.
For whan I se her goodly face
And thenke upon her highé pris,
As though I were in paradis,
I am so ravisshed of the sight,
That speke unto her I ne might
As for the timé, though I wolde.
For I ne may my witte unfolde
To finde o worde of that I mene,
But all it is foryeté clene.
And though I stondé there a mile,
All is foryeté for the while;
A tunge I have and wordés none.
And thus I stonde and thenke alone
Of thing that helpeth ofte nought.
But what I had aforé thought
To speké, whan I comé there,
It is foryete, as nought ne were.
And stond amaséd and assotéd,
That of no thing which I have noted
I can nought than a noté singe,
But all is out of knoulechinge.
Thus what for joy and what for drede
All is foryeten atté nede,
So that, my fader, of this Slouthe
I have you said the pleiné trouthe,
Ye may it, as ye list, redresse.
For thus stant my foryetelnesse
And eke my pusillamité.
Say now forth what ye list to me,

For I wol only do by you."—
"My sone, I have wel herd, how thou
Hast said, and that thou must amende.
For Love his gracé wol nought sende
To that man which dare axé none.
For this we knowen everychone,
A mannés thought withouté speche
God wot, and yet that man beseche
His will is.[1] For withouté bedes
He doth his grace in fewé stedes.
And what man that foryete him selve,
Among a thousand be nought twelve
That wol him take in remembraúnce,
But let him falle and take his chaúnce.
Forthý pull up a besy herte,
My sone, and let no thing asterte
Of Lové fro thy besinesse.
For touching of foryetelnesse,
Which many a love hath set behinde,
A tale of great ensample I finde,
Wherof it is pité to wite
In the manér as it is write.
King Demephon whan he by ship
To Troié ward with felaship
Sailend goth upon his wey,
It hapneth him at Rodepey,
As Eolus him haddé blowe
To londe and rested for a throwe.
And fell that ilké timé thus,
That the doughter of Lígurgús,
Which quené was of the contré,
Was sojournéd in that citee
Within a castel nigh the stronde,
Where Demephon cam up to londe.
Phillis she hight and of yong age
And of statúre and of viságe
She had all that her best besemeth.
Of Demephon right wel her quemeth,[2]
Whan he was come and made him chere.
And he, that was of his manere
A lusty knight, ne might asterte
That he ne set on her his herte,
So that within a day or two
He thought, how ever that it go,
He wolde assaié the fortúne;
And gan his herté to comune
With goodly wordés in her ere,
And for to put her out of fere
He swore and hath his trouthé plight
To be for ever her owné knight.
And thus with her he stille abode
There, while his ship on anker rode,
And had inough of time and space
To speke of love and seché grace.
This lady herd all that he saide,
And how he swore and how he praide,
Which was as an enchauntément
To here, that was as innocent.
As though it weré trouthe and feith
She leveth all that ever he saith,
And as her in fortúné sholde
She graunteth him all that he wolde.
Thus was he for the time in joie,
Til that he shuldé go to Troie,
But tho she madé mochel sorwe
And he his trouthé laid to borwe[1]
To come and if that he live may
Ayein within a monthé day.
And therupon they kisten bothe,
But were hem leef or were hem lothe
To ship he goth, and forth he went
To Troy, as was his first entent.
The daiés go, the monthé passeth,
Her love encreseth and his lasseth;
For him she lefté slepe and mete,
And he his time hath all foryete,
So that this wofull yongé quene,
Which wot nought what it mighté mene,

[1] Although God knows our thoughts, yet his will is that we utter them in prayer.
[2] *Her quemeth*, is agreeable to her.

[1] *To borwe*, in pledge.

A letter send and praid him come
And saith how she is overcome
With strengthe of love in suche a
wise,
That she nought longé may suffise
To liven out of his presénce,
And put upon his consciénce
The trouthé whiche he hath behote,
Wherof she loveth him so hote,
She saith, that if he lenger lette
Of such a day as she him sette,
She shuldé sterven in his Slouthe,
Which were a shame unto his
trouthe.
This letter is forth upon her sonde,
Wherof somdele comfórt on honde
She toke, as she that wolde abide
And waite upon that ilké tide
Which she hath in her letter write.
But now is pité for to wite,
As he did erst, so he foryate
His time eftsone and over-sate.
But she, which mighté nought do so,
The tide awaiteth evermo
And cast her eye upon the see.
Somtimé nay, somtimé ye,
Somtime he cam, somtimé nought.
Thus she disputeth in her thought
And wot nought what she thenké
may.
But fastend all the longé day
She was into the derké night;
And tho she hath do set up light
In a lantérne on high alofte
Upon a toure, where she goth ofte
In hopé that in his commínge
He shuldé se the light brennínge,
Wherof he might his weiés right
To comé where she was by night.
But all for nought, she was deceived,
For Venus hath her hopé weived
And shewéd her upon the sky
How that the day was fasté by,
So that within a litel throwe
The daiés light she mighté knowe;
Tho she beheld the see at large:
And whan she sigh there was no
barge
Ne ship, als fer as she may kenne,
Down fro the tour she gan to renne
Into an herber all her owne,
Where many a wonder wofull mone
She madé, that no life it wist,
As she which all her joié mist,
That now she swouneth, now she
pleigneth,
And all her facé she disteigneth
With terés, whiche as of a welle
The stremés from her eyen felle.
So as she might, and ever in one,
She clepéd upon Demephon
And said: 'Alas, thou slowé wight,
Where was there ever suche a
knight,
That so through his ungentilesse
Of Slouthe and of Foryetelnesse
Ayein his trouthé brak his steven.'[1]
And tho her eye up to the heven
She cast and saide: 'O thou un-
kinde,
Here shalt thou through thy Slouthé
finde,
If that the list to come and se,
A lady dede for love of the,
So as I shall my selve spille,
Whome, if it haddé be thy wille,
Thou mightest savé well inough.
With that upon a grené bough
A ceinte of silke, which she there had,
She knette, and so her self she lad
That she about her white swere[2]
It did, and henge her selven there.
Wherof the goddés were amoved,
And Demephon was so reproved,
That of the goddés providence
Was shapé suche an evidence
Ever afterward ayein the slowe,
That Phillis in the samé throwe[3]

[1] *Steven*, voice. [2] *Swere*, neck.
[3] *Throwe*, space of time.

Was shape into a nutté-tre,
That allé men it mighté se,
And after Phillis philliberd[1]
This tre was clepéd in the yerd,
And yet for Demephon to shame
Into this day it bereth the name.
This wofull chaunce how that it ferde
Anone as Demephon it herde
And every man it hadde in speche,
His sorwe was nought tho to seche,
He gan his Slouthé for to banne,[2]
But it was all to laté thanne.
"Lo, thus, my soné, might thou wite
Ayein this Vice how it is write,
For no man may the harmés gesse,
That fallen through Foryetelnesse,
Wherof that I thy shrift have herd.
But yet of Slouthe how it hath ferd
In other wise I thenke oppose,
If thou have gilt, as I suppose.
Fulfilled of Slouthes exemplaire
There is yet one his secretaire,
And he is clepéd Negligence,
Which woll nought loke his evidence,
Wherof he may beware to-fore.
But whan he hath his causé lore
Than is he wise after the honde,
Whan helpé may no maner bonde
Than atté firsté wold he binde.
Thus evermore he stant behinde,
Whan he the thing may nought amende,
Than is he ware, and saith at ende:
'Ha, wolde god I hadde knowe,'
Wherof bejapéd with a mowe[3]
He goth, for whan the greté stede
Is stolé than he taketh hede
And maketh the stable-doré fast.
Thus ever he pleith an after cast
Of all that he shall say or do.

[1] *Philliberd*, filbert.
[2] *Banne*, put under interdict.
[3] *Mowe*, mouth, grimace.

He hath a maner eke also,
Him list nought lerné to be wise,
For he sette of no vertu prise
But as him liketh for the while,
So feleth he ful ofté guile
Whan that he weneth siker to stonde.
And thus thou might wel understonde,
My sone, if thou art suche in love
Thou might nought come at thin above
Of that thou woldest wel acheve."—
"Min holy fader, as I leve,
I may wel with sauf consciënce
Excusé me of Negligence
Towardés Love in allé wise.
For though I be none of the wise,
I am so truly amoroús,
That I am ever curioús
Of hem that conné best enforme
To knowe and witen all the forme,
What falleth unto Lovés craft.
But yet ne fond I nought the haft
Which might unto the blade accorde.
For never herd I men recorde
What thinge it is that might availe
To winné love withouté faile.
Yet so fer couthe I never finde
Man that by reson ne by kinde
Me couthé teché suche an arte,
That he ne failéd of a parte.
And as toward min owné wit
Contrive I couthé never yit
To finden any sikernesse,
That me might other more or lesse
Of Lové maké for to spede.
For leveth wel withouten drede,
If that there weré suche a wey
As certainly as I shall deie
I hadde it lernéd longe ago;
But I wot wel there is none so.
And nethéles it may wel be
I am so rude in my degré
And eke my wittés ben so dull,

That I ne may nought to the full
Atteigne unto so highe a lore.
But this I dar say overmore,
All though my Wit ne be nought
stronge,
It is nought on my Will alonge;
For that is besy night and day
To lerne all that he lerné may,
How that I mighté Lové winne.
But yet I am as to beginne
Of that I woldé make an ende,
And for I not[1] how it shall wende,
That is to me my mosté sorwe.
But I dare také God to borwe,
As after min entendement
None other wisé negligent
Than I you say have I nought be.
Forthý pur sainté charité
Tell me, my fader, what you
semeth."—
"In good feith, soné, wel me
quemeth,
That thou thy self hast thus acquit
Toward this Vice in which no wit
Abidé may, for in an houre
He lest[2] all that he may laboure
The longé yere, so that men sain
What ever he doth it is in vein.
For through the Slouth of Negli-
gence
There was yet never such sciénce
Ne vertue which was bodely,
That nis destruied and lost therby.
Ensample that it hath be so,
In boke I findé write also.

Phebus, which is the sonné hote,
That shineth upon erthé hote
And causeth every livés helth,
He hadde a sone in all his welth,
Which Pheton hight, and he de-
sireth
And with his moder he conspireth,
The which was clepéd Clemene,
For helpe and counseil, so that he

[1] *Not*, know not. [2] *Lest*, lost.

His faders carté[1] ledé might
Upon the fairé daiés light.
And for this thing they bothé praide
Unto the fader, and he saide,
He wolde wel, but forth with all
Thre points he bad in speciall
Unto his sone in allé wise,
That he him shuldé wel avise
And take it as by wey of lore.
First was, that he his hors to sore
Ne prike; and over that he tolde,
That he the reines fasté holde;
And also that he be right ware
In what manér he lede his chare,
That he mistaké nought his gate,
But upon avisement algate
He shuldé bere a siker eye,
That he to lowé ne to high
His carté drive at any throwe,
Wherof that he might overthrowe.
And thus by Phebus ordenaunce
Toke Pheton into governaunce
The sonnés carté, which he ladde.
But he such veiné glorie hadde
Of that he was set upon high,
That he his own estate ne sigh
Through negligence, and toke none
hede.
So might he wel nought longé spede.
For he the hors withouten lawe
The carté let abouté drawe
Where as hem liketh wantonly,
That atté lasté sodeinly,
For he no reson woldé knowe,
This firy cart he drove to lowe
And fireth all the worlde aboute;
Wherof they weren all in doubte,
And to the god for helpé criden
Of suche unhappés as betiden.
Phebus, which sigh the negligénce,
How Pheton ayein his defence[2]
His chare hath drive oute of the wey
Ordeigneth that he fel awey

[1] *Carte*, chariot.
[2] *Defence*, forbidding.

Out of the cart into the flood
And dreinté. Lo now, how it stood
With him, that was so negligent,
That fro the highé firmament,
For that he woldé go to lowe,
He was anone down overthrowe.
In high estate it is a Vice
To go to lowe, and in servíce
It greveth for to go to high,
Wherof a tale in poesie
I finde, how whilom Dedalus
Whiche hadde a sone and Icharus
He hight, and though hem thoughté lothe
In such prisón they weren bothe
With Minotaurus, that aboute
They mighten no where wenden oute.
So they begonné for to shape
How they the prison might escape.
This Dedalus, which fro his youthe
Was taught and many craftés couthe,
Of fethers and of other thinges
Hath made to flee diversé winges
For him and for his sone also;
To whome he yaf in chargé tho
And bad him thenké therupon,
How that his wingés ben set on
With wex, and if he toke his flight
To high, all sodeinlich he might
Make it to melté with the sonne.
And thus they have her flight begonne
Out of the prison faire and softe.
And whan they weren both alofte,
This Icharus began to mounte
And of the counseil none acompte
He setté whiche his fader taught,
Til that the sonne his wingés caught,
Wherof it malt, and fro the hight
Withouten helpe of any flight
He fell to his destructiön.
And lich to that conditiön
There fallen ofte times fele
For lacke of governaunce in wele
Als wel in love as other wey."—
"Now godé fader, I you prey,
If there be more in this matere
Of Slouthé, that I might it here."—
"My sone, as for thy diligence,
Whiche every mannés consciënce
By reson shuldé reule and kepe,
If that thee list to také kepe,
I wol thee tell aboven alle,
In whom no vertu may befalle,
Whiche yiveth unto the Vices rest
And is of Slouthé the slowest.
Among these other of Slouthés kinde,
Whiche allé labour set behinde,
And hateth allé besinesse,
There is yet one, whiche Idelnesse
Is clepéd, and is the noríce
In mannés kinde of every Vice,
Which secheth esés many folde.
In winter doth he nought for colde;
In somer may he nought for hete;
So wether that he frese or swete,
Or be he in, or be he oute,
He woll ben idel all aboute,
But if he pleié ought at dees.
For who as ever také fees
And thenketh worship to deserve,
There is no lord whome he woll serve
As for to dwelle in his service,
But if it were in suche a wise,
Of that he seeth par aventure,
That by lordship and coverture
He may the moré stondé stille
And use his Idelnesse at wille.
For he ne woll no travail take
To ridé for his ladies sake,
But liveth all upon his wisshes,
And as a cat wold eté fisshes
Withoute weting of his cles,
So wolde he do, but nethéles
He faileth ofte of that he wolde.
"My sone, if thou of suche a molde
Art made, now tell me plein thy shrift."—

"Nay fader, god I yive a yift,
That toward Love, as by my wit
All idel was I never yit,
Ne never shall, while I may go."—
"Now, soné, tellé me than so,
What hast thou done of besiship
To Love and to the ladyship
Of heré which thy lady is?"—
"My fader, ever yet er this
In every place, in every stede,
What so my lady hath me bede,
With all min herte obedient
I have therto be diligent.
And if so is that she bid nought,
What thing that than into my thought
Cometh first, of that I may suffise,
I bowe and profre my servíce.
Somtime in chambre, somtime in halle,
Right so as I se the timés falle,
And whan she goth to heré masse
That timé shall nought overpasse,
That I napproche her ladyhede
In aunter if I may her lede
Unto the chapel and ayein,
Than is nought all my wey in vein.
Somdele I may the better fare,
Whan I, that may nought fele her bare,
May lede her clothéd in min arme.
But afterwarde it doth me harme
Of pure ymaginatión,
For thanne this collatión
I make unto my selven ofte
And say: 'Ha lord, how she is softe,
How she is round, how she is small,
Now woldé God, I hadde her all
Withouté daunger at my wille!'
'And than I sike and sitté stille,
Of that I se my besy thought
Is tornéd idel into nought.
But for all that let I ne may,
Whan I se time another day,
That I ne do my besinesse
Unto my ladies worthinesse.
For I therto my wit affaite[1]
To se the timés and awaite
What is to done, and what to leve.
And so whan time is, by her leve
What thing she bit me don, I do,
And where she bit me gon, I go,
And whan her list to clepe, I come.
Thus hath she fulliche overcome
Min Idelnessé til I sterve,
So that I mot her nedés serve.
For as men sain, nede hath no lawe,
Thus mote I nedely to her drawe;
I serve, I bowe, I loke, I loute,
Min eyé folweth her aboute.
What so she wollé so woll I,
Whan she woll sit, I knelé by,
And whan she stont, than woll I stonde,
And whan she taketh her werk on honde
Of weving or of embrouderie,
Than can I nought but muse and prie
Upon her fingers longe and smale.
And nowe I thenke, and nowe I tale,
And nowe I singe, and nowe I sike,
And thus my contenaunce I pike.[2]
And if it falle, as for a timé
Her liketh nought abidé by me
But busien her on other thinges,
Than make I other tarienges
To drecché forth the longé day,
For me is loth departe away.
And than I am so simple of port,
That for to feigné some desporte
I pleié with her litel hound
Nowe on the bed, nowe on the ground,
Now with the briddés in the cage,
For there is none so litel page
Ne yet so simple a chamberere,
That I ne make hem allé chere,

[1] *Affaite*, bring to fitness.
[2] *Pike*, make peep.

All for they shuldé speké wele.
Thus mow ye se my besy whele,
That goth nought ideliche aboute.
And if her list to riden oute
On pelrinage or other stede,
I comé, though I be nought bede,
And take her in min arme alofte
And set her in her sadel softe
And so forth lede her by the bridel,
For that I woldé nought ben idel.
And if her list to ride in chare,
And than I may therof beware,
Anone I shapé me to ride
Right even by the charés side.
And as I may, I speke amonge,
And other while I singe a songe,
Whiche Ovide in his bokés made,
And said : 'O whiché sorwés glad,
O which wofúll prosperité
Belongeth to the propreté
Of Lové? Who so wold him serve,
And yet therefro may no man swerve,
That he ne mot his lawe obey.'
And thus I ridé forth my wey
And am right besy overall
With herte, and with my body all,
As I have saide you here to-fore.
My godé fader tell therfore
Of Idelnesse if I have gilt."—
"My soné, but thou tellé wilt
Ought elles than I may now here,
Thou shalt have no penauncé here.
And nethéles a man may se,
How now a daiés that there be
Full many of such hertés slowe,
That woll nought besien hem to knowe
What thing Love is, til atté last,
That he with strengthe hem overcast
That malgré hem they mot obey
And done all idelship awey
To servé wel and besiliche.
But, soné, thou art none of sich,
For Lové shall thee wel excuse,
But otherwise if thou refuse
To lové thou might so par cas
Ben idel, as somtimé was
A kingés doughter unavised,
Til that Cupide her hath chastised,
Wherof thou shalt a talé here
Accordant unto this matere.

Of Armenie I redé thus,
There was a king whiche Herupus
Was hote, and he a lusty maide
To doughter had, and as men saide
Her namé was Rosiphelé,
Which tho was of great renomé.
For she was bothé wise and faire
And shuldé ben her faders heire.
But she had o defaulte of Slouthe
Towardés Love, and that was routhe.
For so well couthé no man say
Which mighté set her in the way
Of Lovés occupación
Through none ymaginación;
That scolé woldé she nought knowe.
And thus she was one of the slowe
As of suche hertés besinesse,
Till whanné Venus the goddesse,
Which Lovés Court hath for to reule,
Hath brought her into better reule
Forth with Cupide, and with his might,
For they merveile of suche a wight,
Which tho was in her lusty age
Desireth not of mariáge.
For he, that highé hertés loweth,
With firy dartés whiche he throweth,
Cupidé, whiche of Love is god,
In chastisínge hath made a rod
To drive away her wantonnesse,
So that within a while I gesse
She had on suche a chauncé sporned[1]
That all her mod was overtorned,
Which first she had, of slowe manere.
For thus it felle, as thou shalt here.

[1] *Sporned*, stumbled against.

Whan comé was the month of
May,
She woldé walke upon a day,
And that was er the sonne arist,
Of women but a fewe it wist.
And forth she wenté prively
Unto the park was fasté by,
All softé walkend on the gras,
Till she came there the laundé[1] was,
Through which ther ran a great
rivere.
It thought her faire and saidé:
'Here
I woll abide under the shawe,'
And bad her women to withdrawe
And there she stood aloné stille
To thenké what was in her wille.
She sigh the swoté flourés springe,
She herdé gladdé foulés singe,
She sigh the bestés in her kinde,
The buck, the doo, the hert, the
hinde,
The malé go with the femele.
And so began there a quarele
Betwené Love and her owne herte,
Fro which she couthé nought asterte.
And as she cast her eye aboute,
She sigh clad in one sute a route
Of ladies, where they comen ride
A longe under the wodés side.
On faire amblendé hors they set,
That were all whité, faire and great,
And everychoné ride on side.
The sadels were of suche a pride
With perle and gold so well begone,
So riché sigh she never none.
In kirtles and in copés riche
They weren clothéd alle aliche,
Departed even of white and blewe
With allé lustés that she knewe
They were embrouded over all.
Her bodies weren longe and small,
The beauté fair upon her[2] face
It may none erthly thing deface,

[1] *Laundé*, lawn. [2] *Her*, their.

Corounés on her hede they bere
As eche of hem a quené were,
That all the golde of Cresus halle
The lesté coronall of alle
Ne might have bought after the
worth.
Thus comen they ridéndé forth.
The kingés doughter, which this
sigh,
For pure abasshé drewe her adrigh[1]
And helde her close under a bough
And let hem passen stille inough.
For as her thought in her avise,
To hem that weren of suche a price
She was nought worthy to axen there
Fro whenne they come, or what
they were;
But lever than this worldés good
She wolde have wist how that it
stood
And put her hede a litel out,
And as she lokéd her aboute,
She sigh coménd under the linde
A woman upon an hors behinde.
The hors on which she rode was
black,
All lene and galled upon the back
And halted as he were encloied,[2]
Wherof the woman was annoied.
Thus was the hors in sory plight,
But for all that a sterré whit
Amiddés in her front she hadde.
Her sadel eke was wonder badde,
In which the wofull woman sat.
And nethéles there was with that
A riché bridel for the nones
Of golde and precioúsé stones;
Her coté was somdele to-tore,
About her middel twenty score
Of horsé halters and well mo
There hingen atté timé tho.
Thus whan she came the lady nigh,
Than toke she better hede and sigh

[1] *Adrigh*, aside.
[2] *Encloied*, hurt with a nail in shoeing.

The woman fair was of viságe,
Fresh, lusty, yong and tendre of age.
And so this lady, there she stood,
Bethought her well and understood,
That this, which came ridénde tho,
Tidíngés couthé telle of tho
Whiche as she sigh to-foré ride,
And put her forth and praide abide
And said : 'Ha suster, let me here,
What ben they that ridén now here
And ben so richély arraied ?'
This woman, which came so es-
 maied,[1]
Answerdé with full softé speche
And said : 'Madame, I shall you
 teche,
These are of tho, that whilom were
Servaúnts to love and trouthé bere
There as they had their hertés sette.
Fare well, for I may nought be lette.
Madame, I go to my servíce,
So must I haste in allé wise,
Forthý madamé, yif me leve.
I may nought longé with you leve.'[2]
'Ha, gode suster, yet I prey,
Tell me, why ye be so besey
And with these halters thus begone?'
'Madame, whilom I was one,
That to my fader hadde a king.
But I was slowe and for no thing
Me listé nought to Love obey,
And that I now full sore abey,[3]
For[4] I whilom no lové hadde,
My hors is now feble and badde
Aud all to-tore is min array,
And every yere this fresshé May
These lusty ladies ride aboute,
And I must nedés sue her route
In this manér, as ye now se
And trusse her halters forth with me
And am but as her horsé knave.

[1] *Esmaied*, troubled, but possibly a-Maying, for "esmaier" meant also in old French to crown with green leaves.
[2] *Leve*, remain.
[3] *Abey*, pay for.
[4] *For*, because.

None other office I ne have,
Hem thenketh I am worthý no more,
For I was slowe in Lovés lore
Whan I was able for to lere
And woldé nought the talés here
Of hem that couthen Lové teche.'
'Now tell me than, I you beseche,
Wherof that riché bridel serveth ?'
With that her chere away she
 swerveth
And gan to wepe and thus she tolde :
'This bridel, which ye now beholde,
So riche upon min horsé hed ;
Madame, afore er I was dede,
Whan I was in my lusty life,
There fell into min hert a strife
Of lové, which me overcome,
So that therafter hede I nome
And thought I woldé love a knight ;
That lasté well a fourténight,
For it no lenger mighté laste,
So nigh my life was atté laste.
But nowe alas to laté ware
That I ne had him loved ere,
For deth cam so in hasté by me,
Er I therto had any timé,
That it ne mighté ben acheved.
But for all that I am releved
Of that my will was good therto
That Lové suffreth it be so
That I shall such a bridel were.
Nowe have ye herd all min answere,
To God, madame, I you betake,[1]
And warneth alle for my sake,
Of Lové that they be nought idel,
And bid hem thenke upon my bridel.'
And with that worde all sodeinly
She passeth as it were a skie[2]
All clene out of this ladies sight.
And tho for fere her herte aflight
And saide to her self : 'Helas !
I am right in the samé cas.
But if I live after this day,
I shall amende it if I may.'

[1] *Betake*, entrust, commend.
[2] *Skie*, shadow.

And thus homwárd this lady went
And chaungéd all her first entent
Within her herte, and gan to swere
That she no halters woldé bere.
"Lo sone, here might thou taken hede,
How Idelnesse is for to drede,
Nameliche of love, as I have write.
Fo thou might understonde and wite,
Among the gentil nación
Love is an occupación
Which for to kepe his lustés save
Shold every gentil herté have;
For as the lady was chastised,
Right so the knight may ben avised
Which idel is and woll nought serve
To Love, he may par cas deserve
A greater peiné than she hadde,
Whan she abouté with her ladde
The horsé halters; and forthý
Good is to be waré therby.
But for to loke aboven alle
These maidenés how so it falle,
They shulden take ensample of this,
Whiche I have tolde, for soth it is.
And thilké Love is well at ese,
Which set is upon mariáge,
For that dare shewen the visage
In allé places openly.
A great merveile it is forthý,
How that a maiden woldé lette
That she her timé ne besette
To haste unto that ilké feste,
Wherof the Love is all honeste.
Men may recover loss of good,
But so wise man yet never stood
Which may recover time ilore.
So may a maiden well therfore
Ensample take, of that she straungeth
As thou hast understonde above."—
"My fader, as toward the love
Of maidens for to tellé trouthe,
Ye havé thilké Vice of Slouthe
Me thenketh right wonder wel declared,
That ye the women have nought spared
Of hem that tarien so behinde.
But yet it falleth in my minde
Toward the men, how that ye speke
Of hem that woll no travail seke
In cause of Love, upon deserte,
To speke in wordés so coverte
I not what travail that ye ment."—
"My sone, and after min entent
I woll the tellé what I thought,
How whilom men her lovés bought
Through great travaile in straungé londes,
Where that they wroughten with her hondes
Of armés many a worthy dede
In sondry place, as men may rede.
"That every love of puré kinde
Is first forth drawé, well I finde.
But nethéless yet over this
Deserté doth so, that it is
The rather had in many place.
Forthý who secheth Lovés grace
Where that these worthy women are,
He may nought than him selvé spare
Upon his travail for to serve
Wherof that he may thank deserve;
Where as these men of armés be
Sometime over the Greté See,
So that by londe and eke by ship
He mot travailé for worship
And maké many hastif rodes,
Somtime in Pruse, somtime in Rodes,
And some time into Tartarie,
So that these heralds on him crie:
'Vailant, vailant, lo, where he goth!'
And than he yiveth hem golde and cloth,

So that his famé mighté springe
And to his ladies eré bringe
Some tiding of his worthinesse;
So that she might of his prowesse
Of that she herdé men recorde
The better unto his love accorde
And daunger put out of her mood,
Whan allé men recorden good,
And that she wot well for her sake
That he no travail woll forsake.
"My sone, of this travaile I mene;
Now shrif the, for it shall be sene,
If thou art idel in this cas."—
"My fader ye, and ever was
For as me thenketh truély,
That every man doth more than I
As of this point, and if so is,
That I have ought so done er this,
It is so litel of accompt
As who saith it may nought amount
To winne of love his lusty yifte.
For this I tellé you in shrifte,
That me were lever her lové winne
Than Kaire and all that is therinne.
And for to sleen the hethen alle
I not[1] what good there mighté falle,
So mochel blood though ther be shad.
This finde I writen, how Crist bad
That no man other shuldé slee.
What shulde I winne over the see,
If I my lady lost at home?
But passé they the salté fome
To whom Crist bad they shulden preche
To all the world and his feith teche.
But now they rucken[2] in her nest
And resten as hem liketh best
In all the swetenesse of delices.
Thus they defenden[3] us the Vices
And sit hem selven all amidde;
To sleen and fighten they us bidde
Hem whom they shuld, as the boke saith,
Converten unto Cristés feith.
But herof have I great merveile,
How they wol biddé me traveile.
A Sarazin if I slee shall,
I slee the soulé forth withall,
And that was never Cristes lore.
But now Ho[1] there, I say no more.
But I woll speke upon my shrifte
And to Cupide I make a yifte,
That who as ever pris deserve
Of armés, I wol Lové serve,
As though I shuld hem bothé kepe,
Als well yet wolde I také kepe,
Whan it were timé to abide
And for to travaile and to ride,
For how as ever a man laboúre,
Cupide appointed hath his hoúre.
"For I have herdé tell also,
Achilles left his armés so
Both of him self and of his men
At Troié for Políxenen
Upon her lové whan he felle,
That for no chauncé that befelle
Among the Grekes or up or down
He woldé nought ayein the town
Ben arméd, for the love of her.
And so me thenketh, levé sir,
A man of armés may him reste
Somtime in hopé for the beste,
If he may finde a werré ner;
What shulde I thanné go so fer
In straungé londes many a mile
To ride, and lese at home there while
My love? it were a short beyete[2]
To winné chaffe and lese whete.
But if my lady biddé woldé,
That I for her lové sholdé
Travail, me thenketh truëly,
I mighté flee through out the sky
And go through out the depé see,

[1] *Not*, know not. [2] *Rucken*, squat. [3] *Defenden*, forbid.

[1] *Ho!* was the cry for stopping in the chase.
[2] *Beyete*, gain.

For all ne sette I at a stre,[1]
What thank that I might ellés gete.
What helpeth a man havé mete,
Where drinké lacketh on the borde,
What helpeth any mannés worde
To say howe I travailé faste,
Where as me faileth atté laste
That thing whiche I travailé fore.
O, in good timé were he bore,
That might atteigné suche a mede.
But certés if I mighté spede
With any maner besinesse
Of worldés travail, than I gesse
There shuldé me none idelship
Departen from her ladyship.
But this I se on daiés now,
The blindé god, I wot nought how,
Cupido, which of love is lorde,
He set the thingés in discorde,
That they that lest to love entende
Full ofte he woll hem yive and sende
Most of his grace, and thus I finde,
That he that sholdé go behinde,
Goth many a timé fer to-fore.
So wote I nought right well therfore,
On whether bord that I shall saile.
Thus can I nought my self counseile,
But all I set on aventúre
And am, as who saith, out of cure
For ought that I can say or do;
For evermore I finde it so,
The moré besinesse I lay,
The moré that I knele and pray
With godé wordés and with softe,
The more I am refuséd ofte
With besinesse and may nought
winne,
And in good feith that is great sinne.
For I may say of dede and thought,
That idel man have I be nought,
For how as ever I be deslaied,
Yet evermore I have assaied.
But though my besinessé laste,
All is but idel atté laste,

[1] *Stre*, straw.

For whan theffect is Idelnesse,
I not what thing is besinesse.
Say what availeth all the dede,
Which nothing helpeth atté nede?
For the Fortúne of every fame
Shall of his endé bere a name.
And thus for ought is yet befalle,
An idel man I woll me calle
As after min entendément.
But upon your amendément,
Min holy fader, as you semeth
My reson and my causé demeth."—
"My sone, I have herde of thy
matere,
Of that thou hast thee shriven
here.
And for to speke of idel fare
Me semeth that thou tharst[1] nought
care,
But only that thou might nought
spede.
And therof, sone, I woll thee rede,
Abide and hasté nought to faste,
Thy dedes ben every day to caste,
Thou nost,[2] what chauncé shall
betide.
Better is to waite upon the tide
Than rowe ayein the stremés
stronge.
For though so be thee thenketh
longe,
Par cas the revolución
Of heven and thy condición
Ne be nought yet of one accorde.
But I dare maké this recorde
To Venus, whose prest that I am,
That sithen that I hider cam
To here, as she me bad, thy life,
Wherof thou ellés be giltife,
Thou might herof thy consciénce
Excuse and of great diligence,
Which thou to love hast so dis-
pended,
Thou oughtest wel to be comended.

[1] *Tharst*, needst. [2] *Nost*, knowest not.

But if so be that there ought faile,
Of that thou slouthest to travaile
In armés, for to ben abséńt,
And for thou makest an argument
Of that thou saidest here above,
How Achillés through strength of love
His armés lefté for a throwe,
Thou shalt an other talé knowe,
Whiche is contrarie, as thou shalt wite.
For this a man may findé write,
Whan that knighthodé shall be werred,
Lust may nought thanné be preferred,
The bed mot thanné be forsake
And shield and spere on hondé take,
Which thing shall make hem after glad,
Whan they be worthy knightés made,
Wherof, so as it cometh to honde,
A talé thou shalt understonde,
How that a knight shall armés sue,
And for the while his ese eschue.
"Upon knighthode I redé thus,
How whilom whan the king Nauplus,
The fader of Palamides,
Came for to preien Ulixes
With other Gregois eke also,
That he with hem to Troié go,
Where that the siegé shuldé be,
Anone upon Penelope,
His wife, whom that he loveth hote,
Thenkend, woldé hem nought behote.
But he shope than a wonder wile
How that he shulde hem best beguile,
So that he mighté dwellé stille
At home and weld his love at wille.
Wherof erly the morwe day
Out of his bed where that he lay
Whan he was up, he gan to fare
Into the felde and loke and stare
As he which feigneth to be wode,[1]
He toke a plough where that it stood,
Wherin anone in stede of oxes
He let do yoken greté foxes,
And with great salt the londe he sewe.
But Nauplus, which the causé knewe,
Ayein the sleighté which he feigneth
Another sleight anone ordeigneth.
And fell that time Ulixes hadde
A childe to sone, and Nauplus radde
How men that soné také sholde
And setten him upon the molde,
Where that his fader held the plough
In thilké furgh which he tho drough.
For in such wise he thought assay
Howe it Ulixes shuldé pay,
If that he weré wode or none.
The knightés for this child forth gone,
Telemacus anone was fette
To-fore the plough and even sette,
Where that his fader shuldé drive.
But whan he sigh his childe as blive[2]
He drof the plough out of the way,
And Nauplus tho began to say
And hath half in a japé cried:
'O Ulixés, thou art aspied,
What is all this thou woldest mene?
For openlich it is now sene
That thou hast feignéd all this thing,
Which is great shamé to a king
Whan that for lust of any slouthe
Thou wolt in a quarél of trouthe
Of armés thilke honoúr forsake
And dwelle at home for lovés sake.
For better it were honoúr to winne
Than lové which likínge is inne.
Forthý také worshíp on honde
And ellés thou shalt understonde
These other worthy kingés alle
Of Grecé, which unto thee calle,
Towardés thee wol be right wroth

[1] *Wode*, mad. [2] *As blive*, quickly.

And grevé the par chauncé both,
Which shall be to thee double shame
Most for the hindringe of thy name,
That thou for slouthe of any love
Shalt so thy lustés set above
And leve of armés the knighthode,
Whiche is the prise of thy manhode
And oughté first to be desired.'
"But he, which had his herté fired,
Upon his wife, whan he this herd,
Nought o[1] word there ayein answerd,
But torneth home halving ashamed
And hath within him self so tamed
His herté, that all the sotie
Of lové for chivalerie
He lefte, and be him leef or loth
To Troié with hem forth he goth
That he him mighté nought excuse.
Thus stant it, if a knight refuse
The lust of armés to travaile;
There may no worldés ese availe,
But if worshípé be with all.
And that hath shewéd overall,
For it sit wel in allé wise
A knight to ben of high emprise
And putten allé drede away,
For in this wise I have herd say,
"**The worthy knight** Prothesalay
On his passágé where he lay
Towardés Troié thilké siege
She which was all his owné liege
Laodomie his lusty wife,
Which for his lové was pensife
As he whiche all her herté hadde,
Upon a thing wherof she dradde
A letter for to make him dwelle
Fro Troié send him, thus to telle,
How she hath axéd of the wise
Touchend of him in suche a wise,
That they have done her understonde,
Towardés other how so it stonde,
The destiné it hath so shape,
That he shall nought the deth escape
In cas that he arrive at Troy.
Forthý as to her worldés joy
With all her herté she him preide
And many another cause alleide,
That he with her at home abide.
But he hath cast her letter aside
As he which tho no maner hede
Toke of her wommanisché drede
And forth he goth, as nought ne were,
To Troy, and was the firsté there
Which londeth and toke arrivaile,
For him was lever in the bataile
He saith to deien as a knight
Than for to live in all his might
And be reprovéd of his name.
Lo, thus upon the worldés fame
Knighthode hath ever yet beset,
Which with no cowardis is let.
"**Of kingé Saul** also I finde,
Whan Samuel out of his kinde,
Through that the Phitonesse hath lered,
In Samarié was arered[1]
Long time aftér that he was dede.
The kingé Saul him axeth rede,
If that he shall go fight or none.
And Samuel him said anone:
The firsté day of the bataile
Thou shalt be slain withouté faile
And Jonathas thy sone also.
But how as ever it felle so,
This worthy knight of his corágе
Hath undertaké the viáge
And woldé nought his knighthode let[2]
For no perfll he couthé set;
Wherof that bothe his sone and he
Upon the mounte of Gelboé
Assemblen with her enemies.
For they knighthode of such a pris

[1] *O*, one.

[1] *Arered*, raised up. [2] *Let*, hinder.

By oldé daiés thanné helden,
That they none other thing be-
helden.
And thus the fader for worshíp
Forth with his sone of felaship
Through lust of armés weren dede
As men may in the bible rede,
They whos knighthode is yet in
mínde
And shall be to the worldés ende.
"And for to loken overmore
It hath and shall ben evermore,
That of knighthodé the prowesse
Is grounded upon hardiesse
Of him that dare wel undertake.
And who that wolde ensample take
Upon the forme of knightés lawe,
How that Achilles was forth drawe
With Chiro, which Centaurus hight,
Of many a wonder here he might.
For it stood thilké timé thus,
That this Chiro this Centaurus
Within a largé wildernesse,
Where was león and leonesse,
The lepard and the tigre also
With hert and hindé, buk and doo,
Had his dwellíng as tho befell
Of Peleon upon the hill,
Wherof was thanné mochel speche,
There hath Chiro this child to teche
What time he was of twelve yere
age.
Wherfore to maken his corage
The more hardý by other wey
In the forést to hunt and pley,
Whan that Achilles walké wolde
Centaurus bad that he ne sholde
After no besté make his chas
Which woldé fleen out of his place
As buk and doo and hert and hinde,
With which he may no werré finde.
But tho that wolden him withstonde,
There shuld he with his dart on
honde
Upon the tigre and the león
Purchace and make his venisón,[1]
As to a knight is accordaúnt.
And therupon a covenaunt
This Chiro with Achilles set,
That every day withouten let
He shuldé such a cruel beste
Or sle or wounden atté leste,
So that he might a token bring
Of blood upon his home comíng.
And thus of that Chiro him taught
Achilles such an herté caught,
That he no more a leon drad
Whan he his dart on hondé had
Than if a león were an asse.
And that hath made him for to passe
All other knightés of his dede,
Whan it cam to the greté nede,
As it was afterward wel knowe.
"Lo, thus, my soné, thou might
knowe
That the corágе of hardiesse
Is of knighthodé the prowesse,
Which is to Lové suffisaúnt
Aboven all the remenaunt
That unto Lovés Court pursue.
But who that wol no Slouth eschue
Upon knighthode and nought tra-
vaile
I not what love him shuld availe,
But every labour axeth why
Of some reward, wherof that I
Ensamples couthé tel inough
Of hem that toward lové drough
By oldé daiés, as they shulde."—
"My fader, therof here I
wolde."—
"My sone, it is wel resonáble
In placé which is honourable
If that a man his herté sette,
That than he for no Slouthé lette
To do what longeth to manhede.
For if thou wolt the bokés rede
Of Launcelot and other mo,
There might thou seen how it was tho

[1] *Venison*, hunted game.

Of armés, for they wold atteigne
To Lové which withouten peine
May nought be get of Idelnesse.
And that I také to witnésse
An old cronique in speciall,
The whiche into memoriall
Is writé, for his loves sake
How that a knight shal undertake.

Ther was a king, which Oënes
Was hoten and he under pees
Held Calidoine in his empire
And had a doughter Deianire;
Men wist in thilké timé none
So fair a wight as she was one.
And as she was a lusty wight,
Right so was than a noble knight,
To whom Mercúrie fader was.
This knight the two pillérs of bras,
The whiché yet a man may finde,
Set up in the desért of Ynde,
That was the worthy Hercules,
Whos namé shall be endéles
For the merveiles which he wrought.
This Hercules the lové sought
Of Deianire, and of his thing
Unto her fader which was king
He spake touchénd of mariáge.
The king knowénd his high lignáge
And drad also his mightés sterne
To him ne durst his doughter werne[1]
And nethéles, this he him saide,
How Achelous, er he, first preide
To wedden her, and in accorde
They stood, as it was of recórde.
But for all that this he him graunteth,
That which of hem that other daunteth
In armés, him she shuldé take,
And that the king hath undertake.
This Achelous was a geaúnt,
A subtil man, a déceivaúnt,
Which through magique and sorcerie
Couth all the worlde of trecherie.
And whan that he this talé herde,
How upon that the king answerde,
With Hercules he musté feight,
He trusteth nought upon his sleight
Al onely, whan it cometh to nede;
But that which voideth allé drede
And every noble herté stereth,
The lové that no life forbereth
For his ladý whom he desireth,
With hardiesse his herté fireth,
And send him word withouté faile,
That he woll také the bataile.
They setten day, they chosen felde,
The knightés covered under shelde
To-gider come at timé sette
And eche one is with other mette.
It fel they foughten both on foot,
There was no stone, there was no root,
Whiche mighté letten hem the wey,
But all was voide and take awey.
They smiten strokés but a fewe,
For Hercules, which wolde shewe
His greté strengthe as for the nones,
He stert upon him all at ones
And caught him in his armés stronge.
This geaunt wote he may nought longe
Endure under so hardé bondes,
And thought he wold out of his hondes
By sleight in some manér escape.
And as he couthe him self forshape,
In likenesse of an adder he slipte
Out of his honde and forth he skipte;
And efte, as he that fighté wolle,
He torneth him into a bolle
And gan to belwe in suche a soune,
As though the world shuld al go doune.

[1] *Werne*, refuse.

The grounde he sporneth and he traunceth,
His largé hornés he avaunceth
And cast hem here and there aboute.
But he which stant of hem no doubte
Awaiteth wel whan that he cam
And him by bothé hornes nam
And all at onés he him caste
Unto the grounde and held him faste,
That he ne mighté with no sleight
Out of his hond get upon height,
Till he was overcome and yolde,
And Hercules hath what he wolde.
The kinge him graunteth to fulfille
His axing at his owné wille;
And she, for whom he haddé served,
Her thought he hath her wel deserved.

"Eneas eke within Itaile
Ne had he wonné the bataile
And done his might so besily
Ayein king Turne his enemy,
He haddé nought Laviné wonne,
But for he hath him over ronne
And gete his pris, he gat her love.

"By these ensamples here above
Lo, now, my sone, as I have told,
Thou might wel se, who that is bold
And bar travaile and undertake
The cause of Love, he shall be take
The rather unto Lovés grace;
For comunliche in worthy place
The women loven worthinesse
Of manhode and of gentilesse,
For the gentils ben most desired."—

"My fader, but I were enspired
Through lore of you, I wot no way
What gentilesse is for to say,
Wherof to telle I you beseche."—

"The ground, my soné, for to seche
Upon this diffiniciön
The worldes constituciön
Hath set the name of gentilesse
Upon the fortune of richesse,
Which of long time is falle in age.
Than is a man of high lignage
After the forme as thou might here
But no thing after the matére.
For who that reson understond
Upon richesse it may nought stond,
For that is thing which faileth ofte.
For he that stant to day alofte
And all the worlde hath in his wones,[1]
To morwe he falleth all at ones
Out of richesse into pouerte;
So that therof is no deserte,
Which gentilessé maketh abide.
And for to loke on other side
How that a gentilman is bore,
Adam, whiche allé was to-fore
With Eve his wife, as of hem two,
All was aliché gentil tho;
So that of generaciön,
To maké declaraciön,
There may no gentilessé be.
For to the reson if we se
Of mannés birthé the mesúre,
It is so comun to natúre,
That it yiveth every man aliche,
As well to the pouer as to the riche,
For naked they ben boré bothe;
The lorde hath no more for to clothe
As of him self that ilké throwe,
Than hath the pouerest of the rowe.
And whan they shullen bothé passe,
I not of hem whiche hath the lasse
Of worldés good, but as of charge
The lorde is moré for to charge,
Whan God shall his accompté here,
For he hath had his lustés here.
But of the body which shall deie,
All though there be diversé wey
To deth, yet is there but one ende,
To which that every man shall wende

[1] *Wones*, dwellings.

As well the begger as the lorde
Of o[1] natúre, of one accorde.
She, which our oldé moder is,
The erthé bothé that and this
Receiveth and alich devoureth,
That she to nouther part favoúreth.
So wote I nothing after kinde,
Where I may gentilessé finde,
For lacke of vertue lacketh grace,
Wherof richesse in many place
Whan men best wené for to stonde
All sodeinly goth out of honde:
But vertue set in the coráge,
There may no world be so salváge,
Which might it take and done away
Till whanné that the body deie;
And than he shall be richéd so,
That it may failé nevermo.
So that may well be gentilesse,
Which yiveth so great a sikernesse,
For after the condiciön
Of resonáble entenciön,
The which out of the soulé groweth
And the Vertue fro Vicé knoweth,
Wherof a man the Vice eschueth
Withouté Slouth, and Vertue sueth,
That is a verray gentilman;
And nothing ellés whiche he can
Ne which he hath, ne which he may.
But for all that yet now a day
In Lovés Court to taken hede,
The pouer Vertue shall nought spede,
Where that the riché Vicé woweth.
For selde it is, that Love alloweth
The gentil man withouten good,
Though his conditión be good.
But if a man of bothé two
Be riche and vertuoús also,
Than is he well the moré worth.
But yet to put him selvé forth
He must done al his besinesse,
For nouther good ne gentilesse
May helpen hem whiche idel be.

1 *O*, one.

But who that woll in his degre
Travailé so as it belongeth,
It happeth ofté that he fongeth
Worshíp and esé bothé two.
For ever yet it hath be so,
That love honést in sondry wey
Profíteth, for it doth awey
The Vice, and as the bokés sain,
It maketh curteis to the vilaín
And to the coward hardiesse
It yiveth, so that the verray prowesse
Is causéd upon Lovés reule
To him that can manhodé reule,
And eke toward the womanhede,
Who that therof woll taken hede.
For they the better affaited be
In every thinge, as men may se,
For love hath ever his lustés grene
In gentil folke, as it is sene,
Which thing there may no kind areste.
I trowé, that there is no beste,
If he with lové shulde acqueint,
That he ne woldé make it queint
As for the whilé that it laste.
And thus I conclude atté laste,
That they ben idel, as me semeth,
Whiche unto thing that Lové demeth
Forslouthen that they shulden do;
And over this, my sone, also
After the Vertue morall eke
To speke of Love, if I shall seke,
Among the holy bokés wise,
I findé write in suche a wise
Who loveth nought is here as dede,
For Love above all other is hede,
Whiche hath the Vertues for to lede,
Of all that unto mannés dede
Belongeth. For of idelship
He hateth all the felaship,
For Slouthe is ever to despise,
Whiche in disdeigne hath all apprise,

And that accordeth nought to man.
For he that wit and reson can,
It sit him wel that he travaile
Upon such thing which might availe,
For idelship is nought comended,
But every law it hath defended.[1]
And in ensamplé thereupon
The noble wisé Salomon,
Whiche had of every thinge insight,
Saith: 'As the briddes to the flight
Ben madé, so the man is bore
To labour,' whiche is nought forbore
To hem that thenken for to thrive.
For we, whiché nowe are alive,
Of hem that besy whilom were
Als wel in scole as ellés where
Now every day ensample take,
That if it weré now to make
Thing which that they first founden
out,
It sholdé nought be brought about.
Her[2] livés thanné weré longe,
Her wittés great, her mightés
stronge,
Her hertés full of besinesse,
Wherof the worldés redinesse
In body both and in corâge
Stant ever upon his avauntâge.
And for to drawe into memoire
Her namés both and her histoire,
Upon the vertu of her dede
In sondry bokés thou might rede.
"Of every wisdom the parfit
The highé God of his spirít
Yaf unto men in erthé here
Upon the forme and the matere
Of that he woldé make hem wise.
And thus cam in the first apprise
Of bokés and of allé good
Through hem that whilom under-
stood
The loré which to hem was yive,
Wherof these other that now live
Ben every day to lerné new.

[1] *Defended*, forbidden. [2] *Her*, their.

But er the timé that men sue[1]
And that the labour forth it brought,
There was no corn, though men it
sought,
In none of all the feldés oute.
And er the wisdom cam aboute
Of hem that first the bokés write,
This may wel every wise man wite,
There was great labour eke also.
Thus was none idel of the two:
That one the plough hath undertake
With labour which the hond hath
take;
That other toke to studie and muse
As he which woldé nought refuse
The labour of his wittés alle.
And in this wise it is befalle
Of labour which that they begonne
We be now taught of that we conne.
Her besinesse is yet to sene,
That it stant ever aliché grene,
All be it so the body deie
The name of hem shall never awey.
In the croníqués as I finde
Cham, whos laboúr is yet in minde,
Was he which first the letters fonde
And wrote in Hebreu with his honde,
Of natural philosophý
He found first also the clergý.
Cadmus the letters of Gregois
First made upon his owné chois.
Theges of thing which shal befalle
He was the first augure of alle.
And Philemon by the visâge
Found to descrivé the corâge.
Claudius, Esdras and Sulpicés,
Trismégist, Pyth'g'ras, Frige
Dares,[2]
Menander and Epícurús,
Solinus, Pandas, Josephús

[1] *Sue*, sowed seed.

[2] *Frigidilles* of the MS. is evidently Phrygian Dares, whose Trojan Chronicle was then of high authority. As Epicurus was a friend of Menander's—they were born in the same year—he must be the writer whom the MS. calls Ephiloquorus.

The firsté were of enditoúrs
Of old cronſque and eke auctoúrs.
And Herodot in his sciénce
Of metre, of rime and of cadence
The firsté was of which men note.
And of musique also the note
In mannés voise or softe or sharpe
That founde Jubál. And of the harpe
The mery soune, whiche is to like,
That foundé Paulius with phisique.
Zeuxis found first the portreture,
And Prometheüs the sculptúre,
After what formé that hem thought
The resemblaunce anon they wrought.
Tubal in iron and in stele
Found first the forge and wrought it wele,
And Jadahel, as saith the boke,
First madé nette and fisshes toke.
Of hunting eke he found the chace,
Which now is knowe in many place;
A tent of cloth with corde and stake
He set up first and did it make.
Berconius of cokerie
First madé the delſcacie.
The craft Minerve of wollé fonde
And madé cloth her owné honde.
And Delbora made it of line,[1]
The women were of great engſne.[2]
But thing which yiveth us mete and drinke
And doth the labour for to swinke
To till the londes and set the vines,
Wherof the cornés and the wines
Ben sustenaúncé to mankinde,
In oldé bokés as I finde,
Saturnus of his owné wit
Hath foundé first, and moré yit
Of chapmenhode he found the wey
And eke to coigné the money
Of sondry metal, as it is,
He was the firsté man of this.
But how that metal cam a place

[1] *Line*, linen. [2] *Engſne*, ingenuity.

Through mannés wit and goddés grace
The route of philosóphres wise
Contreveden by sondry wise
First for to get it out of mine
And after for to trie and fine.
And also with great diligence
They foundé thilke experience,
Which clepéd is alconomy,[1]
Wherof the silver multiply
They made, and eke the golde also.
And for to telle howe it is so,
Of bodies seven in speciáll
With fouré spirits joint withall
Stant the substance of this matére.
The bodies whiche I speke of here
Of the planettés ben begonne.
The golde is titled to the Sonne,
The Mone of silver hath his part,
And iron that stond upon Mart,
The leed after Satorne groweth,
And Jupiter the brass bestoweth,
The copper set is to Venús,
And to his part Mercuriús
Hath the quick silver, as it falleth,
The whiche after the boke it calleth
Is first of thilké fouré named
Of spirités which ben proclaimed.
And the spirít, whiche is secounde
In sal ammoniak is founde.
The thriddé spirit sulphur is,
The fourthé suende after this
Arsenicum by name is hote.
With blowing and with firés hote
In thesé thingés, whiche I say,
They worchen by diversé way.
For as the philosóphre tolde,
Of golde and silver they ben holde
Two principal extremities,
To whiche all other by degrees
Of the metalles ben accordaúnt.
And so through kindé resemblaúnt,
That what man couthe awaié take
The rust of which they waxen blacke,

[1] *Alconomy*, alchemy.

And the savoúr of the hardnésse,
They shulden také the likenesse
Of golde or silver parfitly.
But for to worche it sikerly
Betwene the corps and the spirít,
Er that the metall be parfít,
In seven formés it is set
Of all. And if that one be let[1]
The remenaunt may nought availe,
But other wise it may nought faile.
For they by whom this art was
founde,
To every point a certain bounde
Ordeignen, that a man may finde
This craft is wrought by wey of
kinde
So that there is no fallas inne.
But what man that this werk be-
ginne,
He mote awaite at every tide,
So that nothíng be left aside.
First of the distillatiön
Forth with the congelatiön
Soluciön, discentiön,
And kepe in his ententiön
The point of sublimatiön,
And forth with calcinatiön
Of verray approbatiön
Do that there be fixatiön
With tempred hetés of the fire,
Till he the parfit elixire
Of thilké philosóphres stone
May gete, of which that many one
Of philosóphres whilom write.
And if thou wolt the namés wite
Of thilké stone with other two
Whiche as the clerkés maden tho,
So as the bokés it recorden,
The kinde of hem I shall recorden.
"These olde philosóphres wise
By wey of kinde in sondry wise
Thre stonés madé through clergy.[2]
The firste if I shall specify,
Was clepéd *vegetabilis*,

[1] *Let*, impeded. [2] *Clergy*, learning.

Of which the propre vertue is
To mannés helé for to serve
As for to kepe and to preserve
The body fro sikenesses alle,
Till deth of kinde upon him falle.
"The stone secónde I thee behote
Is *lapis animalis* hote,
The whose vertue is propre and
couth
For ere and eye and nase and mouth,
Wherof a man may here and se
And smelle and taste in his degre.
And for to fele and for to go
It helpeth a man, of bothé two
The wittés five he underfongeth
To kepe as it to him belongeth.
"The thriddé stone in speciáll
By name is clepéd *minerall*,
Which the metálles of every mine
Attempreth till that they ben fine,
And pureth hem by such a wey
That all the vicé goth awey
Of rust, of stinke and of hardnésse.
And whan they ben of such clen-
nesse,
This minerá ll, so as I finde,
Transformeth all the firsté kinde
And maketh hem able to conceive
Through his vertúe and to receive
Both in substaúnce and in figúre
Of golde and silver the natúre.
For they two ben thextremities
To whiche after the propreties
Hath every metal his desire
With helpe and comfort of the fire
Forth with this stone, as it is said,
Which to the Sonne and Mone is laid;
For to the redde and to the white
This stone hath power to profite,
It maketh multiplicatiön
Of golde and the fixatiön
It causeth, and of his habite
He doth the werke to be parfite
Of thilke elixir: which men calle
Alconomy, as is befalle

To hem that whilom weré wise.
But nowe it stant all otherwise.
They speken fast of thilké stone,
But how to make it now wot none
After the sothe experiénce.
And nethéles great diligénce
They setten upon thilké dede
And spillen moré than they spede.
For allé way they finde a lette[1]
Which bringeth in pouerte and dette
To hem, that riché were afore.
The loss is had, the lucre is lore,
To get a pound they spenden five,
I not how such a craft shall thrive
In the manér as it is used.
It weré better be refused
Than for to worchen upon wene[2]
In thing which stant nought as they
wene.
But nought forthý, who that it knewe,
The science of him self is trewe
Upon the forme as it was founded,
Wherof the namés yet be grounded
Of hem that first it founden out.
And thus the famé goth about
To such as soughten besinesse
Of vertue and of worthinesse,
Of whom if I the namés calle,
Hermes was one the first of alle,
To whom this art is most applied.
Geber therof was magnified
And Ortolan and Morien,
Among the which is Avicen,
Which found and wrote a great
partie
The practique of alconomie.
Whose bokés pleinly, as they stonde
Upon this craft, few understonde;
But yet to put hem in assay,
There ben full many now a day
That knowen litel what they mene.
It is nought one to wite and wene
In forme of wordes they it trete,
But yet they failen of beyete,

[1] *Lette*, hindrance. [2] *Wene*, expectation.

For of to moche or of to lite
There is algaté found a wite,[1]
So that they folwe nought the line
Of the parfité medicíne,
Which grounded is upon natúre.
But they that writen the scripture
Of Greke, Arabe and of Caldee,
They were of suche auctorité,
That they first founden out the way
Of all that thou hast herd me say,
Wherof the cronique of her lore
Shall stonde in prise for evermore.
But toward ouré marches here
Of the Latíns, if thou wolt here
Of hem that whilom vertuoús
Were and therto laborioús,
Carmenté made of her engine
The firsté letters of Latine,
Of which the tungé Romain cam,
Wherof that Aristarchus nam
Forth with Donat and Dindimus
The firsté reule of scole, as thus
How that Latín shall be compounéd
And in what wise it shall be sounéd,
That every word in his degré
Shall stond upon congruité.
And thilké time at Rome also
Ther was Tullíus Cicero
That writeth upon rethorique,
How that men shuld her wordés
pike
After the forme of eloquence,
Which is, men sain, a great pru-
dénce.
And after that out of Hebrew
Jeromé, which the langage knew,
The Bible in which the lawe is closed
Into Latine he hath transposed.
And many an other writer eke
Out of Caldee, Arabe and Greke
With great laboúr the bokes wise
Translateden. And otherwise
The Latins of hem self also
Her study at thilké timé so

[1] *Wite*, blame.

With great travaile of scolé toke
In sondry formé for to boke,
That we may take her evidences
Upon the lore of the sciences,
Of craftes bothe and of clergie;
Among the whiche in poesie
To the lovérs Ovídé wrote
And taught, if lové be to hote,
In what maner it shulde akele.
"Forthy my sone, if that thou fele,
That Lové wringé the to sore,
Behold Ovide and take his lore."—
"My fader, if they mighté spede
My love, I wolde his bokés rede.
And if they techen to restreigne
My love, it were an idel peine
To lerne a thing which may nought be.
For lich unto the grené tre
If that men take his root awey,
Right so min herté shuldé deie
If that my lové be withdrawe.
Wherof touchénd unto this sawe
There is but onely to pursue
My Love, and Idelship escheue."—
"My godé soné, soth to say,
If there be siker any way
To lové, thou hast said the best.
For who that woll have all his rest
And do no travaile at the nede,
It is no reson that he spede
In Lovés causé for to winne.
For he which dare nothíng beginne,
I not what thinge he shulde acheve.
But over this thou shalt beleve,
So as it sit thee well to knowe,
That there ben other Vices slowe,
Which unto Lové don great lette,
If thou thin hert upon hem sette.
Toward the slowé progeny
There is yet one of compaigny,
And he is clepéd Sompnolence,
Which doth to Slouth his reverence
As he which is his chamberlein,
That many an hunderd time hath lein
To slepé whan he shuldé wake.
He hath with Lové trewes take,
That waké who so waké will,
If he may couche adown his bill
He hath all wowéd what him list,
That oft he goth to bed unkist
And saith, that for no druéry
He woll nought leve his sluggardy.
For though no man it wold allowe,
To slepé lever than to wowe
Is his manér, and thus on nightes,
Whan he seeth the lusty knightes
Revelen where these women are,
Awey he skulketh as an hare
And goth tobed and laith him softe;
And of his Slouth he dremeth ofte,
How that he sticketh in the mire,
And how he sitteth by the fire
And claweth on his baré shankes,
And how he climeth up the bankes
And falleth in the slades[1] depe.
But thanné who so také kepe
Whan he is fall in suche a dreme
Right as a ship ayein the streme
He routeth with a slepy noise
And brustleth as a monkés froise[2]
Whan it is throwe into the panne.
And otherwhilé seldé whanne
That he may dreme a lusty sweven,
Him thenketh as though he were in heven
And as the world were holy his;
And than he speketh of that and this
And maketh his expositiön
After his dispositiön
Of that he wold, in such a wise
He doth to Love all his servise,
I not what thank he shall deserve.
But sone, if thou wolt Lové serve,
I redé that thou do nought so."—
"Ha, godé fader, certés no.
I haddé lever by my trouth,

[1] *Slades*, valleys. [2] *Froise*, pancake.

Er I were set on such a Slouth
And beré such a slepy snout,
Bothe eyen of my hede were out.
For me were better fully deie
Than I of suché sluggardie
Had any namé, God me shielde.
"For certes, fader Genius,
Yet unto now it hath be thus
At allé time if it befelle
So that I mighté come and dwelle
In placé there my lady were,
I was nought slow ne slepy there.
For than I dare well undertake,
That whan her list on nightés wake
In chambre as to caróle and daunce,
Me thenketh I may me more avaunce
If I may gone upon her honde,
Than if I wonne a kingés londe.
For whan I may her hond beclippe,
With such gladnésse I daunce and skippe
Me thenketh I touché nought the floor,
The roo, which renneth on the moor,
Is thanné nought so light as I.
So mow ye witen all forthý,
That for the timé slepe I hate.
And whan it falleth other gate,
So that her liké nought to daunce,
But on the dees to casté chaunce,
Or axe of Lové some demaunde,
Or ellés that her list commaunde
To rede and here of Troilus,—
Right as she wold, or so or thus,
I am all redy to consent.
And if so is, that I may hent
Somtime amonge a good leisír,
So as I dare of my desír
I telle a part, but whan I prey,
Anone she biddeth me go my wey
And saith: 'It is fer in the night:'
And I swere, it is even light.
But as it falleth atté laste,
There may no worldés joié laste,
So mote I nedés fro her wende
And of my wacché make an ende.
And if she thanné hedé toke
How pitouslich on her I loke,
Whan that I shall my levé take,
Her ought of mercy for to slake
Her daunger, which saith ever nay.
But he saith often, 'Have good day,'
That loth is for to take his leve.
Therforé while I may beleve,[1]
I tarie forth the night alonge.
For it is nought on me alonge
To slepé that I so soone go
Till that I mote algaté so,
And thanne I biddé: 'God her se,'
And so down knelende on my kne
I také leve, and if I shall
I kisse her and go forth withall.
And other while, if that I dore,[2]
Er I come fully atté dore,
I torne ayein and feigne a thing,
As though I haddé lost a ring
Or somwhat ellés, for I wolde
Kisse her eftsone, if that I sholde.
But selden is, that I so spede.
And whan I se that I mot nede
Departen, I departe, and thanne
With all my herte I curse and banne
That ever slepe was made for eye.
For as me thenketh I might drie[3]
Withouté slepe to waken ever
So that I shuldé nought dissever
Fro her in whom is all my light.
And than I curse also the night
With all the will of my coráge
And say: 'Away thou black ymáge,
Which of thy derké cloudy face
Makest all the worldés light deface
And causest unto slepe a way,
By which I mot now gone away
Out of my ladies compaignie.
O slepy night, I thee defie,

[1] *Beleve*, remain. [2] *Dore*, dare.
[3] *Drie*, endure.

And woldé that thou lay in presse
With Proserpiné the goddesse
And with Pluto the hellé king.
For till I se the daiés spring,
I setté slepe nought at a risshe.'
And with that worde I sigh and wisshe
And say: 'Ha, why ne were it day,
For yet my lady than I may
Beholdé, though I do no more.'
But slepe,—I not wherof it serveth,
Of which no man his thank deserveth
To get him love in any place,
But is an hindrer of his grace
And maketh hem dede as for a throwe
Right as a stoke were overthrowe.
And so, my fader, in this wise
The slepy nightés I despise
And ever amiddés of my tale
I thenke upon the nightingale,
Which slepeth nought by wey of kinde
For love, in bokés as I finde.
Thus atté last I go to bedde
And yet min herté lith to wedde
With her where as I camé fro,
Though I departe he woll nought so.
There is no lock may shet him out,
Him nedeth nought to gon about
That percé may the hardé wal,
Thus is he with her overall.
And thus my selven I torment,
Til that the dedé slepe me hent.
But thanné by a thousand score
Wel moré than I was to-fore
I am tormented in my slepe,
But that I dreme is nought on shepe,
For I ne thenké nought on wulle,
But I am drecched [1] to the fulle
Of Lové that I have to kepe,
That now I laugh and now I wepe
And now I lese and now I winne

[1] *Drecched*, troubled, vexed.

And now I ende and now beginne.
And other while I dreme and mete,[1]
That I aloné with her mete
And that Daunger is left behinde.
And than in slepe such joy I finde,
That I ne bedé never awake.
But after, whan I hedé take,
And shall arise upon the morwe,
Than is all tornéd into sorwe,
Nought for the cause I shall arise,
But for I mette [2] in suche a wise,
And atté last I am bethought,
That all is vein and helpeth nought,
But yet me thenketh by my wille
I wold have lay and slepé stille
To meten ever of such a sweven,[3]
For than I had a slepy heven."—
"My sone, and for thou tellest so,
A man may finde of time ago,
That many a sweven hath be certain,
All be it so that som men sain
That swevens ben of no credence.
But for to shewe in evidence
That they full ofté sothé thinges
Betoken, I thenke in my writinges
To telle a talé therupon,
Which fell by oldé daiés gone.
"This finde I writen in poesý.
Ceix the king of Troceny
Hadde Alceoné to his wife,
Which as her owné hertés life
Him loveth. And he had also
A brother, which was clepéd tho
Dedalion, and he par cas
Fro kinde of man forshapé was
Into a goshauke for likenésse;
Wherof this king great hevinesse
Hath take and thought in his coráge
To gone upon a pelrinage
Into a straungé region,
Where he hath his devoción
To done his sacrifice and prey
If that he might in any wey

[1] *Mete*, dream. [2] *Mette*, dreamt.
[3] *Sweven*, a dream.

Toward the goddés findé grace
His brothers helé to purchace,
So that he mighté be reformed
Of that he haddé be transformed.
To this purpóse and to this ende
This king is redy for to wende
As he which woldé go by ship.
And for to done him felaship
His wife unto the see him brought
With all her herte, and him besought
That he the time her woldé sain
Whan that he thoughté come ayein.
Within, he saith, two monthés day.
And thus in allé haste he may
He toke his leve and forth he saileth,
Wepend and she her self bewaileth
And torneth home there she cam fro.
But whan the monthés were ago,
The which he set of his comíng,
And that she herdé no tidíng,
There was no caré for to seche
Wherof the goddés to beseche.
Tho she began in many a wise
And to Juno her sacrifice
Above all other most she dede
And for her lord she hath so hede
To wite and knowe how that he ferd,
That Juno the goddesse her herde
Anone, and upon this matere
She badde Yrís her messagere
To Slepés hous that she shal wende
And bid him that he make an ende
By sweven, and shewe all the cas
Unto this lady how it was.
"This Yris fro the highé stage,
Whiche undertake hath the message,
Her reiny copé did upon,
The which was wonderly begone
With colours of divérsé hewe
An hunderd mo than men it knewe,
The heven liche unto a bowe
She bende, and she cam downé lowe
The God of Slepe where that she fond,
And that was in a straungé lond
Which marcheth[1] upon Chimery.
For there, as saith the poesy,
The God of Slepe hath made his hous,
Whiche of entaile is merveilous.
"Under an hill there is a cave
Which of the sonné may nought have,
So that no man may knowe aright
The point betwene the day and night.
There is no fire, there is no sparke,
There is no doré which may charke,[2]
Wherof an eyé shulde unshet,
So that inwárd there is no let.
And for to speke of that withoute,
There stant no great tre nigh aboute,
Wheron there mighté crowe or pie
Alighté for to clepe or crie.
There is no cock to crowé day,
Ne besté none which noisé may
The hille, but all abouté round
There is growénd upon the ground
Poppy, which bereth the sede of slepe,
With other herbés suche an hepe.
A stillé water for the nones
Rennénd upon the smallé stones,
Which hight of Lethés the rivér,
Under that hille in such manér
There is, which yiveth great appetite
To slepe. And thus ful of delite
Slepe hath his hous, and of his couche
Within his chambre if I shall touche
Of hebenus that slepy tre
The bordés all abouté be,
And for he shuldé slepé softe
Upon a fether bed alofte
He lith with many a pilwe of doun,
The chambre is strowéd up and doun

[1] *Marcheth*, borders. [2] *Charke*, creak.

O

With swevenés many a thousand
fold.
Thus came Yrís into this holde
And to the bed, whiche is all black,
She goth, and ther with Slepe she
spake,
And in this wise as she was bede
The message of Junó she dede.
Full ofte her wordés she reherceth,
Er she his slepy erés perceth
With mochel wo. But atté laste
His slombrend eyen he upcaste
And said her, that it shal be do,
Wherof amonge a thousand tho
Within his hous that slepy were
In speciáll he chese out there
Thre, whiché shulden do this dede.
The first of hem, so as I rede,
Was Morpheus, the whose natúre
Is for to také the figúre
Of that personé that him liketh,
Wherof that he ful ofte entriketh[1]
The life which slepé shal by night.
And Ithecus that other hight,
Which hath the vois of every soune,
The chere and the condicioún
Of every life what so it is.
The thriddé suend after this
Is Panthasas, which may transforme
Of every thing the righté forme
And chaunge it in another kinde.
Upon hem thre, so as I finde,
Of swevens stant all thápparénce,
Which other while is evidence
And other whilé but a jape.[2]
But nethéles it is so shape,
That Morpheús by night alone
Appereth unto Alceone
In likenesse of her husébonde
Al naked dede upon the stronde,
And how he dreint[3] in speciáll
These other two it shewen all.
The tempest of the blácké cloude

1 *Entriketh*, deceives. 2 *Jape*, trick, jest.
3 *Dreint*, was drowned.

The wodé[1] see, the windés loude
All this she met,[2] and sigh him
deien,
Wherof that she began to crien
Slepend abeddé there she lay.
And with that noise of her affray
Her women sterten up aboute,
Whiche of her lady were in doubte
And axen her how that she ferde.
And she right as she sigh and herde
Her sweven hath tolde hem every
dele.
And they it halsen[3] alle wele
And sain, it is a token of good;
But til she wist how that it stood,
She hath no comfort in her herte.
Upon the morwe and up she sterte
And to the see where as she met[2]
The body lay withoute lete
She drough, and whanné she cam
nigh
Starke dede, his armés sprad, she
sigh
Her lord fleténd upon the wawe,
Wherof her wittés be withdrawe.
And she which toke of deth no kepe,
Anone forth lepte into the depe
And wold have caught him in her
arme.
This infortúne of double harme
The goddés from the heven above
Beheld, and for the trouthe of love
Whiche in this worthy lady stood,
They have upon the salté flood
Her dreinté lorde and her also
Fro deth to lifé torned so,
That they ben shapen into briddes
Swimmend upon the wawe amiddes.
And whan she sigh her lord livénd
In likenesse of a bird swimménd,
And she was of the samé sort,
So as she mighté do disport
Upon the joié which she hadde,

1 *Wodé*, raging. 2 *Met*, dreamed.
3 *Halsen*, embrace.

Her wingés both abrode she spradde
And him so as she may suffise
Beclipt and kist in suche a wise
As she was whilome wont to do.
Her wingés for her armés two
She toke and for her lippés softe
Her hardé bille, and so ful ofte
She fondeth in her briddés forme,
If that she might her self conforme
To do the plesaunce of a wife
As she did in that other life.
For though she hadde her power lore
Her will stood as it was to-fore,
And serveth him so as she may.
Wherof into this ilké day
To-gider upon the see they wone,[1]
Where many a doughter and a sone
They bringen forth of briddés kinde.
And for men shulden take in minde
This Alceon the trewé quene,
Her briddés yet as it is sene
Of Alceón [2] the namé bere.
"Lo thus, my sone, it may thee stere
Of swevens for to také kepe;
For ofté time a man a slepe
May se what after shall betide.
Forthý it helpeth at some tide
A man to slepe as it belongeth;
But Slouthé no life underfongeth
Whiche is to Love appertenaunt."—
"My fader, upon the covenaunt
I daré wel make this avowe,
Of allé my life into nowe
Als fer as I can understonde
Yet took I never slepe on honde
Whan it was timé for to wake,
For though min eye it woldé take,
Min herte is ever there ayein.
But nethéles to speke it plein
All this that I have said you here
Of my wakínge, as ye may here,
It toucheth to my lady swete,
For other wise I you behete,[1]
In straungé placé whan I go
Me list no thing to waké so.
For whan the women listen play
And I her se nought in the way
Of whome I shuldé merthé take,
Me list nought longé for to wake
But if it be for puré shame
Of that I wolde escheue a name,
That they ne shuld have causé none
To say: 'Ha, wheré goth such one
That hath forlore his contenaunce,'
And thus among I singe and daunce
And feigné lust thereas none is.
For ofté sith I felé this,
Of thought which in min herté falleth,
Whan it is night min hede appalleth,[2]
And that is for I se her nought
Whiche is the waker of my thought.
And thus as timelich as I may
Ful oft, whan it is brodé day,
I take of all these other leve
And go my wey, and they beleve [3]
That seen par cas her lovés there,
And I go forth as nought ne were
Unto my bed, so that alone
I may there liggé, sigh and grone
And wisshen all the longé night,
Til that I see the daiés light.
I not if that be Sompnolence,
But upon youré consciénce,
Min holy fader, demeth ye."—
"My sone, I am well paid [4] with the,
Of slepe that thou the sluggardy
By night in lovés compaignie
Eschuéd hast, and do thy pain
So that thy lové dare nought pleine.
But only slepé helpeth kind
Somtime in phisique as I finde,

1 *Wone*, dwell. 2 *Alceon*, halcyon.

1 *I you behete*, I promise you.
2 *Appalleth*, becomes weak.
3 *Beleve*, remain.
4 *Paid*, pleased.

Whan it is take by mesúre,
But he which can no slepe mesúre
Upon the reule as it belongeth
Ful ofte of sodein chaunce he fongeth
Suche infortúné that him greveth.
But who these oldé bokés leveth
Of Sompnolence howe it is write,
There may a man the sothé wite,
If that he wolde ensample take,
That other while is good to wake;
Wherof a tale in poesý
I thenké for to specifý.
"Ovidé telleth in his sawes,
How Jupiter by oldé dawes
Lay by a maidé whiche Yo
Was clepéd, wherof that Juno
His wife was wrothe and the goddesse
Of Yo torneth the likenesse
Into a cow to gon there oute
The largé feldés all aboute
And gette her mete upon the grene.
And therupon this highé quene
Betoke her Argus for to kepe,
For he was selden wont to slepe;
And yet he had an hunderd eyen,
And all aliché wel they sighen.
Now herke how that he was beguiled.
Mercúry, which was all affiled[1]
This cow to stele, he came desguised
And had a pipé wel devised
Upon the notés of musique,
Wherof he might his erés like.
And over that he had affaited
His lusty talés and awaited
His time. And thus into the felde
He came, where Argus he behelde
With Yo, which beside him went.
With that his pipe anon he hent
And gan to pipe in his mandre
Thing which was slepy for to here.
And in his piping ever amonge
He tolde him such a lusty songe,
That he the fool hath brought a slepe,
There was none eyé that might kepe
His hede, which Mercury of-smote.
And forth withall anone foot hote
He stale the cow whiche Argus kepte,
And all this fel for that he slepte.
Ensample it was to many mo,
That mochel slepe doth ofte wo
Whan it is timé for to wake.
For if a man this Vicé take
In Sompnolence and him delite,
Men shuld upon his doré write
His epitaphe and on his grave,
For he to spille and nought to save
Is shape as though he weré dede.
"Forthý my sone, hold up thin hede
And let no slepe thin eye englue,
But whan it is to reson due."—
"My fader, as touchénd of this
Right so as I you tolde it is,
That ofte abeddé whan I sholde
I may nought slepé though I wolde.
For Love is ever fasté by me,
Which taketh none hede of due timé,
For whan I shall min eyen close,
Anone min hert he woll oppose
And hold his scole in such a wise
Till it be day that I arise,
That selde it is whan that I slepe.
And thus fro Sompnolence I kepe
Min eye. And forthý if there be
Ought ellés more in this degre
Now axeth forth."—"My soné, yis.
For Slouthé, whiche as moder is
The forth drawer and the norice
To man of many a dredful Vice,
Hath yet another, last of alle,
Which many a man hath made to falle
Where that he might never arise,
Wherof for thou thee shalt avise
Er thou so with thy self misfare,

[1] *Affiled*, adapted.

What Vice it is I woll declare.
"Whan Slouth hath don all that he may
To drivé forth the longé day,
Till it becomé to the nede,
Than atté last upon the dede
He loketh how his time is lore,
And is so wo begone therfore
That he within his thought conceiveth
Tristesse, and so him self deceiveth
That he Wanhopé [1] bringeth inne,
Where is no comfort to beginne.
But every joy him is deslaied,
So that within his herte affraied
A thousand timé with one breth
Wepénd he wissheth after deth,
Whan he Fortúné fint adverse.
For than he woll his hope reherse,
As though his world were all forlore,
And saith, 'Alas, that I was bore,
How shall I live? how shall I do?
For now Fortúne is thus my fo,
I wot well God me woll nought helpe,
What shulde I than of joiés yelpe,[2]
Whan there no bote [3] is of my care;
So overcast is my welfare,
That I am shapen all to strife;
Helas, that I nere of this life,
Er I be fullich overtake!'
And thus he woll his sorwe make,
As God him mighté nought availe.
But yet ne woll he nought travaile
To helpe him self at suche a nede,
But sloutheth under suche a drede
Whiche is affermód in his herte
Right as he mighté nought asterte
The worldés wo which he is inne.
Also whan he is falle in sinne,
Him thenketh he is so fer coulpáble,
That god woll nought be merciáble
So great a sinné to foryive,

[1] *Wanhope*, despair. [2] *Yelpe*, boast.
[3] *Bote*, remedy.

And thus he leveth to be shrive.
And if a man in thilké throwe
Wold him counseile, he wol nought knowe
The sothé, though a man it finde.
For Tristesse is of suche a kinde,
That for to mainten his folý,
He hath with him obstínacý,
Which is within of suche a Slouth
That he forsaketh alle trouth
And woll unto no reson bowe.
And yet ne can he nought abowe [1]
His owné skillé, but of hede
Thus dwineth [2] he till he be dede,
In hindring of his owne estate.
For where a man is obstinate,
Wanhopé folweth atté laste,
Whiché may nought longe after laste
Till Slouthé make of him an ende.
But God wot whider he shall wende!
"My sone, and right in such manere,
There be lovérs of hevy chere,
That sorwen moré than is nede,
Whan they be taried of her spede
And conné nought hem selven rede,
But lesen hopé for to spede
And stinten lové to pursue.
And thus they faden hide and hewe
And lustles in her hertés waxe.
Herof it is that I wolde axe,
If thou, my sone, arte one of tho?"—
"Ha, godé fader, it is so,
Outtake o point, I am beknowe,[3]
For ellés I am overthrowe
In all that ever ye have saide;
My sorwe is evermore unteide
And secheth over all my veines.
But for to counseile of my peines,
I can no boté do therto.
And thus withouten hope I go,
So that my wittés ben empeired
And I as who saith am dispeired

[1] *Abowe*, maintain.
[2] *Dwineth*, wastes, pines.
[3] I confess, except as to one point.

To winné love of thilké swete,
Withouté whom, I you behete,
Min herté that is so bestadde
Right inly never may be gladde.
For by my trouth I shall nought lie
Of puré sorwe whiche I drie[1]
For that she saith she will me nought,
With drecchinge[2] of min owné thought
In suche a Wanhope I am falle,
That I ne can unnethés calle
As for to speke of any grace
My ladies mercy to purcháce.
But yet I saié nought for this
That all in my default it is
That I cam never yet in stede
Whan timé was, that I my bede
Ne saide and as I dorsté tolde.
But never found I that she wolde
For ought she knewe of min entent
To speke a goodly worde assent.
And nethéles this dare I say,
That if a sinfull woldé prey
To God of his foryivénesse
With half so great a besinesse
As I have do to my ladý
In lack of axing of mercý,
He shuldé never come in helle.
And thus I may you sothly telle,
Sauf only that I crie and bidde,
I am in Tristesse all amidde
And fulfilléd of desperaunce.
And therof yef me my penaunce,
Min holy fader, as you liketh."—
"My sone, of that thin herté siketh
With sorwe might thou nought amende,
Till Love his gracé woll thee sende,
For thou thin owné cause empeirest
What time as thou thy self despeirest.
I not what other thinge availeth
Of hopé whan the herté faileth,
For suche a sore is incuráble,
And eke the goddés ben vengeáble,

[1] *Drie*, endure. [2] *Drecchinge*, vexing.

And that a man may right well frede,[1]
These oldé bokés who so rede
Of thing which hath befalle er this,
Now here, of what ensample it is.
Whilom by oldé daiés fer
Of Mesé was the king Theucer,
Whiche had a knight to sone Iphis.
Of love and he so mastred is,
That he hath set all his coráge
As to reward of his lignáge
Upon a maide of lowe estate.
But though he were a potestate
Of worldés good, he was subgit
To love and put in suche a plite
That he excedeth the mesúre
Of reson, that him self assure
He can nought. For the more he praid,
The lassé love on him she laid.
He was with love unwise constreignéd,
And she with reson was restreignéd.
The lustés of his herte he sueth,
And she for dredé shame eschueth,
And as she shuldé, toke good hede
To save and kepe her womanhede.
And thus the thing stood in debate
Betwene his lust and her estate,
He yaf, he send, he spake by mouth,
But yet for ought that ever he couth
Unto his spede he found no wey,
So that he cast his hope awey.
Within his hert he gan despeire
Fro day to day and so empeire
That he hath lost all his delite
Of lust, of slepe, of appetite,
That he through strength of lové lasseth,
His wit and reson overpasseth
As he whiche of his life ne rought.[2]
His deth upon him self he sought,
So that by night his wey he nam,
There wisté none where he becam.

[1] *Frede*, feel. [2] *Rought*, recked.

The night was derk, there shone no mone,
To-fore the gatés he cam sone,
Where that this yongé maiden was,
And with this wofull worde, 'Helas,'
His dedly pleintés he began
So stillé that there was no man
It herde, and than he saidé thus:
'O thou Cupide, O thou Venús,
Fortúnéd by whose ordenaunce
Of love is every mannés chaunce,
Ye knowen all min holé hert,
That I ne may your hond astert,
On you is ever that I crie,
And you deigneth nought to plie
Ne toward me your ere encline.
Thus for I se no medicíne
To make an ende of my quarele,
My deth shall be in stede of hele.
Ha, thou my wofull lady dere,
Which dwellest with thy fader here
And slepest in thy bedde at ese,
Thou wost nothing of my disese,
How thou and I be now unmete.
Ha lord, what sweven shalt thou mete?
What dremés hast thou now on honde?
Thou slepest there, and I here stonde,
Though I no deth to thee deserve.
Here shall I for thy lové sterve,
Here shall I a kings soné deie
For love and for no felony;
Where thou therof have joy or sorwe,
Here shalt thou se me dede to morwe.
O herté hard aboven alle,
This deth, which shall to me befalle,
For that thou wol nought do my grace,
Yet shall be tolde in many a place;
That I am dede for love and trouth
In thy defaulte and in thy slouth,
Thy daunger shall to many mo
Ensample be for evermo,
Whan they my wofull deth recorde.'
And with that worde he toke a corde
With which upon the gaté tre
He henge him self, that was pité.
The morwe cam, the night is gone,
Men comen out and sigh anone,
Where that this yongé lord was dede.
There was an hous withouté rede,
For no man knewe the causé why,
There was wepíngé, there was cry.
This maiden, whan that she it herde
And sigh this thing howe it misferde,
Anone she wisté what it ment,
And all the causé how it went
To all the world she tolde it out
And preith to hem that were about
To take of her the vengeaúnce,
For she was cause of thilké chaunce
Why that this kingés sone is spilt.[1]
She taketh upon her self the gilt
And is all redy to the peine
Whiche any man her wold ordeigne.
And but if any other wolde,
She saith, that she her selvé sholde
Do wreché with her owné honde,
Through out the worlde in every londe
That every life[2] therof shall speke
How she her self it shuldé wreke.
She wepeth, she crieth, she swouneth ofte,
She cast her eyen up alofte
And said among full pitously:
'O god, thou wost wel it am I,
For whom Iphis is thus beseine,
Ordeigné so, that men may saine
A thousand winter after this,
How suche a maiden did amis,
And as I diddé do to me
For I ne diddé no pite
To him which for my love is lore,
Do no pité to me therfore.'

[1] *Spilt*, destroyed. [2] *Life*, body.

And with this word she fell to grounde
A swoune, and there she lay astounde.
"The goddés, which her pleintés herd
And sigh how wofully she ferd,
Her life they toke awey anone
And shopen her into a stone
After the forme of her ymáge
Of body both and of visage.
And for the merveile of this thing
Unto this placé came the king
And eke the quene and many mo,
And whan they wisten it was so,
As I have tolde it here above,
How that Iphís was dede for love
Of that he haddé be refused,
They helden allé men excused
And wondren upon the vengeaúnce.
And for to kepé remembraúnce
This faire ymagé maiden liche,
With compaignié noble and riche
With torche and great solempnité
To Salaminé the cité,
They lede and carie forth withall
This dede corps, and saine it shall
Besidé thilke ymágé have
His sepulture and be begrave.[1]
This corps and this ymágé thus
Into the cité to Venús,
Where that goddesse her temple had,
To-gider bothé two they lad.
This ilke ymáge as for mirácle
Was set upon an high pinácle
That allé men it mighté knowe,
And under that they maden lowe
A tombé riché for the nones
Of marbre and eke of jaspre stones,
Wherin that Iphis was beloken
That evermore it shall be spoken.
And for men shall the sothé wite
They have her epitaphé write

[1] *Begrave*, buried.

As thing which shulde abidé stable,
The letters graven in a table
Of marbre were and saiden this:
'Here lith, which sloughe him self, Iphis
For love of Araxarathen,
And in ensample of tho women
That suffren men to deié so,
Her forme a man may se also,
How it is tornéd flesshe and bone
Into the figure of a stone.
He was to neissh[1] and she to harde,
Beware forthý here afterwarde,
Ye men and women, bothé two,
Ensampleth you of that was tho.'
"Lo thus, my sone, as I thee say
It greveth by diversé way
In Desespeire a man to falle,
Which is the lasté braunch of alle
Of Slouthe, as thou hast herd devise,
Wherof that thou thy self avise
Good is, er that thou be deceived
Wher that the grace of hope is weived."—
"My fader, how so that it stonde,
Now have I pleinly understonde
Of Slouthés Court the properté,
Wherof touchénd in my degre
For ever I thenké to beware.
But over this so as I dare
With all min hert I you beseche,
That ye me wolde enforme and teche,
What there is more of your apprise
In Love als well as otherwise,
So that I may me clené shrive."—
My soné, while thou art alive
And hast also thy fullé minde,
Among the Vices, which I finde,
There is yet one such of the Seven
Which all this world hath set uneven
And causeth many thingés wronge
Where he the cause hath underfonge;
Wherof hereafter thou shalt here
The formé bothe and the matére.

[1] *Neissh*, delicate.

Book V.

OF AVARICE.

First whan the highé God began
This worlde and that the kind of man
Was fall into no gret encress,
For worldés good was tho [1] no press
But all was set to the comune,
They speken than of no fortúne
Or for to lese or for to winne,
Till Avaricé brought it inne.
And that was whan the world was woxe
Of man, of hors, of shepe, of oxe,
And that men knewen the monéy,
Tho wenté pees out of the wey
And werré came on every side,
Whiche allé lové laid aside
And of común his propré made,
So that in stede of shovel and spade
The sharpé swerd was take on honde.
And in this wise it cam to londe
Wherof men maden diches depe
And highé wallés for to kepe
The gold which Avarice encloseth.
But all to litel him supposeth,
Though he might all the world purcháse.
For what thing that he may embrace
Of golde, of catel or of londe,
He let it never out of his honde,
But get him more and halt it fast,
As though the world shuld ever last.

[1] *Tho*, then.

So is he lich unto the helle,
For as these olde bokés telle,
What cometh ther in lass or more
It shall departé nevermore.
Thus whan he hath his cofre loken,
It shall nought after ben unstoken [1]
But whan him list to have a sight
Of gold, how that it shineth bright,
That he theron may loke and muse,
For otherwise he dare nought use
To take his part or lasse or more.
So is he pouer, and evermore
Him lacketh that he hath inough.
An oxé draweth in the plough
Of that him self hath no proffite,
A shep right in the samé plite
His wolle bereth, but on a day
An other taketh the flees away.
Thus hath he, that he nought ne hath,
For he therof his part ne tath,[2]
To say how suche a man hath good
Who so that reson understood
It is unproperliché said;
That good hath him and halt him taid [3]
That he ne gladdeth nought withall,
But is unto his good a thrall
And a subgit; thus serveth he
Where that he shuldé maister be:

[1] *Unstoken*, unbarred. [2] *Tath*, taketh.
[3] *Taid*, tied.

Suche is the kinde of thavarous.
"My sone, as thou art amorous,
Tell if thou fare of Lové so."—
"My fader, as it semeth, no,
That avarous yet never I was,
So as ye setten me the cas.
For as ye tolden here above
In full possessiön of love
Yet was I never here to-fore,
So that me thenketh well therfore
I may excusé well my dede.
But of my will withouté drede
If I that tresor mighté gete
It shuldé never be foryete
That I ne wolde it fasté holde,
Till God of Love him selvé wolde
That deth us shuld departe atwo.
For leveth well, I love her so,
That even with min owné life,
If I that sweté lusty wife
Might onés welden at my wille,
For ever I wold holde her stille.
And in this wisé, taketh kepe,
If I her had I wolde her kepe;
And yet no friday wolde I fast,
Though I her kepte and heldé fast.
Fy on the baggés in the kist,
I had inough if I her kist.
For certés if she weré min,
I had her lever than a mine
Of gold, for all this worldes riche
Ne mighté maké me so riche
As she, that is so inly good
I setté nought of other good;
For might I getté such a thing,
I had a tresor for a king,
And though I wolde it fasté holde,
I weré thanné wel beholde.
But I might pipé now with lasse
And suffre that it overpasse,
Nought with my will, for thus I wolde
Ben avaroús if that I sholde.
But fader, I you herdé say,
How thavaroús hath yet some way,
Wherof he may be glad. For he
May, whan him list, his tresor se
And grope and fele it all aboute.
But I full ofte am shet theroute,
There as my worthy tresor is,
So is my life lich unto this
That ye me tolden here to-fore,
How that an oxe his yoke hath bore
For thing that shulde him nought availe;
And in this wise I me travaile.
For who that ever hath the welfare
I wot wel that I have the care,
For I am had and nought ne have
And am as who saith lovés knave.
Now demeth in your owné thought,
If this be avarice or nought."—
"My sone, I have of thee no wonder,
Though thou to servé be put under
With Lové, which to kinde accordeth.
But so as every boke recordeth,
It is to findé no plesaunce
That man above his sustenaunce
Unto the gold shall serve and bowe,
For that may no resón avowe.
But Avaricé nethéles,
If he may geten his encrés
Of gold, that wold he serve and kepe,
For he taketh of nought ellés kepe,
But for to fille his baggés large;
And all is to him but a charge,
For he ne parteth nought withall,
But kepeth it as a servaunt shall,
And thus though that he multiply
His goldé, without tresory
He is, for man is nought amended
With gold but if it be despended
To mannés use, wherof I rede
A tale and take therof good hede
Of that befell by oldé tide,
As telleth us the clerke Ovide.

Bachus, which is the god of wine,
Accordant unto his divine
A prest the which Cillenus hight
He had, and fell so, that by night
This prest was drunke and goth astraied,
Wherof the men were evil apaied
In Phrigilond, where as he went.
But atté last a cherle him hent
With strength of other felaship,
So that upon his drunkeship
They bounden him with cheines faste
And forth they lad him also faste
Unto the king, which highté Mide.
But he that wolde his Vicé hide
This curteis king toke of him hede
And bad, that men him shuldé lede
Into a chambre for to kepe,
Till he of leiser haddé slepe.
And tho this prest was sone unbound
And up a couché fro the ground
To slepe he was laid soft inough.
And whan he woke, the king him drough
To his presénce and did him chere,
So that this prest in such manere
While that him liketh ther he dwelleth,
And al this he to Bachus telleth
Whan that he cam to him ayein.
And whan that Bachus herdé sain
How Mide hath done his curtesy,
Him thenketh, it were a vilany
But he reward him for his dede,
So as he might of his godhede.
Unto this king this god appereth
And clepeth, and that other hereth.
This god to Midé thonketh faire
Of that he was so debonaire
Toward his prest, and bad him say
What thinge it were he woldé pray
He shulde it have, of worldés good.
This king was glad and stillé stood
And was of his axínge in doubte
And all the worlde he cast aboute,
What thing was best for his estate.
And with him self stood in debate
Upon thre pointés, which I finde
Ben levest unto mannés kinde.
The first of hem it is delite,
The two ben worship and profite.
And than he thought, if that I crave
Delite, though I delite may have,
Delite shall passen in my age;
That is no siker avauntage.
For every joié bodely
Shall ende in wo, delite forthý
Woll I nought chese. And if worshíp
I axe and of the world lordshíp,
That is an occupatiön
Of proude ymaginatiön,
Which maketh an herté vein withinne;
There is no certain for to winne,
For lorde and knave is all o wey
Whan they be bore and whan they deie.
And if I profite axé wolde,
I not in what manér I sholde
Of worldés good have sikernesse,
For every thefe upon richesse
Awaiteth for to robbe and stele.
Such good is cause of harmés fele;
And also though a man at ones
Of all the world within his wones[1]
The tresor might have every dele,
Yet had he but one mannés dele
Toward him self, so as I thinke,
Of clothing and of mete and drinke,
For more, out také vanité,
There hath no lord in his degre.
And thus upon these points diverse
Diverselich he gan reherce,
What point it thought him for the best,
But pleinly for to get him rest

1 *Wones*, dwellings.

He can no siker waié cast,
And nethéles yet atté laste
He fell upon the covetise
Of gold, and than in sondry wise
He thought, as I have said to-fore,
How tresor may be soné lore,
And hadde an inly great desir
Touchénde of such recoverír,
How that he might his cause availe
To gete him gold withouté faile.
Within his hert and thus he preiseth
The gold, and saith how that he peiseth
Above all other metal most.
The gold, he saith, may lede an hoste
To maké werre ayein a king,
The gold put under allé thing
And set it whan him list above,
The gold can make of haté love
And werre of pees and right of wrong
And long to short and short to long.
Withouté gold may be no fest,
Gold is the lord of man and best
And may hem bothé beie and selle,
So that a man may sothly telle
That all the world to golde obeieth.
"Forthý this king to Bachus preieth
To graunt him gold, but he excedeth
Mesúré moré than him nedeth.
Men tellen, that the malady,
Which clepéd is ydropesy
Resembled is unto this Vice
By way of kinde of Avarice.
The more ydropesié drinketh,
The more him thursteth, for him thinketh
That he may never drink his fille.
So that there may no thing fulfille
The lustés of his appetite,
And right in such a maner plite
Stant Avarice and ever stood;
The more he hath of worldés good,
The more he wolde it kepé streite
And ever more and more coveite,
And right in such condiciön
Withouté good discreciön
This king with Avarice is smitte,
That all the worlde it mighté witte.
For he to Bachus thanné preide,
That therupon his honde he leide,
It shuldé through his touche anone
Becomé gold; and therupon
This god him graunteth as he bad.
Tho was this kinge of Phrigé glad.
And for to put it in assay
With all the hasté that he may
He toucheth that, he toucheth this,
And in his hond all gold it is;
The stone, the tre, the leef, the gras,
The flour, the fruit, all gold it was.
Thus toucheth he while he may laste
To go, but hunger atté laste
Him toké so, that he must nede
By wey of kinde his hunger fede.
The cloth was laid, the bord was set
And all was forth to-fore him set
His dissh, his cup, his drink, his mete,
But whan he wolde or drinke or ete
Anone as it his mouth cam nigh
It was all gold, and than he sigh
Of Avaricé the folie.
And he with that began to crie
And preidé Bachus to foryive
His gilt and suffre him for to live
And be such as he was to-fore,
So that he weré nought forlore.
This god which herd of this grevaúnce
Toke routhe upon his repentaúnce
And bad him go forth redély
Unto a flood was fasté by,
The which Pactolé thanné hight,
In whiche als clene as ever he might
He shuld him wasshen overall,
And said him thanné that he shall
Recover his first estate ayein.

This king right as he herdé sain
Into the flood goth fro the lond
And wissh him bothé fote and hond,
And so forth all the remenaunt
As him was set in covenaunt.
And than he sigh merveilés straunge,
The flood his colour gan to chaunge,
The gravel with the smalé stones
To gold they torné both atones,
And he was quite of that he hadde,
And thus Fortúne his chauncé ladde.
And whan he sigh his touch awey,
He goth him home the righté wey
And liveth forth as he did er
And put all Avarice afer
And the richesse of gold despiseth
And saith, that mete and cloth suffiseth.
Thus hath this king experiénce,
How foolés done the reverénce
To gold, which of his owné kinde
Is lassé worth than is the rinde
To sustenaunce of mannés food.
And than he madé lawés good
And all his thing set upon skille,
He bad his people for to tille
Her lond and live under the lawe,
And that they shulde also forth drawe
Bestaile and seché none encrees
Of gold, whiche is the breche of pees.
For this a man may findé write,
To-fore the time, er gold was smite
In coigne, that men the florein knewe,
There was wel nighe no man untrewe.
Tho was there nouther shield ne spere
Ne dedly wepen for to bere;
Tho was the town withouten walle,
Whiche nowe is closéd over alle;
Tho was there no brocáge in lond,
Which now taketh every cause on hond.
So may men knowe how the florein
Was moder first of malengín
And bringer in of allé werre,
Wherof this world stant out of herre,[1]
Through the counseil of Avarice,
Whiche of his owné propré Vice
Is as the hellé wonderful,
For it may nevermore be full,
That what as ever cometh therinne
Awey ne may it never winne.
"But soné min, do thou nought so,
Let all suche Avaricé go
And take thy part of that thou hast.
I biddé nought that thou do wast,
But hold largesse in his mesúre.
And if thou se a creätúre,
Which through pouerte is falle in nede,
Yef him some good, for this I rede
To him that wol nought yeven here
What peine he shal have elles where.
There is a pein amongés alle
Benethe in hellé, which men calle
The wofull peine of Tantaly,
Of which I shall thee redely
Devisé how men therin stonde.
In hellé thou shalt understonde
There is a flood of thilk offíce,
Which serveth all for Avaríce.
What man that stondé shall therinne
He stant up even to the chinne,
Above his hede also there hongeth
A fruit which to that peiné longeth,
And that fruit toucheth ever in one
His overlippe, and therupon
Such thirst and hunger him assaileth,
That never his appetite ne faileth.
But whan he wolde his hunger fede
The fruit withdraweth him at nede,
And though he heve his hede on high
The fruit is ever aliché nigh,
So is the hunger wel the more.
And also though him thursté sore
And to the water bowe adown,
The flood in such condiciön

[1] Unhinged.

Avaleth,[1] that his drinke arecche
He may nought. Lo now, whiche a wreche,
That mete and drinke is him so couth
And yet ther cometh none in his mouth!
Lich to the peinés of this flood
Stant Avarice in worldés good,
He hath inough and yet him nedeth,
For his scarcenésse it him forbedeth
And ever his hunger after more
Travaileth him aliché sore,
So is he peinéd overall.
Forthý thy goodés forth withal,
My soné, loké thou despende,
Wherof thou might thy self amende
Both here and eke in other place.
And also if thou wolt purcháce
To be belovéd, thou must use
Largéssé, for if thou refuse
To yivé for thy lovés sake,
It is no reson that thou take
Of lové that thou woldest crave.
Forthý if thou wolt gracé have,
Be graciońs and do largesse,
Of Avarice and [2] the sikenesse
Escheue above all other thinge,
And take ensample of Mide the kinge
And of the flood of helle also,
Where is inough of allé wo.
And though there weré no matére
But onely that we finden here,
Men oughten Avarice eschue;
For what man thilké Vicé sue,
He gete him self but litel rest.
For how so that the body rest,
The hert upon the gold traváileth,
Whom many a nightés drede assaileth.
For though he ligge a beddé naked,
His herte is evermore awaked
And dremeth as he lith to slepe
How besy that he is to kepe
His tresor, that no thefe it stele;
Thus hath he but a wofull wele.
And right so in the samé wise,
If thou thy self wolt wel avise,
There be lovérs of suche inow,
That wollen unto reson bowe
If so be that they come above,
Whan they ben maisters of her love
And that they shulden be most glad
With lové, they ben most bestad,
So fain they wolden holde it all.
Her herte, her eye is overall,
And wenen every man be thefe
To stele awey that hem is lefe;
Thus through her owné fantasy
They fallen into jelousy.
Than hath the ship to-brok his cable
With every winde and is mevable."[1]—

"My fader, for that ye now telle,
I have herd oftetimé telle
Of Jelousy, but what it is
Yet understode I never er this.
Wherfore I woldé you beseche,
That ye me wolde enforme and teche
What maner thing it mighté be."—

"My soné, that is hard to me,
But nethéles as I have herd
Now herke, and thou shalt be answerd.

Among the men lack of manhode
In mariáge upon wif-hode
Maketh that a man him self deceiveth,
Wherof it is that he conceiveth
That ilke unsely maladý,
The whiche is cleped Jelousý,
Of whiche if I the propreté
Shall telle after the nicété
So as it worcheth on a man,—
A fever it is cotidian,
Whiche every day wol come aboute
Where so a man be in or oute,

[1] *Avaleth*, goes lower.

[2] *Of Avarice and*, &c.; And Escheue, &c. See note, page 61. This construction is frequent throughout the poem.

[1] And is to be moved by every wind.

At home if that a man wol wone
This fever is than of comun wone[1]
Most grevous in a mannés eye,
For than he maketh him tote and pry;
Where so as ever his lové go,
She shall nought with her litel toe
Misteppé, but he se it all.
His eye is walkend overall,
Where that she singe or that she daunce,
He seeth the lesté countenaunce;
If she loke on a man aside
Or with him rowne at any tide,
Or that she laugh or that she loure,
His eye is there at every houre.
And whan it draweth to the night,
If she than be withouté light,
Anone is all the gamé shent.
For than he set his parlement
To speke it whan he cometh to bed
And saith: 'If I were now to wed,
I wolde never more have wife.'
And so he torneth into strife
The lust of lovés dueté
And al upon diversité.
If she be fresshe and well arraied,
He saith her banner is desplaied
To clepe in gestes by the way;
And if she be nought wel besey[2]
And that her list nought to be glad,
He bereth on honde that she is mad
And loveth nought her husébonde;
He saith, he may wel understonde,
That if she wolde his compaignie,
She shuldé than afore his eye
Shew all the plesure that she might.
So that by daié ne by night
She not what thing is for the best,
But liveth out of allé rest.
For what as ever him list to sain,
She dare nought speke o worde ayein,
But wepeth and holt her lippés close.
She may wel writé, 'Sans repose,'
The wife, which is to such one maried.
Of allé women be he waried,[1]
For with his fever of jelousý
His eché daiés fantasý
Of sorwe is ever aliché grene,
So that there is no lové sene
While that him list at home abide.
And whan so is he woll out ride,
Than hath he redy his aspy
Abiding in her compaigny
A jangler, an ill mouthéd one,
That she ne may no whider gone
Ne speke o word, ne onés loke,
But he ne wol it wende and croke
And torne after his owne entent,
Though she no thing but honour ment.
Whan that the lord cometh home ayein
The jangler musté somwhat sain.
So what withoute and what withinne
This fever is ever to beginne,
For where he cometh he can nought ende
Til deth of him hath made an ende.
For though so be that he ne here,
Ne se, ne wite, in no manere
But all honoúre and womanhede,
Therof the jelous taketh none hede,
But as a man to Love unkinde
He cast his stafe and as the blinde
And fint defaulté where is none;
As who so dremeth on a stone
How he is laid, and groneth ofte
Whan he lieth on his pilwes softe.
So is there nought but strife and chest,
Whan Lové shuldé make his fest.
I wot the time is ofté cursed,
That ever was the gold unpursed,

[1] *Wone*, custom. [2] *Besey*, clothed.

[1] *Waried*, cursed.

The which was laid upon the boke,
Whan that all other she forsoke
For love of him, but all to late
She pleigneth, for as than algate
She mot forbere and to him bowe,
Though he ne woldé that allowe;
For man is lord of thilké faire,
So may the woman but empeire
If she speke ought ayein his wille,
And thus she bereth her peine stille.
But if this fever a woman take
She shall be wel more hardé shake,
For though she bothé se and here
And finde that there is no matere,
She dare but to her selvé pleigne,
And thus she suffreth double peine.
"Lo thus, my sone, as I have write,
Thou might of jelousié wite
His fever and his condiciön,
Which is full of suspiciön.
But wherof that this fever groweth,
Who so these oldé bokés troweth,
There may he findé how it is.
For they us teche and tellé this,
How that this fever of jelousy
Somdele it groweth of sotý[1]
Of love and somdele of untrust.
For as a sikman lest his lust,[2]
And whan he may no savour gete
He hateth than his owné mete,
Right so this feverous maladý,
Which causéd is of fantasý,
Maketh the jeloús in feble plite
To lese of love his appetite
Through feignéd enformaciön
Of his ymaginaciön.
But finally to taken hede
Men may wel make a liklyhede
Betwene him whiche is avaroús
Of golde and him that is jeloús
Of lové, for in o degre
They stondé both, as semeth me;

[1] *Sotý* (*sottise*), folly.
[2] Loses his enjoyment.

That one wold have his baggés still
And nought departen[1] with his will
And dare nought for the thevés slepe
So faine he wolde his tresor kepe;
That other may nought well be glad,
For he is evermore adrad
Of these lovérs that gone aboute,
In aunter if they put him oute.
So have they bothé litel joy
As wel of love as of money.
"Now hast thou, sone, of my teching
Of jelousy a knouleching,
That thou might understondé this,
Fro whenne he cometh and what he is,
And eke to whom that he is like.
Beware forthý thou be not sike
Of thilké fever, as I have spoke,
For it woll in him self be wroke.
For Lové hateth no thing more,
As men may findé by the lore
Of hem that whilom weré wise,
How that they speke in many wise."—
"My fader, soth is that ye sain;
But for to loké there ayein
Before this timé how it is falle,
Wherof there might ensample falle
To suché men as ben jeloús
In what manér it is grevoús,
Right fain I wolde ensample here."—
"My godé sone, at thy praiere
Of suche ensamples as I finde,
So as they comen now to minde
Upon this point of timé gone,
I thenké for to tellen one.
Ovidé wrote of many thinges,
Among the whiche in his writinges
He told a tale in poesy,
Which toucheth unto jelousy
Upon a certain cas of Love.
Among the goddés al above

[1] *Departen*, distribute.

It felle at thilké timé thus.
The god of fire, which Vulcanus
Is hote and hath a craft forth with
Assignéd for to be the smith
Of Jupiter, and his figúre
Both of viságe and of statúre
Is lothly and malgracious;
But yet he hath within his hous
As for the liking of his life
The fairé Venus to his wife.
But Mars, which of bataillés is
The god, an eye had unto this,
As he which was chivalerous.
It felle him to ben amorous,
And thought it was a great pité
To se so lusty one as she
Be coupled with so lourd[1] a wight,
So that his peiné day and night
He did, if he her winne might.
And she that had a good insight
Toward so noble a knightly lord
In lové fel of his accord.
There lacketh nought but time and place,
That he nis siker of her grace.
But whan two hertés fallen in one,
So wise a wait[2] was never none
That at sometimé they ne mete;
And thus this fairé lusty swete
With Mars hath ofté compaigny.
But thilke unkindé jelousy,
Which evermore the herte opposeth,
Maketh Vulcanús that he supposeth
That it is nought wel overall;
And to him self he said, he shall
Aspié better, if that he may.
And so it felle upon a day,
That he this thing so sleightly ledde,
He founde hem bothé two abedde.
With stronge cheinés he hem bounde,
As he to-gíder hem had founde,
And lefté hem both liggé so
And gan to clepe and crié tho
Unto the goddés all aboute.
And they assembled in a route
Come all at onés for to se,
But none amendés haddé he,
But was rebukéd here and there
Of hem that lovés frendés were,
And saiden that he was to blame,
For if there felle him any shame
It was through his misgovernaunce,
And thus he losté contenaunce
This god and let his causé falle,
And they to scorne him laughen alle.
Forthý my sone, in thine office
Beware, that thou be nought jelous,
Whiche ofté time hath shent the hous."—
"My fader, this ensample is hard,
How such thing to the hevenward
Among the goddés mighté falle.
For there is but o god of alle,
Which is the lord of heven and helle.
But if it liké you to telle
How suché goddés cóme aplace,
Ye mighten mochel thank purchace,
For I shall be wel taught withall."—
"My sone, it is thus overall
With hem, that stonden misbeleved,
That suché goddés ben beleved
In sondry placé sondry wise.
Amongés hem which be unwise,
There is betaken of credence,
Wherof that I the difference
In the manér as it is write
Shall do thee pleinly for to wite.
"Er Crist was bore among us here
Of the belevés that tho were,
In fouré formés thus it was.
They of Caldee as in this cas
Had a belevé by hem selve,
Which stood upon the signés twelve,
Forth eke with the planetés seven,
Whiche as they sighen upon the heven

[1] *Lourd*, dull, heavy. [2] *Wait*, watch.

Of sondry constellación
In her ymaginación
With sondry kerfe and portreture
They made of goddés the figúre.
In thelementes and eke also
They hadden a belevé tho.
And all was that unresonáble,
For thelementes ben servisáble
To man. And ofte of accidence,
As men may se thexperience,
They ben corrupt by sondry way,
So may no mannés reson say
That they ben god in any wise.
And eke if men hem wel avise,
The sonne and mone eclipsen both,
That be hem lef or be hem loth
They suffre, and what thing is passíble[1]
To ben a god is inpossíble.
These elements ben creätúres,
So ben these hevenly figúres,
Wherof may wel be justified,
That they may nought ben deified.
And who that taketh away thonour,
Which due is to the creätoúr,
And yiveth it to the creätúre,
He doth to great a forfeiture.
But of Caldeë nethéles
Upon this feith though it be lesse
They holde afferméd the creaunce,
So that of hellé the penaunce,
As folk which stant out of beleve,
They shall receive, as we beleve.
"Of the Caldees so in this wise
Stant the beleve out of assise.
But in Egipté worst of alle
The feith is fals, how so it falle,
For they diversé bestés there
Honoúr, as though they goddes were.
And nethélesse yet forth withall
Thre goddés most in speciall
They havé forth with a goddesse,
In whome is all her sikernesse.
Tho goddés be yet clepéd thus

[1] *Passible*, capable of suffering.

Orus, Tiphon and Isirus.
They weré brethren allé thre
And the goddesse in her degre
Her suster was and Ysis hight,
Whom Isirus forlay by night
And helde her after as his wife.
So it befell, that upon strife
Tiphon hath Isre his brother slain,
Which had a child to sone, Orain,
And he his faders deth to herte
So toke, that it may nought asterte
That he Tiphón after ne slough,
Whan he was ripe of age inough.
But yet thegipcienés trowe
For all this errour, which they knowe,
That thesé brethern ben of might
To sette and kepe Egípt upright
And overthrowe if that hem like.
But Ysis, as saith the croníque,
Fro Grece into Egipté cam
And she than upon hondé nam
To teche hem for to sowe and ere,
Which no man knew to-foré there.
And whanné thegipcíens sigh
The feldés full afore her eye,
And that the lond began to greine,
Which whilom haddé be bareine,
For therthé bare after the kinde
His dué chargé, this I finde,
That she of berthé the goddesse
Is clepéd, so that in distresse
The women therupon childing
To her they clepe and her offríng
They beren whan that they ben light.
Lo, howe Egipt all out of sight
Fro reson stant in misbeleve,
For lacke of lore as I beleve.
"Among the Grekes out of the wey
As they that reson put awey
There was, as the croníqué saith,
Of misbeleve an other feith,
That they her goddés and goddesses
As who saith token all to gesses
Of suche as weren full of vice,
To whom they madé sacrifice.

"The Highé God, so as they
saide,
To whom they mosté worship laide,
Saturnus hight, and king of Crete
He haddé be. But of his sete
He was put down as he which stood
In frenésy and was so wode [1]
That fro his wife, which Rea hight,
His owné children he to plight [2]
And ete hem of his comune wone.[3]
But Jupiter, which was his sone
And of full age, his fader bonde
And kut of with his owné honde
His genitals, whiche also faste
Into the depé see he caste,
Wherof the Grekes afferme and say
That, whan they weré cast awey
Came Venus forth by wey of kinde.
And of Saturne also I finde,
Howe afterwarde into an ile
This Jupiter him didde exile,
Where that he stood in great mis-
chéfe.
Lo, what a god they maden chefe!
And sithen that suche one was he
Which stood most high in his degre
Among the goddés, thou might know
These other that ben moré low
Ben litel worth, as it is founde.

"For Jupiter was the secoúnde,
Whiche Juno had unto his wife.
And yet a lechour all his life
He was and in avouterie [4]
He wroughté many a trecherie.
And for he was so full of vices,
They clepéd him God of Delices,
Of whom if thou wolt moré wite
Ovidé the poéte hath write.
But yet her sterrés bothé two
Saturne and Jupiter also
They have, although they ben to
blame,
Attitled to her owné name.

[1] *Wode*, mad. [2] *To plight*, plucked to pieces.
[3] *Of his comune wone*, as his usual custom.
[4] *Avouterie*, adultery.

"Mars was an other in that lawe,
The which in Dacé was forth drawe,
Of whom the clerk Vegecius
Wrote in his boke and toldé thus,
Howe he into Itailé came
And such fortuné there he nam,
That he a maiden hath oppressed,
Whiche in her ordre was professed
As she which was the prioresse
In Vestés temple the goddesse,
So was she well the more to blame.
Dame Ylia this ladye name
Men clepe, and eke she was also
The kingés doughter, that was tho,
Which Minitor by namé hight.
So that ayein the lawés right
Mars thilké time upon her that
Remús and Romulus begat,
Whiche after, whan they come in
age,
Of knighthode and of vassellage
Itaile al hole they overcome
And foundeden the greté Rome.
In armés and of suche emprise
They weren, that in thilké wise
Her fader Mars for the merveile
The God is clepéd of Bataile.
They were his children bothé two,
Through hem he toke his namé so,
There was none other causé why.
And yet a sterre upon the sky
He hath unto his name applied,
In which that he is signified.

"An other god they hadden eke,
To whom for counseil they beseke,
The which was brother to Venús,
Apollo men him clepé thus.
He was an hunte upon the hilles,
There was with him no vertue elles
Wherof that any bokés carpe,
But only that he couthé harpe,
Which whan he walkéd over londe
Full ofté time he toke on honde
To get him with his sustenaúnce
For lack of other purveaúnce.

And otherwhile of his falshede
He feigneth him to conne arede
Of thing which afterward shuld falle,
Wherof among his sleightés alle
He hath the leudé[1] folk deceived,
So that the better he was received.
Lo now, through what creaciön
He hath deificaciön
And clepéd is the God of Wit,
To suche as be the foolés yet.
"An other god, to whom they sought,
Mercúrie hight, and him ne rought
What thing he stale, ne whom he slough.
Of sorcery he couthe inough,
That whan he wold him self transforme,
Full ofté time he toke the forme
Of woman and his owné lefte.
So did he well the moré thefte.
A great spekér in allé thinges
He was also and of lesinges
An autor, that men wisté none
An other suche as he was one.
And yet they maden of this thefe
A god which was unto hem lefe,
And clepéd him in tho beleves
The God of Marchants and of Theves.
But yet a sterre upon the heven
He hath of the planetés seven.
But Vulcanus, of whom I spake,
He had a courbe[2] upon the back,
And therto he was hippe-halt,
Of whom thou understondé shalt,
He was a shrewe in al his youth
And he none other vertue couth
Of craft to helpe him selvé with
But only that he was a smith
With Jupiter, whiche in his forge
Diversé thingés made him forge;
So wote I nought for what desire
They clepen him the God of Fire.

[1] *Leudé*, unlearned. [2] *Courbe*, hump.

King of Cicile Ypolitus
A sone he had, and Eolus
He hight, and of his faders graunt
He held by way of covenaunt
The governaunce of every ile
Which was longénd unto Cicile,
Of hem that fro the lond forein
Lay ope the windés alle pleine.[1]
And fro thilke iles into the londe
Full ofté cam the wind to honde;
After the name of him forthý
The windés clepéd Eoly
They were, and he the God of Winde.
Lo now, how this beleve is blinde.
The king of Creté Jupiter,
The samé, whiché I spake of er,
Unto his brother, which Neptune
Was hote, it list him to comune
Parte of his good, so that by ship
He made him stronge of the lordship
Of all the see in tho parties,
Where that he wrought his tirannies,
And the straunge ilés aboute
He wan, that every man hath doubte
Upon his marché[2] for to saile.
For he anone hem wolde assaile
And robbé what thing that they ladden,
His sauf conduit but if[3] they hadden.
Wherof the comun vois aros
In every lond, that suche a los
He caught, all nere it worth a stre,
That he was cleped of the See
The God by name, and yet he is
With hem that so beleve amis.
This Neptune eke was thilke also,
Which was the firsté founder tho
Of noble Troy, and he forthý
Was well the moré letté by.
The lorésman of the shephérdes
And eke of hem that ben nethérdes,
Was of Archade and highté Pan,

[1] Laid up a full store of all the winds.
[2] *Marché*, borders. [3] *But if*, unless.

Of whom hath spoké many a man.
For in the wode of Nonartigne
Encloséd with the trees of pigne
And on the mount of Parasie
He had of bestés the bailie,[1]
And eke beneth in the valéy,
Where thilké river, as men may say,
Which Ladon hightć, made his
cours,
He was the chefe of governours
Of hem that kepten tamé bestes,
Wherof they maken yet the festes
In the citee of Stimfalides.
And forth withall yet nethéles
He taughté men the forth drawíng
Of bestaile and eke the makíng
Of oxen and of hors the same,
How men hem shuldé ride and tame,
Of foulés eke, so as we finde,
Full many a subtil craft of kinde
He found, which no man knew to-
fore.
Men did him worship eke therfore,
That he the first in thilké londe
Was, which the melodië fonde
Of reedés whan they weren ripe,
With double pipés for to pipe.
Therof he yaf the firsté lore,
Till afterward men couthé more;
To every crafte of mannés helpe
He had a redy wit to helpe
Through natural experiénce.
And thus thurh nicé reverence
Of foolés, whan that he was dede,
The foot was tornéd to the hede
And clepen him God of Natúre,
For so they maden his figúre.
"An other god, so as they fele,
Whiche Jupiter upon Semele
Begat in his avouterie,
Whom, for to hide his lecherie
That none therof shall také kepe,
In a mountaigné for to kepe
Which Dion hight and was in Ynde

[1] *Bailie*, custody.

He send, in bokés as I finde,
And he by namé Bachus hight,
Which afterward, whan that he
might,
A wastor was and all his rent
In wine and bordel[1] he despent.
But yet all were he wonder bad
Among the Grekes a name he had,
They clepéd him the God of Wine
And thus a gloton was divine.
"There was yet Esculapius
A god in thilké time as thus.
His craft stood upon surgerie,
But for the luste of lecherie,
That he to Dairés doughter drough,
It fell that Jupiter him slough.
And yet they made him nought
forthý
A god, and wist no causé why.
In Rome he was long timé so
A god among the Romains tho,
For as they saide of his presénce
There was destruied a pestilénce
Whan they to thile of Delphos went;
And that Apollo with him sent
This Esculapiús his sone
Among the Romains for to wone;
And there he dwelté for a while,
Till afterwarde into that ile
Fro when he cam ayeine he torneth,
Where all his life that he sojórneth
Among the Grekes till that he
deiede.
And they upon him thanné leide
His name, and God of Medicíne
He hatte after that ilké line.
"An other god of Hercules
They madé, which was nethéles
A man, but that he was so stronge
In al this world that brode and longe
So mighty was no man as he.
Merveilés twelve in his degre,
As it was couth in sondry londes,
He didé with his owné hondes

[1] *Bordel*, revelry.

Ayein geaúnts and monstres both,
The whiche horríble were and loth.
But he with strength hem overcam,
Wherof so great a price he nam,
That they him clepe amongés alle
The God of Strengthe and to him calle.
And yet there is no reson inne,
For he a man was full of sinne,
Which provéd was upon his ende,
For in a rage him self he brende.
And suche a cruell mannés dede
Accordeth nothing with godhede.
They had of goddés yet an other,
Which Pluto hight, and was the brother
Of Jupiter, and he fro youth
With every word which cam to mouth,
Of any thing, whan he was wroth,
He woldé swere his comun othe
By Lethen and by Flegeton,
By Cochitum and Acheron,
The whiche after the bokés telle
Ben the chefe floodés of the helle;
By Segne and Stige he swore also,
That ben the depé pittés two
Of hellé the most principall.
Pluto these othés over all
Swore of his comun custumaúnce,
Till it befelle upon a chaunce,
That he for Jupiterés sake
Unto the goddés let do make
A sacrifice, and for that dede
One of the pittés for his mede
In hell of whiche I spake of er
Was graunted him, and thus he there
Upon the fortune of this thinge
The namé toke of Hellé Kinge.
"Lo, thesé goddés and well mo
Among the Grekés they had tho,
And of goddésses many one,
Whose namés thou shalt here anone,
And in what wisé they deceiven
The foolés, whiche her feith receiven.
"So as Saturne is soveraine
Of falsé goddés, as they saine,
So is Cybeles of goddésses
The moder, whom withouté gesses
The folké prein, honoúr, and serve
As they the whiche her lawe observe.
But for to knowen upon this,
Fro when she cam and what she is,
Bethincia the contré hight,
Where she cam first to mannés sight.
And after was Saturnés wife,
By whom thre children in her life
She bare, and they were clepéd tho
Juno, Neptunus and Pluto,
The which of nicé fantasý
The people woldé deify.
And for her children weren so
Cybelés thanné was also
Made a goddesse, and they her calle
The Moder of the Goddés alle.
So was that namé boré forth,
And yet the cause is litel worth.
A vois unto Saturné tolde,
How that his owné sone him sholde
Out of his regné put away,
And he because of thilké wey
That him was shapé suche a fate,
Cybele his wife began to hate
And eke her progenië bothe.
And thus while that they weré wrothe
By Philerem upon a day
In his avouterie he lay,
On whom he Jupiter begat.
And thilké child was after that
Which wrought al that was prophecied,
As it to-fore is specified.
So whan that Jupiter of Crete
Was king, a wife unto him mete
The doughter of Cybele he toke,
And that was Juno, saith the boke
Of his deffication
After the fals opinion
That I have tolde, so as they mene.

And for this Juno was the quene
Of Jupiter and suster eke,
The foolés unto hiré seke
And sain, that she is the Goddesse
Of Regnés bothe and of Richesse,
And eke she, as they understonde,
The water nimphés hath in honde
To leden at her owné heste.
And whan her list the sky tempéste
The reinbowe is her messagere.
Lo, which a misbeleve is here
That she goddésse is of the sky,
I wot none other causé why.
"An other goddesse is Minerve,
To whom the Grekes obey and serve.
And she was nigh the greaté lay[1]
Of Triton foundé, where she lay
A child for-cast, but what she was
There knew no man the sothé cas.
But in Aufriqué she was laide
In the manér as I have saide
And caried fro that ilké place
Into an ilé fer in Trace,
The which Pallené thanné hight,
Where a noríce hir kepte and dight.
And after for she was so wise,
That she found first in her avise
The cloth makíng of woll and line,
Men saiden that she was divine,
And the Goddesse of Sapience
They clepen her in that credence.
Of the goddessé, which Pallas
Is clepéd, sondry speché was.
One saith her fader was Pallaunt,
Whiche was in his time a geaunt,
A cruell man, a batailous.
An other saith, how in his hous
She was the causé why he deiede.
And of this Pallas some eke saide
That she was Martés wife, and so
Among the men that weren tho
Of misbeleve in the riot
The Goddesse of Batailés hote

[1] *Lay*, lake.

She was, and yet she bereth the name.
Now loke, how they be for to blame.
"Saturnus after his exile
Fro Creté cam in great perile
Into the londés of Itaile
And there he didé great merveile,
Wherof his namé dwelleth yit.
For he founde of his owné wit
The firsté crafte of plough tillíng,
Of ering[1] and of corn sowing,
And how men shulden setté vines
And of the grapés make wines;
All this he taught. And it fell so
His wife, the which cam with him tho,
Was clepéd Cereres by name,
And for she taught also the same
And was his wife that ilké throwe,
As it was to the people knowe,
They made of Ceres a goddesse,
In whom her tilthé yet they blesse
And sain that Tricolonius
Her soné goth amongés us
And maketh the corn good chepe or dere,
Right as her list, from yere to yere,
So that this wife because of this
Goddesse of Cornés cleped is.
"King Jupiter, which his likíng
Whilom fulfilled in allé thing,
So priveliche about he ladde
His lust, that he his willé hadde
Of Latoná and on her that
Diane his doughter he begat
Unknowen of his wife Juno.
But afterward she knewe it so,
That Latoná for dredé fled
Into an ilé, where she hid
Her wombé which of childe aros.
Thilke ilé clepéd was Delos,
In which Diana was forth brought
And kept so that her lacketh nought.
And after whan she was of age,
She toke none hede of mariáge,

[1] *Ering*, ploughing.

But out of mannés compaigny
She toke her all to venery[1]
In forest and in wildernesse,
For there was all her besinesse
By day and eke by nightés tide
With arwés brode under the side
And bow in honde, of which she slough
And toke all that her list inough
Of bestés which ben chaceable.
Wherof the cronique of this fable
Saith that the gentils most of alle
Worshippen her, and to her calle
And the Goddesse of highé Hilles,
Of grené trees, of fresshé welles
They clepen her in that beleve,
Which that no reson may acheve.
"Prosérpina, which doughter was
Of Cereres, befell this cas:
While she was dwelling in Cicile,
Her moder in that ilké while
Upon her blessing and her hest
Bad that she shuldé ben honést
And lerné for to weve and spinne
And dwell at home and kepe her inne.
But she cast all that lore awey,
And as she went her out to pley
To gader flourés in a pleine,
And that was under the mountaigne
Of Ethna, fell the samé tide
That Pluto cam that waié ride.
And sodeinly, er she was ware,
He toke her up into his chare,[2]
And as they riden in the felde,
Her greté beauté he behelde,
Which was so plesaunt in his eye,
That for to holde in compaignie
He wedded her, and helde her so
To ben his wife for evermo.
And as thou hast to-fore herde telle,
How he was clepéd God of Helle,
So is she clepéd the Goddesse
Because of him, ne more ne lesse.

[1] *Venery*, hunting. [2] *Chare*, car, chariot.

"Lo thus, my sone, as I the tolde
The Grekes whilóm by daiés olde
Her goddés had in sondry wise,
And through the lore of her apprise[1]
The Romains helden eke the same
And in the worshippe of her name
To every god in speciáll
They made a temple forth withall
And eche of hem his yerés day
Attitled hadde. And of array
The temples weren than ordeigned,
And eke the people was constreigned
To come and done her sacrifice.
The prestés eke in her office
Solempné maden thilké festes.
And thus the Grekés lich to bestes
The men in stede of God honoúr,
Which mighten nought hem self soccour
While that they were alivé here.
"And over this as thou shalt here
The Grekes fulfilled of fantasy
Sain eke that of the hilles high
The goddés ben in speciall,
But of her name in generall
They hoten allé Satiry.
"There ben of Nimphés proprely
In the beleve of hem also:
Oréadés they saiden tho
Attitled ben to the montaignes;
And for the wodés in demeines
To kepé tho ben Driadés;
Of fresshé wellés Naiadés;
And of the nimphés of the see
I finde a tale in proprete,
How Dorus whilom king of Grece,
Whiche had of infortúne a piece,
His wife forth with his doughter alle
So as the happés shulden falle
With many a gentilwoman there
Dreint in the salté see they were,
Wherof the Grekés that time saiden
And such a name upon hem laiden,

[1] *Apprise*, teaching.

Nereïdes that they ben hote,
The nimphés whiché that they note
To regne upon the stremés salte.
Lo now, if this belevé halte.
But of the nimphés as they telle,
In every placé where they dwelle
They ben all redy obeisaúnt
As damisellés attendaúnt
To the goddésses, whose servíse
They mote obey in allé wise,
Wherof the Grekes to hem beseke
With tho that ben goddesses eke,
And have in hem a great credénce.
And yet without experience
Saufe onely of illusión,
Which was to hem dampnación.
"For men also that weré dede
They hadden goddés as I rede,
And tho by namé Manes highten,
To whom ful great honoúr they dighten,
So as the Grekés lawé saith,
Which was ayein the righté feith.
"Thus have I tolde a great partie,
But all the holé progenie
Of goddés in that ilké time
To longe it weré for to rime.
But yet of that which thou hast herde
Of misbeleve, howe it hath ferde,
There is a great diversité."—
"My fader, right so thenketh me.
But yet o thinge I you beseche,
Which stant in allé mennés speche,
The God and the Goddesse of Love,
Of whom ye nothing here above
Have told, ne spoken of her fare,
That ye me woldé now declare,
How they first comé to that name."—
"My sone, I have it left for shame,
Because I am her owné prest.
But for they stondé nigh thy brest
Upon the shrifte of thy matere,
Thou shalt of hem the sothé here,
And understond now well the cas.
Venus Saturnés doughter was,
Which allé Daunger put awey
Of Love and found to lust a wey,
So that of her in sondry place
Diversé men fell into grace,
And such a lusty life she ladde,
That she diversé children hadde,
Now one by this, now one by that.
Of her it was that Mars begat
A child which clepéd was Armene,
Of her cam also Andragene,
To whom Mercúrie father was.
Anchises begat Eneás
Of her also, and Ericon
Biten begatte, and therupon
Whan that she sigh ther was none other
By Jupiter her owné brother
She lay, and he begat Cupíde.
And thilké sone upon a tide,
Whan he was come unto his age,
He had a wonder fair viságe
And founde his mother amorous,
And he was also lecherous.
So whan they weren bothe alone,
As he whiche eyen haddé none
To se reson, his mother kist,
And she also that nothing wist
But that whiche to his lust belongeth,
To bene her love him underfongeth.
Thus was he blinde and she unwis.
But nethéles this cause it is
Which Cupide is the god of love,
For he his mother derste love,
And she, which through her lustes fonde
Diversé lovés toke on honde
Wel mo than I the tellé here.
And for she wolde her selvé skere,[1]
She madé comun that disporte
And set a lawe of such a porte
That every woman mighté take
What man her list and nought forsake

[1] *Skere*, clear, free.

To ben as comun as she wolde.
She was the first also which tolde
That women shulde her body selle.
Semiramis so as men telle
Of Venus kepté thilke apprise.
And so did in the samé wise
Of Romé fairé Neabólie,
Which lift her body to Rególie.
She was to every man felawe
And held the lust of thilké lawe
Which Venus of her self beganne,
Wherof that she the namé wanne
Why men her clepen the Goddesse
Of Love and eke of gentilesse,
Of worldés lust and of plesaunce.
"Se now the foulé miscreaunce
Of Grekes in thilké timé tho,
Whan Venus toke her namé so.
There was no cause under the mone
Of which they hadden tho to done
Of wel or wo where so it was,
That they ne token in that cas
A god to helpe or a goddesse,
Wherof to také my witnesse,
"The king of Bragman Dindimus
Wrote unto Alisaundre thus
In blaminge of the Grekés feith
And of the misbeleve he saith
How they for every membre hadden
A sondry god, to whom they spradden
Her armés and of help besoughten.
"Minervé for the hede they soughten,
For she was wise, and of a man
The wit and reson which he can
Is in the cellés of the brain,
Wherof they made her soverain.
"Mercúrie, which was in his dawes
A great spekér of falsé lawes,
On him the keping of the tunge
They laiden, whan they speke or sunge.
"For Bachus was a gloten eke
Him for the throté they beseke,
That he it woldé wasshen ofte
With suoté drinkés and with softe.
The god of shulders and of armes
Was Hercules, for he in armes
The mightiesté was to fight,
To him tho limmés they behight.
The god whom that they clepen Mart
The brest to kepe hath for his part,
For with the herte in his ymage
That he addresse to his corage.
And of the gallé the goddesse,
For she was ful of hastinesse,
Of wrath and light to greve also,
They made and said, it was Juno.
"Cupidé, which the brond of fire
Bare in his hond, he was the sire
Of the stomáck, which boileth ever,
Wherof the lustés ben the lever.
"Thus was dispers in sondry wise
The misbeleve as I devise
With many an ymage of entaile[1]
Of suche as might hem nought availe.
For they withouté livés chere
Unmighty ben to se or here
Or speke or do or ellés fele,
And yet the foolés to hem knele
Whiche is her owné handés werke.
Ha lord, how this beleve is derke
And fer fro resonáble wit,
And nethéles they don it yit.
That was o day a ragged tre
To morwe upon his magesté
Stant in the temple wel besein;
How might a mannés reson sain,
That such a stock may helpe or greve?
But they that ben of such beleve
And unto suché goddés calle,
It shall to hem right so befalle
And failen atté mosté nede.
But if thee list to taken hede

[1] Graven image.

And of the first ymágé.wite,
Petronius therof hath write
And eke Nigargorus also,
And they afferme and writé so,
That Promethéüs was to-fore
And foundé the first craft therfore,
And Cirophánes, as they telle,
Through counseil which was take in helle,
In remembraúnce of his lignage
Let setten up the first ymáge.
Of Cirophánes saith the boke
That he for sorwe which he toke
Of that he sigh his soné dede,
Of comfort knew none other rede
But let do make in remembraúnce
A faire ymáge of his semblaúnce
And set it in the market place,
Which openly to-fore his face
Stood every day to done him ese.
And they that thanné wolde plese
The fader, shulden it obey[1]
Whan that they comen thilké wey.
"And of Ninús king of Assire
I redé, how that in his empire
He was, next after, the secoúnd
Of hem that first ymáges found.
For he right in sembláble cas
Of Belus, which his fader was
Fro Nembroth in the righté line,
Let make of gold and stonés fine
A precïóus ymágé riche
After his fader evenliche,
And therupon a law he sette
That every man of puré dette
With sacrifice and with truáge
Honóuré shuldé thilk ymáge,
So that withinné time it felle
Of Belus cam the name of Belle,
Of Bel cam Belzebub and so
The misbelevé wenté tho.
"The thrid ymágé next to this
Was whan the king of Grece, Apis,
Was dede, they maden a figúre
In resemblaúnce of his statúre.
Of this king Apis saith the boke,
That Serapis his namé toke,
In whom through long continuaúnce
Of misbeleve a great creaúnce
They hadden and the reverence
Of sacrifice and of encence
To him they made. And as they telle
Among the wonders that befelle,
Whan Alisaundre fro Candace
Cam ridend in a wildé place
Under an hille a cave he fond,
And Candalus, whiche in that lond
Was bore and was Candaces sone,
Him told, how that of comun wone
The goddés were in thilké cave.
And he that wolde assay and have
A knoulechinge if it be soth,
Light of his hors and in he goth
And fond therinné that he sought.
For through the fendés sleight him thought
Amongés other goddés mo
That Sérapis spake to him tho,
Whom he sigh there in great array.
And thus the fend fro day to day
The worship of ydolatrie
Drough forth upon the fantasie
Of hem that weren thanné blinde
And couthen nought the trouthé finde.
Thus hast thou herd in what degre
Of Grece, and Egipte and Caldee
The misbelevés whilom stood,
And how so that they be nought good
Ne trewé, yet they sprongen oute,
Wherof the widé worlde aboute
His parte of misbelevé toke.
Til so befelle, as saith the boke,
That God a people for him selve
Hath chose of the lignáges twelve,
Wherof the sothé redely,
As it is write in Genesy,

[1] Make obeisance to.

I thenké telle in suche a wise,
That it shall be to thin apprise.
"After the flood, fro which Noë
Was sauf, the worlde in his degré
Was made as who saith new ayein
Of flour, of fruit, of gras, of grein,
Of beest, of brid and of mankinde,
Whiche ever hath be to God unkinde.
For nought withstonding all the fare
Of that this world was made so bare,
And afterward it was restored,
Among the men was nothing mored[1]
Towardés God of good livíng,
But all was tornéd to likíng
After the flessh, so that foryete
Was he which yaf hem life and mete,
Of heven and erthé creätoúr.
And thus cam forth the great errour,
That they the highé God ne knewe,
But maden other goddés newe,
As thou hast herd me said to-fore.
There was no man that timé bore,
That he ne had after his chois
A god to whom he yaf his vois,
Wherof the misbelevé cam
Into the time of Abraham.
But he found out the rightć wey,
Howe only men shulden obey
The highé God, which weldeth all
And ever hath done and ever shall
In heven, in erth and eke in helle,
There is no tunge his might may telle.
This patriarch to his lignáge
Forbad that they to none ymáge
Encliné sholden in no wise,
But her offrende and sacrifise
With all the holé hertés love
Unto the mighty God above
They shuldé yive and to no mo.
And thus in thilké timé tho
Began that sect upon this erthe,
Whiche of belevés was the ferthe.
Of rightwisnesse it was conceived,
So must it nedés be received

[1] *Mored*, increased.

Of him that alle right is inne,
The highé God, which woldé winne
A people unto his owné feith.
On Abraham the ground he laith
And made him for to multiply
Into so great a progeny,
That they Egipte all over spradde.
But Pharaö with wrong hem ladde
In servitude ayein the pees,
Til God let sendé Moïses
To maké the deliveraunce.
And for his people great vengeaunce
He toke, which is to here a wonder.
The king was slain, the lond put under,
God bad the Reddé See devide,
Which stood upright on every side
And yaf unto his people a wey
That they on foot it passéd drey
And gone so forth into desért,
Where for to kepe hem in covert
The daiés whan the sonné brent
A largé cloude hem over went,
And for to wissen hem by night
A firy piller hem alight.
And whan that they for hunger pleigne,
The mighty God began to reine
Manna fro heven down to grounde,
Wherof that eche of hem hath founde
His foodé such right as him list.
And for they shuld upon him trist
Right as who set a tonne abroche
He percedé the hardé roche
And spronge out water all at wille,
That man and beste hath dronk his fille.
And afterward he yaf the lawe
To Moïses, that hem withdrawe
They shuldé nought fro that he bad.
And in this wisé they be lad,
Til they toke in possessiön
The londés of promissiön,
Where that Caleph and Josué
The marches upon such degre

Departen[1] after the lignáge
That eche of hem as heritage
His purparty[2] hath underfonge.
And thus stood this belevé longe,
Whiche of prophétés was govérned.
And they had eke the people lerned
Of great honoúr that shuld hem falle,
But atté mosté nede of alle
They faileden, whan Crist was bore.
But how that they her feith have lore
It nedeth nought to tellen all,
The matere is so generall.
"Whan Lucifer was best in heven
And oughté most have stonde in even,
Towardes God he toke debate,
And for that he was obstinate
And woldé nought to trouth encline
He fel for ever into ruíne.
"And Adam eke in Paradis,
Whan he stood most in all his pris
After the state of innocence,
Ayein the God brake his defence[3]
And fell out of his place awey.
And right by such a maner wey
The Jewés in her besté plite,
Whan that they sholden most parfite
Have stonde upon the prophecý,
Tho fellen they to most folý
And him which was fro heven come
And of a maid his flessh hath nome
And was among hem bore and fed,
As men that wolden nought be sped
Of Goddés Soné, with o vois
They heng and slough upon the crois,
Wherof the parfite of her lawe
Fro thenné forth hem was withdrawe,
So that they stonde of no meríte,
But in a truage[4] as folk subgíte
Withouté propreté of place
They liven oute of Goddés grace,
Dispers in allé londés oute.
And thus the feith is come aboute,
That whilome in the Jewés stood,
Whiche is nought parfitliché good.
To speke as it is now befalle
There is a feith aboven alle,
In which the trouthe is comprehended,
Wherof that we ben all amended.
"The high almighty magesté
Of rightwisnesse and of pité
The sinné which that Adam wrought,
Whan he sigh time, ayein he bought
And send His Sone fro the heven
To setté mannés soule in even,
Which thanné was so soré fall
Upon the point which was befall
That he ne might him self arise.
"Gregoiré saith in his apprise:
It helpeth nought a man be bore,
If Goddés Soné were unbore,
For thanné through the firsté sinne,
Which Adam whilom brought us inne,
There shulden allé men be lost;
But Crist restoreth thilké lost
And bought it with his flesshe and blood.
And if we thenken how it stood
Of thilké raunson which he paid,
As saint Gregoire it wrote and said,
All was behovely to the man.
For that wherof his wo began
Was after cause of all his welth,
Whan he which is the welle of helth,
The highé creatoúr of life,
Upon the nede of such a strife
So wolde he for his creätúre
Take on him self the forfeitúre
And suffre for the mannés sake.
Thus may no reson wel forsake[1]

[1] *Departen*, divide. [2] *Purparty*, share.
[3] *His defence*, his prohibition (that which was "defendu").
[4] *Truage*, homage.

[1] *Forsake*, deny.

That ilké sinne original
Ne was the cause in speciall
Of mannés worship atté last
Which shall withouten endé last.
For by that causé the godhede
Assembled was to the manhede
In the Virginé, where he nome
Our flesshe and verray man become
Of bodély fraternité,
Wherof the man in his degré
Stant moré worth, as I have told,
Than he stood erst by many fold,
Through baptisme of the newé lawe,
Of which Crist lord is and feláwe.
And thus the Highé Goddés might,
Which was in the Vírgine alight,
The mannés soule has reconciled,
Which haddé longé ben exiled.
So stant the feith upon beleve
Withouté which may non acheve.
But this beleve is so certain
To biggé[1] mannés soule ayein,
So full of grace and of vertú,
That what man clepeth[2] to Jesú
In clené life forth with goode dede,
He may nought faile of Heven mede
Which taken hath the righté feith.
For ellés, as the gospel saith,
Salvaciön there may be none.
And for to preché therupon
Crist bad to his apostles alle,
The whos powér as now is falle
On us that ben of holy chirche,
If we the godé dedés werche;
For feith onlý sufficeth nought
But if good dede also be wrought.
"Now were it good, that thou forthý,
Which through baptismé proprely
Art unto Cristés feith professed,
Beware that thou be nought oppressed
With anticristés Lollárdie.
For as the Jewés prophecie

[1] *Bigge*, buy. [2] Whatever man calls.

Was set of God for avauntáge,
Right so this newé tapinage[1]
Of Lollardïé goth aboute
To setté Cristés feith in doubte.
The saints that weren us to-fore,
By whom the feith was first up bore
That holy chirché stood releved,
They oughten better be beleved
Than thesé whiché that men knowe
Nought holy, though they feigne and blowe
Her Lollardy in mennés ere.
But if thou wolt live out of fere
Such newé lore I rede escheue,
And hold forth right the wey and sue
As thin auncéstres did er this,
So shalt thou nought beleve amis.
Crist wroughté first and after taught
So that the dede his word araught,
He yaf ensample in his persóne
And we tho wordés have alone,
Like to the tree with levés grene
Upon the which no fruit is sene.
"The prest Thoas, which of Minerve
The temple haddé for to serve
And the Palladion of Troy
Kept under keié, for monaie
Of Anthenor whiche he hath nome
Hath suffred Anthenor to come
And the Palladion to stele,
Wherof the worship and the wele
Of the Troiáns was overthrowe.
But Thoas atté samé throwe,
Whan Anthenor this jeuele toke,
Winkendé cast awey his loke
For a deceipte and for a wile,
As he that shuld him self beguile
He hid his eyen fro the sight
And wendé wel that he so might
Excuse his falsé consciënce.
I wot nought if thilke evidence
Now at this time in her estates
Excusé mighté the prelates,

[1] *Tapinage*, secret skulking.

Knowend how that the feith discreseth
And allé morál vertu ceseth
Wherof that they the keiés bere.
But yet hem liketh nought to stere
Her gostlich eyé for to se
The worlde in his adversité;
They wol no laboure undertake
To kepé that hem is betake.[1]
Crist deidé him self for the feith,
But now our ferful prelate saith;
'The life is swete,' and that he kepeth
So that the feith unholpé slepeth,
And they unto her ese entenden
And in her lust her life despenden,
And every man doth what him list.
Thus stant this world fulfilled of mist,
That no man seeth the righté wey.
The wardés of the chirché key
Through mishandlíngé ben miswreint,[2]
The worldés wawe[3] hath welnigh dreint
The ship which Peter hath to stere,
The forme is kept, but the matere
Transforméd is in other wise.
But if they weren gostly wise
And that the prelats weren good,
As they by oldé daiés stood,
It weré thanné litel nede
Among the men to taken hede
Of that they heren Pseudo[4] telle,
Which now is comé for to dwelle
To sowé cockel with the corn
So that the tilthe is nigh forlorn,
Which Crist sew first his owné hond.
Now stant the cockel in the lond,
Where stood whilom the godé greine,
For the prelats now, as men saín,
Forslouthen[1] that they sholden tille.
And that I trowé be the skille[2]
Whan there is lacke in hem above,
The people is straungéd to the love
Of trouth in cause of ignoraunce.
For where there is no purveaunce
Of light, men erren in the derke.
But if the prelats wolden werke
Upon the feith which they us teche,
Men sholden nought her waié seche
Withouté light as now is used;
Men se the charge all day refused
Whiche holy chirche hath undertake.

But who that wolde ensample take,
Gregoire upon his Omelie
Ayein the Slouthe of Prelacie
Compleigneth him and thus he saith:
'Whan Peter, fader of the feith,
At domésday shall with him bring
Judeam, which through his prechíng
He wan, and Andrew with Achay
Shall come his detté for to pay,
And Thomas eke with his beyete
Of Ynde, and Paul the routés grete
Of sondry londés to present,
And we fulfilled of londe and rent
Whiche of this worlde we holden here,
With voidé hondés shall appere,
Touchend our curé spirituall
Whiche is our charge in speciall,
I not what thing it may amounte
Upon thilke ende of our accompte
Where Crist him self is auditour,
Which taketh none hede of vein honoúr.
Thoffice of the chauncéllerie
Or of the kingés tresorie
Ne for ne write ne for ne taile[3]
To warrant may nought than availe.

[1] *Betake*, entrusted.
[2] *Miswreint*, wrenched out of shape.
[3] *Wawe*, wave. [4] *Pseudo*, false.

[1] *Forslouthen*, waste by their slouth.
[2] *Skille*, reason.
[3] *Taile*, tally, used for checking of accounts.

The world which now so wel we trow
Shall make us thanné but a mowe,
So passé we withouté mede,
That we none otherwisé spede
But as we redé that he spedde,
The whiche his lordés besant[1] hadde
And therupon gat none encres.
But at his timé nethéles
What other man his thank deserve
The world so lusty is to serve
That we with him ben all accorded,
And that is wist and well recorded
Throughout this erthe in allé londes;
Let knightés winné with her hondes,
For ouré tungé shall be still
And stande upon the flesshés will;
It were a travail for to preche
The feith of Crist, as for to teche
The folké painim; it woll nought be:
But every prelate holde his see
With allé such as he may gete
Of lusty drinke and lusty mete,
Wherof the body fat and full
Is unto gostly labour dull
And slough to handle thilké plough.
But ellés we ben swifte inough
Toward the worldés Avarice.
And that is as a sacrifice,
Which after that thapostle saith
Is openly ayein the feith
Unto the ydols yove and graunted,
But netheles as it is now haunted
And vertue chaungéd into vice,
So that Largesse is Avarice,
In whose chapitre now we trete."—
"My fader, this matere is bete
So far, that ever while I live
I shall the better hedé yive
Unto my self by many wey.
But over this now wolde I prey
To wité, what the braunches are
Of Avarice, and how they fare
Als well in love as otherwise."—
"My sone, and I the shall devise

[1] *Besant*, a gold coin of Byzantium; talent.

In suche a maner as they stonde,
So that thou shalt hem understonde.
"Dame Avarice is nought soleine,[1]
Which is of gold the capiteine.
But of her Courte in sondry wise
After the scole of her apprise
She hath of servaunts many one,
Wherof that Covetise is one,
Which góth the largé worlde about
To seché thavauntáges out
Where that he may the profit winne
To Avarice and bringeth it inne.
That one halt and that other draweth,
There is no day which hem bedaweth[2]
No more the sonné than the mone,
Whan there is any thing to done,
And namély with Covetise,
For he stant out of all assise
Of resonáble mannes fare
Where he purpóseth him to fare
Upon his lucre and his beyete.
The smallé path, the largé strete,
The furlonge and the longé mile,
All is but one for thilké while.
And for that he is such one holde,
Dame Avarice him hath witholde,[3]
As he which is the principall
Outward,[4] for he is over all
A purveioúr and an espy.
For right as of an hungry py
The storvé bestés ben awaited,
Right so is Covetise affaited
To loké where he may purchace,[5]
For by his will he wolde embrace
All that this widé world beclippeth.
But ever he somwhat overhippeth[6]
That he ne may nought all fulfille
The lustés of his gredy wille.
But where it falleth in a londe,

[1] *Soleine*, single.
[2] *Bedaweth*, awakes.
[3] *Witholde*, held with.
[4] *Outward*, watcher outside.
[5] *Purchace*, get booty.
[6] *Overhippeth*, hops over.

That Covetise in mighty honde
Is set, it is full hard to fede.
For than he taketh none other hede
But that he may purcháce and gete,
His consciénce hath all foryete
And nought what thing it may amounte
That he shall afterwarde accompte.
But as the luce[1] in his degre
Of tho that lassé ben than he
The fisshes gredily devoureth,
So that no water hem soccoúreth,
Right so no lawé may rescowe
Fro him that woll no right allowe.
For where that such one is of might,
His will shall stonde in stede of right.
Thus be the men destruied full ofte,
Till that the greté God alofte
Ayein so great a Covetise
Redresse it in his owné wise.
And in ensample of allé tho
I finde a talé writé so,
The which for it is good to lere
Herafterward thou shalt it here.
"Whan Romé stood in noble plite,
Virgilé, which was tho parfite,
A Mirrour made of his clergie[2]
And sette it in the townés eye
Of marbre on a pillér without,
That they by thritty mile about
By day and eke also by night
In that Mirroúr beholdé might
Her ennemies, if any were,
With all her ordenauncé there
Which they ayein the citee cast.
So that while thilké Mirrour last,
Ther was no lond which might acheve
With werré Romé for to greve,
Wherof was great envïé tho.
And fell that ilké timé so,
That Romé haddé werrés stronge
Ayein Cartáge, and stoden longe
The two citees upon debate.
Cartágé sigh the strong estate
Of Rome in thilké mirrour stonde,
And thought all prively to fonde
To overthrowe it by some wile.
And Hanibal was thilké while
The prince and leader of Cartáge,
Which haddé set all his coráge
Upon knighthode in such a wise
That he by worthy and by wise
And by none other was counseiled,
Wherof the world is yet merveiled
Of the maistrïés that he wrought
Upon the marches which he sought.
And fell in thilké time also,
The kinge of Puilé, which was tho,
Thought ayein Romé to rebelle,
And thus was také the quarelle,
How to destruie the Mirrour.
Of Romé tho was emperoúr
Crassus, which was so covetoús,
That he was ever desiroús,
Of gold to geté the pilage,
Wherof that Puile and eke Cartage
With philosóphres wise and great
Beginne of this matere to treat.
And atté last in this degre
There weren philosóphres thre
To do this thing whiche undertoke;
And therupon they with hem toke
A great tresúre of gold in cofres
To Rome, and thus these philosóphres
To-gider in compaígnie went,
But no man wisté what they ment.
Whan they to Romé comé were,
So privély they dwelté there
As they that thoughten to deceive;
Was none that might of hem perceive
Till they in sondry stedés have
Her gold under the erth begrave
In two tresórs that to beholde
They sholden seme as they were olde.

[1] *Luce*, pike. [2] By his learning.

And so forth than upon a day
All openly in good array
To themperoúr they hem present
And tolden it was her entent
To dwellen under his servíse;
And he hem axeth in what wise.
And they him told in such a plite[1]
That eche of hem had a spirite
The which slepénd anight appereth
And hem by sondry dremés lereth
After the world that hath betid,
Under the grounde if ought be hid
Of old tresór at any throwe,
They shall it in her swevenes[2] knowe.
And upon this conditión
They sain, what gold under the town
Of Rome is hid, they woll it finde,
There shuldé nought beleft behinde
Be so that he the halvé dele
Hem graunt, and he assenteth wele.
And thus cam Sleighté for to dwelle
With Covetise as I the telle.
This emperoúr bad redély,
That they be logéd faste by,
Where he his owné body lay.
And whan it was at morwe day,
That one of hem saith that he mette[3]
Where he a gold hord shuldé fette,
Wherof this emperoúr was glad.
And therupon anone he bad
His minours for to go and mine,
And he him self of that covine
Goth forth withall, and at his honde
The tresor redy there he fonde
Where as they said it shuldé be.
And who was thanné glad but he?
"Upon that other day secounde
They have an other gold hord founde,
Which the secondé maister toke
Upon his sweven and undertoke.
And thus the soth experiénce
To themperour yaf such credénce,

[1] *Plite*, promise. [2] *Swevenes*, dreams.
[3] *Mette*, dreamed.

That all his trust and all his feith
So sikerliche on hem he laith
Of that he found him so releved,[1]
That they ben parfitly beleved,
As though they weré goddés thre.
Now herkeneth the subtilite
The thriddé maister shuldé mete,
Whiche as they saiden was unmete[2]
Above hem all, and couthé most,
And he withouté noise or bost
All privelich, so as he wolde,
Upon the morwe his swevenes tolde
To themperoúr right in his ere
And said him, that he wiste where
A tresor was so plenteoús
Of golde and eke so precioús
Of jeuellés and of rich stones,
That unto all his hors at ones
It were a chargé suffisaunt.
This lord upon this covenaunt
Was glad and axeth where it was:
The maister said, under the glas.
He tolde him eke as for the mine
He wolde ordeigné such engine,
That they the werk shulde undersette
With timber, and withouté lette
Men may the tresor saufly delve,
So that the Mirrour by him selve
Without empeirément shal stonde.
All this the maister upon honde
Hath undertake in allé wey.
This lord, whiche had his wit awey
And was with Covetisé blent,
Anone therto yaf his assent.
And thus they miné forth withall,
The timber set up over all,
Wherof the piller stood upright;
Till it befell upon a night
These clerkés, whan they weré ware
How that the timber only bare
The piller where the Mirrour stood,—

[1] *Releved*, enriched, as by reliefs and fines.
[2] *Unmete*, immeasurably.

Her sleighté no man understood,—
They go by night unto the mine
With pitch, with sulphre and rosine,
And whan the citee was aslepe,
A wildé fire into the depe
They cast among the timber werke,
And so forth while the night was derke
Desguiséd in a pouer array
They passeden the towne er day.
And whan they come upon an hille,
They sighen how the Mirrour felle,
Wherof they madé joy inough,
And eche of hem with other lough
And saiden, 'Lo, what Covetise
May do with hem that be nought wise!'
And that was provéd afterwarde,
For every lond to Romé warde,
Whiche haddé be subgit to-fore,
Whan this Mirroúr was so forlore
And they the wonder herdé say,
Anone begunné disobey
With werrés upon every side.
And thus hath Romé lost his pride
And was defouléd over all.
For this I finde of Hanibal,
That he of Romains in a day
Whan he hem found out of array,
So great a multitudé slough,
That of gold ringes which he drough
Of gentil hondés that ben dede
Busshellés fullé thre I rede
He filled, and made a brigge also
That he might over Tiber go
Upon the corps that dedé were
Of the Romains whiche he slough there.
"But now to speke of the juise,
The which after the Covetise
Was take upon this emperour,
For he destruiéd the Mirrour,
It is a wonder for to here.
The Romains maden a chaiere
And set her emperour therinne
And saiden, for he woldé winne
Of gold the superfluité,
Of golde he shuldé such plenté
Receivé till he saidé 'ho.'
And with gold which they haddé tho
Boilendé hot within a panne,
Into his mouth they pouré thanne.
And thus the thurst of gold was queint
With gold whiche haddé ben atteint.
"Wherof, my soné, thou might here,
Whan Covetise hath lost the stere
Of resonáble governaunce,
There falleth ofté great grevaunce.
For there may be no worsé thing
Than Covetise about a king.
If it in his personé be
It doth the more adversité;
And if it in his counseil stonde
It bringeth all day mischéfe to honde
Of comun harme; and if it growe
Within his court, it woll be knowe,
For thanné shall the king be pilled.[1]
The man, whiche hath his londé tilled,
Awaiteth nought more redély
The hervest, than they gredily
Ne maken thanné warde and wacche
Where they the profit mighten cacche.
And yet full oft it falleth so,
As men may sene among hem tho,
That he which most coveiteth fast
Hath leest avauntage atté last.
For whan fortúne is there ayein,
Though he coveite it is in veine,
The happés ben nought allé liche,
One is made pouer, an other riche,
The court to some it doth profite,
And some ben ever in o plite.
And yet they both aliché sore
Coveité, but fortúne is more

1 *Pilled*, fleeced.

Unto that o part favouráble;
And though it be nought resonáble,
This thing a man may sene al day,
Wherof that I the tellé may
After ensample in remembraúnce,
How every man may take his chaunce
Or of richesse or of pouerte,
How so it stonde of the deserte.
Here is nought every thing acquit,
For oft a man may se this yit
That who best doth lest thank shal have;
It helpeth nought, the world to crave,
Whiche out of reule and of mesúre
Hath ever stonde in aventúre
Als well in court as ellés where;
And how in oldé daiés there
It stood so as the thingés felle,
I thenke a talé for to telle.

"In a croniqué this I rede:
About a kinge as it must nede
There was of knightés and squiérs
Great route and eke of officérs.
Some of long time him hadden served
And thoughten that they have deserved
Avauncément and gone withoute;
And some also ben of the route
That comen but a while agone,
And they avauncéd were anone.
These oldé men upon this thing
So as they durst ayein the king
Among hem self compleignen ofte.
But there is nothing said so softe,
That it ne cometh out at last.
The king it wist anone als fast
As he which was of high prudence.
He shope therfore an evidence
Of hem that pleignen in that cas,
To knowe in whose default it was.
And all within his owne entent,
That no man wisté what it ment
Anone he let two cofres make
Of one semblaunce and of o make,
So lich that no life thilké throwe[1]
That one may fro that other knowe.
They were into his chambre brought,
But no man wot why they be wrought.
And nethéles the king hath bede,
That they be set in privé stede,
As he that was of wisdom sligh.
Whan he therto his timé sigh
All privelich, that none it wist,
His owné hondés that o kist
Of fine golde and of fine perrie,
The which out of his tresorie
Was take, anone he fildé full,
That other cofre of strawe and mull[2]
With stonés meind he filde also.
Thus be they fullé bothé two.
So that erliche upon a day
He bad withinné where he lay
There shuldé be to-fore his bedde
A borde up set and fairé spredde.
And than he let the cofres fet,
Upon the borde and did hem set.[3]
He knew the namés well of tho,
The whiche ayein him grucché so
Both of his chambre and of his halle,
Anone and sendé for hem alle
And saidé to hem in this wise:
'There shall no man his hap despise;
I wot well ye have longé served,
And God wot what ye have deserved.
But if it is along on me
Of that ye unavauncéd be
Or ellés it belonge on you,
The sothé shall be proved now
To stoppé with your evil worde.
Lo here two cofres on the borde,

1 Nobody at that time.
2 *Mull*, dirt, rubbish.
3 And caused them to be set upon the board.

Chese whiche you list of bothé two
And witeth well, that one of tho
Is with tresór so full begon
That if ye happé therupon
Ye shal be riché men for ever.
Now chese and take whiche you is lever.
But be well ware, er that ye take,
For of that one I undertake
There is no maner good therinne
Whereof ye mighten profit winne.
Now goth to-gider of one assent
And taketh your advisément,
For but I you this day avaunce
It stant upon your owné chaunce:
All only in default of grace
So shall be shewed in this place
Upon you allé well and fine,
That no defaulté shall be mine.'
"They knelen all and with one vois
The king they thonken of this chois.
And after that they up arise
And gon aside and hem avise
And atté lasté they accorde,
Wherof her talé to recorde
To what issué they be falle
A knight shall speké for hem alle.
He kneleth down unto the king
And saith, that they upon this thing
Or for to winne or for to lese
Ben all aviséd for to chese.
"Tho toke this knight a yerd on hond
And goth there as the cofres stond
And with thassent of everychone
He laïth his yerde upon one
And saith the king how thilké same
They chese in reguerdón by name,
And preith him that they might it have.
The king, which wold his honour save,
When he hath herd the comun vois
Hath graunted hem her owné chois
And toke hem therupon the key.
But for he wolde it weré say
What good they have as they suppose,
He bad anone the cofre unclose,—
Which was fulfilled with straw and stones,
Thus be they servéd all at ones.
This king than in the samé stede
Anone that other cofre undede,
Where as they sighen great richesse
Wel moré than they couthen gesse.
'Lo,' saith the king, 'now may ye se,
That there is no defaulte in me,
Forthý my self I woll acquite
And bereth ye your owné wite [1]
Of that fortúne hath you refused.'
Thus was this wisé king excused,
And they lefte of her evil speche
And mercy of her king beseche.
"Somdele to this materé like
I finde a tale, how Frederike,
Of Romé that time emperour,
Herde, as he went, a great clamoúr
Of two beggers upon the way,
That one of hem began to say:
'Ha lord, wel may the man be riche,
Whom that a king list for to riche.'
That other said: 'No thingé so,
But he is riche and well bego,
To whom that God wol sendé wele.'
And thus they maden wordés fele,
Wherof this lord hath hedé nome
And did hem bothé for to come
To the paleis where he shall ete,
And bad ordeigné for her mete
Two pastees which he let do make;
A capon in that one was bake,
And in that other, for to winne,
Of floreins all that may withinne
He let do put a great richesse,
And even aliche as man may gesse
Outward they weré bothé two.
This begger was commaunded tho,

[1] *Wite*, blame.

He that which held him to the king,
That he first chese upon this thing.
He sigh hem, but he felt hem nought,
So that upon his owne thought
He chese the capon and forsoke
That other, which his felaw toke.
But whan he wist how that it ferde,
He said aloud, that men it herde:
'Now have I certainly conceived,
That he may lightly be deceived
That tristeth unto mannes helpe.
But wel is him, that God wol helpe,
For he stant on the siker side,
Whiche ellés shuldé go beside.
I se my felaw wel recouer,
And I mot dwellé stillé pouer.
Thus spake the begger his entent,
And pouer he cam and pouer he went,
Of that he hath richessé sought
His infortúne it woldé nought.
So may it shewe in sondry wise
Betwene Fortune and Covetise
The chaunce is cast upon a dee,
But yet full oft a man may see
Inough of suché nethéles
Which ever put hem self in pres
To get hem good, and yet they faile.
"And for to speke of this entaile
Touchend of Love in thy matere,
My godé sone, as thou might here,
That right as it with tho men stood
Of infortúne of worldés good,
As thou hast herd me tell above,
Right so full ofte it stant by Love;
Though thou coveite it evermore
Thou shalt nought have o dele the more,
But only that which the is shape,
The remenaunt is but a jape.
And nethéles inough of tho
There ben that now coveiten so
That where as they a woman se,
To ten or twelvé though there be,
The love is now so unavised
That where the beauté stant assised
The mannes herte anone is there
And rouneth[1] talés in her ere
And saith, how that he loveth streite.
And thus he set him to coveite,
An hundred though he sigh a day,
So wolde he moré than he may.
So for the greté Covetise
Of soty[2] and of fool emprise
In eche of hem he fint somwhat,
That pleseth him, or this or that:
Some one, for she is white of skinne,
Some one, for she is noble of kinne,
Some one, for she hath a rody cheke,
Some one, for that she semeth meke,
Some one, for she hath eyen grey,
Some one, for she can laugh and pley,
Some one, for she is longe and small,
Some one, for she is lithe and tall,
Some one, for she is pale and bleche,
Some one, for she is softe of speche,
Some one, for that she is camused,[3]
Some one, for she hath nought ben used,
Some one, for she can daunce and sing,
So that some thing of his liking
He fint; and though no more he fele
But that she hath a litel hele,
It is inough, that he therfore
Her love; and thus an hundred score,
While they be new, he wolde he had,
Whom he forsaketh she shall be bad.
The blindé man no colour demeth,
But all is one right as him semeth;
So hath his lust no jugément
Whom Covetise of Lové blent.[4]
Him thenketh, to his Covetise,
How all the world ne may suffise,
For by his will he wolde have all,
If that it mighté so befall.
So is he comun as the strete,

[1] *Rouneth*, whisper. [2] *Soty*, folly.
[3] *Camused*, with a curve in the nose.
[4] *Blent*, blinds.

I setté nought of his beyete.
My sone, hast thou such covetise?"—
"Nay fader, such love I despise,
And while I livé shal don ever,
For in good feith yet had I lever
Than to coveite in suche a wey
To ben for ever till I deie
As pouer as Job and lovéles
Out taken one, for havéles
His thonkés[1] is no man alive,
For that a man shulde all unthrive
There ought no wisé man coveite,
The lawé was nought set so streite.
Forthý my self withall to save
Suche one there is I woldé have
And none of all this other mo."—
"My sone, of that thou woldest so,
I am nought wroth; but over this
I woll the tellen howe it is.
For there be men which other wise
Right only for the covetise
Of that they seen a woman riche,
There wol they all her love affiche.
Nought for the beauté of her face,
Ne yet for vertu, ne for grace,
Which she hath ellés right inough,
But for the parke and for the plough
And other thing which therto longeth,
For in none other wise hem longeth
To lové but[2] they profit finde.
And if the profit be behinde,
Her[3] love is ever lesse and lesse,
For after that she hath richesse
Her love is of proportión.
If thou hast such conditión,
My soné, tell right as it is."—
"Min holy fader, nay iwis,
Condición such have I none.
For truly fader, I love one
So well, with all min hertés thought,
That certés though she haddé nought
And were as pouer as Medeá,
Which was exiléd for Creusá,
I wolde her nought the lassé love;
Ne though she were at her above
As was the riché quene Candace,
Which to deservé love and grace
To Alisaundre that was king
Yaf many a worthy riché thing;
Or ellés as Pantasilee,
Which was the quene of Feminee
And great richessé with her nam
Whan she for love of Hector cam
To Troy in rescousse of the town;
I am of such condicióun,
That though my lady of her selve
Were al so riche as suché twelve,
I couthé nought though it were so
No better love her than I do.
For I love in so pleine[1] a wise,
That for to speke of Covetise
As for pouerte or for richesse
My love is nouther more ne lesse.
For in good feith I trowé this,
So covetous no man there is
For why and he my lady sigh
That he through loking of his eye
Ne shuld have such a stroke withinne
That for no gold he mighté winne
He shuldé nought her love asterte
But if he lefté there his herte:
Be so it weré such a man
That couthé skille of a womán.
For there ben men so rudé some
Whan they among the women come
They gon under protectiön,
That love and his affectiön
Ne shal nought take hem by the sleve
For they ben out of that beleve;
Hem lusteth of no lady chere,
But ever thenken there and here
Where that her golde is in the cofre
And wol none other lové profer.

[1] *Haveles his thonkes*, wanting possession, with his own good will.
[2] *But*, unless.
[3] *Her* their.

[1] *Pleine*, full.

But who so wot what love amounteth
And by resón truliche accompteth,
Than may he knowe and taken hede
That all the lust of womanhede
Which may ben in a ladies face
My lady hath, and eke of grace,
If men shuld yiven her apprise
They may wel say how she is wise
And sober and simple of countenaunce,
And all that to good governaunce
Belongeth of a worthy wight
She hath pleinlý. For thilké night
That she was bore as for the nones
Natúré set in her at ones
Beauté with bounté so besein,
That I may well afferme and sain,
I sigh yet never creätúre
Of comlyhede and of fetúre
In any kingés región
Be liche her in comparisón.
And therto, as I have you tolde,
Yet hath she more a thousand folde
Of bounté, and shortlý to telle
She is the puré hede and welle
And mirrour and ensample of good;
Who so her vertues understood
Me thenketh it ought inough suffise
Withouten other Covetise
To lové suche one and to serve,
Which with her cheré can deserve
To be belovéd better iwis
Than she par cas that richest is
And hath of golde a millión.
Suche hath be min opinión
And ever shall. But nethéles
I say she is nought havéles,[1]
That she nis riche and well at ese
And hath inough wherwith to plese
Of worldés good whom that her list.
But o thing wold I wel ye wist,
That never for no worldés good
Min hert unto ward hiré stood,
But only right for puré love,
That wot the highé God above.
Now fader, what say ye therto?"—
"My sone, I say it is wel do.
For take of this right good beleve,
What man that wol him self releve
To love in any other wise
He shall wel finde his Covetise
Shall soré greve him atté laste,
For such a lové may nought laste.
But now men sain in ouré daies
Men maken but a few assaies
But if the causé be richesse,
Forthý the love is well the lesse.
And who that wold ensamples telle
By oldé daiés as they felle,
Than might a man wel understonde
Such lové may nought longé stonde.
Now herken, sone, and thou shalt here
A great ensample of this matere.
To trete upon the cas of love,
So as we tolden here above,
I findé write a wonder thing.
Of Puilé whilom was a king,
A man of high complexion
And yong, but his affection
After the nature of his age
Was yet not falle in his corágé
The lust of women for to knowe.
So it betid upon a throwe,
This lord fell into great sikenesse.
Phisique hath done the besinesse
Of sondry curés many one
To make him hole, and therupon
A worthy maister which there was,
Yaf him counseil upon this cas,
That if he wolde have parfite hele,
He shuldé with a woman dele.
For than he said him redely,
That he shal be al hole therby,
And other wise he knew no cure.
The king, which stood in aventúre
Of life and deth for medicine,
Assented was, and of covine
His steward, whom he trusteth well,

[1] *Havéles*, wanting possessions.

He toke and told him every dele,
How that this maister haddé said.
And therupon he hath him praid
And chargéd upon his legeaúnce,
That he do maké purveaúnce
And badde him, how that ever it
stood,
That he shall sparé for no good,
For his will is right well to pay.
The steward said, he wolde assay.
"But now here after thou shalt
wite,
As I finde in the bokés write,
What Covetise in Lové doth.
This steward, for to tellé soth,
Amongés all the men alive
A lusty lady hath to wive,
Which nethéles for gold he toke
And nought for love, as saith the
boke.
A riché marchaunt of the londe
Her fader was, and he her fonde
So worthély and such richesse
Of worldés good and such largesse
With her he yaf in mariáge,
That only for thilke avauntáge
Of good the steward hath her take,
For lucre and nought for lovés sake.
And that was afterward wel sene.
Nowe herken, what it woldé mene.
This steward in his owné hert
Sigh that his lord may nought astert
His maladië but he have
A lusty woman him to save,
And tho he woldé yive inough
Of his tresor; wherof he drough
Great Covetise into his minde
And set his honour fer behinde.
Thus he whom gold hath oversette
Was trappéd in his owné nette.
The gold hath made his wittés lame,
So that sechénd his owné shame
He rouneth in the kingés ere
And said him that he wisté where
A gentil and a lusty one
Tho was, and thider wold he gone,
But he mote yivé yeftés great,
For but it be through great beyete
Of gold, he said, he shuld nought
spede.
The king him bad upon the nede
That take an hundred pound he
sholde
And yive it wheré that he wolde,
Be so it were in worthy place.
And thus to stonde in lovés grace
This king his gold hath abandóned.
And whan this tale was full rouned,
The steward toke the gold and went
Within his herte and many a went[1]
Of covetisé than he caste,
Wherof a purpos atté laste
Ayein love and ayein his right
He toke and saide, how thilké night
His wife shall liggé by the king.
And goth thenkénd upon this thing
Toward his inn till he cam home
Into the chambre, and than he nome
His wife and tolde her al the cas.
And she, which red for shamé was,
With bothe her hondés hath him
praid
Knelénd and in this wise said,
That she to reson and to skill
In what thing that he biddé will
Is redy for to done his heste
But[2] this thing that were nought
honéste,
That he for gold her shuldé selle.
And he tho with his wordés felle
Forth with his gastly countenaunce
Saith, that she shall done obeisaúnce
And folwe his wille in every place.
And thus through strength of his
manáce
Her innocénce is overladde,
Wherof she was so sore adradde,
That she his will mot nede obey.
And therupon was shape a wey.

[1] *Went*, turn. [2] *But*, except.

When it was nigh upon the day
The steward thanné where she lay
Cam to the bed and in this wise
Hath biddé that she shulde arise.
The king saith: 'Nay, she shall nought go.'
The steward said ayein: 'Nought so,
For she mot gone er it be knowe,
And so I swore at thilké throwe,
Whan I her fetté to you here.'
The king his talé wol nought here
And saith how that he hath her bought
Forthý she shall departé nought,
But who she was he knew nothing.
Tho cam the steward to the king
And praid him that withouté shame
In saving of her godé name
He mighté leaden home ayeine
This lady, and hath told him pleine
How that it was his owné wife.
The king his ere unto this strife
Hath leid, and whan that he it herde,
Well nigh out of his wit he ferde
And said: 'Ha, caitif most of alle,
Where was it ever er this befalle,
That any cokard in this wise
Betoke his wife for covetise.
Thou hast bothe her and me beguiled
And eke thin own estate reviled,
Wherof that buxom unto the
Here after shall she never be.
For this avow to God I make
After this day, if I the take,
Thou shalt be hongéd and to-drawe.
Now loke anone thou be withdrawe,
So that I se the never more!'
This steward thanné drad him sore,
With all the hasté that he may
And fled awey the samé day,
And was exiléd out of lond.

Lo, there a nicé husébond,
Which thus hath loste his wife for ever.
But nethéles she hadde a lever;
The king her weddeth and honoúreth,
Wherof her namé she soccoúreth,
Which erst was lost through covetise
Of him that lad her other wise
And hath him self also forlore.

"My soné, be thou ware therfore,
Where thou shalt love in any place,
That thou no Covetise embrace,
The which is nought of Lovés kinde.
But for all that a man may finde
Now in this time of thilké rage
Full great disese in mariáge,
Whan venim medleth with the sucre
And mariáge is made for lucre
Or for the lust or for the hele,
What man that shall with other dele
He may nought failé to repent."—

"My fader, such is min entent.
But nethéles good is to have,
For good may ofté timé save
The lové which shulde ellés spille.
But God which wot min hertes wille
I dar wel také to witnésse,
Yet was I never for richesse
Beset with mariágé none,
For all min herte is upon one
So frely that in the persone
Stant all my worldés joy alone.
I axé nouther park ne plough,
If I her hadde, it were inough,
Her lové shuldé me suffise
Withouten other Covetise.
Lo now, my fader, as of this
Touchend of me right as it is
My shrifte I am beknowé plein,
And if ye wol ought elles sain
Of Covetise if there be more
In Love, agropeth out the sore.

My soné, thou shalt understonde,
How Covetise hath yet on honde
In speciáll two counseilors,
That ben also his prócurors.
The first of hem is Fals Witnesse,

Which ever is redy to witnesse
What thing his maister woll him hote.[1]
Perjúrie is the second hote,[2]
Which spareth nought to swere an othe
Though it be fals and God be wrothe,
That oné shall fals witnesse bere,
That other shall the thing forswere
When he is chargéd on the boke.
So what with hoke and what with croke
They make her maister ofte winne
And woll nought knowé what is sinne
For Covetise, and thus men sain
They maken many a fals bargaín.
There may no trewé quarel arise
In thilké queste of thilke assise
Where as they two the people enforme.
For they kepe ever o[3] maner forme,
That upon golde her[4] consciénce
They founde and take her evidénce.
And thus with Fals Witnesse and othes
They winne hem meté, drink and clothes.
Right so there be, who that hem knewe,
Of these lovérs ful many untrewe.
Now may a woman finde inow,
That eche of hem whan he shall wowe
Anone he woll his hand down lain
Upon a boke and swere and sain
That he woll feith and trouthé bere.
And thus he profreth him to swere
To serven ever till he deie,
And all is verray trechery.
For whan the soth him selven trieth,
The more he swereth the more he lieth,

[1] *Hote*, command. [2] *Hote*, called.
[3] *O*, one. [4] *Her*, their.

Whan he his feith maketh allthermest,[1]
Than may a woman trust him lest,
For till he may his will acheve,
He is no lenger for to leve.
Thus is the trouth of love exiled,
And many a good womán beguiled.
"And eke to speke of Fals Witnesse
There be now many such I gesse,
That lich unto the provisoúrs
They make her privé procuroûrs
To tell how there is such man,
Which is worthý to love and can
All that a good man shuldé conne,
So that with lesing is begonne
The cause, in which they woll procede.
And al so siker as the Crede
They make of that they knowen fals,
And thus full oft about the hals[2]
Love is of falsé men embraced.
But lové which is so purcháced,
Cometh afterward to litel prise.
Forthý, my sone, if thou be wise,
Now thou hast herd this evidence,
Thou might thin owné consciënce
Oppose, if thou hast be such one."—
"Nay God wot, fader, I am none
Ne never was, for, as men saith,
Whan that a man shall make his feith
His hert and tungé must accorde.
For if so be that they discorde
Than he is fals, and ellés nought,
And I dare say as of my thought
In love it is nought discordáble
Unto my word, but accordáble.
And in this wisé, fader, I
May righté well swere and sauflý,
That I my lady lové well,
For that accordeth every dele;
It nedeth nought to my soth sawe
That I witnessé shuldé drawe

[1] *Alltherme st*, most of all.
[2] *Hals*, neck.

Into this day, for ever yit
Ne might it sinke into my wit
That I my counseil shouldé say
To any wight or me bewrey [1]
To sechen helpe in such manere,
But onely for my lady dere.
And though a thousand men it wiste
That I her love, and than hem liste
With me to swere and to witnésse,
Yet weré that no fals witnésse.
For I dare unto this trouth dwelle,
I love her more than I can telle.
Thus am I, fader, giltéles,
As ye have herde, and nethéles
In youré dome I put it all."—
"My soné, wite in speciall
It shall nought comunliché faile,
All though it for a time availe
That Fals Witnesse his causé spede
Upon the point of his falshede;
It shall well afterward be kid,
Wherof so as it is betid
Ensample of such thingés blinde
In a croniqué write I finde.
The goddesse of the see Thetis,
She had a sone, and his name is
Achilles, whom to kepe and warde,
While he was yonge, and into warde
She thought him saufly to betake
As she which draddé for his sake
Of that was said of prophecie,
That he at Troié sholdé deie
Whan that the citee was belein.
Forthý so as the bokés sain,
She cast her wit in sondry wise,
How she him mighté so desguise
That no man shuld his body knowe.
And so befell that ilké throwe
While that she thought upon this
dede,
There was a king, which Lichomede
Was hote, and he was well begone
With fairé doughters many one
And dwelté fer out in an ile.

[1] *Me bewrey*, disclose myself.

Now shalt thou here a wonder wile.
This quené which the mother was
Of Áchillés, upon this cas
Her sone as he a maiden were
Let clothen in the samé gere,
Which longeth unto womanhede.
And he was yonge and toke none
hede
But suffreth all that she him dede,
Wherof she hath her women bede
And chargeth by her othés alle,
How so it afterward befalle,
That they discover nought this thing,
But feigne and make a knouleching
Upon the counseil which was nome,
In every placé where they come
To telle and to witnéssé this,
Howe he her ladies doughter is.
And right in such a maner wise
She bad they shuld her don servíse,
So that Achilles underfongeth
As to a yong ladý belongeth
Honoúr, servíce and reverénce.
For Thetis with great diligence
Him hath so taught and so affaited
That, how so that he were awaited,
With sobre and goodly contenaunce
He shuld his womanhede avaunce
That none the sothé knowé might,
But that in every mannés sight
He shuldé seme a puré maide.
And in such wise as she him said
Achilles, which that ilké while
Was yonge, upon him selfe to smile
Began, whan he was so besein.
And thus after the bokés sain
With frette of perle upon his hede
All fresshé betwene white and red,
As he which tho was tender of age,
Stood the coloúr in his viságe,
That for to loke upon his cheke
And seen his childly maner eke
He was a woman to beholde.
And than his moder to him tolde,
That she him haddé so begone

By causé that she thoughté gone
To Lichomede at thilké tide,
Where that she said, he shulde abide
Amonge his doughters for to dwelle.
Achilles herd his moder telle
And wisté nought the causé why.
And nethéles full buxomlý
He was redý to that she bad,
Wherof his moder was right glad.
To Lichomede and forth they went,
And whan the king knewe her entent
And sigh this yongé doughter there,
And that it came unto his ere
Of such recórd, of such witnesse,
He haddé right a great gladnésse
Of that he bothé sigh and herde,
As he that wot nought how it ferde
Upon the counseil of the nede.
But for all that king Lichomede
Hath toward him his doughter take
And for Thetís his moder sake
He put her into compaigny
To dwellé with Deïdamy,
His owné doughter the eldést,
The fairest and the comliest
Of al his doughters which he had.
Lo, thus Thetís the causé lad
And lefté there Achilles feigned,
As he which hath him self restreigned
In all that ever he may and can
Out of the maner of a man
And toke his womanisshé chere,
Wherof unto his beddéfere
Deïdamý he hath by night,
Where kindé will him selvé right
After the philosóphres sain,
There may no wight be there ayein.
And it befell that ilké throwe
At Troié, where the siegé lay
Upon the cause of Menelay
And of his quené dame Heleine,
The Gregois hadden mochel peine
All day to fight and to assaile.
But for they mighten nought availe
So noble a citee for to winne
A privé counseil they beginne
In sondry wisé where they treat
And atté laste among the great
They fellen unto this accorde,
That Protheus of his recorde,
Which was an astronomien
And eke a great magicien,
Shulde of his calculatión
Sechen of constellatión
How they the citee mighten gette;
And he, which haddé nought foryete
Of that belongeth to a clerke,
His study set upon this werke.
So longe his wit about he caste,
Till that he founde out atté laste,
But if they hadden Áchilles
Her werré shall ben endéles.
And over that he tolde hem pleine
In what manér he was beseine
And in what place he shall be founde;
So that within a litel stounde[1]
Ulixes forth with Diomede
Upon this point to Lichomede
Agámenon to-gider sente.
But Ulixes, er he forth wente,
Which was one of the mosté wise
Ordeinéd hath in such a wise,
That he the mosté riche array
Wherof a woman may be gay
With him he toké manifolde;
And overmore, as it is tolde,
An harneis for a lusty knight,
Which burnéd was as silver bright,
Of swerde, of plate, and eke of maile,
As though he shuldé do bataile,
He toke also with him by ship.
And thus to-gider in felaship
Forth gone this Diomede and he
In hopé till they mighten se
The placé where Achilles is.
The wind stood thanné nought amis,
But every topsailecole[2] it blewe,
Till Úlixés the marches knewe,

[1] *Stounde*, interval of time, hour.
[2] *Topsailecole. Cole*, in Godefroy's *Dictionnaire de l'Ancienne Langue Française*, is an

Where Lichomede his regné had.
The stirésman so well him lad
That they ben comen sauf to londe,
Where they gone out upon the stronde
Into the burgh, where that they founde
The king; and he which hath facounde,[1]
Ulixes, didé the messáge.
But the counseile of his coráge,[2]
Why that he came, he toldé nought,
But underneth he was bethought
In what manér he might aspie
Achilles fro Deïdamý
And fro these other that there were,
Full many a lusty lady there.
"They plaide hem there a day or two,
And as it was fortúned so,
It fell that time in suche a wise
To Bachus that a sacrifice
These yongé ladies shulden make.
And for the straungé mennés sake
That comen fro the siege of Troy,
They maden well the moré joy.
There was revéll, there was dauncíng,
And every life[3] which couthé sing
Of lusty women in the route
A fressh caróll hath song aboute.
But for all this yet nethéles
The Grekes unknowe of Áchillés
So weren, that in no degre
They couthen wité which was he
Ne by his vois, ne by his pas.
Ulixes than upon the cas
A thing of high prudénce hath wrought.

unexplained word illustrated by this passage: "Se mistrent en barges, et alerent aux salandres, et en prisrent les xvii. et l'une echapa, qui estoit a la *cole*."

[1] *Facounde*, eloquence.
[2] *Corâge*, thought in his heart.
[3] *Life*, body.

For thilk array which he hath brought
To yive among the women there
He let do fetten[1] all the gere
Forth, with a knightés harneis eke.
In all the contré for to seke
Men sholden nought a fairer se.
And every thing in his degré
Endelong upon a bourde he laide.
To Lichomede and than he preide,
That every lady chesé sholde
What thing of allé that she wolde
And take it as by way of yift,
For they hem self it shuldé shift
He saide after her owné wille.
Achilles thanné stood nought stille,
Whan he the brighté helm behelde,
The swerd, the hauberk and the shelde,
His herté fell therto anone,
Of all that other wold he none;
The knightés gere he underfongeth
And thilke array which that belongeth
Unto the women he forsoke.
And in this wise, as saith the boke,
They knowen thanné whiche he was,
For he goth forth the greté pas
Into the chambre where he lay,
Anone and madé no delay,
He armeth him in knightly wise,
That better can no man devise.
And as fortúné shulde falle,
He came so forth to-fore hem alle
As he which tho was glad inough.
But Lichomédé nothing lough[2]
Whan that he sigh how that it ferde.
For than he wisté well and herde
His doughter haddé be forlain.
But that he was so oversein
The wonder overgoth his wit.
For in croníque is writé yit
Thing which shall never be foryete,

[1] *Let do fetten*, caused to be fetched.
[2] *Lough*, laughed.

How that Achilles hath begete
Pirrús upon Deidamý,
Wherof came out the trechery
Of Fals Witnessé when he saide
How that Achilles was a maide.
But that was nothing sené tho,
For he is to the siegé go
Forth with Ulixes and Diomede.
"Lo, thus was provéd in the dede
And fully spoke at thilké while,
If o woman an other beguile
Where is there any sikernesse,
Whan Thetis which was than goddesse
Deidamý hath so bejaped,
I not how it shall bene escaped
With tho womén whose innocence
Is now al day through such credence
Deceivéd ofte as it is sene
With men that such untrouthé mene.
For they ben sligh in suche a wise,
That they by sleight and by queintise
Of fals witnessé bringen inne
That doth hem ofté for to winne
Where they ben nought worthý therto.
Forthy, my soné, do nought so."—
"My fader, as of fals witnésse
The trouth and the matere expresse
Touchénd of love, howe it hath ferde,
As ye have tolde I have well herde.
But for ye saiden other wise,
How thilké Vice of Covetise
Hath yet Perjúrie of his accorde,
If that you list of some recorde
To tellen an other tale also
In Lovés cause of time ago,
What thing it is to be forswore,
I woldé preié you therfore,
Wherof I might ensample take."—
"My godé sone, and for thy sake
Touchend of this I shall fulfill
Thin axing at thin owné will
And the matere I shall declare
How the womén deceived are
Whan they so tendre hertés bere
Of that they heren men so swere.
But whan it cometh unto thassay,
They finde it fals another day,
As Jason did unto Medee,
Which stant yet of auctorité
In token and in memoriall,
Wherof the tale in speciáll
Is in the boke of Troié write,
Which I shall do the for to wite.
"In Grecé whilom was a king,
Of whom the fame and knouleching
Beleveth[1] yet, and Peleús
He highté, but it fell him thus,
That his Fortúne her whele so lad,
That he no childe his owné had
To regnen after his decess.
He had a brother nethéles,
Whose righté namé was Eson,
And he the worthy knight Jason
Begat, the which in every londe
All other passéd of his honde
In armés, so that he the best
Was naméd and the worthiest.
He soughté worship over all.
Now herken, and I tellé shall
An adventúré that he sought,
Which afterward full dere he bought.
There was an ilé, which Colchós
Was clepéd, and therof aros
Great speche in every londe aboute,
That such merveilé was none oute
In all the widé world no where
As tho was in that ilé there.
There was a shepe, as it was tolde,
The which his flees bare all of golde,
And so the goddés had it sette
That it ne might away be fette
By power of no worldés wight.
And yet full many a worthy knight
It had assaiéd as they dorste,
And ever it fell hem to the worste.

[1] *Beleveth*, remains.

But he that wolde it nought forsake
But of his knighthode undertake
To do what thing therto belongeth,
This worthy Jason, sore alongeth
To se the straungé regions
And knowé the conditions
Of other marches where he went.
And for that cause his hole entent
He setté Colchos for to seche
And therupon he made a speche
To Peleús his eme[1] the king.
And he wel paid was of that thing
And shope anone for his passáge
And such as were of his lignáge
With other knightés whiche he chees
With him he toke, and Hercules
Which full was of chiválerie
With Jason went in compaignie,
And that was in the month of May
Whan coldé stormes were away;
The wind was good, the ship was yare,
They toke her leve and forth they fare
Towárd Colchós. But on the way
What hem befelle is long to say,
How Lamedon the king of Troy,
Which oughté well have made hem joy
Whan they to rest a while him preide,
Out of his lond he them congeide.
And so fell the dissentión
Whiche after was destructión
Of that citee, as men may here.
But that is nought to my matere,
But thus the worthy folk Gregois
Fro that king which was nought curtois
And fro his londe with sail updrawe
They went hem forth, and many a sawe
They made and many a great manáce;
Till atté last into that place
Which as they soughté they arrive,

[1] *Eme*, uncle.

And striken sail and forth as blive[1]
They sent unto the king and tolden
Who weren there and what they wolden.

Oëtés, which was thanné king,
Whan that he herdé this tidíng
Of Jason which was comen there,
And of these other what they were,
He thoughté done hem great worshíp.
For they anone come out of ship
And straught unto the king they wente
And by the honde Jason he hente,
And that was at the paleis gate,
So fer the king came on his gate
Toward Jasón to done him chere.
And he, whom lacketh no manere,
Whan he the king sigh in presénce
Yaf him ayein such reverence
As to the kingés state belongeth.
And thus the king him underfongeth
And Jason in his arme he caught
And forth into the hall he straught,
And there they sit and speke of thinges.
And Jason tolde him tho tidinges
Why he was come, and faire him preide
To haste his time, and the king saide:
'Jason, thou art a worthy knight,
But it lieth in no mannés might
To done that thou art comé fore.
There hath bene many a knight forlore
Of that they wolden it assaie.'
But Jason wolde him nought esmaie
And saide: 'Of every worldés cure
Fortúné stant in aventúre,
Paraunter[2] well, paraunter wo.
But how as ever that it go,
It shall be with min honde assaied.

[1] *As blive*, quickly.
[2] *Paraunter*, peradventure

The king tho helde him nought
wel paied,
For he the Grekés soré dredde,
In aunter if Jasón ne spedde
He mighté therof bere a blame,
For tho was all the worldés fame
In Grece as for to speke of armes.
Forthý he drad him of his harmes
And gan to prechen and to prey.
But Jason woldé nought obey,
But said, he wolde his purpos holde
For ought that any man him tolde.
The king whan he these wordés herde
And sigh how that this knight
answérde,
Yet for he woldé make him glad,
After Medea gone he bad,
Which was his doughter, and she
cam
And Jason, which good hedé nam,
Whan he her sigh ayein her goth.
And she, which was him nothing loth,
Welcóméd him into that londe
And softé toke him by the honde
And down they setten bothé same.[1]
She had herd spoken of his name
And of his greté worthinesse,
Forthý she gan her eye impresse
Upon his face and his statúre
And thought, how never creätúre
Was so welfarend as was he.
And Jason right in such degré
Ne mighté nought witholde his loke,
But so good hede on her he toke
That him ne thought under the
heven
Of beauté sigh he never her even
With all that felle to womanhede.
Thus eche of other token hede
Though there no word was of re-
corde,
Her hertés both of one accorde
Ben sette to loven, but as tho
There mighten ben no wordés mo.

[1] *Bothé same*, both together.

The king made him great joy and
fest,
To all his men he yaf an hest,
So as they wolde his thank deserve
That they shulde allé Jason serve
While that he woldé theré dwelle.
And thus the day, shortlý to telle,
With many merthés they dispent,
Till night was come, and tho they
went;
Echone of other toke his leve,
Whan they no lenger mighten leve.[1]
I not[2] how Jason that night slepe,
But well I wot, that of the shepe
For which he cam into that ile
He thoughté but a litel while;
All was Medea that he thought,
So that in many wise he sought
His wit, wakénd er it was day,
Some timé ye, some timé nay,
Some timé thus, some timé so,
As he was steréd to and fro
Of love and eke of his conquést,
As he was holde of his behest.
And thus he rose up by the morwe
And toke him self seint John to
borwe[3]
And saide, he woldé first beginne
At love, and after for to winne
The flees of gold for which he come,
And thus to him good herte he nome.
"Medea right the samé wise
Till day cam, that she must arise,
Lay and bethought her all the night
How she that noble worthy knight
By any waié mighté wedde.
And wel she wist, if he ne spedde
Of thing which he had undertake,
She might her self no purpose take.
For if he deiede of his bataile,
She musté than algaté faile

[1] *Leve*, remain. [2] *Not*, know not.
[3] *Seint John to borwe*, St. John for surety, a common way of invoking a saint in the Middle Ages. Jason swore, like a good knight, by St. John.

To geten him, whan he were dede.
Thus she began to setté rede
And torne about her wittés all
To loke how that it mighté fall,
That she with him had a leisír
To speke and telle of her desír.
And so it fell the samé day
That Jason with that sweté may[1]
To-gider set and hadden space
To speke, and he besought her grace.
And she his talé goodly herde
And afterward she him answérde
And saidé: 'Jason, as thou wilt
Thou might be sauf, thou might be spilt,
For witté well, that never man,
But if he couthé that I can,
Ne mighté that fortúne acheve,
For which thou comest. But as I leve,
If thou wolt holdé covenaunt
To love of all the remenaunt,
I shall thy life and honour save,
That thou the flees of gold shalt have.'
He said: 'Al at your owné wille,
Madame, I shall trulý fulfille
Your hesté, while my life may last.
Thus longe he praid and atté last
She graunteth, and behight him this,
That whan night cometh and it time is
She wolde him sendé certainly
Such one that shulde him prively
Alone into her chambre bringe.
He thonketh her of that tidínge,
For of that grace is him begonne
Him thenketh al other thingés wonne.
"The day made ende and lost his sight
And comen was the derké night,
Whiche all the daiés eyé blent.

[1] *May*, maid.

"Jasón toke leve and forth he went,
And whan he cam out of the prees
He toke to counseil Hercules
And tolde him how it was betid,
And praide it shuldé well ben hid,
And that he woldé loke about
The whilés that he shall be out.
Thus as he stood and hedé name,
A maiden fro Medea came,
The fairest and the wisest eke.
And she with simple chere and meke,
Whan she him sigh, wax all ashamed.
Tho was her talé newe entamed
For sikernesse of mariáge,
She fette forth a riche ymáge,
Was the figúre of Jupitér,
And Jason swore and saidé there,
That also wis god shuld him helpe,
That if Medea did him helpe,
That he his purpose mighté winne,
They shuldé never part atwinne,
But ever while him lasteth life,
He woldé holde her for his wife.
They hadden bothe what they wolde.
And than at leiser she him tolde
And gan fro point to point enforme
Of this bataile and all the forme,
Whiche as he shuldé findé there,
Whan he to thilé[1] comé were.
She saide, at entré of the pas
How Mars, which God of Armés was,
Hath set two oxen sterne and stoute,
That casten fire and flame aboute
Both atté mouth and at the nase,
So that they setten all on blase
What thing that passeth hem betwene.
And furthermore upon the grene
There goth, the flees of gold to kepe,
A serpent which may never slepe.
Thus who that ever it shulde winne,
The fire to stoppe he mot beginne

[1] *Thilé*, the island.

Which that the fiercé bestés caste,
And daunt he mot hem atté laste,
So that he may hem yoke and drive,
And there upon he mot as blive
The serpent with such strength assaile
That he may sleen him by bataile,
Of which he mot the teeth outdrawe,
As it belongeth to that lawe.
And than he must the oxen yoke
Til they have with a plough to-broke
A furgh of lond, in which arow
The teeth of thadder he must sow.
And therof shull arisé knightes
Well arméd at allé rightes;
Of hem is nought to taken hede,
For eche of hem in hastihede
Shall other slee with dethés wounde.
And thus whan they ben laid to grounde
Than mot he to the goddés pray
And go so forth and take his pray.
But if he faile in any wise
Of that ye heré me devise,
There may be set non other wey,
That he ne must algatés deie.
'Now have I told the peril all
I woll you tellen forth withall,'
Quod Medeá to Jason tho,
'That ye shull knowen er ye go
Ayein the venim and the fire,
What shall be the recoverire.
But, siré, for it is nigh day,
Ariseth up, so that I may
Deliver you what thing I have
That may your life and honour save.'
Tho toke she forth a riché tie[1]
Made all of gold and of perrie,
Out of the which she nam a ring,
The stone was worth all other thing.
She saidé, while he wold it were,
There mighté no perıl him dere;[2]
In water may it nought be dreint,
Where as it cometh the fire is queint,

[1] *Tie*, casket. [2] *Dere*, injure.

It daunteth eke the cruel beste,
There may none quad[1] that man areste,
Where so he be on see or londe,
That hath this ring upon his honde.
And over that she gan to sain,
That if a man will ben unsein,
Within his hond hold close the stone
And he may invisible gone.
The ring to Jason she betaught[2]
And so forth after she him taught
What sacrifice he shuldé make.
And gan out of her cofre take
Him thought an hevenly figúre,
Which all by charme and by conjúre
Was wrought, and eke it was through writ
With namés which he shuldé wite,
As she him taughté tho to rede,
And bad him as he woldé spede
Withouté rest of any while,
Whan he were londed in that ile,
He shuldé make his sacrifice
And rede his carect[3] in the wise
As she him taught, on knees down bent
Thre sithés[4] toward orient.
For so shuld he the goddés plese
And win him selven mochel ese.
And whan he had it thriés radde
To open a buïst[5] she him badde,
That she there toke him in present,
And was full of such oignément
That there was fire ne venim none
That shuldé fastné him upon
Whan that he were anoint withall.
Forthý she taught him how he shall
Anoint his armés all aboute,
And for he shuldé nothing doubte
She toke him than a maner[6] glue
The which was of so great vertúe

[1] *Quad*, evil. [2] *Betaught*, entrusted.
[3] *Carect*, written charm.
[4] *Sithés*, times. [5] *Buïst*, box.
[6] *A maner*, a kind of.

That where a man it shuldé cast
It shuldé binde anon so fast
That no man might it done away.
And that she bad by allé way
He shulde into the mouthés throw
Of tho twein oxen that fire blow,
Therof to stoppen the malíce
The glue shall serve of that offíce.
And over that, her oignément
Her ring and her enchauntément
Ayein the serpent shulde him were,[1]
Till he him slee with swerd or spere.
And than he may sauflý inough
His oxen yoke into the plough
And the teeth sowe in such a wise
Till he the knightés se arise,
And eche of other down be laide
In suche a maner as I have saide.
"Lo, thus Medea for Jasón
Ordeineth, and praieth therupon
That he nothíng foryeté sholde,
And eke she praieth him that he wolde,
Whan he hath all his armés done,
To groundé knele and thonke anone
The goddés, and so forth by ese
The flees of golde he shuldé sese.
And whan he had it seséd so,
That than he weré sone ago
Withouten any tarieng.
Whan this was said, into weping
She fel, as she that was throughnome
With love and so fer overcome
That all her worlde on him she sette.
But whan she sigh there was no lette,
That he mot nedés part her fro,
She toke him in her armés two
An hunderd times and gan him kisse
And said: 'O, all my worldes blisse,
My trust, my lust, my life, min hele,
To ben thin helpe in this quarele
I pray unto the goddés alle!'

[1] *Were*, protect.

And with that word she gan down falle
Of swoune, and he her uppé nam,
And forth with that the maiden cam,
And they to bed anone her brought,
And thanné Jason her besought
And to her saide in this manere:
'My worthy lusty lady dere,
Comfórteth you, for by my trouth
It shall nought fallen in my slouth
That I ne woll throughout fulfille
Your hestés at your owné wille.
And yet I hopé to you bringe
Within a whilé such tidínge,
The which shall make us bothé game.'
"But for he woldé kepe her name,
Whan that he wist it was nigh day,
He saide, 'Adewe my sweté may.'
And forth with him he nam his gere
Which as she haddé take him there,
And straught unto his chambre went
And goth to bedde and slepe him hent[1]
And lay that no man him awoke,
For Hercules hede of him toke,
Till it was underne[2] high and more.
And than he gan to sighé sore
And sodeinlich he braide of slepe,
And they than token of him kepe;
His chamberleins ben soné there
And maden redy all his gere,
And he arose and to the king
He went and said how to that thing
For which he cam he woldé go.
The king therof was wonder wo
And for he wolde him fain withdraw,
He told him many a dredefull sawe.
But Jason wolde it nought recorde
And atté lasté they accorde.
Whan that he woldé nought abide,
A bote was redy atté tide,

[1] *Hent*, seized.
[2] *Underne*, time of a light refreshment between breakfast and dinner, or between dinner and supper.

In which this worthy knight of Grece,
Full arméd up at every piece
To his batailé which belongeth,
Toke ore in hond and sore him longeth
Till he the water passéd were.
"Whan he cam to that ilé there,
He set him on his knees down straught
And his carecte, as he was taught,
He rad and made his sacrifice
And sith anoint him in that wise
As Médeá him haddé bede;
And than arose up fro that stede,
And with the glue the fire he queint;
And anone after he atteint
The greté serpent and him slough.
But erst he haddé sorwe inough,
For that serpént made him travaile
So hard and sore of his bataile,
That now he stood and nowe he fell,
For longé time it so befell
That with his swerd and with his spere
He mighté nought that serpent dere,
He was so sherded[1] all aboute
It held all eggé tole[2] withoute,
He was so rude and hard of skin
There might no thingé go therein.
Venim and fire to-gider he cast,
That he Jasón so sore ablast
That if ne were his oignément,
His ring and his enchauntément,
Which Médeá toke him before,
He haddé with that worm be lore.[3]
But of vertú which therof cam
Jasón the dragon overcam
And he anone the teeth out drough
And set his oxen in his plough,
With which he brake a piece of lond
And sewe hem with his owné hond.
Tho might he great merveilé se,
Of every toth in his degré
Sprong up a knight with spere and sheld,
Of which anone right in the feld
Echone slough other, and with that
Jason Medea not foryat,
On both his knees he gan down falle
And yaf thank to the goddés alle.
The flees he toke and goth to bote,
The sonné shineth bright and hote,
The flees of gold shone forth with all,
The water glistred over all.
Medea wept and sighéd ofte
And stood upon a toure alofte;
All privély within her selve,
There herd it nouther ten ne twelve,
She praid and said: 'O, god him spede,
The knight, which hath my maidenhede.'
And ay she loketh toward thile,
But whan she sigh within a while
The flees glistrénd ayein the sonne,
She said: 'Ha lord, now all is wonne,
My knight the feld hath overcome,
Now woldé god, he weré come.
Ha lord, I wold he were alonde.'
But I dare také this on honde,
If that she haddé winges two,
She wold have flowe unto him tho
Straught there he was unto the bote.
The day was clere, the sonné hote,
The Gregois weren in great doubt
The whilé that her lord was out,
They wisten nought what shuld betide,
But waited ever upon the tide
To se what endé shuldé falle.
There stoden eke the nobles alle
Forth with the comunes of the town,
And as they loken up and down,
They weren ware within a throwe
Where cam the bote which they wel knowe,

[1] *Sherded*, scaled. [2] *Egge tole*, edge tools. [3] *Lore*, lost.

And sigh how Jason brought his prey.
And tho they gonnen allé say
And criden allé with o steven :[1]
'Ha, where was ever under the heven
So noble a knight, as Jason is?'
And wel nigh allé saiden this,
That Jason was a fairé knight,
For it was never of mannés might
The flees of gold so for to winne,
And thus to tellen they beginne.
With that the king cam forth anone
And sigh the flees, how that it shone.
And whan Jasón cam to the londe,
The kinge him selvé toke his honde
And kist him and great joy him made.
The Gregois weren wonder glade
And of that thing right merry hem thought
And forth with hem the flees they brought,
And eche on other gan to ligh.[2]
But wel was him that mighté nigh
To se there of the propreté,
And thus they passen the citee
And gone unto the paleis straught.
"Medea, which foryat her nought,
Was redy there and said anon:
'Welcome, O worthy knight Jasón!'
She wolde have kist him wonder fain,
But shamé tornéd her ayein,
It was nought the manere as tho,[3]
Forthý she dorsté nought do so.
She toke her leve, and Jason went
Into his chambre and she him sent
Her maiden to sene how he ferde.
The which whan that she sigh and herde,
How that he haddé faren out
And that it stood well all about,
She tolde her lady what she wist,
And she for joy her maiden kist.

[1] *Steven*, voice. [2] *Ligh*, laugh. [3] *Tho*, then.

The bathés weren than araied
With herbés tempred and assaied
And Jason was unarméd sone
And dide as it befell to done;
Into his bathe he went anone
And wisshe him clene as any bone,
He toke a soppe and out he cam
And on his best array he nam
And kempt his hede whan he was clad,
And goth him forth all merry and glad
Right straught into the kingés halle.
The king cam with his knightés alle
And maden him glad welcomíng.
And he hem toldé tho tiding
Of this and that, how it befell,
Whan that he wan the shepés fell.
Medea whan she was asent[1]
Come soné to that parlément,
And whan she mighte Jason se,
Was none so glad of all as she.
There was no joié for to seche,
Of him made every man a speche,
Some man said oné, some said other,
But though he weré goddés brother
And mighté maké fire and thonder,
There mighté be no moré wonder
Than was of him in that citee.
Echone taught other 'This is he
Whiche hath in his powér withinne
That all the world ne mighté winne!
Lo, here the best of allé good!'
Thus saiden they, that theré stood
And eke that walkéd up and down
Both of the court and of the town.
"The time of souper cam anon,
They wisshen and therto they gon;
Medea was with Jason set,
Tho was there many a deinté fet
And set to-fore hem on the bord,
But none so liking as the word
Which was there spoke among hem two,

[1] *Asent*, sent for.

So as they dorsté speké tho.
But though they hadden litel space,
Yet they accorden in that place
How Jason shuldé come at night,
Whan every torche and every light
Were out, and than of other thinges
They speke aloud for súpposínges
Of hem that stoden there aboute,
For love is evermore in doubte,
If that it be wisly govérned
Of hem that ben of lové lérned.
Whan al was done, that dissh and cup
And cloth and bord and all was up,
They waken while hem list to wake,
And after that they levé take
And gon to beddé for to reste.
And whan him thoughté for the beste,
That every man was fast a slepe,
Jasón, that wolde his timé kepe,
Goth forth stalkénd all privély
Unto the chambre and redely
There was a maidé, which him kept,
Medea woke and no thing slept,
So that they hadden joy inow.
And tho they setten whan and how
That she with him awey shal stele,
With wordés such and other fele.[1]
Whan all was treted to an ende,
Jasón toke leve and gan forth wende
Unto his owné chambre in pees.
There wist it non but Hercules.
"He slept and ros, whan it was time,
And whan it fel towardés prime,
He toke to him such as he triste
In secré, that none other wiste,
And told hem of his counseil there
And saidé that his willé were,
That they to ship had allé thing
So privelich in thevening,
That no man might her[2] dede aspie
But tho that were of compaignie,

[1] *Fele*, many. [2] *Her*, their.

For he woll go withouté leve
And lenger woll he nought beleve,[1]
But he ne wolde at thilké throwe
The king or quené shulde it knowe.
They said, all this shall well be do.
And Jason trusté well therto.
"Medea in the mené while,
Which thought her fader to beguile,
The tresor which her fader hadde
With her all privély she ladde
And with Jasón at timé set
Away she stale and found no let
And straught she goth her into ship
Of Grecé with that felaship.
And theyanone drough up the saile,
And all that night this wascounseil;
But erly whan the sonné shone
Men sigh how that they weré gone
And come unto the kinge and tolde.
And he the sothé knowé wolde
And axeth, where his doughter was.
There was no word, but 'Out alas,
She was ago.'[2] The moder wept,
The fader as a wodeman lept
And gan the timé for to warie[3]
And swore his othe he wold nought tarie,
That with galiote and with galéy
The samé cours the samé wey
Which Jason toke he woldé take,
If that he might him overtake.
To this they saiden allé ye.
Anone as they were atté see
And all as who saith at one worde,
They gone withinné shippés borde,
The sail goth up, and forth they straught,
But none esploit therof they caught,
And so they tornen home ayein,
For all that labour was in vein.
Jasón to Grecé with his pray
Goth through the see the righté way.

[1] *Beleve*, remain. [2] *Ago*, gone.
[3] *Warie*, curse

Whan he there come and men it
tolde,
They maden joié yong and olde.
"Esón whan that he wist of this,
How that his soné comen is
And hath achevéd that he sought
And home with him Medea brought,
In all the widé world was none
So glad a man as he was one.
To-gider ben these lovers tho,
Till that they hadden sonés two
Wherof they weren bothé glade,
And olde Eson great joié made
To seen thencrees of his lignage,
For he was of so great an age
That men awaiten every day
Whan that he shuldé gone away.
Jasón, which sigh his fader olde,
Upon Medea made him bolde
Of art magíqué which she couth,
And praieth her that his faders
youth
She woldé make ayeinward newe.
And she that was towárd him trewe
Behight him that she wolde it do,
Whan that she timé sigh therto.
But what she did in that matére
It is a wonder thing to here,
But yet for the novellérie
I thenké telle a great partie.
"Thus it befell upon a night,
Whan there was nought but sterré
light,
She was vanísshed right as her list,
That no wight but her self it wist.
And that was atté midnight tide;
The world was still on every side,
With open hede and foot all bare
Her hair to-sprad she gan to fare,
Upon her clothés gert she was
All spechélés and on the gras
She glode forth as an adder doth.
None other wisé she ne goth,
Till she came to the fresshé flood,
And there a whilé she withstood,
Thriés she tornéd her aboute
And thriés eke she gan down loute,
And in the flood she wete her hair,
And thriés on the water there
She gaspeth with a drecchinge onde[1]
And tho she toke her speche on
honde.
First she began to clepe and calle
Upwárde unto the sterrés alle,
To winde, to air, to see, to londe
She preide and eke helde up her
honde
To Échatés and gan to crie,
Whiche is goddesse of sorcerie,
She saidé, 'Helpeth at this nede,
And as ye maden me to spede
Whan Jason came the flees to seche,
So help me now, I you beseche!'
With that she loketh and was ware,
Down fro the sky there came a chare,
The which dragóns abouté drowe.
And tho she gan her hede down bowe
And up she stighe and faire and well
She drové forth by chare and wheel
Above in thaire among the skies;
The londe of Crete in tho parties
She sought, and fasté gan her hie,
And therupon the hullés high
Of Othrin and Olimpe also
And eke of other hullés mo
She founde and gadreth herbés
suote,
She pulleth up some by the rote
And many with a knife she shereth
And all into her char she bereth.
Thus whan she hath the hullés
sought,
The floodés there foryate she nought
Eridian and Amphrisos,
Peneie and eke Spercheïdos,
To hem she went and there she
nome
Both of the water and of the fome,
The sonde and eke the smallé stones

[1] *Drecching onde*, troubled breath.

Whiche as she chese out for the
nones,
And of the Reddé See a part
That was behovelich to her art
She toke, and after that about
She soughté sondry sedés out
In feldés and in many greves
And eke a part she toke of leves.
But thing which might her most
availe
She found in Crete and in Thessaile.
In daiés and in nightés nine,
With great travaile and with great
peine
She was purveyed of every piece
And torneth homward into Grece.
Before the gatés of Eson
Her chare she let away to gone
And toke out first that was therinne,
For tho she thoughté to beginne
Such thing as semeth impossſble
And made her selven invisſble,
As she that was with thaire enclosed
And might of no man be desclosed.
She toke up turvés of the londe
Withouté helpe of mannés honde
And heled [1] with the grené gras,
Of whiche an alter made there was
Unto Echates the goddesse
Of art magique and the maistresse.
And este an other to invent,
As she which did her hole intent,
Tho toke she feldwode [2] and ver-
veine,
Of herbés ben nought better tweine,
Of which anone withouté let
These alters ben abouté set.
Two sondry pittés fasté by
She made, and with that hastély
A wether which was black she
slough,
And out therof the blood she drough
And did into the pittés two,
Warm milk she put also therto

[1] *Heled*, covered. [2] *Felwood*, gentian.

With hony meind,[1] and in such wise
She gan to make her sacrifice
And cried and praidé forth withall
To Pluto the god ſnfernál
And to the quené Proserpine.
And so she sought out all the line
Of hem that longen to that craft,
Behindé was no namé last,
And praid hem all, as she well couth,
To graunt Esón his firsté youth.
This olde Esón brought forth was
tho; [2]
Away she bad all other go
Upon perſl that mighté falle,
And with that word they wenten alle
And left hem theré two alone.
And tho she gan to gaspe and gone
And madé signés many one
And said her wordés therupon,
And with spellinge and her charmes
She toke Esón in both her armes
And made him for to slepé fast
And him upon her herbés cast.
The blacké wether tho she toke
And hew the flesshe as doth a coke,
On either alter part she laide,
And with the charmés that she saide
A fire down fro the sky alight
And made it for to brenné light.
And whan Medea sigh it brenne,
Anone she gan to sterte and renne
The firy alters all about.
There was no besté which goth out
More wildé than she semeth there.
Aboute her shulders heng her hair
As though she were oute of her minde
And tornéd to another kinde.
Tho lay there certain wodé cleft
Of which the pieces now and eft
She made hem in the pittés wete
And put hem in the firy hete
And toke the bronde with all the
blase
And thriés she began to rase

[1] *Meind*, mixed. [2] *Tho*, then.

About Esón there as he slept.
And eft with water which she kept
She made a cercle about him thries
And eft with fire of sulphre twies
Full many another thing she dede,
Whiche is nought writen in the stede.
But tho she ran so up and doune
She madé many a wonder soune,
Somtimé lich unto the cock,
Somtime unto the laverock,
Somtimé cacleth as an hen,
Somtimé speketh as don men.
And right so as her jargon straungeth
In sondry wise her formé chaungeth,
She semeth faire and no womán,
For with the craftés that she can
She was as who saith a goddésse,
And what her listé more or lesse
She did, in bokés as we finde,
That passeth over mannés kinde.
But who that woll of wonders here,
What thing she wrought in this matere
To make an ende of that she gan,
Such merveil herdé never man.
"Apointed in the newé mone,
Whan it was timé for to done,
She set a caldron on the fire,
In which was al the hole attire
Whereon the medicíné stood,
Of juse, of water, and of blood,
And let it boile in suche a plite
Till that she sigh the spumé white.
And tho she cast in rinde and rote
And sede and floure that was for bote,
With many an herbe and many a stone
Wherof she hath there many one.
And eke Cimpheiús, the serpént,
To her hath all her scalés lent,
Chelidre her yafe her adders skin,
And she to boilen cast hem in,
And parte eke of the hornéd oule,
The which men here on nightés houle,
And of a raven which was tolde
Of niné hundred winter olde
She toke the hede with all the bille.
And as the medicíne it wille
She toke her after the bowele
Of the seewolf and for the hele
Of Eson, with a thousand mo
Of thingés that she haddé tho.
In that caldrón to-gider as blive
She put and toke than of olíve
A drié braunche hem with to stere,[1]
The which anon gan floure and bere
And waxe all fresshe and grene ayein.
Whan she this vertue haddé sene,
She let the leesté droppe of alle
Upon the baré floure[2] down falle:
Anon there sprong up floure and gras
Where as the droppé fallen was,
And waxe anone all medow grene
So that it mighté well be sene.
Medea thanné knewe and wist
Her medicíne is for to trist[3]
And goth to Eson there he lay
And toke a swerd was of assay,
With which a wounde upon his side
She madé, that there out may slide
The blood withinné which was olde
And sike and trouble and feble and colde.
And tho she toke unto his use
Of herbés all the besté juse
And pouréd it into his wounde,
That made his veinés full and sounde.
And tho she made his woundés close,
And toke his honde, and up he rose.
And tho she yaf him drinke a draught
Of which his youth ayein he caught,
His hede, his herte and his viságe
Lich unto twenty winter age,

[1] *Stere*, stir. [2] *Baré floure*, bare ground. [3] *To trist*, to be trusted.

His horé hairés were away,
And lich unto the fresshé May
Whan passéd ben the coldé shoures,
Right so recovereth he his floures.
"Lo, what might any man devise
A woman shewe in any wise
More hertely love in any stede
Than Medeá to Jason dede.
First she made him the flees to winne,
And after that fro kith and kinne
With great tresór with him she stale,
And to his fader forth with all
His elde hath tornéd into youthe,
Which thing none other woman
couthe.
But how it was to her aquit,
The rémembraúncé dwelleth yit.
King Peleús his eme was dede,
Jasón bare croune upon his hede,
Medea hath fulfilled his will,
But whan he shuld of right fulfill
The trothé which to her afore
He had in thile of Colchos swore,
Tho was Medea most deceived.
For he an other hath received
Which doughter was to king Creon,
Creusá she hight, and thus Jasón,
As he that was to love untrewe,
Medea left and toke a newe;
But that was after sone abought.[1]
Medea with her art hath wrought
Of cloth of golde a mantel riche,
Which semeth worth a kingés riche,[2]
And that was unto Creusa sent
In name of yeft and of presént,
For susterhode hem was betwene.
And whan that yongé fresshé quene
That mantel lappéd her aboute,
Anon therof the fire sprang oute
And brent her bothé flesshe and bon.
Tho cam Medea to Jasón
With both his sonés on her honde
And said, 'O thou of every londe
The most untrewé creätúre,
Lo, this shall be thy forfeitúre.'
With that she both his sonés slough
Before his eye, and he out drough
His swerd and wold have slain her
tho,—
But faréwell, she was ago
Unto Pallas the court above,
Where as she pleigneth upon love,
As she that was with that goddesse,
And he was lefte in great distresse.
"Thus might thou se, what sorwe
it doth
To swere an oth, which is nought
soth,
In Lovés causé namély.
My soné, be well ware forthý
And kepe that thou be nought for-
swore.
For this, whiche I have told to-fore,
Ovídé telleth every dele."—
"My fader, I may leve it wele,
For I have herde it ofté say,
How Jason toke the flees awey
Fro Colchos, but yet herde I nought,
By whom it was first thider brought.
And for it weré good to here,
If that you list at my praiere
To telle I woldé you beseche."—
"My soné, who that woll it seche,
In bokés he may finde it write.
And nethéles, if thou wolt wite
In the manér as thou hast preide,
I shall the tell, how it is saide.
The fame of thilké shepés felle
Whiche in Colchos, as it befelle,
Was all of gold, shal never deie,
Wherof I thenké for to say,
Howe it cam first into that ile.
There was a king in thilké while
Towardés Grece, and Athemas
The cronique of his namé was.
And had a wif, which Philen hight,
By whom, so as Fortúne it dight,
He had of children yongé two.
Frixus the firsté was of tho,

1 *Abought*, paid for. 2 *Riche*, kingdom.

A knavé[1] child right faire with all.
A doughter eke the which men call
Hellen, he haddé by his wife.
But for there may no mannés life
Endure upon this erthé here,
This worthy quene, as thou might
here,
Er that the children were of age,
Toke of her endé the passage
With great worshíp and was be-
grave:[2]
What thing it liketh God to have
It is great reson to ben his.
Forthý this king, so as it is,
With great suffránce it under-
fongeth.
And afterward, as him belongeth,
Whan it was timé for to wedde,
A newé wife he toke to bedde,
Whiche Yno hight and was a maide
And eke the doughter as men saide
Of Cadmé, whiche a king also
Was holde in thilké daiés tho.

Whan Yno was the kingés make
She cast how that she mighté make
These children to her fader loth
And shope a wile ayein hem both,
Which to the king was all unknowe.
A yere or two she let do sowe
The lond with sodé whete aboute,
Wherof no corn may springen oute.
And thus by sleight and by covine
Aros the derth and the famine
Through out the londe in such a wise,
So that the king a sacrifice
Upon the point of this distresse
To Ceres, which is the goddesse
Of corne, hath shape him for to yive,
To loke, if it may be foryive
The mischefe which was in his londe.
But she, which knewe to-fore the
honde[3]
The circumstance of all this thing,

[1] *Knavé*, boy. [2] *Begrave*, buried.
[3] *To-fore the honde*, beforehand.

Ayein the coming of the king
Into the temple hath shape so
Of her accord, that allé tho
Which of the temple prestés were,
Have said and full declaréd there
Unto the king, but if so be
That he deliver the contré
Of Frixus and of Hellen bothe,
With whom the goddés ben so
wrothe
That while tho children ben with-
inne
Such tilthé shall no man beginne
Wherof to get him any corne;
Thus was it said, thus was it sworne
Of all the prestés that there are.
And she which causeth all this fare,
Said eke therto what that she wolde.
And every man than after tolde
So as the quené had hem preide.

"The king, which hath his eré
leide
And leveth[1] all that ever he herde,
Unto her talés thus answerde
And saith, that lever him is to chese
His children bothé for to lese
Than him and all the remenaunt
Of hem which are appertenaunt
Unto the lond whiche he shall kepe.
And bade his wifé to take kepe
In what manére is best to done,
That they deliveréd were sone
Out of this worlde. And she anone
Two men ordeineth for to gone,
But first she made hem for to swere
That they the children shuldé bere
Unto the see, that none it knowe,
And hem therinné bothé throwe.
The children to the see ben lad,
Where in the wise as Yno bad
These men be redy for to do.
But the goddessé which Juno
Is hote appereth in the stede
And hath unto the men forbede

[1] *Leveth*, believes.

That they the children nought ne slee,
But bad hem loke into the see
And taken hede of that they sighen.
There swam a shepe to-fore her eyen,
Whose flees of burnéd gold was all.
And this goddessé forth with all
Commaundeth that withouté let
They shulde anon the children set
Above upon the shepés back.
And all was do, right as she spak,
Wherof the men gone home ayein.
"And fell so, as the bokés sain,
Hellen the yongé maiden tho,
Whiche of the see was wo bego,
For puré drede her hert hath lore,
That fro the shepe which hath her bore,
As she that was swounéndé feint,
She fell and hath her self adreint.
With Frixus and this shepe forth swam,
Till he to thile of Colchos cam,
Where Juno the goddésse he fonde,
Which toke the shepe unto the londe
And set it there in such a wise,
As thou to-fore hast herd devise,
Wherof cam after all the wo,
Why Jason was forsworé so
Unto Medee, as it is spoke."—
"My fader, who that hath to-broke
His trouth, as ye have tolde above,
He is nought worthy for to love
Ne be belovéd, as me semeth.
But every newé lové quemeth
To him that newé fangel is.
And nethéles now after this,
If that you list to taken hede
Upon my shrifté to procede
In Lovés cause ayein the Vice
Of Covetise and Avarice,
What there is more I woldé wite."—
"My soné, this I findé write,
There is yet one of thilké brood,
Which only for the worldés good
To make a tresor of monéy
Put allé consciénce awey.
Wherof in thy confessión
The name and the conditión
I shall here afterward declare,
Which maketh one riche an other bare.

Upon the bench sitténd on high
With Avarice Usure I sigh,
Ful clothéd of his owné suite,
Which after gold maketh chase and suite
With his brocoúrs, that renne aboute
Liche unto racches [1] in a route.
Such lucre is none above grounde,
Which is nought of tho racchés founde.
For where they se beyeté sterte,
That shall hem in no wise asterte
But they it drive into the net
Of lucre, whiche Usúre hath set.
Usúré with the riché dwelleth,
To all that ever he bieth and selleth
He hath ordeinéd of his sleight
Mesúré double and double weight.
Outwárd he selleth by the lasse
And with the more he maketh his tasse,[2]
Wherof his hous is full withinne.
He recheth nought be so he winne,
Though that there leséten or twelve.
His love is all toward him selve
And to none other but he se
That he may winné suché thre.
For where he shall ought yive or lene
He woll ayeinward take a bene
There he hath lent the smallé pese.[3]
And right so there ben many of these
Lovers, that though they love a lite[4]
That scarsly wolde it weie a mite,
Yet wol they have a pound ayein,
As doth Usúre in his bargain.

1 *Racches*, scenting hounds.
2 *Tasse*, heap.
3 Will take a bean where he has lent a pea.
4 *Lite*, little.

But certes such Usúre unliche
It falleth more unto the riche
Als well of love as of beyete
Than unto hem that ben nought grete,
And as who saith ben simple and pouer;
For selden is whan they recouer
But if it be through great deserte,
And nethéles men se pouerte
With pursuíte of contenaunce[1]
Full ofté make a great chevaúnce
And take of love his avauntáge
Forth with the helpe of his brocáge
That maken seme where it is nought.
And thus full ofté is lové bought
For litel what, and mochel take
With falsé weightés that they make.
"Now sone, of that I saide above
Thou wost what Usure is of Love.
Tell me forthy what so thou wilt,
If thou therof hast any gilt?"—
"My fader nay, for ought I here.
For of tho points ye tolden here
I will you by my trouth assure,
My weight of love and my mesúre
Hath be more large and more certeine
Than ever I toke of love ayeine.
For so yet couthe I never of sleighte
To take ayein by double weighte
Of lové more than I have yive.
For also wis mote I be shrive
And have remissión of sinne,
And so yet couth I never winne
Ne yet so mochel soth to sain,
That ever I might have half ayein
Of so full love as I have lent.
And if mine hap were so well went,
That for the hole I might have half,
Me thenketh I were a goddes half.
For where Usuré wold have double,
My conscience is nought so trouble,

[1] *Pursuíte of contenaunce*, continued perseverance.

I biddé never as to my dele
But of the hole an halven dele.
That is none éxcess as me thenketh,
But netheles it me forthenketh.
For well I wot that wol nought be,
For every day the better I se
That how so ever I yive or lene
My love in placé that I mene,
For ought that ever I axe or crave
I can nothíng ayeinwarde have.
But yet for that I wol nought lete
What so befall of my beyete,
That I ne shall her yive and lene
My love and all my thought so clene,
That toward me shall nought beleve.[1]
And if she of her godé leve
Rewardé wol me nought ayein,
I wot the last of my bargein
Shall stonde upon so great a lost,
That I may never more the cost
Recouer in this world till I deie,
So that touchénd of this partie
I may me well excuse and shall;
And for to speké forth withall,
If any brocour for me went
That point come never in min entent,
So that the moré me mervelleth
What thing it is my lady eileth,
That all min herte and all my timé
She hath, and do no better by me.
"I have herd said, that thought is free
And nethéles in priveté
To you, my fader, that bene here
Min holé shrifté for to here,
I dare min herté well disclose
Touchend Usúrie, as I suppose,
Whiche, as ye telle, in love is used.
My lady may nought ben excused
That for o loking of her eye
Min holé herté till I deie
With all that ever I may and can
She hath me wonné to her man,

[1] *Beleve*, remain.

Wherof me thenketh good reson
wolde
That she somdele rewardé sholde,
And yive a part there she hath all.
I not what falle herafter shall,
But into now yet dare I sain
Her listé never yive ayein
A goodly word in such a wise
Wherof min hopé might arise
My greté love to recompense.
I not how she her consciënce
Excusé wol of this Usúre
By largé weight and great mesúre.
She hath my love and I have nought
Of that which I have dere abought,
And with min herte I have it paide,
But all this is asidé laide,
And I go lovélés aboute.
Her oughté stonde in full great
doubte,
Till she redressé suche a sinne
That she wol al my lové winne
And yiveth me nought to livé by.
Nought al so moch as 'grauntmercy'
Her list to say, of which I might
Some of my greté peine alight.
But of this point, lo, thus I fare,
As he that paieth for his chaffare
And bieth it dere and yet hath none,
So mote he nedés pouer gone.
Thus bie I dere and have no love,
That I ne may nought come above
To winne of lové none encrese.
But I me willé nethélese
Touchend Usúre of love aquite,
And if my lady be to wite[1]
I pray to God such grace her sende
That she by time it mot amende."—
"My sone, of that thou hast an-
swérde
Touchend Usure I have al herde,
How thou of love hast wonné smale.
But that thou tellest in thy tale
And thy ladý therof accusest,
Me thenketh tho wordes thou mis-
usest.
For by thin owné knouleching
Thou saist, how she for one loking
Thy holé hert fro the she toke,
She may be such that her o loke
Is worth thine herté many folde,
So hast thou well thin herté solde
Whan thou hast that is moré
worthe.
And eke of that thou tellest forthe,
How that her weight of love uneven
Is unto thine, under the heven
Stood never in even that balaunce
Which stont in lovés governaunce.
Such is the statute of his lawe,
That though thy lové moré drawe
And peise in the balaúncé more,
Thou might nought axe ayein ther-
fore
Of duété, but all of grace.
For Love is Lorde in every place,
There may no lawe him justify,
By reddour ne by compaigny[1]
That he ne wol, after his wille,
Whom that him liketh spede or
spille.
To love a man may well beginne,
But whether he shall lese or winne
That wot no man, til atté last.
Forthý coveité nought to fast,
My soné, but abide thin ende,
Parcas all may to goodé wende.
But that thou hast me tolde and
saide
Of o thing I am right well paide,
That thou by sleighté ne by guile
Of no brocoúr hast otherwhile
Engínéd love, for suché dede
Is soré vengéd as I rede.
"Brocours of lové, that deceiven,
No wonder is though they receiven
After the wrong that they deserven.
For whom as ever that they serven

[1] *To wite*, to blame.

[1] By force or fellowship.

And do plesauncé for a while,
Yet atté last her owné guile
Upon her owné hede descendeth,
Which God of his vengeauncé sendeth.
As by ensample of time ago
A man may finde it hath be so.
"It fell some time, as it was sene,
The highé goddesse and the quene
Juno tho had in compaigny
A maiden full of trechery.
For she was ever in accorde
With Jupiter, that was her lorde,
To get him other lovés newe
Through such brocáge, and was untrewe
All other wisé than him nedeth.
But she, the which no shamé dredeth,
With queinté wordés and with slie
Blent in such wise her ladies eye
As she to whom that Juno trist,
So that therof she nothing wist.
But so privé may be nothíng,
That it ne cometh to knouleching,
Thing done upon the derké night
Is after knowe on daiés light.
So it befell, that atté last
All that this slighé maiden cast
Was overcast and overthrowe.
For as the sothé mot be knowe,
To Juno it was done understonde,
In what manére her husébonde
With fals brocáge hath take usure
Of lové more than his mesure,
Whan he toke other than his wife;
Wherof this maiden was giltife,
Whiche haddé ben of his assent.
And thus was all the gamé shent.
She suffred him, as she mot nede,
But the brocoúr of his misdede,
She which her counseil yaf therto,
On her is the vengeaúncé do;
For Juno with her wordes hote
This maiden, which Eccho was hote,
Reproveth and saith in this wise:
'O traiteresse, of which servíce
Hast thou thin owné lady served,
Thou hast great peiné well deserved
That thou canst maken it so queint.
Thy slighé wordés for to peint
Towardés me that am thy quene,
Wherof thou madest me to wene,
That my husbondé trewé were
Whan that he loveth ellés where
All be it so him nedeth nought.
But upon the it shall be bought
Whiche art privé to tho doínges,
And me full ofte of thy lesínges
Deceivéd hast. Nowe is the day,
That I thy wilé quité may,
And for thou hast to me conceled
That my lorde hath with other deled,
I shall the sette in suche a kinde
That ever unto the worldés ende
All that thou herest thou shalt telle
And clappe it out as doth a belle.
And with that word she was forshape,
There may no vois her mouthe escape:
What man that in the wodés crieth,
Withouten faile Ecchó replieth;
And what word that him lust to sain,
The samé word she saith ayein.
Thus she, which whilome haddé leve
To dwelle in chambre, mot beleve[1]
In wodés and on hillés both,
For such brocáge as wives loth,
Which doth her lordés hertés chaunge
And love in other places straunge.
"Forthý if ever it so befalle
That thou, my sone, amongés alle
Be wedded man, hold that thou hast,
For than all other love is waste;
O wife shal wel to the suffise,
And than if thou for covetise
Of lové woldest axé more,

[1] *Beleve*, remain.

Thou shuldest don ayein the lore
Of alle hem that trewé be."—
"My fader, as in this degré
My consciënce is nought accused,
For I no such brocáge have used
Wherof that lust of love is wonne.
Forthý speke forth, as ye begonne,
Of Avarice upon my shrifte."—
"My sone, I shall the braunches shifte
By order so as they ben set,
On whom no good is wel beset.
Blind Avarice of his lignáge
For counseil and for cousináge
To be witholde ayein Largesse
Hath one, whose name is said Scarsnesse,
The which is keper of his hous
And is so throughout ávarous,
That he no good let out of honde;
Though God him self it woldé fonde,
Of yifté shuld he no thing have.
And if a man it woldé crave,
He musté thanné failé nede
Where God him selvé may nought spede.
And thus Scarsnésse in every place
By reson may no thank purcháce.
And nethéles in his degre
Above all other most privé
With Avarícé stant he this.
For he govérneth that there is
In eche estate of his office
After the reule of thilké vice
He taketh, he kepeth, he halt, he bint,
That lighter is to fle[1] the flint
Than gete of him in hard or neisshe
Only the value of a reisshe
Of good in helping of an other,
Nought though it were his owné brother.
For in the cas of yift and lone
Stant every man for him alone.

[1] *Fle*, flay.

Him thenketh, of his unkindship,
That him nedéth no felaship
Be so the bagge and he accorden,
Him reccheth nought what men recorden
Of him, or be it evil or good,
For all his truste is on his good;
So that alone he falleth ofte,
Whan he best weneth stonde alofte,
Als well in love as other wise.
For love is ever of some reprise
To him that woll his lové holde.
Forthý my sone, as thou art holde
Touchend of this tell me thy shrifte,
Hast thou be scarse or large of yifte
Unto thy lové, whom thou servest.
For after that thou well deservest
Of yifté, thou might be the bet.
For that good holde I well beset
For which thou might the better fare,
Than is no wisdom for to spare.
For thus men sain in every nede,
He was wise that first madé mede.
For where as medé may nought spede,
I not what helpeth other dede.
Full ofte he faileth of his game,
That will with idel[1] hond reclame
His hawke, as many a nicé doth.
Forthý my soné, tell me soth
And say the trouth, if thou hast be
Unto thy love or scarse or fre?"—
"My fader, it hath stondé thus,
That if the tresor of Cresús
And all the golde of Octavien,
Forth with the richesse of Yndien
Of perlés and of riché stones
Were all to-gider min at ones,
I set it at no more accompt
Than wolde a baré straw amount
To yive it her all in a day,
Be so that to that sweté may
It mighté like or more or lesse.
And thus because of my scarsnesse

[1] *Idel*, empty.

Ye may well understond and leve
That I shall nought the worse acheve
The purpos which is in my thought,
But yet I yaf her never nought
Ne therto durst a profre make.
For well I wot she woll nought take,
And yivé woll she nought also,
She is escheue of bothé two.
And this I trowé be the skill
Towardés me, for she ne will
That I have any cause of hope,
Nought al so mochel as a drope.
But toward other as I may se
She taketh and yiveth in such degré,
That as by wey of frendelyhede
She can so kepe her womanhede
That every man speketh of her wele.
But she wol take of me no dele,
And yet she wot wel that I wolde
Yive and do bothé what I sholde
To plesen her in all my might,
By reson this wote every wight.
For that may by no wey asterte,
There she is maister of the herte
She mot be maister of the good.
For god wot wel that all my mood
And all min herte and all my thought
And all my good while I have ought,
Als frely as God hath it yive,
It shall be hers, the while I live,
Right as her list her self commaunde.
So that it nedeth no demaunde
To axe me if I have be scarse
To lové, for as to tho parse[1]
I will answeren and say no."—
"My soné, that is right well do.
For often timés of scarsnesse
It hath ben seen, that for the lesse
Is lost the more, as thou shalt here
A talé, lich to this matere.

Scarsnesse and Love accorden never,.

For every thing is wel the lever
Whan that a man hath bought it dere.
And for to speke in this matere
For sparing of a litel cost
Full ofté time a man hath lost
The largé coté for the hood.
What man that scarse is of his good
And wol nought yive, he shall nought take,
With yift a man may undertake
The highé God to plese and queme,
With yift a man the world may deme.
For every creätúré bore
If thou him yive is glad therfore,
And every gladship, as I finde,
Is comfort unto lovés kinde
And causeth ofte a man to spede;
So was he wise that first yaf mede.
For Medé kepeth Love in hous,
But where the men ben coveitoús
And sparen for to yive a parte,
They knowen nought Cupidés arte.
For his fortúne and his apprise
Disdeigneth allé covetise
And hateth allé nigardie.
And for to loke of this partie
A sothe ensample, howe it is so,
I findé write of Babio,
Which had a love at his menáge,
There was no fairer of her age
And highte Viola by name,
Which full of youth and full of game
Was of her selfe and large and free.
But such an other chinche[1] as he
Men wisten nought in all the londe,
And had affaited to his honde
His servant, the which Spodius
Was hote. And in this wisé thus
The worldés good of suffisaúnce
Was had, but liking and plesaúnce
Of that belongeth to richésse
Of lové stode in great distresse,
So that this yongé lusty wight
Of thing which fell to lovés right

[1] *Tho parse*, those charms.

[1] *Chinche*, miser.

Was evil servéd over all,
That she was wo bego withall.
Til that Cupide and Venus eke
A medicíné for the seke
Ordeiné wolden in this cas;
So as fortúné thanné was
Of love upon the destiné
It fell right as it shulde be.
A fresshe, a free, a frendly man,
That nought of Avarícé can,
Which Croceús by namé hight,
Toward this sweté cast his sight
And there she was cam in presence;
She sigh him large of his despense
And amorous and glad of chere,
So that her liketh well to here
The goodly wordés which he saide,
And therupon of love he praide.
Of lové was all that he ment,
To love and for she shulde assent
He yaf her yiftés ever among.
But for men sain that 'Mede is strong'
It was well sene at thilké tide,
For as it shulde of right betide
This Viola largesse hath take
And the nigárd she hath forsake.
Of Babio she will no more,
For he was grucchend evermore,
There was with him none other fare,
But for to pinche and for to spare,
Of worldés muck to get encres.
So goth the wrecché lovéles
Bejapéd for his Scarsité:
And he that largé was and fre
And set his herté to despende,
This Croceús his bowé bende
Which Venus toke him for to holde,
And shot as ofte as ever he wolde.
"Lo, thus departeth love his lawe,
That what man woll nought be felawe
To yive and spende, as I the telle,
He is nought worthy for to dwelle
In Lovés Court to be relieved.
Forthý my sone, if I be leved,
Thou shalt be large of thy despense."—
"My fader, in my consciénce
If there be any thinge amis,
I wolde amende it after this
Toward my lové namély."—
"My soné, well and redély
Thou saist, so that well paid withall
I am, and further if I shall
Unto thy shrifté specifie
Of Avarice the progenie,
What Vicé sueth after this,
Thou shalt have wonder how it is
Among the folke in any regne,
That such a Vicé mighté regne,
Whiche is comúne at all assaies,
As men may findé now a daies.
The Vicé like unto the Fende,
Which never yet was mannés frende,
And clepéd is Unkindéship,
Of covine and of felaship
With Avarice he is witholde.
Him thenketh he shuld nought ben holde
Unto the moder which him bare.
Of him may never man beware,
He wol nought knowé the merite
For that he wolde it nought aquite,
Which in this worlde is mochel used,
And fewé ben therof excused.
To tell of him is endéles,
But thus I saié nethéles,
Where as this Vicé cometh to londe
There taketh no man his thanke on honde;
Though he with all his mightés serve
He shall of him no thank deserve;
He taketh what any man will yive
But while he hath o day to live
He wol no thíng rewarde ayein,
He gruccheth for to yive o grein
Where he hath take a berné full.
That maketh a kindé herté dull,

To set his trust in such frendship
There as he fint no kindéship.
And for to speké wordés pleine,
Thus here I many a man compleigne
That nowe on daiés thou shalt finde
At nedé fewé frendés kinde.
What thou hast done for hem tofore
It is foryeten as it were lore.[1]
The bokés speken of this Vice
And telle how God of his justice
By way of kinde, and eke natúre
And every liflich creätúre,
The lawe also, who that it can,
They dampnen an unkindé man.
"It is all one, to say Unkinde
As thing which done is ayein Kinde,[2]
For it with Kindé never stood
A man to yielden evil for good.
For who that woldé taken hede,
A beste is glad of a good dede
And loveth thilké creätúre
After the lawe of his natúre
And doth him ese. And for to se
Of this matere auctorité,
Full ofté time it hath befalle;
Wherof a tale amongés alle,
Which is of olde ensamplarie,
I thenké for to specifie.
To speke of an unkindé man
I finde, how whilome Adrian
Of Romé, which a great lorde was,
Upon a day as he par cas
To wodé in his hunting went,
It hapneth at a sodein went,
After the chase as he pursueth,
Through happé, which no man escheueth,
He felle unware into a pit,
Where that it mighté nought be let.
The pit was depe, and he fell lowe,
That of his men none mighté knowe
Where he became, for none was nigh

[1] *Lore*, lost. [2] *Kinde*, nature.

Which of his fall the mischefe sigh.
And thus aloné there he lay
Clepende and criend all the day
For socoure and deliverance,
Till ayein eve it fell per chance,
A while er it began to night,
A pouer man which Bardus hight
Cam forthé walkend with his asse
And haddé gadered him a tasse[1]
Of grené stickés and of drie
To sellé whom that wolde hem bie,
As he which had no livélode
But whan he mighté suche a lode
To towné with his assé carie.
And as it fel him for to tarie
That ilké timé nigh the pit
And hath the trussé fasté knit,
He herde a vois, which criéd dimme,
And he his eré to the brimme
Hath leide and herde it was a man,
Which saide, 'O helpe here Adrian,
And I will yivé half my good!'
The pouer man this understood
As he that woldé gladly win,
And to this lord which was within
He spake and said, 'If I the save,
What sikernessé shall I have
Of covenant, that afterwarde
Thou wolt me yivé such rewarde,
As thou behightest now before?'
That other hath his othés swore
By heven and by the goddés alle,
If that it mighté so befalle
That he out of the pit him brought,
Of all the goodés which he ought[2]
He shall have even halven dele.
This Bardus said, he wolde wele.
And with this worde his asse anon
He let untrussé, and therupon
Down goth the corde into the pit,
To whiche he hath at ende knit
A staff, wherby, he saide, he wolde
That Adrian him shuldé holde.
But it was tho per chauncé falle,

[1] *Tasse*, heap. [2] *Ought*, owned.

Into that pit was also falle
An Apé, which at thilké throwe,
Whan that the cordé cam down lowe,
All sodeinly therto he skipte
And it in both his armés clipte.
And Bardus with his asse anone
Him hath up draw, and he is gon.
But whan he sigh it was an Ape,
He wend all haddé ben a jape
Of faierie, and sore him dradde.
And Adrian eft soné gradde
For helpe and cride and preidé faste.
And he eftsone his cordé caste.
But whan it came unto the grounde,
A great serpént it hath bewounde,
The which Bardus anone up drough.
And than him thoughté wel inough,
It was fantasmé that he herde
The vois, and he therto answerde:
'What wight art thou in goddés name?'
'I am,' quod Adrian, 'the same,
Whose good thou shalt have even halfe.'
Quod Bardus 'Than a goddés halfe
The thriddé time assaie I shall.'
And cast his cordé forth withall
Into the pit, and whan it came
To him, this lord of Rome it name
And therupon him hath adressed
And with his hond ful ofté blessed.
And than he bad to Bardus 'Hale!'[1]
And he, which understood his tale,
Betwene him and his asse all softe
Hath drawe and set him up a lofte
Withouten harm all esély.
He saith not onés 'graunt mercy,'[2]
But straught him forth to the citee
And let this pouer Bardus be.
And nethéles this simple man
His covenaunt, so as he can,
Hath axéd. And that other saide,
If so be that he him upbraide

[1] *Hale*, "Haul up!"
[2] *Graunt mercy*, thank you.

Of ought that hath be spoke or do,
It shall be vengéd of him so
That him were better to be dede.
And he can tho no other rede;
But on his asse ayein he cast
His trusse and hieth homward fast.
And whan that he came home to bed,
He tolde his wife how that he sped.
"But finally, to speke ought more
Unto this lorde he drad him sore,
So that a word ne durst he sain.
And thus upon the morwe ayein
In the manér as I recorde,
Forth with his asse and with his corde
To gader wode, as he did er,
He goth, and whan that he cam ner
Unto the placé where he wolde,
He gan his Ape anone beholde,
Which had gadéréd al aboute
Of stickés here and there a route
And leide hem redy to his honde,
Wherof he made his trusse and bonde.
Fro daie to daie and in this wise
This Apé profreth his servíse,
So that he had of wode inough.
Upon a time and as he drough
Toward the wode, he sigh beside
The greaté gastly serpent glide
Till that she cam in his presénce,
And in her kinde a reverence
She hath him do, and forth withall
A stone more bright than a cristall
Out of her mouth to-fore his way
She let down fall and went away,
For that he shall nought ben adrad.
"Tho was this pouer Bardus glad,
Thonkéndé God, and to the stone
He goth and taketh it up anone
And hath great wonder in his witte
How that the beste him hath aquitte
Where that the mannés sone hath failed
For whom he haddé most travailed.

But all he put in Goddés honde
And torneth home, and what he fonde
Unto his wife he hath it shewed
And they, that weren bothé lewed,
Accorden that he shulde it selle.
And he no lenger woldé dwelle [1]
But forth anone upon the tale
The stone he profreth to the sale;
And right as he him selfe it sette,
The jueller anone forth fette
The golde and made his paiément,
Therof was no delaiement.
Thus whan this stone was bought and sold,
Homwárd with joié many fold
This Bardus goth, and whan he cam
Hom to his hous and that he nam
His gold out of his purs withinne,
He fonde his stone also therinne,
Wherof for joy his herte plaide,
Unto his wife and thus he saide,
'Lo, here my golde,—lo, here my stone!'
His wife hath wonder therupon,
And axeth him how that may be.
'Now by my trouth, I not,' [2] quod he,
'But I dare swere upon a boke
That to my marchant I it toke,
And he it haddé whan I went
So know I nought to what entent
It is now here, but it be grace.
Forthý to morwe in other place
I will it foundé [3] for to selle,
And if it woll nought with him dwelle,
But crepe into my purse ayein,
Than dare I saufly swere and sain,
It is the vertue of the stone.'
"The morwe came, and he is gone
To seche about in other stede
His stone to selle, and so he dede
And lefte it with his chapman there.

[1] *Dwelle*, delay.
[2] *Not*, know not. [3] *Foundé*, try.

But whan that he came ellés where,
In presence of his wife at home,
Out of his purs and that he nome
His golde, he founde his stone withal.
And thus it felle him overal
Where he it solde in sondrie place,
Such was the fortune and the grace.
But so well may nothíng be hid,
That it nis atté lasté kid. [1]
This famé goth abouté Rome
So ferforth, that the wordés come
To themperoúr Justinián,
And he let sendé for the man
And axéd him, how that it was.
"And Bardus tolde him all the cas,
How that the worme and eke the beste,
Al though they madé no beheste,
His travaile hadden well aquit.
But he which had a mannés wit
And made his covenant by mouth
And swore therto all that he couth
To parte and yivé half his good
Hath now foryete how that it stood,
As he which wol no trouthé holde.
This emperoúr al that he tolde
Hath herde and thilke unkindénesse,
He said, he wolde him self redresse.
And thus in court of jugément
This Adrian was than assent, [2]
And the quaréll in audiénce
Declaréd was in the presénce
Of themperoúr and many mo;
Wherof was mochel speché tho
And great wondríng among the press.
But atté lasté nethéless,
For the partië which hath pleigned
The law hath deméd and ordeigned
By hem that were aviséd wele,
That he shal have the halven dele
Throughout of Adrianés good.
And thus of thilke unkindé blood
Stant the memoire unto this day,

[1] *Kid*, made known. [2] *Assent*, sent for.

Wheré that every wise man may
Ensamplen him and take in minde
What shame it is to ben unkinde,
Ayein the which resón debateth
And every creätúre it hateth.
"Forthý my sone, in thy office
I redé flee that ilké Vice.
For right as the croníqué saith
Of Adrian, how he his feith
Foryat for worldés covetise,
Ful oft in suche a maner wise
Of lovers now a man may se
Ful many that unkindé be,
For wel behote and evil last
That is her life,[1] for atté last
Whan that they have her wille do
Her love is sone aftér ago.
What saist thou, soné, to this cas?"—
"My fader, I wil say, Helas,
That ever such a man was bore
Which whan he hath his trouthé swore
And hath of lové what he wolde,
That he at any timé sholde
Ever after in his herté finde
To falsen and to ben unkinde.
"But, fader, as touchénd of me,
I may nought stond in that degre.
For I toke never of lové why
That I ne may wel go therby
And do my profite ellés where
For any spede I findé there,
I dare wel thenken, all about.
But I ne dare nought speke it out,
And if I dorst I woldé pleigne,
That she for whom I suffré peine
And love her ever aliché hote,
That nouther yivé ne behote
In rewardíng of my servíce
It list[2] her in no maner wise.
I wol nought say that she is kinde,
And for to say she is unkinde
That dare I nought by God above
Which demeth every herte of love,
He wot that on min owné side
Shall none unkindéship abide;
If it shall with my lady dwelle,
Therof dare I no moré telle.
Now, godé fader, as it is
Tell me, what thenketh you of this?"—
My sone, of that unkindéship,
The which toward thy ladisship
Thou pleignest, for she woll the nought,
Thou art to blamen of thy thought.
For it may be that thy desire,
Though it brenne ever as doth the fire,
Par cas to her honoúr misset,
Or ellés timé come nought yet
Which stant upon thy destiné.
Forthý my sone, I redé the
Thenk well, what ever the befalle,
For no man hath his lustés alle.
But as thou toldest me before
That thou to love art nought forswore
And hast done non unkindénesse,
Thou might therof thy gracé blesse
And levé nought that cóntinuánce,
For there may be no such grevánce
To love as is Unkindéship.
Wherof to kepé thy worshíp,
So as these oldé bokés tale,
I shall the telle a redy tale.
Now herken and be ware therby,
For I will telle it openly.
"**Minos**, as telleth the poéte,
The which whilóm was king of Crete,
A soné had and Androchee
He hight. And so befell that he
Unto Athenés for to lere
Was sent, and so he bare him there
For that he was of high lignáge,
Such pride he toke in his coráge,

[1] Well promised and ill performed, that is their life.
[2] *List*, pleases.

That he foryeten hath the scoles,
And in riót among the fooles
He diddé many thingés wronge
And uséd thilké life so longe,
Til atté last of that he wrought
He found the mischefe which he sought,
Wherof it fell that he was slain.
His fader, which it herde sain,
Was wroth, and all that ever he might
Of men of armés he him dight
A strong powér and forth he went
Unto Athenés, where he brent
The pleiné contré al aboute.
The cités stood of him in doubte[1]
As they that no defencé had
Ayein the power which he lad.
Egëus which was theré king
His counseil toke upon this thing,
For he was than in the citee,
So that of pees into tretee
Betwene Minós and Egëús
They fell, and bene accorded thus,
That king Minós fro yere to yere
Receivé shal as thou shalt here
Out of Athenés for truáge
Of men that were of mighty age
Personés nine, of which he shall
His willé don in speciall
For vengeaunce of his sonés deth,
None other gracé there ne geth
But for to také the juise,[2]
And that was don in suche a wise.
Upon which stood a wonder cas.
For thilké timé so it was,
Wherof that men yet rede and sing,
King Minos had in his kepíng
A cruel monster, as saith the gest.
For he was half man and half beste,
And Minotaurus he was hote,
Which was begotten in a riote
Upon Pasiphe, his owné wife,
Whil he was out upon the strife
Of thilké greaté siege at Troie.

[1] *Doubte*, fear. [2] *Juise*, judgment.

But she which lost hath allé joie
Whan that she sigh this monster bore
Bad men ordeigne anon therfore.
And fell that ilké timé thus,
There was a clerke, one Dedalus,
Which haddé ben of her assent[1]
Of that her world was so miswent;
And he made of his owné wit,
Wherof the remembraúnce is yit,
For Minotauré suche a hous
That was so stronge and merveilóus
That what man that withinné went,
There was so many a sondry went
That he ne shuldé nought come out,
But gone amaséd all about.
And in this hous to locke and warde
Was Minotaurus put in warde,
That what life[2] that therinné cam,
Or man or beste, he overcam
And slough, and fed him therupon.
And in this wisé many one
Out of Athenés for truage
Devouréd weren in that rage.
For every yere they shope hem so,
They of Athenés er they go
Toward that ilké wofull chaunce
As it was set in ordenaunce,
Upon Fortúne her lot they cast;
Till that Thesëús atté laste,
Which was the kingés soné there
Amongés other that there were,
In thilké yere as it befell
The lot upon his chauncé fell.
He was a worthy knight withall,
And whan he sigh his chauncé fall,
He ferde as though he toke none hede,
But all that ever he might spede
With him and with his felaship
Forth into Crete he goth by ship,
Where that the king Minós he sought
And profreth all that he him ought
Upon the point of her accorde.

[1] *Of her assent*, sent for by her.
[2] *Life*, body; *what life*, whoever.

This sterné king, this cruel lorde,
Toke every day one of the nine
And put into the disciplíne
Of Minotaure to be devoured.
But Theseús was so favoúred
That he was kept till atté last,
And in the meané while he cast
What thing him weré best to do.
And fell, that Ariadné tho,
Which was the doughter of Minós,
And haddé herd the worthy los[1]
Of Theseús and of his might
And sigh he was a lusty knight,
Her holé herte on him she laide.
And he also of love her praide
So ferforth that they were alone,
And she ordeineth than anone
In what manér she shuld him save.
And shopé so, she did him have
A clue of threde of which withinne
First atté dore he shall beginne
With him to také that one ende,
That whan he wold ayeinward wende
He mighté go the samé wey.
And over this so as I say,
Of pitch she toke him a pelote,[2]
The which he shulde into the throte
Of Minotauré casté right.
Such wepon also for him she dight,
That he by reson may nought faile
To make an ende of his bataile.
For she him taught in sondry wise
Till he was knowe of thilke emprise
How he this besté shuldé quelle.
And thus short talé for to telle,
So as this maiden him had taught
Theseús with this monster faught
And smote of his hede, the whiche
    he nam,
And by the thred, so as he cam
He goth ayein, til he were out.
So was great wonder all about;
Minós the tribute hath relesed,

[1] *Los*, praise.
[2] *Toke him a pelote*, gave him a ball.

And so was all the werré cesed
Betwene Athenes and hem of Crete.
"But now to speke of thilké swete
Whose beauté was withouté wan,
This faire maiden Adriane,
Whan that she sigh Theseús sounde
Was never yet upon this grounde
A gladder wight than she was tho.
Theseüs dwelt a day or two
Where that Minós great chere him
    ded.
Theseús in a privé sted
Hath with this maiden spoke and
    rouned,[1]
That she to him was abandoúned;
For he so fairé tho behight[2]
That ever while he livé might
He shuld her také for his wife
And as his owné hertés life
He wolde her love and trouthé bere.
And she, which mighté nought for-
    bere,
So soré lovéth him ayein,
That what as ever he wold sain
With all her herté she beleveth.
And thus his purpos he acheveth,
So that assuréd of his trouthe
With him she went, and that was
    routhe.
Fedra her yongé suster eke,
A lusty maide, a sobre, a meke,
Fulfilléd of all curtesie,
For susterhode and compaignie
Of lové which was hem betwene,
To sen her suster made a quene
Her fader lefte and forth she went
With him which all his first entent
Foryat within a litel throwe,[3]
So that it was all over throwe
Whan she best wend it shuldé stonde.
The ship was blowé fro the londe,
Wherinné that they sailend were.
This Ariadne had mochel fere

[1] *Rouned*, whispered.
[2] *Tho behight*, then promised.
[3] *Throwe*, space of time.

Of that the wind so loudé blewe,
As she which of the see ne knewe,
And praidé for to reste a while.
And so fell that upon an ile
Which Chio highté they ben drive,
Where he to her hath levé yive,
That she shall lond and take her rest,
But that was nothing for her best.
For whan she was to londé brought,
She, which that timé thoughté nought
But allé trouth and toke no kepe,
Hath laid her softé for to slepe,
As she which longe hath ben forwacched.
But certés she was evil macched
And fer from allé lovés kinde.
For moré than the beste[1] unkinde
Theseüs, which no trouthé kept,
While that this yongé lady slept,
Fulfilled of all unkindéship
Hath all foryetc the godéship,
Whiche Ariadné him hadde do,
And bad unto the shipmen tho
Hale up the saile and nought abide,
And forth he goth the samé tide
Towarde Athenes, and her on londe
He lefté, which lay nigh the stronde
Slepéndé til that she awoke.
But whan that she cast up her loke
Toward the stronde and sigh no wight,
Her herté was so sore aflight[2]
That she ne wisté what to thinke
But drough her to the water brinke,
Where she beheld the see at large.
She sigh no ship, she sigh no barge
Als ferforth as she mighté kenne.
'Ha lord,' she saidé, 'which a senne,
As all the world shall after here,
Upon this wofull woman here
This worthy knight hath done and wrought,

[1] *Beste*, beast. [2] *Aflight*, afflicted.

I wend I had his lové bought,
And so deservéd atté nede,
Whan that he stood upon his drede,
And eke the love he me behight.
It is great wonder, how he might
Towardés me now ben unkinde,
And so to let out of his minde
Thing which he said his owné mouth.
But after this, whan it is couth
And drawe into the worldés fame,
It shall ben hindring of his name.
For well he wote, and so wote I,
He yafe his trouthé bodily
That he min honour shuldé kepe.'
And with that word she gan to wepe
And sorweth moré than inough.
Her fairé tresses she to-drough
And with her self toke such a strife,
That she betwene the deth and life
Swounéndé lay full oft amonge.
And all was this on him alonge,
Which was to love unkindé so,
Wherof the wrong shall evermo
Stond in croníque of remembraúnce.
And eke it axeth a vengeaúnce
To ben unkinde in lovés cas
So as Theseüs thanné was,
All though he were a noble knight.
For he the lawe of lovés right
Forfested hath in allé way,
That Ariadne he put away,
Which was a great unkindé dede.
And after this, so as I rede,
Fedra, the which her suster is,
He toke in stede of her, and this
Fell afterward to mochel tene.
For thilké Vice of whiche I mene,
Unkindéship, where that it falleth
The trouthe of mannés hert it palleth
That he can no good dede acquite,
So may he stonde of no merite
Towardés God and eke also
Men clepen him the worldés fo,
For he no moré than the Fende
Unto none other man is frende,

But all toward him self alone.
"Forthý my sone, in thy persone
This Vice above all other fle."—
My fader, as ye techen me,
I thenké don in this matere.
But over this now wold I here,
Wherof I shall me shrivé more."
"My godé sone, as for thy lore,
After the reule of Covetise,
I shall the propreté devise
Of every Vicé by and by.
Now herke and be wel ware therby.
"**In the lignage** of Avarice,
My soné, yet there is a Vice,
His righté name it is Ravine,
Which hath a route of his covine.
Ravine among the maisters dwelleth,
And with his servants as men telleth
Extorción is now witholde.
Ravine of other mennés folde
Maketh his lardér and paieth nought.
For where as ever it may be sought
In his hous there shall no thing lacke,
And that ful ofte abieth the packe
Of pouer men that dwelle aboute;
Thus stant the comune people in doubte,
Which can do none amendément.
For whan him faileth paiément,
Raviné maketh non other skille,
But taketh by strength al that he wille.
So ben there in the samé wise
Lovérs, as I the shall devise,
That whan nought ellés may availe,
Anone with strengthé they assaile
And get of lové the sesine
Whan they se timé, by ravine.
"Forthy my soné, shrive the here,
If thou hast ben a ravinere
Of lové."—"Certes, fader, no,
For I my lady lové so
For though I were as was Pompéy
That all the world me wolde obey,
Or ellés such as Alisaundre,
I woldé nought do suche a sclaunder.
It is no good man, which so doth."—
"In godé feith, sone, thou saist soth.
For he that woll of purveánce
By such a wey his lust avance
He shall it after sore abie,
But if[1] these olde ensamples lie."—
"Now, godé fader, tell me one,
So as ye connen many one,
Touchénd of love in this matere."—
"Now list, my sone, and thou shalt here
So as it hath befall er this
In lovés cause how that it is,
A man to také by ravine
The preié which is feminine.
There was a roial noble kinge,
A riche of allé worldés thinge,
Which of his propre enheritaunce
Athenés had in governaunce,
And whoso thenké therupon,
His namé was king Pandión.
Two doughters had he by his wife,
The which he lovéd as his life.
The firsté doughter Progné hight,
And the secónde, as she well might,
Was clepéd fairé Philomene,
To whom fell after mochel tene.[2]
The fader of his purveánce
His doughter Progné wolde avance,
And yafe her unto mariáge
A worthy king of high lignáge,
A noble knight eke of his honde,
So was he kid[3] in every londe.
Of Tracé he hight Terëús,
The clerke Ovídé telleth thus.

[1] *But if*, unless. [2] *Tene*, sorrow.
[3] *Kid*, made known, renowned.

This Terëús his wife home lad,
A lusty life with her he had
Till it befell upon a tide,
This Progne, as she lay him beside,
Bethought her how it mighté be
That she her suster mighté se;
And to her lorde her will she saide
With goodly wordés and him praide
That she unto her mighté go,
And if it likéd him nought so,
That than he wolde him selvé wende,
Or ellés by some other sende
Which might her deré suster grete
And shape how that they mighten
 mete.
Her lorde anone to that he herde
Yaf his accorde and thus answérde:
'I woll,' he saidé, 'for thy sake,
The wey after thy suster take
My self and bring her, if I may.'
And she with that, there as she lay,
Began him in her armés clippe
And kist him with her softé lippe
And saidé: 'Siré, graunt mercy.'
And he sone after was redý
And toke his levé for to go.
In sory timé did he so.
This Terëús goth forth to shippe
With him and all his felashippe.
By sea the righté cours he nam
Unto the contré till he cam
Where Philoméné was dwellíng,
And of her suster the tiding
He tolde and tho they weren glad
And mochel joie of him they made.
The fader and the moder bothe
To leve her doughter weré lothe
But if they weren in presence,
And nethéles at reverence
Of him that wolde him self travaile,
They woldé nought he shuldé faile,
And that they praiden yive her leve.
And she that woldé nought beleve[1]
In allé hasté made her yare[2]

[1] *Beleve*, stay behind. [2] *Yare*, ready.

Toward her suster for to fare
With Terëús and forth she went.
And he with al his hole entent
Whan she was fro her frendés go
Assoteth of her lové so
His eyé might he nought witholde
That he ne must on her beholde,
And with the sight he gan desire
And set his owné hert a fire.
And fire whan it to tow approcheth
To him anon the strength accro-
 cheth,[1]
Till with his hete it be devoured,
The tow ne may nought be soc-
 coúred.
And so the tirann ravinere,
Whan that she was in his powere,
And he therto sigh time and place,
As he that lost hath all his grace,
Foryate he was a wedded man,
And in a rage on her he ran
Right as a wolf that taketh his pray.
And she began to crie and pray:
'O fader dere, o moder dere,
Now help!' But they ne might it
 here,
And she was of to litel might
Defence ayein so rude a knight
To maké whan he was so wode
That he no reson understode.
But whan she to her selvé come
And of her mischefe hedé nome
And knewe how that she was no
 maide,
With wofull herté thus she saide:
'O thou of allé men the worst,
Where was there ever man that dorst
Do such a dede as thou hast do?
That day shall falle, I hopé so,
That I shall tell out all my fille
And with my speche I shall fulfille
The widé worlde in brede and
 length
That thou hast do to me by strength.

[1] *Accrocheth*, increaseth.

If I among the people dwelle
Unto the people I shall it telle;
And if I be withinné wall
Of stonés closéd, than I shall
Unto the stonés clepe and crie,
And tellen hem thy felonie;
And if I to the wodés wende,
There shall I tellé tale and ende
And crie it to the briddés out,
That they shall here it all about:
For I so loude it shall reherce,
That my vois shall the heven perce,
That it shall soune in Goddés ere.
Ha falsé man, where is thy fere?
O more cruél than any beste,
How hast thou holden thy behest
Which thou unto my suster madest?
O thou, which allé love ungladest
And art ensample of all untrewe,
Now woldé god my suster knewe
Of thin untrouthe, how that it stood!'
And he than as a leon wode [1]
With his unhappy hondés strong
He caught her by the tresses long
With whiche he bondé both her armes,
That was a feble dede of armes,
And to the grounde anone her cast,
And out he clippeth also fast
Her tungé with a paire of sheres.
So what with blode and what with teres,
Out of her eyne and of her mouth,
He made her fairé face uncouth.
She lay swounénd unto the dethe,
There was unnethés any brethe.
But yet whan he her tungé refte,
A litel part therof he lefte.
But she withall no word may soune
But chitre [2] and as a brid jargoune.
And nethéles that wodé hounde
Her body hent up fro the grounde
And sent her there as by his will
She shulde abide, in prison still

[1] *Wode*, madly raging. [2] *Chitre*, chirp.

For ever mo. But now take hede
What after fell of this misdede.
Whan all this mischefe was befalle,
This Terëús, that foule him falle,
Unto his contré home he tigh,[1]
And whan he cam his paleis nigh,
His wife alredy there him kept.
Whan he her sigh, anon he wept,
And that he didé for deceipt,
For she began to axe him streit:
'Where is my suster?' And he saide
That she was dede, and Progne abraide,
As she that was a wofull wife,
And stood betwene her deth and life
Because she herdé such tidíng.
But for she sigh her lord wepíng,
She wendé nought but alle trouth
And haddé wel the moré routh.
The perlés weré tho forsake
To her and blacké clothés take,
As she that was gentil and kinde.
In worship of her susters minde [2]
She made a riche enterément,[3]
For she found none amendément
To sighen or to sobbé more,
So was there guile under the gore.
"Now levé we this king and quene,
And torne ayein to Philomene.
As I began to tellen erst,
Whan she cam into prison ferst,
It thought a kingés doughter straunge
To maké so sodeín a chaunge
Fro welth unto so great a wo.
And she began to thenké tho,
Though she by mouthé nothing praide,
Within her herté thus she saide:
'O thou, almighty Jupitér,
That highé sittest and lokest fer,

[1] *Tigh*, drew.
[2] In reverence to her sister's memory.
[3] *Enterément*, interment, funeral pomp.

Thou suffrest many a wrong doíng,
And yet it is nought thy willíng.
To the there may nothíng ben hid,
Thou wost[1] how it is me betid.
I wolde I haddé nought be bore.
For than I haddé nought forlore
My speche and my virginité.
But godé lord, all is in the,
Whan thou therof wolt do vengeaúnce
And shapé my deliveraúnce!'
And ever among this lady wepte
And thoughté that she never kepte
To be a worldés woman more,
And that she wissheth evermore.
But ofte unto her suster dere
Her herté speketh in this manere
And saide: 'Ha suster, if ye knewe
Of min estate ye woldé rewe
I trowe, and my deliveraúnce
Ye woldé shape, and do vengeaúnce
On him that is so fals a man.
And nethéles, so as I can,
I woll you send some tokening,
Wherof ye shall have knouleching
Of thing I wot that shall you loth
The which you toucheth and me both.'
And tho within a while als tite[2]
She wafe a cloth of silke all white
With letters and ymagery,
In which was all the felony,
Which Terëús to her hath do,
And lappéd it to-gider tho
And set her signet therupon
And sent it unto Progne anon.
The messager which forth it bare,
What it amounteth is nought ware,
And nethéles to Progne he goth
And privély taketh her the cloth
And went ayein right as he cám,
The Court of him none hedé name.
"Whan Progne of Philomené herde
She woldé knowe how that it ferde,
And openeth that the man hath brought
And wot therby what hath be wrought
And what mischefe there is befalle.
In swouné tho she gan down falle,
And efte arose and gan to stonde,
And eft she taketh the clothe on honde,
Beheld the letters and thymáges,
But atté last of suche oultráges
She said, 'Wepíng is nought the bote,'[1]
And swereth, if that she livé mote
It shall be vengéd other wise.
And with that she gan her avise,
How first she might unto her winne
Her suster, that no man withinne,
But only they that weré swore,
It shuldé knowe, and shope therfore,
That Terëús nothíng it wist,
And yet right as her selven list
Her suster was delivered sone
Out of prisón, and by the mone
To Progné she was brought by night.
Whan eche of other had a sight
In chambre there they were alone,
They maden many a pitous mone.
But Progné most of sorwé made,
Which sigh her suster pale and fade
And spechéles and deshonoúred
Of that she haddé be defloured,
And eke upon her lord she thought
Of that he so untruely wrought
And had his espousailé broke,
She maketh a vow it shall be wroke.
And with that word she kneleth down
Weping in great devocioún,
Unto Cupide and to Venus
She praid and saidé thanné thus:

[1] *Wost*, knowest. [2] *Als tite*, promptly.

[1] *Bote*, remedy.

'O ye, to whom no thing asterte[1]
Of Lové may, for every herte
Ye knowe, as ye that ben above
The God and the Goddésse of Love,
Ye witen well, that ever yit
With al min herte and all my wit
I have ben trewe in my degre
And ever thoughté for to be,
And never love in other place
But all onlý the king of Trace
Whiche is my lord and I his wife.
But now alas this wofull strife,
That I him thus ayeinward finde
The most untrewe and most unkinde
That ever in ladies armés lay,
And wel I wot that he ne may
Amend his wronge, it is so great,
For he to litel of me lete
Whan he min owné suster toke
And me that am his wife forsoke.'
Lo, thus to Venus and Cupide
She praid, and furthermore she cride
Unto Apollo the highést
And said: 'O mighty god of rest,
Thou do vengeaúnce of this debate,
My suster and all her estate
Thou wost, and I shall bere a blame
Of that my suster hath a shame,
That Terëús to her I sent.
And well thou wost, that min entent
Was all for worship and for good.
O lord, that yivest the livés food
To every wight, I pray the here
These wofull susters that ben here,
And let us nought to the ben loth,
We ben thin owné women both.'
Thus pleigneth Progne and axeth wreche,
And though her suster lacké speche,
To him that allé thinges wote
Her sorwe is nought the lassé hote.
But he that thanné herd hem two
Him ought have sorwed evermo
For sorwe which was hem betwene.
With signés pleigneth Philomene,
And Progné saith: 'It shal be wreke,
That all the world therof shall speke.'
"And Progne tho sikenessé feigned,
Wherof unto her lord she pleigned
And preith she mote her chambre kepe
And as her liketh wake and slepe.
And he her graunteth to be so.
And thus to-gider ben they two,
That wold him but a litel good.
Now herke hereafter, how it stood
Of wofull auntrés that befelle.
These susters, that ben bothé felle,
And that was nought on hem alonge
But only on the greaté wronge
Which Terëús hem hadde do,
They shopen for to venge hem tho.
This Terëús by Progne his wife
A soné hath, which as his life
He loveth, and Ithſs he hight.
His moder wisté well she might
Do Terëús no moré greve
Than slee his child which was so leve.
Thus she that was as who saith mad
Of wo which hath her overlad,
Without insight of moderhede
Foryat pité and losté drede
And in her chambre privély
This childé without noise or cry
She slough and hewe him all to pieces.
And after with diversé spieces
The flessh whan it was so to-hewe,
She taketh and maketh therof a sewe,[1]
With which the fader at his mete
Was servéd till he had him ete
That he ne wist how that it stood.
But thus his owné flessh and blood

[1] *Asterte*, escape.

[1] *Sewe*, broth, stew.

Him self devoureth ayeine kinde,
As he that was to-fore unkinde.
And than er that he were arise,
For that he shuldé bene agrise
To shewen him the child was dede,
This Philomené toke the hede
Betwene two disshes, and all wrothe
Tho camen forth the susters bothe
And setten it upon the bord.
And Progné than began the word
And saide: 'O werst of alle wicke,
Of consciëncé whom no pricke
May steré, lo, what thou hast do,
Lo, here ben now we susters two.
O raviner, lo here thy prey,
With whom so falslich on the wey
Thou hast thy tirannïë wrought,
Lo, now it is somedele abought
And beter it shall, for of thy dede
The world shall ever sing and rede
In remembraúnce of thy defame,
For thou to love hast done such shame,
That it shall never be foryete.'
With that he sterte up fro the mete,
And shove the bord into the flore,
And caught a swerd anone and swore
That they shulde of his hondés deie.
And they unto the goddés crie
Begunné with so loude a steven,
That they were herde unto the heven,
And in the twinkeling of an eye
The goddés that the mischefe sigh
Her formés chaungéd allé thre.
Echone of hem in his degré
Was torned into a briddés kinde
Diversélich as men may finde.
After thestate that they were inne
Her formés weré set a twinne,
And as it telleth in the tale
The first into a nightingale
Was shape, and that was Philomene,
Which in the winter is nought sene,
For thanné ben the levés falle
And naked ben the busshes alle.
For after that she was a brid
Her will was ever to ben hid
And for to dwelle in privé place,
That no man shuldé sen her face
For shamé which may nought ben lassed
Of thing that was to-foré passed,
And halt her clos the winter day.
But whan the winter goth away
And that natúré the goddesse
Woll of her owné fre largesse
With herbés and with flourés bothe
The feldés and the medewes clothe,
And eke the wodés and the greves
Ben heléd [1] all with grené leves,
So that a brid her hidé may
Betwené March, Aprílle and May,
She that the winter [2] held her clos
For puré shame and nought aros,
Whan that she sigh the bowés thicke
And that there is no baré sticke
But all is hid with levés grene,
To wodé cometh this Philomene
And maketh her firsté yerés flight,
Where as she singeth day and night,
And in her song all openly
She maketh her pleint and saith: 'O why,
O why ne were I yet a maide?'
For so these oldé wisé saide
Which understoden what she ment,
Her notés ben of suche entent.
And eke they said, how in her songe
She maketh great joy and merth amonge
And saith: 'Ha, now I am a brid,
Ha, now my facé may ben hid!'
Thus medleth she with joié wo
And with her sorwé merth also,
So that of lovés maladie
She maketh diversé melodie
And saith: 'Love is a wofull blisse,

[1] *Greves . . heled*, groves . . covered.
[2] *The winter*, during winter.

A wisdom, which can no man wisse,
A lusty fever, a woundé softe.'
This noté she reherseth ofte
To hem which understonde her tale.
"Now have I of this nightingale,
Which erst was clepéd Philomene,
Told all that ever woldé mene
Both of her forme and of her note,
Wherof men may the story note.
And of her suster Progne I finde,
How she was tornéd out of kinde
Into a swalwé swift of wing,
Which eke in winter lith swouning
There as she may no thing be sene,
But whan the world is woxé grene
And comen is the somer tide,
Than fleeth she forth and ginneth to chide
And chitereth out in her langáge
What falshede is in mariáge;
And telleth in a maner speche
Of Terëús the spousé breche.
She wol nought in the wodés dwelle,
For she wold openliché telle,
And eke for that she was a spouse,
Among the folk she cometh to house
To do these wivés understonde
The falshode of her husébonde,
That they of hem beware also,
For there be many untrewe of tho.
"Thus ben the susters briddés both
And ben toward the men so loth,
That they ne woll for puré shame
Unto no mannés hond be tame,
For ever it dwelleth in her minde
Of that they found a man unkinde,
And that was falsé Terëús.
If suché one be amonge us
I not, but his conditiön
Men say in every regiön
Withinné town and eke without
Now regneth comunlich about.
And nethéles in remembraúnce
I woll declare what vengeaúnce
The goddés hadden him ordeigned,
Of that the susters hadden pleigned.
For anone after he was chaunged
And from his owné kindéstraunged,
A lappéwinké made he was
And thus he hoppeth on the gras,
And on his heed there stont upright
A crest in token of a knight,
And yet unto this day, men saith,
A lappéwinke hath lost his feith
And is the brid falsést of alle.
"Beware, my sone, er the so falle,
For if thou be of such covine
To get of lové by ravine
Thy lust, it may the fallé thus,
As it befell of Terëús."—
"My fader, nay, Goddés forbode,
Me weré lever be fortrode,
With wildé hors and be to-drawe,
Er I ayein love and his lawe
Did any thing, or loude or still,
Which weré nought my ladies will.
Men saien that every love hath drede,
So folweth it that I her drede,
For I her love, and who so dredeth,—
To plese his love and serve, him nedeth.
Thus may ye knowen by this skill,
That no Raviné done I will
Ayein her will by such a wey.
But while I live I will obey,
Abiding on her courtesie
If any mercy wolde her plie.[1]
"Forthy my fader, as of this
I wot nought I have do amis.
But furthermore I you beseche,
Some other point that ye me teche,
And axeth forth if there be ought,
That I may be the better taught."—
"Whan Covetise in pouer estate
Stont with him self upon debate

[1] *Plie*, bend, turn.

Through lacke of his misgovernaunce,
That he unto his sustenaunce
Ne can non other waié finde
To get him good, than as the blinde
Which seeth nought what shal after fall,
That ilké Vicé which men call
Of Robbery he taketh on honde,
Wherof by water and by londe
Of thing which other men beswinke[1]
He get him cloth and mete and drinke,
Him reccheth nought what he beginne
Through thefté so that he may winne.
Forthý to maken his purchás
He lith awaitend on the pas,
And what thing that he seeth ther passe
He taketh his parte or more or lasse
If it be worthy to be take,
He can the packés well ransake.
So privély bereth none about
His gold that he ne fint it out,
Or other juell what it be
He taketh it as his propreté
In wodés and in feldés eke.
Thus Robberíë goth to seke
Where as he may his purchas finde.
And right so in the samé kinde
My godé sone, as thou might here,
To speke of love in the matere
And make a verray résemblánce
Right as a thefe maketh chevesance
And robbeth mennés goodes about
In wode and felde where he goth out,
So be there of these lovers some
In wildé stedés[2] where they come
And finden there a woman able
And therto placé covenáble,
Withouté leve er that they fare
They take a parte of that chaffare.

[1] *Beswinke*, obtain by labour.
[2] *Stedes*, places.

But therof wot nothing the wife
At home, which loveth as her life
Her lord and sit all day wisshing
After her lordés home coming.
But whan he cométh home at eve
Anone he maketh his wife beleve,
For she nought ellés shuldé knowe
He telleth her, how his hunt hath blowe
And howe his houndés have well ronne,
And how there shone a mery sonne,
And how his hawkés flowen wele.
But he wol telle her never a dele,
How he to love untrewé was
Of that he robbéd in the pas
And toke his lust under the shawe
Ayein Love and ayein his lawe.
"Which thing, my sone, I the forbede,
For it is an ungoodly dede.
For who that taketh by robberie
His love, he may nought justifie
His cause, and so ful ofté sithe[1]
For onés that he hath ben blithe
He shall ben after sory thries.
Ensamples for such robberies
I findé write as thou shalt here
Accordend unto this matere.
"**I rede, how whilom** was a maide
The fairest, as Ovídé saide,
Which was in hiré timé tho.
And she was of the chambre also
Of Pallas, which is the goddésse
And wife to Marte, of whom prowesse
Is yové to these worthy knightes,
For he is of so greaté mightes,
That he govérneth the bataile;
Withouten him may nought availe
The strongé hond, but he it helpe,
There may no knight of armes yelpe[2]

[1] *Ofté sith*, many times. [2] *Yelpe*, boast.

But he fight under his banere.
But now to speke of my matere
This fairé, fresshé, lusty may[1]
Alone as she went on a day
Upon the strondé for to play,
There came Neptúnus in the way,
Which hath the see in governaunce,
And in his herté such plesaunce
He toke whan he this maiden sigh,
That all his hert aros on high.
For he so sodeinlich unware
Beheld the beauté that she bare,
And cast anone within his hert
That she him shall no way astert.
This maiden which Cornix by name
Was hoté, dredend allé shame,
Sigh that she mighté nought debate,
And well she wist he wolde algate
Fulfill his lust of robberie,
Anone began to wepe and crie
And said, 'O Pallas noble quene,
Shew now thy might, and let be sene,
To kepe and savé min honoúr!'
That word was nought so soné spoke,
Whan Pallas shopé recoverír
After the will and the desire
Of hiré which a maiden was,
And sodeinlich upon this cas
Out of her womanisshé kinde
Into a briddés like I finde
She was transforméd forth withall,
So that Neptunus nothing stal
Of such thing that he wolde have stole.
With fethers blacke as any cole
Out of his armés in a throwe
She fleigh before his eyen a crowe;
Which was to her a more delite
To kepe her maidenhedé white
Under the wede of fethers blacke,
In perles whité than forsake
That[2] no life may restore ayein.
But thus Neptúne his hert in vein
Hath upon robberíe set.
The bird is flowe and he was let
The fairé maid him hath escaped,
Wherof for ever he was bejaped
And scornéd of that he hath lore.
"My soné, be thou ware therfore,
So as I shall the yet devise
Another talé therupon,
Which fell by oldé daiés gone.
King Lichaón upon his wife
A doughter had, a goodly life
And clené maide of worthy fame,
Calistona whose righté name
Was clepéd, and of many a lorde
She was besought, but her accorde
To lové mighté no man winne,
As she whiche hath no lust therinne,
But swore within her hert and saide,
That she woll ever ben a maide.
Wherfore, to kepe her selfe in pees,
With suche as Amadriades
Were clepéd, wodémaidens tho,
And with the nimphés eke also
Upon the spring of fresshé welles
She shope to dwelle and no where elles.
And thus came this Calistoná
Into the wode of Tegeá,
Where she virginité behight
Unto Diane, that on a day
Was priveliche stole away.
For Jupiter through his queintise
From her it toke in suche a wise,
So that it mighté nought be hid.
And therupon it is betid,
Diané, whiche it herdé tell,
In privé place unto a welle
With nimphes al a compaigny
Was come and in a ragery
She saidé, that she bathé wolde,
And bad that every maiden sholde
With her all naked bath also.
And tho began the privé wo.

[1] *May*, maid. [2] *That*, that which.

With shame from her the nimphés fled,
Till whanné that natúre her spedde,
That of a soné, which Archas
Was naméd, she delivered was.
And tho Juno, which was the wife
Of Jupiter, wrothe and hastife
In purpose for to do vengeaúnce,
Came forth upon this ilké chaunce,
And to Calistona she spake
And set upon her many a lacke
And said: 'Ha, now thou art atake,
That thou thy werk might nought forsake.
Ha, thou ungoodly ypocrite,
How thou art greatly for to wite.
Thy greté beauté shall be torned,
Through which that thou hast be mistorned,
Thy largé front, thy eyen gray
I shall hem chaunge in other way,
And all the feture of thy face
In such a wise I shall deface,
That every man the shall forbere.'
With that the likenesse of a bere
She toke and was forshape anone.
Within a time and therupon
Befell, that with a bow in honde
To hunte and gamé for to fonde
Into that wodé goth to play
Her sone Archás, and in his way
It hapneth that this beré came.
And whan that she good hedé name,
Where that he stood under the bough,
She knewe him well and to him drough,
For though she had her formé lore,
The lové was nought lost therfóre
Which kinde hath set under his lawe.
Whan she under the wodé shawe
Her child beheld, she was so glad
That she with both her armés sprad,
As though she were in womanhede,
Toward him come and toke nonc hede
Of that a bow he baré bent.
And he with that an arwe hath hent[1]
And gan to teise[2] it in his bowe,
As he, that can none other knowe
But that it was a besté wilde.
But Jupiter, which woldé shilde
The moder and the sone also,
Ordeineth for hem bothé two
That they for ever weré save.
"But thus, my soné, thou might have
Ensample, and by other wey
In oldé bokés as I rede,
Such robberſe is for to drede,
And namélich of thilke good
Whiche every woman that is good
Desireth for to kepe and holde
As whilom was by daiés olde.
For if thou here my talé wele
Of that was tho, thou might somdele
Of olde ensamples taken hede
How that the floure of maidenhede
Was thilké timé holde in pris.
And so it was, and so it is,
And so it shall for ever stonde,
And for thou shalt it understonde,
Now herken a tale next suend,
How maidenhede is to commend.
Of Rome among the gestes olde
I find, how that Valéry tolde,
That what man tho was emperour
Of Romé he sholde done honour
To the virgin, and in the wey
Where he her mete, he shulde obey
In worship of virginité,
Which tho was a great dignité
Nought onlich of the women tho,
But of the chasté men also
It was commended over all.
And for to speke in speciáll
Touchend of men ensample I finde.

[1] *Hent*, seized. [2] *Trise*, stretch.

"Phirins, which was of mannés kinde
Above all other the fairést
Of Rome and eke the comeliést,
That well was hiré which him might
Beholde and have of him a sight.
Thus was he tempted ofté sore,
But for he woldé be no more
Among the women so coveited,
The beauté of his facé streited
He hath, and thrust out both his eyne,
That allé women whiche it sein
Than afterwarde of him ne rought.
And thus his maidenhede he bought.
"So may I provcoé wel forthý
Above all other under the sky,
Who that the vertues woldé peise,
Virginité is for to preise,
Which as thapocalips recordeth
To Criste in heven best accordeth.
So may it shewé well therfore
As I have tolde it here to-fore,
In heven and eke in erth also
It is accept to bothé two.
Out of his flesshe a man to live
Gregoire hath this ensample yive
And saith: It shall rather be told [1]
Lich to an aungel manyfold
Than to the life of mannes kinde;
There is no reson for to finde,
But only through the grace above,
In flesshé without flesshly love
A man to livé chasté here.
And nethéles a man may here
Of suché that have ben er this,
And yet there ben, but for it is
A vertue which is seldé wonne,
Now I this matter have begonne
I thenké tellen over more,
Which is, my soné, for thy lore,
If that the list to taken hede,
To trete upon the maidenhede.

1 *Told*, accounted.

"The boke saith that a mannés life
Upon knighthode in werre and strife
Is set among his enemies.
The freilé flessh, whose nature is
Ay redy for to sporne and fall,
The firsté foman is of all.
For thilké werre is redy ay,
It werreth night, it werreth day,
So that a man hath never rest.
Forthý is thilké knight the best
Through might and grace of goddés sonde
Which that batailé may withstonde,
Wherof yet dwelleth the memoire
Of hem that whilome the victoire
Of thilké dedly werré hadden,
The high prowessé which they ladden
Wherof the soulé stood amended,
Upon this erth yet is commended.
An emperour by thilké daies
There was, and he at all assaies
A worthy knight was of his honde,
There was none such in all the londe,
But yet for all his vassellage [1]
He stood unwedded all his age,
And in cronique as it is tolde
He was an hundred winter olde.
And haddé ben a worthy knight
Both of his lawe and of his might.
But whan men wolde his knighthood peise
And of his dedes of armés preise
Of that he didé with his hondes,
Whan he the kingés and the londes
To his subjectión put under,
Of all that prise hath he no wonder,
For he it set of none accompte
And said, all that may nought amounte
Ayein a point whiche he hath nome,
That he his flessh hath overcome.

1 *Vassellage*, valour in arms, as in Chaucer's "Knight's Tale" and in Barbour's "Bruce."

He was a virgine, as he said;
On that bataile his pris he laid.
Lo now, my sone, avisé the."—
"Ye, fader, all this may well be.
But if all other didé so,
The world of men were sone ago;[1]
And in the lawe a man may finde
How God to man by wey of kinde
Hath set the world to multiply.
And who that woll him justify,
It is inough to do the lawe.
And nethéles your godé sawe
Is good to kepé, who so may,
I woll nought there ayein say nay."
"**My soné**, take it as I say,
If maidenhed be take away
Withouté lawés ordenaúnce,
It may nought failen of vengeaúnce.
"And if thou wolt the sothé wite,
Behold a talé which is write,
How that the king Agámenon
Whan he the citee of Lesbon
Hath won, a maiden there he fonde
Which was the fairest of the londe
In thilké timé that men wist.
He toke of hiré what him list
Of thing which was most precioús,
Wherof that she was daungeroús.
This fairé maiden clepéd is
Criseid, the doughter of Crisís,
Which was that timé speciáll
Of thilké temple principáll
Where Phebus had his sacrifice,
So was it well the moré vice.
Agámenon was than in way
To Troié ward and toke awey
This maiden, whiche he with him lad,
So greaté lust in her he had.
But Phebus which hath great disdein
Of that his maiden was forlein,
Anone as he to Troié came,

[1] *Ago*, gone.

Vengeaúnce upon this dede he name[1]
And send a comune pestilence.
They soughten than her evidence
And maden calculación,
To knowe in what condición
This deth cam in so sodeinly,
And atté lasté redely
The cause and eke the man they founde,
And forth withal the samé stounde
Agámenon opposéd was,
Whiche hath beknowen all the cas
Of the folíë, which he wrought.
And therupon mercý they sought
Toward the god in sondry wise
With praier and with sacrifice;
The maiden home ayein they sende
And yaf her good inough to spende
For ever while she shuldé live,
And thus the sinné was foryive
And all the pestilencé cesed.
"Lo, what it is to ben encresed
Of lové whiche is evil wonne.
It weré better nought begonne
Than take a thing withouté leve
Which thou must after nedés leve
And yet have malgré forth with all.
Forthý to robben over all
In lovés cause if thou beginne,
I not what esé thou shalt winne.
My soné, be well ware of this,
For thus of robbery it is."—
"My fader, your ensamplarie
In lovés cause of robberie
I have it right well understonde.
But over this how so it stonde,
Yet wol I wite of your apprise,
What thing is more of Covetise.
With Covetisé yet I finde
A servaunt of the samé kinde,
Which Stelth is hote, and micherie[2]
With him is ever in compaignie.
Of whom if I shall tellé soth

[1] *Name*, took. [2] *Micherie*, secrecy.

He stalketh as a pecock doth
And taketh his preié so covérte,
That no man wote it in apérte.
For whan he wot the lord from home
Than woll he stalke about and come,
And what thing he fint in his wey
Whan that he seeth the men awey
He steleth it and goth forth withall
That therof no man knowé shall.
And eke full ofte he goth anight
Withouté mone or sterré light
And with his craft the dore unpiketh
And taketh therinné what him liketh.
And if the doré be so shet,
That he be of his entré let,
He woll in atté window crepe,
And while the lord is fast aslepe,
He steleth what thing him best list,
And goth his wey er it be wist.
Full ofte also by light of day
Yet woll he stele and make assay,
Under the cote his honde he put
Till he the mannés purs have kut
And rifleth that he fint therinne.
And thus he auntreth him to winne
And bereth an horn and nought ne bloweth
For no man of his counseil knoweth
What he may get of his miching,
It is all bile[1] under the wing.
And as an hound that goth to folde
And hath there také what he wolde
His mouth upon the gras he wipeth,
And so with feignéd chere him slipeth,
That what as ever of shepe he strangle
There is no man therof shall jangle
And for to knowen who it dede;
Right so doth stelthe in every stede,
Where as him list his preié take.
He can so well his causé make
And so well feigne and so well glose
That there ne shall no man suppose

[1] *Bile*, bill.

But that he were an innocent,
And thus a mannés eye he blent.
So that this crafte I may remeve[1]
Withouten helpe of any meve.
There be lovérs of that degre,
Which all her lust in priveté
As who saith getten all by Stelth
And ofte atteignen to great welth
As for the timé that it lasteth.
For love awaiteth ever and casteth
How he may stele and cacche his pray
Whan he therto may finde a way.
For be it night, or be it day
He taketh his part, whan that he may,
And if he may no moré do
Yet woll he stele a cuss[2] or two.
"My soné, what saist thou therto,
Telle, if thou diddest ever so."—
"My fader, how?"—"My soné, thus,
If thou hast stolen any cuss
Or other thing which therto longeth,
For no man suché theves hongeth;
Tell on forthý and say the trouth."—
"My fader, nay; and that is routh,
For by my will I am a thefe,
But she that is to me most lefe,
Yet durst I never in priveté
Nought onés take her by the kne
To stele of her or this or that,
And if I durst I wot well what.
And nethéles but if I lie
By stelthé ne by robberie
Of lové, which fell in my thought,
To hire did I never nought;
But as men sain, where hert is failed
There shall no castel be assailed,
But though I haddé hertés ten
And were as stronge as allé men,
If I be nought min owné man
And dare nought usen that I can,

[1] *Remeve*, change to another field of enterprise; from Money to Love.
[2] *Cuss*, kiss.

I may my selvé nought recouer
Though I be never man so pouer.
I bere an herte and here it is,
So that me faileth wit in this
How that I shulde of mine accorde
The servant lede ayein the lorde.
For if my foot wold owhere go,
Or that min hond wolde ellés do,
Whan that min hert is there ayein
The remenaunt is all in vein.
And thus me lacketh alle wele,
And yet ne dare I nothing stele
Of thing which longeth unto love,
And eke it is so high above
I may nought well therto arecche,
But if so be at time of speche
Full selde if than I stelé may
A worde or two and go my way.
Betwene her high estate and me
Comparison there may none be,
So that I fele and well I wote
All is to hevy and to hote
To set on hondé without leve.
And thus I mot algaté leve
To stelé that I may nought take,
And in this wise I mot forsake
To ben a thefe ayein my will
Of thing which I may nought fulfill.
"For that serpént which never slept
The flees of gold so well ne kept
In Colchos, as the tale is tolde,
As my ladý a thousand folde
To kepe her body night and day.
She hath a wardein redy ay,
Which is so wounderfull a wight,
That him ne may no mannés might
With swerd ne with no wepon daunt,
Ne with no sleight of charme enchaunt
Wherof he might be madé tame,
And Daunger is his righté name,
Whiche under lock and under key,
That no man may it stele awey,
Hath al the tresor underfonge
That unto lové may belonge.
The lesté loking of her eye
May nought be stole, if he it sigh;
And who so gruccheth for so lite
He woldé soné set a wite
On him that woldé stelé more.
And that me greveth wonder sore,
For this provérb is ever newe,
That strongé lockés maken trewe
Of hem that wolden stele and pike.
For so wel can there no man slike [1]
By him ne by no other mene,
To whom Daungér wol yive or lene
Of that tresór he hath to kepe.
So though I woldé stalke and crepe
And waite on eve and eke on morwe,
Of Daunger shal I nothing borwe,
And stelé wot wel may I nought.
And thus I am right wel bethought,
While Daunger stont in his office,
Of Stelthé, which ye clepe a Vice,
I shall be gilty never mo.
Therfore I wold he were ago
So fer that I never of him herde
How so that afterward it ferde,
For than I mighté yet par cas
Of lové maké some purchas
By stelth or by some other way,
That now fro me stont fer away.
"But, fader, as ye tolde above,
How Stelthé goth anight for love,
I may nought wel that point forsake,
That ofté timés I ne wake
On nightés whan that other slepe.
But now, I pray you také kepe,
Whan I am loggéd in such wise
That I by nighté may arise
At some windów and loken out
And se the housing al about,
So that I may the chambre knowe
In which my lady, as I trowe,
Lith in her bed and slepeth softe,
Than is min hert a thefe ful ofte,
For there I stondé to behold

[1] Smooth the way.

The longé nightés that ben cold
And thenke on her that lieth there.
But atté lasté whan I finde
That I am fall into my minde,
And se that I have stondé longe
And have no profit underfonge,
Than stalke I to my bed withinne.
And this is all that ever I winne
Of lové, whan I walke on night.
My will is good, but of my might
Me lacketh both and of my grace,
For what so that my thought embrace
Yet have I nought the better ferde.
My fader, lo, now have ye herde
What I by Stelth of Love have do,
And how my will hath be therto;
If I be worthy to penaunce,
I put it to your ordenaunce."—
"My sone, of stelth I the behete,
Though it be for a timé swete,
At ende it doth but litel good,
As by ensample how that it stood
Whilom, I may the tellé now."—
"I pray you, fader, say me how."—
"My sone, of him, which goth by day
By wey of stelthé to assay
In lovés cause and taketh his pray,
Ovídé said, as I shall say,
And in his Methamor he tolde
A talé which is good to holde.
The poet upon this matere
Of Stelthé wrote in this manere.
Venus, which hath the lawe in honde
Of thing which may nought be withstonde,
As she which the tresór to warde
Of lové hath within her warde,
Phebus to love hath so constreigned
That he withouté rest is peined
With all his herté to coveite
A maiden which was warded streite
Withinné chambre and kept so clos
That selden was whan she desclos
Goth with her moder for to play.
Leucothoë, so as men say,
This maiden hight, and Orchamus
Her fader was. And befell thus,
This doughter that was kept so dere
And haddé be from yere to yere,
Upon the whose nativité
Of comeliheed and of beauté
Natúre hath set all that she may,
That lich unto the fresshé May,
Whiche other monthes of the yere
Sourmounteth, so withouté pere
Was of this maiden the fetúre,
Wherof Phebús out of mesúre
Her loveth and on every side
Awaiteth what so may betide.
In his await so longe he lay
Till it befell upon a day
That he through out her chambre wall
Came in all sodeinlich and stall
That thing which was to him so lefe.
But wo the while, he was a thefe,
For Venus, which was enemy
Of thilké lovés michery,
Descovereth all the pleiné cas
To Climené, which thanné was
Toward Phebús his concubine.
And she, to letté the covine
Of thilké lové, dedely wrothe,
To pleign upon this maide she goth
And tolde her fader howe it stood,
Wherof for sorwe well nigh wode
Unto her moder thus he saide:
'Lo, what it is to kepe a maide.
To Phebus dare I nothing speke
But upon her it shall be wreke.'
And bad with that do make a pit,
Wherin he hath his doughter set,
As he that woll no pité have,
So that she was all quike begrave
And deide anone in his presence.
But Phebus, for the reverence

Of that she haddé be his love,
Hath wrought through his powér above
That she sprong up out of the molde
Into a flour, was naméd Golde,
Which stant govérnéd of the sonne.
And thus whan love is evil wonne,
Full ofte it cometh to repentail."—
"My fader, that is no merveile,
Whan that the counceil is bewreied.
For in your tale as it betid,
Venus descovereth all the cas,
And eke also brode day it was
Whan Phebus such a stelthé wrought,
Wherof the maide in blame he brought,
That afterwards he was so lore.
But for ye saiden now to-fore,
How Stelth of Lové goth by night
And doth his thingés out of sight,
Therof me lust also to here
A talé lich to the matere,
Wherof I might ensample take."
"My godé soné, for thy sake,
So as it befell by daiés olde
And so as the poét it tolde,
Upon the nightés michery
Now herken a tale of poesy.
The mightiest of allé men,
Whan Hercules with Eolen,
Which was the love of his coráge,
To-gider upon a pelrinage
Towardé Romé shulden go,
It fell hem by the waié so,
That they upon a day a cave
Within a roché founden have,
Which was reál and glorious
And of entailé curioús,
By name and Thophis it was hote.
The sonné shone tho wonder hote,
As it was in the somer tide.
"This Hercules, which by his side
Hath Eolen his lové there,
Whan they at thilké cavé were,
He said, he thought it for the best,
That she her for the heté rest
All thilké day. And so befell,
This cavé was under the hill
Of Tímolus, which was begrowe
With vinés, and at thilké throwe
Faunus with Saba the goddesse,
By whom the largé wildernesse
In thilké timé stood govérned,
Were in a place, as I am lerned,
Nigh by, which Bachus wodé hight.
"This Faunus toke a great insight
Of Eolen, that was so nigh,
For whan that he her beauté sigh,
Out of his wit he was assoted
And in his herte it hath so noted,
That he forsoke the nimphés alle
And said, he wolde, how so it falle,
Assay an other for to winne,
He set his hertes thought withinne,
And therupon his time awaiteth.
Now take good hede, how love affaiteth
Him which withal is overcome.
Faire Eolen whan she was come
With Hercules into the cave,
She said him, that she woldé have
His clothés of and hire bothe,
And eche of hem shulde other clothe.
And all was do right as she bad,
He hath her in his clothés clad
And cast on her his gulion,
Which of the skin of a leon
Was made, as he upon the wey
It slough, and over this to pley
She toke his greté mace also
And knet it at her girdel tho.
So was she lich the man arraied,
And Hercules than hath assaied
To clothen him in her array.
And thus they japé forth the day,
Till that her souper redy were.
And whan they hadden soupéd there,
They shopen hem to go to rest,
And as it thought hem for the best,

They bad, as for that ilké night,
Two sondry beddés shuld be dight,
Wherin that they to resté gone
Eche by hem self in sondry place.
Fair Eolen hath set the mace
Besides her beddés heved above,
And with the clothés of her love
She helléd[1] all her bed aboute.
And he, which had nothíng in
doubte,
Her wimpel wonde about his cheke,
Her kirtel and her mantel eke
Abrode upon his bed he spredde,
And thus they slepen both a bedde.
And what of travail, what of wine
The servaunts like to dronken swine
Beganné for to routé[2] faste.
This Faunus, which his stelthé caste,
Was thanné comen to the cave
And found, they weren alle save;
Withouté noise and in he went,
The derké night his sighté blent,
And yet it hapned him to go
Where Eolen a beddé tho
Was laid aloné for to slepe.
But for he woldé take kepe
Whose bed it was, he made assay
And of a leon where it lay
The cote he founde and eke he feleth
The mace, and than his hertékeleth,
That theré durst he nought abide;
But stalketh upon every side
And sought abouté with his honde
That other bed, till that he fonde
Where lay bewimpled a viságe.
Tho was he glad in his coráge,
For he her kirtel founde also
And eke her mantel bothé two
Bespred upon the bedde alofte,
And wendé well it weré she.
And thus in stede of Eolé
Anone he profreth him to love,
But he, which sigh a man above,
This Hercules him threw to grounde

[1] *Helléd*, covered. [2] *Routé*, snore.

So soré, that they have him founde
Liggendé there upon the morwe,
And tho was nought a litel sorwe
That Faunus of him selvé made.
But ellés there they were all glade
And loughen him to scorne aboute,
Saba with nimphés all a route
Came down to loke how that it ferde,
And whan that they the sothé herde
He was bejapéd over all.

"My soné, be thou ware with all
In aunter if the so betide
As Faunus didé thilké tide,
Whereof thou might be shaméd so."—

"Min holy fader, certes no.
But if I haddé right good leve,
Such micherie I thenké leve.
My fainté herté woll nought serve,
For malgré wolde I nought deserve
In thilké placé where I love.
But for ye tolden here above
Of Covetise and his pilage,
If there be more of that lignage,
Which toucheth to my shrifte, I
pray,
That ye therof me woldé say,
So that I may the Vice escheue."—

"My sone, if I by order sue
The Vices as they stonde a rowe,
Of Covetisé thou shalt knowe,
There is yet one, which is the last,
In whom there may no Vertue last,
For he with God him self debateth,
Wherof that all the heven him
hateth.

The highé God, which allé good
Purveiéd hath for mannés food
Of clothés and of mete and drinke,
Bade Adam, that he shuldé swinke
To geten him his sustenaunce,
And eke he set an ordenaunce
Upon the lawe of Moïses,
That though a man be havéles,
Yet shall he nought by thefté stele.
But now a daiés there ben fele,

That woll no labour undertake ;
But what they may by stelthé take
They holde it sikerliché wonne.
And thus the lawe is overronne,
Which God hath set, and namély
With hem that so untruëly
The goodés robbe of Holy Chirche.
The thefté, which they thanné wirche,
By name is cleped Sacrilegge,
Ayein the whom I thenke allegge.
Upon three points as we ben taught
Stont Sacrilege, and ellés nought.
The firsté point is for to say,
Whan that a thefe shall stele away
The holy thing from holy place.
The seconde is, if he purcháce
By way of theft an holy thinge
The whiche upon his knowlechinge
Fro holy place away was toke.
The thirdé point, as saith the boke,
Is suche, as whereas ever it be,
In wode, in felde, or in cite,
Shall no man stelé by no wise
That halowed is to the servise
Of God whiche allé thingés wote.
But there is nouther cold ne hote,
Whiche he for God or man woll spare,
So that the body may wel fare
And that he may the world escape,
The heven him thinketh is but a jape
Of his condiciön to telle,
Which rifeleth bothe boke and belle,
So forthwith all the remenaunt
To Goddés hous appurtenaunt,
Where that he shuldé bid his bede,
He doth his theft in holy stede,
And taketh what thing he fint therin.
For whan he seeth that he may win
He wondeth for no cursednesse
That he ne breketh the holinesse
And doth to God no reverence.
For he hath lost his consciënce,
That though the prest therforé curse,
He saith, he fareth nought the worse.
And for to speke it other wise,
What man that lasseth the fraunchise
And taketh of Holy Chirch his pray,
I not what bedés he shall pray
Whan he fro God which hath yive all
The purpartie in speciáll,
Which unto Crist him self is due,
Benimth ; he may nought wel eschue
The peiné comend afterward,
For he hath made his foréward
With sacrileggé for to dwelle,
Which hath his heritage in helle.
"And if we rede of tholde lawe,
I findé write in thilké lawe,
Of princes how there weren thre
Coupáble sore in this degre.
That one of hem was clepéd thus
The proudé king Antiochus ;
That other Nabuzardan hight,
Which of his crueltė behight
The temple to destruie and waste,
And so he did in allé haste ;
The thridde, which was after shamed,
Was Nabugodonósor named,
And he Jerusalem put under
Of sacrilegge and many a wonder
There in the holy temple he wrought,
Which Baltazár his heire abought,
Whan Mane Techel Phares write
Was on the wall, as thou might wite
So as the bible it hath declared.
But for al that it is nought spared
Yet now a day that men ne pille
And maken argument and skille
To sacrilegge as it belongeth,
For what man that there after longeth
He taketh none hede what he doth.
And if a man shall tellé soth,
Of guile and of subtilité
Is none so sligh in his degre

To feigne a thing for his beyete
As is this Vice of whiche I trete.
He can so priveliché pike,
He can so well his wordés slike
To put away suspición,
That in his excusatión
There shall no man defalté finde.
And thus full ofté men be blinde,
That stónden in his word deceived,
Er his queintísé be perceived.
But nethéles yet other while
For all his sleight and all his guile
Of that he wolde his werke forsake,[1]
He is atteint and overtake.
Wherof thou shalte a talé rede,
In Rome as it befell in dede.
Er Romé cam to the creaunce
Of Cristés feith, it fell perchaunce,
Cesár, which tho was emperour,
Him listé for to done honoúr
Unto the temple Apollinis,
And made an ymage upon this,
The which was clepéd Apolló,
Was none so riche in Romé tho[2]
Of plate of golde a berde he hadde,
The which his brest all over spradde
Of golde also withouté faile
His mantell was of large entaile
Beset with perrie[3] all about,
Forth right he straught his finger out
Upon the which he had a ringe,
To seen it was a riché thing
A fine carbuncle for the nones
Most precïóus of alle stones.
"And fell that time in Romé thus
There was a clerke one Lucius,
A courteóur, a famous man,
Of every wit somwhat he can,
Out také that him lacketh reule
His owne estat to guide and reule.
How so it stood of his spekíng,
He was nought wise in his doíng.

[1] *Forsake*, deny. [2] *Tho*, then. [3] *Perrie*, precious stones.

But every riote atté last
Mot nedés falle, and may nought laste.
After the mede of his deserte
So fell this clerke into pouerte
And wisté nought how for to rise,
Wherof in many a sondry wise
He cast his wittés here and ther,
He loketh nigh, he loketh fer,
Till on a timé that he come
Into the temple, and hede he nome
Where that the god Apollo stood,
He sigh the richesse and the good
And thought he woldé by some way
The tresor picke and stele away;
And therupon so sleighly wrought
That his purpóse about he brought,
And went awey unápperceived.
Thus hath the man his god deceived;
His ring, his mantel and his berd,
As he which nothing was aferd,
All privély with him he bare.
And whan the wardeins weren ware
Of that her god despuiléd was,
Hem thought it was a wonder cas
How that a man for any wele
Durst in so holy placé stele,
And namély so great a thing.
This talé came unto the king,
And was through spoken over all.
But for to knowe in speciall,
What maner man hath do the dede,
They soughten helpe upon the nede
And maden calculaciön,
Wherof by demonstraciön
The man was foundé with the good;
In jugément and whan he stood,
The king hath axéd of him thus:
'Say thou, unsely Lucius,
Why hast thou don this sacrilegge?'—
'My lord, if I the cause allegge,
Quod he ayein, me thenketh this,
That I have do nothíng amis.

Thre points ther ben, which I have
do:
Wherof the firsté point stant so,
That I the ring have take away;
As unto that, this woll I say,
Whan I the god behelde about,
I sigh how he his hond straught out
And profred me the ring to yive.
And I, which woldé gladly live
Out of pouerte, through his largesse
It underfang, so that I gesse
As therof I am nought to wite.[1]
And overmore I woll me quite
Of gold that I the mantel toke;
Gold in his kind, as saith the boke,
Is hevy both and colde also.
And for that it was hevy so,
Me thought it was no garnément
Unto the god convenient
To clothen him the somer tide.
I thought, upon that other side,
Howgold is colde, and such a clothe
By reson oughté to be lothe
In winter timé for the chele.
And thus thenkéndé thoughtés fele
As I min eie abouté cast,
His largé berd than atté last
I sigh, and thought anone therfore,
How that his fader him before
Which stood upon the samé place,
Was berdles with a yongly face.
And in such wise, as ye have herde,
I toke away the sonés berde
For that his fader haddé none
To make hem liche, and hereupon
I axé for to ben excused.'
"Lo thus, where sacrileggeis used,
A man can feigne his consciénce
And right upon such evidence
In Lovés cause if I shall trete,
There ben of suché small and great,
If they no leiser finden elles
They wol nought wonden for the
belles,
Ne though they sen the prest at
masse,
That wol they leten overpasse,
If that they finden her love there
They stande and tellen in her ere
And axe of God none other grace
While they ben in that holy place.
But er they gon some avauntáge
There will they have and some
pilláge
Of goodly word or of beheste,
Or ellés they take atté leste
Out of her honde a ring or glove,
So nigh the weder they will hove,
As who saith she shall nought for-
yete
Now I this token of her have gete.
Thus halwe they the highé feste,
Such thefté may no chirch areste,
For all is lefull that hem liketh,
To whom that ellés it misliketh.
And eke right in the selvé kinde
In greaté citees men may finde
This lusty folk that make hem gay
And waite upon the haliday,
In chirches and in minstres eke
They gon the women for to seke,
And where that such one goth about
To-fore the fairest of the route
Where as they sitten all a rewe,
There will he moste his body shewe,
His croket[1] kempt and theron set
An ouché[2] with a chapélet
Or ellés one of grené leves
Which laté came oute of the greves,
All for he shuldé semé fressh.
And thus he loketh on his flessh
Right as an hawke which hath a sight
Upon the fowl there he shall light,
And as he were a fairie
He sheweth him to-fore her eye
In holy placé where they sitte

[1] *To wite*, to blame.

[1] *Croket*, crocquet, a large roll of crossed hair once in the fashion.

[2] *Ouché*, jewel, or jewel setting . . . *greves*, groves.

Al for to make her hertés flitte.
His eyé no where woll abide
But loke and pry on every side
On her and her, as him best liketh,
And other while among he siketh;
Thenketh one of hem 'That was for me!'
And so there thenken two or thre
And yet he loveth none of alle,
But where as ever his chauncé falle;
And nethéles to say a soth
The causé why that he so doth,
Is for to stele an herte or two
Out of the chirche er that he go.
And as I said it here above,
All is that sacrilegge of love,
For well may be he steleth awey
That he never after yeldé may.
Tell me forthý, my sone, anone,
Hast thou do sacrilegge or none
As I have said in this manere?"—
"My fader, as of this matere
I woll you tellen redely
What I have do, but truëly
I may excusé min entent,
That I never yet to chirché went
In such manér as ye me shrive,
For no womán that is on live.
The causé why I have it laft
May be for I unto that craft
Am nothing able for to stele,
Though there be women nought so fele.
But yet woll I nought saié this
Whan I am there my lady is,
In whom lith holy my quaréle,
And she to chirche or to chapéle
Woll go to matins or to messe
That time I waité well and gesse,
To chirche I come, and there I stonde,
And though I take a boke on honde
My contenaunce is on the boke
But toward her is all my loke.
And if so fallé, that I pray
Unto my God and somwhat say
Of *Pater Noster* or of Crede
All is for that I woldé spede,
So that my bede in holy chirche
There mighté some mirácle wirche
My ladies herté for to chaunge,
Which ever hath be to me so straunge;
So that all my devociön
And all my contemplaciön
With all min herte and my corâge
Is only set on her ymáge.
And ever I waite upon the tide
If she loke any thing aside,
That I me may of her avise;
Anone I am with Covetise
So smité that me weré lefe
To be in holy chirche a thefe,
But nought to stele a vestément
For that is nothíng my talént.
But I wol stele if that I might
A glad word or a goodly sight,
And ever my servíce I profre,
And namely whan she woll gone offre,
For than I lede her, if I may.
For somwhat wold I stele away
Whan I beclippe her on the waste,
Yet atté last I stele a taste,[1]
And other whilé 'graunt mercy'
She saith, and so win I therby
A lusty touch, a good worde eke,
But all the remenaunt to seke
Is fro my purpos wonder fer.
So may I say, as I said er,
In holy chirch if that I wowe,
My consciénce I wolde allowe
Be so that up amendément
I mighté get assignément
Where for to spede in other place;
Such sacrilegge I hold a grace.
"And thus, my fader, soth to say
In chirché right as in the way

[1] *Taste*, touch (*tâter*). So a knight might in the old romances taste his horse; or a damsel taste a hero's wound.

If I might ought of lové take
Such hansel have I nought forsake.
But finally I me confesse,
There is in me no halinesse
While I her se in haly stede.
And yet for ought that ever I dede
No sacrilegge of her I toke
But if it were of worde or loke
Or ellés if that I her fredde[1]
Whan I toward offríng her ledde,
Také therof what I take may
For ellés bere I nought away,
For though I wolde ought ellés have
All other thingés ben so save
And kept with such a privilegge
That I may do no sacrilegge;
God wot my willé nethéles.
Though I must nedés kepé pees
And malgré min so let it passe,
My will therto is nought the lasse,
If I might other wise away.
Forthý, my fader, I you pray,
Tell what you thenketh therupon,
If I therof have gilt or none."—
"Thy will, my sone, is for to blame,
The remenaunt is but a game
That I have herd the tellé yit.
But take this lore into thy wit,
That allé thing hath time and stede,
The chirche serveth for the bede,[2]
The chambre is of an other speche;
But if thou wistest of the wreche
How sacrilegge it hath abought,
Thou woldest better ben bethought.
And for thou shalt the more amende,
A tale I will on the despende.
"To alle men as who saith knowe
It is, and in the world through blowe,
How that of Troié Lamedón
To Hercules and to Jasón,
Whan toward Colchos out of Grece
By see sailénd, upon a piece
Of londe of Troié resté preide.

[1] *Fredde*, felt. [2] *Bede*, prayer.

But he hem wrothfully congeide,[1]
And for they found him so villein,
Whan they came into Grece ayein
With power that they getté might
Towardés Troié they hem dight
And there they token such vengeaúnce,
Wherof stant yet the remembraúnce.
For they destruiéd king and all
And leften but the brenté wall,
The Grekes of Troians many slow[2]
And prisoners they toke inow,
Among the whiché there was one
The kingés doughter Lamedon
Esſona the fairé thing,
Which unto Thelamon the king
By Hercules and by thassent
Of all the holé parlément
Was at his willé yove and graunted.
And thus hath Grecé Troié daunted,
And home they torne in such manére.
But after this, now shalt thou here
The cause, why I this talé telle,
Upon the chauncé that befelle.
"King Lamedon, which deidé thus,
He had a sone one Priamus,
Which was nought thilké time at home,
But whan he herd of this, he come
And found how the citee was falle,
Which he began anon to walle
And madé there a citee newe,
That they which other londés knewe
Tho saiden that of lime and stone
In all the world so faire was none.
And on that o side of the town
The king let maken Ylion,
That highé toure, that strongé place,
Which was adrad of no manáce
Of quarele nor of none engíne.
And though men woldé make a mine,
No mannés craft it might approche,
For it was set upon a roche

[1] *Congeide*, expelled. [2] *Slow*, slew.

The wallés of the towne about,
Hem stood of all the world no doubt.[1]
And after the proportioún
Six gatés were there of the town
Of such a forme of such entaile
That hem to se was great merveile.
The dichés weren brode and depe,
A fewé men it mighté kepe
From all the world, as semeth tho
But if[2] the goddés weren fo.
Great prees unto that citee drough,
So that there was of people inough
Of burgeis that therinné dwellen,
There may no mannés tunge tellen,
How that citee was riche and good.
"Whan all was made and all well stood,
King Priamus tho him bethought
What they of Grecé whilom wrought,
And what was of her swerd devoured,
And how his suster deshonoúred
With Thelamon away was lad.
And tho thenkénd he wex unglad
And set anone a parlément
To which the lordés were assent.[3]
In many wisé there was spoke,
How that they mighten bene awroke,
But atté lasté nethéles
They saiden all accorde and pees;
To setten every parte in rest
It thought hem thanné for the best
With resonáble amendément.
And thus was Anthenor forth sent
To axen Esióna ayein
And witen what they wolden sain.
"So passeth he the see by barge
To Grecé for to say his charge,
The which he saidé redely
Unto the lordés by and by.[4]
But where he spake in Grece aboute,
He herdé nought but wordés stoute
And naméliche of Thelamon.
The maiden wolde he nought forgon,
He saidé, for no maner thing,
And bad him gone home to his king,
For theré gat he none amende
For ought he couthé do or sende.
"This Anthenór ayein goth home
Unto his king, and whan he come,
He tolde in Grece of that he herde,
And how that Thelamon answérde,
And how they were at her above,
That they wol nouther pees ne love
But every man shall done his best.
But for men sain, that night hath rest,
The king bethought him all that night,
And erly whan the day was light
He toke counsell of this matére,
And they accorde in this manére,—
That he withouten any let
A certain timé shuldé set
A parlément to ben avised,
And in this wise it was avised.
Of parlément he set a day,
And that was in the month of May.
This Priamus had in his ight[1]
A wife, and Hecuba she hight,
By whom at that time eke had he
Sonés five and doughters thre
Besiden hem and thritty mo,
And weren knightés alle tho[2]
But nought upon his wife begete,
But ellés where he might hem gete
Of women which he haddé knowe.
Such was the world that ilké throwe,
So that he was of children riche
So therof was no man him liche.
Of parlément the day was come.
There ben the lordés all and some,
Tho was pronouncéd and purposed
And all the cause hem was desclosed,

1 *Doubt*, fear.
2 *But if*, unless.
3 *Assent*, sent for, summoned.
4 *By and by*, immediately. "By and by," "presently," "anon," and some other words of promptitude, have grown into senses that express some little delay.

1 *Ight*, possession.
2 *Tho*, those.

How Anthenór in Grecé ferde.
They sitten allé still and herde,
And tho spake every man aboute;
There was alleggéd many a doubte,
And many a proud word spoke also.
But for the mosté parte as tho
They wisten nought what was the beste
Or for to werre or for to reste.
But he that was withouté fere,[1]
Hector, among the lordés there
His talé tolde in suche a wise
And saidé: 'Lordés, ye ben wise,
Ye knowen this als well as I,
Above all other most worthý
Stant now in Grecé the manhod
Of worthinesse and of knighthod.
For who so woll it wel agrope,
To hem belongeth all Europe,
Whiche is the thriddé parte evén
Of all the world undér the hevén.
And we be but of folk a fewe,
So were it reson for to shewe
The peril er we fall therinne.
Bet is to levé than beginne
Thing whichas may nought ben acheved,
He is nought wise, that find him greved
And doth so that his greve be more.
For who that loketh all to-fore
And woll nought se what is behinde,
He may full ofte his harmés finde.
Wick is to strive and have the worse,
We have enchéson for to curse,
This wote I well, and for to hate
The Grekes, but er that we debate
With hem that ben of such a might
It is full good that every wight
Be of him self right well bethought.
But as for me thus say I nought,
For whilé that my life woll stonde,
If that ye také werre on honde,
Fall it to the best or to the werst,

[1] *Fere*, companion, equal.

I shall my selven be the ferst
To greven hem what ever I may.
I woll nought onés saié nay
To thing which that your counceil demeth,
For unto me well more it quemeth
The werré certés than the pees.
But this I saié nethéles,
As me belongeth for to say.
Now shapé ye the besté way.'

"Whan Hector hath said his avís
Next after him tho spake París,
Which was his brother, and alaide[1]
What him best thought, and thus he saide:
'Strong thing it is to suffré wronge,
And suffré shame is moré stronge;
But we have suffred bothé two:
And, for all that, yet have we do
What so we mighté to reforme
The pees, whan we in suche a forme
Sent Anthenór, as ye wel knowe.
And they her greté wordés blowe
Upon her wrongfull dedés eke,
And he that woll him self nought meke
To pees and list no reson take,
Men sain resón him wol forsake.
For in the multitude of men
Is nought the strengthé, for with ten
It hath be sene in true quaréle
Ayein an hunderd falsé dele
And had the better, of Goddés grace.
Thus hath befalle in many place.
And if it like unto you alle,
I will assay how so it falle
Our enemies if I may greve,
For I have caught a gret beleve
Upon a point I wol declare.

'This ender day as I gan fare
To hunt unto the greté herte
Which was to-fore min houndés sterte,
And every man went on his side

[1] *Alaide*, alleged.

Him to pursue, and I to ride
Began to chase, and soth to say,
Within a while, out of my way
I rode, and nisté where I was,
And slepé caught me and on the
grasse
Beside a welle I laid me down
To slepe, and in a visión
To me the god Mercúrie cam,
Goddesses thre with him he nam
Minervé, Venus and Juno,
And in his honde an appel tho
He helde of gold with letters write.
And this he didé me to wite
How that they put hem upon me,
That to the fairest of hem thre
Of gold that appel shulde I yive.
With ech of hem tho was I shrive
And eche one fairé me behight.[1]
But Venus said, if that she might
That appel of my yifté gete,
She wolde it nevermore foryete;
And saide, how that in Grecé londe
She woldé bring into min honde
Of all this erthé the fairést:
So that me thought it for the best
To her and yaf the appel tho.
Thus hope I well if that I go
That she for me woll so ordeigne
That they matéré for to pleigne
Shull have or that I come ayein.
Nowe have ye herd that I woll sain,
Say ye what stant in your avis.'—
And every man tho saidé his,
And sondry causes they recorde,
But atté lasté they accorde
That Paris shall to Grecé wende.
And thus the parlement toke ende.
"Cassandra whan she herd of this,
The which to Paris suster is,
Anone she gan to wepe and weile
And said: 'Alas, what may us eile,
Fortúné with her blindé whele
Ne woll nought let us stondé wele,
For this I dare well undertake,
That if París his waié take,
As it is said that he shall do,
We ben for ever than undo.'—
The which—Cassandra thanné hight
In all the world as it bereth sight,—
In bokés as men findé write,
Is that Sibille of whom ye wite,[1]
That allé men yet clepen sage.
Whan that she wist of this viáge,
How Paris shall to Grecé fare,
No woman mighté worsé fare
Ne sorwé moré than she did.
And right so in the samé stede
Ferd Helenus which was her brother,
Of prophecy and such another,
And all was holdé but a jape,
So that the purpos which was shape,
Or were hem lefe or were hem lothe,
Was holde, and into Grece he goth,
This Paris, with his retenaunce.
And as it fell upon his chaunce,
Of Grece he londeth in an ile,
And him was told the samé while
Of folk which he began to freine,[2]
Tho was in thilé quene Heleine,
And eke of contrés there about
Of ladies many a lusty rout,
With mochel worthy people also.
And why they comen thider tho
The causé stood in such a wise
For worship and for sacrifice
That they to Venus wolden make,
As they to-fore had undertake,
Some of good will, some of behest,
For thanné was her highé fest
Within a temple which was there.
Whan Paris wisté what they were,
Anone he shope his ordenaúnce
To gone and done his obeisaúnce
To Venus on her haliday
And did upon[3] his best array.

[1] *Fairé behight*, promised fairly, made fair promises.

[1] *Wite*, know. [2] *Freine*, make inquiry. [3] *Did upon*, put on.

With great richesse he him be-
hongeth
As it to such a lord belongeth,
He was nought arméd netheles,
But as it were in londe of pees.
And thus he goth forth out of ship
And taketh with him his felaship;
In such manere as I you say
Unto the Temple he helde his way.
"Tidíngé, which goth over all
To greate and smallé forth withall,
Come to the quenés ere and tolde
How Paris come, and that he wolde
Do sacrificé to Venús.
And whan she herdé tellé thus,
She thought, how that it ever be,
That she woll him abide and se.
"Forth cometh París with glad
viságe
Into the Temple on pelrinage,
Where unto Venus the goddesse
He yiveth and offreth great richésse
And praieth her that he praié wolde.
And than aside he gan beholde,
And sigh where that this lady stood,
And he forth in his fresshé mood
Goth there she was, and made her
chere
As he well couth in his manére,
That of his wordés such plesaunce
She toke, that all her aqueintaunce
Als ferforth as the herté lay
He stale er that he went away.
So goth he forth and toke his leve
And thought anone, as it was eve,
He woldé done his sacrilegge,
That many a man shulde it abegge.[1]
Whan he to ship ayein was come
To him he hath his counseil nome[2]
And all deviséd the matere
In such a wise as thou shalt here.
Withinné night all privély
His men he warneth by and by
That they be redy arméd sone

[1] *Abegge*, abye, pay for. [2] *Nome*, taken.

For certain thing whiche is to done.
And they anone ben redy alle
And echone other gan to calle
And went hem out upon the stronde
And toke a purpos there on londe
Of what thing that they wolden do,
Toward the Temple and forth
they go.
So fell it of devociön
Heleine in contemplaciön
With many an other worthy wight
Was in the Temple and woke all
night
To bid and pray unto thymáge
Of Venus, as was than uságe,
So that París right as him list
Into the Temple er they it wist
Came with his men all sodeinly.
And all at onés set askry[1]
In hem which in the Temple were,
For tho was mochel people there,
But of defencé was no bote,
So suffren they that suffre mote.
París unto the quené wente
And her in both his armés hente
With him and with his felaship
And forth they bere her into ship.
Up goth the saile, and forth they
went,
And suche a wind Fortúne hem sent,
Till they the haven of Troié caught,
Where out of ship anone they
straught
And gone hem forth toward the town,
The which came with processión
Ayein Paris to sene his pray.
And every man began to say
To Paris and his felaship
All that they couthen of worshíp,
Was none so litel man in Troy
That he ne madé merthe and joy
Of that París had wonne Heleine.
But all that merthe is sorwe and
peine

[1] *Askry*, screaming.

To Helenus and to Cassandre.
For they it tolden[1] shame and sclaundre
And loss of all the comun grace,
That Paris out of haly place
By stelth hath take a mannés wife,
Wherof that he shall lese his life,
And many a worthy man therto,
And all the citee be fordo
Which never shall be made ayein.
And so it fell, right as they sain,
The sacrileggé which he wrought
Was causé why the Gregois sought
Unto the town and it belay
And wolden never part away
Till what by sleight and what by strength
They had it wonne in brede and length
And brent and slain that was withinne.
" Now se, my soné, which a sinne
Is sacrilegge in haly stede.
Beware therfore, and bid thy bede[2]
And do nothíng in haly chirche
But that thou might by reson wirche.
And eke take hede of Áchillés,
Whan he unto his lové chees
Polfxená that was also
In haly Temple of Ápolló,
Which was the causé why he deide
And all his lust was laid aside.
And Troilus upon Creseide
Also his firsté lové laide
In haly place, and how it ferde
As who saith all the world it herde.
Forsake he was for Diomede,
Such was of love his lasté mede.
" Forthý my sone, I woldé rede
By this ensample as thou might rede
Seche ellés where thou wilt thy grace
And ware thee well, in haly place,
What thou to lové do or speke

[1] *Tolden*, accounted, reckoned.
[2] *Bid thy bede*, pray thy prayer.

In aunter if it so be wreke[1]
As thou hast herd me tell to-fore,
And take good hede also therfore.
Upon the forme of Avarice
More than of any other Vice
I have devided in parties
The braunches, which of compaignies
Through out the world in generall
Be now the leders over all
Of Covetise and Perjurie,
Of Fals Brocáge and Usurie,
Of Scarsenesse and of Unkindeship,
Which never drough to felaship,
Of Robberie and of Privé Stelth,
Which done is for the worldés welth,
Of Ravine and of Sacrilegge,
Which maketh the conscience agregge;[2]
All though it may richésse atteigne,
It floureth but it shall not greine
Unto the fruit of rightwisnesse.
But who that woldé do Largesse
Upon the reule as it is yive,
So might a man in trouthé live
Toward his God and eke also
Toward the World, for bothé two
Largesse awaiteth, as belongeth
To neither part that he ne wrongeth.
He kepeth him self, he kepeth his frendes,
So stant he sauf to both his endes;
That he excedeth no mesure,
So well he can him self mesure:
Wherof, my soné, thou shalt wite[3]
So as the philosophre hath write,
" Betwene the two extremités
Of Vicé stont the propertés
Of Vertue, and to prove it so
Take Avarice and take also
The Vice of Prodegalité,
Betwene hem Liberalite,

[1] *Wreke*, avenged.
[2] *Agregge*, feel overburdened.
[3] *Wite*, know.

Which is the Vertue of Largesse,
Stant and govérneth his noblesse.
For tho two Vices in discorde
Stond ever, as I find of recorde;
So that betwene her two debate
Largessé reuleth his estate,
For in such wise as Avarice,
As I to-fore have told the Vice,
Through streit holdíng and through scarsnesse
Stant as contrairé to largesse,
Right so stant Prodegalité
Revers, but nought in such degre.
For so as Avarícé spareth
And for to kepe his tresor careth,
That other all his own and more
Ayein the wisé mannés lore
Yiveth and despendeth here and there,
So that him reccheth never where;
While he may borwe he woll despende
Till atté last he saith: 'I wende.'[1]
But that is spoken all to late,
For than is pouerte at the gate
And taketh him even by the sleve,
For erst woll he no wisdom leve.
And right as Avarice is sinne,
That wold his tresor kepe and winne,
Right so is Prodegalité.
But of Largesse in his degre,
Which even stant betwene the two,
The highé God and man also
The vertue eche of hem commendeth.
For he him selven first amendeth,
That over all his namé spredeth,
And to all other where it nedeth
He yiveth his good in such a wise
That he maketh many a man arise
Which ellés shuldé fallé low.
Largéssé may nought be unknowe,
For what lond that he regneth inne,
It may nought failé for to winne
Through his deserté love and grace,
Where it shall faile in other place.
And thus, betwene to moch and lite,
Largessé, which is nought to wite,[1]
Holt ever forth the middel way.
But who that torné wol away
Fro that to Prodegalité,
Anone he left the propreté
Of Vertu and goth to the Vice.
For in such wise as Avarice
Leseth for scarsenesse his good name,
Right so that other is to blame,
Which through his wast mesúre excedeth.
For no man wot what harm that bredeth
But mochel joié ther betideth,
Where that Largesse an herté guideth.
For his mesúre is so govérned,
That he in bothé parts is lerned
To God and to the World also,
He doth resón to bothé two.
The pouer folk of his almesse
Relievéd ben in the distresse
Of thurst of hunger and of colde,
Ne yift of him was never solde
But frely yive, and nethéles
The mighty God of his encres
Rewardeth him of double grace,
The heven he doth him to purchase
And yiveth him eke the worldés good.
And thus the coté for the hood
Largessé taketh, and yet no sinne
He doth, how so that ever he winne.
What man hath hors, men yiven him hors,
And who ne hath, of him no force,[2]
For he may thenne on foté go;
The world hath ever stondé so.
But for to loken of the tweie,

[1] *I wende*, I will turn (over a new leaf), will change my way.

[1] *To wite*, to be blamed.
[2] *No force*, no matter.

A man to go the siker weie,
Bet is to yivé than to take,
With yifte a man may frendés make,
But who that taketh or great or small,
He taketh a chargé forth with all
And stant nought fre til it be quit.
So for to deme in mannés wit,
It helpeth more a man to have
His owné good than for to crave
Of other men and make him bonde
Wher ellés he may stond unbonde.
Senec counseileth in this wise
And saith: 'But if the good suffice
Unto the liking of the will,
Withdrawe thy lust and hold the still
And be to thy good suffisaúnt,
For that thing is appurtenaunt
To trouthe and causeth to be fre
After the reule of charité,
Which first beginneth of him selve.
For if thou richest other twelve,
Wherof thou shalt thyself be pouer,
I not what thank thou might recouer.
While that a man hath good to yive,
With greaté routés he may live
And hath his frendés over all,
And everich of him tellé shall,
The while he hath his fullé packe
They say, 'A good feláw is Jacke.'
But whan it faileth atté last,
Anone his prise they overcast,
For than is there none other lawe,
But 'Jacké was a good felawe.'
Whan they him pouer and nedy se,
They let him passe and fare well he;
Al that he wend of compaignie
Is thanné torned to folie.
"But now to speke in other kinde
Of Love, a man may suché finde,
That where they come in every rout,
They cast and wast her love about
Till all her time is overgone,
And thanné have they lové none.
For he that loveth over all,
It is no reson that he shall
Of love have any propreté.
Forthý my sone, avisé the,
If thou of love hast ben to large;
For suche a man is nought to charge.
And if it so be, that thou hast
Despended al thy time in wast
And set thy love in sondry place,
Though thou the substaunce of thy grace
Lese at the last, it is no wonder,
For he that put him selven under
As who saith comun over all,
He leseth the lové speciall
Of any one, if she be wise.
For lové shall nought bere his prise
By reson, whan it passeth one.
So have I sen full many one,
That were of lové wel at ese,
Which after fell in great disese
Through wast of lové, that they spent
In sondry places where they went.
Right so, my sone, I axe of the,
If thou with prodegalité
Hast here and there thy lové wasted?"—
"My fader, nay, but I have tasted
In many a place as I have go,
And yet love I never one of tho
But for to drivé forth the day.
For leveth well, my hert is ay
Withouté mo for evermore
All upon one, for I no more
Desiré but her love alone.
So make I many a privé mone,
For well I fele I have despended
My longé love and nought amended
My spede, for ought I findé yit.
If this be wast, unto your wit,
Of love and prodegalité,
Now, godé fader, demeth ye.
But of o thing I woll me shrive,
That I shall for no lové thrive
But if her self me woll releve."—
"My soné, that I may well leve,[1]

[1] *Leve*, believe.

And nethéles me semeth so
For ought that thou hast yet misdo
Of timé whiché thou hast spended,
It may with gracé ben amended.
For thing which may be worth the
cost
Perchaunce is nouther wast ne lost,
For what thing stant on aventúre
That can no worldés creätúre
Tell in certain how it shall wende
Till he therof may sene an ende.
So that I note[1] as yet therfore,
If thou, my sone, hast wone or lore.
For ofté time, as it is sene,
Whan somer hath lost all his grene
And is with winter wast and bare,
That him is left nothíng to spare,—

[1] *Note*, know not.

All is recovered in a throwe;
The coldé windés overblowe,
And stilléd ben the sharpé shoures,
And sodeinlich ayein his floures
The somer happneth, and is riche,
And so parcas thy grace is liche.
My soné, though thou be now pouer
Of lové, yet thou might recouer."—
"My fader, certés graunt mercý,
Ye have me taught so redilý,
That ever while I livé shall
The bet I may be ware with all
Of thing which ye have said er this.
But evermore how that it is
Toward my shrifte as it belongeth,
To wit of other points me longeth,
Wherof that ye me wolden teche
With all min herte I you beseche."

Book VI.

OF GLUTTONY.

The greté sinne originall,
Which every man in general
Upon his birth hath envenímed,
In Paradis it was mistimed,
Whan Adam of thilke appel bote,
His sweté morcel was to hote,
Which dedly[1] madé the mankinde.
And in the bokés as I finde
This Vicé, which so out of reule
Hath set us all, is clepéd Gule,
Of which the braunchés ben so great
That of hem all I wol nought treat,
But only as touchénd of two
I thenké speke and of no mo.
Wherof the first is Dronkéship
Which bereth the cuppé felaship.
Ful many a wonder doth this Vice,
He can make of a wisman nice,
And of a fool that him shall seme
That he can all the lawé deme
And yiven every jugémént
Which longeth to the firmament
Both of the sterre and of the mone.
And thus he maketh a great clerk sone
Of him that is a lewdé man.
There is no thing, whiche he ne can
While he hath dronkéship on honde,
He knoweth the see, he knoweth the stronde,
He is a noble man of armes,—
And yet no strength is in his armes.

[1] *Dedly*, mortal.

There he was stronge inow to-fore
With dronkéship it is forlore,
And all is chaungéd his estate
And wext anone so feble and mate,[1]
That he may nouther go ne come,
But all to-gider he is benome[2]
The power both of honde and fote
So that algate abide he mote,
And all his wittés he foryete.
The which is to him such a lete[3]
That he wot never what he doth,
Ne which is fals ne which is soth,
Ne which is day ne which is night,
As for the time he knoweth no wight[4]
That he ne wot so moch as this—
What maner thing him selven is
Or he be man or he be beste.
That holde I right a sory feste,
Whan he that reson understode
So sodeinlich is woxé wode
Or elles lich the dedé man
Which nouther go ne speké can.
Thus ofte he is to beddé brought,
But where he lith yet wot he nought,
Till he arise upon the morwe
And than he saith, 'O, which a sorwe
It is for to be drinkéles,'
So that half drunke in such a rees
With drié mouth he sterte him up
And saith, 'Now *baillez ça* the cuppe.'

[1] *Mate*, dull, flat.
[2] *Benome*, deprived of.
[3] *Lete*, hindrance.
[4] *No wight*, no whit.

That made him lese his wit at eve
Is than a morwe all his beleve,
The cuppe is all that ever him pleseth
And also that him most diseseth,
It is the cuppé whom he serveth,
Which allé carés from him kerveth
And all the balés to him bringeth.
In joy he wepeth, in sorwe he singeth,
For dronkéship is so divers
It may no whilé stonde invers,
He drinketh the wine, but atté last
The wine drinketh him and bint him fast
And laith him drunké by the walle
As him which is his bondé thralle
And all in his subjectión.
And lich to such condición
As for to speke it otherwise
It falleth, that the mosté wise
Ben other while of Love adoted
And so bewhappéd and assoted [1]
Of dronken men that never yit
Was none which half so lost his wit
Of drinke, as they of such thing do
Which cleped is the jolif wo,
And waxen of her owné thought
So drunké that they knowé nought,
What reson is, or more or lesse.
Such is the kinde of that siknesse,
And that is nought for lacke of braine,
But Love is of so great a maine [2]
That where he taketh a herte on honde,
There may no thing his might withstonde.
The wisé Salomon was nome,
And strongé Sampson overcome,
The knightly David him ne might
Rescoué that he with the sight
Of Bersabé ne was bestade.
Virgile also was overlade,
And Aristotle was put under.

1 *Bewhappéd and assoted*, knocked over and besotted.
2 *Maine*, strength.

"Forthy my sone, it is no wonder,
If thou be drunke of Love amonge,
Which is above all other stronge.
And if so is that thou so be,
Tell me thy shrift in privété,
It is no shame of such a thewe
A yong man to be dronkelewe.
Of such phisíque I can a parte,
And as me semeth by that arte
Thou shuldest by phisonomý
Be shapen to that maladý
Of lové drunk, and that is routhe."—
"Ha, holy fader, all is trouthe
That ye me telle, I am beknowe,
That I with Love am so bethrowe [1]
And al min herte is so through sunke
That I am veriliché drunke,
And yet I may both speke and go.
But I am overcomé so
And tornéd fro my self so clene
That oft I wot nought what I mene,
So that excusen I ne may
My herté fro the firsté day
That I cam to my lady kith. [2]
I was yet sobre never sith,
Where [3] I her se or se her nought;
With musing of min owné thought
Of lové which min herte assaileth
So drunke I am that my wit faileth
And all my braine is overtorned,
And my maneré so mistorned,
That I foryete all that I can
And stondé like a maséd man,
That ofté whan I shuldé play
It maketh me drawe out of the way
In solein [4] placé by my selve,
As doth a laborér to delve
Which can no gentilmannés chere, [5]
Or ellés as a lewdé frere,
Whan he is put to his penaunce,

1 *Bethrowe*, cast down.
2 *Cam kith*, became known.
3 *Where*, whether.
4 *Solein*, single.
5 Who knows nothing of the good manners of a gentleman.

Right so lese I my contenaunce.
And if it nedés so betide,
That I in compaigný abide,
Where as I musté daunce and singe
The hové-daunce[1] and carolinge,
Or for to go the newé fote,
I may nought wel heve up my fote,
If that she be nought in the way.
For than is all my merth away,
And waxe anone of thought so full,
Wherof my limmés ben so dull,
I may unethés[2] gon the pas.
For thus it is and ever was,
Whan I on suché thoughtés muse,
The lust and merthé that men use,
Whan I se nought my lady by me,
All is foryeté for the timé
So ferforth that my wittés chaungen
And allé lustés fro me straungen,
That they sain allé truélý
And sweré, that it am nought I.
For as the man which ofté drinketh
The wine that in his stomack sinketh
Wexth drunke and witles for a
throwe,
Right so my lust is overthrowe,
And of min owné thought so mate[3]
I waxé, that to min estate
There is no limmé will me serve,
But as a drunken man I swerve
And suffre such a passiön,
That men have great compassiön
And everich by him self merveileth
What thing it is that me so eileth.
Such is the maner of my wo,
Which timé that I am her fro,
Till efte ayein that I her se.
But than it were a nicété
To tellé you how that I fare.
For whan I may upon her stare,
Her womanheed, her gentilesse,
Min hert is full of such gladnesse
That overpasseth so my wit

[1] *Hové-daunce*, court dance.
[2] *Unethés*, not easily.
[3] *Mate*, dull, dead.

That I wot never where it sit,
But am so drunken of that sight
Me thenketh for the time I might
Right sterté through the holé wall.
And than I may well, if I shall,
Both singe and daunce and lepe
about
And holdé forth the lusty rout.
But nethéles it falleth so
Full ofté that I fro her go
Ne may, but as it were a stake
I stonde, avisément to take
And loke upon her fairé face,
That for the while out of the place
For all the world ne might I wende.
Such lust comth than into my
minde,
So that withouté mete and drinke
Of lusty thoughtés which I thinke,
Me thenketh I mighté stonden ever.
And so it weré to me lever
Than such a sighté for to leve,
If that she woldé yive me leve
To have so mochel of my will.
And thus thenkénd I stondé still
Withouté blenching of min eye,
Right as me thoughté that I sigh
Of paradis the mosté joy.
And so there while I me rejoy;
Unto min herte a great desire
The which is hoter than the fire
All sodeinliche upon me renneth,
That all my thought withinné bren-
neth
And am so ferforth overcome
That I not where I am become,
So that among tho hertés stronge
In stede of drinke I underfonge
A thought so swete in my coráge,
That never piment[1] ne vernage[2]
Was half so sweté for to drinke.
For as I wolde, than I thinke,

[1] *Piment*, wine with a third part of honey spiced with powder of cloves, mace, cinnamon, cubebs, and galingale.
[2] *Vernage*, a white wine.

As though I were at min above,
For so through drunke I am of love,
That all that my sotïé demeth
Is soth as than it to me semeth.
And while I may tho thoughtés kepe
Me thenketh as though I were aslepe
And that I were in Goddés barme.[1]
But whan I se min owné harme
And that I sodeinliche awake
Out of my thought and hedé take
How that the sothé stant in dede,
Than is my sikernesse in drede
And joié tornéd into wo,
So that the hete is all ago
Of such sotie as I was inne.
And than ayeinward I beginne
To take of love a newé thorst,
The which me greveth alltherworst,
For thanné cometh the blanché fever
With chele and maketh me so to
chever[2]
And so it coldeth at min herte,
That wonder is how I asterte[3]
In suche a point that I ne deie.
For certés there was never keie
Ne frosen ïs upon the walle
More inly cold than I am alle.
And thus suffre I the hoté chele
Which passeth other peinés fele,
In colde I brenne and frese in hete
And than I drinke a bitter swete
With drié lippe and eyen wete.
Lo, thus I temper my diete
And take a draught of such relés[4]
That all my wit is hertéles
And all min herté there it sit
Is as who saith withouté wit,
So that to prove it by resón
In making of comparisón
There may no differéncé be
Betwen a drunken man and me,
But all the werst of everychone
Is ever that I thurst in one,

[1] *Barme*, bosom.
[2] *Chever*, shiver.
[3] *Asterte*, escape.
[4] *Relés*, relish.

The moré that my herté drinketh
The more I may, so that me
thinketh,
My thurst shall never be acqueint.[1]
God shieldé that I be nought dreint
Of such a superfluité.
For well I fele in my degre
That all my wit is overcast,
Wherof I am the more agast
That in defaulte of ladyship
Perchaunce in such a dronkéship
I may be dead er I beware.
For certés, fader, this I dare
Beknowe and in my shrifté telle,
But[2] I a draught have of that welle
In which my deth is and my life,
My joy is tornéd into strife,
That sobre shall I never worthe,[3]
But as a drunken man forworthe,[4]
So that in londé, where I fare,
The lust is lore of my welfare,
As he that may no boté finde.
But this me thenketh a wonder kinde,
As I am drunke of that I drinke
Of thesé thoughtés that I thinke
Of which I findé no reles,
But if I mighté nethéles
Of suche a drinke as I coveite
So as me list have o receite,
I shulde assobre[5] and faré wele.
But so Fortúne upon her whele
On high me deigneth nought to sette,
For evermore I finde a lette.
The botéler is nought my frend
Which hath the keié by the bend.[6]
I may well wissh and that is waste,
For well I wot so fressh a taste,
But if my gracé be the more,
I shall assaié nevermore.
Thus am I drunke of that I se,
For tasting is defended me,

[1] *Acqueint*, quenched.
[2] *But*, unless.
[3] *Worthe*, become.
[4] *Forworthe*, perish.
[5] *Assobre*, become sober.
[6] The key on his girdle, or band.

And I can nought my selven staunche,
So that, my fader, of this braunche
I am giltif, to tellé trouth."—
"My soné, that me thenketh routh.
For lovédrunke is the mischefe
Above all other the moste chefe,
If he no lusty thought assay
Which may his sory thurst allay,
As for the timé yet it lesseth
To him which other joié misseth.
"Forthy my sone, aboven all
Think well how so it the befall,
And kepe thy wittés that thou hast
And let hem nought be drunke in wast.
But nethéles there is no wight,
That may withstondé Lovés might.
But why the cause is, as I finde,
But that there is diversé kinde
Of lovédrunké: why men pleigneth
After the court which all ordeigneth,
I will the tellen the manére,
Now list, my sone, and thou shalt here.
For the fortune of every chaunce
After the goddés purveaunce
To man it groweth from above,
So that the spede of every love
Is shapé there, er it befalle.
For Jupiter aboven alle,
Which is of goddes soverain,
Hath in his celler, as men sain,
Two tonnés full of lové drinke
That maketh many an herté sinke
And many an herte also to flete,[1]
Or of the soure or of the swete.
That one is full of such piment,
Which passeth all entendément
Of mannés wit if he it taste,
And maketh a jolif herte in haste.
"That other bitter as the galle,
Which maketh a mannés herté palle,
Whose dronkéship is a siknesse
Through feling of the bitternesse.
Cupide is botéler of bothe,
Which to the leve and to the lothe
Yiveth of the swete and of the soure,
That somé laugh and somé loure.
But for so much as he blinde is
Full ofté time he goth amis
And taketh the baddé for the good,
Which hindreth many a mannés food
Withouté cause and furthereth eke.
So be there some of lové seke
Which ought of reson to ben hole,
And somé comé to the dole
In happe and as hem selven lest[1]
Drinke undeservéd of the best.
"And thus this blindé botélere
Yiveth of the trouble in stede of chere
And eke the chere in stede of trouble.
Lo, how he can the hertés trouble
And maketh men drunke al upon chaunce
Withouté lawe of governaunce.
If he drawe of the sweté tonne,
Than is the sorwe all overronne
Of lovédrunke, and shall nought greven
So to be drunken every even,
For all is thanné but a game.
But whan it is nought of the same
And he the better tonné draweth,
Such dronkéship an herté gnaweth
And febleth all a mannés thought,
That better him were have drunké nought
And all his brede have eten drie,
For than he lest his lusty wey
With dronkéship and wot nought whider
To go, the waies ben so slider,
In whiche he may par cas so falle
That he shall breke his wittés alle.

[1] *Flete*, float, swim.

[1] *Lest*, please.

And in this wisé men be drunke
And the drinké they have drunke.
But allé drinken nought alike,
For some shall singe and some shal sike,
So that it me no thing mervesleth,
My sone, of lové that the eyleth.
For wel I knowé by thy tale,
That thou hast drunken of the dwale[1]
Which bitter is, till God the sende
Such gracé that thou might amende.
But soné, thou shalt bid and pray
In such a wise as I shall say,
That thou the lusté well atteigne
Thy wofull thurstes to restreigne
Of Love and tasté the swetenesse,
As Bachus did in his distresse,
Whan bodeliché thurst him hent
In straungé londés, where he went.
"This Bachus sone of Jupiter
Was hote,[2] and as he wenté fer
By his fadérs assignément
To make a wer in Orient
And great powér with him he ladde,
So that the higher hond he hadde
And victoire of his enemies
And torneth homward with his prise.
In suche a contré which was drie
A mischefe fell upon the wey,
As he rode with his compaigny
Nigh to the strondés of Lubie,
There mighté they no drinké finde
Of water ne of other kinde,
So that him self and all his hoste
Were for default of drinke almoste
Distruiéd, and than Bachus praid
To Jupiter, and thus he said:
'O highé fader, that seest all,
To whom is reson that I shall
Beseche and pray in every nede,
Behold, my fader, and take hede
This wofull thurst that we be inne,
To staunche and graunt us for to winne
And saufe unto the contré fare
Where that our lusty lovés are
Waiténd upon our home coming.'
And with the vois of his praying,
Which herd was to the goddés high,
He sigh anone to-fore his eye
A wether which the grounde hath sporned,
And where he hath it overtorned,
There sprang a wellé fressh and clere,
Wherof his owné botélere
After the lustés of his will
Was every man, to drinke his fill.
And for this ilké greté grace
Bachus upon the samé place
A riché temple let arere,
Which ever shuldé stondé there
To thursty men in remembraúnce.
"Forthý, my sone, after this chaunce
It sit the well to taken hede
So for to pray upon thy nede,
As Bachus praidé for the well.
And thenke as thou hast herd me tell
How grace he gradde[1] and grace he had,
He was no fool that first so rad.
For selden get a domb man londe,
Take that provérbe, and understonde
That wordés ben of vertue gret.
Forthý to speké thou ne let
And axe and pray erelý and late
Thy thurst to quenche, and thenke algate,
The boteler which bereth the key
Is blinde, as thou hast herd me say.
And if it mighté so betide,
That he upon the blindé side
Par cas the sweté tonne araught,

[1] *Dwale*, nightshade. [2] *Hote*, called.

[1] *Gradde*, cried for.

Than shalt thou have a lusty draught
And waxe of lovédrunké sobre.
And thus I redé thou assobre
Thin herte in hope of suche a grace,
For dronkéship in every place
To whether sidé that it torne
Doth harme and maketh a man to
sporne [1]
And ofté falle in suche a wise,
Where he par cas may nought arise.
"And for to loke in evidence
Upon the sothe experiénce
So as it hath befall er this,
In every mannés mouth it is
How Tristram was of lové drunke
With Bele Isoldé, whan they drunke
The drink which Brangweine hem
betok
Er that king Mark his eme her toke
To wife, as it was after knowe.
And eke, my sone, if thou wolt knowe
As it hath fallen over more
In lovés cause, and what is more
Of dronkéshippé for to drede
As it whilom befell in dede,
Wherof thou might the better
escheue
Of drunké men that thou ne sue
The compaigný in no manere,
A great ensample thou shalt here.
This finde I write in poesy
Of thilké faire Ypotasy,
Of whose beauté there as she was
Spake every man. And fell par cas,
That Pirothóus so him spedde,
That he to wife her shuldé wedde,
Wherof that he great joié made.
And for he wolde his lové glade
Ayein the day of mariáge
By mouthé bothe and by messáge
His frendés to the fest he praid,
With great worshíp and as men said
He hath this yongé lady spoused.
And whan that they were allé housed
And set and servéd atté mete,
There was no wine, which may
begete
That there ne was plentý inough.
But Bachus thilké tonné drough,
Wherof by way of dronkéship
The greatest of the felaship
Were out of reson overtake,
And Venus, which hath also take
The causé most in speciall,
Hath yive him drinké forth with all
Of thilké cuppé whiche exciteth
The lust wherin a man deliteth.
And thus by double weié drunke
Of lust that ilké firy funke [1]
Hath made hem as who saith half
wode, [2]
That they no reson understode
Ne to none other thing they seen
But hiré which to-fore her eyen
Was wedded thilké samé day;
That fresshé wife, that lusty may
Of her it was all that they thoughten
And so ferforth her lustés soughten
That they the whiché naméd were
Centauri, at the festé there
Of one assent, of one accorde,
This yongé wife malgré her lorde
In suche a rage away forth ladden,
As they which none insight ne
hadden
But only to her drunké fare,
Which many a man hath made
misfare
In love als wel as other wey.
Wherof, if I shall moré say
Upon the nature of this Vice,
Of custume and of exercise
The mannés grace how it fordoth,
A talé, which was whilom soth
Of foolés that so drunken were,
I shall reherce unto thin ere.
I rede in a cronísqué thus
Of Galba and of Vitelliús,

[1] *Sporne*, strike with the foot; stumble.

[1] *Funke*, touchwood, spark. [2] *Wode*, mad.

The which of Spainé bothé were
The greatest of all other there,
And bothe of o conditión
After the dispositión
Of glotony and dronkéship,
That was a sory felaship.
For this thou might wel understonde,
That man may nought well longé stonde
Which is wine drunke of comun use,
For he hath loré the vertues
Wherof that Reson shuld him clothe,
And that was sen upon hem bothe.
Men sain there is non evidence
Wherof to knowe a difference
Betwene the drunken and the wode,
For they ben never nouther gode;
For where that wine doth wit awey
Wisdome hath lost the righté wey,
That he no maner Vicé dredeth;
No moré than a blind man thredeth
His nedel by the sonnés light,
No more is Reson than of might
Whan he with dronkeship is blent.
And in this point they weren shent
This Galba both and eke Vitelle
Upon the cause as I shall telle,
Wherof good is to taken hede.
For they two through her dronkenhede
Of witlés excitatión
Oppresséd all the nación
Of Spainé, for all foul usaúnce,
Which done was of continuaúnce
Of hem which all day drunké were.
There was no wife ne maiden there
What so they were or faire or foule
Whom they ne taken to defoule,
Wherof the lond was often wo.
And eke in other thingés mo
They wroughten many a sondry wronge.
But how so that the day be longe,
The derké night cometh atté last.
God woldé nought they shulden last,
And shope the lawe in suche a wise
That they through dome to the juise
Ben dampnéd for to be forlore.
But they that hadden be to-fore
Enclined to allé drunkenesse,
Her endé thanné bare witnésse;
For they in hopé to assuage
The peine of dethe upon the rage
That they the lassé shulden fele,
Of winé let fill full a mele
And drunken till so was befall
That they her strengthés losten all
Withouten wit of any braine,
And thus they ben half dedé slaine,
That hem ne greveth but a lite.
"My sone, if thou be for to wite
In any point which I have said,
Wherof thy wittes bene unteid,
I redé clepe hem home ayein."—
"I shall do, fader, as ye sain,
Als ferforth as I may suffise.
But well I wot that in no wise
The dronkéship of Love awey
I may remué by no wey,
It stant nought upon my fortúne.
But if you listé to comúne
Of the secóndé glotony,
Which clepéd is Delscacý,
Wherof ye speken here to-fore,
Beseche I woldé you therfore."—
My sone, as of that ilké Vice
Which of all other is the norice,
And stant upon the retenue
Of Venus, so as it is due,
The propreté how that it fareth
The boke herafter now declareth.

Of this chapitre, in which we trete,
There is yet one of such diete
To which no pouer may atteigne,
For all is past as paindemaine[1]
And sondry wine and sondry drinke
Wherof that he woll ete and drinke

[1] *Past as paindemaine*, diet unattainable by the poor; all pastry, as fine white bread, &c.

His cokés ben for him affaited,
So that his body is awaited
That him shall lacké no delite
Als ferforth as his appetite
Suffiseth to the metés hote.
Wherof the lusty Vice is hote
Of gulé the Delscacý,[1]
Which all the holé progeny
Of lusty folke hath undertake
To fedé while that he may take
Richessé, wherof to be founde.
Of abstinence he wot no bounde,
To what proffit it shuldé serve.
And yet phisique of his conserve
Maketh many a restauración
Unto his recreación,
Which woldé be to Venus lefe.
Thus for the point of his relefe
The coke which shal his mete array
But he the bet his mouth assay
His lordés thank shall ofté lèse
Er he be servéd to the chese.
For there may lacké nought so lite[2]
That he ne fint anone a wite,[3]
For but his lust be fully served
There hath no wight his thank deserved,
And yet for mannés sustenaunce
To kepe and holde in governaunce
To him that woll his helé gete
Is none so good as comun mete.
For who that loketh on the bokes,
It saith, confectión of cokes
A man him shuldé well avise
How he it toke and in what wise.
For who that useth that he knoweth
Full selden siknesse on him groweth,
And who that useth metés straunge
Though his natúre empeire and chaunge
It is no wonder, levé sone,
Whan that he doth ayein his wone[4]
To také metes and drinkés newe,
The which it shulde alwey eschewe
For in phisqué this I finde,
That Usance is the seconde Kinde.[1]
"And right so chaungeth his estate
He that of Love is delicate,
For though he haddé to his honde
The besté wife of all the londe
Or the fairésté love of alle,
Yet wolde his herte on other falle
And thinke hem more delicioús
Than he hath in his owné hous.
Men sain it is now ofté so,
Avise hem well, that they so do,
And for to speke in other way
Full ofté time I have herd say,
That he which hath no love acheved
Him thenketh that he is nought relieved
Though that his lady make him chere,
So as she may in good manere
Her honour and her namé save,
But he the surplus mighté have;
Nothing withstanding her estate,
Of lové moré delicate,
He set her chere at no delite
But he have all his appetite.
"My sone, if it with the be so,
Tell me?"—"Min holy fader, no.
For delicate in such a wise
Of Love, as ye to me devise,
Ne was I never yet giltife.
For if I haddé suche a wife,
As ye speke of, what shulde I more?
For than I woldé never more
For lust of any womanhede
Min herte upon none other fede.
And if I did, it were a waste.
But all withouté such repaste
Of lust as ye me tolde above,
Of wife or yet of other love,
I faste and may no fodé gete,
So that for lack of deintie mete

[1] Delicacy of the gullet. [2] *Lite*, little.
[3] *Wite*, blame. [4] *Wone*, custom.

[1] Use is second Nature.

Of whiche an herté may be fedde,
I go fasténdé to my bedde.
But might I getten as ye tolde
So mochel that my lady wolde
Me fedé with her glad semblaunt,
Though me lacke all theremenaunt,
Yet shulde I somdele ben abeshed[1]
And for the timé wel refreshed.
But certes, fader, she ne doth;
For in good feith to tellé soth
I trowé, though I shuldé sterve,
She woldé nought her eyé swerve
My herté with one goodly loke
To fede, and thus for such a coke
I may go fasting evermo.
But if so is that any wo
May fede a mannés herté wele,
Therof I have at every mele
Of plenté moré than inough.
But that is of him self so tough,
My stomack may it nought defie.[2]
Lo, such is the Delfcacie
Of Lové which min herté fedeth,
Thus have I lacke of that me nedeth.
But for all this yet nethéles,
I say, I am nought giltéles,
That I somdele am delicate.
For ellés were I fully mate
But if that I some lusty stounde
Of comfort and of esé founde
To take of lové some repast;
For though I with the fullé taste
The lust[3] of Lové may nought fele,
Min hunger otherwise I kele
Of smalé lustés whiche I pike,
And for a timé yet they like,
If that ye wisten, what I mene."—
"Now, godé soné, shrive the clene
Of suché deinties as ben good
Wherof thou takest thin herté food."—
"My fader, I you shall reherce,
How that my fodés ben diverse,
So as they fallen in degre.
One feding is of that I se,
An other is of that I here,
The thridde, as I shall tellen here,
It groweth of min owné thought.
And ellés shulde I livé nought,
For whom that faileth food of herte
He may nought well the dethe asterte.
"Of sight is all my firsté food,
Through which min eye of allé good
Hath that to him is accordaúnt
A lusty fodé suffisaúnt.
Whan that I go toward the place
Where I shall se my ladies face,
Min eyé, whiche is loth to faste,
Beginneth to hunger anone so faste
That him thenketh of an houré thre,
Till I there come and he her se.
And than after his appetite
He taketh a food of such delite,
That him none other deintie nedeth,
Of sondry sightés he him fedeth.
He seeth her face of such coloúr
That fressher is than any floúr;
He seeth her front is large and pleine
Withouté frounce of any greine;
He seeth her eyen liche an heven;
He seeth her nasé straughte and even;
He seeth her rudde upon the cheke;
He seeth her reddé lippés eke;
Her chinne accordeth to the face,
All that he seeth is full of grace;
He seeth her necké rounde and clene,
Therinné may no bone be sene;
He seeth her handés faire and white,
For all this thingé without wite
He may se naked atté leste,
So is it well the moré feste
And well the more delfcacie
Unto the feding of min eye.
He seeth her shapé forth with all,
Her body rounde, her middel small,

[1] *Abeshed*, astonished.
[2] *Defie*, digest.
[3] *Lust*, pleasure, in no bad sense; so lusty = the German "lustig."

So well begone with good array,
Which passeth all the lust of May
Whan he is most with softé shoures
Full clothéd in his lusty floures.
With suché sightés by and by
Min eye is fed, but finallý,
Whan he the port and the manere
Seeth of her womanisshé chere,
Than hath he such delite on honde
Him thenketh he might stillé stonde
And that he hath full suffisaunce
Of livelode and of sustenaunce
As to his part for evermo.
And if it thought all other so,
Fro thenné wolde he never wende
But there unto the worldés ende
He wolde abide, if that he might,
And feden him upon the sight.
For though I mighté stonden ay
Into the time of domésday
And loke upon her ever in one,
Yet whan I shuldé fro her gone
Min eyé wolde, as though he faste,
Ben hunger storven also faste
Till eft ayein that he her see,
Such is the nature of min eye.
There is no lust so deintéfull,
Of which a man shall nought be full
Of that the stomack underfongeth,
But ever in one min eyé longeth;
For loke, how that a goshawk tireth,[1]
Right so doth he, whan that he pireth
And toteth on her womanhede,
For he may never fully fede
His lust, but ever a liche sore
Him hungreth, so that he the more
Desireth to be fed algate.
And thus min eye is made the gate
Through which the deinties of my
thought
Of lust ben to min herté brought.
Right as min eyé with his loke
Is to min herte a lusty coke

[1] *Tireth*, tears and plucks in feeding, as a bird of prey.

Of Lovés fodé delicate,
Right so min ere in his estate,
Whereas min eyé may nought
serve,
Can well min hertés thank deserve
And feden him fro day to day
With suché deintés, as he may.
For thus it is, that over all
Where as I come in speciáll
I may here of my lady prise:
I here one say, that she is wise;
An other saith, that she is good;
And some men sain, of worthy blood
That she is come, and is also
So fair, that no where is none so;
And some men preise her goodly
chere:
Thus every thing that I may here
Which souneth to my lady good,
Is to min ere a lusty food.
And eke min ere hath over this
A deinty festé, whan so is
That I may here her selven speke,
For than anone my faste I breke
On suché wordés as she saith,
That full of trouth and full of feith
They ben, and of so good disporte,
That to min eré great comfórte
They done as they that ben delices.
For all the metés and the spices
That any Lumbard couthé make
Ne be so lusty for to take
Ne so ferforth restauratife
I say as for min owné life,
As be the wordés of her mouth.
For as the windés of the south
Ben most of allé debonaire,
So whan her list to speké faire
The vertue of her goodly speche
Is verrily min hertés leche.[1]
And if it so befall amonge
That she carole upon a songe,
Whan I it here I am so fed
That I am fro my self so led

[1] *Leche*, physician.

As though I were in Paradis,
For certes as to min avis,
Whan I here of her vois the steven[1]
Me thenkth it is a blisse of heven.
And eke in otherwise also
Ful ofté time it falleth so
Min eré with a good pitaunce
Is fed of reding of romaunce
Of Ydoine and of Amadas,
That whilom weren in my cas,
And eke of other many a score,
That loveden longe er I was bore;
For whan I of her lovés rede,
Min eré with the tale I fede
And with the lust of her histoire.
Somtime I drawe into memoire
How sorwe may nought ever last,
And so cometh hope in atté last,
Whan I none other fodé knowe.
And that endureth but a throwe,
Right as it were a chery feste.
But for to compten atté lest,
As for the whilé yet it eseth
And somdele of min hert appeseth.
For what thing to min eré spredeth,
Which is plesaunt, somdele it fedeth,
With wordés such as he may gete,
My lust in stede of other mete.
"Lo thus, my fader, as I you say
Of lust the which min eye hath see
And eke of that min ere hath herde,
Full ofte I have the better ferde.
And tho two bringen in the thridde,
The which hath in min herte amidde
His placé také to array
The lusty fodé whiche assay
I mote, and namélich on nightes,
Whan that me lacketh allé sightes,
And that min hering is awey,
Than is he redy in the wey
My reré souper[2] for to make,
Of which min hertés fode I take.
"This lusty cokés name is hote

[1] *Steven*, voice, sound.
[2] *Reré souper*, a supper after supper for the luxurious who sat up late.

Thought, which hath ever his pottés hote
Of lové boilend on the fire
With fantasy and with desire,
Of which er this full ofte he fed
Min herté whan I was a bed.
And than he set upon my borde
Both every sight and every worde
Of lust which I have herd or seen.
But yet is nought my fest all plein,
But all of woldés and of wisshes
Therof have I my fullé disshes,
But as of feling and of taste
Yet might I never have o repaste.
And thus as I have said a-forn,
I lické hony on the thorn,
And as who saith upon the bridel
I chewé, so that all is idel,
As in effect the fode I have.
But as a man that wolde him save
Whan he is sike by medicíne,
Right so of lové the famíne
I fonde in all that ever I may
To fede, and drivé forth the day
Till I may have the greté fest
Which all min hunger might arest.
"Lo, suché ben my lustes thre,
Of that I thenké, here and se,
I take of lové my fedíng
Withouté tasting or felíng,
And as the plover doth of aire
I live, and am in good espeire
That for no such delícacý
I trowe I do no glotený.
And nethéles to your avis,
Min holy fader, that ben wis,
I recommaundé min estate
Of that I have ben delicate."—
"My sone, I understondé wele
That thou hast told here every dele,
And as me thenketh by thy tale
It ben delités wonder smale
Wherof thou takest thy lovés fode.
But, sone, if that thou understode,
What is to ben deliciońs,

Thou woldest nought ben curioús
Upon the lust of thin estate
To ben to soré delicate
Wherof that thou resón excede;
For in the bokés thou might rede,
If mannés wisdom shall be sued
It oughté wel to ben escheued
In Love als well as other way;
For as these haly bokés say,
The bodély delíces alle
In every point how so they falle
Unto the soulé done grevaúnce.
And for to take in remembraúnce
A tale accordaunt unto this,
Which of great understanding is
To mannés soulé resonáble,
I thenke tell and is no fable.
"**Of Cristés word** who wol it rede
How that this Vice is for to drede
In thevangile it telleth pleine,
Which mote algaté be certeine
For Crist him self it bereth witnésse.
And though the clerke and the clergesse
In Latin tunge it rede and singe
Yet for the moré knoulechinge
Of trouthé, which is good to wite,
I shal declare as it is write
In English, for thus it began.
"**Crist saith**: There was a riché man,
A mighty lord of great estate,
And he was eke so delicate
Of his clothíng that every day
Of purpure and bisse[1] he made him gay
And ete and drank therto his fill
After the lustés of his will
As he which all stode in delice
And toke none hede of thilké Vice.
And as it shuldé so betide,
A pouer lazér upon a tide
Came to the gate and axéd mete.

[1] *Bisse*, finest linen.

But theré might he nothing gete
His dedely hunger for to staunche,
For he which had his fullé paunche
Of allé lustés atté borde
Nedeigneth nought to speke a worde
Onlich a crummé for to yive
Wherof the pouer mighté live
Upon the yift of his almesse.
Thus lay this pouer in great distresse
A colde and hungry at the gate,
Fro which he mighté go no gate
So was he wofully besene.
And as these haly bokés sain,
The houndés comen fro the halle,
Where that this siké man was falle,
And as he lay there for to deie,
The woundés of his maladý
They licken, for to done him ese.
But he was full of such disese
That he may nought the deth escape.
But as it was that timé shape
The soulé fro the body passeth,
And he whom nothing overpasseth,
The highé God up to the heven
Him toke, where he hath set him even
In Abrahamés barme[1] on high,
Where he the hevens joié sigh
And had all that he havé wolde.
And fell as it befallé sholde,
This riché man the samé throwe
With sodein deth was overthrowe
And forth withouten any went[2]
Unto the helle straught he went,
The fende into the fire him drough
Where that he haddé peine inough
Of flamé which that ever brenneth.
And as his eye abouté renneth,
Toward the heven he cast his loke,
Where that he sigh and hedé toke
How Lazar set was in his see
Als fer as ever he mighté see
With Abraham, and than he praide
Unto the patriarch and saide:

[1] *Barme*, bosom. [2] *Went*, turning.

'Send Lazar down fro thilké sete
And do that he his finger wete
In water, so that he may droppe
Upon my tungé for to stoppe
The greté hete in which I brenne.'
But Abrahám answérdé thenne
And saidé to him in this wise:
'My soné, thou the might avise
And take into thy remembraúnce
How Lazar haddé great penaúnce
While he was in that other life.
But thou in all thy lust jolife
The bodely delícés soughtest,
Forthý so as thou thanné wroughtest,
Now shalt thou také thy rewarde
Of dedely peine here afterwarde
In hellé, which shall ever last.
And this Lazar now atté last
This worldés peine is overronne,
In heven and hath his life begonne
Of joié which is endéles.
But that thou praiest nethéles,
That I shall Lazar to the sende
With water on his finger ende
Thine hoté tungé for to kele,
Thou shalt no suché graces fele,
For to that foulé place of sinne
For ever in which thou shalt ben inne,
Cometh none out of this placé thider
Ne none of you may comen hider,
Thus be ye parted now a-two.'
The rich ayeinward cridé tho:
'O Abraham, sithe it so is,
That Lazar may nought do me this
Whiche I have axéd in this place,
I woldé pray an other grace.
For I have yet of bretherne five
That with my fader ben a-live
To-gider dwellend in one hous,
To whom, as thou art gracïoús,
I praié, that thou woldest sende
Lazar, so that he mighté wende
To warne hem how the worlde is went,
That afterward they benought shent
Of suché peinés as they deie.
Lo, this I praie and this I crie,
How I may nought my self amende.'
The patriarche anone suende
To this praiér answérdé: 'Nay,'
And saide him, how that every day
His bretheren mighten knowe and here
Of Moïses on erthé here
And of prophétés other mo,
What hem was best. And he saith: 'No,
But if there might a man arise
From deth to life in suche a wise
To tellen hem how that it were,'
He saidé, 'than of puré fere
They shulden well beware therby.'
Quod Abraham: 'Nay sikerly,
For if they now will nought obey
To such as techen hem the wey
And all day preche and all day telle
How that it stant of heven and helle,
They woll nought thanné taken hede
Though it befellé so in dede
That any dede man weré arered,
To ben of him no better lered
Than of an other man alive.'
"If thou, my soné, canst descrive
This tale, as Crist him self it tolde,
Thou shalt have causé to beholde
To se so great an evidence,
Wherof the sothe experience
Hath shewéd openlich at eye,
That bodély delícacý
Of him which yiveth none almesse,
Shall after falle in great distresse.
And that was sene upon the riche,
For he ne wolde unto his liche
A crummé yiven of his brede,
Than afterward whan he was dede
A droppe of water him was werned.[1]
Thus may a mannés wit be lerned
Of hem that so delités taken

[1] *Werned*, denied.

Whan they with deth ben overtaken,
That erst was swete is thanné soure.
But he that is a governoúr
Of worldés good, if he be wise,
Within his herte he set no prise
Of all the worlde, and yet he useth
The good that he nothíng refuseth,
As he which lord is of the thinges,
The ouches and the riché ringes,
The cloth of gold and the perrie
He taketh, and yet delícacíe
He leveth though he wear all this.
The beste meté that there is
He eteth, and drinketh the besté drinke,
But how that ever he ete or drinke
Delícacié he put awey
As he which goth the righté wey
Nought only for to fede and clothe
His body, but his soulé bothe.
But they that taken other wise
Her lustés, ben none of the wise,
And that whilom was shewéd eke,
If thou these oldé bokés seke.
"That man that wolde him well avise,
Delícacý is to despise
Whan Kinde accordeth nought withall,
Wherof ensample in speciall
Of Nero whilom may be tolde,
Whiche ayein kindé manifolde
His lustés toke, till atté last,
That God him wolde all overcast,
Of whom the cronique is so plein,
Me lust no more of him to sain.
And nethéles for glotony
Of bodély delícacý
To knowe his stomack how it ferde,
Of that no man to-foré herde
Which he within him self bethought,
A wonder subtil thing he wrought.
Thre men upon electión
Of age and of complexión
Lich to him self by allé way
He toke towardés him to play,
And ete and dranke as well as he,
Therof was no diversité.
For every day whan that they ete
To-fore his owné bord they sete,
And of such mete as he was served,
All though they had it nought deserved,
They token service of the same.
But afterward all thilké game
Was into wofull ernest torned.
For whan they weré thus sojórned,
Within a time at after-mete
Nero, which haddé nought foryete
The lustés of his frele estate,
As he which all was delicate
To knowé thilke experiénce,
The men let come in his presence.
And to that one the samé tide
A courser that he sholdé ride
Into the felde anone he bad,
Wherof this man was wonder glad
And goth to pricke and praunce about.
That other, while that he was out,
He laide upon his bed to slepe.
The thriddé, which he woldé kepe
Within his chambre faire and softe,
He goth now up now down ful ofte,
Walkénd apace, that he ne slepte
Till he which on the courser lepte,
Was comen fro the felde ayein.
Nero than, as the bokés sain,
These men did done take allé thre
And slough hem for he woldé se
The whose stomáck was best defied.[1]
And whan he hath the sothé tried,
He found that he which goth the pas
Defiéd best of allé was,
Which afterward he uséd ay.
And thus what thing unto his pay
Was most plesánt, he lefté none;
With every lust he was begone

[1] *Was defied*, had digested.

Wherof the body mighté glade,
For he no abstinencé made;
But althermost of erthly thinges
Of women unto the likínges
Nero set all his holé herte,
For that lust shuld him nought asterte.
Whan that the thurst of love him caught
Where that him list he toke a draught,
He spareth nouther wife ne maide,
That such another, as men saide,
In all this world was never yit.
He was so drunke in all his wit
Through sondry lustés which he toke,
That ever while there is a boke
Of Nero men shall rede and sing
Unto the worldés knouleching.
"My gode sone, as thou hast herde,
For ever yet it hath so ferde,
Delícacý in Lovés cas
Withouté reson is and was.
For where that love his herté set
Him thenketh it might be no bet,
All though it be nought fully mete
The luste of love is ever swete.
Lo, thus to-gider of felaship,
Delícacý and dronkéship,
Wherof Reson stant out of herre,[1]
Have made full many a wise man erre
In Lovés causé most of all.
For than how so that ever it fall
Wit can no reson understonde,
But let the governauncé stonde
To Will, which thanné wexeth so wilde
That he can nought him selven shilde
Fro the perfll, but out of fere
The way he secheth here and there,
Him reccheth nought upon what side,

[1] *Out of herre*, off its hinges.

For ofté time he goth beside
And doth such thing withouté drede,
Wherof him oughté wel to drede.
But whan that Love assoteth sore,
It passeth allé mennés lore,
What lust it is that he ordeigneth
There is no mannés might re-streigneth,
And of God taketh he none hede,
But lawéles withouté drede,
His purpos for he wolde acheve,
Ayein the points of the beleve
He tempteth heven, erth and helle,
Here afterward as I shall telle.
"Who dare do thing, which Love ne dare?
To Love is every lawe unware,
But to the lawés of his hest
The fissh, the fowl, the man, the beste
Of all the worldés kindé louteth.
For Love is he which nothing doubteth,[1]
In mannés herté where he sit
He compteth nought toward his wit
The wo no moré than the wele,
No more the heté than the chele,
No more the weté than the drie,
No more to livé than to deie,
So that to-foré ne behinde
He seeth no thíng but as the blinde.
Withoute insight of his corâge
He doth merveilés in his rage
To what thing that he wol him drawe.
There is no God, there is no lawe
Of whom that he taketh any hede,
But as Bayárd the blindé stede
Till he falle in the dicche a midde
He goth there no man will him bidde,
He stant so ferforth out of reule,
There is no wit that may him reule.
And thus to tell of him in soth,
Full many a wonder thing he doth,
That weré better to be laft,

[1] *Doubteth*, feareth.

Among the whiche is wicché craft,
That some men clepen sorcerý,
Which for to winne his druerý [1]
With many a circumstaunce he useth,
There is no point which he refuseth.
The craft, which that Saturnus fonde,
To maké prickés in the sonde,
That geomauncé clepéd is,
Ful oft he useth it amis;
And of the flood his ydromaúnce;
And of the fire the piromaúnce:
With questiöns echone of tho
He tempteth ofte, and eke also
Aëromaunce in jugément
To Love he bringeth of his assent.
For thesé craftés as I finde
A man may do by way of kinde
Be so it be to good entent.
But he goéth all other went,[2]
For rather er he shuldé faile
With nigromaunce he wolde assaile
To make his incantación
With hote subfumigación,
Thilke art which specular [3] is hote
And used is of comun rote
Among paiéns which that craft eke,[4]
Of whiche is auctor Thosz the Greke,
He wercheth one and one by rowe.
Razel is nought to him unknowe,
The Salomónés Candary,
His Ydeác, his Eutony,
The figure and the boke withall
Of Balamuz and of Ghenball,
The seale and therupon thymáge
Of Thebith for his avauntáge
He taketh, and some what of Gibere,
Which helplich is to this matere.
Babylla to her sonés seven
Which hath renouncéd to the heven,
With Cernés bothé square and rounde,
He traceth ofte upon the grounde,
Makénd his invocatión.
And for full énformatión
The scolé, which Honorius
Wrote, he pursueth. And lo, thus
Magique he useth for to winne
His love, and spareth for no sinne.
And over that of his sotý
Right as he secheth sorcerý
Of hem that ben magiciéns,
Right so of the naturiéns
Upon the sterrés from above
His wey he secheth unto love
Als fer as he hem understondeth.
In many a sondry wise he fondeth,
He maketh ymáge, he maketh sculptúre,
He maketh writíng, he maketh figúre,
He maketh his calculatións,
He maketh his demonstratións,
His hours of astronomý
He kepeth as for that partý
Which longeth to the inspectión
Of love and his affectión,
He wolde into the hellé seche
The devel him selvé to beseche
If that he wisté for to spede
To gete of love his lusty mede.
Where that he hath his herté set
He biddé never faré bet,
Ne wit of other heven more.
My sone, if thou of such a lore
Hast ben er this, I rede the leve."—
"Min holy fader, by your leve
Of all that ye have spoken here
Which toucheth unto this matere,
To tellé soth right as I wene,
I wot nought o word what ye mene.
I woll nought say if that I couth
That I nolde in my lusty youth
Beneth in helle and eke above
To winné with my ladies love

1 *Druerý*, love.
2 *Went*, turning, cross way.
3 *Specular*, miswritten "spatula" in MS. The chapter "De Speculatoria" follows that on Geomancy in Cornelius Agrippa, "De Vanitate Scientiarum."
4 *Eke*, increase, extend.

Done al that ever that I might.
For therof have I none insight
Where afterward that I become
So that I wonne and overcome
Her lové which I most coveite."—
"My soné, that goth wonder streite.
For this I may well tellé soth,
There is no man the which so doth
For all the craft that he can caste,
That he ne bieth it atté laste.
For often he that will beguile
Is guiléd with the samé guile,
And thus the guiler is beguiled,
As I finde in a boke compiled
To this matére an olde histoire,
The which comth now to my memoire
And is of great ensemplary
Ayein the vice of sorcery,
Wherof none endé may be good.
But how whilóm therof it stood,
A talé which is good to knowe
To the, my sone, I shall beknowe.
Among hem, which at Troié were,
Ulixes at the siegé there
Was one by name in speciáll
Of whom yet the memoriáll
Abit, for while there is a mouthe
For ever his namé shall be couthe.
He was a worthy knight and king
And clerk knowénd of every thing,
He was a great rethorien,
He was a great magicien;
Of Tullius the rethorique,
Of king Zorastes the magique,
Of Tholomé thastronomy,
Of Plato the philosophy,
Of Daniel the slepy dremes,
Of Neptune eke the water stremes,
Of Salomon and the proverbes,
Of Macer all the strength of herbes,
And the phisique of Ypocras,
And lich unto Pithagoras
Of surgery he knew the cures.
But some what of his aventúres,
Which shall to my matere accorde,
To the, my sone, I will recorde.
"This king, of which thou hast herd sain,
From Troy as he goth home ayein
By ship, he found the see diverse
With many a windy storm reverse.
But he through wisdom which he shapeth
Ful many a great períl escapeth,
Of whiche I thenké tellen one,
How that malgré the nedel and stone
Wind-drive he was all sodeinly
Upon the strondés of Cilly,
Where that he must abide a while.
Twey quenés weren in that ile
Calipso naméd and Circes.
And whan they herde, how Úlixés
Is londed there upon the rive,
For him they senden also blive.[1]
With him such as he wolde he nam
And to the court to hem he cam.
These quenés were as two goddésses
Of art magiqué sorcerésses,
That what lord come to that rivage,
They make him love in such a rage
And upon hem assoté so,
That they woll have, er that he go,
All that he hath of worldés good.
Ulixes well this understood,
They couthé moch, he couthé more.
They shape and cast ayein him sore
And wrought mańy a subtil wile
But yet they might him nought beguile;
But of the men of his navie
They two forshope[2] a great partie,
May none of hem withstonde her hestes:
Some part they shopen into bestes,
Some part they shopen into foules,

[1] *Rive*, shore; *also blive*, very quickly; *nam*, took.
[2] Those two (queens) transformed.

To berés, tigres, apés, oules,
Or ellés by some other wey,
Ther might no thíng hem disobey,
Such craft they had abové kinde.
But that art couthé they nought finde
Of which Ulixes was deceived,
That he ne hath hem alle weived
And brought hem into such a rote [1]
That upon him they bothe assote.
And through the science of his arte
He toke of hem so well his parte
That he begat Circes with childe,
He kepte him sobre and made hem wilde,
He set him selvé so above
That with her good and with her love,
Who that therof be leve or loth,
All quite into his ship he goth.
Circes to-swollé bothé sides
He left, and waiteth on the tides,
And straught throughout the salté fome
He taketh his cours and comth him home,
Where as he found Penelopé,
A better wife there may none be,
And yet there ben inough of good.
But who her goodship understood
Fro first that she wifehodé toke,
How many lovés she forsoke
And how she bare her all about
Therewhilés that her lord was out,
He mighté make a great avaunt,
Amonges all the remenaunt,
That she was one of all the best.
Well might he set his herte in rest,
This king, whan he her founde in hele.
For as he couthe in wisdom dele,
So couthé she in womanhede.
And whan she sigh withouten drede
Her lord upon his owné grounde,
That he was comé sauf and sounde,

[1] *Rote*, practice; routine, as in the phrase "repeat by rote."

In all this world ne mighté be
A gladder woman than was she.
"The famé which may nought be hid
Throughout the londe is soné kid,
Her king is comen home ayein;
There may no man the fullé sain
How that they weren allé glad
So mochel joy of him they made;
The presents every day be newed,
He was with yiftés all besnewed,
The people was of him so glad
That though none other man hem bad
Taillage upon hem self they sette,
And as it were of puré dette
They yive her goodés to the king.
This was a glad home welcomíng.
"Thus hath Ulixes what he wolde,
His wife was such as she be sholde,
His people was to him subgite,
Him lacketh nothing of delite.
"But Fortune is of such a fleight
That whan a man is most on height
She maketh him rathest for to falle,
There wot no man what shall befalle.
The happés over mannés hede
Ben hongé with a tender threde;
That provéd was on Ulixés,
For whan he was most in his pees
Fortúné gan to make him werre
And set his welthe al out of herre.
Upon a day as he was mery,
As though there might him no thing dery, [1]
Whan night was come he goth to bedde,
With slepe and both his eyen fedde.
And while he slept he met a sweven,
Him thought he sigh a statue even
Which brighter than the sonné shone.
A man it seméd was it none,

[1] *Dery*, hurt.

But yet it was as in figúre
Most lich to mannés creätúre.
But as of beauté hevenlich
It was most to an aungel lich,
And thus betwene aungél and man
Beholden it this king began,
And suche a lust toke of the sight,
That fain he wolde, if that he might,
The forme of that figúre embrace.
And goth him forth toward that place
Where he sigh that ymágé tho,
And takth it in his armés two
And it embraceth him ayein
And to the king thus gan it sain:
'Ulixes, understond wel this,
The token of our acqueintaunce is
Here afterward to mochel tene;
The lové that is us betwene,
Of that we now such joié make,
That one of us the deth shall take,
Whan timé cometh of destiné,
It may none otherwisé be.'
Ulixes tho began to pray
That this figúré wolde him say
What wight he is, that saith him so.
This wight upon a speré tho
A pensel[1] which was well begone
Embrouded, sheweth him anone,
Thre fisshes all of o coloúr
In maner as it were a toúre
Upon the pensel weré wrought.
Ulixes knew this token nought
And praith to wite, in some partie,
What thinge it mighté signifie.
'A signe it is,' the wight answerde,
'Of an empire;' and forth he ferde
All sodeinly, whan he that said.
"Ulixés out of slepe abraid,
And that was right ayein the day,
That lenger slepen he ne may.
Men sain, a man hath knouleching
Save of him self of allé thing;

[1] *Pensel*, a small banner hanging from a lance.

His owné chauncé noman knoweth,
But as Fortúne it on him throweth.
Was never yet so wise a clerk,
Which mighté knowe all Goddés werk,
Ne the secrét which God hath sette
Ayein a man may nought be lette.
Ulixes though that he be wise,
With all his wit in his avise
The more that he his sweven acompteth
The lasse he wot what it amounteth.
For all his calculatión
He seeth no demonstratión
As pleinly for to knowe an ende.
But nethéles, how so it wende,
He drad him of his owné sone;
That maketh him well the more astone
And shope therfore anone withall
So that withinné castell wall
Thelemachum his sone he shette
And upon him strong warde he sette.
The sothé further he ne knewe,
Till that Fortúne him overthrewe.
But nethéles for sikernesse,
Where that he mighté wit and gesse
A placé strengest in his londe,
There let he make of lime and sonde
A strengthé where he wolde dwelle,
Was never man yet herdé telle
Of suche an other as it was.
And for to strength him in that cas
Of all his lond the sikerest
Of servants and the worthiest
To kepen him withinné warde
He set his body for to warde;
And madé such an ordenaunce
For lové, ne for áqueintaúnce,
That were it erely were it late
They shuldé let in at the gate
No maner man, what so betid,
But if so were him self it bid.
"But all that might him nought availe,

For whom Fortúné wol assaile
There may be no such résisténce
Which mighté make a man defénce,
All that shall be, mot fall algate.
This Circes whiche I spake of late,
On whom Ulixés hath begete
A child, though he it have foryete,
Whan timé came, as it was wone,
She was deliverd of a sone,
Which clepéd is Thelogonus.
This child whan he was boré thus
About his moder to full age
That he can reson and langáge
In good estate was drawé forth.
And whan he was so mochel worth
To stonden in a mannés stede,
Circes his mother hath him bede,
That he shall to his fader go
And told him all to-gider tho
What man he was that him begat.
And whan Thelogonus of that
Was ware, and hath full knouleching
How that his fader was a king,
He praith his moder fairé this
To go where that his fader is.
And she him graunteth that he shall,
And made him redy forth with all.
"It was that timé such usaunce,
That every man the conoissaunce
Of his contré bare in his honde,
Whan he went into straungé londe.
And thus was every man therfore
Wel knowé, where that he was bore,
For espiáll and mistrowínges
They didé thanné suché thinges
That every man might other knowe.
So it befell that ilké throwe
Thelogonus, as in this cas,
Of his contré the signé was
Thre fisshes, which he shuldé bere
Upon the penon of a spere.
And whan that he was thus arraied
And hath his harneis all assaied,
That he was redy every dele,
His moder bad him faré wele
And said him, that he shuldé swithe[1]
His fader grete a thousand sithe.
Thelogonus his moder kist
And toke his leve, and where he wist
His fader was, the waié name,
Till he unto Nachaié came,
Which of that lond the chefe citee
Was clepéd, and there axeth he
Where was the kinge and how he ferde.
And whan that he the sothé herde,
Where that the king Ulixes was,
Alone upon his hors great pas
He rode him forth, and in his honde
He bare the signal of his londe
With fisshes thre, as I have tolde,
And thus he went unto that holde
Where that his owné fader dwelleth.
The causé why he comth, he telleth
Unto the kepers of the gate,
And wolde have comen in there at,
But shortly they him saidé nay.
And he als faire as ever he may
Besought and toldé hem of this,
How that the king his fader is.
But they with proudé wordés great
Began to manace and to threte
But[2] he go fro the gaté fast
They wolde him take and setté fast.
Fro wordés unto strokés thus
They felle, and so Thelogonus
Was soré hurte and well nigh dede,
But with his sharpé sperés hede
He maketh defence, how so it falle,
And wan the gate upon hem alle
And hath slain of the besté five.
And they ascriden also blive
Through out the castell all about;
On every sidé men come out,
Wherof the kingés herte affiight,
And he with all the hast he might
A speré caught and forth he goth
As he that was nigh wode for wroth.

[1] *Swithe*, strongly. [2] *But*, unless.

He sigh the gatés full of blood,
Thelogonus and where he stood
He sigh also, but he ne knewe
What man it was, but to him threwe
His spere, and he sterte out a side,
But destiné which shall betide,
Befell that ilké timé so,
Thelogonus knew nothing tho
What man it was that to him caste,
And while his owné speré laste,
With all the signé therupon,
He cast unto the kinge anon
And smot him with a dedly wounde.
Ulixes fell anone to grounde,
Tho every man, 'The king! the king!'
Began to cry, and of this thing
Thelogonus which sigh the cas
On knes he fell and saide: 'Alas,
I have min owné fader slain!
Now wolde I deié wonder fain,
Now sle me who that ever will,
For certés it is right good skill.'[1]
He crieth, he wepeth, he saith therfore:
'Alas, that ever was I bore,
That this unhappy destiné
So wofully comth in by me!'
This king, which yet hath life inough,
His herte ayein to him he drough
And to that vois an ere he laide
And understood all that he saide
And gan to speke and saide on high:
'Bring me this man.' And whan he sigh
Thelogonus, his though he sette
Upon the sweven which he mette,[2]
And axeth, that he mighté se
His spere, on which the fisshes thre
He sigh upon the pensel wrought.
Tho wist he well, it faileth nought,
And bad him that he telle sholde
Fro whenne he came and what he wolde.
Thelogonus in sorwe and wo
So as he mighté toldé tho
Unto Ulixes all the cas,
How that Circés his moder was,
And so forth said him every dele,
How that his moder grete him wele,
And in what wisé she him sent.
Tho wist Ulixes what it ment,
And toke him in his armés softe
And all bledéndé kist him ofte
And saidé: 'Soné, while I live,
This infortúne I the foryive.'
After his other sone in hast
He send, and he began him hast
And cam unto his fader tite.[1]
But whan he sigh him in such plite,
He wold have ronne upon that other
Anone and slain his owné brother,
Ne haddé be that Ulixés
Betwene hem made accorde and pees,
And to his heir Thelemachus
He bad that he Thelogonus
With all his power shuldé kepe
Till he were of his woundés depe
All hole, and than he shulde him yive
Lond where upon he mighté live.
Thelemachus whan he this herde,
Unto his fader he answérde
And saide, he woldé don his wille.
So dwellé they to-gider stille
These brethren, and the fader sterveth.
"Lo, wherof sorcerié serveth.
Through sorcerý his lust he wan,
Through sorcerý his wo began,
Through sorcerý his love he chese,
Through sorcerý his life he lese.
The child was gete in sorcerý,
The which did all his feloný,

[1] *Skill*, reason.
[2] *Sweven* . . *mette*, dream . . dreamed.

[1] *Tite*, quickly.

Thing which was ayein kindé wrought
Unkindéliche it was abought:
The child his owné fader slough,
That was unkindéship inough.
"Forthý take hede how that it is,
So for to winné love amis,
Which endeth all his joy in wo.
For of this arte I find also,
That hath be do for Lovés sake,
Wherof thou might ensample take,
A great cronique emperiall
Which ever into memoriall
Among the men, how so it wende,
Shall dwellé to the worldés ende.
The highé creatór of thinges,
Which is the king of allé kinges,
Full many wonder worldés chaunce
Let slide under his sufferaúnce,
There wot no man the causé why
But he, the which is Almightý.
And that was provéd whilóm thus,
Whan that the king Nectánabús,
Which had Egipté for to lede,
But for he sigh to-fore the dede
Through magique of his sorcerie,
Wherof he couth a great partie,
His enemies to him coménd,
Fro whom he might him nought defend,
Out of his owné lond he fledde
And in the wise as he him dredde
It fell, for all his wicchécraft,
So that Egipte him was beraft.
And he desguiséd fledde away
By ship and held the righté way
To Macedoiné, where that he
Arriveth at the chefe citee.
Thre yomen of his chambre there
All only for to serve him were,
The which he trusteth wonder wele
For they were trewe as any stele.
And hapneth that they with him ladde
Parte of the besté good he hadde,
They také logginge in the town
After the dispositioún,
Where as him thoughté best to dwelle.
He axeth than and herdé telle
How that the kingé was out go
Upon a werre he haddé tho.
But in that citee thanné was
The quené which Olimpias
Was hote and with solempnité
The feste of her nativité,
As it befell, was thanné holde.
And for her lust to be beholde
And preiséd of the people about
She shope her for to riden out
At after-mete all openly.
Anone were allé men redý,
And that was in the month of May.
This lusty quene in good array
Was set upon a mulé white,
To sene it was a great delite
The joié that the citee made.
With fresshé thingés and with glade
The noble town was all behonged,
And every wight was sore alonged
To se this lusty lady ride.
There was great merth on allé side
Where as she passeth by the strete,
There was ful many a timbre bete
And many a maidé caroléndé.
And thus through out the town pleiénde
This quene unto the pleiné rode,
Where that she hovéd and abode
To se diversé gamés pley,
The lusty folk joust and tourney.
And so forth every other man
Which pleié couth his pley began
To plesé with this noble quene.
"Nectánabús came to the grene
Amongés other and drough him nigh.
But whan that he this lady sigh
And of her beauté hedé toke,
He couthé nought witholde his loke

To se nought ellés in the felde,
But stood and only her behelde.
Of his clothínge and of his gere
He was unliche all other there,
So that it hapneth atté laste
The quene on him her eyé caste
And knew that he was straunge anone.
But he behelde her ever in one
Withouté blenching of his chere.
She toke good hede of his manére
And wondreth why he didé so,
And bad men shuldé for him go.
He came and did her reverénce.
And she him axeth in silénce
From whenne he cam and what he wolde.
And he with sobre wordés tolde,
He saith: 'Madame, a clerk I am
To you and in messáge I cam
The whiche I may nought tellen here,
But if it liketh you to here,
It mot be said so privélý
Where none shall be but ye and I.
"Thus for the time he toke his leve.
The day goth forth till it was eve
That every man mot leve his werk.
And she thought ever upon this clerk,
What thing it is that he wold mene.
And in this wise abode the quene
And passeth over thilké night,
Till it was on the morwé light.
She sendé for him, and he came,
With him his astrolabe he name,[1]
Which was of finé gold precioús
With points and cercles merveiloús.
And eke the hevenly figúres
Wrought in a boke full of peintúres
He toke this lady for to shewe
And tolde of eche of hem by rewe
The cours and the condition.
And she with great affection

[1] *Name*, took.

Sate still and herdé what he wolde.
And thus whan he seeth time he tolde
And feigneth with his wordés wise
A tale and saith in such a wise:
'Madamé, but a while ago,
Where I was in Egipté tho
And rad in scole of this science,
It fell into my consciénce
That I unto the temple went
And there with all min hole entent
As I my sacrificé dede
One of the goddés hath me bede
That I you warné privelý,
So that ye maké you redý,
And that ye be nothíng agast,
For he such love hath to you cast,
That ye shull bene his owné dere
And he shall be your beddéfere
Till ye conceive and be with childe.'
And with that word she wax all milde
And somdele red became for shame
And axeth him that goddés name,
Which so woll done her compaigny.
And he said: 'Amos of Luby.'
And she saith: 'That may I nought leve,
But if I se a better preve.'
'Madamé,' quod Nectánabús,
'In token that it shall be thus
This night for enformatión
Ye shall have an avisión,
That Amos shall to you appere
To shewe and teche in what manere
The thing shall afterward befalle.
Ye oughten well aboven alle
To maké joy of such a lorde.
For whan ye ben of one accorde
He shall a sone of you begete
Which with his swerd shall win and gete
The widé worlde in length and brede,
All erthly kingés shall him drede.
And in such wise I you behote
The god of erthe he shall be hote.'
'If this be soth,' tho quod the quene,

'This night, thou saiest, it shall be sene.
And if it falle into my grace,
Of god Amos that I purchace
To take of him so great worship,
I wol do the such ladiship,
Wherof thou shalt for evermo
Be riche.' And he her thonketh tho
And toke his leve and forth he went.
She wisté litel what he ment.
For it was guile and sorcerý
All that she toke for prophecý.
Nectánabús throughout the day
Whan he cam home where as he lay
His chambre by him self betoke
And overtorneth many a boke
And through the craft of artemáge[1]
Of wexe he forgéd an ymáge.
He loketh his equaciόns
And eke the constellaciόns,
He loketh the conjunctiόns,
He loketh the receptiόns,
His signe, his houre, his áscendént,
And draweth Fortúne of his assent.
The name of quene Olimpias
In thilke ymágé written was
Amiddés in the front above.
And thus to winne his lust of love
Nectánabús this werk hath dight.
And whan it cam withinné night,
That every wight is fall aslepe,
He thought he wolde his timé kepe
As he, whiche hath his houre apointed.
And thanné first he hath anointed
With sondry herbés that figúre
And therupon he gan conjúre,
So that through his enchantément
This lady, which was innocent
And wisté nothing of this guile,
Met[2] as she slepté thilke while,
How fro the heven came a light,
Whiche all her chambre madé light.

[1] *Artemage*, Art Magic. [2] *Met*, dreamed.

And as she loketh to and fro,
She sigh, her thought, a dragon tho,
Whose scherdés[1] shinen as the sonne,
And hath his softé pas begonne
With all the cheré that he may
Toward the bed there as she lay,
Till he came to the beddés side.
And she lay still and nothing cride,
For he did all his thingés faire
And was courteís and debonaire.
And as he stood her fasté by,
His forme he chaungeth sodeinly,
And the figúre of man he nome
To her and into bed he come,
And she was wonder glad withall.
Nectánabús, which causeth all
Of this metredé[2] the substaunce,
Whan he sigh time his nigromaúnce
He stint and nothing moré saide
Of his carecte, and she abraide
Out of her slepe and leveth wele
That it is soth than every dele
Of that this clerke her haddé tolde,
And was the glader many folde
In hope of suche a glad metréde
Which after shall befalle in dede.
She longeth sore after the day,
That she her sweven tellé may
To this guiloúr in privété,
Which knewe it al so well as she.
And nethéles on morwe sone
She left al other thing to done
And for him send, and all the cas
She tolde him pleinly as it was
And saidé, how than well she wist
That she his wordes mighté trist,
For she founde her avisiόn
Right after the conditiόn
Which he her haddé told to-fore,
And praid him hertély therfore,
That he her holdé covenant
So forth of all the remenant,

[1] *Scherdes*, scales.
[2] *Metredé*, dream-counsel.

That she may through his ordenaúnce
Towardés god do such plesaúnce,
That she wakéndé might him kepe
In such wise as she met[1] a slepe.
And he that couth of guile inough,
Whan he this herd, for joy he lough
And saith: 'Madame, it shall be do.
But this I warné you therto,
This night whan that he comth to play,
That there be no life[2] in the way
But I that shall at his liking
Ordeiné so for his comíng
That ye ne shull nought of him faile.
For this, madame, I you counseile,
That ye it kepé so privé,
That no wight ellés but we thre
Have knouleching how that it is;
For ellés might it fare amis
If ye did ought that shulde him greve.'
And thus he makth her to beleve
And feigneth under guilé feith.
But nethéles all that he saith
She troweth. And ayein the night
She hath within her chambre dight,
Where as this guiler fasté by
Upon this god shall privély
Awaite, as he makth her to wene.
And thus this noble gentil quene,
Whan she most trusted, was deceived.

"The night come, and the chambre is weived,
Nectánabús hath take his place,
And whan he sigh the time and space,
Through the deceipt of his magíque
He put him out of mannés like
And of a dragon toke the forme,
As he, which wolde him all conforme
To that she sigh in sweven er this;
And thus to chambre come he is.
The quené lay a bed and sigh
And hopeth ever as he cam nigh,

[1] *Met*, dreamed. [2] *No life*, no body.

That he god of Lubíë were,
So hath she well the iessé fere.
But for he wold her more assure,
Yet efte he chaungeth his figure
And of a wether the likenésse
He toke in signe of his noblésse,
With largé hornés for the nones
Of finé gold and riché stones.
A corone on his heved he bare
And sodeinlich, er she was ware,
As he whiche alle guilé can,
His forme he torneth into man.
All though she were in part deceived,
Yet for all that she hath conceived
The worthiest of allé kithe,
Which ever was to-fore or sithe
Of conquest and chiválerie,
Só that through guile and sorcerie
There was that noble knight begonne,
Which all the worlde hath after wonne.
Thus fell the thing which fallé sholde,
Nectánabús hath that he wolde,
With guile he hath his lové sped,
With guile he came into the bed,
With guile he goth him out ayein.
He was a shrewéd chamberlein
So to beguile a worthy quene,
And that on him was after sene.
But nethéles the thing is do,
This falsé god was soné go
With his deceipt and helde him close,
Till morwe cam that he arose,
And tho, whan time and leiser was,
The quené tolde him all the cas
As she that guilé none supposeth,
And of two points she him opposeth.
One was, if that this god no more
Woll come ayein, and overmore
How she shall stonden in accorde
With king Philíppe her owné lorde,

When he comth home and seeth her grone.
'Madame,' he saith, 'let me alone,
As for the god I undertake
That whan it liketh you to take
His compaigný at any throwe,
If I a day to-fore it knowe
He shall be with you on the night,
And he is well of such a might
To kepé you from allé blame.
Forthý comforté you, madame,
There shall none other causé be.'
Thus toke he leve and forth goth he.
And tho began he for to muse
How he the quené might excuse
Toward the king of that is falle,
And found a craft amongés alle,
Through which he hath a see foule daunted[1]
With his magíque and so enchaunted,
That he flew forth whan it was night
Unto the kingés tenté right,
Where that he lay amidde his hoste.
"And whan he was a-slepé most,
With that the see foule to him brought,
An other charmé which he wrought
At home within his chambre still,
The kinge he torneth at his will,
And maketh him for to dreme and se
The dragon and the priveté
Which was betwene him and the quene.
And over that he made him wene
In sweven that the god Amós,
Whan he up fro the quene aros,
Toke forth a ring wherin a stone
Was set and gravé therupon
A sonne, in which, whan he cam nigh,
A leon with a swerd he sigh.
And with that prent, as he so mette,[2]
Upon the quenés wombe he sette
A seal, and goth him forth his way;
With that the sweven went away.
And tho began the king awake
And sigheth for his wivés sake
Where as he lay within his tent,
And hath great wonder what it ment.
With that he hasted him to rise
Anone and sent after the wise,
Among the whiché there was one,
A clerke, his name is Amphione,
Whan he the kingés sweven herde,
What it betokneth he answérde
And saith: 'As sikerly as the life
A god hath laien by thy wife
And got a soné which shall winne
The world and all that is withinne.
As leon is the king of bestes
So shall the world obey his hestes,
Which with his swerd shal al be wonne
Als fer as shineth any sonne.'
"The king was doubtif of this dome,
But nethéles whan that he come
Ayein into his owné lond,
His wife with childé great he fond;
He mighté nought him selven stere
That he ne made her hevy chere.
But he which couthe of allé sorwe,
Nectánabús, upon the morwe
Through the deceipt of nigromaúnce
Toke of a dragon the semblaúnce
And where the king sat in his halle,
Cam in rampénd among hem alle
With such a noise and such a rore,
That they agast were all so sore
As though they shuldé deie anone.
And nethéles he greveth none,
But goth toward the deis on high.
And whan he cam the quené nigh,
He stint his noise and in his wise
To her he profreth his servíce
And laith his hede upon her barme,
And she with goodly chere her arme
About his necke ayeinward laide,

[1] A sea-fowl tamed. [2] *Mette*, dreamed.

And thus the quené with him plaide
In sight of allé men about.
And atté last he gan to lout
And óbeisaúnce unto her make,
As he that wolde his levé take.
And sodeinly his lothely forme
Into an egle he gan transforme,
And fligh and set him on a raile,
Wherof the king had great merveile.
For there he pruneth him and piketh,
As doth an hawk whan him wel liketh,
And after that him self he shoke,
Wherof that all the halle quoke,
As it a terremoté[1] were.
They saiden alle, god was there,
In suche a rees and forth he fligh.
"The king which all this wonder sigh,
Whan he cam to his chambre alone,
Unto the quené made his mone
And of foryivenesse he her praide.
For than he knew well, as he saide,
She was with childé with a god.
"Thus was the king withouté rod
Chastiséd and the quene excused
Of that she haddé ben accused.
And for the greater evidence
Yet after that in the presénce
Of king Philip and other mo,
Whan they ride in the feldés tho,
A fesaunt came before her eye
The whiche anone, as they her sigh
Fleéndé, let an ey[2] down falle,
And it to-brake to-fore hem alle.
And as they token therof kepe,
They sigh out of the shellé crepe
A litel serpent on the grounde,
Which rampeth all abouté rounde,
And in ayein he woll have wonne,
But for the brenning of the sonne
It mighté nought, and so it deide.
And therupon the clerkés saide:
'As the serpént, when it was out,

[1] *Terremoté*, earthquake. [2] *Ey*, egg.

Went environ the shelle aboute
And mighté nought torne in ayein,
So shall it fallen in certein,—
This child the world shall environe
And above allé the corone
Him shall befall, and in yonge age
He shall desire in his coráge,
Whan all the worlde is in his honde
To torne ayein unto the londe
Where he was bore, and in his wey
Howeward he shall with poison dey.'
"The king whiche al this sigh and herde
Fro that day forth how so it ferde
His jalousie hath all foryete.
But he, whiche hath the child begete,
Nectánabús in privité
The time of his nativité
Upon the constellatión
Awaiteth and relatión
Maketh to the quene, how she shall do,
And every houre appointeth so
That no minúte therof was lore.
So that in duë time is bore
This childe, and forthwith therupon
There fellen wonders many one;
Of terremote unfverséle;
The sonné toke coloúr of stele
And lost his light; the windés blewe
And many strengthés overthrewe;
The see his propré kindé chaungeth
And all the worlde his formé straungeth;
The thunder with his firy leven
So cruel was upon the heven,
That every erthely creätúre
Tho thought his life in aventúre.
The tempest atté lasté ceseth,
The child is kepte, his age encreseth,
And Alisaúndre his name is hote;
To whom Calistre and Aristote
To techen him philosophý
Entenden, and astronomý
With other thingés which he couth,

Also to teche him in his youth
Nectánabús toke upon honde.
But every man may understonde
Of sorcerý, how that it wende,
It woll him selvé prove at ende,
And namély for to beguile
A lady which withouté guile
Supposeth trouth all that she hereth.
But often he that evil stereth,
His ship is dreint therin amidde,
And in this cas right so betidde.
Nectánabús, upon a night
Whan it was faire and sterré light,
This yongé lord lad upon high
Above a toure, where as he sigh
The sterrés such as he accompteth,
And saith what eche of hem amounteth,
As though he knewe of allé thing.
But yet hath he no knouleching
What shal unto him self befalle.
Whan he hath tolde his wordés alle,
This yongé lord than him opposeth
And axeth if that he supposeth
What deth he shul him selvé dey.
He saith: 'Or fortune is awey
And every sterre hath lost his wone,
Or ellés of min owné sone
I shall be slain, I may nought fle.'
Thought Alisaundre in priveté:
'Herof this oldé dotard lieth.'
And er that other ought aspieth
All sodeinlich his oldé bones
He shof over the wall at ones
And saith him: 'Lie down there a part!
Wherof now serveth all thin art?
Thou knewe all other mennés chaunce
And of thy self hast ignoraunce;
That thou hast said amonges alle
Of thy persone is nought befalle.'
"Nectánabús, which hath his dethe,
Yet while him lasteth life and brethe
To Alisaundre he spake and said
That he with wrong blame on him laid.
Fro point to point and all the cas
He tolde, how he his soné was.
Tho he which sory was inough,
Out of the dich his fader drough
And tolde his moder how it ferde,
In counseil and whan she it herde,
And knew the tokens which he tolde,
She nisté[1] what she saié sholde,
But stood abasshed as for the while
Of this magíque and all the guile.
She thought, how that she was deceived,
That she hath of a man conceived
And wende a god it haddé be.
But nethéles in such degre
So as she might her honour save
She shope the body was begrave.
And thus Nectánabús abought
The sorcerïé, which he wrought,
Though he upon the creätúres
Through his carectés and figúres
The maistry and the power hadde
His Creätór to nought him ladde,
Ayein whose lawe his craft he useth,
Whan he for lust his god refuseth
And toke him for the devels craft.
Lo, what profit is him belaft:
That thing, through which he wend have stonde,
First him exiléd out of londe
Which was his own, and from a king
Made him to be an underling,
And sithen to deceive a quene,
That torneth him to mochel tene,
Through lust of love he gat him hate,
That endé couth he nought abate
His oldé sleightés which he cast,
Yonge Alisaundre him overcast;
His fader which him misbegat
He slough, a great mishap was that.

[1] *Nisté*, knew not.

But for o mis an other mis
Was yolde, and so full ofte it is.
Nectánabús his craft miswent,
So it misfell him er he went.[1]
I not what helpeth that clergý [2]
Which maketh a man to do foly,
And namélich of nigromaúnce,
Which stont upon the miscreaúnce.
"And for to se more evidence
Zorastes, which thexperience
Of art magíqué first forth drough,
Anone as he was bore he lough,
Which token was of wo suínge,
For of his owné controvínge
He found magíque and taught it forth,
But all that was him litel worth.
For of Surrie a worthy king
Him slewe and that was his endíng.
But yet through him this craft is used,
And he through all the world accused,
For it shall never well acheve
That stont nought right with the beleve.
But lich to wolle is evil sponne,
Who leseth him self hath litel wonne,
An ende proveth every thing.
"Saül, which was of Jewés king,
Up peine of deth forbad this arte,
And yet he toke therof his parte.
The Phitonisse in Samarý
Yaf him counseil by sorcerý,
Which after fell to mochel sorwe,
For he was slain upon the morwe.
To conné mochel thing it helpeth,
But of to moché no man yelpeth.[3]
So for to loke on every side,
Magíqué may nought well betide.
"Forthý my sone, I woll the rede,
That thou of these ensamples drede,
That for no lust of erthly love
Thou seché so to come above
Wherof as in the worldés wonder
Thou shalt for ever be put under."—
"My godé fader, graunt mercý.
For ever I shall beware therby
Of Lové what me so befalle
Such sorcerý aboven alle.
Fro this day forth I shall escheue,
That so ne woll I nought pursue
My lust of Lové for to seche.
But this I woldé you beseche
Besidé that me stant of Love,
As I you herdé speke above,
How Alisaundre was betaught
Of Aristotle and so well taught
Of all that to a king belongeth,
Wherof my herté soré longeth
To wité what it woldé mene.
For by resón I woldé wene,
But if I herde of thingés straunge,
Yet for a time it shuldé chaunge
My peine and lissé me somdele."—
"My godé soné, thou saiest wele.
For wisdom, how that ever it stonde,
To him that can it understonde
Doth great profít in sondry wise;
But touchend of so high a prise,
Which is nought unto Venus knowe,
I may it nought my selvé knowe,
Which of her Court am all forth drawe
And can no thing but of her lawe.
But nethéles to knowé more
As wel as thou me longeth sore.
And for it helpeth to comúne
All be they nought to me comune,
The scolés of philosophý
Yet thenk I for to specifý
In boke as it is comprehended,
Wherof thou mightest ben amended.
For though I be nought all cunníng
Upon the forme of this writíng,
Some part therof yet I have herde,
In this matere how it hath ferde.

[1] *Went*, weened. [2] *Clergy*, learning. [3] *Yelpeth*, boasts.

Book VII.

HOW A KING WAS TAUGHT.

I Genius the prest of love,
My sone, as thou hast praid above,
That I the scolé shall declare
Of Aristotle and eke the fare
Of Alisaundre, how he was taught,
I am somdele therof destraught.
For it is nowight the matere
Of lové, why we sitten here
To shrivé so as Venus badde,
But nethéles for it is gladde,
So as thou saist, for thin apprise
To here of suché thingés wise,
Wherof thou might thy timé lisse,
So as I can, I shall the wisse.
For Wisdom is at every throwe
Above all other thing to knowe
In Lovés cause and ellés where.
Forthý my sone, unto thin ere,
Though it be nought in the registre
Of Venus, yet of that Calistre
And Aristotle whilom write
To Alisaundre, thou shalt wite.
But for the lorés ben diverse
I thenké first to the reherce
The nature of philosophý,
Which Aristotle of his clergy
Wise and experte in the Sciénces,
Declaréd thilke intelligénces,
As of the points in principall.
Wherof the first in speciáll
Is Theorîqué, which is grounded
On him which al the worlde hath founded,
Which comprehended al the lore.
And for to loken overmore
Next of Sciénces the secoúnde
Is Rhetoriqué, whose facounde
Above all other is eloquent.
To telle a tale in jugément
So well can no man speke as he.
The lasté Science of the thre
It is Practiqué, whose offîce
The Vertu trieth fro the Vice
And techeth upon godé thewes [1]
To fle the compaigny of shrewes,[2]
Which stant in diposición
Of mannes fre electión.
Practique enformeth eke the reule,
How that a worthy King shall reule
His realmé both in werre and pees.
Lo, thus danz [3] Aristotelés
These thre Sciénces hath devided
And the natúre also decided
Wherof that eche of hem shall serve.
The firsté, which is the conserve
And keper of the remenaunt,
As that which is most suffisaunt
And chefe of the philosophy,
If I therof shall specify,
So as the philosóphre tolde,
Now herke and kepe that thou it holde.

[1] *Thewes*, manners, morals.
[2] *Shrewes*, evil men.
[3] *Dans*, Dominus, applied to a Graduate in Arts.

"Of theoriqué principall
The philosóphre in speciáll
The propretés hath détermíned,
As thilké which is enlumíned
Of wisdom and of high prudence
Above all other in his science,
And stant departed upon thre.
The first of which in his degre
Is clepéd in philosophy
The Science of Theology,
That other naméd is Phisíque,
The thridde is said Mathématíque.
Theology is that science,
Which unto man yiveth evidence
Of thing which is nought bodely,
Wherof men knowé redely
The High Almighty Trinité,
Which is o God in Unité
Withouten ende and béginníng
And Creatór of allé thing,
Of erthe, of heven and of helle,
Wherof as oldé bokés telle
The philosóphre in his resón
Wrote upon this conclusión,
And of his writing in a clause
He clepeth God the Firsté Cause,
Which of him self is thilké good
Withouté whom nothíng is good,
Of which that every creätúre
Hath his beíng and his natúre.
After the being of the thinges
There ben thre formés of beínges.
"Thing, which began and endé shall,
That thing is clepéd temporall.
There is also by other way
Thing which began and shall nought dey
As soulés that ben spirituell,
Her being is perpetuell.
But there is one above the sonne
Whose timé never was begonne
And endelés shall ever be,
That is the God, whose magesté
All other thingés shall govérne,
And his Beíng is sempiterne.
The God, to whom that all honoúr
Belongeth, he is Creatoúr.
And other ben his creätúres,
He commaundeth the natúres
That they to him obeién allé.
Withouten him, what so befallé,
Her might is none and He may[1] all:
The God was ever and ever shall,
And they begonne of his assente.
The timés allé be present
To God, and to hem alle unknowe,
But what him liketh that they knowe.
Thus both an aungel and a man,
The which of all that God began
Be chefe, obeién Goddes might,
And He stont endélés up right.
To this Sciéncé ben privé
The Clerkés of Divinité,
The which unto the people prechen
The feith of Haly Chirche and techen,
Which in one cas upon beleve
Stant moré than they conné preve
By wey of argument sensíble.
But nethéles it is credíble
And doth a man great medé have
To him that thenketh him self to save.
Theology in such a wise
Of highé Science and apprise
Above all other stant unlike
And is the first of Theorique.
"Phisique is after the secónde,
Through which the philosóphre hath fonde
To techen sondry knoulechinges
Upon the bodeliché thinges
Of man, of beste, of herbe, of stone,
Of fisshe, of foule, of everichone
That ben of bodély substaúnce,
The nature and of the substaunce.
Through this Sciénce it is full sought,
Which vaileth and which vaileth nought.

[1] *May*, has power over.

"The thridde point of Theorique,
Which clepéd is Mathématſque,
Devided is in sondry wise
And stant upon divers apprise.
The ferst of whiche is Arsmetique,[1]
And the secónd is said Musique,
The thridde is eke Geometrie,
Also the forth Astronomie.
"Of Arsmetſqué the matere
Is that of which a man may lere,
What algorisme[2] in nombre amounteth,
Whan that the wiséman accompteth
After the formal propreté
Of algorismés a, be, ce.
By which multiplicatión
Is made and diminutión
Of sommés by thexperiénce
Of this art and of this sciénce.
"The seconde of mathématſque,
Which is the Science of Musique,
That techeth upon Harmonie
A man to maké melodie
By vois and soune of instrument
Through notés of accordément,
The whiché men pronounce alofte;
Now sharpé notés and now softe
Now highé notés and now lowe,
As by the gamme[3] a man may knowe,
Which techeth the prolación
Of note and the conditión.
Mathematique of his Sciénce
Hath yet the thridde intelligénce
Full of wisdóm and of clergie
And clepéd is Geometrie,
Through which that a man hath the sleight
Of length, of brede, of depth, of height
To knowé the proporción
By verray calculación
Of this Science. And in this wise
These oldé philosóphres wise
Of all this worldés erthé rounde
How large, how thické was the grounde,
Contrivéd in thexperiénce,
The cercle and the circumferénce
Of every thing unto the heven
They setten point and mesure even.
"Mathématſque above the erth,
Of High Sciénce above, the ferth
Which speketh upon Astronomie
And techeth of the sterrés high,
Beginning upward fro the mone.
But first, as it was for to done
This Aristotle in other thing
Unto this worthy yongé king
The kinde of every elemént,
Which stant under the firmamént,
How it is made and in what wise
Fro point to point he gan devise.
"He, which natúreth every kinde,
The mighty God, so as I finde,
Of Man, which is his creätúre,
Hath so devided the nature
That none till other well accordeth.
And by the cause it so discordeth
The life, which feleth the siknesse,
May stond upon no sikernesse.
"Of therthé, which is colde and dry,
The kinde of man Maléncoly
Is clépéd, and that is the firste,
The most ungoodlich and the werste.
What man hath that complexiön,
Full of ymaginatiön
Of dredés and of wrathfull thought,
He fret him selven all to nought.
"The water, which is moist and colde,
Maketh Fleumé,[1] which is manifolde, [sic: "[folde," printed as turnover]
Foryetel, slow and wery sone
Of every thing whiche is to done.
What man that taketh his kind of thair,
He shall be light, he shall be fair.

[1] *Arsmetique*, Arithmetic.
[2] *Algorisme*, Algebra.
[3] *Gamme*, gamut.

[1] *Fleumé*, phlegm of the phlegmatic temperament.

For his complexión is blood,
Of allé there is none so good,
Where as he hath love undertake,
Wronge is it, if that he forsake.
"The first of his condición
Appropreth the complexión,
Whose propretes ben drie and hote,
Which in a man is coler[1] hote.
It maketh a man ben enginous
And swifte of fote and eke irous.[2]
Of conteke and fool hastifnesse
He hath a right great besinesse.
After the kinde of thelement
Thus stant a mannés kindé went[3]
As touchend his complexión
Upon sondrý división
Of dry, of moist, of chele, of hete,
And eche of hem his owné sete
Appropred hath within a man.
And first to telle as I began
The Splen is to Maléncolý
Assignéd for herbérgerý.[4]
"The moisté Fleumé with the colde
Hath in the Lungés for his holde
Ordeinéd him a propre stede
To dwellé there as he is bede.
"To the Sanguíne Complexión
Natúre of his inspectión
A propre hous hath in the Liver
For his dwellíngé made deliver.[5]
"The drié Coler with his hete
By wey of kinde his propre sete
Hath in the Gallé, where he dwelleth,
So as the philosóphre telleth.
"Now over this is for to wite,
As it is in phisíqué write
Of Liver, of Lunge, of Galle, of Splen,
They all unto the herté ben
Servaúnts, and eche in his office
Entendeth to don him servíce,
As he, which is chefe lord above.
The Liver maketh him for to love,
The Lungé yiveth him wey of speche,
The Gallé servéth to do wreche,
The Splen doth him to laugh and play
Whan all unclennesse is away.
Lo, thus hath eche of hem his dede
To susteignen hem and fede.
In time of recreatión
Nature hath in creatión
The Stomack for a comun coke
Ordeinéd so, as saith the boke:
The Stomack coke is for the hall
And boileth meté for hem all
To make hem mighty for to serve
The Herté, that he shall nought sterve.
For as a King in his empire
Above all other is lorde and sire,
So is the Herté principall,
To whom Resón in speciáll
Is yove as for the governaunce.
"And thus natúre his purveaúnce
Hath made for man to liven here.
But God which hath the Soulé dere
Hath forméd it in other wise
That can no man pleinlý devise.
But as the clerkés us enforme,
That lich to God it hath a forme,
Through which figúre and which likenésse
The Soule hath many an high noblesse
Appropred to his owné kinde.
But oft her wittés ben made blinde
Al onelich of this ilké pointe,
That her abiding is conjointe
Forth with the body for to dwelle.
"That one desireth toward helle,
That other upward to the heven;
So shall they never stonde in even
But if the Flessh be overcome
And that the Soule have holy nome[1]

1 *Coler*, choler, bile.
2 *Irous*, given to anger, choleric.
3 *Kindé went*, natural turn or bent.
4 The Spleen is assigned to Melancholy for its place of lodging.
5 *Deliver*, free, supple.

1 *Holy nome*, wholly taken.

The governaunce, and that is selde
While that the Flessh him may bewelde.
All erthely thing which God began,
Was only made to servé man,
But he the Soul all onely made
Him selven for to serve and glade.
All other bestés that men finde
They serve unto her owné kinde,
But to Resón the Soulé serveth,
Wherof the man his thank deserveth
And get him with his workés good
The perduráble livés food.
" Of what matere it shall be tolde
A talé liketh many folde
The bet if it be spoké pleine,
Thus thenke I for to torne ayeine
And tellen plenerly therfore
Of therthé, wherof now to-fore
I spake, and of the water eke,
So as these oldé bokés speke,
And setté properly the bounde
After the forme of mappemounde,[1]
Through which the ground by pur-parties
Departed is in thre parties,
That is Asie, Aufríque, Europe,
The which under the heven cope
As fer as streccheth any ground
Begripeth all this erthé round.
But after that the highe wreche [2]
The water weiés let out seche
And overgo the hillés high,
Which every kindé madé deie
That upon middel erthé stood
Out také Noë and his blood,
His sonés and his doughters thre
They weren sauf and so was he.
Her namés, who that redé right,
Sem, Cham, Japhét the brethern hight,
And whanné thilke almighty honde
Withdrough the water fro the londe
And all the ragé was away
And erthé was the mannés way,
The sonés thre, of which I tolde,
Right after that hem selvé wolde,
This world departé they begonne.[1]
" Asía, which lay to the sonne
Upon the marche of orient,
Was graunted by commúne assent
To Sem, which was the sone eldést,
For that partïé was the best
And double as moch as other two.
And was that timé bounded so,
Wher as the flood which men Nile calleth,
Departeth fro his cours and falleth
Into the see Aléxandrine,
There taketh Asie first sesíne [2]
Toward the west, and over this
Of Canahim, where the flood is
Into the Greté See renn énd,
Fro that into the worldés end
Estwarde Asie it is algates
Till that men comen to the gates
Of Paradis, and theré ho.[3]
And shortly for to speke it so
Of orient in generall
Within his bounde Asié hath all.
" And than upon that other side
Westwárde, as it fell thilké tide,
The brother, which was hoté Cham,
Unto his parte Aufríqué nam.
Japhét Európé tho toke he;
Thus parten they the worlde on thre.
But yet there ben of londés fele [4]
In occident as for the chele,
In oriente as for the hete,
Which of the people be forlete
As lond desérte, that is unáble,
For it may nought ben habitáble.

[1] *Mappemounde*, Mappa Mundi, map of the world.
[2] *The highe wreche*, the vengeance of God.

[1] They began to divide this world.
[2] *Sesíne*, seizin, possession.
[3] *Ho*, stop. [4] *Fele*, many.

"The water eke hath sondry bounde,
After the lond where it is founde,
And taketh his name of thilké londes
Where that it renneth on the strondes.
But thilké see, which hath no wane,
Is clepéd the Great Oceane,
Out of the which arise and come
The highé flodés all and some.
Is none so litel wellé spring,
Which there ne taketh his béginníng,
And lich a man that lacketh breth
By wey of kindé so it geth
Out of the see and in ayein,
The water, as the bokés sain.
"Of Elements the propretés
How that they stonden by degres,
As I have told now might thou here,
My godé sone, all the matere
Of erthe, of water, aíre and fire.
And for thou saist, that thy desire
Is for to witen overmore
The forme of Aristotles lore,
He saith in his entendément
That yet there is an Element
Above the foure, and is the fifte
Set of the highe Goddes yifte,
The which that *orbis* clepéd is.
And therupon he telleth this,
That as the shellé hole and sounde
Encloseth all abouté rounde
What thing within an ey[1] belongeth,
Right so this *orbis* underfongeth
These Eleméntés everychone
Which I have spoke of one and one.
"But over this now take good hede,
My soné, for I wol procede
To speke upon Mathématíque,
Which grounded is on Theorique.
The Science of Astronomy
I thenke for to specify,
Withouté which to tellé pleine

[1] *Ey*, egg.

All other Science is in veine
Toward the scole of erthly thinges.
For as an egle with his winges
Fleeth above allé that men finde,
So doth this Science in his kinde.
"Benethe upon this erthé here
Of allé thingés the matere,
As tellen us they that ben lerned,
Of thing above it stont govérned,
That is to sain of the planétes
The chelés bothe and eke the hetes,
The chaunces of the worlde also,
That we Fortúné clepen so
Among the mennés nación,
All is through constellación;
Wherof that some man hath the wele,
And some men have diseses fele
In love as well as other thinges.
The state of realmés and of kinges
In time of pees, in time of werre,
It is conceivéd of the sterre.
And thus saith the Naturien,
Whiche is an Astronomien.
But the Divine saith other wise,
That if men weré good and wise
And plesant unto the Godhede
They shulden nought the sterrés drede.
For o man if him well befalle
Is moré worth than ben they alle
Towardés him that weldeth all.
But yet the lawe origináll,
Which he hath set in the natúres,
Mot worchen in the creätúres,
That therof may be none obstácle
But if[1] it stonde upon miracle
Through praier of some haly man.
And forthý so as I began
To speke upon Astronomy
As it is write in the clergý,
To telle how the planétés fare,
Some parte I thenké to declare,
My sone, unto thin audiénce.

[1] *But if*, unless.

"Astronomy is the Sciénce
Of wisdom and of high conning
Which maketh a man have knouleching
Of sterrés in the fermament,
Figúré, cercle and movemént
Of eche of hem in sondry place,
And what betwene hem is of space,
How so they move or stondé fast,
All this it telleth to the last.
Assembled with Astronomy
Is eke that ilke Astrology,
The which in jugéménts accompteth
Theffect what every sterre amounteth.
And how they causen many a wonder
To the climáts[1] that stond hem under.
And for to telle it moré pleine
These oldé philosóphres saine
That *orbis* which I spake of er
Is that which we fro therthe afer
Beholde, and firmament it calle,
In which the sterrés stonden alle,
Among the which in speciáll
Planetés seven principáll
There ben, that mannés sighte demeth
By thorizont as to us semeth.
And also there ben Signés twelve,
Which have her cercles by hem selve
Compásséd in the zodiaque
In which they have her places take,
And as they stonden in degre
Her cercles more or lassé be
Made after the proportión
Of therthé, whose condición
Is set to be the foundamént
To susteigne up the firmamént.
And by this skill a man may knowe,
The moré that they stonden lowe
The moré ben the cercles lasse,
That causeth why that somé passe
Her düé cours to-fore an other.

[1] *Climáts*, regions, climes.

But now, my levé deré brother,
As thou desirest for to wite
What I finde in the bokés write,
To telle of the Planetés Seven
How that they stonde upon the heven,
And in what point that they ben in,
Take hedé, for I woll begin,
So as the philosóphre taught
To Alisaundre and it betaught,
Wherof that he was fully taught
Of wisdom which was him betaught.
"Beneth all other stant the Mone,
The which hath with the See to done
Of flodés high and ebbés lowe
Upon his chaunge it shall be knowe.
And every fissh which hath a shelle
Mote in his governaúncé dwelle
To wexe and wane in his degre,
As by the Mone a man may se,
And all that stant upon the grounde
Of his moistúre it mot be founde.
All other sterrés, as men finde,
Ben shinend of her owné kinde
Out take onlý the moné light,
Which is nought of him selvé bright,
But as he taketh it of the Sonne.
And yet he hath nought all full wonne
His light that he nis somdele derke.
But what the let is of that werke
In almagest[1] it telleth this.
The Monés cercle so lowe is,
Wherof the Sonne out of his stage
Ne seth him nought with full viságe
For he is with the ground beshaded,
So that the Mone is somdele faded
And may nought fully shiné clere.
But what man under his powere
Is bore, he shall his placé chaunge
And seché many londés straunge.

[1] *Almagest*, Ptolemy's collection of the observations of the old astronomers.

And as of this condición
The Monés disposición
Upon the londe of Alemaigne
Is set, and eke upon Britaigne,
Which is now clepéd Engelonde,
For they travaile in every londe.
"Of the Planetés the secónde
Above the Mone hath take his bonde
Mercúre, and his natúre is this,
That under him who that bore is,
In boke he shall be studiós
And in writingé curiós
And slowe and lustles to travaile
In thing whiche ellés might availe.
He loveth ese, he loveth rest,
So is he nought the worthiést.
But with somdelé besinesse
His hert is set upon richésse.
And as in this condición
Theffect and disposición
Of this Planete and of his chaunce
Is most in Borgone and in Fraunce.
Next to Mercure as woll befalle
Stant that Planeté which men calle
Venús, whose constellación
Govérneth all the nación
Of lovers, where they spede or none,
Of which I trowé thou be one.
But whiderward thin happés wende,
Shall this Planété shewe at ende,
As it hath do to many mo,
To somé wel, to somé wo.
And nethéles of this Planéte
The most partý is softe and swete.
"For who that therof taketh his berth
He shall desiré joy and merth,
Gentíl, curtéis and debonaire
To speke his wordés softe and faire,
Such shall he be by wey of kinde.
And over all where he may finde
Plesaúnce of love, his herté boweth
With all his might and ther he woweth.
Venus of lové the goddésse
Is clepéd, but of wantonesse
The climate of her lechery
Is most comúne in Lumbardy.
"Next unto this Planéte of love
The brighté Sonne stant above,
Which is the hinderer of the night
And furtherer of the daiés light,
As he which is the worldés eye,
Through whom the lusty compaignie
Of foulés by the morwé singe,
The freshe flourés sprede and springe,
The highétre the ground beshadeth,
And every mannés herté gladdeth.
And for it is the Hede Planete,
How that he sitteth in his fete,
Of what richésse, of what nobléy
These bokés telle, and thus they say.
"Of golde glistrend spoke and whele
The sonne his carte [1] hath faire and wele,
In whiche he sitte, and is coróned
With brighté stonés environed,
Of which if that I speké shall
There be to-fore in speciáll
Set in the front of his coróne
Thre stonés, which that no persóne
Hath upon erthe, and the first is
By namé clepéd licuchis.
That other two be clepéd thus
Astrices and ceramius.
In his coróne, also behinde,
By oldé bokés as I finde,
There ben of worthy stonés thre
Set ech of hem in his degre,
Wherof a cristall is that one,
Which that coróne is set upon.
The seconde is an adamant.
The thridde is noble and avenaúnt,
Which clepéd is ydríades.
And over this yet nethéles

[1] *Carte*, chariot.

Upon the sidés of the werke,
After the writing of the clerke,
There sitten fivé stonés mo,
The smaragdine is one of tho,
Jaspis and elitropius
And vendides and jácinctus.
Lo, thus the coróne is beset,
Wherof it shineth well the bet,
And in such wise his light to sprede
Sit with his diadéme on hede
The sonné shinend in his carte.
And for to lede him swithe and
smarte
After the brighté daiés lawe
There ben ordeinéd for to drawe
Four hors his chare and him withall,
Wherof the namés telle I shall.
Erſtheús the first is hote,
The which is red and shineth hote,
The second Acteós the bright,
Lampés the thriddé courser hight,
And Philogéus is the ferth,
That bringen light unto this erth
And gone so swifte upon the
heven,
In foure and twenty hourés even
The carté with the brighté sonne
They drawé, so that over ronne
They have under the cercles high
All middel erthe in suche an hie.[1]
"And thus the sonne is over all
The Chefe Planéte imperiall,
Above him and beneth him thre
And thus betwene hem regneth he
As he that hath the middel place
Among the Seven, and of his face
Be glad all erthly creätúres
And taken after the natúres
Her ese and recreación.
And in his constellación
Who that is bore in speciáll,
Of good will and of liberall
He shall be founde in allé place
And also stonde in mochel grace
Toward the lordés for to serve
And great proffite and thank de-
serve.
And over that it causeth yit
A man to be subtil of wit,
To worch in golde, and to be wise
In every thing which is of prise.
But for to speken in what coste
Of all this erth he regneth moste,
As for wisdóm it is in Grece,
Where is appropred thilké spiece.
"Mars the planété bataillous
Next to the sonné glorioús
Abové stant and doth merveiles
Upon the fortune of batailes.
The conqueroúrs by daiés olde
Were unto this planété holde.
But who that his nativité
Hath take upon the propreté
Of Martés disposición
By wey of constellación,
He shall be fiers and fool hastife
And désiroús of werre and strife.
But for to tellen redely
In what climáte most communly
That this Planéte hath his effecte,
Said is, that he hath his aspecte
Upon the Haly Londe so cast,
That there is no pees stedéfast.
"Abové Mars upon the heven
The Sixté Planete of the Seven
Stant Jupiter the delicate,
Which causeth pees and no debate.
For he is clepéd the Planéte,
Which of his kindé softe and swete
Attempreth all that to him longeth.
And whom this Planete under-
fongeth
To stonde upon his regiment,[1]
He shall be meke and paciént
And fortunate to marchandý
And lusty to delſcacý
In every thing which he shall do.
This Jupiter is cause also

[1] *Hie*, haste.

[1] *Regiment*, rule.

Of the sciénce of lighté werkes,
And in this wisé tellen clerkes
He is the planete of delices.
But in Egipte of his offíces
He regneth most in speciáll,
For there be lustés over all
Of all that to this life befalleth.
For there no stormy weder falleth,
Which mighté grevé man or beste,
And eke the londe is so honéste,
That it is plenteoús and pleine,
There is no idel ground in veine.
And upon such felicité
Stant Jupiter in his degre.
" The highest and aboven alle
Stant that Planété, which men calle
Satúrnus, whose complexión
Is colde, and his condición
Causeth malíce and cruelté
To him the whose nativité
Is set under his governaúnce.
For all his werkés ben grevaúnce
And enemý to mannés hele,
In what degre that he shall dele.
His climate is in orient,
Where that he is most violent.
" Of the Planetes by and by,
How that they stonde upon the sky,
Fro point to point as thou might here
Was Alisaundre made to lere.
But over this touchénd his lore
Of thing that they him taughté more
Upon the scolés of clergý,
Now herken the philosophy.
" He which departeth day fro night,
That oné derke that other bright,
Of seven daiés made a weke;
A month of fouré wekés eke,
He hath ordeinéd in his lawe;
Of monthés twelve and eke forth-drawe
He hath also the longé yere.
And as he set of his pówére
Accordaunt to the daiés seven
Planétés seven upon the heven,
As thou to-fore hast herd devise,
To speké right in such a wise
To every monthé by him selve
Upon the heven, of signés twelve
He hath after his ordinall
Assignéd one in speciáll,
Wherof so as I shall rehercen
The tidés of the yere diversen.
But pleinly for to make it knowe
How that the signés sit a rowe,
Eche after other by degré
In substaunce and in propreté
The zodiáqué comprehendeth
Within his cercle and it appendeth.
" The firste of whiché nethéles
By name is clepéd Ariés,
Which lich a wether of statúre
Resembled is in his figúre.
And as it saith in almageste
Of sterrés twelve upon this beste
Ben set, wherof in his degre
The wombe hath two, the heved hath thre,
The taile hath seven, and in this wise,
As thou might heré me devise,
Stant Aries, which hote and drie
Is of him self, and in partie
He is the réceipt and the hous
Of mighty Mars the batailous.
And overmore eke as I finde
The Creatór of alle kinde
Upon this Signé first began
The world, whan that he madé man,
And of this constellación
The verray operación
Availeth, if a man therinne
The purpose of his werk beginne,
For than he hath of propreté
Good spede and great felicité.
" The twelvé monthés of the yere
Attitled under the powére
Of thesé twelvé signés stonde,
Wherof that thou shalt understonde
This Aries out of the twelve
Hath Marche attitled for him selve,

Whan every brid shall chese his make,
And every nedder and every snake
And every reptile which may move,
His might assaieth for to prove
To crepen out ayein the sonne,
Whan Ver[1] his seson hath begonne.
"Taurus the seconde after this
Of Signés which figúréd is
Unto a bullé, drie and colde,
And as it is in bokés tolde
He is the hous appurtenaunt
To Venus somdele déscordaúnt.
This bulle is eke with sterrés set,
Through which he hath his hornés knet
Unto the taile of Aries,
So is he nought there sterrélés.
Upon his brest eke eightétene
He hath, and eke as it is sene
Upon his tail stonde other two.
His month assignéd eke also
Is Averil, which of his shoures
Minístreth way unto the floures.
"The thriddé Signe is Gemini,
Which is figúréd redely
Lich to two twinnés of man kinde,
That naked stonde. And as I finde,
They ben with sterrés wel bego,
The heved hath parte of thilké two,
That shine upon the bullés taile,
So ben they both of o parasle.
But on the wombe of Gemini
Ben fivé sterrés nought forthý.
And eke upon the fete be twey,
So as these oldé bokés say,
That wisé Tholomeus wrote.
His propre monthé wel I wote
Assignéd is the lusty May,
Whan every brid upon his lay
Among the grené levés singeth,
And love of his pointúré stingeth
After the lawés of natúre

1 *Ver*, the Spring.

The youthe of every creätúre.
"Cancér after the reule and space
Of Signés halt the forthé place.
Like to the crabbe he hath semblaúnce
And hath unto his retinaúnce
Sixtené sterrés, wherof ten,
So as these oldé wisé men
Descrive, he bereth on him to-fore
And in the middle two before
And four he hath upon his ende,
Thus goth he sterréd in his kende.
And of him self is moist and colde
And is the propre hous and holde
Which apperteineth to the Mone
And doth what longeth him to done.
The month of Juin unto this Signe
Thou shalte after the reule assigne.
"The fifté Signe is Leo hote,
Whos kinde is shapé drie and hote,
In whom the Sonne hath herbergage.
And the semblaúnce of his ymáge
Is a león, which in baillie
Of sterrés hath his purpartie,
The fouré which as Cancer hath
Upon his endé, Leo tath
Upon his heved, and thanné neste
He hath eke foure upon his breste,
And one upon his tail behinde.
In oldé bokés as we finde.
His propre month is Juil by name,
In which men pleien many a game.
"After Leó Virgó the nexte
Of Signés clepéd is the sexte,
Wherof the figure is a maide,
And as the philosóphre saide,
She is the welth and the rising,
The lust, the joy and the liking
Unto Mercure. And soth to say
She is with sterrés well beseie,
Wherof Leó hath lent her one,
Which sit on high her heved upon.
Her wombe hath five, her fete also
Have other five, and ever mo

Touchénd as of complexión
By kindly dispositión
Of drie and cold this maiden is.
And for to tellen over this
Her month as thou shalte understonde,
Whan every felde hath corne in honde
And many a man his backe hath plied,
Unto this signe is Augst applied.
"After Virgó to reknen even
Libra sit in the nombre of seven,
Which hath figúre and resemblaúnce
Unto a man which a balaunce
Bereth in his honde as for to weie,
In boke and as it may be seie.
Diversé sterrés to him longeth,
Wherof on heved he underfongeth
First thre, and eke his wombe hath two,
And down beneth eight other mo.
This signe is hote and moisté both,
The whiché thingés be nought loth
Unto Venús, so that alofte
She resteth in his hous full ofte,
And eke Saturnus often hied
Is in this signe and magnified.
His propre month is said Septembre,
Which yiveth men cause to remembre,
If any sore be left behinde
Of thing which grevé may to kinde.
"Among the Signés upon height
The signé, whiche is nombred eight,
Is Scorpio, which as felón
Figúréd is a Scorpión.
But for all that yet nethélesse
Is Scorpio nought sterrélesse.
For Libra graunteth him his ende
Of eighté sterrés, where he wende,
The which upon his heved assised
He bereth, and eke there ben devised
Upon his wombé sterrés thre
And eight upon his taile hath he.
Which of his kinde is moist and colde
And unbehovely manyfolde.
He harméth Venus and empeireth,
But Mars unto his hous repeireth,
But ware whan they to-gider dwellen.
His propre monthe is, as men tellen,
Octobre, which bringeth the kalende
Of Winter, that cometh next suénde.
"The ninth signe in Novembre also,
Which folweth after Scorpio,
Is clepéd Sagittarius,
The whos figúre is markéd thus;
A monstre with a bowe on honde,
On whom that sondry sterrés stonde,
Thilke eight of whiche I spake tofore,
The which upon the tail ben lore
Of Scorpio the heved all faire
Be spreden of the Sagittaire,
And eight of other stonden even
Upon his wombe, and other seven
There stonden on his tail behinde,
And he is hote and drie of kinde.
To Jupiter his hous is fre.
But to Mercure in his degre,
For they be nought of one assent,
He worcheth great empeirément.
This signe hath of his propreté
A monthé, whiche of duëté
After the seson that befalleth
The ploughés oxe in winter stalleth.
And fire into the halle he bringeth
And thilké drinke of which men singeth,
He torneth must into the wine,
Than is the larder of the swine.
That is Novembre which I mene,
Whan that the leef hath lost his grene
"The tenthé Signé drie and colde,
The which is Capricornus tolde,
Unto a gote hath resemblaúnce.
For whosé love and áqueintaúnce
Within his housé to sojorne
It liketh well unto Satorne.

But to the Mone it liketh nought,
For no profít is theré wrought.
This Signe as of his propreté
Upon his heved hath sterrés thre
And eke upon his wombé two
And twey upon his taile also.
Decembre after the yerés forme,
So as the bokés us enforme,
With daiés shorte and nightés longe
This ilké Signe hath underfonge.
"Of tho that sitte upon the heven
Of Signés in the nombre elleven
Aquariús hath take his place
And stant well in Satornés grace,
Which dwelleth in his herbergage.
But to the Sonne he doth oultrage.
This Signe is verraily resembled
Lich to a man which halte assembled
In either honde a water spout,
Wherof the stremés rennen out.
He is of kindé moist and hote,
And he that of the stérres wote
Saith, that he hath of sterrés two
Upon his heved, and bene of tho
That Capricorn hath on his ende.
And as the bokés maken minde
That Tholoméus made him selve,
He hath eke on his wombé twelve,
And twey upon his endé stonde.
Thou shalte also this understonde,
The frosty coldé Janevere,
Whan comen is the newé yere,
That Janus with the double face
In his chare hath take his place
And loketh upon bothé sides
Some dele toward the winter tides,
Some dele toward the yere suénde,
That is the monthé belongénde
Unto this Signe, and of his dole
He yiveth the firsté primerole.[1]
"The twelfthé, which is last of alle
Of signés, Piscis men it calle,
The which, as telleth the scriptúre,
Bereth of two fisshes the figúre.

[1] *Primerole*, primrose.

So is he colde and moist of kinde,
And eke with sterrés as I finde
Beset in sondry wise, as thus
Two of his ende Aquarius
Hath lent unto his heved, and two
This Signe hath of his owne also
Upon his wombe, and over this
Upon his ende also there is
A nombre of twenty sterrés bright,
Which is to sene a wonder sight.
Toward this signe into his hous
Comth Jupiter the glorioús,
And Venus eke with him accordeth
To dwellen, as the boke recordeth.
The Month unto this signe ordeined
Is Februar, which is bereined.
And with londflodés in his rage
At fordés letteth[1] the passage.
"Now hast thou herd the propreté
Of Signes, but in his degré
Albumazare yet over this
Saith, so as therthé parted is
In fouré, right so ben devised
The signés twelve, and stonde assised
That eche of hem in his partie
Hath his climate to justifie.
Wherof the firsté regiment
Toward the parte of orient
From Antióche and that contré
Govérnéd is of Signés thre,
That is Cancér, Virgó, Leó.
And towarde occident also
From Armeny, as I am lerned,
Of Capricorne it stant govérned,
Of Piscis and Aquarius.
And after hem I findé thus
Southward fro Alisaundré forth
Tho Signés, whiché most ben worth
In governaúnce of that doaire,[2]
Libra they ben and Sagittaire
With Scorpio, which is conjoint
With hem to stonde upon that point
Of Constantnople the cité,
So as the bókés tellen me.

[1] *Letteth*, hinders. [2] *Doaire*, province.

The last of this división
Stant untoward Septemtrion,
Where as by wey of purveiaúnce
Hath Aries the governaúnce
Forth with Taurús and Gemini.
Thus ben the Signés proprely
Devided, as it is reherced,
Wherof the londés ben diversed.
"**Lo thus, my sone**, as thou might here,
Was Alisaundre made to lere
Of hem that weren for his lore.
But now to loken overmore
Of other sterrés how they fare
I thenke hereafter to declare,
So as king Alisaundre in youth
Of him that suché signés couth
Enforméd was to-fore his eye
By night upon the sterrés sigh.
"Upon sondry creäción
Stant sondry operación,
Some worcheth this, some worcheth that;
The fire is hote in his estate
And brenneth what hemayatteigne,
The water may the fire restreigne,
The which is colde and moist also.
Of other thinge it fareth right so
Upon this erthe among us here.
And for to speke in this manére
Upon the heven, as men may finde
The sterrés ben of sondry kinde
And worchen many sondry thinges
To us that bene her underlinges.
Among the whiché forth withall
Nectánabús in speciáll,
Which was an astronomien
And eke a great magicien
And undertake hath thilke emprise,
To Alisaundre in his apprise
As of magíqué naturele
To knowe, enformeth him somdele
Of certein sterrés what they mene,
Of which he saith there ben fiftene.
And sondrily to everichone
A gras belongeth and a stone,
Wherof men worchen many a wonder
To setté thing bothe up and under.
"To telle right as he began
The firsté sterre Aldeboran,
The clerest and the most of alle,
By righté namé men it calle,
Which liche is of condition
To Mars and of complexión
To Venus, and hath therupon
Carbunculum his propre stone.
His herbe is Anabulla named,
Which is of great vertúe proclamed.
"The seconde is nought vertulés
Clota, or ellés Pliades
It hatte and of the Monés kinde
He is. And also this I finde,
He taketh of Mars complexión,
And lich to such condition
His stone appropred is Cristall,
And eke his herbe in speciall
The vertuoús Fenél it is.
"The thriddé, which comth after this,
Is hote Algol the cleré rede,
Whiche of Satorne as I may rede
His kindé taketh and eke of Jove
Complexión to his behove.
His propre stone is Diamaunt,
Which is to him most áccordaunt.
His herbé, which is him betake,
Is hote Eléborum the blacke.
"So as it falleth upon lot
The fourthé sterre is Alhaiot,
Which in the wise as I saide er
Of Satorne and of Jupiter
Hath take his kinde, and therupon
The Saphir is his propre stone,
Marrubium his herbe also,
The which accorden bothé two.
"And Canis major in his like
The fifté sterre is of magíque,
The whosé kinde is Venerien,
As saith this astronomien.

His propre stone is said Berille,
But for to worche and to fulfille
Thing which to this Sciéncé falleth,
There is an herbé, which men calleth
Saveine, and that behoveth nede
To him that woll his purpos spede.
"The sixté suende after this
By namé Canis minor is.
The which sterre is Mercuriáll
By wey of kinde, and forth withall
As it is writen in the carte
Complexión he taketh of Marte.
His stone and herbe as saith the scole
Ben Achatés and Primerole.
"The seventh sterre in speciáll
Of this Sciénce is Ariall,
Which sondry nature underfongeth.
The stone which propre unto him longeth,
Gorgonza proprelý it hight.
His herbe also, which he shall right,
Upon the worching as I mene
Is Celidoiné fresshe and grene.
"Sterre Ala corvi upon height
Hath take his place in nombre of eight,
Which of his kindé mot performe
The will of Marte and of Satorne,
To whom Lapacia the gret
Is herbé, but of no beyete.
His stone is Honochinus hote,
Through which men worchen great riote.
"The ninthé sterréfaire and wele
By name is hote Alaëzele,
Which taketh his propre kindé thus
Bothe of Mercure and of Venus.
His stone is the grene Emeraude
To whom is yoven many a laude.
Saulge is his herbe appurtenaunt
Aboven all the remenaunt.
"The tenthé sterre is Almareth,
Which upon life and upon deth
Through kinde of Jupiter and Marte
He doth what longeth to his parte.
His stone is Jaspe and of Plantaine
He hath his herbé soveraine.
"The sterre eleventh is Venenas,
The whose natúre is, as it was,
Take of Venús and of the Mone
In thing which he hath for to done.
Of Adamaunt is that perrie,
In whiche he worcheth his maistrie.
Thilke herbe also, which him befalleth,
Cicorea the boke him calleth.
"Alpheta in the nombre sit
And is the twelfté sterré yit,
Of Scorpio which is govérned,
And taketh his kinde as I am lerned
And hath his vertue in the stone
Which cleped is Topazion.
His herbé propre is Rosmarine,
Which shapen is for his covine.
"Of thesé sterrés which I mene,
Cor Scorpionis is thrittene,
The whos natúré Mart and Jove
Have yoven unto his behove.
Hís herbe is aristolochý,[1]
Which folweth his astronomy.
The stoné which this sterre alloweth,
Is Sardis which unto him boweth.
"The sterré which stant next the last,
Natúre of him this namé cast
And clepen him Botercadent,
Which of his kind obediént
Is to Mercure and to Venus.
His stone is said Crisolitus.
His herbe is clepéd Satureie,
So as these oldé bokés saie.
"But now the lasté sterre of alle
The Taile of Scorpio men calle,
Which to Mercure and to Satorne
By wey of kindé mot retorne

[1] *Aristolochý*, miswritten "astrology." Cornelius Agrippa, *De Occult. Phil.*, Lib. I., cap. 32, gives the plants under *Cor Scorpionis* as Aristolochia and Crocus.

After the preparatión
Of dúë constellatión.
The Calcidoine unto him longeth
Which for his stone he underfongeth.
Of Majoran his herbe is grounded.
Thus have I said how they ben founded
Of every sterre in speciáll,
Which hath his herbe and stone withall,
As Hermes in his bokés olde
Witnéssé bereth, of that I tolde.
"Now hast thou herd, in suche a wise
These noble philosóphres wise
Enformeden this yongé king
And made him have a knouleching
Of thing which first to the partie
Belongeth of philosophie,
Which Theorîqué clepéd is,
As thou to-fore hast herde er this.
But now to speke of the secónde,
Whiche Aristotle hath also founde
And techeth how to speké faire,
Whiche is a thing full necessaire
To counterpeisé the balaunce,
Where lacketh other suffisaunce.
"Above all erthly creätúres
The Highé Maker of natúres
The Word to man hath yove alone,
So that the speche of his persone
Or for to lese, or for to winne
The hertés thought which is withinne,
May shewé what it woldé mene.
And that is no where ellés sene
Of kindé with none other beste.
So shulde he be the more honést,
To whom God yaf so worthy a yifte,
And loké well that he ne shifte
His Wordés to none wicked use,
For Word the techer of vertuse
Is clepéd in philosophy.
Wherof touchéndé this party
Is rhetorîqué the sciénce
Appropred to the reverence
Of Wordés that ben resonáble.
And for this art shall be vailáble
With goodly wordés for to like
It hath Gramaire, it hath Logiqúe,
That serven both unto the speche.
Gramairé first hath for to teche
To speke upon congruité.
Logique hath eke in his degre
Betwene the trouthe and the falshode
The pleiné wordés for to shode,[1]
So that nothing shall go beside
That he the right ne shall decide,
Wherof full many a great debate
Reforméd is to good estate
And pees susteignéd up alofte
With esy wordés and with softe,
Where strengthé shuldé let it falle.
The philosóphre amongés alle
Forthý commendeth this sciénce,
Which hath the reule of eloquence.
In stone and gras vertúe there is,
But yet the bokés tellen this,
That Worde above all erthly thinges
Is vertuoús in his doinges,
Where so it be to evil or good.
For if the Wordés semen good
And be well spoke at mannés ere
Whan that there is no trouthé there,
They done full oft full great deceipt.
For whan the Word to the conceipt
Descordeth in so double a wise,
Such Rhetorîque is to despise
In every place and for to drede.
"For of Ulixes thus I rede,
As in the boke of Troy is founde,
His eloquence and his facoúnde
Of goodly wordés which he tolde
Hath made that Anthenor him solde
The town whiche he with treson wan.
Worde hath beguiléd many a man,
With word the wildé beste is daunted,

[1] *Shode*, divide, discriminate.

With word the serpent is enchaunted,
Of wordés mong the men of armes
Ben woundés heléd with the charmes,
Where lacketh other medicíne
Worde hath under his disciplíne
Of sorcerié the carectes.
The wordés ben of sondry sectes,
Of evil and eke of good also.
The wordés maken frende of fo,
And fo of frende, and pees of werre,
And werre of pees, and out of herre
The word the worldés cause entriketh
And reconcileth who on him liketh.
The worde under the cope of heven
Set every thing or odde or even.
With word the Highé God is plesed,
With word the wordés ben appesed.
The softé word the loudé stilleth,
Where lacketh good the word fulfilleth
To make amendés for the wronge.
Whan wordés medlen with the songe,
It doth plesauncé well the more.
But for to loke upon the lore,
How Tulliús his rhetoríque
Componeth, there a man may pike
How that he shall his wordés set.
How he shall lose, how he shall knet,
And in what wise he shall pronounce
His talé pleiné without frounce.
Wherof ensample if thou wilt seche,
Take hede and rede whilom the speche
"Of Julius and Cicero,
Which consul was of Romé tho,
Of Caton eke, and of Silene
Behold the wordés hem betwene,
Whan the tresón of Cateline
Discovered was, and the covine
Of hem that were of his assent
Was knowe and spoke in parlement,
And axéd howe and in what wise
Men sholden done him to juíse.
Silanus first his talé tolde
To trouth and as he was beholde
The comun profit fòr to save,
He saide how treson shuldé have
A cruel dethe. And thus they speke,
The consul both and Caton eke,
And saiden that for suche a wronge
There may no peiné be to stronge.
But Julius with wordés wise
His talé tolde all other wise,
As he which wolde her dethe respíte,
And foundeth howe he might excite
The juges through his eloquénce
Fro deth to torné the senténce
And set her hertés to pité.
Now tolden they, now toldé he:
They speken pleine after the lawe;
But he the wordés of his sawe
Coloúreth in an other wey
Spekénd. And thus betwene the twey
To trete upon this jugément
Made eche of hem his argument.
Wherof the talés for to here
There may a man the scolé lere
Of Rhetoríqué the eloquence,
Whiche is the seconde of Science
Touchéndé to Philosophie,
Wherof a man shall justifie
His wordés in dispútesón
And knette upon conclusión
His argument in suche a forme,
Which may the pleiné trouthe enforme
And the subtíl cautéle abate,
Whiche every true man shall debate.
"The firsté, whiche is Theorique,
And the secóndé Rhetorique
Sciénces of Philosophy,
I have hem tolde as in party,
So as the philosóphre it tolde
To Alisaundre. And now I wolde

Tell of the thriddé, what it is,
The which Practíqué clepéd is.
"Practíqué stant upon thre thinges
Toward the governaunce of kinges.
Wherof the firste Ethique is named,
The whose Sciéncé stant proclamed
To teche of vertue thilké reule,
How that a King him self shall reule
Of his morál conditión
With worthy dispositión,
Of good livíng in his persónc,
Which is the chefe of his corónc.
It maketh a kinge also to lerne
Howe he his body shall govérne,
Howe he shall wake, how he shall slepe,
How that he shall his helé kepe
In mete, in drinke, in clothing ekc.
There is no wisdom for to seke
As for the reule of his persone,
The which that this sciénce allone
Ne techeth as by wey of kinde
That there is nothing left behinde.
"That other point, which to practique
Belongeth, is Ecónomiquc,
Which techeth thilké honesté,
Through which a King in his degré
His wife and child shal reule and guie
So forth with all the compaignie
Which in his houshold shall abide,
And his estate on every side
In such manéré for to lede
That he his houshold ne mislede.
"Practíque hath yet the thridde apprise,
Which techeth how and in what wise
Through his purveiéd ordenaunce
A King shall set in governaunce
His realme, and that is Policie
Which longeth unto Regalie
In time of werre, in time of pees,
To worship and to good encrees
Of clerke, of knight, and of marchaunt,
And so forth all the remenaunt
Of all the comun people about
Withinné burgh and eke without
Of hem that ben artificers,
Whiche usen craftes and mestiérs,
Whose art is clepéd mechanique;
And though they ben nought allé like,
Yet nethéles how so it falle,
O[1] lawé mot govérne hem alle,
Or that they lese, or that they winne,
After the state that they ben inne.
"Lo, thus this worthy yongé king
Was fully taught of every thing
Which mighté yive entendément
Of good reule and good regiment
To suche a worthy prince as he.
But of verráy necessité
The philosóphre him hath betake
Five points, which he hath undertake
To kepe and holde in observaúnce
As for the worthy governaúnce
Which longeth to his Regalic
After the reule of Policie.
"To every man belongeth lore,
But to no man belongeth more
Than to a King which hath to lede
The people als for his kinghede.
He may hem bothé save and spille,
And for it stant upon his wille
It sit him well to ben avised
And the vertúes which are assised
Unto a Kingés regiment[2]
To take in his entendément,
Wherof to tellen as they stonde
Hereafterward now woll I fonde.
Among the Vertues one is chefe
And that is Trouthé, which is lefe
To God and eke to man also.
And for it hath ben ever so,
Taught Aristotle as he well couth

[1] *O*, one. [2] *Regiment*, rule.

To Alisaundre, how in his youth
He shulde of Trouthé thilké grace
With all his holé herte embrace,
So that his word be trewe and pleine
Toward the world, and so certeine
That in him be no double speche.
For if men shuldé Trouthé seche
And found it nought within a King,
It were an unsitténdé[1] thing.
The worde is token of that within,
There shall a worthy king begin
To kepe his tunge and to be trewe,
So shall his price ben ever newe.
Avise him every man to-fore
And be well ware, er he be swore,
For afterwarde it is to late
If that he wolde his word debate.
For as a King in speciáll
Above all other is principáll
Of his powér, so shulde he be
Most vertuoús in his degre.
And that may well be signified
By his coróne and specified.
"The gold betokneth excellence,
That men shuld done him reverence
As to her legé soveraine.
The stonés, as the bokés saine,
Commended ben in treble wise.
First they ben hard and thilke assise
Betokeneth in a King constaúnce,
So that there shall no variaúnce
Be found in his condición.
And also by descriptión
The vertue whiche is in the stones,
A verray signe is for the nones
Of that a king shall ben honést
And holdé trewely his behest
Of thing which longeth to kinghede.
The brighté colour, as I rede,
Which is in the stonés shinénd,
Is in figúre betokenénd
The cronique of this worldés fame
Which stant upon his godé name.

[1] *Unsittendé*, unbecoming.

The cercle, which is rounde aboute
Is token of all the londe aboute,
Which stant under his gerarchie,
That he it shall well kepe and guie.
And for that Trouthe how so it falle
Is the Vertue Soveraine of alle
That longeth unto regiment,
A talé which is evident
Of Trouthe in commendación,
Toward thin enformación,
My sone, herafter thou shalt here
Of a cronſque in this matere.

As the cronique it doth reherce,
A soldan whilom was of Perse,
Which Daires hight, and Ytaspis
His fader was. And sothe it is,
That through wisdóm and high prudénce
More than for any reverénce
Of his lignáge as by descent
The regne of thilke empire he hent.
And as he was him selfé wise
The wisé men he held in prise,
And sought hem out on every side
That toward him they shulde abide.
Among the whiché thre there were,
That most servíce unto him bere
As they which in his chambre lighen
And all his counceil herd and sighen.
Her namés ben of straungé note,
Harpaghes was the firsté hote,
And Manachaz was the secóunde,
Zorobabel, as it is founde
In the cronſqué, was the thridde.
This soldan what so him betidde
To hem he tristé most of alle,
Wherof the case is so befalle:
This lord, which hath conceiptés depe,
Upon a night whan he hath slepe,
As he which hath his wit disposed,
Touchend a point hem hath opposed.
The kingés questiön was this,
Of thingés thre which strongest is,

The Wine, the Woman or the King?
And that they shulde upon this thing
Of her answére avised be,
He yaf hem fully daiés thre
And hath behote hem by his feith
That who the besté reson saith
He shall receive a worthy mede.
"Upon this thing they token hede
And stoden in dispútesón,
That by divérs opinión
Of arguments that they have holde
Harpaghes first his talé tolde
And said, how that the strength of kinges
Is mightiest of allé thinges.
For King hath power over man,
And man is he which reson can,
As he which is of his natúre
The mosté noble creätúre
Of allé tho that God hath wrought.
And by that skill it semeth nought,
He saith, that any erthly thing
May be so mighty as a King.
A King may spille, a King may save,
A King may make of lorde a knave
And of a knave a lord also,
The power of a King stant so,
That he the lawés overpasseth.
What he woll maké lasse he lasseth,
What he woll maké more he moreth.
And as a gentil faucon soreth,
He fleeth that no man him reclameth,
But he alone all other tameth
And stant him self of lawé fre.
Lo, thus a Kingés might, saith he,
So as his reson can argúe,
Is strengest and of most valúe.
"But Manachaz saith other wise,
That Wine is of the more emprise,
And that he sheweth by this way.
The Wine full ofté taketh away
The reson fro the mannés herte,
The Wine can make a creple sterte
And a deliver[1] man unwelde,
It maketh a blind man to behelde
And a bright eÿéd semé derke,
It maketh a lewdé man a clerke,
And fro the clerkés the clergý
It taketh awey, and cowardy
It torneth into hardiésse,
Of avarice it maketh largesse.
The Winé maketh eke the good blood,
In which the soulé, which is good,
Hath chosen her a resting place
While that the life her woll embrace.
And by this skillé Manachaz,
Answéréd hath upon this cas
And saith, that Wine by wey of kind
Is thing which may the hertés bind
Well moré than the Regalie.
"Zorobabel for his partie
Said as him thoughté for the best,
That Women ben the mightiest.
The Kinge and the Vinour also
Of Women comen bothé two.
And eke he said, how that manhede
Through strengthe unto the womanhede
Of lové, where he woll or none,
Obeié shall, and therupon
To shewe of Women the maistrie
A talé whiche he sigh with eye
As for ensample he toldé this.
"How Apemen, of Besazis
Which doughter was, in the paleis
Sittend upon his highé deis,
Whan he was hottest in his ire
Toward the great of his empire,
Cyrus the King tiraunt she toke.
And only with her goodly loke
She made him debonaire and meke,
And by the chin and by the cheke
She luggeth him right as her list,
That now she japeth and now she kist

[1] *Deliver*, free of movement, lithe.

And doth with him what ever her liketh.
Whan that she loureth than he siketh,
And whan she gladeth he is glad.
And thus this King was overlad
With hiré which his lemman was.
"Among the men is no solas
If that there be no Woman there,
For but if that the Woman were
This worldés joié were awey.
Through hem men finden out the wey
To knighthode and to worldés fame,
They make a man to dredé shame
And honour for to be desired.
Through the beauté of hem is fired
The dart of which Cupídé throweth,
Wherof the jolif peiné groweth
Which al the worlde hath under fote.
A Woman is the mannés bote,
His life, his deth, his wo, his wele.
And this thing may be shewéd wele,
How that Womén ben good and kinde,
For in ensample thus I finde.
"Whan that the duke Admetus lay
Sike in his bed, that every day
Men waiten whan he shuldé dey,
Alcest his wife goth for to prey
With sacrifice unto Minerve,
As she which woldé thank deserve,
To wite answére of the goddesse,
How that her lorde of his sikenesse,
Wherof he was so wo beseine,
Recover might his hele ayeine.
Lo, thus she cride and thus she praide,
Till atté last a vois her saide,
That if she woldé for his sake
The maladíe suffre and take
And deie her self, he shuldé live.
Of this answere Alcest hath yive
Unto Minervé great thonkíng,
So that her dethe and his livíng
She chese with all her hole entent,
And thus accorded home she went.
Into the chambre whan she came,
Her housébonde anone she name
In bothe her armés and him kist,
And spake unto him what her list.
And therupon within a throwe
The goodé wife was overthrowe
And deied, and he was hole in haste.
So may a man by reson taste,
How next after the God above
The trouth of Women and the love,
In whom that allé grace is founde,
Is mightiest upon this grounde
And most behovely manyfolde.
"Lo, thus Zorobabel hath tolde
The tale of his opinión.
But for fináll conclusión,
What strengest is of erthly thinges
The Wine, the Women or the Kinges,
He saith, that Trouthe above hem alle
Is mightiest, how ever it falle.
The Trouthe how so it ever come
May for no thíng ben overcome.
It may well suffre for a throwe,
But atté last it shall be knowe.
The proverbe is, who that is trewe,
Him shall his whilé[1] never rewe.
For how so that the causé wende
The trouthe is shameles atté ende.
But what thing that is trouthélés
It may nought well be shamélés,
And shamé hindereth every wight.
So proveth it, there is no might
Withouté Trouthe in no degre.
And thus for trouthe of his decré
Zorobabel was most commended,
Wherof the questión was ended
And he receivéd hath his mede
For Trouthé, which to mannés nede
Is most behovelich over all.
Forthý was Trouthe in speciáll

[1] *Whilé*, time.

The firsté point in observaúnce
Betake unto the governaúnce
Of Alisaundre, as it is saide;
For therupon the ground is laide
Of every Kingés regiment,
As thing which most conveniént
Is for to set a king in even
Bothe in this worlde and eke in heven.

"**Next after Trouthé** the secounde
In Policie as it is founde,
Which serveth to the worldés fame
In worship of a Kingés name,
Largesse it is, whose privilege
There may non avaríce abrege.
The worldés good was first comúne,
But afterward upon Fortúne
Was thilké comun profit cessed.
For whan the people stood encressed
And the lignáges woxen great,
Anone for singular beyete
Drough every man to his partie,
Wherof come in the first envíe
With great debate and werrés stronge,
And last among the men so longe
Till no man wisté who was who
Ne which was frende ne which was fo.
Till atté laste in every londe
Within hem self the people fonde,
That it was good to make a King
Which might appesen all this thing
And yivé right to the lignáges
In parting of her heritáges
And eke of all her other good.
And thus above hem allé stood
The King upon his regaly,
As he which hath to justify
The worldés good fro covetise.
So sit it well in allé wisé
A King betwene the more and lesse
To sette his herte upon Largesse
Toward him self and eke also
Towarde his people. And if nought so,
That is to sain, if that he be
Toward him selfé large and fre
And of his people take and pille,
Largessé by no wey of skille
It may be said, but Avarice,
Which in a Kinge is a great Vice.

"A King behoveth eke to fle
The Vice of Prodegalité,
That he mesúre in his expence
So kepé that of indigence
He may be sauf. For who that nedeth,
In all his werk the wors he spedeth.
As Aristotle upon Chaldee
Ensample of great auctorité
Unto king Alisaundre taught
Of thilké folk that were unsaught [1]
Toward her King for his pillage.
Wherof he bad in his corage
That he unto thre points entende
Where that he wolde his good despende.

"First shulde he loke how that it stood
That all were of his owné good
The yiftés which he woldé yive,
So might he wel the better live.

"And eké he must taken hede
If there be cause of any nede
Which oughté for to be defended,
Er that his goodés ben despended.

"He mote eke as it is befalle
Amongés other thingés alle
Se the desértés of his men,
And after that they ben of ken
And of estate and of meríte
He shall hem largélich aquite,
Or for the werre, or for the pees,
That none honoúr fall in decrees
Which mighté torne into diffame,

[1] *Unsaught*, out of accord (First English, saht, peace, reconcilement).

But that he kepe his godé name,
So that he be nought holde unkinde.
For in cronſque a tale I finde,
Which speketh somdele of this matere,
Herafterward as thou shalte here.
"In Romé to pursue his right
There was a worthy pouer knight
Which came aloné for to sain
His causé, when the court was plein
Where Julius was in presénce.
And for him lacketh of despense
There was with him none advocate
To maké plee for his estate.
But though him lacké for to plede
Him lacketh nothing of manhede.
He wisté well his purse was pouer,
But yet he thought his right recouer,
And openly pouerte aleide
To themperoúr, and thus he saide:
'O Julius, lord of the lawe,
Behold, my counseil is withdrawe
For lacke of gold to thine office
After the lawés of justice.
Help, that I haddé counseil here
Upon the trouthe of my matere.'
And Julius with that anone
Assignéd him a worthy one.
But he him self no word ne spake.
This knight was wroth and found a lake[1]
In themperoúr, and saidé thus:
'O thou unkindé Julius,
Whan thou in thy batailé were
Up in Aufrique, and I was there,
My might for thy rescousse I did
And putté no man in my stede.
Thou wost what woundés there I had,
But here I findé the so bad,
That the ne list to speke o worde
Thine owné mouth, nor of thin horde
To yive a florein me to helpe.
How shulde I thanné me beyelpe[2]
Fro this day forth of thy largesse,
Whan such a great unkindénesse
Is found in suche a lorde as thou?'
This Julius knew well inough
That all was soth which he him tolde.
And for he woldé nought ben holde
Unkind, he toke his cause on honde,
And as it were of Goddés sonde,
He yaf him good inough to spende
For ever unto his livés ende.
"And thus shuld every worthy king
Take of his knightés knouleching
Whan that he sigh they hadden nede,
For every service axeth mede.
But other, which have nought deserved
Through vertue but of japés served,
A King shall nought deservé grace,
Though he be large in suche a place.
"It sit well every king to have
Discretión whan men him crave,
So that he may his yifté wite;
Wherof I finde a talé write,
How Cinichus a poueré knight
A sommé which was over might,
Praied of his king Antigonus.
The kinge answerdé to him thus
And said, how such a yifté passeth
His pouer estate. And than he lasseth
And axeth but a litel peny,
If that the king wold yive him any.
"The king answérd, it was to small
For him which was a lord réall,
To yive a man so litel thinge,
It were unworship in a kinge.
"By this ensample a King may lere,
That for to yive is in manere,
For if a King his tresor lasseth
Without honoúr and thankeles passeth,
Whan he him self woll so beguile
I not who shall compleigne his while

[1] *Lake*, lack. [2] *Beyelpe*, boast.

Ne who by right him shall releve.
But nethéles this I beleve
To helpé with his owné londe
Belongeth every man his honde
To set upon necessité.
"And eke his Kingés realté
Mote every legé man comfórte
With good and body to supporte,
Whan they se causé resonáble.
For who that is nought entendáble
To holde upright his Kingés name,
Him oughté for to be to blame.
"Of Policie and over more
To speke in this matéré more
So as the philosóphre tolde,
A King after the reule is holde
To modifie and to adresse
His yiftés upon such largesse
That he mesúré nought excede.
"For if a King fall into nede,
It causeth ofté sondry thinges,
Whiche are ungoodly to the kinges.
What man will nought him self mesúre,
Men seen ful ofté that mesúre
Him hath forsake. And so doth he
That useth prodegalité,
Which is the moder of pouérte,
Wherof the londés ben desérte.
And namély whan thilké vice
About a King stant in office
And hath witholde of his partý
The covetoúsé flaterý
Which many a worthy King deceiveth,
Er he the fallace apperceiveth
Of hem that serven to the glose.
For they that connen plese and glose
Ben, as men tellen, the norices
Unto the fostring of the Vices,
Wherof full ofté nethéles
A King is blaméd giltéles.
A Philosóphre, as thou shalt here,
Spake to a King of this matére
And said him well how that flatroúrs
Coupáble were of thre erroúrs.
One was toward the goddes high,
That weren wroth of that they sigh,
The mischefe which befallé sholde
Of that the falsé flatrour tolde
Toward the King. Another was,
Whan they by sleight and by fallas
Of feignéd wordés make him wene
That black is white and blew is grene
Touchend of his condición.
For whan he doth extorción
With many an other Vicé mo,
Men shall nought finden one of tho
To grucche or speké there ayein,
But holden up his oile[1] and sain,
That all is well what ever he doth.
And thus of fals they maken soth,
So that her Kingés eye is blent
And wot nought how the worlde is went.
The thridde erroúr is harm commune,
With which the people mot commúne
Of wrongés that they bringen inne.
And thus they werchen treble sinne
That ben flatroúrs about a king.
There mighté be no worsé thing
About a kingés regaly,
Than is the Vice of Flatery.
And nethéles it hath ben used
That it was never yet refused,
As for to speke, in Court Reáll.
For there it is most speciáll
And may nought longé be forbore.
But whan this Vice of hem is bore
That sholden the Vertúes forth bringe,
And Trouthe is tornéd to Lesinge,
It is, as who saith, ayein kinde,
Wherof an old ensample I finde.
"Among these other talés wise
Of philosóphres in this wise

1 *His oile*, his affirmation.

I rede, how whilom two there were
And to the scolé for to lere
Unto Athenés fro Cartáge
Her frendés whan they were of age,
Hem sende. And there they stoden longe
Till they such lore have underfonge
That in her timé they surmounte
All other men, that to accompte
Of hem was tho the greté fame.
The first of hem his righté name
Was Diogénes thanné hote,
In whom was foundé no riote.
His felaw Aristippus hight,
Which mochel couthe and mochel might.
But atté lasté soth to sain
They bothé tornen home ayein
Unto Cartáge and scolé lete.
This Diogénes no beyete
Of worldés good or lasse or more
Ne soughté for his longé lore,
But toke him only for to dwelle
At home. And as the bokés telle,
His house was nigh to a rivére
Beside a brigge, as thou shalt here.
There dwelleth he and taketh his rest,
So as it thought him for the best,
To studie in his philósóphie,
As he which woldé so defie
The worldés pompe on every side.
"But Aristippe his boke aside
Hath laid, and to the court he wente,
Where many a wile and many a wente[1]
With flaterý and wordés softe
He caste and hath compasséd ofte
How he his princé mighté plese.
And in this wise he gate him ese
Of veine honoúr and worldés good,
The londés reule upon him stood.
The king of him was wonder glad,
And all was do what thinge he bad,

1 *Wente*, turn.

Bothe in the courte and eke without
With flaterý he brought about
His purpos of the worldés werke,
Which was ayein the state of clerke,
So that philosophý he lefte
And to richésse him self uplefte.
Lo, thus had Aristippe his will.
But Diogénes dwelté still
At home and lokéd on his boké.
He soughté nought the worldes croke
For veine honoúr ne for richesse,
But all his hertés besinesse
He setté to be vertuoús.
And thus within his owné hous
He liveth to the suffisaúnce
Of his havíng. And fell perchaunce,
This Diogéne upon a day,
And that was in the month of May,
Whan that these herbés ben holsóme,
He walketh for to gader some
In his gardin, of which his joutes[1]
He thoughté have, and thus aboutes
Whan he hath gadred what him liketh,
He set him thanné downe and piketh
And wisshe his herbés in the flood
Upon the which his gardin stood
Nigh to the brigge, as I tolde ere.
And hapneth while he sitteth there,
Cam Aristippus by the strete
With many hors and routés grete
And straught unto the brigge he rode
Where that he hovéd and abode,
For as he cast his eyé nigh
His felaw Diogéne he sigh,
And what he dede he sigh also,
Wherof he saidé to him so:
'O Diogéné, God the spede.
It weré certés litel nede
To sitten here and wortés pike
If thou thy princé couthest like[2]

1 *Joutes* or *jotes*, beets; also legumes used in old cookery.
2 *Like*, please.

So as I can in my degre.'
'O Aristippe,' ayein quod he,
'If that thou couthest so as I
Thy wortés piké truélý,
It were als litel nede or lasse
That thou so worldly wol compasse
With flaterſë for to serve,
Wherof thou thenkest to deserve
Thy princés thank and to purcháce
How thou might stonden in his grace
For getting of a litel good.
If thou wolt take into thy mood
Resón, thou might by reson deme,
That so thy princé for to queme[1]
Is nought to reson accordaúnt,
But it is greatly descordaunt
Unto the scolés of Athene.'
"Lo, thus answerdé Diogéne
Ayein the clerkés flaterie.
But yet men sene thessamplerie
Of Aristippe is well received
And thilke of Diogéne is weived.
Office in court and gold in coffre
Is now, men sain, the philosóphre
Which hath the worship in the halle.
But flaterſë passeth alle
In chambre whom the court avaunceth.
For upon thilké lot it chaunceth
To be belovéd now a day.
"I not if it be ye or nay,
How Danté the poéte answerde
To a flatrour, the tale I herde.
Upon a strife betwene hem two
He said him, there ben many mo
Of thy servauntés than of min.
For the poéte of his covine
Hath none that woll him cloth and fede,
But a flatroúr may reule and lede
A king with all his londe about.
So stant the wisé man in doubt
Of hem that to folſë drawe,
For such is now the comun lawe.

[1] *Queme*, please.

But as the comune vois it telleth,
Where now that flaterſë dwelleth
In every londe under the sonne,
There is full many a thing begonne
Which weré better to be lefte;
That hath be shewed now and efte
"**But if a prince** him woldé reule
Of the Romains after the reule
In thilké time as it was used,
This Vicé shuldé be refused
Wherof the princes ben assoted.
But where the pleiné trouth is noted,
There may a princé wel conceive
That he shall nought him self deceive
Of that he hereth wordés pleine,
For him ther nought[1] by reson pleigne
That warnéd is er him be wo.
And that was fully provéd tho,
Whan Romé was the worldés chefe,
The sothésaier tho was lefe,
Which woldé nought the trouthé spare
But with his wordés plaine and bare
To themperoúr his sothés tolde,
As in croníque it is witholde,
Here afterwarde as thou shalt here
Accordend unto this matere.
"To se this olde ensemplarie,
That whilom was no flaterie
Toward the princes, wel I finde,
Wherof so as it comth to minde,
My sone, a tale unto thin ere,
While that the worthy princes were
At Rome, I thenke for to telle.
For whan the chaunces so befelle,
That any emperoúr as tho
Victórie had upon his fo
And so forth came to Rome ayein,
Of treble honoúr he was certaín,
Wherof that he was magnified.
"The first, as it is specified,

[1] *Nought*, ought not.

Was, whan he cam at thilké tide,
The chare, in which he shuldé ride
Four whité stedés sholdé drawe;
Of Jupiter by thilké lawe
The cote he shuldé were also.
His prisonérs eke sholden go
Endlong the chare on either honde,
And all the noble of the londe
To-fore and after with him come
Ridénd and broughten him to Rome
In token of his chivalrie,
And for none other flaterie.
And that was shewéd forth withall
Where he sat in his chare reäll
Beside him was a ribald set
Which had his wordés so beset
To themperoúr in all his glorie
He saidé: 'Take into memórie,
For all this pompe and all this pride
Let no justícé gon aside,
But know thy self, what so befalle.
For men seen ofté timé falle
Thing which men wendé siker stonde.
Though thou victórie have on honde,
Fortúné may nought stonde alwey;
The whele perchaunce another day
May torne and thou might overthrowe,
There lasteth nothing but a throwe.'

"With thesé wordés and with mo
This ribald, which sat with him tho,
To themperoúr his talé tolde.
And overmore what ever he wolde
Or were it evil or were it good
So plainly as the trouthé stood,
He spareth nought but speketh it out.
And so might every man about,
The day of that solempnité,
His talé tellen as wele as he
To themperoúr all openlý.
And all was this the causé why,
That while he stood in his noblesse
He shulde his vanité represse
With suché wordés as he herde.

"Lo now, how thilké time it ferde
Toward so high a worthy lorde.
For this I finde eke of recórde,
Which the cronique hath auctorized,
What emperoúr was entronized
The firsté day of his coróne,
Where he was in his reäl throne
And helde his fest in the paleis
Sitténd upon his highé deis,
With all the lust that may be gete
Whan he was gladest at his mete,
And every minstrell haddé pleide
And every disour haddé saide
What most was plesant to his ere,
Than atté lasté comen there
His masons for they sholden crave
Where that he woldé be begrave,
And of what stone his sepultúre
They sholden make, and what sculptúre
He wolde ordeigné therupon.
Tho was there flaterie none
The worthy princes to bejape,
The thing was otherwisé shape
With good counséile; and otherwise
They were hem selven thanné wise
And understoden well and knewen;
Whan suché softé windés blewen
Of flaterý into her ere
They setten nought her hertés there.
But whan they herdé wordés feigned
The pleiné trouth it hath desdeigned[1]
Of hem that weren so discrete.
So toke the flaterer no beyete
Of him that was his princé tho.
And for to proven it is so,
A talé, which befell in dede,
In a cronique of Rome I rede.

Cesár upon his reäll throne
Where that he sat in his persone
And was highést in all his pris,
A man which wolde make him wise

[1] Feigned words undervalued the plain truth in men of such discernment.

Fell down knelénd in his presence
And did him such a reverence
As though the highé God it were.
Men hadden great merveilé there
Of the worshípé which he dede.
This man aros fro thilké stede
And forth withall the samé tide
He goth him up and by his side
He set him down as pere and pere
And saide, 'If thou that sittest here
Art God which allé thingés might,
Than have I do worshíp aright
As to the God; and other wise,
If thou be nought of thilke assise,
But art a man suche as am I,
Than may I sit the fasté by,
For we be bothe of oné kinde.'
" Cesár answérde and saide: 'O blinde,
Thou art a fol, it is well sene
Upon thy self. For if thou wene
I be a God, thou dost amis
To sit where thou seést God is.
And if I be a man also,
Thou hast a great folíë do,
Whan thou to such one as shall deie
The worship of thy God awey
Hast yiven so unworthily.
Thus may I provê redely,
Thou art nought wise.' And they that herde,
How wisely that the king answérde,
It was to hem a newé lore,
Wherof they dradden him the more,
And broughten nothing to his ere
But if it trouthe and reson were.
So ben there many in such a wise,
That feignen wordés to be wise
And all is verray flateryѓ
To him which can it well aspy.
" The kindé flatrour can nought love
But for to bring him-self above,
For how that ever his maister fare,
So that him self stonde out of care
Him reccheth nought. And thus ful ofte
Deceivéd ben with wordés softe
The kingés that ben innocent.
Wherof as for chastíëment
The wisé philosóphre saide:
'What king that so his tresure laide
Upon such folke, he hath the lesse
And yet ne doth he no largesse
But harmeth with his owné honde
Him self and eke his owné londe.
And that by many a sondry wey,
Wherof if that a man shall sey
As for to speke in generall
Where such thing falleth over all
That any king him self misreule,—
The philosóphre upon his reule
In speciáll a causé set
Whiche is and ever hath be the let
In governaúnce about a king
Upon the mischefe of the thing,
And that, he saith, is Flateryѓ,
Wherof to-fore as in partyѓ,
What Vice it is, I have declared.
For who that hath his wit bewared[1]
Upon a flatrour to beleve,
Whan that he weneth best acheve
His godé world, it is most fro.
And for to proven it is so
Ensamples there ben many one,
Of whiche if thou wolt knowen one,
It is behovely for to here
What whilom fell in this matere.

Among the kingés in the bible
I finde a tale and is credíble
Of him, that whilom Achab hight,
Which had all Israel to right.
But who that couthé glosé softe
And flater, such he set alofte
In great estate and made hem riche.
But they that speken wordés liche
To trouthe and wolde it nought forbere
For hem was none estate to bere,

1 *Bewared*, spent.

The courte of suché toke none hede.
Till atté last upon a nede,
That Benedab kinge of Surïe,
Of Israel a great partïe,
Which Ramoth Galaäd was hote,
Hath sesé́d. And of that rióte
He toke counseïle in sondry wise,
But nought of hem that weren wise.
And nethéles upon this cas
To strengthen him, for Josephas
Which thanné was kinge of Judee
He sendé for to come, as he
Which through frendshïp and alli-
aúnce
Was next to him of áqueintáúnce.
For Joram sone of Josaphath
Achabbés doughter wedded hath,
Which highté fairé Godelie.
And thus cam into Samarý
King Josaphat, and he found there
The king Achâb. And when they
were
To-gider spekend of this thing,
This Josaphat saith to the king,
How that he woldé gladly here
Some true prophét in this matere,
That he his counseil mighté yive
To what point it shall be adrive.
And in that timé so befell
There was such one in Israel,
Which set him all to flaterý,
And he was clepéd Sedechý,
And after him Achâb hath sent.
And he at his commaundément
To-fore him cam, and by a sleight
He hath upon his heved on height
Two largé hornés set of bras,
As he whiche all a flatrour was,
And goth rampénd as a león
And cast his hornés up and down
And bad men ben of good espeire,
For as the hornés percen thaire
He saith, withouten resisténce,
So wist he well of his sciénce
That Benedab is discomfíte.

Whan Sedechy upon this plite
Hath told this tale unto his lorde,
Anone they were of his accorde
Prophétés falsé many mo
To bere up oile [1] and allé tho
Affermen that which he hath tolde;
Wherof the king Achâb was bolde
And yaf hem yiftés all aboute.
But Josaphat was in great doubte
And held fantósme all that he herde,
Praiénd Achâb how so it ferde,
If there were any other man,
The which of prophecïë can,
To here him speke er that they gone.
Quod Achab thanné: 'There is one,
A brothel, which Micheas hight.
But he ne comth nought in my sight
For he hath long in prison laien,
Him likéd never yet to saien
A goodly word to my plesaúnce.
And nethéles at thine instaúnce
He shall come out, and than he may
Say as he saidé many a day;
For yet he saidé never wele.'
Tho Josaphat began some dele
To gladen him in hope of trouthe,
And bad withouten any slouthe
That men him shuldé fette [2] anone.
And they that weren for him gone
Whan that they comen where he was
They tolden unto Micheás
The manere how that Sedechý
Declaréd hath his prophecý.
And therupon they pray him faire
That he woll saié no contraire
Wherof the king may be desplesed,
For so shall every man be esed,
And he may helpe him self also.
Micheas upon trouthé tho
His herté set and to hem saith—
All that belongé to his feith

[1] *To bere up oile*, to sustain the affirmation (of Zedekiah). *Oil* or *oile* is an old form of *oui*, yes. "*Oil, par ma foi, sire, oil mult volontiers*," says each of the false prophets to Ahab. See note, p. 366.

[2] *Fette*, fetch.

And of none other feignéd thing
That woll he tell unto the king,
Als fer as God hath yive him grace.
Thus came this prophete into place,
Where he the kingés willé herde.
And he therto anone answérde
And saide unto him in this wise:
'My legé lord, for my servíce,
Which trewe hath stonden ever yit,
Thou hast me with prisón aquite.
But for all that I shall nought glose
Of trouthe als far as I suppose;
And as touchénd of thy bataile
Thou shalt nought of the sothé faile.
For if it liké the to here,
As I am taught in that matere,
Thou might it understondé sone.
But what is afterward to done
Avisé the, for this I sigh,
I was to-fore the throne on high,
Where all the world me thoughté
stode,
And there I herde and understode
The vois of God with wordés clere
Axénd and saide in this manere:
'In what thing may I best beguile
The king Achab?' And for a while
Upon this point they speken fast.
Tho said a spirit atté last:
'I undertaké this emprise.'
And God him axeth in what wise.
'I shall,' quod he, 'deceive and lie
With flaterénde prophecie
In suché mouthés as he leveth.'
And he which allé thing acheveth,
Bad him go forth and do right so.
And over this I sigh also
The noble people of Israël
Dispers as shepe upon an hill
Without a keper unarraied.
And as they wente about astraied,
I herde a vois unto hem sain:
'Goth home into your hous ayein,
Till I for you have better ordeigned.'
Quod Sedechié: 'Thou hast feigned
This tale in angring of the king.'
And in a wrathe upon this thing
He smote Micheen upon the cheke;
The king him hath rebukéd eke;
And every man upon him cride.
Thus was he shent on every side
Ayein and into prison ladde,
For so the kinge him selvé badde.
The trouthé mighté nought ben
herde;
But afterward as it hath ferde,
The dedé proveth his entent.
Acháb to the batailé went,
Where Benedab for all his shelde
Him slough, so that upon the felde
His people goth about astray.
But God, which allé thingés may,
So doth that they no mischefe have.
Her king was dede and they ben
save,
And home ayein in Goddes pees
They wente, and all was founde les[1]
That Sedechý hath said to-fore.
So sit it wel a king therfore
To loven hem that trouthé mene.
For atté last it will be sene,
That flaterý is nothing worth.
"But now to my materé forth
As for to speken overmore
After the philosóphres lore,
The thriddé point of policy
I thenké for to specify.
"**What is a lond**, where men
be none?
What ben the men which are allone
Without a kingés governaunce?
What is a king in his legeaunce
Where that there is no lawe in londe?
What is to také lawe on honde,
But if the jugés weren trewe?
These oldé worldés with the newe
Who that woll take in evidence
There may he se thexperiénce
What thing it is to kepé lawe

[1] *Les*, leasings, untruth.

Through which the wrongés be withdrawe
And rightwisnessé stant commended,
Wherof the regnés ben amended.
For where the lawé may comúne,
The lordés forth with the comúne
Eche hath his propré duëté.
And eke the kingés reälté
Of bothe his worship underfongeth,
To his estate as it belongeth,
Whiche of his highé worthinesse
Hath to govérné rightwisnesse,
As he which shall the lawé guide.
And nethéles upon some side
His power stant above the lawe
To yivé both and to withdrawe
The forfet of a mannés life.
But thingés which are excessife
Ayein the lawe he shal nought do
For lové ne for hate also.
"The mightés of a king be gret.
But yet a worthy king shall let
Of wrong to done all that he might,
For he which shall the people right,
It sit wel to his regalý
That he him self first justify
Towardés God in his degré.
For his estate is ellés fre
Toward all other in his persóne,
Sauf only to the God alone
Which woll him self a king chastise
Where that none other may suffise.
"So were it good to taken hede
That first a king his owné dede
Betwene the Vertue and the Vice
Redresse, and than of his justíce
So set in even the balaúnce
Towardés other in governaúnce,
That to the pouer and to the riche
His lawés mighten stonden liche,
He shall excepté no persone.
But for he may nought all him one
In sondry places do justíce,
He shall of his reäl offíce
With wise consideratión
Ordeigne his deputatión
Of suché jugés as ben lerned,
So that his people be govérned
By hem that trué ben and wise.
For if the lawe of covetise
Be set upon a jugés honde,
Wo is the people of thilké londe.
For wrong may nought him selven hide.
But ellés, on that other side,
If lawé stondé with the right
The people is glad and stant upright,
Where as the lawe is resonáble,
The comun people stant meváble,
And if the lawé torne amis,
The people also mistornéd is.
"And in ensample of this matere
Of Maximin a man may here,
Of Romé which was emperoúr,
That whan he made a governoúr
By wey of substitución
Of province or of región,
He woldé first enquire his name
And lete it openly proclame
What man he were, or evil or good.
And upon that his namé stood
Enclined to vertue or to vice,
So wolde he set him in offíce,
Or ellés put him all awey.
Thus held the lawe his righté wey,
Which found no let of covetise.
The world stood than upon the wise,
As by ensample thou might rede
And holde it in thy minde I rede.
In a cronique I findé thus,
How that Gaiús Fabriciús,
Which whilom was consúl of Rome
By whom the lawés yede and come,
Whan the Sampnités to him brought
A somme of gold and him besought
To don hem favour in the lawe,
Toward the gold he gan him drawe
Wherof in allé mennés loke
A part up in his honde he toke,

Which to his mouth in allé haste
He put it for to smelle and taste
And to his eye and to his ere,
But he ne found no comfort there.
And than he gan it to despise
And tolde unto hem in this wise:
'I not what is with gold to thrive,
Whan none of all my wittés five
Find favour ne delite therinne.
So is it but a nicé sinne
Of gold to ben to covetoús.
But he is riche and glorious
Which hath in his subjectión
Tho men which in possessión
Ben riche of gold, and by this skill,
For he may all day whan he will
Or be hem lefe or be hem lothe
Justícé done upon hem bothe.'
"Lo, thus he said. And with that worde
He threw to-fore hem on the borde
The gold out of his honde anone,
And said hem, that he woldé none.
So that he kept his liberté
To do justíce and equité,
Withouté lucre of such richesse.
There ben now fewe of suche I gesse.
For it was thilké timés used,
That every jugé was refused
Which was nought frend to comun right,
But they that wolden stonde upright
For trouthe onlý to do justíce
Preferréd were in thilke offíce
To deme and jugé comun lawe,
Which now men sain is all withdrawe.
"To sette a lawe and kepe it nought
There is no comune profit sought.
But above allé nethéles
The lawé which is made for pees
Is good to kepé for the best,
For that set allé men in rest.

The rightful emperoúr Conráde
To kepé pees such lawé made
That none withinné the cité
In destorbaúnce of unité
Durst onés meven a matere.
For in his time as thou might here,
What point that was for lawé set
It shuldé for no good be let[1]
To what personé that it were.
And this brought in the comun fere
Why every man the lawé dradde,
For there was none which favour hadde.

So as these oldé bokés sain,
I findé write, how a Romain,
Which consul was of the pretoire,
Whose namé was Carmidotoire,
He set a lawé for the pees
That none, but he be wepenles,
Shall come into the counseil hous,
And ellés as malicioús
He shal ben of the lawé dede.
To that statúte, and to that rede
Accorden alle, it shall be so,
For certein causé which was tho.
Now list, what fell therafter sone.
This consul haddé for to done
And was into the feldés ride.
And they him haddé longe abide,
That lordés of the counseil were,
And for him sende, and he cam there
With swerd begert, and hath foryete
Till he was in the counseil sete.
Was none of hem that madé speche
Till he him self it woldé seche,
And founde out the default him selve.
And than he saide unto the twelve
Which of the Senate weren wise:
'I have deservéd the juíse
In hasté that it were do.'
And they him saiden allé no,
For well they wist it was no vice,
Whan he ne thoughté no malice

[1] *For no good be let*, be stayed for no money consideration.

But onlich of a litel slouth.
And thus they leften as for routh
To do justíce upon his gilte,
For that he shuldé nought be spilte.
And whan he sigh the maner how
They wolde him save, he made a vow
With manful herte, and thus he saide,
That Romé shuldé never abraide
His heires whan he were of dawe [1]
That her auncéstre brake the lawe.
Forthý er that they weren ware,
Forthwith the samé swerde he bare
The statute of his lawé kepte,
So that all Rome his dethe bewepte.
"**In other place** also I rede,
Where that a juge his owné dede
He wol nought venge of lawé broke,
The king it hath him selven wroke.
The greté king, which Cámbisés
Was hote, a jugé lawéles
He found, and into rémembraúnce
He did upon him such vengeaúnce:
Out of his skin he was beflain
All quick, and in that wisé slain,
So that his skin was shape all mete
And nailéd on the samé sete,
Where that his soné shuldé sitte:
Avise him if he woldé flitte
The lawé for the covetise,
There sigh he redy his juíse.
"Thus in defalte of other juge
The king mote otherwhilé juge
To holden up the righté lawe.
And for to speke of tholdé dawe
To take ensample of that was tho,
I finde a talé write also,
How that a worthy prince is holde
The lawés of his londe to holde,
First for the highé Goddes sake
And eke for that him is betake
The people for to guide and lede,
Which is the charge of his kinghede.

[1] *Whan he were of dawe*, when his days were ended.

"**In a cronique** I redé thus
Of the rightfull Ligurgiús,
Which of Athénés princé was,
How he the lawe in every cas
Wherof he shulde his people reule,
Hath set upon so good a reule
In all this world that cité none
Of lawé was so well begone;
Forth with the trouthe of governaunce
There was among hem no distaunce,
But every man hath his encrees;
There was withouté werré pees,
Without envíé lové stood;
Richesse upon the comune good
And nought upon the singuler
Ordeinéd was; and the powér
Of hem that weren in estate,
Was sauf; wherof upon debate
There stood no thíng, so that in reste
Might every man his herté reste.
"And whan this noble rightfull king,
Sigh how it ferde of all this thing
Wherof the people stood in ese,
He which for ever woldé plese
The highé God whose thank he sought,
A wonder thing than he bethought
And shope, if that it mighté be,
How that his lawe in the cité
Might afterward for ever laste.
And therupon his wit he caste,
What thing him weré best to feigne,
That he his purpose might atteigne.
A parlément and thus he set
His wisdom where that he beset
In audience of great and smale,
And in this wise he tolde his tale:
'God wote, and so ye woten alle,
Here afterward how so it falle,
Yet into now my will hath be
To do justíce and equité
In forthring of común profíte,

Such hath ben ever my delite.
But of o thing I am beknowe,
The which my will is that ye knowe.
The lawé which I toke on honde,
Was all to-gider of Goddés sonde
And no thinge of min owné wit,
So mote it nede enduré yit
And shall do lenger, if ye will,
For I wol tellé you the skill.
The god Mercurius and no man
He hath me taught all that I can
Of suché lawés as I made,
Wherof that ye ben allé glad.
It was the god and no thíng I,
Which did all this, and now forthý
He hath commaunded of his grace,
That I shall come into a place
Which is foreín, out in an ile,
Where I mot tarie for a while
With him to speke and he hath bede.
For as he saith, in thilké stede
He shall me suché thingés telle
That ever while the world shal dwelle
Athénés shall the better fare.
But first er that I thider fare,
For that I woldé that my lawe
Amongés you ne be withdrawe
There whilés that I shall be oute,
Forthý to setten out of doubte
Both you and me, thus wol I pray,
That ye me wolde assure and say
With such an othe as ye woll take,
That eche of you shall undertake
My lawés for to kepe and holde.'
"They saiden allé, that they wolde.
And there upon they swore here othe,
That fro that timé that he goth
Till he to hem be come ayeine
They shuld his lawés well and pleine
In every point kepe and fulfill.
Thus hath Ligurgius his will,
And toke his leve and forth he went.
But list now well to what entent
Of rightwisnessé he did so.
For after that he was ago,
He shope him never to be founde:
So that Athénés, which was bounde,
Never after shuldé be relesed,
Ne thilké godé lawé cesed,
Which was for comun profit set.
And in this wise he hath it knet,
He which the commun profite sought,
The king his owne estate ne rought.[1]
To do proffte to the comúne
He toke of exile the fortúne
And lefte of princé thilke office
Only for love and for justíce,
Through which he thought, if that he might,
For ever aftér his deth to right
The cité which was him betake.
Wherof men ought ensample take
The godé lawés to avaunce
With hem which under governaunce
The lawés havé for to kepe.
For who that woldé také kepe
Of hem that firsté lawés founde,
Als fer as lasteth any bounde
Of londe her namés yet ben knowe.
And if it liké the to knowe
Some of her namés, how they stonde,
Now herke and thou shalt understonde.

Of every bienfait the merite
The God him self it woll aquite.
And eke full ofte it falleth so,
The worlde it woll aquite also,
But that may nought ben even liche.
The God he yiveth the heven riche,
The world yifth only but a name
Which stant upon the godé fame
Of hem that done the godé dede.
And in this wisé double mede
Receiven they that done well here,
Wherof if that the list to here
After the fame as it is blowe,
There might thou well the sothé knowe,

[1] *Rought*, cared for.

How thilke honesté besinesse
Of hem that first for rightwisnesse
Among the men the lawés made,
May never upon this erthé fade.
For ever while there is a tunge,
Her namés shall be rede and sunge
And holde in the cronſqué write,
So that the men it sholden wite
To speké good, as they well oughten,
Of hem that first the lawes soughten
In forthring of the worldés pees.
Unto the Hebrews was Moisés
The first, and to thegipciéns
Mercurius, and to Trojéns
First was Numa Pompilius,
To Athénés Ligurgius
Yave first the lawe, and to Gregois,
Foroneus hath thilké vois,
And Romulus to the Romains;
For suché men that ben vilains,
The lawe in such a wise ordeigneth,
That what man to the lawé pleigneth,
Be so the jugé stond upright,
He shall be servéd of his right.
And so ferforth it is befalle
That lawe is come among us alle,
God leve it moté well bene holde,
As every king therto is holde.
For thing whiche is of kingés set,
With kingés ought it nought be let.
What king of lawé taketh no kepe
By lawe he may no regné kepe.
Do lawe away, what is a king?
Where is the right of any thing,
If that there be no lawe in londe?
This ought a king well understonde,
As he which is to lawé swore,
That if the lawé be forbore
Withouten execución,
It maketh a lond torne up so down,
Which is unto the king a sclaundre.
Forthý unto king Alisaundre
The wisé philosóphre bad
That he him selvé first be lad
Of lawe, and forth than over all
To do justíce in generall,
That all the widé lond aboute
The justice of his lawé doubte,[1]
And thanné shall he stonde in rest.
For therto lawe is one the best
Above all other erthly thing
To make a legé drede his king.
"But how a king shall gete him love
Toward the highé God above
And eke among the men in erthe
This nexté point, which is the ferthe
Of Aristotles lore, it techeth,
Wherof who that the scolé secheth
What policíë that it is
The boke reherceth after this.

It nedeth nought that I delate
The pris which preiséd is algate
And hath bene ever and ever shall,
Wherof to speke in speciáll
It is the vertue of Pité,
Through which the highé magesté
Was steréd, whan his sone alight
And in Pité the world to right
Toke of the maidé flessh and blood.
Pité was cause of thilké good,
Wherof that we ben allé save.
Well ought a man Pité to have
And the vertue to set in prise,
Whan he him self whiche is All Wise
Hath shewéd why it shall be preised.
Pité may nought be counterpeised
Of tirannſë with no peise.
For Pité maketh a king curteise
Both in his worde and in his dede.
It sit well every legé drede
His king, and to his hest obey.
And right so by the samé wey
It sit a king to be pitóus
Toward his people and graciós
Upon the reule of governaúnce,
So that he worché no vengeaúnce
Which may be clepéd cruelte.
Justícé which doth equité

[1] *Doubte*, fear, reverence.

Is dredful, for he no man spareth
But in the lond, where Pité fareth
The king may never faile of love,
For Pité through the grace above
So as the philosóphre affermeth,
His regne in good estate confermeth.
Thapostel Jamés in this wise
Saith, what man shuldé do juíse
And hath not Pité forth with all,
The dome of him which demeth all
He may him self ful soré drede,
That him shall lacke upon the nede
To findé Pité whan he wolde.
For who that Pité woll beholde,
It is a point of Cristés lore;
And for to loken overmore
It is behovely, as we finde,
To reson and to lawe of kinde.
Cassiódore in his aprise telleth:
'The Regne is sauf, where Pité dwelleth.'
And Tullius his tale avoweth
And saith: What king to Pité boweth
And with Pité stont overcome,
He hath that shilde of gracé nome
Which to the kingés yiveth victoire.
"Of Alisaundre in his histoire
I rede, how he a worthy knight
Of sodein wrath and not of right
Forjugéd hath, and he appelleth.
And with that word the king quareleth
And saith: 'None is abové me.'
'That wote I wel my lorde,' quod he,
Fro thy lordshíp appele I nought,
But fro thy Wrath in all my thought
To thy Pité stant min appele.'
The king, which understode him wele,
Of puré Pité yave him grace.
And eke I rede in other place
Thus saidé whilom Constantine:
'What emperoúr that is encline
To Pité for to be servaunt,
Of all the worldés remenaunt
He is worthý to ben a lord.'
"**In olde bokés** of recorde
Thus finde I write of ensamplaire:
Trajan the worthy debonaire,
By whom that Romé stood govérned,
Upon a time, as he was lerned
Of that he was to fámiliér,
He saide unto that counceller
That for to ben an emperoúr
His wil was nought for vein honoúr
Ne yet for reddour[1] of justice,
But if he might in his offíce
His lordés and his people plese.
Him thought it were a greater ese
With love her hertés to him drawe,
Than with the drede of any lawe.
For whan a thing is do for doubte,
Ful ofte it cometh the wors aboute;
But where a kinge is pietoús
He is the moré gracioús,
That mochel thrift him shall betide
Which ellés shuldé torne aside.
"**To do pité**, support, and grace
The philosóphre upon a place
In his writíng of daiés olde
A tale of great ensample tolde
Unto the king of Macedoine,
How betwene Kaire and Babeloine,
Whan comen is the somer hete,
It hapneth two men for to mete
As they shulde entren in a pas
Where that the wildernessé was.
And as they wenten forth spekénde
Under the largé wodés ende,
That o man axeth of that other:
'What man art thou, my levé brother?
Which is thy creaunce and thy feith?'
'I am paién,' that other saith,
'And by the lawé which I use,
I shall nought in my feith refuse
To loven alle men aliche,
The pouer both and eke the riche;

[1] *Reddour* (*roideur*), rigour.

Whan they ben glad I shall be glad,
And sory whan they ben bestad;
So shall I live in unité
With every man in his degré:
For right as to my self I wolde,
Right so toward al other I sholde
Be gracïoús and debonaire.
Thus have I told the soft and faire
My feith, my lawe, and my creaúnce.
And if the list for aqueintaunce,
Now tell, what maner man thou art?'
And he answérde upon his part:
'I am a Jewe, and by my lawe
I shall to no man be felawe
To kepe him trouth in word ne dede
But if he be withouté drede
A verray Jew right as am I.
For ellés I may trewély
Bereve him bothé life and good.'
"The paien herde and understood
And thought it was a wonder lawe;
And thus upon her sondry sawe
Talkénde bothé forth they went.
The day was hote, the sonné brent,
The paien rode upon an asse,
And of his catell more and lasse
With him a riché trusse he ladde.
"The Jew, which all untrouthé hadde
And went upon his feet beside,
Bethought him how he mighté ride,
And with his wordés sligh and wise
Unto the paien in this wise
He said: 'O, now it shall be sene
What thing it is thou woldest mene.
For if thy lawé be certaín,
As thou hast tolde, I dare well saín
Thou wolt beholdé my destresse,
Which am so full of werinesse
That I ne may unethé go,
And let me ride a mile or two
So that I may my body ese.'
The paien wold him nought displese
Of that he spake, but in pité
It list him for to knowe and se
The pleinté which that other made.
And for he wolde his herté glade,
He light and made him nothing straunge,
Thus was there made a newé chaunge.
The paien goth, the Jewe alofte
Was set upon his assé softe.
So gone they forth carpénde faste
On this and that, till atté laste
The paien mighté go no more
And praide unto the Jew therfore
To suffre him ride a litel while.
The Jew, which thought him to beguile,
Anone rode forth the greté pas
And to the paien in this cas
He saidé: 'Thou hast do thy right
Of that thou haddest me behight
To do succoúr upon my nede,
And that accordeth to the dede,
As thou art to the lawé holde.
And in such wise, as I the tolde,
I thenke also for my partie
Upon the lawe of Jewerie
To worche and do my duëté.
Thin assé shall go forth with me
With all thy good, which I have sesed,
And that I wot thou art disesed
I am right glad and nought mispaid.'
And whan he hath these wordés said,
In allé haste he rode away.
"This paien wot none other way,
But on the grounde he kneleth even,
His handés up unto the heven,
And said: 'O highe sothfastnesse,
That lovest alle rightwisnesse,
Unto thy dome, lorde, I appele,
Beholde and demé my queréle
With humble herte I the beseche,
The mercy bothe and eke the wreche

I set all in thy jugément.'
And thus upon his marrément
This paien hath made his preiere.
And than he rose with drery chere
And goth him forth, and in his gate
He cast his eye about algate
The Jewe if that he mighté se.
But for a time it may nought be,
Till atté last ayein the night,
So as God wolde he went aright
As he which held the highé wey,
And than he sigh in a valley,
Where that the Jewé liggend was,
All bloody, dede upon the gras,
Which straungled was of a leon.
And as he lokéd up and down,
He found his assé fasté by
Forth with his harneis redely
All hole and sound as he it lefte
Whan that the Jewe it him berefte :
Wherof he thonkéd God knelende.
"Lo, thus a man may knowe at ende,
How the pitoús pité deserveth.
For what man that to Pité serveth,
As Aristotle it bereth witnésse,
God shall his fomen so represse,
That they shall ay stond under fote.
Pité men sain is thilké rote
Wherof the vertues springen alle.
What infortúné that befalle
In any lond, lack of Pité
Is cause of thilke adversité ;
And that alday may shewe at eye,
Who that the world discretely sigh.
Good is that every man therfore
Take hede of that is said to-fore.
For of this tale and other inowe
These noble princes whilom drowe
Her evidence and her apprise,
As men may finde in many a wise,
Who that these oldé bokés rede.
And though they ben in erthé dede,
Her godé namé may nought deie
For Pité which they wold obey
To do the dedés of mercý.
And who this talé redelý
Remembre, as Aristótle it tolde,
He may the will of God beholde
Upon the point as it was ended,
Wherof that Pité stood commended,
Whiche is to Charité felawe,
As they that kepen both o lawe.
"Of Pité for to speké pleine,
Which is with mercy well beseine,
Full ofte he woll him selvé peine
To kepe an other fro the peine.
For Charité the moder is
Of Pité, which nothíng amis
Can suffre if he it may amende.
It sit to every man livénde
To be pitoús, but none so wele
As to a king, which on the whele
Fortúne hath set aboven all.
For in a king, if so befalle
That his pité be ferme and stable,
To all the londe it is vailable
Only through grace of his persone.
For the pité of him alone
May all the largé roialme save.
So sit it wel a king to have
Pité. For this Valeiré tolde
And said, how that by daiés olde
Codrus, which was in his degree
King of Athénés the citee,
A werre he had ayein Dorence.
And for to take his evidence,
What shall befalle of the bataile,
He thought he wolde him first counseile
With Ápolló, in whom he triste,
Through whose answeré thus he wiste
Of two points that he mighté chese,—
Or that he wolde his body lese
And in bataile him selvé deie,
Or ellés the secónde wey
To seen his people discomfíte.
But he, which Pité hath parfite

Upon the point of his beleve,
The people thoughté to releve
And chese him selvé to be dede.
Where is now such another hede
Which woldé for the limmés die?
And nethéles in some partie
It ought a kingés herté stere
That he his legé men forbere.
And eke toward his enemíes
Full ofte he may deservé prise
To take of Pité remembraunce ·
Where that he mighté do vengeaúnce.
For whan a king hath the victoire
And than he drawe into memoire
To do pité in stede of wreche
He may nought fail of thilké speche
Wherof arist the worldés fame,
To yive a prince a worthy name.
"I rede, how whilom that Pompéy,
To whom that Romé must obey,
A werré had in jeopartie
Ayein the king of Armenie,
Which of long time him haddé greved.
But atté last it was acheved,
That he this king discomfit hadde
And forth with him to Romé ladde
As prisonér, where many a day
In sory plite and pouer he lay,
The coróne on his hede deposed,
Withinné wallés fast enclosed.
And with full great humilité
He suffreth his adversité.
Pompeié sigh his paciénce
And toke pité with consciénce,
So that upon his highé deis
To-fore all Rome in his paleis,
As he that wolde upon him rewe,
Let yive him his coróné newe
And his estate all full and pleine
Restoreth of his regne ayein
And said, 'it was more goodly thing
To maké than undone a king,
To him which power had of bothe.'
Thus they, that weren bothé wrothe,
Accorden hem to finall pees.
And yet justícé nethélees
Was kept and in nothíng offended,
Wherof Pompéy is yet commended.
There may no king him self excuse
But if justíce he kepe and use,
Which, for to escheué crueltė,
He mote attempre with Pité.
Of crueltė the feloný
Engendred is of tiranný,
Ayein the whose conditión
God is him self the champión
Whose strengthé may no man withstonde.
For ever yet it hath so stonde
That God a tiraunt over ladde.
But where Pité the reiné ladde
There mighté no fortúné last,
Which was grevoús. But atté last
The God him self it hath redressed.
Pité is thilké vertue blessed,
Which never let his maister falle.
But Crueltė though it so falle
That it may regné for a throwe,
God woll it shall ben over throwe,
Wherof ensamples ben inough
Of hem that thilké merel drowe.[1]
Of cruelte I redé thus,
Whan the tiránt Leoncius
Was to thempíre of Rome arrived,
Fro which he hath with strengthé prived
The pietoús Justinián,
As he which was a cruel man,
His nase of and his lippés both
He kutté, for he wolde him loth
Unto the people and make unable.
But he which all is merciáble,
The highé God ordeineth so,
That he within a time also,

[1] *Thilke merel drowe*, suffered that pain. *Traire la merele*, in old French, meant to expose oneself to danger, endure pain or fatigue (Godefroy).

Whan he was strongest in his ire,
Was shoven out of his empire.
Tiberius the power hadde
And Rome after his will he ladde,
And for Leonce in suche a wise
Ordeineth that he toke juise
Of nase and lippés bothé two,
For that he did another so
Which moré worthy was than he.
Lo, which a fall hath Crueltè,
And Pité was set up ayein.
For after that the bokés sain,
Terbellis king of Bulgarie
With helpe of his chivalerie
Justinian hath unprisóned
And to thempire ayein coróned.
"In a cronique I finde also
Of Siculus, which was eke so
A cruel king like the tempést,
The whom no pité might arest.
He was the first, as bokés say,
Upon the see which found galéy
And let hem maké for the werre,
As he which all was out of herre[1]
Fro pité and misericorde,
For therto couthe he nought accorde;
But whom he mighté slain he slough,
And therof was he glad inough.
He had of counseil many one,
Among the whiché there was one,
By namé which Perillus hight.
And he bethought him, how he might
Unto the tirant do likíng.
And of his own ymaginíng
Let forge and make a bulle of bras,
And on the sidé cast there was
A doré, where a man may inne
Whan he his peiné shall beginne
Through firé which that men put under.
And all this did he for a wonder,
That whan a man for peiné cride,
The bull of bras, which gapeth wide,
It shuldé seme as though it were
A bellewing in a mannés ere
And nought the crieng of a man.
But he which alle sleightés can,
The Devil that lith in hellé fast,
Him that it cast hath overcast,
That for a trespas which he dede
He was put in the samé stede,
And was him self the first of alle
Which was into that peiné falle
That he for other men ordeigneth.
There was no man that him compleigneth.
Of tyranný and crueltè
By this ensample a king may se
Him selfe and eke his counseil bothe,
How they ben to mankindé lothe
And to the God abhominàble.
Ensamples that ben concordáble
I finde of other princes mo,
As thou shalt here of time ago.
"The grete tirant Dionise,
Which mannés life set of no prise,
Unto his hors full ofte he yafe
The men in stede of corne and chafe.
So that the hors of thilké stood[1]
Devoureden the mannés blood,
Till fortune atté lasté came
That Hercules him overcame,
And he right in the samé wise
Of this tiránt toke the juíse.
As he till other men hath do
The samé deth he deied also,
That no pité him hath socoúred
Till he was of his hors devoured.
"Of Lichaón also I finde,
How he ayein the lawe of kinde
His hostés slough and into mete
He made her bodies to ben ete
With other men within his hous.
But Jupiter the glorioús,
Which was commeved of this thing,
Vengeaúnce upon this cruel king

[1] *Out of herre*, unhinged, broken away.

[1] *Stood*, stud.

So toke that he fro mannés forme
Into a wolfe him let transforme.
And thus the cruelté was kid
Which of long timé he hath hid.
A wolfe he was than openly,
The whose natúré prively
He had in his condición.
And unto this conclusión
That tiranny is to despise,
I finde ensample in sondry wise
And namélich of hem full ofte,
The whom Fortúne hath set alofte
Upon the werrés for to winne.
But how so that the wrong beginne
Of tirannẏ́, it may nought laste,
But suche as they done atté laste
To other men suche on hem falleth.
For ayein suché pité calleth
Vengeaúncé to the God above.
For who that hath no tendre love
In saving of a mannés life,
He shall be foundé so giltife
That whan he woldé mercy crave,
In time of nede he shall none have.
"Of the natúré this I finde,
The fiercé león in his kinde,
Which goth rampénd aftér his pray,
If he a man finde in his way
He woll him slain if he withstonde.
But if the man couth understonde
To fall anone to-fore his face
In signe of mercy and of grace,
The leon shall of his natúre
Restreigne his ire in such mesúre
As though it were a besté tamed,
And torne awey halfíng ashamed,
That he the man shall nothing greve.
How shuldé than a prince acheve
The worldés grace, if that he wolde
Destruie a man whan he is yolde
And stant upon his mercy all?
"But for to speke in speciáll
There have be such and yet there be,
Tiraunts, whose hertés no pité
May to no point of mercy ply,
That they upon her tiranny
Ne gladen hem the men to slee.
And as the rages of the see
Ben unpitoús in the tempést,
Right so may no pité arest
Of cruelté the great oultráge,
Which the tiraúnt in his coráge
Engendred hath, wherof I finde
A talé, which cometh now to minde.
I rede in oldé bokés thus,
There was a duke, which Spertachus
Men clepe, and was a werrioúr,
A cruel man, a conqueroúr
With strongé power which he lad.
For this conditión he had,
That where him hapneth thė victoire,
His lust and all his mosté gloire
Was for to slee and nought to save.
Of raunsom wolde he no good have
For saving of a mannés life,
But all goth to the swerde and knife
So lefe him was the mannés blood.
And nethéles yet thus it stood,
So as Fortúne abouté went,
He fell right heire as by descent
To Pers and was corónéd king.
And whan the worship of this thing
Was falle, and he was kinge of Perse,
If that they weren first diverse,
The tiranníés which he wrought,
A thousand fold wel more he sought
Than afterward to do malíce,
Till God vengeaúnce ayein the vice
Hath shapé. For upon a tide,
Whan he was highest in his pride,
In his rancoúr and in his hete,
Ayein the quene of Massegete,
Which Thamarís that timé hight,
He madé werre all that he might.
And she which wolde her lond defende
Her owné sone ayein him sende
Which the defence hath undertake,
But he discomfit was and take.

And whan this king him had in honde,
He wol no mercy understonde,
But did him sleen in his presénce.
The tiding of this violence
Whan it cam to the moders ere,
She sende anone ay widé where
To suché frendés as she had,
A great powér till that she lad
In sondry wise, and tho she cast
How she this king may overcast.
And atté last accorded was,
That in the daunger of a pas,
Through which this tiraunt shuldé pas,
She shope his power to compas
With strength of men by such a wey
That he shall nought escape awey.
And whan she haddé thus ordeigned,
She hath her owné body feigned
For fere as though she woldé flee
Out of her londe. And whan that he
Hath herde how that this lady fledde,
So fast after the chace he spedde,
That he was founde out of array.
For it betid upon a day
Into the pas whan he was falle,
Thembusshéments to-breken alle
And him beclipt on every side,
That flee ne might he nought aside.
So that there weren dede and take
Two hundred thousand for his sake
That weren with him of his hoste.
And thus was laid the greté boste
Of him and of his tiranny.
It halp no mercy for to cry
To him which whilom didé none.
For he unto the quene anone
Was brought, and whan that she him sigh,
This word she spake and said on high:
'O man, which óut of mannés kinde
Resón of man hast left behinde
And livéd worsé than a beste
Whom pité mighté nought areste;
The mannés blood to shede and spille,
Thou haddest never yet thy fille,
But now the lasté time is come,
That thy malíce is overcome;
As thou till other men hast do,
Now shall be do to the right so.'
Tho bad this lady that men sholde
A vessel bringe, in which she wolde
Se the vengeaúnce of his juíse
Which she began anone devise,
And toke the princes which he ladde,
By whom his chefe counséil he hadde.
And while hem lasteth any breth,
She made hem bledé to the deth
Into the vessel where it stood,
And whan it was fulfild of blood,
She casté this tiraúnt therinne
And said him: 'Lo, thus might thou winne
The lustés of thine appetite.
In blood was whilom thy delite,
Now shalt thou drinken all thy fille.'
And thus onlich of Goddes wille
He which that wolde him selven straunge
To pité, found mercý so straunge
That he withouté grace is lore.
"So may it shewé well therefore,
That crueltè hath no good ende.
But pité how so that it wende
Maketh that God is merciáble,
If there be causé resonáble,
Why that a King shall be pitoús.
But ellés if he be doubtoús
To sleen in cause of rightwisnesse,
It may be said no pitousnesse
But it is pusillamité,
Whiche every princé shuldé flee.
For if pité mesúre excede,
Knighthodé may nought wel procede

To do justíse upon the right.
For it belongeth to a knight
As gladly for to fight as reste
To set his legé people in reste
Whan that the werre upon hem falleth.
For than he mote as it befalleth
Of his knighthode as a león
Be to the people a champión
Withouten any pité feigned.
For if manhodé be restreigned,
Or be it pees or be it werre,
Justicé goth all out of herre,
So that knighthode is set behinde.
"Of Aristotles lore I finde,
A King shall maké good viságe
That no man knowe of his coráge
But all honoúr and worthinesse.
For if a King shall upon gesse
Withouté verray causé drede,
He may be liche to that I rede,—
And though that be liche to a fable,
Thensample is good and resonáble.
"As it by olde daiés fell,
I redé whilóm that an hill
Up in the londés of Archade
A wonder dredfull noise it made.
For so it fell that ilké day,
This hill on his childingé lay.
And whan the throwés on him come,
His noisé lich the day of dome
Was ferefull in a mannés thought
Of thing which that they sighé nought.
But well they herden all aboute
The noise of which they were in doubte,
As they that wenden to be lore
Of thing which thanné was unbore.
The nere this hill was upon chaunce
To taken his deliveraunce,
The more unbuxomlich he cride;
And every man was fled aside
For drede and left his owné hous.
And atté last it was a mous
The which was bore and to norice
Betake. And tho they helde hem nice,
For they withouté causé dradde.
Thus if a King his herté ladde
With every thing that he shall here,
Ful ofte he shuldé chaunge his chere
And upon fantasíë drede
Whan that there is no cause of drede.
Oracé to his princé tolde,
That him were lever that he wolde
Upon knighthode 'Achillem sue
In time of werré than escheue
So as Thersites did at Troy.
Achilles al his holé joy
Set upon armés for to fight;
Thersites sought all that he might
Unarméd for to stonde in reste.
But of the two it was the beste,
That Áchillés upon the nede
Hath do, wherof his knightlihede
Is yet commended overall.
King Salomon in speciáll
Saith: 'As there is a time of pees,
So is a timé nethéles
Of werre, in whiche a prince algate
Shall for the comun right debate
And for his owné worship eke.
But it behoveth nought to seke
Only the werré for worship,
But to the right of his lordship
Which he is holdé to defende
Mote every worthy prince entende
Betwene the simplesse of pité
And the foolhaste of crueltć.
Where stant the verray hardiesse,
There mote a king his herte adresse,
Whan it is timé to forsake
And whan time is also to take
The dedly werrés upon honde,
That he shall for no dredé wonde[1]
If rightwisnessé be withall.
For God is mighty over all

[1] *Wonde*, turn aside.

To furtheren every mannés trouthe;
But it be through his owné slouthe,
And namély the kingés nede
It may nought failé for to spede.
For he stant oné for hem alle,
So mote it well the better falle.
And wel the moré God favoúreth,
Whan he the comun right socoúreth.
And for to se the soth in dede,
Behold the bible and thou might rede
Of great ensamples many one,
Wherof that I wil tellen one.
"Upon a time as it befell
Ayein Judé and Israël,
Whan sondry kingés comé were
In purpos to destruié there
The people which God kepté tho,
It stood in thilké daiés so,
That Gedeon, which shuldé lede
The Goddés folk, toke him to rede
And sende in all the lond aboute,
Till he assembled hath a route
With thritty thousand of defence
To fight and maké resistence
Ayein the which hem wolde assaile.
And nethéles that o bataile[1]
Of thre that weren enemis,
Was double more than was all his,
Wherof that Gedeon him drad,
That he so litel people had.
But he which allé thing may helpe,
Where that there lacketh mannés
helpe,
To Gedeon his aungel sent
And bad, er that he further went,
All openly that he do cry
That every man in his party
Which wolde after his owné will
In his delite abidé still
At home in any maner wise
For purchace or for covetise,
For lust of love or lacke of herte,
He shuldé nought abouté sterte
But holde him still at home in pees.

[1] *Bataile*, army.

Wherof upon the morwe he lees
Wel twenty thousand men and mo
The which after the cry ben go.
Thus was with him but only left
The thriddé parte, and yet God eft
His aungel send and saidé this
To Gedeon: 'If it so is
That I thin help shall undertake,
Thou shalt yet lassé people take
By whom my will is that thou spede.
Forthý to morwe take good hede
Unto the flood whan ye be come,
What man that hath the water nome
Up in his hande and lappeth so,
To thy part chese out allé tho,
And him which wery is to swinke
Upon his wombe and lith to drinke
Forsake, and put hem al awey.
For I am mighty allé wey
Where as me list min help to shewe
In godé men though they be fewe.
"This Gedeon awaiteth wele
Upon the morwe and every dele,
As God him bad, right so he dede.
And thus ther leften in that stede
With him thre hundred and no mo,
The remenaunt was all ago.
Wherof that Gedeon mervéileth
And therupon with God counséileth
Pleining as ferforth as he dare.
And God, which wolde he weré ware
That he shall spede upon his right,
Hath bede him go the samé night
And take a man with him to here
What shall be spoke in this matere
Among the hethen enemies,
So may he be the moré wise,
What afterwarde him shall befalle.
This Gedeon amongés alle
Phara, to whom he tristé most,
By night toke toward thilké host,
Which loggéd was in a valey,
To heré what they wolden say.
Upon his fote and as he ferde
Two Sarazins spekénd he herde.

Quod one: 'Arede my sweven[1]
aright,
Whiche I met[2] in my slepe to-night.
Me thought I sigh a barly cake,
Which fro the hille his wey hath take
And comé rollend down at ones,
And as it weré for the nones
Forth in his cours so as it ran
The kingés tent of Madian,
Of Amalech, of Amorie,
Of Amon and of Jebuseie
And many another tenté mo
With greté noise as me thought tho
It threw to grounde and over cast
And all his host so sore agast,
That I awoke for puré drede.'
'This sweven can I well arede,'
Quod thother Sarazin anone,
'The barly cake is Gedeon,
Which fro the hill down sodeinly
Shall come and setté such askry
Upon the kingés and us both,
That it shall to us allé lothe.
For in such drede he shall us bringe,
That if we haddé flight of winge,
The wey one fote in our despeire
We sholden leve and flee in thaire.[3]
For there shal nothing him with-
stonde.'
Whan Gedeon hath understonde
This tale, he thonketh God of alle,
And privelich ayein he stalle,
So that no life[4] him hath perceived.
And than he hath fullý conceived,
That he shall spede. And therupon
The night suénd he shope to gone
This multitúdé to assaile.
Now shalt thou here a great
merveile,
With what wisdómé that he wrought.
The litel people which he brought
Was none of hem that he ne hath
A pot of erthe, in whiche he tath
A light brennínġ in a cressét,
And eche of hem eke a trompét
Bare in his other hond beside.
And thus upon the nightés tide
Duke Gedeón whan it was derke
Ordeineth him unto his werke,
And parteth than his folke in thre
And chargeth hem that they ne flee,
And taught hem how they shuld
askrý
All in o vois par compaigný.
And what worde eke they shuldé
speke,
And how they shulde her pottés
breke
Echone with other, whan they herde
That he him selvé first so ferde.
For whan they come into the stede,
He bad hem do right as he dede.
And thus stalkéndé forth a pas
This noble duke whan timé was
His pot to-brake and loude askríde,
And tho they breke on every side.
The trompé was nought for to seke,
He blewe and so they blewen eke
With such a noise amonge hem
alle,
As though the heven shuldé falle.
The hill unto her vois answérde.
This hoste in the valéy it herde
And sigh how that hill was alight,
So what of hering and of sight
They caughten such a sodein fere,
That none of hem be lefté there.
The tentés holy they forsoke
That they none other good ne toke,
But only with her body bare
They fledde, as doth the wildé hare.
And ever upon the hill they blewe
Till that they sighen time and knewe
That they be fled upon the rage.
And whan they wiste their avaun-
táge,
They fell anone unto the chace.

[1] *Sweven*, dream. [2] *Met*, dreamt.
[3] In our despair we should leave the way of going on foot, and fly in the air.
[4] *No life*, nobody.

"Thus might thou se, how Goddes grace
Unto the godé men availeth.
But elles ofté time it faileth
To such as be nought well disposed.
This talé nedeth nought be glosed,
For it is openliché shewed,
That God to hem that ben well thewed
Hath yove and graunted the victoire,
So that thensample of this histoire
Is good for every King to holde.
First in himself that he beholde
If he be good of his living,
And that the folk which he shal bring
Be good also, for than he may
Be glad of many a mery day
In what that ever he hath to done.
For he which sit above the mone
And allé thing may spill and spede
In every cause and every nede,
His godé King so well adresseth,
That all his fomen he represseth,
So that there may no man him dere.
And also well he can forbere
And suffre a wicked king to falle
In hondés of his fomen alle.
"Now furthermore if I shall sain
Of my matere and torne ayein
To speke of Justice and Pité
After the reule of Realté,
This may a King well understonde,
Knighthodé mot be take on honde
Whan that it stant upon the nede,
He shall no rightfull causé drede,
No more of werré than of pees,
If he woll stondé blaméles.
For suche a cause a king may have,
That better him is to slee than save;
Wherof thou might ensample finde.
The highé maker of mankinde
By Samuel to Saül bad,
That he shall nothing ben adrad
Ayein king Agag for to fight.
For this the Godhede him behight,
That Agag shall be overcome.
And whan it is so ferforth come,
That Saül hath him descomfite,
The God bad maké no respíte,
That he ne shulde him sleen anone.
But Saül let it overgone
And didé nought the Goddés heste.
For Agag made a great beheste [1]
Of raunsom which he woldé yive.
King Saül suffreth him to live
And feigneth pité forth withall.
But he which seeth and knoweth all,
The highé God, of that he feigneth
To Samuel upon him pleigneth,
And send him word for that he lefte
Of Agag that he ne berefte
The life, he shall nought only deie
Him self, but fro his Regalie
He shall be put for evermo,
Nought he but eke his heire also,
That it shall never come ayein.
"Thus might thou se the sothé plein,
That of to moch and of to lite
Upon the princes stant the wite. [2]
But ever it was a Kingés right
To do the dedés of a knight.
For in the hondés of a King
The dethe and life is all o thing
After the lawés of justíce;
To sleen, it is a dedly vice
But if a man the deth deserve.
And if a king the life preserve
Of him which oughté for to deie,
He sueth nought thensamplarie,
Which in the bible is evident,
How David in his testament,
Whan he no lenger mighté live,
Unto his sone in charge hath yive,
That he Joáb shall sleen algate.
And whan Davíd was gone his gate,
The yongé wisé Salomone

[1] *Beheste*, promise.
[2] *Wite*, blame.

His faders hesté did anone
And slew Joáb in such a wise,
That they that herden the juſse
Ever after dradden him the more.
And God was eke well paid therfore
That he so wolde his herté ply
The lawés for to justify.
And yet he kepté forth withall
Pité, so as a princé shall,
That he no tirannſë wrought.
He found the wisdom which he sought,
And was so rightfull nethéles
That all his life he stood in pees,
That he no dedly werrés had,
For every man his wisdom drad.
And as he was him selvé wise,
Right so the worthy men of prise
He hath of his counséil witholde,
For that is every princé holde
To make of such his retenue
Which wisé ben, and to remue
The foolés. For there is no thing,
Which may be better about a king
Than counseil, which is the substaúnce
Of all a kingés governaúnce.
"**In Salomon** a man may se,
What thing of most necessité
Unto a worthy King belongeth,
Whan he his kingdom underfongeth.
God bad him chesé what he wolde
And saide him that he havé sholde
What he wold axe, as of o thing.
And he, which was a newé king,
Forth therupon his boné [1] praide
To God, and in this wisé saide:
'O king, by whom that I shall regne,
Yive me Wisdóme that I my regne
Forth with the people which I have
To thin honóur may kepe and save.'
Whan Salomon his bone hath taxed,
The God of that which he hath axed
Was right well paid and graunteth sone
Nought all onlý that he his bone
Shall have of that, but of richesse,
Of hele, of pees, of high noblesse,
Forth with Wisdóm at his axinges,
Which stant above all other thinges.
"But what king woll his regné save,
First him behoveth for to have
After the God and his beleve
Such counseil which is to beleve [1]
Fullfild of trouth and rightwisnesse.
But above all in his noblésse
Betwene the reddour and pité
A king shall do suche equité
And setté the balaunce in even,
So that the highé God in heven
And all the people of his nobley
Loënge [2] unto his namé say.
For most above all erthly good,
Where that a king him self is good,
It helpeth; for in other wey
If so be that a king forswey, [3]
Full oft er this it hath be sain,
The comun people is overlain
And hath the Kingés sin abought [4]
All though the people agulté nought.
Of that the King his God misserveth,
The people taketh that he deserveth;
Here in this world, but ellés where
I not how it shall stondé there.
Forthý good is a king to triste
First to him self, as he ne wiste
None other help but God allone,
So shall the reule of his persone
Within him self through providénce
Ben of the better consciénce.
And for to finde ensample of this

[1] *Bone*, boon.

[1] *Beleve*, remain. [2] *Loënge*, praise.
[3] *Forswey*, become remiss, not awake to his duty.
[4] *Abought*, paid for, suffered for.

A tale I rede, and soth it is.
"*In a cronique* it telleth thus,
The King of Romé Luciús
Within his chambre upon a night
The steward of his hous a knight
Forth with his chamberlein also
To counseil haddé bothé two,
And stoden by the chiménée
To-gider spekend allé thre.
And hapneth that the Kingés fole
Sat by the fire upon a stole,
As he that with his babel[1] plaide,
And yet he herde all that they saide,
And therof toké they non hede.
The King hem axeth what to rede
Of such matére as cam to mouth.
And they him tolden as they couth.
Whan all was spoke of that they ment,
The King with all his hole entent
That atté last hem axeth this,
What King men tellen that he is
Among the folk touchénd his name,
Or it be pris, or it be blame,
Right after that they herden sain
He bad hem for to telle it plein,
That they no point of soth forbere
By thilké feith that they him bere.
"The steward first upon this thing
Yaf his answére unto the King
And thoughté glose in this matére
And said, als fer as he can here,
His name is good and honouráble.
Thus was the steward favouráble,
That he the trouthé plein ne tolde.
The King than axeth, as he sholde,
The chamberlein of his avise,
And he, that was subtil and wise
And somdele thought upon his feith,
Him tolde, how all the people saith,
That if his counseil weré trewe,
They wisté thanné well and knewe,
That of him self he shuldé be
A worthy King in his degré.

[1] *Babel*, bauble.

And thus the counseil he accuseth
In party, and the king excuseth.
"The fool, which herde of all the cas,
What time as Goddés willé was,
Sigh, that they saiden nought inough,
And hem to scorné bothé lough,
And to the king he saidé tho:
'Sir king, if that it weré so
Of wisdome in thin owné mode,
That thou thy selven weré good,
Thy counseil shuldé nought be bad.'
The king therof merveilé had,
Whan that a fool so wisely spake,
And of him self found out the lacke
Within his owné consciënce.
And thus the foolés evidence,
Which was of goddés grace enspired,
Maketh, that good counseil was desired.
He put awey the viciós
And toke to him the vertuós.
The wrongfull lawés ben amended,
The londés good is well despended,
The people was no more opressed
And thus stood every thing redressed.
For where a king is propre wise
And hath such as him selven is
Of his counséil, it may nought faile,
That every thing ne shal availe.
The Vices thanné gone awey,
And every Vertu holt his wey,
Wherof the highé God is plesed
And all the londés folke is esed.
For if the comun people cry
And than a king list nought to ply
To heré what the clamour wolde,
And other wisé than he sholde
Desdaineth for to done hem grace,
It hath be seen in many place,
There hath befallé great contraire,
And that I finde of ensamplaire.

"After the deth of Salomone,
Whan thilké wisé king was gone
And Roboás in his persóne
Receivé shuldé the coróne,
The people upon a parlemént
Avised were of one assent
And all unto the king they preiden
With comun vois and thus they saiden:
'Our legé lord, we the beseche,
That thou receive our humble speche
And graunt us that which reson will
Or of thy grace or of thy skill.
Thy fader, while he was alive
And mighté bothé graunt and prive,
Upon the werkés which he had
The comun people streité lad,
Whan he the temple madé newe.
Thing which men never afore knewe
He brought up than of his talláge,
And all was under the viságe
Of werkés which he madé tho.
But now it is befallé so,
That all is made right, as he saide,
And he was riché whan he deide.
So that it is no maner nede,
If thou therof wolt taken hede,
To pilen of the people more,
Which long time hath be grevéd sore.
And in this wise as we the say,
With tender herté we the prey,
That thou relessé thilké dette,
Which upon us thy fader sette.
And if the liké to done so,
We ben thy men for evermo
To gone and comen at thin heste.'
"The King, which herdé this requeste,
Saith, that he woldé ben avised,
And hath therof a time assised,
And in the while as he him thought
Upon this thing counseil he sought.
And first the wisé knightés olde,
To whom that he his talé tolde,
Counseillen him in this manére,
That he with love and with glad chere
Foryive and graunt all that is axed
Of that his fader haddé taxed.
For so he may his regne acheve
With thing which shall hem litel greve.
"The King hem herd and over passeth
And with these other his wit compásseth
That yongé were and nothing wise.
And they these oldé men despise
And saiden: 'Sir, it shall be shame
For ever unto thy worthy name,
If thou ne kepé nought thy right,
While thou art in thy yongé might,
Which that thin oldé fader gat.
But say unto the people plat,
That while thou livest in thy londe,
The lesté finger of thin honde
It shall be stronger over all,
Than was thy faders body all.
And thus also shall be thy tale,—
If he hem smote with roddés smale,
With scorpións thou shalt hem smite.
And where thy fader toke a lite,
Thou thenkest také mochel more,
Thus shalt thou make hem dredé sore
The greté hert of thy coráge,
So for to holde hem in servage.'
"This yongé king him hath conformed
To done as he was last enformed,
Which was to him his undoíng.
For whan it came to the spekíng,
He hath the yongé counseil holde,
That he the samé wordés tolde
Of all the people in audiénce.
And whan they herden the senténce
Of his malíce and the manáce,
Anone to-fore his owné face

They have him oultrely refused
And with full great reproveaccused.
So they beginné for to rave,
That he was faine him self to save.
For as the wildé wodé rage
Of windés maketh the see salvage
And that was calm bringth into wawe,
So for defalt and grace of lawe,
The people is steréd all at ones
And forth they gone out of his wones,
So that of the lignáges twelve,
Two tribus onely by hem selve
With him abiden and no mo.
So weré they for evermo
Of no retorne without espeire
Departed fro the rightfull heire
Of Israel with comun vois.
A king upon her owné chois
Among hem self anone they make
And have her yongé lord forsake.
A pouer knight Jeróboás
They toke and lefté Roboás,
Which rightfull heire was by descent.
Lo, thus the yongé causé went,
For that the counseil was nought good
The regné fro the rightfull blood
Ever afterward devided was.
So may it proven by this cas,
That yong counséil, which is to warme,
Or men beware, doth ofté harme.
Old agé for the counseil serveth,
And lusty youth his thank deserveth
Upon the travail which he doth.
And bothé for to say a soth
By sondry causé for to have,
If that he will his regné save,
A king behoveth every day,
That one can and that other may
Be so the kinge hem bothé reule,
Or ellés all goth out of reule.
"And upon this matere also
A questión betwene the two
Thus writen in a boke I fonde,
Where[1] it be better for the londe
A King him selvé to be wise
And so to bere his owné prise,
And that his counseil be nought good;
Or otherwise if it so stood,
A King if he be viciós
And his counséil be vertuós:
It is answerde in suche a wise,
That better it is that they be wise,
By whom that the counséil shall gone.
For they be many, and he is one,
And rather shall an oné man
With fals counséil, for ought he can,
From his wisdóme be made to fall,
Than he aloné shuld hem all
Fro vices into vertue chaunge,
For that is well the moré straunge.
Forthý the lond may well be glad,
Whose king with good counséil is lad,
Which set him unto rightwisnesse,
So that his highé worthinesse
Betwene the reddour and pité
Doth mercy forth with equité.
A king is holden over all
To pité, but in speciall
To hem, where he is most beholde,
They shulde his pité most beholde
That ben the leges of the londe,
For they ben ever under his honde
After the goddés ordenaúnce
To stonde upon his governaúnce.
Of themperour Anthonius
I find, how that he saidé thus:
'Lever him weré for to save
One of his legés than to have
Of enemies a thousand dede.'
And thus he lernéd as I rede
Of Cipio, which haddé be
Consul of Rome. And thus to se

[1] *Where*, whether.

Divers ensamples how they stonde,
A King, which hath the charge on
honde
The comun people to govérne,
If that he woll, he may well lerne
Is none so good to the plesaúnce
Of God, as is good governaúnce.
And every governaúnce is due
To pité; thus I may argue
That pité is the foundement
Of every Kinges regiment.
If it be medled with justice,
They two remeven allé Vice
And ben of Vertue most vailable
To make a Kingés regné stable.
"Lo, thus the fouré points to-fore
In Governaunce as they ben bore
Of Trouthé first and of Largesse,
Of Pité forth with Rightwisnesse,
I have hem tolde. And over this
The fifté point, so as it is
Set of the reule of Policý,
Wherof a king shall modefy
The fleshly lustés of natúre,
Now thenke I telle of such mesure,
That bothé kindé shall be served
And eke the lawe of God observed.
"It sit a man by wey of kinde
To lové, but it is nought kinde
A man for love his wit to lese.
For if the month of Juil shall frese
And that December shall be hote,
The yere mistorneth wel I wote.
To seen a man from his estate
Through his sotý effeminate
And levé that a man shall do,
It is as hose above the sho
To man, which ought nought to be
used.
But yet the world hath oft accused
Full greté princes of this dede,
How they for love hem self mislede,
Wherof manhodé stood behinde
Of olde ensamples as men finde.
These olde gestes tellen thus,
That whilom Sardanapallus,
Which held all hole in his empire
The greté kingdom of Assire,
Was through the slouth of his
coráge
Fall into thilké firy rage
Of lové which the men assoteth,
Wherof him self he so rióteth,
And wax so ferforth womanissh,
That ayein kinde, as if a fissh
Abidé wold upon the londe,
In women suche a luste he fonde,
That he dwelt ever in chambre still
And only wrought after the will
Of women, so as he was bede,
They taughten him a lace to braide
And weve a purs and to enfile
A perle. And fell that ilké while,
One Arbactus the prince of Mede
Sigh how this king in womanhede
Was fallé fro chiválerié,
And gate him helpe and compaignie
And wroughté so that atté last
This king out of his regne he cast,
Which was undone for ever mo.
And yet men speken of him so,
That it is shamé for to here;
Forthý to love is in manere.
For where a prince his lustés sueth,
That he the werré nought pursueth,
Whan it is timé to bene armed,
His contré stant full ofté harmed,
Whan thenemiés ben woxé bolde,
That they defencé none beholde.
Full many a londe hath so be lore,
As men may rede oft time afore
Of hem that so her eses soughten,
Which after they full dere aboughten.
To mochel ese is nothing worth,
For that set every vicé forth
And every vertue put a backe,
Wherof pris torneth into lacke,
As in cronique I may reherse,
Which telleth, how the king of Perse
That Cyrus hight, a werré hadde

Ayein the people which he dradde
Of a contré which Lidos hight.
But yet for ought that he do might
As in bataile upon the werre,
He had of hem alway the werre.[1]
And whan he sigh and wist it wele,
That he by strengthé wan no dele,
Than atté last he cast a wile
This worthy people to beguile
And toke with hem a feignéd pees,
Which shuldé lasten endelees,
So as he saide in wordés wise,
But he thought all in other wise.
For it betid upon the cas
Whan that this people in resté was
They token eses many folde,
And worldés ese as it is tolde
By way of kinde is the norſce
Of every lust which toucheth vice.
Thus whan they were in lustés falle,
The werrés ben forgotten alle.
Was none which woldé the worshſp
Of armés, but in idelship
They putten besinesse away
And token hem to daunce and play,
And every man doth what him liste.
But whan the king of Perse it wiste,
That they unto folie entenden,
With his powér, whan they lest
wenden,
More sodeinly than doth the thunder
He came for ever and put hem under.
And thus hath lecherſë lore
The londé which had be to-fore
The best of hem that weré tho.
"And in the bible I finde also
A talé lich unto this thing,
How Amalech the paien king,
Whan that he mighté by no wey
Defend his londe and put awey
The worthy people of Israel,
This Sarazin, as it befell,
Through the counsell of Balaäm
A rout of fairé women nam,

[1] *The werre,* the worse.

That lusty were and yonge of age,
And bad hem gon to the lignage
Of these Hebrews. And forth they
went
With eyen grey and browés bent
And well arraiéd everychone.
And whan they comé were anone
Among thebrews, was none in sight
But cacché who that cacché might,
And grace anone began to faile,
That whan they comen to bataile,
Than afterward in sory plite
They weré take and discomfite,
So that within a litel throwe,
The might of hem was overthrowe,
That whilom weré wont to stonde,
Till Phineës the cause on honde
Hath také this vengeaúncé last.
But than it ceséd atté last.
For God was paid of that he dede,
For where he found upon a stede
A couple which misferdé so
Throughout he smote hem bothé two
And let hem ligge in mennés eye,
Wherof all other which hem sigh
Ensampled hem upon the dede
And praiden unto the godhede
Her oldé sinnés to amende.
And he which wold his mercy sende
Restoréd hem to newé grace.
Thus may it shewe in sondry place
Of chastété how the clennésse
Accordeth to the worthinesse
Of men of armés over all.
But most of all in speciáll
This vertue to a King belongeth,
For upon his fortúne it hongeth
Of that his lond shall spede or spill.
Forthý but if a King his will
Fro lustés of his flessh restreigne,
Ayein him self he maketh a treigne,
Into the whiche if that he slide,
Him weré better go beside.
For every man may understonde
How for a timé that it stonde,

It is a sory lust to like,
Whose endé maketh a man to sike[1]
And torneth joiés into sorwe.
The brighté sonné by the morwe[2]
Beshineth nought the derké night;
The lusty youth of mannés might,
In agé but it stondé wele,
Mistorneth all the lasté whele.
"That every worthy prince is holde
Within him self him self beholde
To se the state of his persóne
And thenke, how there be joiés none
Upon this erthé made to last,
And how the flesshé shall at last
The lustés of his life forsake,
Him ought a great ensample take
Of Salomon, Ecclesiaste,
The fame of whom shall ever laste,
That he the mighty God forsoke,
Ayein the lawé whan he toke
His wivés and his concubines,
Of hem that weré Sarazines,
For which he did ydolatrie.
For this I rede of his sotý,
She of Sidoiné so him ladde,
That he knelénd his armés spradde
To Astrathen with great humblésse,
Which of her lond was the goddesse.
And she that was of Moabite
So ferforth made him to delite
Through lust, which al his wit devoureth,
That he Chamos her god honoúreth.
An other Amonite also
With love him hath assoted so,
Her god Moloch that with encense
He sacreth and doth reverence
In such a wise as she him bad.
Thus was the wisest overlad
With blindé lustés which he sought.
But he it afterward abought.
"For Achiás Selonités,

[1] *Sike*, sigh.
[2] The bright morning sun.

Which was prophét, er his deces,
While he was in his lustés alle,
Betokeneth what shall after falle.
For on a day, whan that he mette
Jeróboam, the knight he grette[1]
And bad him that he shulde abide
To heré what him shall betide.
And forth withall Achias cast
His mantel of, and al so fast
He kut it into pieces twelve,
Wherof two parts toward him selve
He kept, and all the remenaunt,
As God hath set his covenaunt,
He toke unto Jeróboás
Of Nabal which the soné was
And of the kingés court a knight.
And said him, 'Such is Goddés might,
As thou hast sene departed[2] here
My mantel, right in such manere
After the deth of Salomon
God hath ordeinéd therupon,
This regné than he shall devide,
Which timé thou shalt eke abide,
And upon that división
The regne, as in proporción
As thou hast of my mantel take,
Thou shalt receive I undertake.'
O, which a sinné violent,
Wherof so wise a king was shent,
That he vengeaúnce of his persóne
Was nought inough to take alone,
But afterward, whan he was passed,
It hath his heritágé lassed,
As I more openly to-fore
The talé tolde; and thus therfore
The philosóphre upon this thing
Writ and counséiled to a king,
That he the forfete of luxure
Shall tempre and reule of such mesure
Which be to kindé suffisaúnt
And eke to reson accordaúnt,
So that the lustés ignoraúnce

[1] *Grette*, greeted.
[2] *Departed*, divided.

Be cause of no misgovernaúnce,
Through which that he be overthrowe
As he that woll no reson knowe.
"For of Antónie thus I rede,
Which of Sevérus was the sone,
That he his life of comun wone
Yaf holy unto thilké vice,
And ofté time he was so nice,
Wherof natúre her hath compleigned
Unto the God, which hath desdeigned
The werkés which Antónie wrought
Of lust which he full sore abought;
For God his forfete hath so wroke,
That in cronique it is yet spoke.
But for to také rémembraúnce
Of speciáll misgovernaúnce
Through covetise and injustíce
Forth with the remenaunt of vice,
I finde a tale, as thou shalt here,
Which is thensample of this matere.
So as these oldé gestés sain,
The proudé tírannísh Romaín
Tarquinius, which was than king
And wrought manÿ a wrongful thing,
Of sonés he had many one,
Among the which Arrons was one
Lich to his fader in maneres,
So that within a fewé yeres
With treson and with tiranny
They wonne of londe a great partÿ
And token hede of no justíce,
Which dúë was to her offíce
Upon the reule of governaúnce.
But al that ever was plesaúnce
Unto the flesshés lust they toke.
And fell so, that they undertoke
A werré, which was nought acheved,
But often time it had hem greved,
Ayein a folk which thanné hight
The Gabiens, and all by night
Thus Arrons whan he was at home
In Rome a privé place he nome
Within a chambre and bete him selve
And made him woundés ten or twelve
Upon the backe, as it was sene.
And so forth with his hurtés grene
In all the hasté that he may
He rode and cam that other day
Unto Gabíë the citee
And in he went. And whan that he
Was knowe, anone the gatés shette,
The lordés all upon him sette
With drawé swerdés upon honde.
And Arrons wolde hem nought withstonde,
And saide: 'I am here at your wille,
As lefe it is that ye me spille,
As if min owné fader dede.'
And forth within the samé stede
He praide hem that they woldé se;
And shewéd hem in what degré
His fader and his brethren bothe,
Which as he saidé weren wrothe,
Him haddé beten and reviled
And out of Rome for ever exiled.
And thus he made hem to beleve
And saide, if that he might acheve
His purpos, it shall well be yolde
Be so that they him helpé wolde.
Whan that the lordés haddé sene,
How wofully he was besene,
They toké pité of his greve.
But yet it was hem wonder leve
That Rome him had exiléd so.
The Gabiens by counseil tho
Upon the goddés made him swere,
That he to hem shall trouthé bere
And strengthen hem with all his might.
And they also him hath behight
To helpé him in his quarélc.
They shopé thanné for his hele
That he was bathéd and anoint
Till that he was in lusty point,

And what he woldé than he had,
That he all hole the cite lad
Right as he wolde him self devise.
And than he thought him in what wise
He might his tirannïé shewe,
And to his counseil toke a shrewe [1]
Whom to his fader forth he sent.
In his messáge and he tho went
And praied his fader for to say
By his avise and finde a wey
How they the cité mighten winne
While that he stood so well therinne.
And whan the messagér was come
To Rome and hath in counseil nome
The king, it fell perchauncé so
That they were in a gardin tho,
This messager forth with the king.
And whan he haddé told the thing
In what maneré that it stode,
And that Tarquínus understode
By the messáge how that it ferde,
Anone he toke in honde a yerde,
And in the gardin as they gone
The lilie croppés one and one
Where that they weren sprongen out
He smote of as they stood about,
And said unto the messagére:
'Lo, this thing which I do now here
Shall be in stede of thin answére.
And in this wise as I me bere,
Thou shalte unto my soné telle.'
And he no lenger woldé dwelle,
But toke his leve and goth withall
Unto his lorde and tolde him all,
How that his fader haddé do.
Whan Arrons herde him tellé so,
Anone he wisté what it ment,
And therto sette all his entent
Till he through fraude and trecherý
The princes hevedés of Gabý
Hath smiten of and all was wonne.
His fader cam to-fore the sonne

[1] *Shrewe*, plotter of evil.

Into the town with the Romains
And toke and slew the citezeins
Withouté reson or pité,
That he ne spareth no degré.
And for the spede of this conquést
He let do make a riché fest
With a solempné sacrifice
In Phebus temple, and in this wise,
Whan the Romains assembled were
In presence of hem allé there,
Upon thaltér whan all was dight
And that the firés were alight,
From under thalter sodeinly
An hidous serpent openly
Cam out and hath devouréd all
The sacrifice, and eke withall
The firés queint, and forth anone,
So as he cam so is he gone
Into the depé ground ayein.
And every man began to sain,
'Ha lord, what may this signify?'
And therupon they pray and cry
To Phebus, that they mighten knowe
The cause. And he the samé throwe
With gastly vois, that all it herde,
The Romains in this wise answérde
And said, how for the wickednesse
Of pride and of unrightwisnesse
That Tarquin and his sone hath do
The sacrifice is wasted so,
Which mighté nought ben acceptáble
Upon such sinne abhomináble.
And over that yet he hem wisseth
And saith, that which of hem first kisseth
His moder, he shall také wreche
Upon the wronge. And of that speche
They ben within her hertés glade,
Though they outwárd no semblaunt made.
There was a knight, which Brutus hight,
And he with all the haste he might

To groundé fell and there he kiste,
But none of hem the causé wiste,
But wenden that he haddé sporned
Perchaunce and so was overtorned.
But Brutus all an other ment,
For he knew well in his entent,
How therthe of every mannés kinde
Is moder. But they weren blinde
And sighen nought so fer as he.
But whan they leften the citee
And comen home to Rome ayein,
Than every man, which was Romain
And moder hath, to her he bende
And kist, and eche of hem thus wende
To be the first upon the chaunce
Of Tarquin for to do vengeaúnce,
So as they herden Phebus sain.
But every time hath his certain,
So must it nedés than abide,
Till afterward upon a tide
Tarquinius made unskilfully
A werré, which was fasté by,
Ayein a town with wallés stronge,
Which Ardeá was clepéd longe,
And cast a siegé there about
That there may no man passen out.
So it befell upon a night
Arrons, which had his souper dight,
A parte of the chiválerie
With him to suppe in compaignie
Hath bede. And whan they comen were
And setten at the suppé there,
Among her other wordés glade
Arrons a great spekíngé made,—
Who haddé tho the besté wife
Of Rome? And thus began a strife,
For Arrons saith he hath the best.
So janglen they withouten reste,
Till atté last one Collatine,
A worthy knight and was cousine
To Arrons, said him in this wise:
'It is,' quod he, 'of none emprise
To speke a word, but of the dede
Wherof it is to taken hede.
Anone forthý this same tide
Lepe on thy hors and let us ride,
So may we knowé bothé two
Unwarely what our wivés do,
And that shall be a trewe assay.'
"This Arrons saith nought onés nay.
On horséback anone they lepte
In such manere and nothing slepte
Ridéndé forth till that they come
All privelich withinné Rome,
In strangé place and down they light
And take a chambre out of sight.
They be desguised for a throwe,
So that no life [1] hem shuldé knowe:
And to the paleis first they sought
To se what thing these ladies wrought,
Of whiche Arrons had made his vaunt.
And they her sigh of glad semblaunt
All full of merthés and of bordes.[2]
But among all her other wordes
She spake nought of her husébonde.
And whan they had all understonde
Of thilké placé what hem list,
They gone hem forth that none it wist
Besidé thilké gate of bras,
Colláceá which clepéd was,
Where Collatin hath his dwellíng.
There founden they at home sittíng
Lucrece his wife all environéd
With women which were abandóned
To werche, and she wrought eke withall
And bad hem haste and said: 'It shall
Be for min husébondes were,
Which with his swerd and with his spere
Lith at siëge in great disese,
And if it shulde him nought displese,
Now woldé God, I had him here.

[1] *No life*, no body. [2] *Bordes*, jests.

For certes till that I may here
Some good tidíng of his estate,
My herte is ever upon debate.
For so as allé men witnesse,
He is of such an hardiesse,
That he can nought him selvéspare,
And that is all my mosté care
Whan they the wallés shulde assaile.
But if my wisshes might availe,
I wolde it were a groundles pit
Be so the siegé were unknit,
And I my huséhondé sigh.'
With that the water in her eye
Arose, that she ne might it stoppe,
And as men sene the dew bedroppe
The levés and the flourés eke,
Right so upon her whité cheke
The wofull salté terés felle.
"Whan Collatin hath herde her telle
The mening of her trewé herte,
Anone with that to her he sterte
And saidé: 'Lo, my goodé dere,
Now is he comé to you here
That ye most loven as ye sain.
And she with goodly chere ayein
Beclipt him in her armés smale.
And the coloúr which erst was pale
To beauté thanné was restored
So that it mighté nought be mored.
The kingés soné, which was nigh,
And of this lady herde and sigh
The thingés as they ben befalle,
The reson of his wittés alle
Hath lost, for love upon his parte
Cam than and of his firy darte
With such a wounde him hath through smite,
That he must nedés fele and wite
Of thilké blindé maladý,
To which no cure of surgery
Can helpé. But yet nethéles
At thilké time he helde his pees
That he no countenaúncé made
But openly with wordés glade,
So as he couthe in his manere,
He spake and madé frendely chere
Till it was timé for to go.
And Collatin with him also
His levé toke, so that by night,
With all the hasté that they might,
They riden to the siege ayein.
But Arrons was so wo besein
With thoughtés which upon him runne
That he all by the brodé sunne
To beddé goth nought for to reste,
But for to thenke upon the beste
And the fairésté forth with alle,
That ever he sigh or ever shalle,
So as him thought in his corágе
Where he portreieth her ymáge.
First the fetúrés of her face,
In which natúre had allé grace
Of womanlý beauté beset
So that it mighté nought be bet.
And how her yelwe hair was tressed
And her attire so wel adressed.
And how she spake, and how she wrought,
And how she wepte, and how she thought,
That he foryeten hath no dele
But all it liketh him so wele
That in the wordé nor in dede
He lackéd nought of womanhede.
"And thus this tiranníssé knight
Was soupled, but nought half aright,
For he none other hedé toke,
But that he might by sommé croke,
All though it were ayein her wille,
The lustés of his flessh fulfille,
Which lové was nought resonáble;
For wher honoúr is remevable,
It oughté well to ben avised.
But he, which hath his lust assised
With melléd[1] love and tirannie,
Hath found upon his trecherie

[1] *Melléd*, mingled.

A wey the which he thenketh to
holde,
And saith, 'Fortúne unto the bolde
Is favoráble for to helpe.'
And thus within him self to yelpe,
As he which was a wilde man
Upon his treson he began.
And up he sterte, and forth he wente
On horsébacke, but his entente
There knew no wight, and thus he
name
The nexté waié, till he came
Unto Collaceá the gate
Of Rome, and it was somdele late
Right even upon the sonné sette.
And he which haddé shape his nette
Her innocéncé to betrappe,
And as it shuldé tho mishappe,
As privelich as ever he might
He rode and of his hors alight
To-foré Collatinés inn
And all frendélich goth him in,
As he that was cousín of house.
And she which is the goodé spouse,
Lucrecé, whan that she him sigh,
With goodly cheré drewe him nigh
As she which all honoúr supposeth
And him so as she dare opposeth
How it stood of her husébonde.
And he tho did her understonde
With talés feignéd in this wise
Right as he wolde him self devise
Wherof he might her herté glade,
That she the better cheré made.
Whan she the gladdé wordés herde
How that her housébondé ferde.
And thus the trouthé was deceived
With slie tresón which was received
To hiré which mente allé good.
For as the festés thanné stood,
His souper was right wel arraied,
But yet he hath no word assaied
To speke of love in no degré.
But with covért subtilité
His frendly speches he affaiteth,
And, as the tigre, his time awaiteth
In hopé for to cacche his pray.

"Whan that the bordés were awey
And they have soupéd in the halle,
He saith that slepe is on him falle,
And praith, he moté go to bedde.
And she with allé hasté spedde
So as her thought it was to done,
That every thing was redy sone.
She brought him to his chambre tho
And toke her leve, and forth is go
Into her owné chambre by.
And she that wendé certainly
Have had a frend then had a fo,
Wherof fell after mochel wo.

"This tiraunt though he lié softe
Out of his bedde aros full ofte
And goth about and laid his ere
To herken till that allé were
To beddé gone and slepten faste.
And than upon him self he caste
A mantel and his swerde all naked
He toke in honde, and she unwaked
A beddé lay. But what she mette,[1]
God wot, for he the dore unshette
So privély that none it herde,
The softé pas and forth he ferde
Into the bed where that she slepte,
All sodeinly and in he crepte.
And her in bothe his armés toke.
With that this worthy wife awoke,
Which through tendrésse of woman-
hed
Her vois hath lost for puré drede,
That o word speké she ne dare.
And eke he bad her to beware,
For if she madé noise or cry,
He said, his swerd lay fasté by
To sleen her and her folke about.
And thus he brought her herte in
doubt,
That lich a lamb whan it is sesed
In wolvés mouth, so was disesed
Lucrecé, who lay dede oppressed.

1 *Mette*, dreamed.

And he, which all him hadde adressed
To lust, toke thanné what him liste
And goth his wey, that none it wiste,
Into his owné chambre ayein
And clepéd up his chamberlein
To horsé lept and forth he rode.
And she, which in her bed abode,
Whan that she wist he was agone,
She clepéd after light anone
And up aros long er the day
And cast awey her fressh array,
As she which hath the world forsake,
And toke upon the clothés blacke.
And ever upon continuíng,
Right as men se a wellé spring,
With eyen full of wofull teres
Her hair hangénd about her eres
She wepte, and no man wisté why.
But yet among full pitouslý
She praiéd that they nolden drecche[1]
Her husébondé for to fecche
Forthwith her fader eke also.
Thus be they comen bothé two,
And Brutus cam with Collatine,
Which to Lucrecé was cousíne,
And in they wenten allé thre
To chambre, where they mighté se
The wofullest upon this molde,
Which wepte as she to water sholde.
The chambre dore anone was stoke,[2]
Er they have ought unto her spoke.
They sigh her clothés all disguised,
And how she hath her self despised
Her haire hangénd unkemt about.
But nethéles she gan to lout
And knele unto her husébonde.
And he, which fain wold understonde
The causé why she faréd so,
With softé wordes axéd tho:
'What may you be,[3] my godé swete?'
And she, which thought her self unmete

[1] *Drecche*, delay. [2] *Stoke*, barred.
[3] What may be to you? How is it with you?

And the lest worth of women alle,
Her woful cheré let down falle
For shame and couthe unnethés[1] loke,
And they therof good hedé toke
And praiden her in allé way,
That she ne sparé for to say
Unto her frendés what her eileth,
Why she so sore her self bewaileth,
And what the sothé woldé mene.
And she, which hath her sorwe grene,
Her wo to tellé thanne assaieth,
But tendre shame her word delaieth,
That sondry timés as she mente
To speke upon the point she stente.
And they her beden ever in one
To tellé forth, and there upon,
Whan that she sigh she musté nede,
Her tale betwené shame and drede
She toldé, nought withouté peine.
And he, which wolde her wo restreigne,
Her husébond, a sory man,
Comfórteth her all that he can
And swore, and eke her fader both,
That they with hiré be nought wroth
Of that is do ayein her wille,
And praiéden her to be stille,
For they to her have all foryive.
But she, which thoughté nought to live,
Of hem woll no foryivénesse
And said, of thilké wickednesse,
Which was to hiré body wrought,
All were it so she might it nought,
Never afterward the world ne shall
Reproven her, and forthwithall,
Er any man therof be ware,
A naked swerd, the which she bare
Within her mantel prively,
Betwene her hondés sodeinly
She toke, and through her hert it throng,
And fell to ground, and ever among,

[1] *Unnethés*, hardly (not easily).

Whan that she fell, so as she might,
Her clothés with her hond she right,
That no man downward fro the knee
Shuld any thinge of her then se.
Thus lay this wife honestély,
All though she diedé wofully.
Tho was no sorwe for to seke,
Her husbonde and her fader eke
A swoune upon the body felle.
There may no mannés tungé telle,
In which anguishé that they were.
But Brutus, which was with hem there,
Toward him self his herté kept
And to Lucrece anone he lept,
The bloody swerde and pulleth out
And swore the goddés al about
That he therof shall do vengeaunce.
And she tho made a countenaúnce
Her dedly eye and atté laste
In thonking as it were up cast,
And so behelde him in the wise
While she to loké may suffise.
And Brutus with a manly herte
Her husébonde hath made up sterte
Forth with her fader eke also
In allé haste and said hem tho,
That they anone withouté lette
A beré for the body fette.
Lucrece and therupon bledénd
He laide and so forth out criénd
He goth unto the market place
Of Rome. And in a litel space
Through cry the cité was assembled,
And every mannés herté trembled
Whan they the soth herde of the cas.
And thereupon the counseil was
Take of the great and of the smale.
And Brutus tolde hem all the tale.
And thus cam into remembraúnce
Of sinné the continuaúnce
Which Arrons haddé do to-fore,
And eke long time er he was bore
Of that his fader haddé do,
The wrong came into placé tho,
So that the comun clamour tolde
The newé shame of sinnés olde.
And all the town began to cry:
'Awey, awey the tiranny
Of lechery and covetise!'
And atté last in such a wise
The fader in the samé while
Forth with the soné they exile
And taken better governaunce.
"But yet an other remembraúnce
That rightwisnesse and lechery
Accorden nought in compaigny
With him that hath the lawe on honde,
That may a man well understonde,
As by a talé thou shalt wite
Of olde ensample as it is write.
"At Romé whan that Appius,
Whose other name was Claudius,
Was governour of the citee,
There fell a wonder thing to se
Touchend a gentil maide, as thus,
Whom Livius Virginius
Begeten had upon his wife.
Men saiden, that so faire a life
As she was nought in all the town.
This famé, which goth up and down,
To Claudius came in his ere,
Wherof his thought anone was there,
But she stood upon mariáge.
A worthy knight of great lignáge,
Iliciús which thanné hight,
Accorded in her faders sight
Was that he shulde his doughter wedde.
But er the cause were fully speddc,
Her fader, which in Romanie
The leding of the chivalrie
In governaunce hath undertake,
Upon a werré which was take,
Goth out with all the strength he hadde
Of men of armés which he ladde.
So was the mariágé left

And stood upon accord till eft.
"The King, which herdé telle of this,
How that this maide ordeined is
To mariágé, thought another,
And haddé thilké time a brother,
Which Marchus Claudius was hote,
And was a man of such riote
Right as the King him selvé was;
They two to-gider upon this cas
In counseil founden out the wey,
That Marchus Claudius shall sey
How she by wey of covenaunt
To his servíce apurtenaunt
Was hole, and to none other man.
And there upon he saith he can
In every point witnéssé take,
So that she shall it nought forsake.[1]
Whan that they hadden shapé so
After the lawé which was tho,
While that her fader was absént,
She was somonéd and assént[2]
To come in presence of the King,
And stood in answere of this thing.
Her frendés wisten allé wele
That it was falshede every dele,
And comen to the Kinge and saiden
Upon the comun lawe and praiden
So as this noble worthy knight,
Her fader, for the comun right
In thilké time, as was befalle,
Lay for the profit of hem alle
Upon the wildé feldés armed,
That he ne shuldé nought ben harmed
Ne shaméd while that he were out.
And thus they praiden all about.
"For all the clamour that he herde
The King upon his lust answerde
And yaf hem only daiés two
Of respit. For he wendé tho,
That in so short a time appere
Her fader might in no manere.
But as therof he was deceived,
For Livius had all conceived
The purpos of the King to-fore,
So that to Rome ayein therfore
In allé hast he came ridénd
And left upon the feld liggend
His host till that he came ayein.
And thus this worthy capitain
Appereth redy at his day,
Where all that ever reson may
By lawe in audience he doth,
So that his doughter upon soth
Of that Marchús her had accused
He hath to-fore the Court excused.
"The King, which sigh his purpos faile,
And that no sleighté might availe,
Incombred of his lustés blinde
The lawé torneth out of kinde,
And halfe in wrath as though it were
In presence of hem allé there
Deceivéd of concúpiscénce
Yaf for his brother the senténce
And bad him that he shuldé sese
This maide and make him well at ese.
But all within his own entent
He wist how that the causé went,
Of that his brother hath the wite
He was him selven for to wite.[1]
But thus this maiden haddé wronge
Which was upon the King alonge,
But ayein him was none apele,
And that the fader wisté wele.
Wherof upon the tirannie,
That for the lust of lecherie
His doughter shuldé be deceived,
And that Ilicius was weived
Untruly fro the mariáge,
Right as a leon in his rage,
Which of no dredé set accompt
And not what pité shuldé amount,
A naked swerde he pulléd out,
The which amongés all the rout

[1] *Forsake*, deny. [2] *Assént*, sent for.

[1] Of that for which his brother had the blame he was himself to be held guilty.

He thresté through his doughters side,
And all aloudé thus he cride:
'Lo, take her there thou wrongfull king,
For me is lever upon this thing
To be the fader of a maide,
Though she be dede, than if men saide
That in her life she weré shamed
And I therof were evil named.'
Tho bad the king men shulde areste
His body, but of thilké heste
Like to the chacéd wildé bore
The houndés whan he feleth sore
To-throweth and goth forth his wey,
In such a wisé for to sey
This worthy knight with swerd in honde
His weié made, and they him wonde,[1]
That none of hem his strokés kepte,
And thus upon his hors he lepte
And with his swerd droppénd of blood,
The which within his doughter stood,
He cam thereas the power was
Of Rome and tolde hem all the cas
And said hem, that they mighten lere
Upon the wronge of this matere,
That better it weré to redresse
At home the great unrightwisnesse,
Than for to werre in straungé place
And lese at home her owné grace.
For thus stant every mannés life
In jeopartïé for his wife
And for his doughter if they be
Passénd an other of beauté.
Of this merveilé which they sigh
So apparaúnt to-fore her eye,
Of that the king him hath misbore,
Her othés they have allé swore
That they woll stondé by the right.
And thus of one accorde upright
To Rome at onés home ayein

[1] *Wonde*, fear.

They torne and shortly for to sain
This tirannïé cam to mouth,
And every man saith what he couth,
So that the privé trecherý,
Which set was upon lechery,
Cam openly to mannés ere,
And that brought in the comun fere,
That every man the perill dradde
Of him that so hem overladde.
For they, or that[1] it worsé falle,
Through comun counseil of hem alle
They have her wrongful King deposed,
And hem in whom it was supposed
The counseil stood of his ledíng,
By lawe unto the dome they bring,
Where they receiven the penaúnce
That longeth to such governaúnce.
And thus thunchasté was chastised;
Wherof they mighten ben avised
That sholden afterward govérne,
And by this evidéncé lerne
How it is good a Kinge eschue
The lust of vice and vertue sue.

To make an ende in this partie,
Which toucheth to the policie
Of chasteté in speciáll,
As for conclusión finall
That every lust is to eschue
By great ensample I may argue,
Howe in Ragés a town of Mede
There was a maide, and as I rede,
Sarra she hight, and Raguël
Her fader was. And so befell
Of body bothe and of visage
Was none so faire of the lignáge
To seche among hem all, as she,
Wherof the riche of the citee
Of lusty folk, that couthen love,
Assoted were upon her love
And axén hiré for to wedde.
One was which atté lasté spedde,
But that was moré for likíng
To have his lust than for weddíng,

[1] *Or that*, before.

As he within his herté caste,
Whiche him repenteth atté laste.
For so it fell the firsté night,
That whan he was to beddé dight
As he which no thíng God besecheth,
But all onlý his lustés secheth,
Asmod, which was a fend of helle
And serveth as the bokés telle
To tempte a man in such a wise,
Was redy there, and thilke emprise
Whiche he hath set upon delite
He vengeth than in such a plite
That he his neck hath writh atwo.
This yongé wife was sory tho,
Which wisté nothing what it ment.
And nethéless yet thus it went
Nought only for this firsté man,
But after right as he began,
Six other of her husébondes
Asmod hath take into his hondes,
So that they all abeddé deiede,
Whan they her hond toward her leide,
Nought for the lawe of mariáge,
But for that ilké firy rage
In which that they the lawe excede.
For who that woldé taken hede
What after fell in this matere,
There might he well the sothé here
Whan she was wedded to Thobie,
And Raphäel in compaignyý
Hath taught him how to be honést.
Asmod wan nought at thilké fest,
And yet Thobý his willé hadde,
For he his lust so godely ladde
That bothé lawe and kinde is served,
Wherof he hath him self preserved
That he fell nought in the senténce.
Of which an open evidence
By this ensample a man may se,
That whan likíng in the degre
Of mariágé may forswey,
Well ought him than in other wey
Of lust to be the better avised.
For God the lawés hath assised
As well to reson as to kinde,
But he the bestés woldé binde
Only to lawés of natúre,
But to the mannés creätúre
God yaf him reson forth withall
Wherof that he natúré shall
Upon the causes modify,
That he shall do no lechery,
And yet he shall his lustés have,
So ben the lawés bothé save
And every thing put out of sclaunder,
As whilom to king Alisaundre
The wisé philosóphre taught,
Whan he his firsté loré caught,
Nought only upon chasteté,
But als upon alle honesté.
Wherof a King him self may taste,
How trewe, how large, how juste, how chaste
Him ought of reson for to be
Forth with the vertue of pité.
Through which he may great thank deserve
Toward his God, that he preserve
Him and his people in allé welthe
Of pees, richésse, honoúr and helthe
Here in this worlde and ellés eke.
"My sone, as we to-foré speke
In shrifté, so as thou me saidest,
And for thin ese, as thou me praidest,
Thy lové throwés for to lisse,
That I the woldé telle and wisse
The forme of Aristotles lore,
I have it said, and somdele more
Of other ensamples to assaie
If I thy peinés mighte alaie
Through any thing whiche I can say."—
"Do wey, my fader, I you pray;
Of that ye have unto me tolde
I thonké you a thousand folde;
The talés sounen in min ere,
But yet min herte is ellés where;

I may my selvé nought restreigne
That I nam ever in lovés peine.
Such loré couthe I never gete,
Which mighté maké me foryete
O point, but if so were I slepte,
That I my tidés ayeine kepte
To thenke of love and of his lawe,
That herté can I nought withdrawe.
Forthý, my godé fader dere,
Leve and speke of my matere
Touchénd of Love as we begonne,
If that there be ought over ronne
Or ought foryete or left behinde
Which falleth unto Lovés kinde,
Wherof it nedeth to be shrive,
Now axeth, so that while I live
I might amende that is amis."—
"My godé deré soné, yis.
Thy shrifté for to maké plein,
There is yet moré for to sain
Of Lové which is unavised.
But for thou shalt be well avised
Unto thy shrifte as it belongeth,
A point which upon lové hongeth
And is the laste of allé tho,
I woll the telle, and thanné 'ho.'[1]

[1] Then stop.

Book VIII.

The mighty God, which unbegonne
Stant of him self and hath begonne
All other thingés at his will,
The heven him listé to fulfill
Of alle joié, where as he
Sit enthronízéd in his see
And hath his aungels him to serve,
Such as him liketh to preserve
So that they mowé nought forswey,
But Lucifer he put awey
With al the route apostazíed
Of hem that ben to him allíed,
Which out of heven into helle
From aungels into fendés felle,
Where that there is no joy of light,
But moré derk than any night,
The peiné shall ben endéless.
And yet of firés nethéles
There is plenté, but they ben blacke,
Wherof no sighté may be take.
"Thus whan the thingés ben befalle,
That Luciferés Court was falle
Where dedly pride hem hath conveied,
Anone forthwith it was purveied
Through him which allé thingés may,
He made Adám the sixté day
In Paradise, and to his make
Him liketh Eve also to make
And bad hem cresce and multiply.
For of the mannés progeny
Which of the woman shall be bore,
The nombre of aungels which was lore
Whan they out fro the blissé felle
He thoughté to restore, and fille
In heven thilké holy place
Which stood tho voide upon his grace.
But as it is well wist and knowe,
Adám and Evé but a throwe,
So as it shuld of hem betide,
In Paradise at thilké tide
Ne dwelten, and the causé why
Write in the boke of Genesý
As who saith allé men have herde,
How Raphaël the firy swerde
In hondé toke and drove hem out
To gete her livés food about
Upon this wofull erthé here.
Metodré saith to this matere,
As he by revelaciön
It had upon avisiön
How that Adám and Eve also
Virginés comen bothé two
Into the world and were ashamed
Till that natúre hath hem reclaimed
To love and taught hem thilké lore
That first they kiste and over more
They done that is to kindé due,
Wherof they hadden faire issue.
A soné was the firste of alle,
And Chaim by namé they him calle.

Abél was after the secoúnde
And in the geste as it is founde
Natúré so the causé ladde,
Two doughters eke dame Evé hadde,
The firsté clepéd Calmaná
Was, and that other Delborá.
Thus was mankindé to beginne,
Forthý that time it was no sinne
The suster for to take the brother,
Whan that ther was of chois non other.
To Chaim was Calmaná betake,
And Delboram hath Abel take,
In whom was geté nethéles
Of worldés folk the first encres.
Men sain that nedé hath no lawe,
And so it was by thilké dawe
And laste unto the seconde age,
Till that the greté water rage
Of Noë, which was said the flood,
The world, which than in sinné stood,
Hath dreint, out také livés eight.
Tho was mankinde of litel weight.
Sem, Cam, Japhét, of thesé thre,
That ben the sonés of Noë,
The worlde of mannés natión
Into multiplicatión
Was tho restoréd new ayein
So ferforth as these bokés sain,
That of hem thre and her issúe
There was so large a retenúe
Of nations seventy and two,
In sondry place eche one of tho
The widé world have enhábíted.
But as natúre hem hath excíted,
They token thanné litel hede
The brother of the susterhede
To weddé wivés, till it cam
Into the time of Abraham,
Whan the thridde agé was begonne,
The nedé tho was overonne,
For there was people inough in londe.
Then atté first it came to honde,
That susterhede of mariáge
Was tornéd into cousináge,
So that aftér the righté line
The cousin weddeth the cousine.
For Abraham er that he deied
This charge upon his servaunt leied
To him and in this wisé spake,
That he his soné Isaäc
Do weddé for no worldés good,
But only to his owné blood.
Wherof the servaunt as he badde,
Whan he was dede, his sone hath ladde
To Bathuël, where he Rebecke
Hath wedded with the whité necke.
For she, he wisté well and sigh,
Was to the childé cousin nigh.
"And thus as Abraham hath taught,
Whan Isaäc was God betaught,
His soné Jacob did also
And of Labán the doughters two,
Which was his eme,[1] he toke to wife
And gate upon hem in his life,
Of her firsté which highté Lie,
Six sonés of his progenie,
And of Rachél two sonés eke;
The remenaunt was for to seke,
This is to sain of fouré mo,
Wherof he gate on Bala two
And of Zelpha he had eke twey.
And thesé twelve, as I the say,
Through providence of God him selve
Ben said[2] the Patriarkes Twelve.
Of whom as afterward befel
The tribés twelf of Israël
Engendred were, and ben the same,
That of Hebréws tho hadden name,
Which of sibred[3] in aliaunce
For ever kepten thilke usaunce
Most comunly, till Crist was bore.
But afterward it was forbore
Among us that ben baptized.
For of the lawé canonized

[1] *Eme*, uncle. [2] *Said*, named. [3] *Sibred*, kindred.

The Pope hath bodé to the men,
That none shall wedden of his kin
Ne the secóndé ne the thriddé.
But though that Holy Chirche it
bidde,
So to restreigné mariáge,
There ben yet upon lovés rage
Ful many of suché now a day,
That taken where they také may.
For lové, whiche is unbesein
Of allé reson, as men sain,
Through sotie and through niceté
Of his voluptuosité
He spareth no condición
Of kin ne yet religión.
My soné, thou shalt understonde,
That such delite is for to blame.
Forthý if thou hast be the same
To love in any such manere,
Tell forth therof and shrive the
here."—
"My fader, nay, God wot the
sothe,
My faire is nought in such a bothe,
So wilde a man yet was I never,
That of my kin, or leve or lever,
Me listé love in such a wise.
And eke I not for what emprise
I shulde assote upon a nonne,
For though I had her lové wonne
It might into no prise amounte,
So therof set I none accompte.
Ye may well axe of this and that,
But sothly for to tellé plat,
In all this world there is but one,
The which my herte hath over gone.
I am toward all other fre."—
"Full well, my soné, now I se
Thy word stant ever upon o place,
But yet therof thou hast a grace,
That thou the might so well excuse
Of lové, such as some men use,
So as I spake of now to-fore.
For all such time of love is lore,
And lich unto the bitter swete,
For though it thenke a man first
swete,
He shall well felen atté laste,
That it is soure and may nought laste.
For as a morcel envenimed,
So hath such love his lust mistimed,
And great ensamples many one
A man may findé therupon.
"**At Romé first** if we begin,
There shal I find howe of this sin
An emperoúr was for to blame,
Gaius Caligula by name,
Which of his owné susters thre
Berefté the virginité,
And did hem out of londe exile.
But afterward within a while
God hath beraft him in his ire
His life, and eke his large empire.
"Of this sotý also I finde
Amon his suster ayein kinde,
Which highte Thamar, he forlay,
But he that lust another day
Aboughté, whan that Absolon
His owné brother there upon,
Of that he had his suster shent,
Toke of that sinné vengément
And slough him with his owné honde.
And thus thunkinde unkindé fonde.
"And for to se more of this thing
The bible maketh a knouleching,
Wherof thou might take evidence
Upon the soth experiénce.
Whan Lothés wife was overgone
And shape unto the salté stone,
As it is spoke unto this day,
By both his doughters than he lay.
And so the cause about he ladde,
That eche of hem a soné hadde,
Moab the first and the secoúnde
Amon; of which as it is founde
Cam afterward to great encres
Two natións. And néthelés
For that the stockés were ungood,
The braunches mighten nought ben
good.

For of the falsé Moabites
Forth with the strength of Amonites,
Of that they weren first misget,
The people of God was ofte upset
In Israël and in Judee,
As in the bible a man may se.
"Lo thus, my soné, as I the say,
Thou might thy selvé be besay
Of that thou hast of other herde,
For ever yet it hath so ferde,
Of lovés lust if so befalle
That it in other placé falle
Than it is of the lawé sette.
He, which his love hath so besette
Mote afterward repent him sore,
And every man is others lore.
Of that befell in time er this,
The present timé which nowe is
May ben enforméd how it stood,
And také that him thenkéth good
And levé that which is nought so.
But for to loke of time ago,
How lust of love excedeth lawe,
It oughté for to be withdrawe.
For every man it shuldé drede
And namélich in his sibrede,
Which torneth ofte to vengeaúnce,
Wherof a tale in rémembraúnce,
Which is a long process to here,
I thenke for to tellen here.
Of a cronique in daiés gon,
The which is cleped Panteón,
In lovés cause I redé thus,
How that the great Antiochus,
Of whom that Antioché toke
His firsté name, as saith the boke,
Was coupled to a noble quene,
And had a doughter hem betwene.
But such fortúné cam to honde,
That deth, which no kind may withstonde
But every life it mote obey,
This worthy quené toke awey.
The king, which madé mochel mone,
Tho stood as who saith all him one
Withouté wife, but nethéles
His doughter which was perélés
Of beauté dwelt about him stille.
But whan a man hath welth at wille
The flesshe is frele and falleth ofte,
And that this maidé tendre and softe
Whiche in her faders chambre dwelte
Within a timé wist and felte,
It helpeth nought all though she wepe,
For they that shulde her body kepe
Of women were absent as than,
And thus this maiden goth to man.
The wildé fader thus devoureth
His owné flessh, which none socoúreth,
And that was cause of mochel care.
But after this unkindé fare
Out of the chambre goth the king.
And she lay still and of this thing
Within her self such sorwe made
There was no wight, that might her glade,
For fere of thilke horríble vice.
With that came inné the norice,
Which fro childhode her haddé kepte
And axeth if she haddé slepte,
And why her cheré was unglad.
But she, which hath ben overlad
Of that she mighté nought be wreke,
For shamé couth unethés speke.
And nethéles mercý she praide
With weping eye and thus she saide:
'Helas, my suster, wailoway,
That ever I sigh this ilké day.
My worldés worship is berefte.'
With that she swouneth now and efte
And ever wissheth after deth,
So that welnigh her lacketh breth.
"That other, which her wordés herde,
In comfortíng of her answérde,
'Whan thing is do, there is no bote.
So suffren they that suffren mote.

There was none other, which it wist.'
Thus hath this king all that him list
And such delite he toke there in,
Him thoughté that it was no sin.
And she durst him no thing withsay.
But Famé, which goth every way,
To sondry regnés all aboute
The greaté beauté telleth oute
Of such a maide of high parágc.
So that for love of mariáge
The worthy princes come and sende,
As they the which all honour wende
And knew nothíng how that it stode.
"The fader whan he understode
That they his doughter thus be-
sought,
With all his wit he cast and sought
How that he mighté finde a lette,
And such a statute than he sette
And in this wise his lawé taxeth,
That what man that his doughter
axeth,
But if he couthe his questión
Assoile[1] upon suggestión
Of certein thingés that befelle,
The which he wolde unto him telle,
He shulde in certein lese his hede.
And thus there weré many dede,
Her hedés stonding on the gate,
Till atté lasté long and late
For lacke of answere in this wise
The remenaunt that weren wise
Escheueden to make assay.
"Till it befell upon a day
Appollinus the prince of Tire,
Which hath to love a great desire,
A yonge, a fresh, a lusty knight,
As he lay musing on a night
Of the tidíngés, which he herde,
He thought assay how that it ferde.
He was with worthy compaignie
Arraiéd and with good navie
To ship he goth, the winde him
driveth,
And saileth till that he arriveth
Sauf in the porte of Antioche.
He londeth and goth to approche
The kingés court and his presence.
"Of every natural sciénce
Whiche any clerké couth him teche
He couth inough, and in his speche
Of wordés he was eloquént.
And whan he sigh the king presént,
He praieth he mote his doughter
have.
The king ayein began to crave
And tolde him the condición,
How first unto his questión
He mote answere and failé nought,
Or with his heved it shall be bought.
And he him axeth, what it was.
"The king declareth him the cas
With sterné loke and stordy chere,
To him and said in this manere:
'With felony I am upbore,
I ete, and have it nought forlore.
My moders flesh, whose husébondé,
My fader, for to seche I fonde,
Which is the sone eke of my wife.
Herof I am inquisitife.
And who that can my talé save
Al quite he shall my doughter have.
Of his answere and if he faile,
He shall be dede withouté faile.
Forthý my soné, quod the king,
Be wel aviséd of this thing,
Which hath thy life in jeopartie.
Appollinus for his partie
Whan he that questión had herde,
Unto the king he hath answérde
And hath rehercéd one and one
The points and saidé therupon:
'The questión, which thou hast
spoke,
If thou wolt that it be unloke,
It toucheth all the privété
Betwene thin owné child and the
And stant all hole upon you two.'
The king was wonder sory tho

[1] *Assoile*, solve.

And thought, if that he said it out,
Than were he shaméd all about.
With slighé wordés and with felle
He saith: 'My sone, I shall the telle,
Though that thou be of litel wit,
It is no great merveile as yit,
Thin agé may it nought suffise.
But loké wel thou nought despise
Thin owné life, for of my grace
Of thritty daiés full a space
I graunté the, to ben avised.'
"And thus with leve and time assised
This yongé princé forth he wente
And understode wel what it mente.
Within his herte as he was lered,
That for to maken him afered
The kinge his time hath so delaied,
Wherof he drad and was amaied
Of treson that he deié sholde
For he the king his sothé tolde.
And sodeinly the nightés tide,
That moré wolde he nought abide,
Al privély his barge he hente
And home ayein to Tire he wente.
And in his owné wit he saide,
For drede, if he the king bewraide
He knew so wel the kingés herte
That deth ne shulde he nought asterte,[1]
The king him woldé so pursue.
But he that wolde his deth escheue
And knewe all this to-fore the honde,
Forsake he thought his owné londe,
That theré wolde he nought abide.
For wel he knew that on some side
This tiraunt of his felonie
By some manere of trecherie
To greve his body woll nought leve.
"Forthý withouten taking leve
As privelich as ever he might
He goth him to the see by night,
Her shippés ben with wheté laden,
Her takil redy tho they maden

[1] *Asterte*, escape.

And haleth sail and forth they fare.
But for to tellen of the care,
That they of Tiré baren tho,
Whan that they wist he was ago,
It is a pité for to here.
They losten lust, they losten chere,
They toke upon hem such penaúnce,
There was no song, there was no daunce,
But every merthe and melodý
To hem was than a maladý,
For unlust of that aventúre.
There was no man which toke tonsúre,
In dolfull clothés they hem clothe.
The bathés and the stewés bothe
They shetten in by every wey.
There was no life which listé pley
Ne take of any joié kepe,
But for her legé lord to wepe,
And every wight said as he couth:
'Helas, the lusty floure of youth,
Our prince, our heved, our governóur,
Through whom we stonden in honóur,
Withouté the comúne assent,
That sodeinly is fro us went!'
Such was the clamour of hem alle.
"But se we now what is befalle
Upon the firsté talé pleine
And torné we therto ayeine.
"Antiochus the greté sire,
Which full of rancour and of ire
His herté bereth so as ye herde
Of that this prince of Tire answerde,
He had a felow bacheler,
Which was his privé counseiler
And Taliart by name he hight.
The king a strong poisón him dight
Within a buist[1] and gold therto,
In allé haste and bad him go
Straught unto Tire and for no cost
Ne sparé till he haddé lost
The princé which he woldé spill.[2]
And whan the king hath said his will

[1] *Buist*, box. [2] *Spill*, destroy.

This Taliart in a galéy
With all the haste he toke his wey.
The wind was good, they saileth blive,
Till he toke lond upon the rive
Of Tire and forth with all anone
Into the burgh he gan to gone
And toke his inne and bode a throwe.
But for he woldé nought be knowe,
Desguiséd than he goth him out.
He sigh the weping all about
And axeth, what the causé was.
And they him tolden all the cas,
How sodeinlý the prince is go.
And whan he sigh that it was so
And that his labour was in veine
Anone he torneth home ayeine
And to the king whan he cam nigh
He tolde of that he herde and sigh,
How that the prince of Tire is fled,
So was he come ayein unsped.
The king was sory for a while
But whan he sigh that with no wile
He might acheve his crueltė,
He stint his wrath and let him be.
"But over this now for to telle
Of adventúrés that befelle
Unto this prince, of which I tolde,
He hath his righté cours forth holde
By stone and nedel till he cam
To Tharse, and ther his londe he
nam.
A bourgeis riche of golde and fee
Was thilké time in that citee,
Which clepéd was Strangulio,
His wife was Dionſse also.
This yongé prince, as saith the boke,
With him his herbergágé toke.
And it befell that citee so
Beforé time and than also
Through strongé famin whiche hem
lad
Was none that any wheté had.
Appollinús, whan that he herde
The mischefe, how the citee ferde,
All frelich of his owné yifte
His whete among hem for to shifte,
The which by ship he haddé brought,
He yave, and toke of hem right
nought.
But sithen first this world began,
Was never yet to such a man
More joié made, than they him made.
For they were all of him so glade
That they for ever in rémembraúnce
Made a figúre in résemblaúnce
Of him and in a comun place
They set it up, so that his face
Might every maner man beholde
So as the citee was beholde,
It was of laton [1] over gilt.
Thus hath he nought his yifté spilt.
"Upon a timé with a route
This lord to pleié goth him oute
And in his way of Tire he mette
A man, which on his knees him grette,
And Hellican by name he hight,
Which praide his lord to have in-
sight
Upon him self and said him thus,
How that the great Antiochus
Awaiteth if he might him spille.
That other thought and helde him
stille
And thonkéd him of his warníng
And bad him tellé no tidíng,
Whan he to Tire cam home ayeine,
That he in Tharse him haddé seine.
"Fortúne hath ever be muáble
And may no whilé stondé stable.
For now it higheth, now it loweth,
Now stant upright, now over-
throweth,
Now full of bliss and now of bale,
As in the telling of my tale
Here afterward a man may lere,
Which is great routhé for to here.
"This lord, which woldé done
his best,

[1] *Laton*, latten, an alloy of copper with tin; the material of ancient church brasses.

Within him self hath litel rest
And thought he wolde his placé
chaunge
And seke a contré moré straunge.
Of Tharsiens his leve anone
He toke and is to shippé gone.
His cours he nam with saile updrawe,
Where as Fortúné doth the lawe
And sheweth as I shall reherce
How she was to this lord diverse,
The which upon the see she ferketh.[1]
The winde aros, the wether derketh,
It blew and madé such tempést,
None anker may the ship arest,
Which hath to-broken all his gere.
The shipmen stood in such a fere,
Was none that might him self
bestere,
But ever awaite upon the lere[2]
Whan that they sholden drenche
at ones.
There was inough within the wones
Of weping and of sorwe tho.
The yongé king maketh mochel wo
So for to se the ship travaile,
But all that might him nought availe.
The mast to-brake, the sail to-rofe,[3]
The ship upon the wawés drofe,
Till that they se the londés coste,
Tho made a vow the leste and moste,
Be so they mighten come a londe.
But he which hath the se on honde,
Neptunus, woldé nought accorde,
But all to-brake cable and corde,
Er they to londé mighte approche.
The ship to-clef upon a roche
And all goth down into the depe.
But he that allé thing may kepe
Unto this lord was merciáble
And brought him sauf upon a table[4]
Which to the londe him hath upbore,
The remenaunt was all forlore.
Herof he madé mochel mone.

1 *Ferketh*, hastens. 2 Wait to learn.
3 *To-rofe*, was riven to shreds.
4 *Table*, plank.

"Thus was this yongé lorde alone
All naked in a pouér plite.
His colour which was whilom white
Was than of water fade and pale,
And eke he was so sore a cale,[1]
That he wist of him self no bote,
It helpe him no thing for to mote[2]
To gete ayein that he hath lore.
But she which hath his deth forbore,
Fortúné, though she woll nought
yelpe,[3]
All sodeinly hath sent him helpe
Whan him thought allé grace awey.
There came a fissher in the wey
And sigh a man there naked stonde.
And whan that he hath understonde
The cause, he hath of him great
routh
And onlich of his pouér trouth
Of suché clothés as he hadde
With great pité this lord he cladde.
And he him thonketh as he sholde
And saith him that it shall be yolde,[4]
If ever he gete his state ayein,
And praieth, that he wolde him sain
If nigh were any town for him.
He saidé: 'Ye, Pentopolim,
Where bothé king and quené
dwellen.'
Whan he this talé herdé tellen,
He gladdeth him and gan beseche,
That he the wey him woldé teche.
And he him taught. And forth he
went
And praidé God with good entent
To sende him joy after his sorwe.
"It was nought passéd yet mid-
morwe,[5]
Than thiderward his wey he nam,
Where sone upon the none he cam.
He eté such as he might gete,
And forth anone whan he had ete,

1 *A cale*, a cold. 2 *Mote*, sue.
3 *Yelpe*, boast. 4 *Yolde*, repaid.
5 *Midmorwe*, half way between sunrise and noon.

He goth to se the town about,
And cam there as he found a rout
Of yongé lusty men withall.
And as it shuldé tho befall,
That day was set of such assise,
That they shulde in the londés gise
As he herde of the people say
Her comun gamé thanné pley.
And criéd was, that they shuld come
Unto the gamés all and some
Of hem that ben deliver [1] and wight
To do such maistry as they might.
They made hem naked as they sholde,
For so that ilké gamé wolde
And it was tho custume and use,
Amongés hem was no refuse.
The floure of all the town was there
And of the court also there were,
And that was in a largé place
Right even before the kingés face,
Whiche Artestrates thanné hight.
The pley was pleied right in his sight,
And who most worthy was of dede
Receive he shulde a certain mede
And in the citee bere a price.
"Appollinus which ware and wise
Of every gamé couth an ende,
He thought assay how so it wende.
And fell among hem into game,
And there he wanne him such a name,
So as the king him self accompteth,
That he all other men surmounteth
And bare the prise above hem alle.
The king bad that into his halle
At souper time he shall be brought.
And he cam than and lefte it nought,
Withouté compaignŷ alone.
Was none so semelich of persone,
Of visage and of limmés bothe,
If that he haddé what to clothe.
At souper timé nethéles

[1] *Deliver*, supple. Chaucer's Squire was "wonderly deliver and grete of strength."

The king amiddés all the pres
Let clepe him up amonge hem alle
And bad his mareshall of his halle
To setten him in such degré
That he upon him mighté se.
The king was soné sette and served,
And he which had his prise deserved
After the kingés owné worde,
Was made begin a middel borde
That bothé king and quene him sigh.
He sette and cast about his eye,
And sigh the lordés in estate
And with him self wax in debate
Thenkénd of what he haddé lore,
And such a sorwe he toke therfore,
That he sat ever still and thought,
As he which of no meté rought.
"The king behelde his hevinesse
And of his greté gentilesse
His doughter which was faire and good
And atté bord before him stood,
As it was thilké time uságe,
He bad to go on his misságe
And foundé[1] for to make him glad.
And she did as her fader bad
And goth to him the softé pas
And axeth whenne and what he was,
And praith he shulde his thoughtés leve.
"He saith: 'Madamé, by your leve.
My name is hote Appollinus,
And of my richesse it is thus,
Upon the see I have it lore.
The contré where as I was bore,
Where that my lond is and my rente,
I lefte at Tire whan that I wente,
The worship there of which I ought
Unto the God I there betought.'
And thus to-gider as they two speke,
The térés ran down by his cheke.
The king, which therof toke good kepe,
Had great pité to se him wepe

[1] *Foundé*, try.

And for his doughter send ayein
And praid her faire and gan to sain
That she no lenger woldé drecche,[1]
But that she wolde anone forth fecche
Her harpe and done all that she can
To gladdé with that sory man.
And she to done her faders hest
Her harpé set and in the feste
Upon a charé which they sette
Her self next to this man she sette.
With harpé both and eke with mouthe
To him she did all that she couthe
To make him chere, and ever he siketh,
And she him axeth how him liketh.
'Madamé, certés well,' he saide,
'But if ye the mesúré plaide
Which, if you list, I shall you lere,
It were a glad thing for to here.'
'Ha, levé siré,' tho quod she,
'Now take the harpe and let me se,
Of what mesúré that ye mene.'
"Tho praith the king, tho praith the quene,
Forth with the lordés all arewe,
That he some merthé woldé shewe.
He taketh the harpe and in his wise
He tempreth, and of suche assise
Singend he harpeth forth withall
That as a vois celestiall
Hem thought it sounéd in her ere,
As though that he an aungel were.
They gladen of his melodý,
But most of all the company
The kingés doughter, which it herde,
And thought eke of that he answérde
Whan that it was of her apposed,
Within her hert hath well supposed
That he is of great gentilesse;
His dedés ben therof witnesse
Forth with the wisdome of his lore,
It nedeth nought to seché more.

[1] *Drecche*, delay.

He might nought havé such manere,
Of gentil blood but if he were.
Whan he hath harpéd all his fill
The kingés hesté to fulfill,
Away goth dish, away goth cup,
Down goth the bord, the cloth was up,
They risen and gone out of halle.
"The king his chamberlein let calle
And bad, that he by allé wey
A chambre for this man purvey,
Which nigh his owné chambre be.
'It shall be do, my lord,' quod he.
"Appollinus, of whom I mene,
Tho toke his leve of king and quene
And of the worthy maide also,
Which praid unto her fader tho,
That she might of the yongé man
Of tho sciénces which he can,
His loré have. And in this wise
The king her graunteth his apprise,
So that him self therto assent.
Thus was accorded er they went
That he with all that ever he may
This yongé fairé freshé may [1]
Of that he couthé shulde enforme.
And ful assented in this forme
They token leve as for that night.
"And whan it was on morweright,
Unto this yongé man of Tire
Of clothés and of good attire
With gold and silver to despende
This worthy yongé lady sende.
And thus she made him well at ese,
And he with all that he can plese
Her serveth well and faire ayeine.
He taught her till she was certeine
Of harpé, citole and of riote [2]
With many a tune and many a note,
Upon musíque, upon mesúre,
And of her harpé the temprure

[1] *May*, maid.
[2] *Citole*, a stringed instrument played with the fingers; *riote*, rote, three-stringed fiddle played with a bow.

He taught her eke, as he well couth.
But as men sain that frele is youth,
With leiser and continuaunce,
This maidé fell upon a chaunce,
That love hath made him a quarele
Aycine her youthé fresh and frele,
That malgré where[1] she wold or nought,
She mot with all her hertés thought
To love and to his lawe obey.
And that she shall full sore abey,
For she wot never what it is.
But ever among she feleth this,
Thenkend upon this man of Tire,
Her herte is hote as any fire,
And otherwise it is acale.[2]
Now is she red, now is she pale
Right after the conditión
Of her ymaginatión.
But ever among her thoughtés alle,
She thoughté, what so may befalle,
Or that she laugh, or that she wepe,
She wolde her godé namé kepe
For fere of womanisshé shame.
But what in ernest, what in game,
She stant for love in such a plite
That she hath lost all appetite
Of mete and drinke, of nightés rest,
As she that not[3] what is the best.
But for to thenken all her fille
She helde her ofté timés stille
Within her chambre and goth nought out.
The king was of her life in doubt,
Which wisté nothing what it ment.
"But fell a time, as he out went
To walke, of princes sonés thre
There came and fellé to his knee,
And eche of hem in sondry wise
Besought and profreth his servíce,
So that he might his doughter have.
The king, which wold her honour save,

[1] *Where*, whether.
[2] *Acale*, acold.
[3] *Not*, knows not.

Saith, she is sike, and of that speche
Tho was no timé to beseche,
But eche of hem to make a bille
He bad and write his owné wille,
His name, his fader and his good.
And whan she wist how that it stood,
And had her billés oversein,
They shulden have answere ayein.
Of this counseil they weren glad
And writen as the king hem bad,
And every man his owné boke
Into the kingés hond betoke.
And he it to his doughter sende
And praide her for to make an ende
And write ayein her owné honde,
Right as she in her herté fonde.
"The billés weren well received,
But she hath all her lovés weived
And thoughté tho was time and space
To put her in her faders grace
And wrote ayein and thus she saide:
'The shamé which is in a maide
With speché dare nought be unloke,
But in writíng it may be spoke.
So write I to you, fader, thus,
But if I have Appollinus,
Of all this world what so betide
I woll non other man abide.
And certes if I of him faile
I wot right well withouté faile
Ye shull for me be doughterles.'
This letter came, and there was pres
To-fore the king there as he stode.
And whan that he it understode,
He yave hem answere by and by.
But that was done so privély,
That none of others counseil wiste.
They toke her leve, and where hem liste,
They wenté forth upon her wey.
"The king ne woldé nought bewrey
The counseil for no maner high,[1]
But suffreth till he time sigh.

[1] *High*, for *hie*, haste.

And whan that he to chambre is
come,
He hath unto his counseil nome
This man of Tire and lete him se
The letter, and all the privété
The which his doughter to him sente.
And he his kne to groundé bente
And thonketh him and her also.
And er they wenten than a two
With good herte and with good
corâge
Of full love and full mariâge
The kinge and he ben hole accorded,
And after, whan it was recorded
Unto the doughter how it stood,
The yifte of all this worldés good
Ne shuld have made her half so
blithe.
And forthwithall the kinge als swithe,
For he woll have her good assent,
Hath for the quene her moder sent.
The quene is come, and whan she
herde
Of this matere how that it ferde,
She sigh debate she sigh disese
But if she wolde her doughter plese,
And is therto assented ful,
Whiche is a dedé wonderful,
For no man knew the sothé cas,
But he him self, what man he was.
And nethéles so as hem thought
His dedés to the sothé wrought,
That he was come of gentil blood,
Him lacketh nought but worldés
good,
And as therof is no despeire,
For she shall be her faders heire
And he was able to govérne,
Thus woll they nought the lové werne[1]
Of him and hiré by no wise,
But all accordéd they devise
The day and time of mariâge,
Where love is lorde of the corage.
Him thenketh longe er that he spede,

[1] *Werne*, forbid.

But atté laste unto the dede
The time is come, and in her wise
With great offrénd and sacrifice
They wedde and make a riché fest,
And every thing was right honést
Withinné hous and eke without.
It was so done, that all about
Of great worshíp and great noblesse
There criéd many a man largesse
Unto the lordés high and loude.
The knightes, that ben yonge and
proude,
They jesté[1] first and after daunce.
The day is go, the nightés chaunce
Hath derkéd all the brighte sonne.
This lord hath thus his lové wonne.
"Now have I tolde of the spou-
sailes.
But for to speke of the merveiles,
Which afterward to hem befelle,
It is a wonder for to telle.
"It fell a day they riden out
The kinge and quene and all the rout
To pleién hem upon the stronde,
Where as they seen toward the londe
A ship sailénd of great array;
To knowé what it mené may,
Till it be comé they abide.
Than se they stonde on every side
Endlong the shippés bord to shewe
Of penouncéls a riché rewe.
They axen whenne the ship is come.
Fro Tire, anone answérdé some.
And over this they saiden more
The causé why they comen fore
Was for to seche and for to finde
Appollinus, which is of kinde
Her legé lord. And he appereth
And of the talé whiche he hereth
He was right glad, for they him tolde,
That for vengeaúnce, as God it wolde,
Antiochus as men may wite
With thunder and lightning is for-
smite.

[1] *Jesté*, joust.

His doughter hath the samé chaunce.
So be they both in o balaunce.
Forthý, our legé lord, we say
In name of all the lond and pray,
That left all other thing to done
It liké you to comé sone
And se your owné legé men
With other that ben of your ken
That live in longing and desire
Till ye be come ayein to Tire.
This tale after the king it had
Pentapolim all oversprad.
There was no joié for to seche,
For every man it had in speche
And saiden all of one accorde:
'A worthy king shall ben our lorde;
That thought us first an hevinesse
Is shape us now to great gladnésse.'
Thus goth the tiding over all.
"But nede he mot that nedé shall.
Appollinus his levé toke,
To God and all the lond betoke[1]
With all the people longe and brode,
That he no lenger there abode.
"The king and quené sorwe made,
But yet somdele they weren glade
Of such thing as they herden tho.
And thus betwene the wele and wo
To ship he goth, his wife with childe,
The which was ever meke and milde
And woldé nought departe him fro,
Such lové was betwene hem two.
Lichorida for her office
Was také, which was a norice,
To wendé with this yongé wife,
To whom was shape a wofull life.
Within a time, as it betid,
Whan they were in the see amid,
Out of the north they sigh a cloude,
The storme aros, the windés loude
They blewen many a dredefull blast,
The welken was all overcast.
The derké night the sonne hath under,
There was a great tempést of thunder.
The mone and eke the sterrés bothe
In blacké cloudés they hem clothe,
Wherof her brighté loke they hide.
This yongé lady wept and cride
To whom no comfort might availe,
Of childé she began travaile
Where she lay in a caban close.
Her wofull lord fro her arose,
And that was long er any morwe,
So that in anguish and in sorwe
She was delivered all by night
And deiede in every mannés sight.
"But netheles for all this wo
A maidé child was boré tho.
"Appollinus whan he this knewe,
For sorwe a swoune he overthrewe
That no man wist in him no life.
And whan he woke, he saide: 'Ha, wife,
My joy, my lust and my desire,
My welth and my recoverire,
Why shall I live, and thou shalt deie?
Ha, thou Fortúne, I the defie,
Now hast thou do to me thy werst.
Ha, herté, why ne wolt thou berst,
That forth with her I mighté passe?
My painés weré well the lasse.
In such wepíng and suché crie
His dedé wife which lay him by
A thousand sithés he her kiste,
Was never man that sigh ne wiste
A sorwe to his sorwe liche,
Was ever among upon the liche.[1]
He fell swounénde as he that thought
His owné deth, which he besought
Unto the goddés all above
With many a pitous word of love.
But suché wordés as tho were
Yet herdé never mannés ere,
But only thilké which he saide.
The maister shipman came and praide

[1] *Betoke*, commended, entrusted.

[1] *The liche*, the body (of his dead wife).

With other such as ben therinne,
And sain that he may nothing winne
Ayein the deth, but they him rede
He be well ware and také hede,
The see by wey of his natúre
Receivé may no creätúre
Within him self as for to holde
The which is dede. Forthý they wolde,
As they counseilen all about,
The dedé body casten out.
For better it is, they saiden all,
That it of hiré so befall,
Than if they shulden allé spille.
"The king, which understode her will
And knew her counseil that was trewe,
Began ayein his sorwe newe
With pitous hert and thus to say:
'It is all reson that ye pray.
I am,' quod he, 'but one alone,
So wolde I nought for my persone
There fellé such adversité.
But whan it may no better be
Doth thanné thus upon my worde,
Let make a coffre stronge of borde,
That it be firm with led and piche.'
Anone was made a coffre siche
All redy brought unto his honde.
And whan he sighe and redy fonde
This coffre made and well englued,
The dedé body was besewed
In cloth of gold and laid therinne.
And for he wolde unto her winne
Upon some coste [1] a sepulture,
Under her heved in adventúre
Of gold he laidé sommés great
And of juéls a strong beyéte
Forth with a letter, and said thus:
'I, king of Tire, Appollinus
Doth allé maner men to wite,
That here and se this letter write,
That helpélés withouté rede
Here lith a kingés doughter dede,
And who that hapneth her to finde
For charité take in his minde
And do so that she be begrave
With this tresór which he shal have.'
"Thus whan the letter was full spoke,
They have anone the coffre stoke
And bounden it with iron faste,
That it may with the wawés laste,
And stoppen it by such a wey
That it shall be withinné drey,
So that no water might it greve.
And thus in hope and good beleve
Of that the corps shall well arrive,
They cast it over borde as blive.
"The ship forth on the wawés went.
The prince hath chaungéd his entent,
And saith, he woll nought come at Tire
As thanné, but all his desire
Is first to sailen unto Tharse.
The windy storm began to scarse,
The sonne arist, the weder clereth,
The shipman which behindé stereth,
Whan that he sigh the windés saught,
Towardés Tharse his cours he straught.
"But now to my matere ayein,
To telle as oldé bokés sain
This dedé corps of whiche ye knowe
With winde and water was forth throwe,
Now here, now there, till atté last
At Ephesim the see upcast
The coffre and all that was therinne.
Of great merveilé now beginne
May heré who that sitteth still.
That God woll savé may nought spill.
Right as the corps was throwe a londe,
There cam walkénd upon the stronde
A worthy clerke and surgién
And eke a great phisicién,

[1] *Coste*, coast.

Of all that lond the wisest one,
Which highté maister Cerimon.
There were of his disciples some.
This maister is to the coffre come,
He peiseth there was somwhat in
And bad hem bere it to his inne,
And goth him selvé forth with all.
All that shall fallé, fallé shall.
"They comen home and tarie nought.
This coffre into his chambre is brought,
Which that they findé fasté stoke,
But they with craft it have unloke.
They loken in, whereas they founde,
A body dede, which was iwounde
In cloth of gold, as I said ere.
The tresor eke they founden there
Forth with the letter, which they rede.
And tho they token better hede.
Unsowéd was the body sone,
As he that knewe what was to done,
This noble clerk with allé haste
Began the veinés for to taste.[1]
And sigh her agé was of youthe;
And with the craftés which he couthe
He sought and found a signe of life.
With that this worthy kingés wife
Honestély they token out
And maden firés all about.
They laid her on a couché softe,
And with a sheté warméd ofte
Her coldé brest began to hete,
Her herte also to flacke[2] and bete.
This maister hath her every jointe
With certain oil and balsme anointe,
And put a liquour in her mouthe
Which is to fewé clerkes couthe,
So that she covereth atté laste.
And first her eyen up she caste,
And whan she more of strengthé caught,
Her armés bothé forth she straught,

[1] *Taste*, try by touch. [2] *Flacke*, flutter.

Held up her hond and pitouslý
She spake and saidé: 'Where am I?
Where is my lord, what world is this?'
As she that wot nought how it is.
But Cerimon that worthy leche
Answerde anone upon her speche
And said: 'Madamé, ye ben here,
Where ye be sauf, as ye shall here
Hereafterward, forthý as now
My counseil is, comfórteth you.
For tristeth wel, withouté faile,
There is no thing which shall you faile,
That ought of reson to be do.'
Thus passen they a day or two;
They speke of nought as for an ende,
Till she began somdele amende,
And wist her selven what she mente.
"Tho for to knowe her hole entente
This maister axeth all the cas,
How she cam there, and what she was.
'How I came heré, wote I nought,'
Quod she, 'but wel I am bethought
Of other thingés all about
Fro point to point,' and tolde him out
Als ferforthly as she it wiste.
And he her tolde how in a kiste
The see her threwe upon the londe,
And what tresór with her he fonde,
Which was all redy at her will,
As he that shope him to fulfill
With al his might what thing he shuld.
She thonketh him that he so wolde,
And all her herté she discloseth
And saith him well that she supposeth,
Her lord be dreint, her childe also.
So sigh she nought but allé wo.
Wherof as to the world no more
Ne woll she torne and praieth therfore,

That in some temple of the citee
To kepe and holde her chastetė
She might among the women dwelle.
Whan he this talé herdé telle
He was right glad, and made her knowen
That he a doughter of his owen
Hath, which he woll unto her yive
To servé while they bothé live,
In stede of that which she hath loste;
All only at his owné coste
She shall be rendred forth with her.
She saith, 'Graunt mercy, levé sir,
God quite it you, there I ne may.'
And thus they drivé forth the day
Till timé cam that she was hole.
And tho they take her counseil hole
To shape upon good ordenaúnce
And make a worthy purveaúnce
Ayein the day whan they be veiled.
And thus whan that they were counseiled,
In blacké clothés they hem clothe
This lady and the doughter bothe
And yolde hem to religión.
The feste and the professión
After the reule of that degré
Was made with great solempnité,
Where as Diane is sanctified.
Thus stant this lady justified
In ordre where she thenketh to dwelle.

"But now ayeinward for to telle,
In what plite that her lord stood inne.
He saileth till that he may winne
The haven of Tharse, as I saide ere.
And whan he was arrivéd there,
Tho it was through the cité knowe,
Men mighté se within a throwe
As who saith all the towne at ones.
They come ayein him for the nones
To yiven him the reverénce,
So glad they were of his presénce.
And though he were in his coráge
Diseséd, yet with glad viságe
He made hem chere and to his inne,
Where he whilom sojournéd in,
He goth him straught and was received.
And whan the press of people is weived,
He taketh his host unto him tho
And saith, 'My frend Strangulio,
Lo thus and thus it is befalle.
And thou thy self art one of alle,
Forth with thy wife, which I most trist,
Forthý if it you bothé list,
My doughter Thaisé by your leve
I thenké shall with you beleve
As for a time, and thus I pray
That she be kept by allé way,
And whan she hath of agé more,
That she be set to bokés lore.
And this avow to God I make,
That I shall never for her sake
My berdé for no liking shave
Till it befallé that I have
In covenáble time of age
Besette her unto mariáge.

"Thus they accorde, and all is well.
And for to resten him somdele
Yet for a while he ther sojórneth,
And than he taketh his leve and torneth
To ship and goth him home to Tire,
Where every man with great desire
Awaiteth upon his coming.
But whan the ship cam in sailing
And they perceiven it is he,
Was never yet in no citee
Such joié made, as they tho made,
His hert also began to glade
Of that he seeth his people glad.
Lo, thus Fortúne his hap hath lad,
In sondry wise he was travailed.
But how so ever he be assailed,
His latter endé shall be good.

"And for to speke how that it stood

Of Thaise his doughter, wher she dwelleth,
In Tharse as the cronîqué telleth
She was well kept, she was well loked,
She was wel taught, she was wel boked,
So well she sped her in her youth
That she of every wisdom couth,
That for to seche in every londe
So wise an other no man fonde
Ne so well taught at mannés eye.
But wo worth ever false envý.
For it befell that timé so,
A doughter hath Strangulio,
The which was clepéd Philotenné.
But Famé, which woll ever renne,
Came all day to her moders ere
And saith, wher ever her doughter were
With Thaisé set in any place
The commun vois the commun grace
Was all upon that other maide,
And of her doughter no man saide.
Who was wroth but Dionísé than?
Her thought a thousand yere till whan
She mighté be of Thaisé wreke
Of that she herdé folk so speke.
And fell that ilké samé tide,
That dede was trewé Lichoride
Whiche haddé be servaúnt to Thaise,
So that she was the wors at ese.
For she hath thanné no servíse
But onely through this Dioníse
Which was her dedlich enemy.
Through puré treson and envý
She that of allé sorwe can
Tho spake unto her bondéman
Which clepéd was Theophilus
And made him swere in counseil thus,
That he such time as she him set
Shall come Thaisé for to fet
And lede her out of allé sight
Where that no man her helpé might
Upon the strondé nigh the see,
And there he shall this maiden slee.
This cherlés hert is in a traunce,
As he which drad him of vengeaúnce
Whan timé comth an other day.
But yet durst he nought saié nay,
But swore and said he shall fulfill
Her hestés at her owné will.
"The treson and the time is shape,
So fell it that this cherlish knape[1]
Hath lad this maiden where he wold
Upon the stronde, and what she sholde
She was adrad, and he out braide
A rusty swerde and to her saide:
'Thou shalt be dede.' 'Alas,' quod she,
'Why shall I so?' 'Lo thus,' quod he,
'My lady Dionise hath bede,
Thou shalt be murdred in this stede.'
This maiden tho for feré shrighte
And for the love of God Allmighte
She praith that for a litel stoundé
She mighté knele upon the grounde
Toward the heven for to crave,
Her wofull soule if she may save.
And with this noise and with this cry,
Out of a bargé fasté by,
Which hid was there on scomer-faré,[2]
Men sterten out and weren ware
Of this felón, and he to go,
And she began to crié tho,
'Ha, mercy, help for Goddes sake,'
Into the bargé they her take,
As thevés shulde, and forth they went.
Upon the see the wind hem hent
And malgré where they wolde or none
To-fore the weder forth they gone,
There halp no sail there halp none ore
Forstorméd and forblowen sore

[1] *Knape*, lad.
[2] *Scomer-fare*, ? for lying in wait in creeks, from some word having its root in *sca* or *scu*, to cover and conceal, whence *skua*, *scedulo*, shadow?

In great peril so forth they drive,
Till atté lasté they arrive
At Miteléné the citee.
In haven sauf and whan they be
The maister shipman made him boune[1]
And goth him out into the towne
And profreth Thaisé for to selle.
One Leonin it herdé telle,
Which maister of the bordel was,
And bad him gon a redy pas
To fecchen her, and forth he went
And Thaise out of his barge he hent
And solde her to the bordel tho.
No wonder is though she be wo
Clos in a chambre by her self.
Eche after other ten or twelf
Of yongé men in to her went.
But suche a gracé God her sent,
That for the sorwe which she made,
Was none of hem which power had
To done her any vilainy.
"This Leonin let ever aspy
And waiteth after great beyete,
But all for nought, she was forlete,
That no man woldé theré come.
Whan he therof hath hede nome
He sent his man, but so it ferde,
Whan he her wofull pleintés herde
And he therof hath také kepe,
Him listé better for to wepe
Than don ought ellés to the game.
And thus she kepte her self fro shame
And kneléd down to therthe and praide
Unto this man and thus she saide:
'If so be, that thy maister wolde
That I his gold encresé sholde
It may nought fallé by this wey,
But suffre me to go my wey
Out of this hous where I am in,
And I shall make him for to win
In some place ellés of the town,
Be so it be of religioun,

[1] *Boune*, ready.

Where that honésté women dwelle.
And thus thou might thy maister telle,
That whan I have a chambre there
Let him do cry ay widé where,
What lord that hath his doughter dere
And is in will that she shall lere
Of such a scolé that is trewe,
I shall her teche of thingés newe
Whiche as none other woman can
In all this londe.' And tho this man
Her tale hath herde he goth ayein
And tolde unto his maister plein,
That she hath saide. And therupon,
Whan that he sigh beyeté none
At the bordél because of hire,
He bad his man to gon and spire
A placé where she might abide,
That he may winne upon some side
By that she can. But atté lest
Thus was she sauf of this tempést.
"He hath her fro the bordel take,
But that was nought for Goddés sake,
But for the lucre, as she him tolde.
Now comen tho that comen wolde,
Of women in her lusty youth
To here and se what thing she couth.
She can the wisdome of a clerke,
She can of any lusty werke
Which to a gentil woman longeth.
And some of hem she underfongeth
To the citole and to the harpe,
And whom it liketh for to carpe
Proverbés and demaundés sligh
An other such they never sigh
Which that sciéncé so well taught,
Wherof she greté yiftés caught,
That she to Leonin hath wonne.
And thus her name is so begonne
Of sondry thingés that she techeth,
That all the londé to her secheth
Of yongé women for to lere.
"Now letté we this maiden here

And speke of Dionise ayeine
And of Theophile the vilaine
Of which I spake of now to-fore,
Whan Thaisé shulde have be forlore.
This falsé cherle to his ladý
Whan he cam home all prively,
He saith, 'Madamé, slain I have
This maidé Thaise, and is begrave
In privé place, as ye me bede.
Forthy, madamé, taketh hede
And kepe counsell, how so it stonde.'
This fend, which hath this understonde,
Was glad and weneth it be soth.
Now herke, hereafter how she doth.
She wepeth, she sorweth, she compleigneth,
And of sikenessé which she feigneth,
She saith, that Thaisé sodeinly
By night is dede, as she and I
To-gider lien nigh my lorde.
She was a woman of recórde,
And all is levéd that she saith.
And for to yive a moré feith,
Her husébonde and eke she bothe
In blacké clothés they hem clothe,
And make a great enterrément.
And for the people shall be blent
Of Thaise as for the rémembraúnce,
After the reál[1] olde usaunce
A tumbe of laton noble and riche
With an ymáge unto her liche
Liggénd abové therupon
They made and set it up anon.
Her epitaphe of good assise
Was write about, and in this wise
It spake: 'O ye, that this beholde,
Lo, here lieth she, the which was holde
The fairest and the floure of alle,
Whose namé Thaïsis men calle.
The king of Tire Appollinus
Her fader was, now lieth she thus.

[1] *Reál*, regal.

Fourtené yere she was of age,
Whan deth her toke to his viage.'
Thus was this falsé treson hid,
Which afterward was widé kid,
As by the tale a man shall here.
But to declaré my matere
To Tire I thenké torne ayein
And telle as the croníqués sain.
Whan that the king was comen home
And hath left in the salté fome
His wife which he may nought foryete,
For he some comfort woldé gete
He let sommone a parlément,
To which the lordés were assent.[1]
And of the time he hath ben out,
He seeth the thingés all about;
And tolde hem eke, how he hath fare,
While he was out of londé fare,
And praide hem allé to abide,
For he wolde at the samé tide
Do shapé for his wivés minde[2]
As he that woll nought ben unkinde.
Solempné was that ilke office,
And riché was the sacrifice,
The festé reálly[3] was holde.
And therto was he well beholde:
For suche a wife as he had one
In thilké daiés was there none.
"Whan this was done, than he him thought
Upon his doughter, and besought
Such of his lordés as he wolde,
That they with him to Tharsé sholde
To fet his doughter Thaisé there,
And they anone all redy were.
To ship they gone and forth they went
Till they the haven of Tharsé hent.
They londe and faile of that they seche,
By coverture and sleight of speche.
This falsé man Strangulio
And Dionise his wife also,

[1] *Assent*, summoned.
[2] In memory of his wife.
[3] *Reálly*, royally.

That he the better trowé might,
They ladden him to have a sight,
Where that her tombé was arraied,
The lassé yet he was mispaied.
And nethéles so as he durst,
He curseth and saith all the worst
Unto Fortúne, as to the blinde,
Which can no siker weié finde,
For she him neweth ever amonge
And medleth sorwe with his songe.
But sithe it may no better be,
He thonketh God and forth goth he
Sailéndé toward Tire ayeine.
But sodeinly the winde and reine
Began upon the see debate,
So that he suffre mote algate
The lawé, which Neptúne deineth,
Wherof full ofté time he pleigneth
And held him wel the more esmaied
Of that he hath to-fore assaied.
So that for puré sorwe and care
Of that he seeth this world so fare,
The reste he leveth of his cabán,
That for the counseil of no man
Ayein therin he noldé come
But hath beneth his placé nome,
Where he wepénd alloné lay
There as he sigh no light of day.
"And thus to-fore the wind they drive
Till longe and laté they arrive
With great distresse, as it was sene,
Upon this town of Mitelene,
Which was a noble cité tho.
And happneth thilké timé so,
The lordés both and the commúne
The highé festés of Neptune
Upon the strond at the rivage,
As it was custume and usage,
Solempneliché they besigh.
"Whan they this straungé vessel sigh
Come in, and hath his saile avaled,[1]
The town therof hath spoke and taled.
The lord which of that cité was,
Whose name is Athenagoras,
Was there and said, he woldé se
What ship it is, and who they be
That ben therin. And after sone,
Whan that he sigh it was to done,
His bargé was for him arraied,
And he goth forth and hath assaied.
He found the ship of great array,
But what thing it amounté may,
He sigh they maden hevy chere,
But well him thenketh by the manere,
That they be worthy men of blood,
And axeth of hem how it stood.
And they him tellen all the cas,
How that her lord fordrivé was,
And what a sorwé that he made
Of which there may no man him glade.
He praieth that he her lord may se.
But they him tolde it may nought be,
For he lith in so derke a place
That there may no wight sen his face.
But for all that, though hem be loth,
He found the ladder and down he goth
And to him spake, but none answér
Ayein of him ne might he bere,
For ought that he can do or sain.
And thus he goth him up ayein.
"Tho was there spoke in many wise
Amongés hem that weren wise,
Now this, now that, but atté last
The wisdom of the town thus cast,
That yongé Thaisé were assent.
For if there be amendément
To gladdé with this wofull king,
She can so moch of every thing
That she shall gladen him anone.
"A messager for her is gone.
And she came with her harp on honde
And saide hem, that she woldé fonde

[1] *Avaled*, lowered.

By allé weiés that she can,
To gladdé with this sory man.
And what he was, she wiste nought.
But all the ship her hath besought
That she her wit on him despende
In aunter if he might amende,
And sain, 'It shall be well aquit.'
Whan she hath understonden it,
She goth her down, there as he lay,
Where that she harpeth many a lay
And lich an aungel sang with alle.
But he no moré than the walle
Toke hede of any thing he herde.
And whan she sigh that he so ferde,
She falleth with him unto wordes,
And telleth him of sondry bordes,
And axeth him demaundés straunge
Wherof she made his herté chaunge,
And to her speche his ere he laide
And hath merveile, of that she saide.
For in provérbe and in probléme
She spake and bade he shuldé deme
In many a subtil questión.
But he for no suggestión
Which toward him she couthe stere
He woldé nought o word answere,
But as a mad man atté laste,
His heved wepíng awey he caste
And half in wrath he bad her go.
But yet she woldé nought do so,
And in the derké forth she goth,
Till she him toucheth, and he wroth
And after hiré with his honde
He smote. And thus whan she
him fonde
Diseséd, courteisly she saide:
'Avoy my lorde, I am a maide.
And if ye wisté what I am,
And out of what lignáge I cam,
Ye woldé nought be so salváge.'
With that he sobreth his corágе
And put awey his hevy chere.
But of hem two a man may lere,
What is to be so sibbe of blood.
None wist of other how it stood,
And yet the fader atté last
His herte upon this maidé cast,
That he her loveth kindély,
And yet he wisté never why;
But all was knowe er that they went.
For God, which wote her hole entent,
Her hertés both anone descloseth.
This king unto this maide opposeth
And axeth first, What is her name,
And where she lernéd all this game,
And of what kin that she was come?
And she, that hath his wordés nome,
Answereth and saith: 'My name
is Thaise,
That was sometimé well at ese.
In Tharse I was forthdrawe and
fedde,
There lernéd I till I was spedde
Of that I can. My fader eke
I not[1] where that I shulde him seke,
He was a king, men toldé me.
My moder dreint was in the see.'
Fro point to point all she him tolde,
That she hath longe in herté holde,
And never dursté make her mone,
But only to this lord allone,
To whom her herté can nought hele,[2]
Torne it to wo torne it to wele,
Torne it to good torne it to harme.
And he tho toke her in his arme.
But such a joy as he tho made
Was never sene; thus be they glade
That sory hadden be to-forne.
Fro this day forth Fortúne hath
sworne
To set him upward on the whele;
So goth the world; now wo, now wele.
"This king hath foundé newé
grace,
So that out of his derké place
He goth him up into the light.
And with him cam that sweté wight
His doughter Thaise, and forth anone
They bothe into the caban gone

[1] *Not*, know not. [2] *Hele*, conceal.

Which was ordeinéd for the kinge.
And there he did of all his thinge
And was arraiéd reálly,
And out he cam all openly
Where Athenagoras he fonde
The which was lorde of all the
londe.
He praieth the king to come and se
His castell bothe and his citee.
And thus they gone forth all in fere,
This king, this lord, this maiden
dere.
This lord tho made hem riché feste
With every thing which was
honéste
To plesé with this worthy kinge,
Ther lacketh hem no maner thinge.
But yet for al his noble array
Wifeles he was unto that day,
As he that yet was yonge of age.
So fell there into his coráge
The lusty wo, the gladdé peine
Of lové which no man restreigne
Yet never might as now to-fore.
This lord thenketh all his world
forlore
But if the king woll done him grace.
He waiteth time he waiteth place
Him thought his herté woll to-breke,
Till he may to this maidé speke
And to her fader eke also
For mariáge. And it fell so,
That all was do, right as he thought,
His purpos to an ende he brought,
She wedded him as for her lorde;
Thus be they alle of one accorde.
"Whan al was do right as they
wolde,
The kinge unto his soné tolde
Of Tharsé thilké treterie,
And said, how in his compaignie
His doughter and him selven eke
Shall go vengeaúncé for to seke.
The shippés weré redy sone.
And whan they sigh it was to done
Withouté let of any went,[1]
With saile up drawé forth they wente
Towardés Tharse upon the tide.
But he that wot what shall betide,
The highe God which wolde him
kepe,
Whan that this king was faste a slepe
By nightés time he hath him bede
To saile unto another stede;
To Ephesim he bad him drawe,
And as it was that timé lawe,
He shall do there his sacrifice.
And eke he bad in allé wise,
That in the temple amongés alle
His Fortune, as it is befalle,
Touchend his doughter and his wife
He shall beknowe upon his life.
The king of this avisión
Hath great ymaginación
What thinge it signifié may.
And nethéles whan it was day
He bad cast anker and abode.
And while that he on anker rode,
The wind, which was to-foré
straunge,
Upon the point began to chaunge
And torneth thider as it shulde.
Tho knewe he well, that God it wolde,
And bad the maister make him yare,
To-fore the wind for he wold fare
To Ephesim, and so he dede.
And whan he came into the stede,
Where as he shuldé londe, he londeth
With all the haste he may, and
fondeth
To shapen him in suche a wise,
That he may by the morwe arise
And done after the maundément
Of him, which hath him thider sent.
And in the wisé that he thought,
Upon the morwe so he wrought.
His doughter and his sone he nome
And forth unto the temple he come

[1] *Let of any went*, hindrance of any turning aside.

With a great route in compaigný
His yiftés for to sacrifý.
The citezeins tho herden say
Of such a king that came to pray
Unto Diané the goddésse
And lefte all other besinesse,
They comen thider for to se
The king and the solempnité.
"With worthy knightés environed
The king him self hath abandóned
Into the temple in good entente.
The dore is up and in he wente,
Whereas with great devoción
Of holy contemplación
Within his herte he made his shrifte.
And after that a riché yifte
He offreth with great reverénce,
And there in open audiénce
Of hem that stoden all about
He tolde hem and declareth out
His hap such as him is befalle;
There was no thing foryete of alle.
His wife, as it was Goddés grace,
Which was professéd in the place
As she that was abbéssé there,
Unto his tale hath laid her ere,
She knew the vois and the viságe,
For puré joy as in a rage
She straught unto him all at ones
And fell a swoune upon the stones
Wherof the temple flore was paved.
She was anone with water laved,
Till she came to her self ayein.
And thanné she began to sain:
'Ha, blessed be the highé sonde,
That I may se min huséбonde,
Which whilom he and I were one.'
The king with that knewe her anone
And toke her in his arme and kist,
And all the town thus sone it wist.
Tho was there joié manyfold,
For every man this tale hath told
As for miráclc, and were glade.
But never man such joié made
As doth the king which hath his wife.
And whan men herde how that her life
Was savéd and by whom it was,
They wondren all of suche a cas.
Through all the londe arose the speche
Of maister Cerimon the leche
And of the curé which he dede.
The king him self tho hath him bede
And eke this quené forth with him,
That he the town of Ephesim
Woll leve and go where as they be,
For never man of his degre
Hath do to hem so mochel good.
And he his profite understood
And graunteth with hem for to wende.
And thus they maden there an ende
And token leve and gone to ship
With all the holé felaship.
"This king, which now hath his desire,
Saith he woll holde his cours to Tire.
They hadden wind at willé tho
With topsail-cole,[1] and forth they go.
And striken never till they come
To Tire wher as they haven nome,
And londen hem with mochel blisse.
There was many a mouth to kisse,
Eche oné welcometh other home.
But whan the quene to londé come
And Thaise her doughter by her side,
The joié which was thilké tide
There may no mannés tungé telle.
They saiden all, 'Here cometh the welle
Of alle womanisshé grace.'
The king hath take his reäl place,
The quene is into chambre go;
There was great feste arraiéd tho.
Whan timé was they gone to mete,
All oldé sorwés ben foryete,
And gladen hem with joiés newe.
The descoloúréd palé hewe

[1] See note, page 253.

Is now become a ruddy cheke,
There was no merthé for to seke,
But every man hath what he wolde,
The king as he well couthe and sholde
Maketh to his people right good chere,
And after sone, as thou shalt here,
A parlément he hath sommóned,
Where he his doughter hath coróned
Forth with the lorde of Mitelene,
That one is king, that other quene.
And thus the faders ordenaunce
This londe hath set in governaunce,
And saidé that he woldé wende
To Tharsé for to make an ende
Of that his doughter was betraied,
Wherof were allé men well paied,
And said, how it was for to done.
"The shippés weren redy sone.
A strong powér with him he toke,
Up to the sky he cast his loke
And sigh the wind was covenáble.
They hale up anker with the cable,
They sail on high, the stere on honde,
They sailen till they come a londe
At Tharsé nigh to the citee.
And whan they wisten it was he,
The town hath done him reverence.
He telleth hem the violence,
Which the tretoúr Strangulio
And Dionise him haddé do
Touchénde his doughter, as ye herde.
And whan they wisté how it ferde,
As he which pees and lové sought,
Unto the town this he besought
To done him right in jugément.
Anone they weré both assent
With strengthe of men, and comen sone,
And as hem thought it was to done,
Atteint they weré by the lawe
And deméd for to honge and drawe
And brent and with the wind to-blowe,
That all the world it mighté knowe.
And upon this condición
The dome in execución
Was put anone withouté faile.
And every man hath great merveile,
Whiche herdé tellen of this chaunce,
And thonketh Goddés purveaunce,
Which doth mercý forth with justíce.
Slain is the mordrer and mordrice
Through verray trouth of rightwisnesse,
And through mercý sauf is simplesse
Of hiré whom mercý preserveth;
Thus hath he wel that wel deserveth.
"Whan all this thing is done and ended,
This king which lovéd was and frended,
A letter hath, which came to him
By shippé fro Pentapolim,
In which the lond hath to him write
That he wolde understonde and wite,
How in good minde and in good pees
Dede is the kinge Artestrates,
Wherof they all of one accorde
Him praiden, as her legé lorde,
That he the letter wol conceive
And come his regné to receive
Which God hath yove him and Fortúne.
And thus besoughté the commúne
Forth with the greté lordés alle.
This king sigh how it was befalle,
Fro Tharse and in prosperité
He toke his leve of that citee
And goth him into ship ayein.
The wind was good, the se was plein,
Hem nedeth nought a riff to slake,[1]
Till they Pentapolim have take.
The lond which herde of that tidíng
Was wonder glad of his comíng.
He resteth him a day or two
And toke his counseil to him tho

[1] To slacken a reef.

And set a time of parlément,
Where all the londe of one assent
Forth with his wife have him coroned,
Where allé good him was foisoned.[1]
"Lo, what it is to be well grounded,
For he hath first his lové founded
Honestélich as for to wedde,
Honestélich his love he spedde
And haddé children with his wife,
And as him list he lad his life.
And in ensaumple his life was write,
That allé lovers mighten wite
How atté last it shal be sene
Of lové what they wolden mene.
For se now, on that other side,
Antiochus with all his pride
Which set his love unkindély,
His ende he haddé sodeinly
Set ayein kinde upon vengeaúnce,
And for his lust hath his penaúnce.
"Lo thus, my soné, might thou lere,
What is to love in good manere,
And what to love in other wise.
The mede ariseth of the servíce,
Fortúné though she be nought stable,
Yet at somtime is favourable
To hem that ben of lové trewe.
But certés it is for to rewe
To se love ayein kindé falle,
For that maketh sore a man to falle,
As thou might of to-foré rede.
Forthý my sone, I woldé rede
To let all other love awey,
But if it be through such a wey
As love and reson wold accorde."—
"My fader, how so that it stonde,
Your tale is herde and understonde,
As thing which worthy is to here,
Of great ensample and grete matere,
Wherof, my fader, God you quite.
But in this point my self aquite

[1] *Foisoned*, poured out profusely.

I may right wel, that never yit
I was assoted in my wit,
But onely in that worthy place
Where allé lust and allé grace
Is set, if that Daunger ne were,
But that is all my mosté fere.
I not what ye Fortúne accompte,
But what thing Daunger may amounte
I wot wel, for I have assaied.
For whan min hert is best arraied
And I have all my wit through sought
Of lové to beseche her ought,
For all that ever I skillé may
I am concluded with a nay,
That o silláble hath over throwe
A thousand wordés on a rowe
Of suche as I best speké can,
Thus am I but a lewdé man.
But fader, for ye ben a clerke
Of lóve, and this matere is derke
And I can ever lenger the lasse
But yet I may nought let it passe,
Your holé counseil I beseche,
That ye me by some weié teche,
What is my best, as for an ende."—
"My sone, unto the trouthé wende
Now woll I for the love of the
And lete all other trifles be.
"The moré that the nede is high,
The more it nedeth to be sligh
To him which hath the nede on honde.
I have well herd and understonde,
My sone, all that thou hast me saied
And eke of that thou hast me praied.
Nowe at this timé that I shall
As for conclusión fináll
Counseil upon thy nedé set,
So thenke I finally to knet
Thy causé where it is to-broke,
And make an ende of that is spoke.
For I behighté the that yift
First whan thou come under my shrift,

That though I toward Venus were,
Yet spake I suché wordés there,
That for the presthode which I have,
Min order and min estate to save,
I saide, I wolde of min office
To vertu moré than to vice
Encline and teché the my lore.
Forthý to speken overmore
Of Lové which the may availe,
Take Lové where it may nought faile.
For as of this which thou art in,
By that thou seest it is a sinne,
And sinné may no prise deserve,
Withouté prise and who shall serve
I not what profit might availe.
Thus folweth it, if thou travaile
Where thou no profit hast ne prise
Thou art toward thy self unwise,
And sith thou mightest lust atteine,
Of every lust the ende is peine
And every pein is good to flee.
So it is wonder thing to se
Why such a thing shall be desired.
The moré that a stock is fired
The rather[1] into ashe it torneth.
The fote which in the weié sporneth
Full ofte his heved hath overthrowe.
Thus Love is blinde and can nought knowe
Where that he goth till he be falle.
Forthý but if it so befalle
With good counsell that he be lad,
Him oughté for to ben adrad.
For counseil passeth allé thing
To him which thenketh to ben a king.
And every man for his partý
A kingdom hath to justifý,
That is to sain, his owné dome.
If he misreulé that kingdóme,
He lest him self, and that is more,
Than if he losté ship and ore
And all the worldés goód with all.
For what man that in speciáll

[1] *Rather*, sooner.

Hath nought him self, he hath nought ellés,
No more the perlés than the shelles,
All is to him of o value—
Though he had all his retenue
The widé world right as he wolde—
Whan he his hert hath nought witholde
Toward him self, all is in vein.
And thus, my sone, I woldé sain,
As I said er, that thou arise
Er that thou falle in such a wise
That thou ne might thy self rekever;
For Lové, which that blind was ever,
Maketh all his servaunts blinde also.
"My sone, and if thou have be so,
Yet it is timé to withdrawe
And set thin hert under that lawe
The which of Reson is govérned
And nought of Will. And to be lerned
Ensamples thou hast many one
Of now and eke of timé gone,
That every lust is but a while.
And who that woll him self beguile,
He may the rather be deceived.
My soné, now thou hast conceived
Somwhat of that I woldé mene,
Here afterward it shall be sene,
If that thou leve upon my lore.
For I can do to the no more,
But teché the the righté way.
Now chese, if thou wilt live or deie."—
"**My fader**, so as I have herde
Your talé, but it were answérde,
I weré mochel for to blame.
My wo to you is but a game,
That feleth nought of that I fele.
The feling of a mannés hele
May nought be likened to the herte;
I wot that though I wolde asterte
And ye be fre from all the peine
Of lové wherof I me pleine,
It is right esy to commaunde.

The hert which fre goth on the launde
Not[1] of an oxé what him eileth,
It falleth oft a man merveileth
Of that he seeth another fare.
But if he knew himself the fare
And felt it as it is in soth,
He shuldé do right as he doth
Or ellés wors in his degré.
For wel I wote and so do ye,
That love hath ever yet ben used,
So mote I nedés ben excused.
But fader, if ye woldé thus
Unto Cupide and to Venús
Be frendly toward my quarele,
So that my herté were in hele
Of lové which is in my breste,
I wot wel than a better preste
Was never made to my behove.
But all the whilé that I hove
In none certein betwene the two,
And not where[2] I to well or wo
Shall torné, that is all my drede,
So that I not what is to rede.
But for finâll conclusión
I thenke a supplicación
With pleiné wordés and expresse
Write unto Venus the goddesse,
The which I praié you to bere
And bring ayein a good answere."
Tho was betwene my prest
and me
Debate and great perplexeté.
My Reson understode him wele
And knewe it was soth every dele
That he hath said, but nought forthý
My Will hath no thing set ther by.
For touching of so wise a porte
It is unto love no disporte.
Yet mighté never man beholde
Resón, where Lové was witholde,[3]
They be nought of o governaunce.
And thus we fellen in distaunce
My prest and I, but I spake faire

[1] *Not*, knows not.
[2] *Not where*, know not whether.
[3] *Witholde*, held with.

And through my wordés debonaire
Than atté lasté we accorden,
So that he saith, he woll accorden
To speke and stond upon my side
To Venus both and to Cupide,
And bad me write what I wolde.
And said me truly that he sholde
My letter bere unto the quene.
And I sat down upon the grene
Fulfilléd of Loves fantasy
And with the terés of min eye
In stede of inke I gan to write
The wordés which I wol endite
Unto Cupide and to Venus,
And in my letter I saide thus:—

The wofull peine of lovés
maladie,
Ayein the which may no phisíque
availe, [sotie,
Min hert hath so bewhappéd with
That wheré so that I reste or travaile
I finde it ever redy to assaile
My reson, which that can him nought
defende.
Thus seche I help wherof I might
amende.

First to Natúre if that I me com-
pleine,
There finde I how that every creätúre
Somtime a yere[1] hath love in his
demaine,
So that the litel wrenne in his mesúre
Have yet of kinde a love under his
cure.
And I but one desiré, which I misse,
And thus but I hath every kinde his
blisse.

The reson of my wit it overpasseth,
Of that Natúré teché me the wey
To love and yet no certein she
compásseth

[1] At some time in each year.

How shal I spede; and thus betwen the twey
I stonde and not[1] if I shall live or dey.
For though Resón ayein my will debate,
I may nought flee that I ne love algate.

Upon my self this ilké talé come,
How whilom Pan, which is the god of kinde,
With Lové wrestled and was overcome,
For ever I wrestle and ever I am behinde,[2]
That I no strength in all min herté finde
Wherof that I may stonden any throwe,
So fer my wit with love is overthrowe.

Whom nedeth help, he mot his helpé crave
Or helpéles he shall his nedé spille.
Pleinly throughsought my wittés al I have,
But none of hem can help after my wille.
And al so well I mighté sité stille
As pray unto my lady of any helpe,
Thus wote I nought wherof my self to helpe.

Unto the greté Jove and if I bid
To do me grace of thilké swetétonne
Which under key in his cellér amid
Lith couchéd, that Fortúne is overronne;
But of the bitter cuppe I have begonne,
I not how ofte, and thus finde I no game,
For ever I axe and ever it is the same.

I se the world stond ever upon eschaunge,
Now windés loudé, now the weder softe,
I may se eke the greté moné chaunge,
And thing which now is low is eft alofte;
The dredful werrés into pees ful ofte
They torne, and ever is Daunger in o place,
Which woldé chaunge his Will to do me grace.

But upon this the greté clerk Ovíde,
Of Lové whan he maketh rémembraúnce,
He saith: Ther is the blindé god Cupide,
The which hath love under his governaúnce
And in his hond with many a firy launce
He woundeth ofté where he woll nought hele,
And that somdele is cause of my quarele.

Ovíde eke saith, that lové to performe
Stant in the hond of Venus the goddésse,
But whan she taketh counseil with Satorne
There is no grace, and in that time I gesse
Began my love, of which min hevinesse
Is now and ever shall, but if I spede,
So wot I nought my self what is to rede.

Forthý to you, Cupide and Venus both,
With all min hertés obeisaúnce I pray,
If ye were atté firsté timé wroth,

1 *Not*, know not.

2 For e'er I wrestl' and e'er I am behind. So in last line of next stanza but one, "e'er" . . . "e'er."

Whan I began to loven, I you say,
Now stint, and do thilké Fortúne away,
So that Daungér, which stant of retenue
With my ladý, his placé may remue.

O thou Cupidé, god of lovés lawe,
That with thy dart brennénd hast set a fire
My herté, do that woundé be withdrawe,
Or yivé me salve, suche as I desire.
For service in thy court withouten hire
To me which ever yet have kept thin heste,
May never be to lovés lawe honeste.

O thou, gentilé Venus, lovés quene,
Withouté gilt thou dost on me thy wreche,
Thou wost my pein is ever alich grene
For love, and yet I may it nought arecche.[1]
Thus wolde I for my lasté word beseche
That thou my love aquite as I deserve,
Or ellés do me pleinly for to sterve.

Whan I this supplicación
With good deliberación,
In suche a wise as ye now wite,
Had after min ententé write
Unto Cupide and to Venús,
This presté which hight Geniús
It toke on hondé to presente.
On my message and forth he wente
To Venus for to wit her wille.
And I bode in the placé stille
And was there but a litel while
Nought full the mountance of a mile,
Whan I behelde and sodeinlý
I sigh where Venus stood me by.
So as I might, under a tree
To grounde I felle upon my knee
And preid her for to do me grace.
She cast her chere upon my face
And as it were halving a game
She axeth me, what wás my name.
'Madame,' I saidé, 'Iohan Gower.'
'Now Iohan,' quod she, 'in my power
Thou must as of thy lové stonde.
For I thy bill have understonde
In which to Cupide and to me
Somdele thou hast compleignéd the;
And somdele to Natúre also,
But that shall stonde among you two
For therof have I nought to done,
For Natúre is under the mone
Maistresse of every livés kinde,
But if so be that she may finde
Some holy man that woll withdrawe
His kindely lust, ayein her lawe.
But seldéwhan it falleth so,
For fewé men there ben of tho.
But of these other inowé be,
Whiche of her owné nicité
Ayein Natúre and her office
Deliten hem in sondry vice
Wherof that she full oft hath pleigned;
And eke my Court it hath disdeigned
And ever shall, for it receiveth
None such that kindé so desceiveth.
For all onlich of gentil love
My Court stant allé Courts above
And taketh nought into retenue
But thing which is to Kindé due.
For ellés it shall be refused,
Wherof I holdé the excused.
For it is many daiés gone,
That thou amongés hem were one
Which of my court shall be witholde,
So that the more I am beholde
Of thy disesé to commúne
And to remüé that Fortune

[1] *Arecche*, reach to.

Which many daiés hath the greved.
But if my counseil may be leved,
Thou shalt be eséd er thou go
Of thilke unsely jolif wo
Wherof thou saist thin hert is fired.
But as of that thou hast desired
After the sentence of thy bill,
Thou must therof done at my will
And I therof me woll avise.
For be thou hole, it shall suffice;
My medicine is nought to seke
The which is holsome to the seke,
Nought all perchaunce as ye it wolde
But so as ye by reson sholde,
Accordaunt unto lovés kinde.
For in the plite which I the finde,
So as my Court it hath awarded,
Thou shalt be duëly rewarded.
And if thou woldest moré crave,
It is no right that thou it have.'
Venus, which stant withouté lawe,
In none certeine, but as men drawe
Of rageman upon the chaunce,
She laith no peise in the balaunce,
But as her liketh for to weie
The trewé man full ofte aweie
She put, which hath her gracé bede,
And sette an untrue in his stede.
Lo, thus blindlý the world she demeth
In Lovés cause, as to me semeth,
I not what other men wold sain
But I algate am so beseine,
And stonde as one amonges alle
Which am out of her gracé falle.
It nedeth také no witnesse,
For she, which said is the goddesse
To whether parte of love it wende,
Hath set me for a finall ende
The point wherto that I shall holde.
For whan she hath me well beholde
Halving of scorne she saidé thus:
"Thou wost well that I am Venús,
Which all onlý my lustés seche.
And well I wot though thou beseche
My lové lustés ben there none
Which I may take in thy persone,
For lovés lust and lockés hore
In chambre accorden nevermore.
And though thou feigne a yong corage,
It sheweth well by thy viságe,
That oldé grisel is no fole.
There ben full many yerés stole
With the and other suché mo
That outward feignen youthé so
And ben within of pouer assay.
'My herté wolde, and I ne may,'
Is nought belovéd now a daies.
Er thou make any such assaies
To love, and faile upon thy fete,
Bet is to maké *beau retrete*.'
" My sone, if that thou well bethought,
This toucheth the, foryete it nought,
The thing is tornéd into 'was,'
The which was whilome grene gras
Is welkéd heie as timé now.
Forthy my counseil is, that thou
Remembre well how thou art olde."
Whan Venus hath her talé tolde,
And I bethought was all aboute,
And wisté wel withouten doubte
That there was no recoverire,
And as a man the blase of fire
With water quencheth, so ferde I.
A coldé me caught sodeinly;
For sorwe that my herté made
My dedly facé pale and fade
Becam, and swoune I fel to grounde.
And as I lay the samé stounde
Ne fully quick, ne fully dede,
Me thought I sigh to-fore min hede
Cupídé with his bowé bent
And like unto a parlément
Which were ordeinéd for the nones,
With him cam all the world atones
Of gentil folke, that whilom were
Lovérs, I sigh hem alle there

Forth with Cupíde in sondry routes.
Min eye and as I cast aboutes
To know among hem who was who,
I sigh where lusty youthé tho,
As he which was a capitein
To-fore all other upon the plein
Stood with his routé well begon,
Her hedes kempt, and therupon
Garlóndés, nought of o colour,
Some of the lefe some of the floure,
And some of greté perles were.
The newé guise of Beawmé there
With sondry thingés well devised
I sigh, wherof they be queintised.
It was all lust that they with ferde.
There was no song that I ne herde
Which unto lové was touchíng,
Of Pan and all that was likíng,
As in pipíng of melodie
Was herde in thilké compaignie,
So loudé that on every side
It thought as all the heven cride
In suche accorde and suche a soune
Of bombarde and of clarioúne
With cornemúse and with shalméle,
That it was half a mannés hele
So glad a noisé for to here.
  And as me thought in this manere
All fresshe I sigh hem springe and daunce,
And do to love her entendaúnce
After the lust of youthés hest,
There was inough of joy and fest.
For ever among they laugh and pley
And putten care out of the wey,
That he with hem ne sat ne stode.
And over this I understode,
So as min ere it might arecche,
The mosté matere of her speche
It was of knighthode and of armes,
And what it is to ligge in armes
With lové whan it is acheved.
  There was Tristram, which was beleved
With Bele Isolde, and Lancelot
Stode with Gunnór, and Galahot
With his ladý, and as me thought,
I sigh where Jason with him brought
His lové, which Creüsa hight.
And Hercules which mochel might
Was theré bering his great mace,
And most of all in thilké place
He peineth him to maké chere
With Eölen which was him dere.
Theseüs though he were untrewe
To love, as allé women knewe,
Yet was he theré nethéles
With Fedra which to love he ches.
Of Grece eke there was Thelamon,
Which fro the kingé Lamedon
At Troy his doughter reft away
Eseönen as for his pray,
Which také was whan Jason cam
Fro Colchos and the citee nam
In vengeaunce of the firsté hate
That made hem after to debate
Whan Priamus the newé town
Hath made. And in avisioún
Me thoughté that I sigh also
Hector forth with his brethern two,
Him self stood with Pantasilee,
And next to him I mighté see,
Where Paris stood with faire Heleine,
Which was his joié soveraine.
And Troilus stood with Creseide.
But ever among although he pleide,
By semblaunt he was hevy chered.
For Diomede, as him was lered,
Claimeth to be his partenére.
And thus full many a bachelere,
A thousand mo than I can sain,
With youth I sigh there well besein
Forth with her lovés glad and blith.
  And some I sigh, which ofte sith
Compleignen hem in sondry wise,
Among the which I sigh Narcise
And Piramus, that sory were.
The worthy Greke also was there,
Achilles, which for lové deied.
Agámenon eke as men saied,

And Menelay the King also
I sigh with many an other mo
Which hadden be fortúnéd sore
In lovés cause. And overmore
Of women in the samé cas
With hem I sigh where Dido was
Forsaké which was with Enee.
And Phillis eke I mighté see,
Whom Demophon deceivéd hadde,
And Adriagne her sorwe ladde,
For Theseús her suster toke
And her unkindély forsoke.
I sigh there eke among the pres
Compleigning upon Herculés
His firsté lové Deianire,
Which set him afterward a fire.
Medea was there eke and pleigneth
Upon Jasón for that he feigneth
Withouté cause and toke a newe,
She saidé, 'Fie on all untrewe!'
I sigh theré Deſdamie,
Which haddé lost the compaignie
Of Áchillés, whan Diomede
To Troy him fet upon the nede.
Among these other upon the grene
I sigh also the wofull quene
Cleópatrás, which in a cave
With serpents hath her self begrave
All quick,[1] and so she was to-tore
For sorwe of that she haddé lore
Antónie, which her love hath be.
And forth with her I sigh Tisbé,
Which on the sharpé swerdés pointe
For lové deied in sory pointe.
And as min ere it mighté knowe,
She saidé, 'Wo worth alle slowe.'
The pleint of Progne and Philomene
There herde I what it woldé mene,
How Tereús of his untrouthe
Undid hem both, and that was routhe.
And next to hem I sigh Canace,
Which for Machair her faders grace
Hath lost and deied in wofull plite.

[1] *Begrave all quick*, buried alive.

And as I sigh in my spiríte,
Me thought amongés other thus
The doughter of king Priamus,
Polſxena, whom Pirrus slough,
Was there and madé sorwe inough,
As she which deide gilteles
For love, and yet was lovéles.
And for to také the desporte
I sigh there some of other porte,
And that was Circes and Calipse,
That couthen do the moné clipse,
Of men and chaungé the liknesse,
Of artmagíqué sorceresse,
They helde in hondé many one
To lové, where they wolde or none.
But above allé that there were
Of women I sigh fouré there,
Whose name I herdé most commended.
By hem the court stode all amended.
For where they comen in presénce
Men diden hem the reverénce
As though they hadden ben goddésses
Of all this world or emperesses.
And as me thought an ere I laid
And herde, how that these other said:
'Lo, thesé ben the fouré wives,
Whose feith was provéd in her lives
For in ensample of all good
With mariágé so they stood
That Famé, which no great thing hideth
Yet in croníque of hem abideth.'
  Penelope that one was hote,
Whom many a knight hath loved hote
While that her lorde Ulixes laie
Full many a yere and many a daie
Upon the greté siege of Troy:
But she which hath no worldés joy
But only of her husébonde,
While that her lord was out of londe,
So well hath kept her womanhede,
That all the world therof toke hede

And namélich of hem in Grece.
That other woman was Lucrece,
Wife to the Romain Collatine.
And she constreignéd of Tarquine
To thing which was ayein her will,
She woldé nought her selven still,
But deide only for drede of shame
In keping of her godé name,
As she which was one of the beste.
The thridde wife was hote Alceste,
Which whan Admetus shuldé die
Upon his greté maladie,
She praied unto the goddés so,
That she receiveth all the wo
And deied her self to yive him life,—
Se where this were a noble wife!
The ferthé wife which I there sigh,
I herde of hem that weré nigh,
How she was cleped Alcfone,
Which Cefx hiré lord allone
And to no mo her body kepte,
And whan she sighe him dreint, she lepte
Into the wawés where he swam,
And there a see foule she becam.
And with her wingés him besprad
For lové that she to him had.
  Lo, thesé fouré weren tho,
Which I sigh as me thoughté tho
Among the greté compaignie,
Which lové haddé for to gie.[1]
But Youthé, which in speciáll
Of Lovés court was maréshall,
So besy was upon his lay,
That he none hedé where he lay
Hath take. And than as I beheldе,
Me thought I sigh upon the felde,
Where Eldé came a softé pas
Toward Venús, there as she was,
With him great compaignie he ladde,
But nought so fele as Youthé hadde.
The mosté part were of great age,
And that was sene in her viságe,
And nought forthý, so as they might,

[1] *Gie*, guide.

They made hem yongly to the sight.
But yet herde I no pipés there
To maké merth in mannés ere,
But the musíque I mighté knowe
For oldé men, which souned lowe
With harpe and lute and with citole
The hové daunce and the carole,[1]
In suche a wise as love hath bede,
A softé pas they daunce and trede,
And with the women otherwhile
With sobre chere among they smile,
For laughter was there none on high.
And nethéles full well I sigh
That they the moré queint it made
For love in whom they weren glade.
And there me thought I mighté see
The king Davíd with Bersabee,
And Salomon was nought withoute
Passing an hundred in a route
Of wivés and of concubines;
Jewesses eke and Sarazínes
To him I sigh all entendaúnt,
I not where he were suffisaúnt.
But nethéles for all his wit
He was attachéd with that writ
Which Lové with his hond enseleth,
From whom none erthly man appeleth.
And over this, as for no wonder,
With his león, which he put under,
With Dálilá Sampsón I knewe,
Whos love his strength all overthrewe.
I sigh there Aristotle also,
Whom that the quene of Grece al so
Hath bridled, that in thilké time
She made him such a silogime,
That he foryate all his logique,
There was none arte of his practique,
Through which it mighté ben excluded,
That he ne was fullý concluded

[1] *Hové daunce*, court dance. *Carole*, an old round dance.

To love and did his obeisaunce.
And eke Virgile of áqueintaúnce
I sigh, where he the maiden praid
Which was the doughter, as men said,
Of themperoúr whilom of Rome.
Sortés and Plato with him come,
So did Ovídé the poete.
I thoughté than how love is swete
Which hath so wisé men reclamed,
And was my self the lasse ashamed
Or for to lese or for to winne
In the mischefe that I was inne,
And thus I lay in hope of grace.
And whan they comen to the place,
Where Venus stood and I was falle,
These oldé men with o vois alle
To Venus praiden for my sake.
And she that mighté nought forsake
So great a clamour as was there,
Let pité come into her ere
And forth with all unto Cupide
She praieth that he upon his side
Me woldé through his gracé sende
Some comfort, that I might amende
Upon the cas which is befalle.
And thus for me they praiden alle
Of hem that weren old aboute,
And eke some of the yongé route,
Of gentilésse and puré trouth
I herde hem tel it was great routh,
That I withouten help so ferde.
And thus me thought I lay and herde.
Cupídé, which maie hurt and hele
In Lovés cause, as for min hele
Upon the point which him was praid
Cam with Venús where I was laid
Swounénd upon the grené gras.
And as me thought anone there was
On every sidé so great pres,
That every life began to pres,
I wot nought wel how many score,
Suche as I spake of now to-fore,
Lovers, that comen to beholde,
But most of hem that weren olde.
They stoden there at thilké tide
To se what endé shall betide
Upon the cure of my sotie.
Tho might I heré great partie
Spekénd, and eche his own avis
Hath tolde, one that another this.
But among allé this I herde,
They weren wo that I so ferde,
And saiden that for no rióte
An oldé man shuld nought assote.
For as they tolden redely
There is in him no causé why,
But if he wold him self be nice,
So were he well the moré nice.
And thus desputen some of tho,
And somé saiden no thíng so,
But that the wildé lovés rage
In mannés life forbereth none age,
While there is oilé for to fire
The lampe is lightly set a fire
And is full hard er it be queint,
But only if he be some seint,
Which God preserveth of his grace.
And thus me thought in sondry place,
Of hem that walken up and down
There was divers opinioún.
And for a whilé so it laste,
Till that Cupidé to the laste,
Forth with his moder full avised
Hath déterminéd and devised,
Unto what point he woll descend.
And all this time I was liggénd
Upon the ground to-fore his eyen.
And they that my disesé sighen
Supposen nought I shuldé live.
But he which woldé thanné yive
His gracé, so as it maie be,
This blindé god which may nought se
Hath gropéd till that he me fonde.
And as he putté forth his honde
Upon my body, where I lay,
Me thought a firy lancegay
Which whilom through my hert he cast
He pulleth out, and al so fast

As this was do, Cupidé nam
His wey; I not where he becam;
And so did all the remenaunt
Which unto him was entendaunt
Of hem that in avisión
I had a revelación,
So as I toldé now to-fore.
But Venus wenté nought therfore,
Ne Genius, which thilké time
Abiden bothé fasté by me.
And she, which may the hertés binde
In lovés cause and eke unbinde,
Er I out of my traunce arose,
Venús, which helde a buisté close
And woldé nought I sholdé deie,
Toke out, more colde then ony keie
An oignément, and in such point
She hath my wounded hert anoint,
My temples and my reins also.
And forth with all she toke me tho
A wonder mirrour for to holde,
In which she bad me to beholde
And také hede of that I sigh;
Wherin anone min hertés eye
I cast and sigh my colour fade,
Min eien dim and all unglade,
My chekés thinne, and all my face
With elde I mighté se deface,
So riveled and so wo besein
That there was no thing full ne plein.
I sigh also min hairés hore,
My will was tho to se no more,
On which for there was no plesaunce.
And than into my rémembraúnce
I drough min oldé daiés passed,
And as resón it hath compassed,
I made a likenesse of my selve
Unto the sondry monthés twelve,
Wherof the yere in his estate
Is made, and stant upon debate,
That lich til other none accordeth.
For who the timés wel recordeth,
And than at Marche if he beginne,
Whan that the lusty yere comth inne
Till Augst be passéd and Septembre,
The mighty youth he may remembre,
In which the yere hath his deduit[1]
Of grass, of lefe, of floure, of fruit,
Of corne, and of the winy grape.
And afterward the time is shape
To frost, to snow, to wind, to rain,
Till eft that March be come ayein.
The Winter woll no Somer knowe,
The grené lefe is overthrowe,
The clothéd erth is thanné bare,
Despuiléd is the somer fare,
That erst was hete is thanné chele.
And thus thenkéndé thoughtés fele
I was out of my swoune affraid,
Wherof I sigh my wittés straid
And gan to clepe hem home ayein.
And whan Reson it herde sain
That lovés ragé was awey,
He cam to me the righté wey
And hath remeved the sotie
Of thilke unwisé fantasie
Wherof that I was wont to plein,
So that of thilké firy pein
I was made sobre and hole inough.
Venus beheld me than and lough
And axeth, as it were in game,
"What lové was?" And I for shame
Ne wisté what I shulde answere.
And nethéles I gan to swere
That "By my trouth I knewe him nought,"
So fer it was out of my thought,
Right as it haddé never be.
"My godé soné," tho quod she,
"Now at this time I leve it wele,
So goth the fortune of my whele.
Forthý my counseil is, thou leve."—
"Madame," I saidé, "by your leve,
Ye weten well, and so wote I,
That I am unbehovély
Your Court fro this day for to serve.
And for I may no thank deserve,

[1] *Deduit*, delight.

And also for I am refused,
I praié you to ben excused.
And nethéles as for to lasté,
While that my wittés with me laste,
Touchendé my confessión,
I axe an absolutión
Of Genius, er that I go."
The prest anone was redy tho,
And saidé: "Sone, as of thy shrifte,
Thou hast full pardon and foryifte.
Foryete it thou, and so will I."
"Min holy fader, graunt mercý,"
Quod I to him, and to the quene
I fell on knees upon the grene,
And toke my levé for to wende.
But she, that woldé make an ende,
As therto, which I was most able,
A paire of bedés blacke as sable
She toke and heng my necke about.
Upon the gaudés all without
Was write of gold *pur reposer*.
"Lo," thus she said, "Iohan Gower,
Now thou art atté lasté caste.
Thus have I for thin esé caste
That thou no more of lové seche.
But my will is, that thou beseche
And pray hereafter for the pees,
And that thou make a plein relees
To love which taketh litel hede
Of oldé men upon the nede,
Whan that the lustes ben awey,
Forthy to the nis but o wey,
In which let Reson be thy guide.
For he may sone him self misguide,
That seeth nought the perill to-fore.
" My soné, be well ware therfore
And kepe the sentence of my lore
Tarie thou in my court no more,
But go there vertue moral dwelleth,
Where ben thy bokés, as men telleth,
Which eof long timé thou hast write.
For this I do the well to wite,
If thou thin helé wolt purcháce
Thou might nought maké sute and chace
Where that the game is nought provâble,
It were a thing unresonáble,
A man to be so overseie.
Forthý take hede of that I saie.
For in the lawe of my commune
We be nought shapé to commune,
Thy self and I, never after this.
Now have I said all that there is
Of love, as for thy final ende.
Adieu, for I mot fro the wende."[1]

[1] MS. Harl. 3490:
And grete well Chaucer, whan ye mete,
As my disciple and my poete.
For in the floures of his youth,
In sondry wise, as he well couth,
Of dittees and of songes glade,
The which he for my sake made,
The lond fulfilled is over all,
Wherof to him in speciall
Above all other I am most holde.
Forthy now in his daies olde
Thou shalt him telle this message,
That he upon his later age
To sette an end of all his werke,
As he, which is min owne clerke,
Do make his testament of love,
As thou hast do thy shrifte above,
So that my court it may recorde.
Madame, I can me well accorde,
Quod I, to telle as ye me bidde.
And with that worde it so betidde
Out of my sight all sodeinly,
Enclosed in a sterry sky,
Up to the heven Venus straught.
And I my righte waie sought
Home fro the wode and forth I wente,
Where as with al min hole entente
Thus with my bedes upon honde
For hem that true love fonde
I thenke bidde while I live,
Upon the point which I am shrive.
He, which withinne daies seven
The large world forth with the heven
Of his eternal providence
Hath made and thilke intelligence
In mannes soule resonable,
Wherof the man of feture
Of alle erthly creature
After the soule is immortall,

And with that word all sodeinly
Enclosed in a sterred sky
Venús, which is the quene of love,
Was take into her place above,
More wist I nought where she becam.
And thus my leve of her I nam.
And forth with al that samé tide
Her Prest, which woldé nought abide,
Or be me lefe or be me loth,
Out of my sighté forth he goth.
And I was left withouten helpe,
So wist I nought wherof to yelpe,
But only that I haddé lore
My time and was sorfe therfore.

To thilke lord in speciall
As he, which is of alle thinges
The creator and of the kinges
Hath the fortune upon honde
His grace and mercy for to fonde,
Upon my bare knees I pray,
That he my worthy king convey
Richard by name the secounde,
In whom hath ever yet be founde
Justice medled with pite,
Largesse forth with charite,
In his persone it may be shewed,
What is a king to be well thewed
Touching of pite namely,
For he yet never unpetously
Ayein the leges of his londe
For no defaute which he fonde
Through cruelte vengeaunce sought.
As though the worldes chaunce in brought
Of infortune great debate,
Yet was he nought infortunate,
For he, which the fortune ladde,
The highe god him overspradde
Of his justice and kept him so,
That his estate stood evermo
Sauf as it oughte wel to be
Lich to the sonne in his degre,
Which with the cloudes up alofte
Is derked and beshadewed ofte,
But how so that it trouble in thaire
The sonne is ever bright and faire
Within him self and nought unpeired,
All though the weder be despeired,
The heved planete is nought to wite.
My worthy prince, of whom I write,
Thus stant he with him selve clere
And doth what lith in his powere,
Nought only here at home to seke
Love and accorde, but outward eke,
As he, that save his people wolde.
So ben we alle well beholde
To do service and obeisaunce
To him, which of his high suffraunce
Hath many a great debate appesed
To make his lege men ben esed,
Wherefore that his cronique shall
For ever be memoriall
To the loenge of that he doth.
For this wote every man in soth,
What king that so desireth pees,
He taketh the way which Criste ches,
And who that Christes weies sueth,
It proveth well that he escheueth
The vices and is vertuous,
Wherof he mot be gracious
Toward his god and acceptable.
And so to make his regne stable
With all the will that I may yive
I pray and shall while that I live,
As I which in subjection
Stonde under the protection
And may my selven nought bewelde,
What for sikenesse and what for elde,
Which I receive of goddes grace,
But though me lacke to purchace
My kinges thank as by deserte,
Yet the simplesse of my pouerte
Unto the love of my legeaunce
Desireth for to do plesaunce.
And for this cause in min entent
This pouer book here I present
Unto his highe worthinesse
Write of my simple besinesse,
So as sikenesse it suffre wolde,
And in such wise as I first tolde,
Whan I this boke began to make,
In some partie it may be take
And for to laugh and for to pley,
And for to loke in other wey
It may be wisdom to the wise,
So that somedele for good apprise,
And eke somedele for lust and game
I have it made for thilke same.

And thus bewhapéd in my thought,
Whan all was tornéd into nought,
I stood amaséd for a while,
And in my self I gan to smile,
Thenkend upon the bedés blacke,
And how they weren me betake
For that I shuldé bid and praie.
And whan I sigh none other waie,
But only that I was refused,
Unto the life whiche I had used
I thoughté never torne ayein.
And in this wisé soth to sain
Homward a softé pas I went,
Where that with all min hole entent,
Upon the point that I am shrive,
I thenke biddé while I live.

He, which withinné daiés seven
This largé worlde forth with the heven,
Of his eternal providence
Hath made, and thilke intelligence
In mannés soulé resonáble
Hath shapé to be perduráble,
Wherof the man of his fetúre
Above all erthly creätúre
After the soule is immortáll,
To thilké lorde in speciáll,
As he which is of allé thinges
The Creätór and of the kinges
Hath the fortúnés upon honde,
His grace and mercy for to fonde,
Upon my baré knees I praie,
That he this londe in siker waie
Woll set upon good governaunce.
For if men take in remembraunce,
What is to live in unité,
There is no state in his degré,
That ne ought to desiré pes,
Withoute which it is no les
To seche and loke into the past,
There may no worldés joié last.
First for to loké the clergie,
Hem oughté well to justifie
Thing which belongeth to their cure,
As for to praie and to procure
Our pees toward the heven above,
And eke to setté rest and love
Among us on this erthé here;
For if they wrought in this manere
After the reule of charité
I hopé that men sholden se
This lond amende.
And over this
To seche and loke how that it is
Touchénd of the chivalérie,
Which for to loke in some partie
Is worthie for to be commended
And in some part to be amended,
That of her largé retenue
The lond is full of maintenue,
Which causeth that the comun right
In fewé contres stont upright.
Extorción, contek, ravine
Witholdé ben of that covine.
All day men heré great compleint
Of the disese, of the constreint,
Wherof the people is sore oppressed,
God graunt it moté be redressed.
For of knighthodé thorder wolde,
That they defende and kepé sholde
The comun right and the fraunchise
Of Holy Chirche in allé wise,
So that no wicked man it dere,
And therof serveth shielde and spere.
But for it goth now other waie,
Our gracé goth the more awaie.
And for to loken overmore,
Wherof the people pleignen sore
Toward the lawes of our londe,
Men sain that trouth hath broke his bonde
And with brocáge is gone awey,
So that no man can se the wey,
Where for to findé rightwisnesse.
And if men sech in sikernesse
Upon the lucre of marchandie,
Compassément and trecherie

Of singulár profít to winne,
Men sain is cause of mochel sinne,
And namely of división,
Which many a noble worthy town
Fro welth and fro prosperité
Hath brought to great adversité;
So were it good to ben all one.
For mochel gracé therupon
Unto the citees shuldé fall,
Which might availé to us all,
If these estates amended were,
So that the Vertues stoden there,
And that the Vices were away,
Me thenketh I dorste thanné say,
This londes gracé shulde arise.
  But yet to loke in other wise,
There is a state, as ye shall here,
Above all other on erthé here,
Which hath the londe in his balaunce;
To him belongeth the legeaunce
Of clerke, of knight, of man of lawe,
Under his honde all is forthdrawe
The marchaunt and the laborer,
So stant it all in powér
Or for to spille, or for to save.
But though that he such power have,
And that his mightés ben so large,
He hath hem nought withouten charge
To which that **every king** is swore.
So were it good, that he therfore
First unto rightwisnesse entende,
Wherof that he him self amende
Toward his God, and levé vice,
Which is the chefe of his office.
And after all the remenaunt
He shall upon his covenaunt
Govérne and lede in such a wise,
So that there be no tirannise
Wherof that he his people greve.
Or elles may he nought acheve
That longeth to his Regalie.
For if a king will justifie
His londe and hem that ben withinne,
First at him self he mot beginne
To kepe and reule his own estate,
That in him self be no debate
Toward his God. For otherwise
Ther may none erthly King suffise
Of his kingdóm the folk to lede,
But he the King of Heven drede.
For what King sette him upon pride
And taketh his lust on every side
And will nought go the righté weie,
Though God his gracé cast aweie,
No wonder is, for atté last
He shall well wite it may nought last,
The pompé whiche he secheth here.
But what King that with humble chere
After the Lawe of God escheueth
The Vices, and the Vertues sueth,
His gracé shall be suffisaúnt
To governe all the remenaúnt,
Which longeth unto his dueté;
So that in his prosperité
The people shall nought be oppressed,
Wherof his namé shall be blessed
For ever and be memoriall.

  And now to speke as in finall
Touchéndé that I undertoke
In English for to make a boke
Which stant betwene ernést and game,
I have it made as thilké same,
Which axé for to be excused,
And that my boke be nought refused
Of leréd men whan they it se
For lack of curiosité;
For thilké scole of eloquence
Belongeth nought to my sciénce,
Upon the forme of rhetorique
My wordes for to peint and pike,
As Tullius somtimé wrote.
But this I knowe and this I wote,
That I have do my trewé peine
With rudé wordés and with pleine

In all that ever I couthe and might,
This boke to write as I behight,
So as siknésse it suffer wolde.
And also for my daiés olde
That I am feble and impotent,
I wot nought how the worlde is went,[1]
So pray I to my lordés alle,
Now in min age, how so befalle,
That I mot stonden in her grace.
For though me lacké to purchace
Her worthy thank, as by deserte,
Yet the simplésse of my pouerte
Desireth for to do plesaúnce
To hem under whose governaunce
I hopé siker to abide.
But now, upon my lasté tide,
That I this boke have made and write,
My Musé doth me for to wite
And saith, it shall be for my beste,
Fro this day forth to také reste,
That I no more of lové make,[2]
Which many a herte hath overtake
And overtornéd as the blinde
Fro reson into lawe of kinde,

[1] *Went*, turned.
[2] *Make*, write poetry.

Where as the wisdom goth aweie
And can nought se the righté weie
How to govérne his own estate,
But every day stant in debate
Within him self and can nought leve.

And thus forthy my finall leve
I také now for evermore
Withouté making[1] any more
Of love and of his dedly hele,
Which no phisicien can hele.
For his natúre is so divers,
That it hath ever some travers
Or of to moch or of to lite,
That pleinly may no man delite,
But if him faile or that or this.
But thilké Lové, which that is
Within a mannés herte affirmed
And stant of Charité confirmed,
Such Love is goodly for to have,
Such Lové may the body save,
Such Lové may the soule amende,
The Highe God such Love us sende
Forth with the remenaunt of grace,
So that above in thilké place,
Where resteth Love and alle Pees,
Our joie may ben endélés.

[1] *Making*, writing poems.

Explicit iste liber, qui transeat obsecro liber,
Ut sine livore vigeat lectoris in ore.
Qui sedet in scamnis celi det, ut ista Johannis
Perpetuis annis stet pagina grata Britannis.

BALLANTYNE PRESS: EDINBURGH AND LONDON.

MORLEY'S UNIVERSAL LIBRARY—*continued.*

32. **THE HISTORY OF THOMAS ELLWOOD.** Written by Himself.
33. **EMERSON'S ESSAYS, REPRESENTATIVE MEN, AND SOCIETY AND SOLITUDE.**
34. **SOUTHEY'S LIFE OF NELSON.**
35. **DE QUINCEY'S OPIUM-EATER, SHAKSPEARE, GOETHE.**
36. **STORIES OF IRELAND.** By MARIA EDGEWORTH.
37. **THE PLAYS OF ARISTOPHANES.** Translated by FRERE.
38. **SPEECHES AND LETTERS.** By EDMUND BURKE.
39. **THOMAS À KEMPIS' IMITATION OF CHRIST.**
40. **POPULAR SONGS OF IRELAND.** Collected by THOMAS CROFTON CROKER.
41. **THE PLAYS OF ÆSCHYLUS.** Translated by R. POTTER.
42. **GOETHE'S FAUST.** The Second Part.
43. **FAMOUS PAMPHLETS.**
44. **SOPHOCLES.** Translated by FRANCKLIN.
45. **TALES OF TERROR AND WONDER.**
46. **VESTIGES OF THE NATURAL HISTORY OF CREATION.**
47. **THE BARONS' WARS, &c.** By MICHAEL DRAYTON.
48. **COBBETT'S ADVICE TO YOUNG MEN.**
49. **THE BANQUET OF DANTE.** Translated by ELIZABETH P. SAYER.
50. **WALKER'S ORIGINAL.**
51. **POEMS AND BALLADS BY SCHILLER.**
52. **PEELE'S PLAYS AND POEMS.**
53. **HARRINGTON'S OCEANA.**
54. **EURIPIDES—ALCESTIS, &c.**
55. **ESSAYS.** By WINTHROP MACKWORTH PRAED.
56. **TRADITIONAL TALES.** ALLAN CUNNINGHAM.
57. **HOOKER'S ECCLESIASTICAL POLITY.** Books I.—IV.
58. **EURIPIDES—THE BACCHANALS, and other PLAYS.**
59. **WALTON'S LIVES OF DONNE, WOTTON, HOOKER, GEORGE HERBERT, &c.**
60. **ARISTOTLE ON GOVERNMENT.**
61. **EURIPIDES—HECUBA, and other PLAYS.**
62. **RABELAIS' HEROIC DEEDS OF PANTAGRUEL.** Books III., IV., and V.
63. **A MISCELLANY.**

GEORGE ROUTLEDGE AND SONS,

LONDON, GLASGOW, MANCHESTER, AND NEW YORK.